Paul Moorcraft is a graduate of the Universities of Swansea, Lancaster, Cardiff and South Africa. His PhD thesis was a study of the Rhodesian war. A former senior instructor at the Royal Military Academy, Sandhurst, he pursued postgraduate studies in Israel and at the University of Rhodesia. He lectured variously in history, politics and international relations at the Universities of Zimbabwe, Cape Town, Natal and the Witwatersrand. Dr Moorcraft also worked as a freelance correspondent for such journals as *Time, International Defence Review, Army* and *Janes's Defence Weekly* in all the countries of southern Africa. He was a political columnist for both the former Johannesburg *Sunday Express* and *The Star*, South Africa's biggest English daily newspaper. His books include *A Short Thousand Years,* (with Dr Peter McLaughlin) *Chimurenga: The War in Rhodesia* and *Travelling to War* to be published by Brassey's. He has also worked as an independent film producer in Africa and Asia, specialising in war documentaries. Paul Moorcraft is currently teaching journalism at Deakin University in Australia.

AFRICAN NEMESIS

War and Revolution in Southern Africa

(1945-2010)

Nemesis: 1) in Greek mythology the goddess of vengeance; 2) any agency of retribution and vengeance; 3) righteous wrath; 4) in popular parlance, comeuppance.

AFRICAN NEMESIS

War and Revolution in Southern Africa (1945-2010)

by Paul L Moorcraft

BRASSEY'S (UK) LTD

LONDON • WASHINGTON

First English edition 1990
Paper edition 1994

UK editorial offices: Brassey's 33 John Street, London WC1N 2AT
orders: Marston Book Services, PO Box 87, Oxford OX2 0DT

USA orders: Macmillan Publishing Company, Front and Brown Streets, Riverside, NJ 08075

Distributed in North America to booksellers and wholesalers by the Macmillan Publishing Company, NY 10022

Library of Congress Cataloging in Publication Data
available

British Library Cataloguing in Publication Data
A catalogue record for this book is available from the British Library

ISBN 1-85753-140-X Paper

Front cover photographs: Nelson Mandela *(International Defence and Aid Fund for Southern Africa)*; Swazi Warriors *(Paul Moorcraft)*; Soldiers of the South African Defence Force on the Angolan border *(Paul Moorcraft)*.

Printed in Great Britain by BPCC Wheatons Ltd, Exeter

CONTENTS

A REVERSE TREK?

Futures are not what they used to be. The world has been hard to keep up with since the first edition of this book was published. In 1990, a period of great political flux, I was confident or stupid enough to look ahead 20 years. This paperback edition is being published to coincide with the first one-person, one-vote election in South Africa. When Nelson Mandela was released from prison in February 1990 universal franchise still seemed a world away.

The Soviet Union has disappeared. It was a kind of alter ego, a demon which nourished Pretoria's paranoia. It was no coincidence that the failed ideologies of Soviet communism and apartheid crumbled at the same time. America became the only superpower, but did not know what to do with that power, especially in Africa. Washington had just led a massive international coalition during the Gulf War, but American forces were bogged down and humiliated fighting tribal warlords in Somalia.

Except for occasional media circuses Africa began to slide off the economic and political map. Except for South Africa, the western media grew even more bored with Africa's perennial catastrophes. There had been a surfeit, it seemed, of distended bellies and wild-looking guerrillas waving battered AKs. Compassion fatigue and frustration with the more egregious black kleptocrats finally encouraged what some optimists called the 'second wave of liberation' in Africa. After telling Pretoria for decades to free Mandela and introduce one person, one vote, some African states started to think about releasing their own political prisoners and ending the one-party systems. Zambia voted out Kenneth Kaunda. And for a while Angola looked like the ballot could replace the bullet. But Unita rejected the election results and resumed the war. Mozambique also groped for a political compromise to end its 30 years of blood-letting. In December 1991 I returned to central Mozambique to make a short TV documentary. The clock had been put back 300 years.

A few commentators raised the possibility of states which had collapsed almost completely, such as Mozambique or Somalia, returning to the temporary governance of the former colonial powers, under the aegis of the UN. This was not so bizarre: the International Monetary Fund and the World Bank had recolonised parts of the African economy. Whether or not Africa has a real chance to set its own house in order, it faces the same dilemma as Eastern Europe: can embryonic democracies take the really tough decisions needed to save the economy without slipping back into dictatorship?

Despite the eccentric international history of South Africa, apartheid has always primarily been an issue for Africans. Opposition to Pretoria had been the only thing the Organisation of African Unity could agree upon. The war against the Boers had been the main excuse for the dictatorships and secret police terrors in many of the frontline states; South Africa's democratisation was contagious. But so was the warfare. Nearly all the black-white colonial conflicts had turned into 'black-on-black' civil wars. Would post-apartheid South Africa suffer the same fate as Angola or Mozambique?

South Africa, as the regional superpower, is the key to the economic and political salvation of the whole of southern and central Africa. Yet a black-ruled and vigorous South Africa (or Azania) is everything the neighbouring states have desired, and dreaded. They wanted liberation, but feared the republic's power. That was part of the reason for their ambiguity about ending sanctions. The ending of sanctions destroyed a legion of vested interests. Sanctions were almost the *raison d'être* of the Commonwealth. For too long, belief in sanctions had been seen as a litmus test of morality. They withered away and South African sports teams could compete internationally. That was the chief pay-off for many whites for the demise of apartheid. For businessmen the transition from siege economy to open economy is likely to be painful, although the African National Congress will have to do pretty poorly to hobble the economy as comprehensively as apartheid did.

All the legal pillars of grand apartheid have collapsed. But until April 1994 Archbishop Desmond Tutu, a 63-year-old Nobel laureate, was still disenfranchised, while an illiterate and unemployed 18-year-old Afrikaner railway worker could vote. Entrenched by decades of apartheid privilege, the white 13 per cent of the population owned more than 87 per cent of the country's land and formal businesses. The registers of the 100 biggest companies had only 40 black directors among them.

South Africa is a much better place in 1994 than it was in 1990. That is a morally comfortable perspective for foreign observers. It is also a much more dangerous place for the locals. Over 13,000 political murders have been committed since Mandela came out of prison. The feral youngsters in the townships are demanding their 'liberation dividends'. Many blacks regard the double act of Mandela and President F W de Klerk as a sell-out. Both reforming lawyers received Nobel prizes, but VCRs did not fall like rain on Soweto. The election campaign is bound to lead to extravagant ANC promises: the chasm between hope and reality is likely to swallow up Mandela. Probable beneficiaries will be the Pan Africanist Congress, a much under-rated party.

What happens after the 1994 elections and an ANC-dominated (temporary) coalition? R W Johnson was the most incisive critic of my predictions in the first edition. He attacked one of my major themes – to use Johnson's words – as 'one final great *Götterdämmerung* struggle by white South Africa against all-comers'. My postscript, however, showed a swing in the opposite direction. When Mandela was released I was infected by the euphoria.

I tipped the coup against Mikhail Gorbachev, but the assassination of Chris Hani scuttled my plans for him to succeed Mandela. The mantle will fall perhaps on Cyril Ramaphosa, although as I write this the TV is showing bullets careering around the ears of Ramaphosa and Joe Slovo. I fear, however, that although I might have erred with some superficial aspects, the underlying themes of my projections still stand. The external siege has been lifted, but the white siege psychosis has been intensified. Whites in Johannesburg continue to compete for the title of the world's greatest wall-builders.

I described four likely scenarios: negotiated settlement; a holding operation; degenerative collapse; and revolution. I suggested that the future could be a mix of these four alternatives. The negotiated settlement has, surprisingly, dominated ... so far. There is important evidence of a holding operation, too. The concern with federal options and checks and balances within a new constitution are (understandable) elements in the white desire to retain some power in the transition. So far there has been no revolution, but some of the townships in the Transvaal and large swathes of Natal fit into my definition of degenerative collapse. Assassination is becoming a national sport in South Africa.

From 1990-94 the ANC and the National Party have conducted a love –hate affair. The transition depends upon the survival of both Mandela and de Klerk, and their strange relationship. But the odd-couple diplomacy has increasingly caused the ANC and NP to lose both left and right wings of their parties. On the left the PAC and other black consciousness groups are feeding off the disenchantment with the ANC. On the right Buthelezi's Inkatha and the *Afrikaner Weerstandsbeweging* have confirmed one of South Africa's oldest clichés: that the Zulus and the Afrikaners would unite to resist domination by other tribes. A minority of Zulus and Afrikaners support these parties, but the majority of the defeated Afrikaners opposed the old Union of South Africa, an imperial imposition. The blacks, especially the Zulus, were not even consulted. 'South Africa' was an artificial and unpopular colonial creation. Why should it survive in its present form?

The most important theme of *African Nemesis* was the potential role of the military in South Africa's transition. Since the book was published considerable evidence has surfaced of police involvement in a so-called Third Force fomenting 'black-on-black' violence. There has also been evidence of army and police hostility to President de Klerk's sweeping changes, especially in the military and intelligence systems.

My analyses of the Rhodesian and the Portuguese security forces suggested a tendency for military reformers to back a political solution to endemic violence. And that sometimes meant intervention by the military to curb the more bellicose politicians. There was a coup in Lisbon and almost one in Salisbury. I had always thought that white military resistance to a settlement would be important, despite what most academic observers opined. Eugene Terreblanche has been a music-hall Hitler and a comic, albeit a dangerous one. General Constand Viljoen, in contrast, is a serious contender for the 'man on horseback'. (Unlike the AWB leader, Viljoen can usually manage to stay on a horse.) The general, a former head of the South Africa Defence Force, could poll more white votes than the National Party. The tens of thousands of conservative English-speaking South Africans, as well as ex-Rhodesians and the large Portuguese-speaking community, were looking for a right-winger who was less of an exclusivist Afrikaner demagogue than Terreblanche. Along with conservative allies in the homelands (particularly in KwaZulu) and among the Indian and coloureds, Viljoen could be the man to negotiate with the future President Mandela (if the ANC leader survives).

The key issue will be autonomy for Afrikaners. Desire for secession in Natal and a white homeland elsewhere are integral to the conservatives' holding operation. It is not just racial or tribal. Ideology intrudes mightily. The wilder shores of the ANC still want large-scale redistribution of land, nationalisation and people's courts. The popularity of the South African Communist Party is not unexpected in a society where the dispossessed equate apartheid with capitalism.

Where will South Africa be in 2010? President Ramaphosa and Prime Minister Viljoen meet in Mandela City (formerly Johannesburg). Buthelezi is still in self-imposed exile. The Federation of South African States is 12 years old. Viljoen's Free State, in a generous reversal of apartheid, comprises 21 per cent of the country, incorporating parts of the Cape, Orange Free State and Transvaal. Viljoen's army had helped the Federation forces to destroy the last cells of the so-called 'Werewolf' white resistance on the Witwatersrand. That was ten years ago, in 2000. That was the last of the fighting. Now Ramaphosa, Viljoen – whose shock of unruly white hair and portliness make him look like Paul Kruger – and Mahendra Patel, the ANC's economic *wunderkind*, are planning how to revamp the economic alliance with the neighbouring states. All have become economic satellites. All have prospered, except Mozambique . . . I could go on, but I think I have made my point. Fanciful? Maybe. Utopian? Probably. A peaceful reverse trek (to a non-black majority whitestan) might ensure survival for the Afrikaners. It would be an ironic fulfilment of apartheid, if they got 13 per cent of the dustiest land in the northern Cape.

Despite the end of external siege, many whites are retreating into an internal siege. So are many beleaguered blacks in the townships. Whatever the elections decide, the results are likely to make the Xhosas, Zulus and Afrikaners even more prickly about their tribal aspirations. It may not be politically correct, but it is foolish to ignore primeval fears in Africa. A negotiated federation – how loose a federation, loose enough to be a confederation? – is far better than the creeping Lebanonisation, prefigured by the current levels of violence. Pretoria could become a second Beirut, another Sarajevo.

Cynical Johannesburgers frequently deploy black humour to alleviate the pressures of their brash, ugly, lively and well-armed city. Bill Clinton, Boris Yeltsin and Nelson Mandela are engaged in a long conversation with Jehovah. Clinton asks how long it will take for his country to solve its problems. 'Not in your administration,' says the Lord, 'but in the next one.' Yeltsin asks the same question. 'Not in your lifetime, but in the lifetime of your children,' says God. When Mandela asks, God sighs and replies: 'Not in my lifetime.'

Paul Moorcraft

Deakin University, Australia
February 1994.

PREFACE

This book is about military power in southern Africa since 1945. It also discusses the various political, economic, social and psychological issues, where they are directly relevant to warfare in the region. This is no moral tract. Rather, it attempts to be a dispassionate account which does not skirt the hypocrisy of both white and black antagonists.

There are very many books about South Africa. Most, however, have an implicit or explicit axe to grind. The majority are infused with righteous indignation about apartheid; a minority are written by apologists of white rule. I have tried to give both sides of the equations, not only in South Africa, but in all the "frontline" states. Such a comprehensive endeavour would not normally be accommodated in a single volume. I hope the reader will forgive my temerity in attempting to do so. I have ventured to maintain a narrative pace, while also weaving in the history of the various wars, and provide a strategic analysis. I have tried very hard not to take sides. The book contains, however, a more detailed study of the machinery of white power in southern Africa. Pretoria is, after all, the central player on the crowded stage.

The first part of the book (Chapters 2-4) sets the scene for the rise of South Africa as a regional superpower. Chapters 5-8 consider Pretoria's involvement in the "colonial" wars in Angola, Namibia, Mozambique and Rhodesia. Chapter 9 discusses the polarisation of the conflict between the frontline states and southern redoubts of white supremacy. Chapters 10-14 consider in detail apartheid's "second front", the wars of destabilisation in South Africa's neighbouring states. Chapter 15 turns to the central issue: the rise of black resistance in the white heartland, the apartheid republic. Chapters 16-18 are concerned with the current military situation in South Africa. In Chapter 19 I stick my neck out. The chapter attempts to peer into the future by extrapolating from past and current military and political trends.

The style of the book may be deemed a trifle eclectic. As an observer who lived and worked for more than a decade in all the southern African states as a journalist, documentary film-maker and academic, I have essayed to marry reportage and analysis. Hence, for example, the use of two "cameos" of travels along the Angolan border and through Renamo-controlled territory in Mozambique. I have not overburdened, I hope, the text with references. Occasionally, attributions have been omitted to protect a source of information. I have generally provided references when they are available in English. Better-known quotations and facts have sometimes not been sourced, nor information available in other languages, especially Portuguese and Afrikaans. Such references can be pursued in the specialist texts in English which can be found in the select bibliography and end-notes. For convenience's sake, I have employed the South African group terminology of black, coloured (mixed-race), Indian (Asian) and white. This does not, of course, infer any endorsement of apartheid. Unless I have qualified the term, "black" usually refers to Asian, coloured and black Africans.

Finally, it should be noted that this book was completed at a time of considerable flux in southern African (and world) politics. When *African Nemesis* was started, in mid-1988, there was a log jam in the region. A number of dramatic events erupted around me as I was in the process of finishing this work. The partial Angolan settlement led to Namibian independence. P W Botha was displaced by F W de Klerk. Serious efforts were being made to end the civil wars in Angola and Mozambique. Most significant, however, were the steps leading up to the release of Nelson Mandela. His freedom, as the concluding chapters suggest, will change the future of the entire region. It is, therefore, a fascinating, if dangerous, time to complete a book on southern Africa. No doubt, some of my controversial predictions will be proved wrong by the time this book is generally available. Nevertheless, the general thrust of the analysis will, I trust, stand the test of time. I sincerely hope that it will provide a durable guide for those who wish to understand the long, tortuous route to peace in this troubled region.

Paul Moorcraft
Altea, Spain
1989

ACKNOWLEDGEMENTS

I should like to acknowledge some of the people who directly helped me to produce this book. Professor Jack Spence kindly read the draft before publication. He has been a mentor to this wayward pupil since his undergraduate days. Thanks are due also to: Jenny Shaw of Brassey's for her moral support; Jane Gregory, my tough-minded literary agent; and my wife, Susan, who suffered with me during the year-long gestation. Francis Ainley advised me on computer techniques.

Others helped me more indirectly over the years: my colleagues when I taught at the University of Rhodesia/Zimbabwe (especially Dr Peter McLaughlin, Professor Marshall Murphree and Dr Ariston Chambati), the University of Natal (especially Sandy Johnston), the University of Cape Town (especially Professor Robert Schrire) and the University of the Witwatersrand; Tim Lambon, a resolute ex-soldier, who gave me so much courage in numerous adventures, especially in Mozambique and Afghanistan; Marie Bruyns, the South African filmmaker, who taught me so much about the Afrikaner establishment; Denis Beckett, the editor of *Frontline* magazine, who tried so hard to make me an optimist about South Africa; Ken Owen, the editor of the former *Sunday Express*, and Harvey Tyson, the editor of *The Star*, for allowing me to learn on the job by writing a weekly political column in their newspapers; Fred van der Merwe, who supported my first four books on southern Africa; Ben Mugabe; Deon Fourie, professor and colonel, who supervised my doctorate on the Rhodesian war while hardly agreeing with anything I wrote; and, finally, Ken Flower, the former director-general of the Central Intelligence Organisation, who not only kept me out of jail, but whose family also showed me great kindness. All the mistakes are, of course, my own.

I wish also to acknowledge the permission to quote from various copyright material: Denis Beckett's articles in *Frontline* magazine; Jesmond Blumenfeld's article, "Western Economic Policy Towards South Africa . . .", in *International Affairs Bulletin,* 11:3, 1987; J M Coetzee's novel,

Waiting for the Barbarians, Penguin, Harmondsworth, 1982; Rodney Davenport's *South Africa: A Modern History*, Macmillan, Johannesburg, 1987; Stephen Davis, *Apartheid's Rebels*, Yale University Press, New Haven, 1987; material from the *Financial Mail*, Johannesburg; Philip Frankel's *Pretoria's Praetorians*, Cambridge University Press, Cambridge, 1984; Joseph Hanlon, *Apartheid's Second Front: South Africa's War against its Neighbours*, Penguin, Harmondsworth, 1986, reproduced by permission of Penguin Books Ltd; Simon Jenkins, "America and South Africa," *The Economist*, 30 March 1985; Peter Katjavivi, *A History of Resistance in Namibia*, Currey, London, 1988; John Marcum, "Regional Security in Southern Africa: Angola," *Survival*, 30:1, January/February 1988; Thomas Pakenham's *The Boer War*; Willem Steenkamp, *Borderstrike*, Butterworths, Durban, 1983; Frederick van Zyl Slabbert's *The Last White Parliament*, Strydom, Melville, 1985.

Photo credits are acknowledged with the photographs. Generally, those without credits were taken by the author. I thank Harvey Tyson, the editor of *The Star*, not only for permission to quote from his newspaper, but also for the right to reproduce the cartoon work of Dave Anderson and Abe Berry.

ABBREVIATIONS

AA: Anti-aircraft

AKTUR: Action Front for the Retention of Turnhalle Principles

ANC: African National Congress

APCs: Armoured Personnel Carriers

AWB: *Afrikaner Weerstandsbeweging*

AZAPO: The Azanian Peoples' Organisation

BCM: Black Consciousness Movement

BOSS: Bureau for State Security

BSAP: British South Africa Police

CF: Citizen Force

COIN: Counterinsurgency

ComOps: Combined Operations HQ (Rhodesia)

CONSAS: Constellation of Southern African States

COSAS: Congress of South African Students

COSATU: Congress of South African Trade Unions

CP: Conservative Party (South Africa)

CUSA: Council of Unions of South Africa

DGS: *Direcçao Geral de Segurança,* Portuguese security police

DONS: Department of National Security

DTA: Democratic Turnhalle Alliance

ECM: Electronic counter-measures

EPG: Eminent Persons Group

FALA: *Forças Armadas para a Libertação de Angola*, the Unita army

FAPLA: *Forças Armadas Populares para a Libertação de Angola*

FNLA: *Frente Nacional de Libertação de Angola*

FPLM: *Forcas Populares de Libertação de Moçambique*

Frelimo: *Frente de Libertação de Moçambique*

JMC: Joint Management Centre

LLA: Lesotho Liberation Army

MDM: Mass Democratic Movement

MFA: *Movimento das Forcas Armadas*, Armed Forces Movement

MK: *Umkhonto we Sizwe*

MNR: See Renamo

MPC: Multi-Party Conference

MPLA: *Movimento Popular de Libertação de Angola*

NIS: National Intelligence Service.

NP: National Party

NSMS: National Security Management System

NUM: National Union of Mineworkers

PAC: Pan-Africanist Congress

PF: Patriotic Front

PF: Permanent Force

PFP: Progressive Federal Party

PIDE: *Policia Internacional de Defesa do Estado*

PLAN: People's Liberation Army of Namibia

Renamo: *Resistência Nacional Moçambicana*

RF: Rhodesian Front

SABC: South African Broadcasting Corporation

SACP: South African Communist Party

SADCC: The Southern African Development Coordination Conference

SADF: South African Defence Force

SAM: Surface-to-air missile

SAP: South African Police

SB: Security Branch (Rhodesia)

SNASP: *Serviço Nacional de Segurança Popular*

SP: Security Police (South Africa)

SSC: State Security Council

SWANU: South West African National Union

SWAP: South West Africa Police

SWAPO: South West Africa People's Organisation

SWATF: South West Africa Territory Force

TTL: Tribal Trust Lands (Rhodesia)

UANC: United African National Council

UDF: United Democratic Front

UDF: Union Defence Force

UDI: Unilateral Declaration of Independence

Unita: *União Nacional para a Independência Total de Angola*

UNTAG: United Nations Transition Assistance Group

ZANLA: Zimbabwe African National Liberation Army

ZANU: Zimbabwe African National Union

ZANU(PF): Zimbabwe African National Union (Patriotic Front)

ZAPU: Zimbabwe African People's Union

ZIPRA: Zimbabwe People's Revolutionary Army.

ZNA: Zimbabwe National Army

GLOSSARY

aldeamentos: Strategic villages introduced by the Portuguese to separate the black population from the guerrillas.

apartheid: Literally, a policy of "separateness"; official policy of racial segregation practised in South Africa since 1948.

assimilado: A black in the Portuguese colonial territories who had satisfied very stringent educational and cultural requirements.

auxiliary: Ex-guerrillas who were affiliated to the Rhodesian forces.

Azania: The name adopted for South Africa by the Pan-Africanist Congress.

Bantu: Language group spoken by the vast majority of the indigenous population in central/southern Africa. Given an ethnic/racial identification in South Africa, it became a derogatory term for blacks.

bantustan: A homeland for the different "tribal nations" of South Africa, the cornerstone of old-style apartheid.

bittereinder: Afrikaners who did not want to sign the peace agreement that ended the Boer war in 1902. Also applied to contemporary last-ditchers.

Boer: Literally a "farmer", but came to be applied to all Afrikaners. Often derogatory.

Broederbond: A secret society to promote Afrikaner interests.

Chimurenga: From the Shona word meaning "resistance". Applied first to the war against the settlers in the 1890s, and then to the war of the 1970s.

comrades: Young black radicals in the South African townships.

contact: Military engagement.

contact group: Five Western states, USA, Britain, France, West Germany and Canada, which negotiated with Pretoria over Namibian independence.

cuca shop: Small local stores, especially in northern Namibia.

fire force: Highly mobile Rhodesian heliborne troops.

Flechas: Elite group of Portuguese troops in Mozambique.

frontline: The major southern African states aligned against apartheid.

House of Assembly: White chamber in South Africa's tricameral parliament.

House of Delegates: Indian chamber of parliament.

House of Representatives: Coloured chamber of parliament.

impis: Zulu regiments or a large group of African warriors..

Indaba: Zulu word for meeting or discussion. Often applied to projected multiracial merger of Natal and KwaZulu.

Inkatha ***(yeNkululeko ye Sizwe):*** Zulu cultural/political party led by Chief Gatsha Buthelezi.

Koevoet: Paramilitary police counterinsurgency unit in Namibia.

kragdadig: Afrikaans term for "hard-line".

Laager: Literally, a defensive circle of oxwagons. Later applied to the defensive mentality of Afrikaners.

Liqoqo: Royal council in Swaziland.

mestiço: A person of mixed white and black ancestry.

mujiba: A young boy or girl who acts as a scout and helper to guerrillas. Term usually applied to the Rhodesian war.

necklacing: The practice of killing alleged collaborators with a tyre, filled with petrol, which is then placed around the victim's neck and set alight.

pass laws: Former South African laws which prevented black people from living and working in certain areas. Repealed in 1986.

platteland: Afrikaans term for the rural areas.

Poqo: A Xhosa word which means "alone" or "pure". The military wing of the PAC, especially in the 1960s.

povo: Portuguese word for the common people or the "masses", used extensively in the Mozambique and Rhodesian wars.

protected villages: Guarded settlements in Rhodesia to prevent the peasantry from supporting the guerrillas.

sjambok: A whip.

stick: Rhodesian term for small patrol, often of six men.

total onslaught: The purported international communist conspiracy to attack South Africa.

townships: Areas of settlement for non-white groups, usually situated near "white" urban areas or towns to serve as a convenient workforce. Townships are sometimes also referred to as "locations".

uitlander: Literally, an outsider. An Afrikaans word for a foreigner.

Umkhonto we Sizwe: The military wing of the ANC.

verkrampte (adj. ***verkramp):*** An Afrikaans term for an ultra-conservative or "narrow" person.

Verligte (adj. ***verlig):*** Liberal or "enlightened" person.

Voortrekker: An Afrikaner/Boer pioneer who *trekked* (travelled) north with the Great Trek.

witdoeke: Literally, "white cloths", worn by conservative vigilantes in the Cape to distinguish them from the comrades. Then applied to the conservative groups as a whole.

CHRONOLOGY

1652: Jan van Riebeeck lands at the Cape.
1806: Britain reoccupies the Cape
1836: The Great Trek begins
1838: Battle of Blood River
1867: Diamond mines opened in Griqualand West
1880-1881: First Boer war
1884: Germany annexes South West Africa
1886: Gold mines opened on the Witwatersrand
1890: Pioneer column reaches Salisbury, Rhodesia
1895: Jameson raid
1899-1902: Second Boer war
1910: Union of South Africa formed
1912: ANC founded
1914-1918: First World War
1939-1945: Second World War
1948: National Party in power, establishes apartheid
1950-1953: Korean war
1960: Sharpeville massacre; banning of ANC and PAC. First state of emergency.
1961: South Africa becomes a republic, leaves Commonwealth. Uprising in northern Angola. Beginning of armed struggle in South Africa.
1964: Rivonia trial. Guerrilla war begins in Mozambique
1965: UDI
1966: SWAPO begins its armed struggle
1974: Coup in Lisbon
1975: Mozambique and Angola become independent
1976-1977: Soweto uprising
1977: Steve Biko murdered
1980: Independence of Zimbabwe
1983: UDF formed to oppose tricameral parliament

1984: Nkomati agreement
1984-1986: "Unrest" throughout South Africa
1985: Second state of emergency declared.
1986: Third state of emergency
1988: Agreement on Angola and Namibia
1989: UN-monitored elections in Namibia. F W de Klerk wins South African election.
1990: Release of Nelson Mandela. Unbanning of ANC, PAC and SACP.

LIST OF FIGURES

LIST OF MAPS

PAX PRETORIA

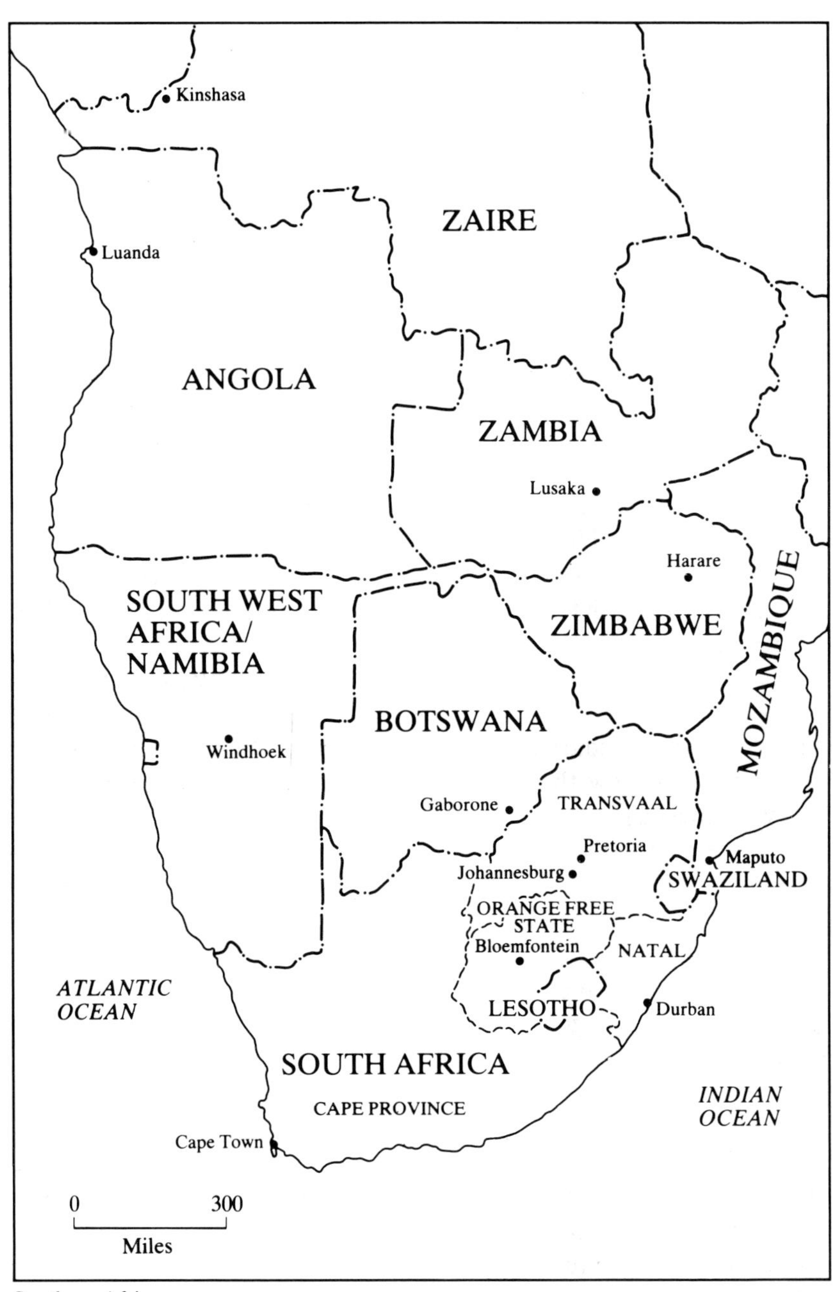

Southern Africa

1

South Africa versus the world

He looked about 13, but he was a soldier. His bush hat was much too big for him. So was the AK he cradled. His tattered Unita uniform was hanging on his small, spindly frame. The boy-soldier sat on a captured Russian truck, which stood waiting in the shimmering heat of the Angolan-Namibian border. A fresh-faced South African soldier, only a few years older than the Unita boy, offered him a cigarette.

"He's too young to smoke," said a fellow South African gruffly.

"If he's old enough to carry a gun, he's old enough to smoke," replied the fresh-faced youth.

This incident, in August 1986, was one of many poignant moments witnessed by the writer. The passing exchange reflects not only the tragedy of the wars in southern Africa, and its almost total embrace of the young, but also how the fate of all the countries in the region have become enmeshed.

The core of the subcontinent is South Africa. The very name conjures up images of hate, passion, pity, fear, war and righteous indignation. To the left, South Africa excites the same emotions as the Spanish civil war. A straightforward case of good versus evil. To the right, the holy war against Pretoria is an example of double standards, the envy directed against a millionaire general by the penniless privates of a ramshackle continent.

The conflict in this strange, fascinating, achingly beautiful land is, however, far more complex than these stereotypes imposed from the distant comfort of the West would suggest. There is little room for knee-jerk moralising. Perhaps sympathy might be in order for *all* the inhabitants of this sociologist's paradise but statesman's hell. Americans and Britons, at least, should approach the South African civil war with some caution. As *The Times* editorialised in 1982: "We have our racial problems too. We are not holier than P W Botha; we are merely luckier."(1)

Amid all the sound and fury about apartheid, South Africa has almost ceased to be a geographical entity: it is more a *condition*.(2) It is no longer a country, but "a map of the mind" in which anyone can find his own place.(3)

Apartheid is usually branded a monstrous failure. In three respects, however, apartheid has "worked". First of all, it has worked psychologically. As intended, it has kept the races physically and emotionally apart. As a South African writer put it: "White South Africans tend to profess an undying love for a country they hardly know, whose people often frighten them, and whose stark beauty they constantly try to change in imitation of Europe."(4) To be in Africa, yet also a part of Europe is the essential paradox of the ruling Afrikaners. To survive, they have usually opted for ideological isolation. Close contact with their fellow black countrymen, or with the rest of the world for that matter, threatened to shatter their tribal icons. As a South African businessman noted: "Afrikaners *need* to be in a laager. When things are going smoothly, they *provoke* aggression in order to make one."(5) If this is true, then international sanctions will nourish both the Afrikaners' self-image and their truculence.

Secondly, in economic terms, apartheid has worked for the whites. In the 1960s and 1970s apartheid amounted to a cargo cult on a grand scale. By the beginning of the 1990s, however, the economy of the racist state was beginning to break down under the strains of war, sanctions and internal social pressures.

Thirdly, apartheid has fashioned a highly efficient defence force. South Africa became a regional superpower, a military and economic giant while remaining a moral pygmy.

This study examines South Africa's intervention in her neighbours' wars and the battle against white supremacy at home. It also addresses the "How long will South Africa survive?" debate. There is a further paradox about white power in South Africa. To observers on the outside it often looks as if the regime is about to fall to the inevitable onrush of revolution. Yet viewed from the inside it appears to be devastatingly powerful. The latter impression is reinforced if the visitor has arrived not from Europe, but from the more derelict black states to the north.

The book analyses in detail the military and political nexus throughout southern Africa. It also attempts to answer a fundamental question: will the war in South Africa lead to revolution? If not, what are the possible alternatives? The answer to these questions are of worldwide significance, not least because the conflict could result in the first victory of a guerrilla movement in a nuclear-armed state.

References and notes:
1. Editorial, *The Times*, 9 March 1982.
2. C Hope, *White Boy Running*, Secker and Warburg, London, 1988, p. 241.
3. A Sampson, *Black and Gold*, Hodder and Stoughton, London, 1987, p. 15.
4. K Owen, "The Way Forward: The Press," in G Jacobs, (ed), *South Africa: The Road Ahead*, Ball, Johannesburg, 1986, p. 231.
5. Discussion with author, 1988. A "laager" is a defensive circle of oxwagons.

2

Pax Britannica

The region until 1945

Pax Britannica is perhaps a misnomer: southern Africa's history is drenched in bloodshed. (1) The epic began as a struggle between white settlers and the indigenous tribes, and then developed, in the nineteenth century, as a Boer/Afrikaner conflict with British imperialism. In the twentieth century both British and Afrikaner historians turned history into myth to suit their own ends. Afrikaner writers tended to re-create their own past to fit their racist ideology: a mixture of right-wing nationalism and Calvinistic Christianity. In dominating the blacks, Afrikaner nationalists liked to think they were fulfilling God's will. On the other side, the Kiplingesque notions of British imperial "race patriotism" had something in common with the Soviet communism of half a century later: "an innocent optimism, a facile disregard for unwelcome truths, an instinct to simplify and categorize, and a dreadful taste in propaganda". (2) War, nationalism and a sense of manifest destiny made Afrikaners paranoiacally independent. The enmity of British imperialism and, after 1948, world opinion merely reinforced the Afrikaner tribe's determination to stand alone, if necessary. God, paradoxically, would give them the strength to justify their belief in Darwin's survival of the fittest. Afrikaner society, despite its imperial links, developed largely in isolation from the mainstreams of western thought. It rejected or corrupted three of the four most dynamic twentieth-century impulses: liberalism, democracy and socialism. The fourth, nationalism, emerged as a crude form of national socialism founded on white tribal exclusivism. (3)

The contemporary political and military issues analysed in detail later in this book have their roots, of course, in the struggles of the past. Boer, Briton and black fought each other in a farrago of alliances until the twentieth century; then South African whites tended to coalesce in joint opposition to black demands for equal rights. Despite public nods to the (sometimes) more liberal sentiments in London, the colonial and local English-speaking authorities laid the legal foundations of racial discrimination in the region. The Afrikaners, especially after the upset National Party victory in 1948, developed the previous discriminatory acts into a cohesive system called "apartheid" ("separateness"). Conventional wisdom held that the British won the Anglo-Boer war and lost the peace to republican Afrikanerdom. But until 1948 and, arguably, afterwards (notwithstanding the flutter in Whitehall because of the 1948 election results) Britain found in South Africa's white governments entirely satisfactory collaborators in safeguarding imperial/British economic and strategic interests.

Inside southern Africa these interests were defended primarily by the gun. In this frontier society, the morality of using force against black opponents was not extensively debated. But there has been continual debate on the safest and most efficient application of military power. The arguments about using black troops began in the eighteenth century. The commando military structure, the basis of the current "area force" system, can also be traced back to the early settler period. Irregular warfare, the issue of national service for whites, the political role of Afrikaner generals, the search for foreign allies and, above all, the military containment of the *swart gevaar*, the black threat, have been constant themes of South African history.

Frontier wars

Permanent white settlement began in 1652 when Jan van Riebeeck established a victualling station for the Dutch East India Company. Afrikaners like to compare 1652 with the earlier Pilgrim Fathers. Unlike the religious ideals of the American settlers, the Dutch motivation was entirely commercial. The Cape of Good Hope provided fresh produce for merchantmen on the long, hazardous sea route to the riches of the East. The company's settlement expanded and intermittent wars against the indigenous Khoikhoi and San (Bushmen) peoples ensued. This set the pattern for the next 300 years as more and more frontier wars were fought against black tribesmen. The nature of the company's tiny colony changed as new immigrants arrived: French, Germans and, after 1820, English settlers. In 1795 the British took over temporary control from the Dutch, but it was only at the end of the Napoleonic wars, in 1815, that Britain, for the price of £6 million, took formal possession of the Cape. The Cape station was a major outpost on the way to the jewel of the Empire, India. The English were often insensitive overlords who regarded the Dutch, or Boers and Afrikaners as they came to be known, as obstinate and inferior: "bold, bloody-minded, sanctimonious outdoor people", as one not unsympathetic British historian called them. (4) Afrikaners were excluded from jury service because of their language (Dutch which evolved into Afrikaans), forced to accept English-speaking ministers in their churches and were incensed by courts which encouraged black servants to give evidence against their masters. In sum, Boers resented paying taxes for the privilege of being browbeaten. Then the British abolished slavery, without fair compensation in Boer opinion.

This inspired a seminal event in Afrikaner history: the Great Trek. In modern Afrikaner nationalist historiography, the Great Trek and apartheid became almost historical synonyms. (5) In the mid-1830s thousands of Boers fled British control. Since there were no navigable rivers in the region, in their heavy oxwagons they sought refuge and independence in the African interior. According to a recent South African study:

> ...the Trek was, at bottom, inspired by a desire to escape from distant authorities which seemed to be both wrongly motivated and at the same time more effective than any other that the frontiersmen had previously known...[the expansion north and later eastwards] was, in its essentials, a story of black-white confrontation in which the white man, with his superior weapons and notion of individual ownership, his theodolite and his title deed, generally gained at the expense of the black. Black chiefdoms seldom became involved in inter-white quarrels, whereas the advancing whites were often able to exploit the divisions in black societies which developed all too frequently as a direct result of the initial loss of land. (6)

Some of the pioneers, or Voortrekkers, travelled north-eastwards into Natal to set up an independent republic. There, a small band of trekkers, led by Piet Retief, was treacherously slaughtered by Dingane, the Zulu king. Dingane ordered his impis to wipe out the remaining Boer laagers. The loose organisation of the Boer commandos and the incessant rivalry between them had aided the Zulu onslaught. The Voortrekker presence in Natal might have been completely eliminated but for Andries Pretorius (the eponym of Pretoria). He organised his commando of 500 Boers (and some Englishmen from Port Natal) into a disciplined force. On 15 December 1838 the trekkers laagered in a strong defensive position on the banks of the Ncome river. The next day the Zulu army, over 10,000 strong, wasted itself in heroic but futile assaults on the well-defended laager. Cannon and musket fire ravaged the Zulu ranks, which broke and ran when mounted Boers charged from the laager to complete the rout of the demoralised impis. To quote *The Oxford History of South Africa*, the Battle of Blood River "was a classic example of the devastating superiority of controlled force, by resolute men from a defensive position, over Africans armed with assegais and spears, however numerous and brave".

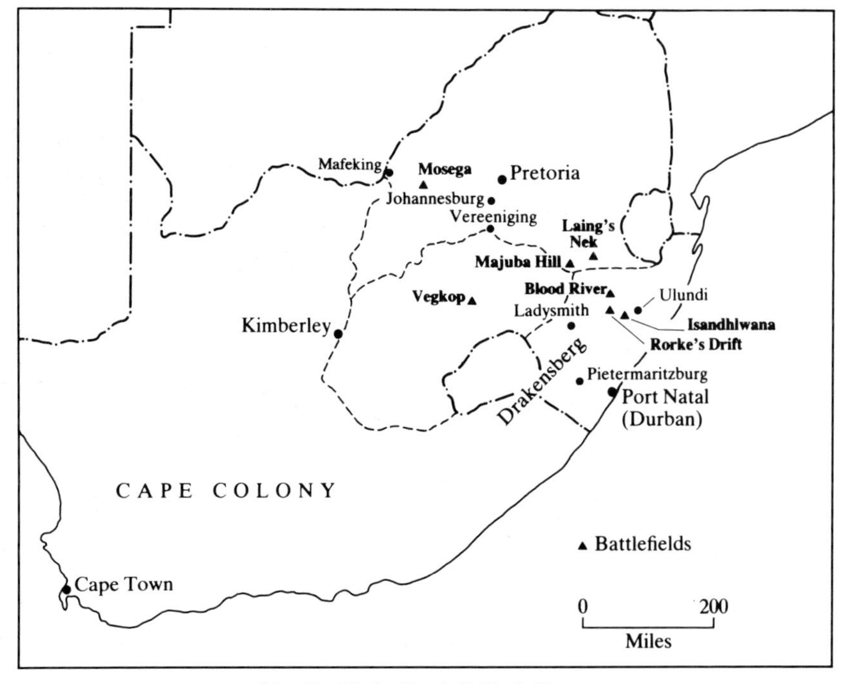

MAP 2 Major Battlefields & Sieges

Blood River, as much as the Great Trek, became enshrined in Afrikaner mythology. Before the battle, the Boers had sworn a covenant with God that if they were victorious they would honour this day for ever as a thanksgiving. So 16 December—the calendar opposite of 16 June when contemporary blacks celebrate the Soweto uprising—became the "day of the vow". From this event a whole series of myths emerged: that Blood River saved the Great Trek; that it marked the birth of the Afrikaner nation; and that the battle was a symbol of white Christianity's triumph over black heathens. Blood River was run in tandem with the fundamental Afrikaner myth: that there were no blacks in South Africa

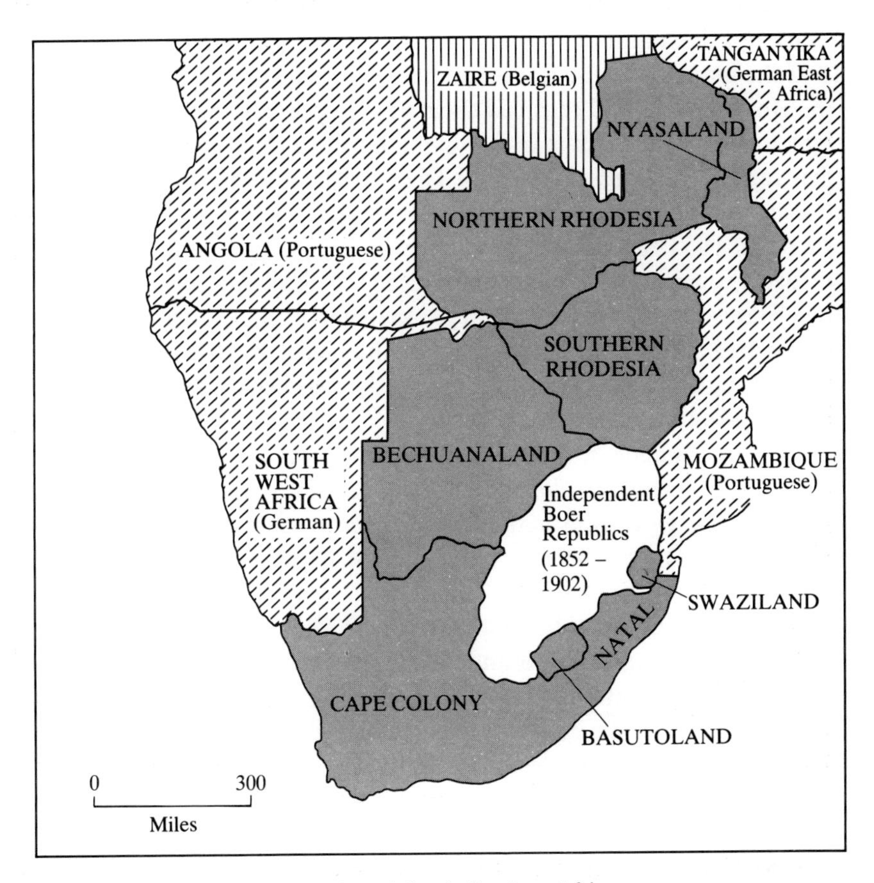

MAP 3 Colonialism in Southern Africa

when van Riebeeck arrived (apart from a few Bushmen); blacks were said to have moved south as the whites moved north, ignoring the evidence of hundreds of years of black settlement in the Cape. In short, argued Afrikaner nationalists, God had sided with them at Blood River, proof that He had called upon the Afrikaner *volk* (people) to keep South Africa white. (7)

In 1838 the trekkers had created a myth and temporarily defeated the Zulus, but the might of the British Empire proved too strong a force. By 1842 the majority of the Boers had been ejected from Natal by the British. Most of them had retraced their steps over the Drakensberg mountains to rejoin their compatriots living on the Transvaal highveld with their republicanism and Jehovah. The British annexed the Transvaal in 1848 (and again in 1871), but then released their grip in 1854 (and 1881). In 1854 the British reluctantly recognised the independence of the two fledgeling Afrikaner republics in the Transvaal and the Orange Free State. There was (temporary) independence, but little peace. The poorly organised republics squabbled amongst themselves—they even reached the brink of war in 1857—and the conflict with the local black tribes continued unabated. Then in 1867 diamonds were discovered near the confluence of the Vaal and Orange rivers where the diamond town of Kimberley was destined to rise. Fortune-hunters from the four corners of the globe, but mainly from Britain, rushed into the area and threatened to overwhelm the small, conservative Afrikaner communities.

The Transvaal republic, which claimed the diamond fields, found itself in dire economic straits and the campaigns against the Pedi tribe in the eastern Transvaal had fared badly. This was the chance the British had been waiting for. Lord Carnarvon, the British colonial secretary, had long cherished the design of unifying the Afrikaner states with Natal and the Cape to form a British-dominated federation. In 1877 Britain annexed the Transvaal under the pretext that it was unable to govern itself or contain the Zulu threat from the southeast. The Boers offered only token resistance.

Another major obstacle confronting British plans for a South African federation was the still-menacing Zulu army, now led by Cetshwayo. Blood River had revealed that the Zulu military machine, though effective against African opposition, was too inflexibly offensive. Yet the British, who were soon to clash with the Zulus, were themselves weakened by outmoded tactics. Cetshwayo was reluctant to be drawn into the complex tangle of Anglo-Boer relations, but the presence of the impis was anathema to the British, particularly Sir Bartle Frere, the new governor of the Cape. Frere issued the Zulu king an impossible ultimatum which would have meant dismantling the whole structure of his kingdom. When Cetshwayo not surprisingly refused, Frere launched an invasion.

The Zulu war of 1879 composed a pattern which became almost compulsory for the later military campaigns of the Empire: the opening tragedy, the heroic redemption and the final crushing victory. (8) The tragedy was Isandhlwana. Six companies of the 2nd Warwickshire Regiment were entirely wiped out. In all, 858 Britons and 470 men from native levies were killed. It was the worst British military disaster since the Afghan retreat of 1842. The heroic redemption came at Rorke's Drift where 110 Britons gallantly warded off waves of charges by 4,000 Zulu warriors. Six months later Lord Chelmsford, determined to redeem his reputation after Isandhlwana, staged a crushing victory at the Zulu capital of Ulundi. The imperial forces formed up in the classic formation, the hollow square, four deep with fixed bayonets, with guns and Gatlings at each corner. There was no digging in, no Boer laager. "They'll only be satisfied," said Chelmsford, thinking of his critics in London, "if we beat them fairly in the open." The Zulus flung themselves in suicidal waves against the walls of disciplined rifle fire. Not a single warrior got within 30 yards of the redcoat square. When the impis

PLATE 2.1 A laager, a defensive circle of wagons. (The Battle of Vechtkop.) *(Africana Museum.)*

faltered, Chelmsford unleashed the cavalry, the 17th Lancers. Zulu power was broken. Zululand was divided up and later incorporated into the Natal colony.

Isandhlwana had revealed British vulnerability to the world; the Boers could not fail but take heart at the pricking of the myth of the British Lion's invincibility. And they had a powerful new leader, Paul Kruger, "a coarse man, a man of spittoons and pipe smoke, home-spun philosophies on the stoep, religious bigotry: but so absolute were his principles, and so profound his sense of Afrikanerness, that he moved among his people like a prophet". (9) At the end of December 1880, the Transvaal Boers launched their first war of independence, perhaps the first modern national liberation struggle against foreign colonialists in southern Africa. No retributive British victory rescued imperial prestige this time: the three-month war was ignominy from start to finish. The British army, facing its first "European" foe since the Crimea, was disastrously defeated at the Battle of Majuba in February 1881. Overwhelmed by "arrogance and sun", as the poet Roy Macnab put it, and the revolutionary guerrilla tactics of individual rifle fire, 280 Britons were killed for the loss of one Boer. The Transvaal became independent once more, although the South African Republic, as it became known, was still bound by a vague British "suzerainty". It was the only occasion in the Victorian Empire when the British negotiated a settlement from the loser's side of the table. It was not the end of Boer struggle, but the beginning. And it was an indication that a unified South Africa would emerge only by force, British or Boer, or later, perhaps, black.

In 1886 gold was discovered in the Transvaal, on the Witwatersrand. The area was to become the largest single producer of gold in the world. The "red-necked blimps of the Brutish Empire" had seized the diamonds; the gold would be next. Initially, the gold rush brought prosperity to the South African Republic, but it also brought an influx of gold-hungry *uitlanders* (outsiders) who threatened to destroy the traditional political fabric of the young republic. *Uitlander* grievances, both real and imagined, grew. Britain's *fin de siècle* imperialists, particularly British High Commissioner Sir Alfred Milner and that visionary freebooter, Cecil Rhodes, could not resist exploiting *uitlander* demands for franchise rights in the Transvaal. Paul Kruger, however, had no illusions about British intentions: "It is not the vote, but my country that you want."

With the connivance of senior members of the British government, Rhodes plotted an *uitlander* rising against Kruger, but the premature Jameson raid in 1895 undermined his plans. The Jameson debacle fired

Afrikaner nationalism from Cape Town to the Limpopo: in the following year an alliance was made between the Transvaal republic and the Orange Free State. The Jameson raid had given the republics a genuine reason to rearm, but this escalation also gave currency to those in British circles who asserted that Kruger was trying not only to preserve his republic, but to construct a "dominion of Afrikanerdom" throughout southern Africa. As the haggling reached a climax in 1899, the Boers were faced with a stark choice: to reform themselves out of existence or to fight. But Kruger was not "bluffing up to the cannon's mouth": he chose to fight rather than surrender his sovereignty.

The first twentieth-century war

The Anglo-Boer war, or the *Tweede Vryheidsoorlog*, the "Second War of Independence" as Afrikaners call it, began on 11 October 1899. This conflict proved to be the British Empire's Vietnam. The imperium was potentially doomed the moment the Boers showed how a professional British army could be outwitted by a relatively small number of determined guerrillas. Britain was ill-prepared for this clash of wills: her troops marched into the first twentieth-century war ready to fight with nineteenth-century tactics. The mounted, highly mobile Boers, with their magazine-loading Mausers and their devastating "Long Tom" artillery, soon drove the imperial forces into siege positions at Ladysmith, Kimberley and Mafeking. Mafeking, in particular, soon became world-famous as the town that resisted the Boers for seven long months. Its paladin was the commander, Robert Baden-Powell. He later founded the Boy Scouts, but behaved abysmally towards the town's blacks, whom he reduced to starvation by keeping the garrison's whites comfortably fed.*

The war became one of attrition. Eventually, the Empire fielded over 450,000 men; the Boers could never muster more than 35,000. It was, therefore, inevitable that the British would win the conventional aspects of the war. Lord Kitchener, the hero of Omdurman, smashed into the Boer republics and captured the main towns. In reply, the Boers resorted to guerrilla tactics. The Boer commandos were more than a match for Britain's unwieldy war machine, which was quite unused to this sort of mobile, irregular war. The Boers sabotaged railway lines, the main means of supply, and learned how to turn retreat into assault by suddenly turning on their exhausted pursuers.

*That, at least, was the judgement of Pakenham's *The Boer War*; Tim Jeal's recent work, *Baden-Powell*, refutes this allegation.

The Boer war is often called the last of the gentleman's wars. Yet the British commanders, caught off-balance by the Afrikaners' unorthodox tactics, often reacted with brutality. Kitchener intensified his scorched earth policy by burning down farms and herding women and children into refugee camps. These were called "concentration" camps after the *reconcentrado* camps used by Spain in her Cuban colony. Disease killed thousands of Afrikaner noncombatants, especially undernourished children in the squalid camps. Emily Hobhouse, the Jane Fonda of her day, carried the cause to the British public. Her personal crusade fuelled the anti-war movement led by David Lloyd George, the Liberal leader. International criticism finally stung the imperial government into allowing the Boers to negotiate a peace settlement. Britain had won a savage war and introduced a moderate peace, which was signed at Vereeniging in May 1902, despite the passionate opposition of Afrikaner *bittereinders* who wanted to fight on. And so the young republics were herded back under the British flag.

In money and lives, no British war since 1815 had been so prodigal. Milner had been a dedicated warmonger: his little Armageddon had cost the lives of over 22,000 imperial troops and 7,000 Boer combatants. As many as 28,000 Boers died in the camps, of whom about 22,000 were

PLATE 2.2 Boer war commandos: three generations. *(Africana Museum.)*

under 16. Many Africans suffered too: over 14,000 died in separate camps for African prisoners. (10) The Afrikaners might have forgiven Britain's heavy-handed treatment in the Cape, their expulsion from Natal, the shifty seizure of the Kimberley diamond mines, even the notorious Jameson raid, but the bodies of concentration camp victims were to be dragon's teeth, sowing a fierce and bitter xenophobia among Afrikaners. And what was this barbarous and unnecessary war intended to achieve? "It was all for the gold mines," says a British Tommy in Thomas Pakenham's sweeping classic on the war. (11) Maybe he was right. The British parliament rewarded Kitchener with a £50,000 victory purse, which he immediately cabled his brokers to invest in South African goldmining stocks. And, according to Pakenham, the arrogant imperial generals failed to heed the military lessons of the tragedy:

> The central tactical lesson of the Boer War eluded them. The reason for those humiliating reverses was not the marksmanship of the Boers, nor their better guns or rifles, nor the crass stupidity of the British generals—all myths which British people found it convenient to believe. It was that the smokeless, long-range, high-velocity, small-bore magazine bullet from rifle or machine-gun—plus the trench—had decisively tilted the balance against attack and in favour of defence. (12)

They would soon learn the lesson the hard way in Flanders.

The Union's wars

Despite the very bitter heritage of the Boer war, the four colonies of South Africa reconciled themselves to unity. In 1910 the Union of South Africa was formed. But this was not quite the federation that Milner and his ilk had imagined. Milner's arithmetic for anglicising the old republics in a new imperial unit rested on one crucial foundation: the inflow of British immigrants. For decades, Afrikaners bred prolifically and contrived to let in only a small number of immigrants. Through sheer numbers (and political determination) Afrikaners came to dominate the South African state, a lesson which they now fear will be applied by blacks, not Britons. Afrikaners have argued also that they hold the land by right of conquest. In fact, the black tribes and kingdoms were overcome mainly by imperial forces and the economic revolution introduced by the Randlords, the foreign mining magnates.

The 1910 Union enshrined the principle of white rule in southern Africa. In effect, the London government traded its half-hearted protection of "native" interests for the sake of Anglo-Boer reconciliation, greed for gold and imperial strategy. In 1912 the Union Defence Force (UDF) was established, merging both the Boer commando and the British regimental traditions. An imperial garrison tarried until 1921, although British influence remained paramount in the local armed forces until 1948. Yet the bitterness of the Boer war never died. As the South African writer, William Plomer, noted: "Out of that bungled unwise war/ An alp of unforgiveness grew."

Many Afrikaners, including members of the UDF, were reluctant to fight on behalf of the Empire that had just defeated them. The litmus test was German South West Africa. Many Boers regarded Germany as a friendly power, especially after its support during the 1899-1902 war. The crunch came in 1914 when the King of England declared war on Germany on behalf of the Empire. Prime Minister Louis Botha, a former Boer general, promised to invade South West Africa. Botha sent a telegram to one of his Boer war comrades to take up arms and drew the reply: "Certainly, but on which side do we fight?" Some senior military commanders, veterans of the recent anti-British war, rose in revolt. Generals "Manie" Maritz, Christiaan de Wet and Koos de la Rey summoned the faithful from their old commandos. After 150 rebels and 132 members of the UDF were killed, the revolt was stamped out by the loyalist sections of the UDF. The Afrikaner rebellion was over, but new martyrs had been added to the nationalist pantheon. (13)

Despite the internal frictions, UDF troops conquered South West Africa: the Germans surrendered in July 1915. The UDF was then sent to German East Africa, where they fought a protracted war against the wily German commander, General Paul von Lettow-Vorbeck. South African troops also fought in the Middle East and in Flanders. For South Africa, the most famous battle on the Western Front took place at Delville Wood, where in a few long days the UDF suffered 2,815 casualties. In November 1918 the carnage caused by the deadly trinity of wire, trenches and machine guns was over. To the allied side South Africa had contributed 190,000 white and 60,000 "non-white" soldiers, as well as 25,000 non-white auxiliaries. For gallantry on the battlefield, South Africans earned 13 Victoria Crosses. At home, the blacks who had volunteered—encouraged in some cases by the African National Congress (then the South African Native National Congress)—received scant reward or political concessions for their service to the country.

In the inter-war period the UDF saw action on the domestic front: in 1922, when it crushed the Bondelswart rebellion in South West Africa and the white mineworkers' revolt on the Rand. The imperial government helped build up a local air force with the gift of a 100 aircraft. Despite various attempts to set up a South African navy in this period, the Royal Navy dominated the Cape route from its base in Simonstown (leased from 1921 until 1975).

Within less than a generation after the war to end all wars, the call to arms sounded again. And, like the Allies, South Africa was almost completely unprepared. The cabinet and parliament split along the old tribal fault-lines on whether to stay neutral or fight, but a decision to join the Allies was taken in parliament by 80 votes to 67. The prime minister, General J B M Hertzog, who was in favour of neutralism, resigned and General Jan Smuts took over the premiership for the second time. The more conservative nationalists veered even more to the right in open sympathy with Hitler; some of them, including the future prime minister, B J Vorster, were interned. There was no conscription during the war, because of Afrikaner resistance. But a massive recruiting drive took place. Over 200,000 uniformed South Africans joined up, of whom about 9,000 were killed. Blacks volunteered in their tens of thousands. Despite the official policy that they should remain noncombatants, many took an active part in the fighting, especially in North Africa. Black leaders were more guarded in their support this time: they were cynical about the Atlantic Charter's freedoms being extended to southern Africa. During the 1942 scare that the Japanese might invade, Smuts talked about training and arming a non-European army, but the plan was quietly dropped as the Axis threat waned. South Africans of all races fought with gallantry and distinction, proving particularly excellent as pilots in the North African and European theatres. One of their most famous operations was during the 1944 "Warsaw Concerto", when South Africans flew Liberators to drop supplies to the Polish underground army besieged in the capital by Nazi forces. Of the 41 planes flown by South African squadrons, 11 were shot down in the vain attempt to relieve the garrison.

After the Second World War, South Africa rallied to the Western side in the Cold War: its pilots once more distinguished themselves during the Berlin Blockade (1948-49) and the see-saw war in Korea (1950-53). In the immediate post-war period Jan Smuts strode the Western stage as a world statesman. He had been a key figure in the creation of the League of Nations, and he played a major role in the establishment of the United Nations. This remarkable man was a visionary to be sure, but his ideals were also tinged with cynical attempts to extend white *Lebensraum* in Africa, especially in the League of Nations' "mandated" territory in South West Africa. He had also hoped to swop German

East Africa for Mozambique south of the Zambezi. He intended as well that Southern Rhodesia and the British protectorates (modern-day Botswana, Lesotho and Swaziland) would also fall into the Union's lap. Then Pretoria would control a territory three times its size before the Second World War. (14) As a Western elder statesman and friend of Winston Churchill, Smuts attended the opening conference of the UN in San Francisco in April 1945. It was Smuts who drafted the original declaration of aims in the preamble of the UN Charter, with its soaring words sanctifying human rights. Ironically, Smuts created a massive stick which would drive his country from the community of nations. At home, he had no vision: his race policy was a muddled paternalism subordinated to the unshakeable principle that white interests must always come first. Even if Smuts, distracted as he was by international events, had tried to practise at home what he preached abroad, he would not have been able to carry his fellow Afrikaner leaders, who were obsessed with domestic racial issues.

Soon the Nazi sympathisers in the National Party would rise to power. In futile counterpoint, some of the returning soldiers who had fought in the name of democracy and human equality adopted more liberal attitudes, which were to surface in ex-servicemen's organisations such as the Springbok Legion and the Torch Commando. It would be to no avail. Racial policy hardened. In the UN General Assembly, in December 1946, Mrs Pandit of India lambasted South Africa's racial discrimination. Even then, Dr A B Xuma, the ANC leader, was busy lobbying UN delegates. Soon South Africa, the honoured ally, was to be branded a "polecat among nations". Britain, it is true, held the line in the Security Council. But the trumpets were sounding the imperial retreat for *Pax Britannica*, especially in Africa. Elsewhere on the continent, the other colonial empires began their recessionals in haste, or slowly and in anger. From these winds of war and change, a new great power was to emerge in southern Africa. It was to be a harsh imperium based upon the naked assertion of white power: the *Pax Pretoria*.

References and notes:

1. See Appendix 1 for a summary of the wars in the region.
2. J Morris, *Heaven's Command*, Penguin, Harmondsworth, 1986, p. 422.
3. For a brilliant analysis of Afrikaner political thought, see W de Klerk, *The Puritans in Africa*, Penguin, Harmondsworth, 1976. For a comparison of Nazi and Afrikaner ideologies, see B Bunting, *The Rise of the South African Reich*, Penguin, Harmondsworth, 1969.
4. Morris, *op. cit.*, p. 50.
5. For a concise summary of the debate on the Great Trek, see P Colenbrander, "Putting the Great Trek back into Context," *The Star*, (weekly edition), 13 April 1988.

6. T Davenport, *South Africa: A Modern History*, Macmillan, Johannesburg, 1987, pp. 53 and 124. This quotation summarises Davenport's views on the Great Trek and the later British expansion into the Eastern Cape.
7. For a summary of the debate on Blood River, see J de Villiers, "Blood River: the Myth that led to more Myths," *The Star*, (weekly edition), 23 February 1988.
8. Morris, *op. cit.*, pp. 431-38.
9. *Ibid.*, p. 440.
10. Davenport, *op. cit.*, p. 221.
11. T Pakenham, *The Boer War*, Ball, Johannesburg, 1982.
12. *Ibid.*, p. 574.
13. For a sympathetic appraisal of Boer sentiments in this period, see J Meintjes, *De La Rey: Lion of the West*, Keartland, Johannesburg, 1966.
14. Davenport, *op. cit.*, pp. 275-6.

3

Winds of change and war

40 years in the wilderness

In 1945, South Africa was a small military power, still nestling in the protective bosom of an exhausted British Empire. At the UN, Jan Smuts epitomised the country's international respectability. But, after 1948, the paragon was destined to become a pariah. The South African government, once in the vanguard of the lobby which insisted that League of Nations' economic sanctions were the best guarantee of collective security, even to the extent of urging an oil embargo against Italy in 1935, today finds itself the object of an unprecedented range of UN sanctions. (1)

The UN began its long-running vendetta with criticisms of Pretoria's treatment of its Indian community, then the illegal control of South West Africa, and later the SADF's attacks on neighbouring states. But the single main cause of world obloquy has been apartheid. There is no doubt that many of the tirades have been based upon sanctimonious ignorance, ceremonial angst and downright double standards. Other obnoxious regimes, however, may be no less repressive, and the behaviour of their police no less outrageous, but no other state has based its oppression so "legally" and so overtly on race. Pretoria is condemned because its policy is both impolitic and immoral. Universal public opinion cannot but agree with William Faulkner's famous remark: "To live anywhere in the world today and be against equality because of race or colour is like living in Alaska and being against snow."

There are many, perhaps too many, political histories of apartheid, often very polemical in tone. The concern here is primarily with a military, not moral, analysis, in so far as such a distinction is feasible. Nevertheless, the implicit core of the military conflicts detailed later is the system of apartheid, racial discrimination and domination founded upon a spurious but ornately legalised basis. Afrikaners set themselves a Herculean task: "a womb-to-tomb surveillance plan for the subjugated population".(2) Only Hitler and Stalin attempted social engineering on so audacious a scale. But they had the manpower. Critics might allege that Israelis are actually trying something of a similar nature in Palestine today, but in Israel, Pretoria's favourite paradigm, Jews outnumber, just, the Arabs in the occupied territories. History, of course, is more than a numbers game, but demography does count, especially in South Africa.

Apartheid tried to command the waves to stop: 30 million are classified at birth and, usually, for life; eight million black citizens have been denationalised; at least 3.5 million—except for a tiny fraction, all blacks, coloureds and Asians —have been physically removed, or "relocated", as Afrikaner bureaucrats put it, often to the impoverished, cramped 13% of the country, the homelands allocated to the 75% majority of the population. African politics has traditionally been about land: pushing so many land-hungry people, often rooted in ancestral terrain, into such small rural and urban ghettoes was bound to encourage revolutionary trends, even if all tribal, ideological, class or racial factors were miraculously removed. The UN talks, with justification, about this "crime against humanity", a term which has been abused by overuse. Yet to black—and not a few white—Africans, apartheid is the same anathema as the Holocaust is to Jews. Apartheid, the slave trade and the Holocaust have become near-synonyms of human evil.

Afrikaners are not uniquely evil people. The architects of apartheid saw it as a rational, even idealistic, segregationist alternative to an unacceptably integrated future. The homelands, to the racialist philosophers who helped foster apartheid, were deemed to be the black counterpart of Afrikaner nationalism. Blacks were not thought fit to vote in white South Africa, but they could vote in their tribal bantustans to reinforce, in the sham parliaments, the oligarchs selected by Pretoria. If Pretoria had shared the land proportionately, many foreign critics might have been more inclined to accept partition—as in India, Palestine, Korea or Germany—as a stalemate resolution of endemic tension. But Pretoria did not proceed to the logical extension of apartheid, a white homeland, and ended up using military power to retain an unequal patrimony. (3)

Afrikaners were to pay a huge price for their misplaced idealism and selfish cruelty. In 1988 the National Party celebrated 40 years in power. The opposition white Progressive Federal Party asked "What is there to celebrate?" and launched a campaign to advertise the "40 years in the wilderness". It pointed out the following:

Emigration: In 1948 the National Party ended a white immigration scheme that brought 51,000 people to South Africa in one year. In 1988 the government announced that 11,174 (mainly skilled) white South Africans had emigrated (although thousands more whites were still entering the country, mainly from Zimbabwe and Britain).

Sport: In 1948 South Africans won two gold, one silver and one bronze medal at the Olympic games. In 1988 Zola Budd was pilloried because she had once been a South African citizen.

Bureaucracy: In 1948 South Africa managed with 12 cabinet ministers and 153 MPs. In 1988 Pretoria was augmenting the 144 cabinet ministers and 1,369 MPs of the various tricameral and homeland parliaments.

The Economy: In 1948 Pretoria loaned war-weary Britain £80 million. In 1988 it was estimated that in three years R18 billion in private capital had been lost to South Africa because of disinvestment. Official foreign government and UN sanctions had increased that tally by many more billions.

Defence: Within four months of taking office in 1948, the minister of defence disarmed the South African Cape Corps and the Native Military Corps, both of which had distinguished themselves in World War Two. He also forbad them to wear their military uniforms. Some, 40 years later, had not received their military pensions, because they had been denationalised into the homelands. By 1988 the African National Congress had welcomed tens of thousands of young blacks and coloureds who were all too eager to put on battledress.

Fewer and fewer South African whites wanted to listen to such mournful comparisons. The white "liberal" opposition had been reduced to a feuding rump in parliament; its traditional English-speaking supporters had crossed over in droves to join the National Party, or even the far-right Conservative Party, after 1987 the official opposition. So what of 40 years of international pressures, sanctions and moral crusades? As many critics had feared, the Afrikaner rulers had become even more intransigent and the South African Defence Force (SADF), the successor of the Union Defence Force, was the mightiest military machine on the continent. But that was only part of the picture: South Africa had become a military giant with feet of clay. Incessant wars on the borders and intermittent domestic insurrections, as in the late British Empire, had caused South Africa to suffer from imperial overstretch. Like all profligate empires, the *Pax Pretoria* was beginning to collapse under its own weight. Empires tend to show signs of crumbling at the edges, even though the rot usually starts at home. "Far-called our navies melt away," wrote Kipling, as Britain entered its Edwardian twilight. By 1988 the South African navy had practically ceased to exist as far as a "blue-water strategy", capable of a conventional defence of the Cape sea route, was concerned. And, as we shall see, there were many other vulnerable points.

International pressures on South Africa were based upon a number of assumptions. The most obvious was that neither the black neighbouring states, as they became independent, nor the indigenous black majority were strong enough to overwhelm the well-armed white minority on their own. Short of joint military intervention by the great powers, isolation and sanctions, it was argued, would help history along and persuade the white rulers that timeous political negotiation, rather than eventual military surrender, was in their own best interest. The economic, political, military and, perhaps most important, the psychological dimensions have been enmeshed in a sustained and complex international debate. (4) South Africa became a political football for many campaigners to kick towards their own, often vastly different, goals.

South Africa in the late 1980s was a little like the USSR in the late 1940s, militarily strong on the ground and in the air and armed with an embryonic nuclear arsenal, but beleaguered, looking out on the world over an expanse of brittle satellites, totalitarian, paranoid, motivated in part by ideology, reliant upon its army, police, its reserves of gold and scarce minerals, its helot workforce, and deluded both by its own propaganda and real and imagined external hostility into believing in a cosmic cleavage: advanced civilisation versus the foreign onslaught. The crucial difference is that the Kremlin's leaders evinced the conviction, probably sincerely, that time and history were on their side in this titanic struggle. Pretoria's Manichean vision, aptly summarised as a "total onslaught [which] equates the 'red peril' with the 'black peril', and defence of apartheid with defence of Western Christian values", lacked such crucial confidence. (5) South Africa's white supremacists were fast using up their future.

The gathering storm

In 1945 the African National Congress was an insignificant organisation, and the KGB had far more important things on its mind than Pretoria's racial eccentricities. The Russians did make a play for a piece of Africa when Foreign Minister Molotov demanded not only a Soviet mandate over ex-Italian Libya, but also Russian control over the ex-Italian Eritrean port of Massawa (which it later accomplished through its support of the radical Dergue regime in Ethiopia in the 1970s). Elsewhere, colonial Africa, and Asia, afforded Moscow many opportunities. The Soviet Union was in the business of franchising revolutions, so Khrushchev rushed to sponsor "wars of national liberation" in the 1950s and 1960s. Initially, Moscow usually sought influence rather than real estate. It had many advantages: it was not tainted with the original sin of (conventional) imperialism; its superpower status, ideology and industrialisation offered a model to African socialists; and it did not have to contend with squeamish liberal public opinion at home. It could provide little economic help, but it poured in a cornucopia of cheap, simple and reliable small-arms. In later years, Africans found the Russians to be tactless colonisers. The second generation of African leaders carped about minimal economic assistance, and Soviet opportunism, especially in grabbing natural resources such as fishing rights and minerals, the very neo-imperialism which Moscow branded as a Western evil. The Soviets lost ground when they propped up the continent's nastiest tyrants such as Idi Amin and Francisco Macías Nguema of Equatorial Guinea. But it took nearly 40 years for many Africans to conclude that the Russians were alarmingly powerful, ruthless, arrogant, communist *and* white, after all. China, of course, was a useful radical alternative. The Chinese were not white and were more empathetic towards fellow underdeveloped countries, but they had less money to spare even than the Russians.

In the first flush of decolonisation in Africa, however, the Russians were often the only reliable military backers for revolutionaries. Moscow's great ally in the scramble to decolonise was the USA. Washington did as much as Moscow to undermine Britain's often half-hearted attempts to hang on to its imperial possessions. Equally important was the hostility to empire among the European left, particularly in Britain: the concept of imperialism as a "civilising mission", so characteristic of the past, and South Africa's present, was forgotten. Both Russia and America tended to define African developments in East-West ideological terms. The new African nations were expected to choose sides in the Cold War. In essence, the old imperial powers, more knowledgeable and cynical about the nuances of African politics, eschewed such simplistic options. They tended to see African events in terms of the North/South divide, sometimes black versus white, but not usually East versus West. Washington might have characterised its failures in the Angolan civil war as "losing" Angola as it lost China; the Europeans, on the other hand, judged America's Angolan policy in 1976 as prudent, if unusual, restraint. In South Africa's case, Britain combined sanctimonious moral disapproval with the uninhibited pursuit of economic self-interest. The north Europeans, of course, were always more ready to provide moral condemnation of white racists (and blankets and food to their victims), while the more cynical southern Europeans emphasised unabashed commercial interests. France, typically, buttered its bread on both sides: it managed in the 1960s to build up its military and economic ties with francophone Africa while also playing a major role in the modernisation of the South African Defence Force. (6)

In the immediate post-war period, the more conservative elements in French and British society were intensely irritated by Washington's criticisms of their colonial policies and, indeed, by the alleged Americanisation of Western Europe. In Paris, for example, the National Assembly tried to ward off creeping Americanisation by outlawing the import and sale of Coca-Cola. Yet, despite the very major disagreements over colonial policies, the Western powers usually closed ranks in the face of Cold War confrontations, not least in the UN Security Council. There the powerful veto was wielded by the British and Americans to protect South Africa from the increasingly hostile array of newly independent third world states. Pretoria was also shielded by its membership of the British Commonwealth. Pretoria, however, disapproved of Britain's invasion of the Suez Canal Zone in 1956, because it provided the ideal opportunity for the USSR to bring Africa into the Cold War arena. Egypt's leader, Abdul Nasser, turned to Moscow after his humiliation at the hands of the Anglo-French and Israeli forces. Then Russia backed Nkrumah's Ghana and in 1958 Sékou Touré's Guinea. Soviet advance was impeded by the relatively graceful French and British imperial retreat from Africa, which became more an issue of timetables than principles. The important exceptions were Algeria and Rhodesia. The mayhem, however, induced by Belgium's precipitous exit from the Congo did provide an opportunity for Soviet meddling, although Moscow lacked the military throwpower, then, to intervene decisively.

The Congo debacle radicalised the new balance of forces in the UN General Assembly, where the Afro-Asian blocs had risen from 15 out of 50 members in 1956 to 73 out of 125 in 1965. The rowdy newcomers increasingly sided with Moscow and Peking, especially in the ritual denunciation of Pretoria. The Sharpeville massacre of March 1960, although not like the calculated slaughter of Indians at Amritsar in 1919, raised the tempo of the UN's righteous indignation. It was also the year that Harold Macmillan, the British premier, delivered his famous "wind of change" speech in Cape Town. That was to be the last visit of a

PLATE 3.1 P. W. Botha; General Magnus Malan; Ian Smith; P. K. van der Byl. *(Former Rhodesian Ministry of Information)*

British prime minister to the pariah. Despite Macmillan's (gentle) warning, London refused to accede to the UN's calls for economic boycotts. In 1961 South Africa felt compelled to leave the Commonwealth. In that year it also became a republic. In 1963 the UN slapped a ban on the sales of arms to South Africa. The ban was not (yet) mandatory. In the same year the Organisation of African Unity (OAU) was set up, even though its title was the ultimate misnomer. Despite the incessant backbiting, the OAU emerged as an important forum for the verbal assault on apartheid, the only issue which all the members could (nearly) always agree upon. In the following year South Africa was pushed out of active participation in the General Assembly, which continued to hammer away at the new republic's occupation of South West Africa/Namibia.

Rhodesia's illegal declaration of independence in 1965 sharpened the UN's focus on southern Africa. Pretoria blamed the collapse of the British-sponsored federations in east and central Africa on the evils of African nationalism and communist intrigue, but the ambiguity of British colonial policy was the more likely culprit. In both areas Britain had vacillated between the themes of responsible government for whites and trusteeship for blacks. As a result, the Kenyans were denied what Rhodesian whites got in the 1920s. Despite the influence of the Kenyan settlers' lobby, and because of the Mau-Mau emergency (from 1952-1960), it was impossible for London to grant self-government to Kenya's 60,000 settlers. In the end Pretoria faced not two white-dominated federations, but five black republics, all hostile, except for docile Malawi, and a rebellion to succour in Rhodesia. South Africa was now castigated at the UN for its economic and military aid to the "bunch of cowboys" in Salisbury. And the former British protectorates (later Botswana, Lesotho and Swaziland) also escaped Pretoria's political, if not economic, clutches.

Tar Babies

Nevertheless, trade with South Africa was more important to the Western powers than UN resolutions, especially as white power seemed firmly entrenched in southern Africa. This was the conclusion drawn in 1969 by President Richard Nixon and his security advisor, Henry Kissinger. Kissinger used to joke about his former Vietnam policies. "We will not repeat the same old mistakes," he would say, then pause for effect and add, "We will make our own." He was true to his word in South East Asia as well as in Africa. In 1969 he had backed the key decisions that originated from the National Security Study Memorandum (NSSM) 39. The memorandum tried to find a compromise which would allow America to avoid having to choose between white and black Africa, a perennial theme of US African policy. The essence of NSSM 39 (in fact, option two of the study) was that black states should not be heedlessly upset—although the ANC called the study an "infamous document"—but trade with South Africa would continue. The white republic was virulently anti-communist, wasn't it? And, unlike South Vietnam, it could fight its own battles, provided it secured some foreign arms. This gelled precisely with the so-called Nixon doctrine which was then in vogue: the doctrine encouraged pro-Western states to defend themselves with American help, but not with American troops. South Africa was, therefore, a useful ally and so was Portugal. The Portuguese Azores could prove vital in the shipment of arms to Israel (as the Yom Kippur war verified). NATO weapons were happily deployed by the Portuguese in their African wars. And South Africa's secret service, the Bureau for State Security (BOSS), had close ties with the CIA. Pretoria was not only a major trading partner, but amenable in other ways, such as helping the National Aeronautics and Space Administration to set up a moonshot-tracking station in South Africa. And Rhodesia? Why treat it like a leper? Rhodesian sanctions were not apparently working, so why should a pro-capitalist government like Nixon's penalise American businessmen in the name of a policy that had failed? This applied especially to the strategic metal chrome. After all, the Russians were surreptitiously buying the supposedly sanctioned ore and then reselling it to Washington at a tidy profit. Why should Americans buy this more expensive "Russian" chrome when they could get a better bargain from pro-Western Rhodesia, and at a good discount? (In 1971, with the passage in Congress of the Byrd Amendment, the USA traded openly in chrome with Salisbury.)

A section of NSSM 39 read:

> The whites are here to stay, and the only way that constructive change can come is through them. There is no hope for the blacks to gain the political rights they seek through violence... which will only lead to chaos and increased opportunities for the communists...We can, through selective relaxation of our stance toward the white regimes, encourage some modification of their current racial and colonial policies...Our tangible interests form a basis for our contacts in the region, and these can be maintained at an acceptable political cost. (7)

The National Security Council obviously discussed this important policy decision in a fog of ignorance. Vice-President Spiro "Ted" Agnew praised the South Africans for having achieved independence with a declaration modelled on America's, until Nixon gently suggested, "Ted, you mean Rhodesia, don't you?" (8) A dismayed State Department quoted the story of Brer Fox who made a Tar Baby to catch Brer Rabbit: each time Brer Rabbit hit the Tar Baby, he became more stuck to it. So they dubbed it the "Tar Baby Option". The name and the policy stuck as well. (9) John Chettle, the South Africa Foundation representative in Washington, said the policy's "ambition ...was to cover itself so thickly in grease that nobody could get hold of it".

After this green light, US support for the whites became overt. In March 1971 the US Export-Import Bank changed its policy to allow long-term loans to Pretoria. IBM and ITT supplied computers and other electronic equipment to the SADF. Between 1967 and 1972 the USA sold 1,376 aircraft of various types to the ex-pariah, including ten big C-130 troop carriers. In 1972 NATO secretly requested its supreme allied commander in the Atlantic to devise plans to protect the Cape sea route, in collaboration with Pretoria. From 1972 NATO helped to furnish sophisticated electronic equipment for Project Advocate, a huge surveillance and communications base near Simonstown. In March 1974 the French and South African navies held joint manoeuvres. (10) Even when Britain announced her withdrawal from the Simonstown base in October 1974, NATO officials hinted to Pretoria that contingency plans for the allied defence of the Cape would not be affected. Pretoria desperately wanted *formal* membership of NATO or some South Atlantic equivalent. That would have been political dynamite for the West. But the secret military accords, from Pretoria's perspectives, were a lot better than nothing. (11)

Despite the stickiness of the Tar Baby option, the tide of events was moving against South Africa. In 1972 the pro-South African regime in the Malagasy Republic was overthrown by radicals furious at the Pretoria connection. Then the Portuguese coup proved both Kissinger and the Tar Baby option wrong. Russia had lain relatively low in Africa after the Congo crisis, a tendency reinforced perhaps by the humiliation endured during the Cuban missiles drama of 1962. While the Portuguese armies retreated from Mozambique and Angola, the ancient monarchy in Ethiopia was usurped by the savage Dergue, which became dependent upon Soviet arms and Cuban troops. Russia was ousted from Somalia in 1977, but there were much bigger pickings in next-door Ethiopia, Somalia's enemy. After the largest airlift in African history and the biggest

African battles since the desert war of the 1940s, Russian generals and their Cuban allies broke the back of a Somalian army they had created a few years before. Then the USSR helped the Ethiopian army to stamp on, but not out, Cuba's former allies among the rebels fighting for Eritrean independence. The Soviets proved themselves inconsistent allies, but supreme opportunists. Washington, traumatised by its defeat in Vietnam, stood and gawked while Moscow chalked up crushing victories in Angola and Ethiopia. African states could not but be impressed by Russia's mailed fist.

Before 1974 the odd African revolution had fallen into Moscow's lap. After 1974, especially in southern Africa, the Kremlin perceived a consistently advantageous revolutionary pattern. The Russians placed—

> ...a special faith in the men and regimes coming to power in Ethiopia, Mozambique and Angola. These were revolutions, as the Soviets judged them, made of stiffer stuff, in part because they were won in armed struggle, led by men who bore arms rather than pamphlets, and in part because they faced real and powerful external threats that would keep them from growing soft. For five years, from 1974 to 1979, Soviet excitement mounted. (12)

Pretoria was more than perturbed by these developments. Angola and Mozambique were now ideological enemies and potential military threats. The SADF had retreated from the Angolan civil war in early 1976, "stabbed in the back" by America, according to Pretoria. Britain had pulled out of the Simonstown agreement and France reneged on its arms deals with South Africa. Kissinger's hectic "shuttle diplomacy" had not ended the war in Rhodesia; it escalated after the abortive Geneva conference of late 1976. Moreover, the dramatic Soweto revolt had coincided with Kissinger's would-be peace brokerage. Nor had any progress been made in ending the war in northern Namibia. By the end of 1976 Kissinger was out of a job as secretary of state, and South Africa had secured few tangible political gains from the Nixon doctrine. True, some important military equipment had been obtained, but, according to R W Johnson, Kissinger's diplomacy had involved the manipulation (downwards) of the gold price—the mainstay of the South African economy—particularly during the big squeeze on Ian Smith in mid-1976. (13) Earlier, Nixon, forced ultimately by the deficit financing of the Vietnam war, allowed the gold price to float above the traditional $35 an ounce. The upwards movement—$220 an ounce when Nixon resigned—helped South Africa during the international recession induced by the 1973 massive OPEC oil-price hikes and the supply problems caused by the Arab oil embargo against Pretoria. As Johnson acknowledged, by 1974 the US had several reasons for wanting to depress the gold price (such as reducing the value of Russian gold sales, hostility towards French fiscal policy and asserting the primacy of the dollar) which may not have been concerned directly with Kissinger's African adventures. (14) Nonetheless, IMF gold auctions had helped push the gold price down to $107 by July 1976. South Africa's gold was no longer an apparently invulnerable hedge against international economic pressure or recession. The fall of the Shah of Iran in 1979 jabbed another vulnerable pressure point: oil supplies.

Moreover, in 1977, a Democrat, President Jimmy Carter, entered the White House determined to take a tougher line on Rhodesia and apartheid. His vociferous black ambassador, Andrew Young, rode shotgun on the new African policy. Young went so far as to call the Cubans a "stabilising force" in Africa, which was too much for such conservative African leaders as Zaire's Mobutu. Pretoria, especially, regarded Carter as held in thrall to the black American vote. Pik Botha expressed the angry mood of his government when he said: "Must I pay the price of Mr Young's hatred of white America?"

Carter had other counsellors. His national security adviser, Zbigniew Brzezinski, was as hostile as Kissinger to Soviet penetration of Africa. On occasions, particularly after the 1978 invasion of Shaba province of Zaire from Angola and the bestial slaughter of whites in Kolwezi, Carter turned on the Russians. If they could use proxy forces in Africa—the Cubans—so could America. The USA assisted the rapid deployment of French and Belgian troops in Zaire and the 1978 invasion was repelled. The French legionnaires became the West's Cubans. Paris, too, was determined to counter Soviet encroachment, especially in francophone Africa. Yet Carter continued to confuse friend and foe alike. At the beginning of his presidency he scoffed at the Soviet menace: Americans, he advised, should throw away their "inordinate fear" of communism. In this he was Young's alter ego. But, later, as Soviet adventurism increased, notably after the invasion of Afghanistan, Carter chose to echo Brzezinski. The president appeared to be not the conductor of American foreign policy but rather the arbiter, at best, or, at worst, merely the inconsistent mouthpiece for the traditionally contentious interests within the CIA, State Department, White House and Congress. Carter came to resemble the ancient Roman Crassus, who employed a private fire brigade *and* an arson squad. To many Americans, Carter looked as though he could not control unruly members of his own family, let alone contain a rampant superpower rival. No wonder the Russians thought 1974-1979 were wonderful years in Africa.

They were lean years for Pretoria. In 1977 Vice-President Walter Mondale told John Vorster, the South African prime minister, at a meeting in Vienna, that South Africa should have one man, one vote, the ultimate insult to Pretoria; and Young had described the South African government as "illegitimate". But by the end of Carter's presidency the harsh rhetoric was muted. The Democrats' idealism had lost its bloom after South Africa had restabilised after Soweto, just as John Kennedy's passion for Africa faded once the furore of the Sharpeville emergency had died down. In essence, until 1984, American foreign policy concentrated on the East-West dimension of conflict in southern Africa. All applied the Tar Baby option in practice: as long as US investment in South Africa was large and profitable, and as long as white supremacy looked secure, then no US foreign policy would rock the boat by putting African liberation before, firstly, the containment of Soviet penetration, secondly, the protection of trade and strategic minerals and thirdly, and least important, the defence of the Cape sea route. There was a gut feeling in Washington that it was better to stick with familiar allies, whatever their nature, as long as they were anti-communist. And was Pretoria worse than the dictators in Haiti, Chile or the Philippines?

Pretoria survived Carter's foreign policy. The outcry over the callous police murder of black consciousness leader Steve Biko in 1977 had prompted world condemnation and the UN mandatory arms embargo. A domestic political and financial scandal, dubbed "Muldergate", which revealed gross corruption in the citadel of Afrikaner power, toppled Vorster and led to P W Botha becoming prime minister. The former defence minister brought his generals into the central decision-making process via the reconstituted State Security Council, which came to run the country behind a parliamentary facade. P W Botha's containment policy rested upon a total strategy to defeat the black/communist threat. A central pillar was to be a pliant black leader, Abel Muzorewa, as leader of Zimbabwe-Rhodesia. A moderate Zimbabwe was supposed to join P W Botha's pet scheme, a "constellation" of southern African states. Robert Mugabe's victory in the 1980 election, however., was a deathblow to the constellation. It was also a major setback for Moscow, which had assiduously promoted Mugabe's main rival, Joshua Nkomo. Mugabe, who owed a debt of loyalty to the Chinese for arming and training his guerrillas, now led a state with a relatively modern industrial base and a large, battle-tested army. Zimbabwe emerged as the most militant, and articulate, frontline enemy of apartheid. The early 1980s introduced a decade of major destabilisation of the frontline states by the SADF. Wars consumed Angola and Mozambique, where

South Africa nourished insurgent armies fighting the Soviet-sponsored Marxist governments. This was a novelty. In the 1980s it was America's turn to sponsor liberation struggles around the world, all aiming to overturn status quo powers armed by the Russians. The tables, it seemed, were being turned.

Destructive engagement?

One of the architects of this turnabout was Ronald Reagan, who replaced Carter's zig-zags with a big-budget war on Russia's "evil empire". The new "Reagan doctrine" bolstered support for anti-Marxist guerrillas, most notably in Angola. Reagan's election, and the Conservative victory in the UK in 1979, came as sweet music to the ears of the hard men in Pretoria. For a while, the heat was off apartheid.

Washington's new approach to southern Africa was dubbed "constructive engagement", a stickier version of the old Tar Baby. Its prime exponent was Assistant Secretary of State Chester Crocker: "with a precisely trimmed mustache and a banker's caution with words, he was guarded, remote, resolutely non-telegenic". (15) Yet, to its many critics, Crocker's policy was a curious concept: only the minority regime could end minority rule, provided not too much pressure was applied. To the "sandbox right" in the USA, Crocker was a dangerous liberal, but to

PLATE 3.2 Constructive Engagement: large mural of Jonas Savimbi and Ronald Reagan overlooking parade ground in Jamba, the Unita "capital".

the anti-apartheid lobby he was Pretoria's ally. He was neither. Nonetheless, the ban on non-military exports for use by the SADF and the South African Police was lifted. US loans, powerful computers and nuclear-related technology started to flow into the republic. Despite the escalating economic and military campaigns against the frontline states, destabilisation in short, the SADF was a "lobby of modernising patriots", in Crocker's words, which would assist P W Botha's reform programme. But could apartheid be reformed, or was its abolition the only way to end the root cause of conflict in southern Africa? The success of constructive engagement was predicated upon real political change in South Africa. Domestic reforms there were—although critics said they were merely cosmetic—but the wars in Angola and Mozambique and the insurrection at home intensified. And a settlement in Namibia, the immediate goal of US policy in the region, looked like a distant mirage. So Pretoria had to supply some political ammunition to its right-wing allies in London and Washington: hence the constant stream of promises of change. As one veteran observer, Stanley Uys, noted: "Diplomats are always looking for glimmers of hope. They have to find a reason for doing nothing. So Pretoria has a special department to supply glimmers." (16)

To the army of Western opponents, constructive engagement was appeasement. Sticks were needed, not carrots dangled as rewards for mere glimmers. As one such critic wrote: "Washington bolstered Pretoria's capacity to delay at home and intervene abroad, emboldening the hawks and postponing the day of reckoning." (17) But, as with Nixon's administration, Reagan intuitively rejected further sanctions. He argued that South Africa combined large mineral resources, skilled technology, stable capitalist economics and good transportation, all of which was sorely needed in southern Africa. Blacks in South Africa and the neighbouring states would suffer if mandatory sanctions were imposed. So the argument ran. But, as with the military rationale for the Cape route, the more Pretoria traded on its strategic advantages, the more her trading partners in Africa and Europe resolved to find alternatives. The more leverage was attempted, the more likely the lever was to bend. (18). That principle worked both ways. If South Africa overplayed its hand over the strategic importance of the Cape and scarce minerals (especially chrome, manganese, platinum and vanadium), her enemies did the same with the embargoes on oil and arms. South Africa simply looked for alternative supplies and built up her domestic infrastructure to produce a successful indigenous arms industry and oil-from-coal technology.

By mid-1984 South Africa looked as if it had weathered the worst of the storms, because of its economic and military strength and the Reagan doctrine. Pretoria had forced Mozambique to sign the humiliating Nkomati non-aggression pact and Washington started to pour in arms to Jonas Savimbi, South Africa's ally in Angola. At home, P W Botha had introduced the big glimmer, a tricameral parliament for Indians, coloureds and whites. But there was one ingredient missing in Pretoria's containment diplomacy: the acquiescence of the black majority in South Africa. They had been totally left out of the new tricameral "dispensation". This startling omission was a major cause of the massive insurrection which spread throughout South Africa in late 1984 and continued until 1986.

Winnie Mandela, the wife of the ANC leader Nelson Mandela, put her finger on it: "Constructive engagement," she said, meant telling blacks to call off the struggle because "the bosses are working it out". (19) The struggle was very much on again, both locally and internationally. As in Vietnam, dramatic television footage of the revolt in South Africa brought the apartheid drama nightly into American homes and, once again, into Congress. Daily anti-apartheid demonstrations and, more seriously, the resulting business disinvestment became the current American fads. The anti-apartheid holy-rollers encouraged Congress to pass a series of new sanctions measures, which even Reagan could not halt. Even Margaret Thatcher, a heroic figure in Pretoria, was forced to concede to Commonwealth pressures to introduce further "tiny" sanctions. As stubborn as any Boer, Thatcher more than Crocker held the line against comprehensive measures.

Nevertheless, P W Botha was in deep trouble. The local business community bayed for his resignation, as private US disinvestment, not UN sanctions, rocked the South African economy. A national state of emergency continued to discourage foreign bankers, even after the two-year black "unrest" petered out in late 1986 because of draconian laws and severe repression by the security forces. The ANC had wound up its faltering armed struggle to capitalise on, not control, the revolt. More effectively, it capitalised, too, on the international pressures on Pretoria, even after the blanket of censorship banished the TV cameras from the unrest areas. The ANC gradually made itself respectable in the West. US and UK officials started talking publicly with the "terrorists". The diplomats were hedging their bets, although not changing sides. But it all helped to augment the ANC's credibility. That, as much as changing the hard hearts of Afrikanerdom, was perhaps the fundamental aim of sanctions.

"New thinking"

Paradoxically, the Russians also started to talk openly with Pretoria. Clandestinely, South Africa and the USSR had long operated a cosy arrangement to sell their gold and diamonds, once a near-monopoly they jointly manipulated. (20) But Mikhail Gorbachev's "new thinking" in foreign policy introduced a fluidity in international relations. (21) *Glasnost* threatened the touchstones of South African as much as NATO security systems. As Georgi Arbatov, the Kremlin's best-known America-watcher, suggestively observed: "We are going to do something terrible to you—we are going to deprive you of an enemy." (22) Russia not only withdrew her army from Afghanistan (in early 1989) but also helped to set in motion an agreement to pull out Cuban troops from Angola, and hence secure Namibian independence. It seemed as though Crocker's patient years of toil had paid off. And Soviet experts began to muse publicly that evolutionary change, not violent revolution, was likely in South Africa. Had both the Russian and the South African totalitarians lost faith in history? Had Marx been displaced by another great German philosopher: Clausewitz? Had pragmatism replaced ideology?

So what had 40 years of pressure achieved? Some fundamentals had changed. The logic of economic ties, strategic links and an intellectual climate in favour of free-trade had permeated the chancelleries of the West. Criticism of apartheid emanated initially from small exiled groups and the left wing. The early calls for sanctions had come from countries with nothing to lose, and, sometimes, with something to gain. But by the late 1980s the old assumptions had withered, for a number of reasons. The 1984-86 uprising had concentrated world attention on Pretoria's misdeeds. The relative importance of the South African gold-based economy had declined. South Africa's share of the European Community's and United States' exports slipped to less than 1% by the early 1980s, although for some individual European countries, such as the UK, South Africa was still an important trading partner. The pressures to disinvest, the "hassle" factor, made many multinationals decide that South African profits were not worth the political and economic costs. The Cape route had always been an overblown stragetic argument. Few military analysts expected the Russians to resort to World War Two naval stratagems to blockade supply lines, particularly in the Gorbachev era. And, it was commonly argued, a stable black regime in Pretoria could be a more reliable supplier of strategic minerals than one run by Afrikaner *bittereinders* prepared to pull down the economic pillars on their own heads.

> In short, the earlier coincidence of interests between Western and South African policy-makers with regard to the need for gradual political change in the Republic was beginning to break down. It was not that any serious policy-maker in the West wanted to see a violent revolution in this country but the South African insistence on 'evolutionary change' was beginning to look more and more like a smoke screen for avoiding the truly fundamental changes which, in the long run, were necessary to protect Western interests. (23)

Even in the conservative administrations of the West, the tide of popular opinion was rushing against Pretoria. The often sensational, and sensationalised, TV coverage of the unrest, endlessly repeated once the curtain of almost total censorship fell, Archbishop Desmond Tutu's emotive appeals to end apartheid and, above all, the dismally ham-fisted behaviour of the South African government, especially towards the Commonwealth peace mission of 1986, and the famously bungled Rubicon speech by President Botha, all helped to conjure up an image of an irredeemably ruthless, savagely inept regime. The old selling points—that blacks would suffer most from economic embargoes, that South Africa should not be singled out for its human rights abuses, and that it stood as a bastion of anti-communism—all looked desperately thin. The imposition of sanctions against the Polish military government and Libya further undermined some of the substantial arguments against deploying more pressure on Pretoria, as did the panoply of existing measures, particularly those that had had some meliorative effects, as in the case of the sporting bans. Nevertheless, by the end of the 1980s, compulsory comprehensive UN sanctions were not, yet, on the political agendas of South Africa's main Western trading partners.

The Afrikaner government has paid an enormous economic price for its stubborn, if often understandable, reluctance to bend its knee to international demands. But, in 1989, it was firmly in the political saddle. The men on horseback, the soldier-imperialists in the State Security Council, had called many of the shots in the 1980s. Military power had been the bedrock of the minority regime. So it is to Pretoria's armed forces that we now turn our attention. How did South Africa, despite the continuous drumbeat of world condemnation, become the single most powerful military machine on the African continent?

References and notes:

1. S Pienaar, "South Africa from Paragon to Pariah," *International Affairs Bulletin*, Johannesburg, 9:3, 1985. See also, D Geldenhuys, "South Africa's International Isolation," *International Affairs Bulletin*, 11:1, 1987.
2. R Cohen, *Endgame in South Africa*, Currey/UNESCO, London, 1986, p. 9.

3. For a discussion of the partition theme, see P Moorcraft, "Towards the Garrison State," in F Clifford-Vaughan, (ed), *International Pressures and Political Change in South Africa*, Oxford University Press, Cape Town, 1978.
4. For an early collection of articles on the debate, see Clifford-Vaughan, *op. cit.*
5. J Hanlon, *Beggar Your Neighbours*, Catholic Institute for International Relations, London, 1986, p. 8.
6. This paragraph has drawn heavily on Michael Howard's illuminating essay, "Europe, the Superpowers and Africa," *International Affairs Bulletin*, 6:3, 1982.
7. See *South Africa: Time Running Out*, The Report of the Study Commission on US Policy Towards Southern Africa, University of California, Berkeley, 1981, pp.351-2.
8. A Sampson, *Black and Gold*, Hodder and Stoughton, London, 1987, p. 118.
9. A Lake, *The 'Tar Baby' Option*, Columbia University Press, New York, 1976.
10. R Johnson, *How Long Will South Africa Survive?*, Macmillan, Johannesburg, 1977, pp. 58-9, 214.
11. According to South African sources, the British cut all military communications at the same time. The line literally went dead; no notice was given. This caused a number of problems for the Royal Navy. On one occasion, a British ship docked at Cape Town suffering from mechanical failures, including a breakdown in its communications systems. The captain asked the South African navy to assist in sending a top secret message to London. He was told to use the post office. The Simonstown severance signified the end of formal military ties with Britain, and caused much bitterness in Pretoria. Immediately after the naval knot was cut, P W Botha turned to Admiral "Flam" Johnson, during the weekly defence meeting with the SADF commanders, and said in English to the Anglophilic admiral: "What of your old English friends now?" Johnson had no reply. Author's interview with Johnson, 1978. For an important revision of the conventional view, see G Berridge and J Spence, "South Africa and the Simonstown Agreements," in J Young, (ed), *The Foreign Policy of Churchill's Peace-Time Administration,* University of Leicester, Leicester, 1987.
12. R Legvold, "The Soviet Threat to Southern Africa," *International Affairs Bulletin*, 8:1, 1984, p. 10.
13. R Johnson, *op. cit.*, For an interesting view on the influence of South African gold (and uranium) on British policy, see A Verrier, *The Road to Zimbabwe*, Cape, London, 1986.
14. R Johnson, p. 216.
15. J Lelyveld, *Move Your Shadow*, Joseph, London, 1986, p. 232.
16. Quoted in Sampson, *op. cit.*, p 104.
17. W Minter, "Destructive Engagement: The United States and South Africa in the Reagan Era," in P Johnson and D Martin, (eds), *Destructive Engagement*, Zimbabwe Publishing, Harare, 1986, p. 294.
18. See T Davenport, *South Africa: A Modern History*, Macmillan, Johannesburg, 1987, pp. 493-9, for a useful summary of the debate.
19. Quoted in Lelyveld, *op. cit.*, p. 233.
20. K Campbell, *Southern Africa in Soviet Foreign Policy*, Adelphi Paper No. 227, International Institute for Strategic Studies, London, 1987/8, pp. 37-46.
21. S Bialer, "'New Thinking' and Soviet Foreign Policy," *Survival*, July/August, 1988.
22. Quoted in *Time*, 23 May 1988.
23. J Blumenfeld, "Western Economic Policy towards South Africa: Empty Rhetoric or Real Interest," *International Affairs Bulletin*, 11:3, 1987, p. 15.

4

The rise of a regional superpower

The search for allies

The core strategy of the National Party government has always been the preservation of white rule by any means. Its military nightmare was the possible conjunction of a massive internal insurrection and an external invasion. The latter seemed unlikely, but all domestic revolts were crushed with utmost vigour. Both threats, however, were combined in Pretoria's ideological perspective: internal unrest has been viewed as the instrument of an international communist conspiracy. One of the first major measures of the apartheid regime was the passage of the Suppression of Communism Act in 1950, which outlawed the tiny, pro-Moscow South African Communist Party. In 1960 the ANC and the Pan-Africanist Congress were also banned. Although internal security was the prime concern, Pretoria felt that this was best achieved by posturing as the Western world's chief ally in the Cold War, especially in Africa.

Although South Africa was a minor element in the East-West confrontation, Pretoria developed what Kenneth Grundy called the equivalent of the Ptolemaic theory of the universe: just as the planets, sun and stars were once thought to revolve around the earth, so South Africa imagined itself to be the epicentre of the "free world's" war on communism. (1) Although apartheid came to provide the most convenient excuse for Soviet penetration of Africa, Pretoria's sense of its own importance was grotesquely exaggerated. The apartheid regime wanted to be the centre of attention, as a pro-capitalist bastion, so as to lock the NATO powers into the defence of white supremacy.

But such diplomatic arabesques prompted a supreme irony. Afrikaner nationalists had long been committed to jettisoning defence ties with its former imperial overlord. Anglophile English-speaking officers were hounded out of the armed forces, which caused the South African chief of the general staff to resign. Yet, at the same time, Pretoria was trying to entice Britain into a joint security pact. Initially it suggested an African Defence Organisation, a would-be southwards extension of NATO to include South Africa and the colonial powers. The British Labour government, despite its commitment to decolonisation, was not averse to the military (and gold and uranium) connections. Pretoria accepted a provisional invitation to join the ill-fated, British-sponsored Middle East Defence Organisation; but MEDO proved abortive, partly because of objections to possible South African participation. The sole concrete achievement of Pretoria's strategic soliciting was the 1955 Simonstown agreement with Britain. This agreement, not a formal defence pact, specifically excluded a British commitment to internal security. In the spirit of Pretoria's apparent willingness to help Britain in the Middle East, South Africa purchased 68 British Centurion tanks and various aircraft between 1955 and 1959. Also, 36 Sabre jets were obtained from Canada. So Pretoria had secured some hardware and joint naval exercises with the Royal Navy, but the goal of a military alliance slipped further away. Although both Labour and Tory administrations allowed British arms to reach South Africa, a formal pact was politically impossible because of apartheid.

Hence emerged Pretoria's love-hate relationship with the West, and Britain in particular. South Africa frequently talked of standing alone, flirted with armed neutrality and even suggested overtures to Red China, but in the end its threats of unfaithfulness could never be consummated because Pretoria needed the West for arms and for psychological reassurance. Moreover, Moscow's identification of South Africa as part of the imperialist camp reinforced Pretoria's self-image. At this stage the West had it both ways. In the event of world war, South Africa would have little alternative but to place its military facilities at the disposal of its old allies. This situation guaranteed Pretoria's availability without the political costs demanded by a formal alliance.

The ambivalence towards the West persisted. It was probably best expressed in John Vorster's famous statement of August 1977 when he said that the end result of American pressure on southern Africa "would be exactly the same as if it were subverted by the Marxists". "In the one case," he argued, "it will come about as a result of brute force. In the other case, it will be strangulation by finesse." (2) Yet, however much South Africa disliked Washington's policies, there was still the acknowledgement that the US "remains the leader of the West and ... only America stands between the continued freedom of mankind and slavery," in the words of Foreign Minister Pik Botha. (3)

But in 1960 South Africa was militarily puny. She had a small, obsolete military structure and no formal pact. Although disconcerted by the rapid pace of decolonisation, Pretoria did not feel threatened externally. Rather, the Sharpeville massacre and the ensuing state of emergency prompted a renewed concern with internal security. If the 1950s were characterised by a search for military alliances, the first half of the 1960s was one of military introversion: the decision was made to build up a large modern defence force, committed initially to internal security. The army was rapidly enlarged. The permanent force (PF), the regular command and training nucleus for the expansion of the reserve citizen force (CF), was increased from 9,000 in 1960 to 15,000 in 1964. Almost 20,000 national servicemen were in training in 1964, a tenfold increase over the number trained in 1960. Compulsory military service replaced the selective ballot system in 1967. By 1969 South Africa had 200,000 armed and trained men. (4) But this new force needed better equipment. Under the Simonstown agreement, Britain supplied a small fleet of second-hand frigates and 15 Buccaneer aircraft. (5) After 1964 London imposed an arms embargo and the French stepped in quickly. Pretoria now had the chance to develop its conventional and counter-insurgency capabilities. The army got the lion's share of the booming defence budget. French armoured cars boosted the army's strength, but the air force also received new Mirage jets, helicopters and missile systems. Three Daphné class submarines were delivered to the navy in 1971-72. Much of this new hardware was assembled from kits or built under licence in South Africa from largely imported components, mainly on the basis of licences from French, Italian and Belgian companies. Small arms were purchased from or via Portugal, Spain, Greece and Eastern European states. The domestic production of teargas, napalm and ammunition was begun with the assistance of mainly British-based companies. America continued to be a major supplier. In the fiscal years 1981-83, for example, the State Department authorised commercial sales of more than $28.3 million-worth of military-related equipment to Pretoria. In addition, aircraft worth $556 million, technically for civilian use, but in many cases suitable for military adaption, were sold during 1980-82. (6)

Pretoria flexed its new muscles not only at home, but also in covert involvement in the wars in Rhodesia, Mozambique and Angola. Stung by criticisms about these adventures and particularly its illegal retention of Namibia, Pretoria continued to manifest its "sometimes bewildering dualism" towards the West. (7) Pretoria kept on stressing that its arms build-up was a commitment to Western goals and its readiness to join an enlarged NATO. Yet the reality of standing alone began to sink in, especially as the Western "allies" grew increasingly reluctant to provide arms, above the counter, for this lonely stance. Hence Pretoria's growing interest in scouting around for new allies—in Latin America, Israel and Taiwan.

The precariousness of South Africa's position was dramatised by the invasion of Angola in 1975–76. This epitomised to Pretoria both the communist threat and Western unreliability. The UN arms embargo of 1977 and the domestic insurrection of 1976–77 all helped to convince the Afrikaner leadership, if they needed convincing, that South Africa was now facing a total communist onslaught. And the answer, decided Pretoria, was a "total strategy".

Total Strategy

The concept of a total national strategy was developed in a number of defence white papers in the 1970s. In essence, it articulated the notion of a world communist conspiracy aimed at South Africa. Thus, the fundamental problem was perceived as not the manifold injustices to blacks, but Kremlin intrigue. And the purported solution was a total economic, political, psychological and military mobilisation of the state's resources to defeat this onslaught. As with the Bolshevik concept of capitalist encirclement in the 1920s, there was just enough truth to the notion to lend it some credibility. That little bit of truth was ruthlessly manipulated by the government's increasing domination of the media. And, as in Rhodesia, the perceived illegality of the international conspiracy implied that black nationalist guerrillas and politicians were not freedom-fighters, but criminal tools of foreign agents.

Although the military response became the primary reaction to the threats, political reform was also included; the axiomatic mixture was supposed to be 80% political and 20% military. But because of the threat-oriented politics of white survival, the characteristic emphasis on military and police repression swallowed up the belated political initiatives. Reform for blacks, essentially the formation of a co-opted black middle class, in itself a highly dubious strategy, always came a poor second.

The intellectual substance of the total strategy was essentially the writings of André Beaufre and John McCuen writ large and awkwardly applied to South Africa.(8) As Philip Frankel has noted:

> ...total strategy selectively interprets the world in the narrow, dialectic and melodramatic terms with which white South Africa is so familiar, confusing communism, nationalism, dissidence, subversion, racism and imperialism into an interpenetrable melange from which only the security of the white state emerges as constant and paramount...Total strategy at its present level of development is no exception to the general rule that most proto-ideologies developed by soldiers are primitive, transparently self-rationalizing and largely devoid of any practical positive content. Total strategy is important in generating and justifying siege psychologies and structures through which the Defence Force can accumulate social power. (9)

The implementation of total strategy did indeed mark the growing influence, although not necesarily the dominance, of the military in South African society. The concept was assiduously fostered by Defence Minister P W Botha, and his successor, General Magnus Malan. Botha revived the State Security Council (SSC), originally established in 1972, and made it the central organ of his counter-revolution. Run like a politburo, it became more important than the cabinet. Perhaps 70% of its members and staff were drawn from the security forces. As we shall see later, the SSC constructed throughout the country a shadow, parallel administration, called the National Security Management System. The restructuring of the Afrikaner security network did not solve the intractable domestic political grievances; they became worse. But the SSC did help to coordinate the growth and deployment of the burgeoning war machine. Military strategy became an end in itself. The 20% solution became god, and the 80% political input almost disappeared amid the gunsmoke. Clausewitz was duly turned on his head.

New weapons

Pretoria spent a lot of money quickly on the SADF. In 1960 the defence budget was R44 million; the 1988–89 budget was R8.09 billion. The police, a paramilitary formation, saw its budgetary vote expand from R129 million to R1.8 billion in the same period. True, the economy was growing rapidly and could absorb some of the strains before the sanctions and disinvestment of the 1980s; and inflation played a part. But even allowing for the latter, the astounding growth in defence expenditure was a heavy burden on the state. Even then the official figures excluded the Namibian defence costs as well as the large secret intelligence funds. Of course, many totalitarian states officially undersell their defence spending. UN estimates put the figure at 35% higher than the official SADF estimates. (10) It has been estimated that between

20-25% of the total national budget—at least R20 million a day—went on defence. (11)

Much of this expenditure was used to buy or develop weapons systems, coordinated by the Armaments Corporation of South Africa (Armscor). (12) Armscor is a paradox, a state corporation run almost exclusively by private enterprise. Once, private enterprise, dominated largely by English-speaking capitalists, had been portrayed as part of the onslaught, but under P W Botha it became part of the counter-revolutionary machinery; though it would be simplistic to describe this symbiosis as a sinister military-industrial complex, for many of the entrepreneurs developed serious misgivings about government strategies and were in some cases fund-raisers for the white liberal opposition. (13) The industrialists also frequently criticised the government about the distortions caused to the economy by excessive defence spending, particularly the insistence on costly import substitution for political not economic reasons. Nonetheless, there were big profits to be made.

Pretoria obtained its arms in a number of ways. As was noted earlier, in the 1960s and 1970s South Africa shopped on the open market for goods from the NATO allies. Between 1960 and 1983 the French were the biggest suppliers. The most important weapons purchased or licensed were Panhard armoured cars, Alouette, Frelon and Puma helicopters, Mirage fighters, the three submarines and the Franco-South African development of the Cactus (Crotale) surface-to-air missile system. As R W Johnson drily observed, "For such a haul as this Pretoria might well have been willing to pay in blood. As it was, she paid in gold which, as was well known, Gaullists preferred."(14) The deals continued for a time even after the French socialists came to power.(15) The British firms Marconi and EMI established electronic components subsidiaries in South Africa which produced military goods. Such subsidiaries were used to circumvent the arms embargo. British Leyland (SA) produced vehicles for the SADF and ICI South Africa, wholly owned then by its parent company in the UK, helped to establish an explosives factory.(16) Many NATO countries ignored or sidestepped the UN restrictions, as did Israel and Taiwan more openly. The SADF's acquisitions from the Jewish state have been especially important: for example, the Reshef and Aliyah class fast-attack boats and their accompanying missile systems, RPV pilotless reconnaissance drones and assistance with the modification of the ageing Mirages (from experience gained with the Israeli Kfir and aborted Lavi aircraft projects).(17) Before covert Israeli cooperation, the South African Atlas Aircraft Corporation had built a range of aircraft under licence, first the

PLATE 4.1 Mirage 111 EZ; Minister class strike craft; Alpha XH1 prototype helicopter; G–6 self-propelled gun; Eland armoured car (SADF).

Impala from Italy's Aermacchi MB-326 and then the French Mirage F-1AZ.

Increasingly Armscor and its subsidiaries were forced to resort to subterfuge: military deals through third parties via front companies or purchase of equipment with nominally "civilian" use. Perhaps the most spectacular and best documented breach of the arms embargo was the acquisition of the US/Canadian-designed 155mm howitzer, which was used to such effect in the fighting in Angola in the late 1980s, but also, in various configurations, became such a money-spinner for Armscor when it moved into the export market. (18)

The arms market has always been renowned for its utter cynicism. One British arms merchant symbolised this truism when he commented:

> We were able to sell them [the South Africans] some helicopters because they were half-French. And they're of course the deadliest machines against natives. When the South Africans came through with an order for patrol boats we told them to redraft the order to make it look as if they were for civilian use—"Surely you must have some *black* fishing boats that need protecting." (19)

By and large, Armscor officials and South African intelligence agents seemed to have operated with great ingenuity, and many bribes, some of which, allegedly, went into Switzerland, not weaponry for the fatherland. Another arms salesman noted: "They're just like other Africans; they all want to get their money out." (20) During the late 1970s there had been a degree of corruption and embezzlement associated with the disgraced Information Department, but P W Botha cleaned up much of the mess when he streamlined defence procurement after 1978. (21) On the whole, Armscor has been a remarkable success story for South Africa. Its adaption, invention and sheer chicanery have resulted in excellent weapons such as the G-6 self-propelled 155mm cannon and the 127mm Valkiri multiple rocket-launcher. Many Warsaw Pact and NATO weapons are not suited to the terrain, structure or skills of smaller armies in developing countries. More important, the SADF has successfully tested and proved Armscor products in combat. Thus, not only has the UN arms embargo, in some areas, backfired, but Armscor has moved into the top league of arms exporters, selling its wares under the slogan, "Born in necessity and tested under fire". African countries, such as Morocco, have bought the impressive Ratel range of infantry combat vehicles. Sri Lanka purchased a series of mine-resistant armoured troop carriers. Iraq bought the 155mm guns. (22) And one newspaper claimed that the Armscor frequency-hopping radios "amazed Britsh soldiers who captured them from the Argentines [during the Falklands war]". (23)

Armscor became the largest single exporter of manufactured goods in South Africa, with sales to 23 countries valued at $2 billion per year (in 1988). It ranked perhaps fifth in the world league of defence contractors. It had ten wholly owned subsidiaries with 23,000 employees and 975 private sector subcontractors supporting a total of 90,000 employees. Efficiency was achieved because of its unusual status as the sole procurement authority for the SADF and as the systems management organisation for all projects. It was producing more than 4,000 items, including 140 types of munition. (24)

Pretoria liked to boast that South Africa was 95% self-sufficient in weaponry. But was this true? That boast, partly intended to boost white morale, tried to demonstrate that further economic and defence sanctions would not work and, crucially, it was a bluff to disguise the foreign expertise and components that were still creating the so-called home-made weaponry. In fact, despite the undeniable skills in adaption to local conditions, and the tenacity in circumventing sanctions, the arsenal is highly derivative and still vulnerable to a strictly enforced arms embargo, especially from the fellow members of the league of the desperate, Israel and Taiwan. South Africa has an urgent military shopping list, as the war in Angola indicated in the 1980s. The South African air force, for example, was alarmed by the competition from the Mig-23s and Su22s and the integrated Soviet defence systems of radar, anti-aircraft artillery and surface-to-air missiles. The navy desperately needs large surface ships such as modern frigates as well as new submarines, although Pretoria has intimated that it might build the latter (at great cost and, probably, with German designs). The SADF had no replacements for long-range maritime reconnaisance aircraft when the aged Shackletons were finally phased out in the early 1980s. The air force has 30 Dakotas, probably the largest surviving fleet in the world. Some of these venerable old warriors, dubbed "Dackletons", have been used by 35 Squadron, based in Cape Town, as crude substitutes for the Shackletons. "The squadron is in fact quite proud of having 'modernised' from a 30-year-old aircraft to one ten years older," wrote a South African defence expert.(25)

The very professional air force is in much better shape than the navy. It has not only adapted some of its 20-year-old Mirage 111s, with Israeli help, to produce the Cheetah fighter, not in full production by 1989, but also a range of experimental helicopters, the Puma XTP1, based on its French namesake, and the Alpha XH1, based on the Alouette 111. The

Alpha, apparently, was not entirely successful, as it proved unstable, and so it is not yet scheduled for production. Even the more successful Puma adaption pales alongside the Russian Hind gunships it is supposed to contend with. In short, the SADF and Armscor have come a long way, despite the embargoes, but cannot compete, nor be expected to, with the up-to-date weapons systems supplied to the frontline states by the USSR. The South Africans are said to be developing a cruise missile, and some of the avionics and electronic counter-measures, courtesy of Israeli designers, are very sophisticated. But the SADF desperately needs more and better combat and transport helicopters and fighters. (26) It has other less pressing vulnerabilities too. The Olifant MK1A, the army's main battle tank, is based upon the British Centurion purchased from Britain in the late 1950s, and additional ones procured, in various states of repair, from Jordan and India in the 1970s. It is not up to current NATO specifications, but it has proved useful against the older generation of Soviet tanks operating in Angola. The South African army's tactics, anyway, are built around highly mobile, wheeled, not tracked, armoured vehicles. But the point remains: despite all the bravura, the SADF faces a future of serious hardware deficiencies. And the arms embargoes are likely to get worse. Originally, Pretoria's hunt for Western arms was a means to secure a political certificate of respectablity, to "get pregnant" by the Western powers, as one Pentagon official tartly observed. In the 1990s, if conventional conflict on the Angolan scale is repeated, the SADF will require state-of-the-art hardware, from any source, if it is to survive.

Nuclear weapons

South Africa's nuclear programme began in the closing days of the Second World War when, at the request of the USA and Britain, a secret study of the country's uranium resources was commissioned. (27) The US supplied Pretoria with its first nuclear reactor, Safari 1, which became operational at Pelindaba in 1965. Thereafter, Britain, France and West Germany, the latter prohibited from developing nuclear weapons on its *own* territory, helped to construct Pretoria's nuclear capacity. (28) Israel has been frequently alleged to have assisted in the process of turning South Africa's civilian nuclear programme into a military one. In 1979 the CIA reportedly concluded that a joint Israeli-South African nuclear test had occurred in the South Atlantic on 22 September. (29) Pretoria refused to sign the Non-Proliferation Treaty, and is often reckoned by experts to have a nuclear arsenal of perhaps 20 "atomic" bombs.

By emulating Israel's "bomb in the basement" strategy, Pretoria has, perhaps, boosted its deterrent posture. Afrikaner leaders like to hint at the possession of the nuclear option from time to time but, as a political policy, such an option may be a dubious asset. In military terms, where are the targets for such a bomb? (30) And, secondly, why should Israel risk its political capital by collaborating with Pretoria in this field? Experts have suggested that, although it is unnecessary to test an atomic bomb by exploding it, the Israelis were developing a hydrogen bomb, which cannot be built safely or reliably without a test explosion. Thermonuclear devices can be much smaller, with a much higher explosive yield than atom bombs, and they produce less fallout. Technically, in the world of Dr Strangelove, they are "more deliverable". South Africa, like Israel, is said to have been working on "small" tactical nuclear weapons. (31) In 1988 rumours circulated in South Africa that tactical nuclear weapons had been positioned to deter a putative Cuban invasion of Namibia. Whether that was fact or officially leaked fiction to deter Cuban adventurism is impossible to ascertain. In 1989 there were (unconfirmed) reports that the SADF was about to test a nuclear-capable ballistic missile with a range of 900 miles. The missile was said to be a modification of the Israeli Jericho 11. It was also suggested that South Africa was preparing to test a more advanced Israeli missile, the Shavit, with a range of 2,000 miles. This could bring states as far away as Kenya in range of such a missile fired from South Africa. (32)

South Africa has had all the ingredients to join the nuclear weapons club: the technology, the delivery systems, the political will, the cash and the perception of local threat; and, presumably, enough diplomatic sense to keep such weapons quietly in the basement. There is a mountain of circumstantial evidence that Pretoria has its bomb, but no conclusive proof. If South Africa is a member of this dangerous club, would she ever, *in extremis*, use the ultimate weapon?

There is also evidence that Pretoria has produced chemical weapons and other weapons banned by international conventions. In 1968 South Africa announced that it had begun the domestic manufacture of napalm. And defoliants were used regularly on the Angolan border to establish free-fire zones. In the 1980s the UN accused the SADF of deploying poison gases in both Angola and Mozambique, but little satisfactory evidence has been provided.

The SADF's structure

The style of the SADF is inherited from remnants of the British regimental traditions superimposed with the heritage of the Boer commandos of the nineteenth century. The SADF's largest service, the army, is essentially a militia force which relies on the core permanent force (PF) members to train and lead the national service personnel, who provide the bulk of the standing army, and the citizen force (CF) of part-time soldiery to provide the reserves of fighting strength. The navy, the air force and the medical services, the other three wings of the SADF, since they are more technology intensive, rely more heavily on full-time personnel. And, in practice, the special forces could also be said to represent an independent fifth wing of the SADF. (For a detailed breakdown of the SADF structure, see Appendix 2.)

The SADF likes to think that it is similar to Switzerland's citizen army, although this is difficult to reconcile with the fact that it is fighting largely a civil war where 75% of the population are not full citizens. Only whites are conscripted, but blacks, Indians and coloureds can, and do, volunteer, although, perhaps, mainly from economic, not patriotic, motives.

The army is geared to two main threats. Counterinsurgency is to be met first by the police and local commandos. (33) This is the first line of "area defence". If the threat is serious, the standing army (the PF plus national servicemen and elements of the CF) would form a reaction force for a conventional response. This has been the pattern for major offensives in Angola.

The standing armed forces stood at 103,500 in 1989, according to the International Institute for Strategic Studies. But the SADF can also count on an array of allied forces, of varying quality and commitment. These include the various police forces, homeland armies and (in 1989) the South West African Territory Force. The full mobilisation figure is usually estimated at around 425,000, but in an extreme emergency, such as a full-scale invasion, it might be possible to mobilise as many as 800,000 trained men (and women) using all reserves and auxiliaries. That is a lot more than the total of all the mobilised forces of the front-line opponents plus the ANC and the current tally of Eastern bloc troops and advisers in the region.

The conventional forces are shaped very much like their Western counterparts in NATO. Their uniforms and equipment would seem familiar, if sometimes a little quaint, to any NATO officer. Our hypothetical NATO observer would recognise some of the tactics learnt from the Rhodesian army, and the flamboyant style, copied somewhat self-consciously, of the Israelis. The SADF, however, although not as formal as British regiments, is decidely more hidebound than the Israelis. (Ex-Rhodesians who joined the SADF found the formality rather tedious. A "prayer meeting" in Rhodesian army slang meant a drinks party; in the SADF, which takes God and country very seriously, the regular prayer meetings mean just that.) Despite its multiracial and officially bilingual composition, the SADF is Afrikaner-dominated. Official rules to the contrary, Afrikaans is the prevailing language and culture. It is a no-nonsense force: there is no talk of unions or hairnets for long hair as in some of the more liberal NATO military establishments. Unlike the US army in Vietnam, drugs are not a major problem. And the "fragging" of unpopular officers is unheard of.

In short, the SADF is a battle-hardened, efficient and, by and large, a well-motivated force. Its counterinsurgency campaigns in Namibia were executed with almost textbook precision in *military* terms and, given its procurement problems, the army performed well in the battles in Angola in the 1980s. But what is it fighting for? By any military yardstick, the SADF is highly professional. No armed force, however, can solve the political issue of apartheid.

Assessment

Despite its frantic search for allies, the South African government has ended up on its own, with a probable apartheid bomb in the basement, that has already, in political terms, blown up in its face. Even its fellow pariah, Israel, has officially distanced itself by applying sanctions. (34) The old arguments, the Cape sea route and the resource war thesis, have helped but a little. (35) The Iran-Iraq war, much nearer the oil interests of the superpowers, suggested that international cooperation, not renewed Cold War, can result from mutual great power concern with mineral resources. The Soviets are equally enmeshed in the global economy and, as Jack Spence noted, Russia is dependent on Western technology, which is one of the many constraints on any attempt to promote a resource denial strategy, especially in southern Africa. (36)

In the 1980s, Pretoria, while wedded to the total strategy, played down the total onslaught theme partly because its alarmist nature proved somewhat counterproductive, not least in boosting the ANC on the left and, on the right, the Conservative Party, which lambasted P W Botha for being soft on the communist threat. Yet, after decades of official propaganda, the idea of the red menace has become deeply internalised in the Afrikaner collective psyche, not least among members of the security forces, particularly in the police. This was especially counterproductive as the Botha regime tried to backtrack on some elements of apartheid doctrine with its reform programme. The right-wing organisations grew in strength as they replayed precisely the former

National Party song to a growing army of voters who were led to believe that Botha and his new English-speaking allies were betraying the *volk*. The reform elements of the total strategy depended fundamentally upon sanitising primitive apartheid so as to create a black labour aristocracy in the urban areas. A co-opted black middle class and the near-feudal ruling elites in the homelands were supposed to drive a wedge between the ANC and its supporters. They did not.

As all good counterinsurgency texts preached, Botha did centralise his counter-revolutionary strategy in his imperial presidency operating through the SSC. This might have been more effective if the centralised machine had proffered an "...alternative vision of society (an essential requirement for any government attempting to compete for popular support against its opponents). Short-term military tactics became long-term strategy, and the prospects of a political solution recedes still further."(37)

Like the white minority in Rhodesia, Pretoria could offer no viable alternative to its hostage black majority. As De Tocqueville had warned, reform is always the most dangerous period for a repressive government. For the restless black masses the reforms of the 1980s always came too late. The repeal of the hated pass laws would have been welcomed in the 1960s. By the 1980s political power was all that seemed to matter.

Even if a convincing political programme had been fashioned as part of the total strategy, it would have demanded a high degree of resolve and unity among the Afrikaner *Herrenvolk*. During most of their war, Rhodesians exhibited this in the crucial areas of effective counter-insurgency: competent security forces, an efficient and honest civil service, and high morale among the majority of the ruling group. P W Botha, however, split Afrikaner ranks. His civil service remained an ultra-conservative, often bungling leviathan which frequently obstructed the reform measures. Only the SADF remained as a trusted and competent tool of Botha's imperium.

Yet even the SADF was riddled with paradoxes. The armed bureaucrats in the SSC tended to be moderate at home, but militant abroad; domestic reformers (up to a point), but hawkish destabilisers in the neighbouring states. Despite the SADF's attempts to forge a multiracial army, for practical and propaganda reasons, and to the fury of the Conservative Party, it still continued to build up tribal forces in both the "independent" and non-independent homelands. Although it emphasised the combat efficiency of its black soldiers, promotion opportunities for blacks and, often, English-speaking South Africans were impeded by the Afrikaner caste system. And, for all the spirited forays to secure modern weaponry, the key component of military counterinsurgency, accurate intelligence, began to dry up as the angry "comrades" mercilessly rounded upon blacks accused of collaboration with the regime. Even the much-vaunted security police informer network began to break down in the mid-1980s.

The SADF was supposed to hold the ring to allow time for the politicians to settle the "political problem". Far-reaching reform, it was said, would have to wait until the unrest was crushed. But the state of emergency, declared first in 1985, and the wars on the borders continued. The jackboot became the symbol of short-term and long-term "solutions".

Nonetheless, the militarisation of South African policy-making must be seen in perspective. Although civil-military relations are analysed in a later chapter, it is important to note that, although military influence in Pretoria was very important, it was not always decisive. The concept of a "creeping coup" is a little too simplistic. As a number of writers have observed, even with hidden costs, expenditure on the armed forces has been fairly modest compared with states such as Israel and Taiwan. (38) And, according to IISS figures, the percentage of GDP spent on the military actually decreased from 4% (1984) to 3.8% (1986). The comparative figures in Israel, where civilian control of the military was not generally in question, were 22.4% of the GDP to 18.9% in the same period. The British figures were 5.5% (1984) and 4.9% (1986). And, despite the current rapid growth of the police, by Western standards South Africa has been under-policed in terms of policemen-to-population ratios. The structure, however, of apartheid society, especially the separate black group areas, physically designed to be easily contained by security forces, has provided extra control measures which do not exist in democratic countries. Nor can figures alone represent the phobias and militarisation of an increasingly gun-happy white population upon whom the financial and conscription burdens weigh so heavily.

So, despite its pariah status, Pretoria had built a powerful defence apparatus by the late 1980s. It would be naive, however, to paint a demonic picture of a rampant military junta, slavering behind a civilian facade and gobbling up the country's wealth and future while stamping out all protests. There is no doubt about the ruthlessness of the apartheid regime, but the image of an SS state portrayed by many anti-apartheid organisations does a disservice to accurate analysis. The interplay between the military and civilian elites has often been very subtle and complex. This will be demonstrated in the following account of South African strategies in the wars in the neighbouring states. Pretoria sought first to uphold colonial rule. Then it deployed its economic power as both a club and a magnet to maintain its regional dominance once its neighbours had broken free from white rule. Throughout the region Pretoria sought to buy hegemony with gold and cheap black labour. Whenever that failed, the *swaardmag* (sword-power) of the SADF would be thrust deep into the fragile polities. But for how long? Was the SADF holding the ring for an eventual political settlement or was it rather the pin in the grenade of all-out war in southern Africa?

References and notes:

1. K Grundy, *The Militarization of South African Politics*, Oxford University Press, Oxford, 1988, p. 13.
2. Quoted in *The Star*, 30 August 1977.
3. *Debates of the House of Assembly*, 19 May 1980, column 6628.
4. For an informative background on this period, see D Geldenhuys, *South Africa's Search for Security Since The Second World War*, South African Institute for International Affairs, Johannesburg, 1978 and R Jaster, *South Africa's Narrowing Security Options*, Adelphi Paper No. 159, International Institute for Strategic Studies, London, 1980, pp. 9-21.
5. The Buccaneers were the centre of a major political controversy in Britain which, in the event, they were hardly worth, according to R Johnson, *How Long Will South Africa Survive?*, Macmillan, Johannesburg, 1977, p. 40. By 1973 no less than six had crashed and the remaining planes were grounded for some time. South African pilots preferred the Mirage and tended to regard the Buccaneer in the same light that their Luftwaffe counterparts regarded the unlucky Starfighter.
6. G Cawthra, *Brutal Force*, International Defence and Aid Fund, London, 1986, pp. 16, 96.
7. The phrase is Geldenhuys's, *op. cit.*, p. 7.
8. A Beaufre, *An Introduction to Strategy*, Faber and Faber, London, 1963 and *Strategy of Action*, Faber and Faber, London, 1967; J McCuen, *The Art of Counter-Revolutionary War*, Faber and Faber, London, 1968.
9. P Frankel, *Pretoria's Praetorians*, Cambridge University Press, Cambridge, 1984, pp.69, 174. For a comparison with the development of the siege mentality and military strategy in Rhodesia, see P Moorcraft, "The Fall of the Republic: The Collapse of White Power in Rhodesia, 1976-1980," Unpublished doctoral thesis, University of South Africa, 1987.
10. Quoted in the *Weekly Mail*, 27 March 1986.
11. M Evans and M Phillips, "Intensifying Civil War: The Role of the South African Defence Force," in P Frankel, N Pines and M Swilling, (eds), *State, Resistance and Change in South Africa*, Croom Helm, London, 1988, p.123.
12. Armscor was formed out of a merger of the Armaments Production Board (established in 1964) and the Armaments Development and Production Corporation (1968). For a general history of Armscor, see J McWilliams, *Armscor: South Africa's Arms Merchant*, Brassey's, London, 1989.
13. P Moorcraft, "The Military-Industrial Complex under Siege," in B Cooling, (ed), *War, Business and World Military-Industrial Complexes*, Kennikat, Port Washington, 1981.
14. Johnson, *op. cit.*, p. 40.
15. Cawthra, *op. cit.*, p. 91.
16. *Ibid.*, p. 90.

17. See B Beit-Hallahmi, *The Israeli Connection*, Tauris, London, 1987. See also, A Guelke, "An Alliance of Pariahs," *Southern African Review of Books*, Spring 1988. The published range of estimates of annual Israeli supplies to Pretoria is wide: from $50 million to the SIPRI yearbook's $300 million (1987).
18. Cawthra, p. 94; "SA's Reply to the Soviets' Big Guns," *The Star*, (weekly edition), 2 February 1988.
19. Quoted in A Sampson, *The Arms Bazaar*, Hodder and Stoughton, London, 1977, p. 167.
20. Quoted in A Sampson, "The Long Reach of the Arms Men," *The Observer*, 4 February 1979.
21. For the details of the Information scandal and the arms connection, see M Rees and C Day, *Muldergate*, Macmillan, Johannesburg, 1980; R Leonard, *South Africa at War*, Hill, Westport, 1983, pp. 131-97.
22. B Nelan, "The Armsmaker an Embargo Built," *Time*, 9 May 1988.
23. *The Cape Times*, 10 June 1983, quoted in A Minty, "South Africa's Military Build-up: The Region at War," in P Johnson and D Martin, (eds), *Destructive Engagement*, Harare Publishing, Harare, 1986, p. 197.
24. *Jane's Defence Weekly*, 21 January 1988.
25. H-R Heitman, *South African Arms and Armour*, Struik, Cape Town, 1988, p. 170.
26. See "Embargo May Leave Us Vulnerable in the Air," *The Star* (weekly edition), 30 March 1988.
27. Cawthra, p. 106.
28. Z Cervenka and B Rogers, *The Nuclear Axis*, Friedmann, London, 1978; B Rogers, "The Nuclear Threat from S.Africa," *Africa*, January 1981; A Minty, "South Africa's Nuclear Capability: The Apartheid Bomb," in Johnson and Martin, *op. cit.*
29. Cawthra, p. 108.
30. For an early assessment of the nuclear option, see P Moorcraft, "The Nuclear Option Mushrooms," *The Sunday Tribune*, 31 July 1977, and "*Kernwapens SAse Keuse*," *Beeld*, 26 July 1977.
31. R Nordland, "The Nuclear Club," *Newsweek*, 11 July 1988.
32. D Braun, "SA-Israel 'in Joint Missile Test' in Cape," *The Star*, (weekly edition), 28 June 1989; M Walker, "S Africa About to Test Medium-Range Missile," *The Guardian*, 21 June 1989.
33. "Commando" has a specific connotation in southern Africa. It does not denote specialised professional forces, but rather the concept of the Boer farmer-soldier who volunteered to fight, with his horse and rifle, at his own expense. For a summary of the strategy, tactics and structure of the SADF, see P Moorcraft, "Defending the Indefensible," *Army*, 39:3, March 1989, and "The Adversary Within," *Army*, 39:4, April 1989.
34. A Whitley, "The Parting of the Pariahs," *Business Day*, 31 March 1987.
35. For a thoughtful debunking of South Africa's arguments concerning the Cape sea route, see C Coker, "South Africa's Strategic Importance: A Reassessment," *Journal of the Royal United Services Institute*, December 1979. For a South African viewpoint, see C McEwan, *Lifeline or Strategic Backwater*? The Southern African Freedom Foundation, Sandton, 1979.
36. J Spence, *The Soviet Union, the Third World and Southern Africa*, South African Institute of International Affairs, Johanesburg, 1988.
37. *Ibid.*, p. 18.
38. For example, L Schlemmer, "South Africa's National Party government," in P Berger and B Godsell, (eds), *A Future South Africa*, Human and Rousseau/Tafelberg, Cape Town, 1988. For an incisive revisionist view on militarisation, see A Seegers, "The Military in South Africa: A Comparison and Critique," *South Africa International*, 16:4, April 1986.

THE COLONIAL WARS

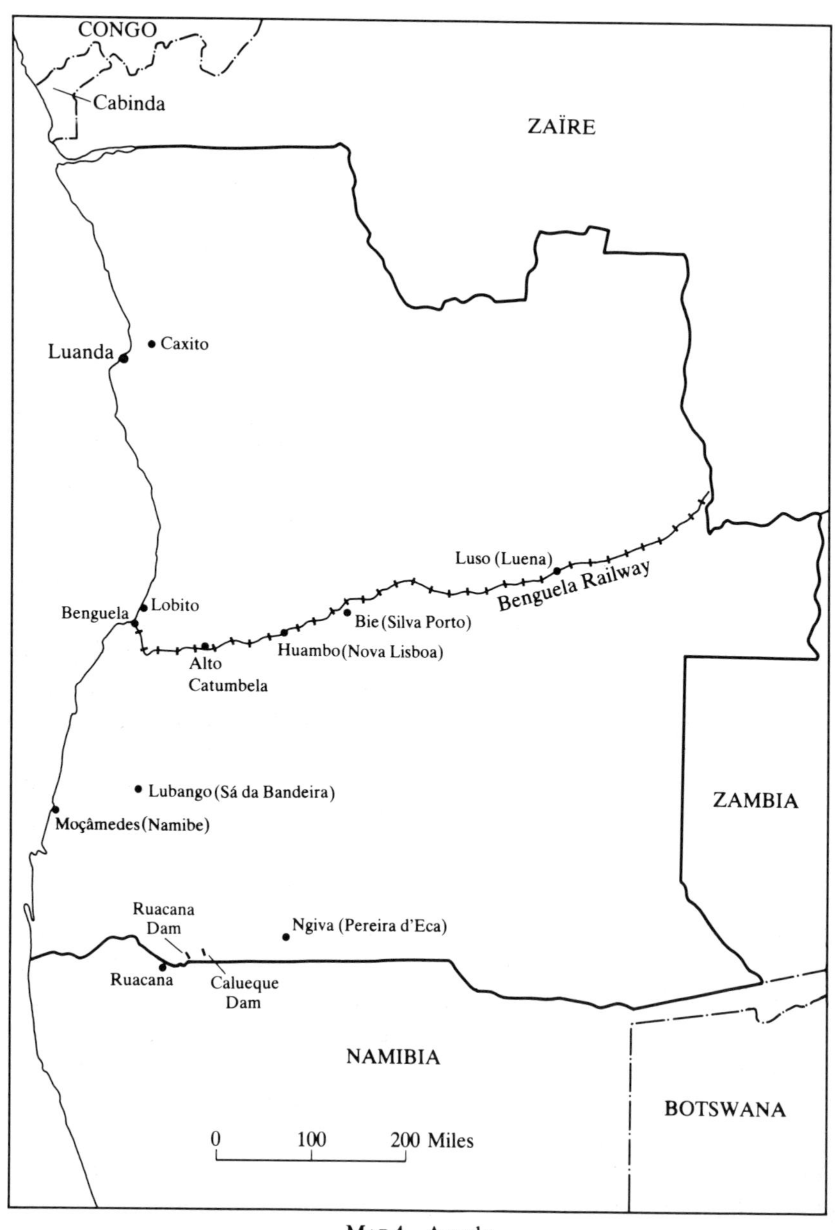
CONGO
Cabinda
ZAÏRE
Luanda
Caxito
Luso (Luena)
Benguela Railway
Benguela
Lobito
Bie (Silva Porto)
Huambo (Nova Lisboa)
Alto
Catumbela
Lubango (Sá da Bandeira)
Moçâmedes (Namibe)
ZAMBIA
Ruacana
Dam
Ngiva (Pereira d'Eca)
Ruacana
Calueque
Dam
NAMIBIA
BOTSWANA
0 100 200 Miles

MAP 4 Angola

5

Angola (1961-1976)

The buffer states

The survival of the white "buffer" colonies in Angola, Rhodesia and Mozambique was a vital element of Pretoria's defence strategy throughout the 1960s and early 1970s. Secretly in the Portuguese territories and more overtly in Rhodesia, South African security forces provided men, equipment and intelligence to their increasingly beleaguered white allies. Lisbon might have insisted that her African possessions were "overseas provinces" of metropolitan Portugal, not colonies, and Ian Smith's UDI might have converted the erstwhile self-governing colony of Southern Rhodesia into a rebel republic; nonetheless, the guerrilla struggles waged against the Portuguese and white Rhodesians fitted into the mould of African anti-colonial wars.

The civil war in South Africa, not a colony but a recognised—if reviled—sovereign state, was to assume a different pattern. Nevertheless, the political and military experiences in these "colonial wars" were destined to help shape the future conflict in the heartland of white supremacy. In three of her neighbours Pretoria was forced to swallow the victory of what it perceived as its most radical Marxist opponents. Accordingly, the South African government became even more determined to prevent an action replay in South West Africa/Namibia.

The long Angolan war was to prove the most costly in terms of SADF lives lost and commitment of military hardware. The saga entailed, initially, the political defeat of Pretoria's Portuguese allies in the colonial war (1961-75), then the debacle of the South African invasion (1975-76), the rapid decline of Pretoria's guerrilla protégé, Jonas Savimbi (1976-80), and the expensive and dangerous series of conventional battles to defend his military resurrection (1985-88). In Mozambique, Pretoria backed Portugal to win, then—reluctantly—strained to reach a *modus vivendi* with the new black rulers. After 1980, however, Pretoria stoked the fires of civil war by supporting the *Resistência Nacional Moçambicana* (Renamo) against the Maputo government. Next door, Rhodesia demanded 15 years of political attention and military largesse from Pretoria, although South Africa's support frequently wavered.

From the perspective of black South Africans, African nationalism had triumphed over white fire power in Portuguese Africa and Rhodesia; Namibia and South Africa were next on the inevitable march of freedom. The guerrilla movements committed to overturning the remaining relics of white domination adapted their tactics from the lessons learnt in these neighbouring wars. The South African government, however, argued ferociously that each of these conflicts was *sui generis*. They set no precedent. To ensure this, the battle-hardened South African military machine improved and expanded. Like its opponents, the SADF had learnt from the wars: the highly successful counterinsurgency campaign in Namibia was an excellent example of how to contain guerrillas by *military* means, although Pretoria did not win the political war there.

So long as white rule looked firm in Pretoria's buffer states, Pretoria was prepared to bolster their war efforts. Once the tides of war began to turn, the South African government launched into a frantic search for the ever-elusive black "moderate" alternatives (Savimbi or Bishop Abel Muzorewa were two such options). Failing that, Pretoria's policy was to debilitate its enemies by economic and military means. This "destabilisation" took its most dramatic form in the encouragement or creation of surrogate guerrilla movements in Angola, Mozambique, Zimbabwe and Lesotho. When necessary, these proxies could count on continuous armed intervention by the SADF (Angola) or intermittent raids (Mozambique).

Thus, South African grand strategy was initially to keep the white-ruled neighbours strong; then Pretoria tried to keep her black-governed neighbours as militarily weak and economically dependent as possible. The colonial *cordon sanitaire* became a cordon of post-independence instability. Underpinning this racist contrast was a complex web of political intrigue and military force. How Pretoria reacted to the destruction of its buffers is considered in the following survey of military events in four key territories: Angola, South West Africa/ Namibia, Mozambique and Rhodesia.

Portuguese withdrawal

After 400 years of African empire, the Portuguese were in no mood to sail with the new winds of change. Not least because during the 1960s, amid the onset of insurgency, Angola enjoyed an economic boom. The exploitation of new oilfields, the expansion of diamond mining, and rich revenues from coffee boosted the confidence of the more than 300,000 white settlers. This bonanza was not shared equally with black Angolans. Portugal claimed, often with apparent sincerity, that racial discrimination did not exist in her African domains, but the more privileged *mestiços* (mixed blood) and *assimilados* (assimilated or "civilised" Africans) constituted a miniscule portion of society. (1) The "uncivilised" remainder suffered under a harsh regime of racial injustice, sometimes not far removed from the days when Angola was a penal colony. True, there were many poor whites too (often recent immigrants), and there were some examples of rapid black mobility (for instance, a black Angolan general). It has been observed, somewhat caustically, that racial integration in Angola reflected the downward mobility of the Portuguese rather than the upward mobility of blacks. Nevertheless, the overall pattern was one of white privilege and black oppression. Harsh labour laws and poor schooling were two of the most resented aspects of alien rule. Lack of schools militated against blacks achieving the educational qualifications required to attain *assimilado* status. By 1961 only 1% of blacks was "assimilated". Any signs of black, or white, Angolan disaffection were rooted out rapidly by the secret police, *Polícia Internacional de Defesa do Estado* (PIDE), later known as the DGS. PIDE was no exception to the maxim that the secret police are usually the most (sometimes only) efficient arm of the totalitarian state. Despite the gradual liberalisation in the metropole, the semi-fascist Salazarist regime in Lisbon, for historic and economic reasons, refused to loosen the grip on the African colonies. As Marcello Caetano, Salazar's successor, put it: "Without Africa we would be a small nation; with Africa we are a big power." Fledgeling nationalist movements did emerge in the late 1960s in Angola, Mozambique and Guinea-Bissau, mostly led by *mestiços* and *assimilados*, the very embryonic "moderate", middle-class allies which the authorities hoped to buy off with privileges.

In 1961, most of these nationalists had been driven underground or into exile in neigbouring black states and Portugal. Thus, in March 1961, when the night of the long knives came—often quite literally—to the settlers of northern Angola, the Portuguese security forces were caught entirely off-guard. Marauding bands of Africans armed with machetes and old muskets attacked isolated white settlements and plantations in the Uige region. Gradually, the violence spread until by June it affected much of northwestern Angola. Only 3,000 Portuguese troops were stationed in the whole of Angola, and none were deployed in the north. By August the Portuguese had 17,000 troops in the field, aided by white vigilantes who exacted merciless reprisals for the earlier savagery. The uprising lasted six months, during which time perhaps 50,000 blacks were killed and 700 whites. The whites resumed their hold on Angola, but the foundations of the empire had been shaken.

The 1961 uprising had been organised—"organised" is a loose term for much of the often random racial slaughter—in part by an Angolan exile group based in the recently independent Belgian Congo. The group, led by Holden Roberto, a somewhat effete chairbound warrior, was initially styled the *Uniao das Populações de Angola* (UPA), but it became better known later as the FNLA (*Frente de Libertação de Angola*). Exploiting local land grievances of the Bakongo people, who straddled both sides of the ill-defined border, the UPA hoped that the violence would prompt the Portuguese to depart as hastily as the Belgians had scuttled from the Congo. The Portuguese, however, chose to fight... and to reform their archaic empire. After years of "colonialism by neglect", the authorities abolished compulsory labour, and launched a widespread programme of social, educational and economic development. But there was to be no change in the political status quo. Lisbon reaffirmed that the African "provinces" were inalienable parts of Portugal. The insurgents fought on; not only in Angola but elsewhere. In January 1963 the guerrilla war in Guinea-Bissau began. In Mozambique, the *Frente de Libertação de Moçambique* (Frelimo) commenced its war of independence in September 1964.

By 1970 Portugal had 150,000 troops in Africa, with 60,000 of them stationed in Angola. For the poorest country in Western Europe, it was no mean feat to contain the guerrillas in remote areas, far from the main towns and major farming areas where the vast majority of the settlers were concentrated. But it was the divisions among the nationalists as much as Portuguese organisation (or often lack of it) which determined the course of these colonial wars. The colonialists frequently manipulated traditional inter-tribal animosities so as to divide and rule. Suppression, exile, infiltration and assassinations, frequently, but not always, perpetrated by the secret police—who put the blame on rival nationalist factions—all took their toll. As the most distinguished historian of the Angolan revolution, John Marcum, has suggested: "clandestinity left its mark too. Decimated by infiltrators and corroded by insecurities and tensions of underground politics, Angola's nationalists became obsessively distrustful of everyone, including each other." The major nationalist parties spent as much time fighting each other as trying to defeat their mutual Portuguese foes. Sometimes, guerrillas would cooperate with the Portuguese to inflict local reversals on rival factions.

Roberto's UPA, founded in 1957 in Leopoldville, aimed initially at restoring the old Kongo kingdom. Despite proclaiming national objectives, its support derived largely from the 700,000 Bakongo tribespeople of the north. The bloody drama of 1961 garnered Roberto backing from Tunisia and Algeria, and recognition from the OAU, as well as covert military assistance from the CIA. Roberto rarely ventured into the field in Angola, preferring instead to enjoy the nightlife in Leopoldville and to concentrate on his successful real estate ventures in Zaire. Emulating the style of his brother-in-law, General Mobutu, perhaps the most corrupt leader in Africa, Roberto ran the UPA/FNLA as a personal fiefdom. Riddled with poor morale, venality and splits, the FNLA's half-hearted armed forays petered out by the mid-1960s.

The *Movimento Popular de Libertação de Angola* (MPLA) was founded in 1956. It had a more secure intellectual, but not military, basis. Its elite mostly comprised *mestiços* and some whites with links to the banned Angolan Communist Party, which was in turn connected to the Portuguese communists. The MPLA attracted a mainly middle class following among civil servants and students in the capital Luanda and in the Kimbundu region. Later, the MPLA was to recruit heavily but not exclusively from the 1,400,000-strong Mbundu tribe. Its leader was Agostinho Neto, a doctor with a (successful) penchant for poetry, who was driven into exile. His movement, also riven by factionalism, was forced to shift its offices from Paris to Conakry, to Leopoldville, to Brazzaville, and, briefly, to Lusaka. After meeting Neto in 1965, that most romanticised of revolutionaries, Che Guevara, provided a small corps of Cuban military instructors. The USSR also contributed some assistance. It later (in 1973) despaired of the MPLA's military performance, only to recharge its support to counter Chinese intervention in Angola.

The third leading protagonist was Jonas Savimbi, a soldier imbued with ever-shifting ideologies, but a charismatic leader and talented guerrilla tactician.(3) He broke from the FNLA in 1964. Two years later he formed the *União Nacional para a Independência Total de Angola* (Unita).The new movement drew its main strength from the Ovimbundu people, about two million-strong and Angola's largest tribe. Unlike Neto and Roberto, Savimbi spent most of his time leading his troops in the field. Scorning—initially—the public relations of the politics of exile, he secured little foreign support. His guerrillas were few in number and poorly trained and equipped. Except for brief periods of Zambian assistance, he could not rely upon a regular sanctuary.

As the war progressed, all three parties tried to capitalise on their relationships with fickle foreign patrons in order to counteract their frequently dismal military performance against the Portuguese army. Roberto and Savimbi, sometimes in concert, often in conflict, received aid not only from the USA, France and Britain, but also from the People's Republic of China, Rumania, North Korea and later, most significantly, from South Africa. Some oberver saw this alliance as "pro-Western", while others strained to call it "pro-Chinese". The MPLA, on the other hand, ranged equally widely across the political spectrum: the USSR, Cuba, Sweden, Denmark and Nigeria. It also recruited to its side the former Katangese mercenaries loyal to Moise Tshombe. To many this was the "pro-Soviet" side, while others dubbed it the "non-aligned" contingent. Thus, a pattern emerged, to persist during the post-independence civil war, where the favoured party was portrayed as enjoying broad ethnic and national support, and the other side was characterised as surrogates of foreign imperialism (classically, Russian or South African). In fact, none of the three movements could be legitimately or intelligently defined by the ideology or interests of their patrons. Instead, each was an expression of internal Angolan differences based upon a melange of historical, ethno-linguistic, regional and personal factors. Foreign meddling, however, played a crucial role in the war's outcome.(4)

Theoretically, the FNLA was the strongest military force. In 1971 Roberto claimed to control up to 8,000 guerrillas, although less than 1,000 were active at one time inside Angola. Indeed, during the final years of the colonial war, the FNLA plunged into a military decline. In 1970, Unita—operating in the south—was estimated by the Portuguese to have no more than 300 insurgents. Whereas the MPLA at the same time had approximately 1,500 men in-country, with two to three times that number outside. (Nationalist figures were frequently wildly inaccurate; Portuguese estimates were usually much nearer the mark.) The MPLA began its campaign by infiltrating the oil-rich Cabinda enclave in 1963-64, but it could not break through northern Angola to reach the Kimbundu areas where its support was strongest.In 1966 it switched to the east, using Zambia as a base. But a series of Portuguese offensives between 1968 and 1973, as well as the withdrawal of Zambian backing, and the splitting of the MPLA into three warring factions, resulted in major military reversals for the MPLA by 1973.

As in many African guerrilla wars, the insurgents were frequently their own worst enemies. Many of their initial advantages were squandered. The terrain was frequently suitable for insurgency. The FNLA, for example, operated along a 1300-mile frontier of swamp, mountains and jungle, while the MPLA forces in the eastern Moxico region could range over a vast plateau of savannah and forest covering 151,000 square miles. But the great distances also hampered the guerrillas, who could never match the logistics of their conventional opponents. The weather also worked both ways. In the south the style of campaign often depended upon the season. The dry season (usually April to September) facilitated conventional vehicle-borne troop movement, with clear skies for air support. In the rainy season, Angola's dirt roads turned into quagmires. The extra foliage in the bush provided more cover for the insurgents. Water was then plentiful and low cloud deterred aerial interdiction.

The long frontiers were porous, so the key neighbouring sanctuary states, the Congo Republic, Zaire and Zambia, provided convenient infiltration routes from external bases. The first 300 MPLA cadres were trained in Algeria; later MPLA units also received instruction in Bulgaria, Czechoslovakia and the Soviet Union. In addition, some of these states, as well as the OAU, offered important diplomatic assistance in the propaganda war. Internally, the guerrillas' political warfare was less effective. All the insurgent groups in the three Portuguese African territories attempted to set up "liberated" zones and to politicise the inhabitants. The most successful was the *Partido Africano da Independência de Guiné e Cabo Verde* (PAIGC) in Guinea-Bissau, which formally established a government in its extensive liberated areas in 1973. The least effective was the FNLA which concentrated almost exclusively on military action. This was one of the reasons for the breakaway of Unita which set a high priority on political education. Internecine feuds within and between the Angolan movements, often deliberately exacerbated by their external mentors, resulted in a failure to evolve an overall military strategy, let alone a concerted political programme.

Most of the guerrilla activities consisted of short-range incursions by relatively small groups, which, after operations, returned to their sanctuaries...if they had survived. Both sides, however, tended to avoid direct confrontation. Indeed, the Angolan war has been characterised as "mines versus helicopters", with relatively few "contacts" on the ground. In 1970, for example, mines accounted for perhaps as many as 50% of Portuguese casualties. Guerrilla weaponry was initially basic. Typically, they carried Simonov automatic rifles and the ubiquitous and hardy AK-47s. Russian 82mm medium mortars, 75mm cannons and various types of "bazookas" were also deployed. In the final stages of the war the weaponry became more sophisticated. In 1973, for example, the PAIGC was successfully operating ground-to-air missiles.

Caught off-guard in 1961, the Portuguese security forces were slow to consolidate their position after the savagery of their initial reprisals. Until troop levels were built up, their strategy was defensive and hesitant. By 1967, however, some 75% of the metropolitan army was overseas. By 1970, with 150,000 troops stationed in Africa, this deployment, in proportion to the Portuguese population as a whole, was five times greater than that of the USA's in Vietnam in the same year.

The Portuguese struggled to quarantine insurgency in the remote areas. For political reasons, the Portuguese were reluctant to engage in a full-scale cross-border strategy to wipe out insurgency bases in their sanctuaries. Already there were pressures from within the NATO alliance and regular condemnation at the UN. Nonetheless, numerous border infringements did take place and Portugal also manipulated Zambian dependence upon the Benguela rail-link, which traversed central Angola to the sea. The army tried to cut the supply routes from the sanctuaries and to destroy the internal bases with a regular series of coordinated sweeps. Airpower, using napalm and defoliants, was combined with swamping targets with ground patrols. Vital to these tactics were the newly introduced helicopters. By 1971, 60 Alouette helicopters were deployed. Delving into their NATO arsenal, the Fiat G91s, American F-84 Thunderjets and Lockheed P-2Vs were used for offensive air support, although the F-86 Sabre was withdrawn from African service in 1967 because of American insistence. The guerrillas had little to deter Portuguese air power. Thus, Lisbon could claim that Operation Attila in 1971, for example, had eliminated half the insurgents operating in eastern Angola.

With the exception of elite units, the Portuguese forces tended to lack an offensive spirit. They relied upon their (out-dated) technological superiority over their opponents. The Rhodesian army, which frequently cooperated with the Portuguese in Mozambique, adopted a much more aggressive hands-on approach by a continuous and forceful use of small foot patrols to engage the enemy regularly in the bush. Rhodesian "troopies" frequently derided their colonial allies for taking siestas in the afternoon while on operations, and for the habitual use of the *pica* (a sharpened stick) to probe for mines ahead of patrols. Some of these primitive methods were very effective. The Portuguese would suspend empty beer bottles on wires around their outposts as early warning devices. They were often just as effective as modern American sensors, which were anyway not available to the Portuguese. And, like the Rhodesians in the 1970s and the South Africans in Namibia in the 1980s, the Portuguese used cavalry quite successfully. Three squadrons were deployed from 1966. Supplied by air, horses could patrol vast areas. In the flat terrain of southern Angola, a mounted soldier had the advantage of silent mobility and elevated observation. Although troops normally dismounted to engage the enemy, many guerrillas displayed an extra wariness of horse-soldiers. Besides this psychological factor, the horse itself was also an (unfortunate) shock absorber in mine warfare.

In contrast to the reluctant conscript troops, elite formations of volunteers, often with a large component of black soldiers, such as the *Grupos Espeçiais*, the airborne *Grupos Espeçiais de Paraquedist* and the *Commandos Africanos* achieved very high kill rates. Perhaps as many as 40% of Portuguese forces in Angola were comprised of black Angolans, often recruited from tribal groups hostile to local rival groups which favoured the nationalists. Also, many captured guerrillas and deserters, "given offers they could not refuse", were "turned" and used to penetrate their former bases.

A major element of Portuguese strategy was the concentration of population in strategic hamlets or defended villages. Approximately one million blacks were resettled in these villages or *aldeamentos*. Allied to this was a prodigious road-building programme: 5,000 miles of roads were constructed in Angola by 1974, partly to avoid mines, but also to provide the infrastructure for the "social promotion" policy. As one official said: "Revolt starts where the road ends". Clinics, cattle-dips and schools were rapidly developed in the rural areas; the number of schools in Angola increased from 3,589 in 1967 to 5,000 by 1972. Improvements there certainly were, but the "hearts and minds" campaign could not alter the political alienation felt by the majority of blacks. Resettlement was largely a failure. To Africans, it appeared as just another phase in the cycle of destruction of traditional life, "a chronicle which began with slavery, continued through the pacification wars and contract labour period, and finally ended with the forced resettlement programme during the war".(5) A minority of traditional tribal chiefs, with reasons to fear guerrilla intimidation, may have welcomed the protection afforded by resettlement, but many Africans translated resettlement as land-grabbing by the white farmers. Even when a military rationale dominated, rather than selfish land expropriation, guerrillas often infiltrated the system and used the various types of protected villages as sources of food and information.

The Portuguese army, in the end, was not defeated in Africa. By 1974, even the most successful insurgency, in Guinea-Bissau, had resulted (arguably) in a stalemate. The verdict on the Angolan war may perhaps be a "low-intensity stalemate". And, in Mozambique, the Portuguese could posssibly have defeated the insurgency—Kenya might have been a parallel—if the war had continued. One British military historian concluded: "In many respects it was a considerable achievement for the Army of arguably the poorest and least developed country in Western Europe to fight three wars simultaneously for such a prolonged period without suffering military defeat."(6)

The strains induced by the African wars, however, played a part, albeit not a predominant part, in destroying the civil-military balance in the metropole. The ensuing coup of April 1974 destroyed almost overnight the historic "mission" in Africa and turned the armed forces into an impotent debating society. Troops in the field refused to fight. The costs had already been enormous: the proportion of the national budget spent on defence had risen from approximately 25% in 1960 to a peak of 48% in 1968. Only in Angola was indigenous production sufficient to fund a large portion (50%) of the local war effort. Revenue from the oil-fields, the diamond and iron-ore mines and the coffee and cotton plantations were drained away to fund the counterinsurgency campaigns. The Portuguese admitted to a total of 3,265 men killed in action in Africa, although independent observers suggest that the real figure was four times that number. Guerrilla casualties were much higher still.(7)

The Portuguese armed forces were the exception to the European pattern: they alone revolted against fighting the "war of the flea" in the colonies. Officers will risk their lives, it is said, but never their careers. General Antonio de Spinola, the army's deputy chief of staff, was an exception. In his book, *Portugal and the Future*, published in February 1974, he stated clearly that the African wars as a whole could never be won militarily. This monocled warrior, a public hero after his campaigns in Guinea-Bissau, tried to emulate Charles de Gaulle during the Algerian crisis. Yet Spinola did not want to grant total independence to the African possessions; he hoped instead to create a "Lusitanian" federation of self-governing states. Although his views on the futility of the wars were shared by the majority of the officer corps, he was sacked. Reinstalled as head of the military junta after the coup, he was outmanoeuvred by officers with more radical opinions.(8) The endgame for the Portuguese forces was their supervision of the transfer to full independence of the African territories. One series of wars was ending, but a much more bloody saga was about to begin.

The transition from colonial war to civil war

At the time of the Lisbon coup, the FNLA possessed the strongest armed forces. But Roberto, the revolutionary entrepreneur, was a poor general. The Zairean army stepped in to quash a mutiny against his erratic leadership in 1972 at Kinkuzu, the FNLA's main military base in the country. Thereafter, Zairean regulars beefed up the FNLA's fire power and discipline (even though the word "disciplined" has never been applied to the Zairean army). In June 1974 an advance party of Chinese instructors arrived in Kinkuzu. Arms from Peking soon followed. During September, as Portuguese troops disengaged, FNLA forces established an occupied zone in northeastern Angola.

The FNLA appeared strong, only because the rival nationalist movements were so weak. The MPLA had fragmented into three quarrelling groups. One was led by Daniel Chipenda, a man of many parts: he was a former inside-forward for the Benfica football club, a holder of the 1970 Lenin Centenary prize and the erstwhile commander of the (collapsed) eastern front. (Neto denied he was a war hero, and insisted he was a diabetic, drunkard, diamond-smuggler and bank-robber. He was, however, eventually rehabilitated by the MPLA and made the ambassador to Egypt.) In his spare time, he developed political aspirations. The dashing Chipenda forged an alliance with Roberto and led 3,000 of his men into battle in his own tribal areas in the south. This handed the FNLA a nationwide military option for the first time. Fearing that the Chinese would steal a march on them, the Russians resumed their military backing for Neto in October. "His" MPLA now made some headway in remobilising its political support in Luanda and the surrounding Kimbundu area. More important was the sympathy shown him by socialists and communists in Lisbon, as well as local Portuguese officials in Luanda. The overall military commander in Angola, Admiral Rosa Coutinho, sent to Luanda after the coup, was an energetic supporter of Neto. Nonetheless, MPLA activism was physically limited to central Angola. The Bakongo in the north and the Ovimbundu in the south were reluctant to commit themselves to Neto's party.

In the central highlands, Savimbi controlled perhaps as many as 6,000 poorly armed guerrillas. China had donated small quantities of arms to Savimbi, who had at one stage, after receiving training in China, declared himself a Maoist. But Peking did not have the same intervention-capacity as Moscow. So Savimbi tried to maximise his local advantages among the Ovimbundu people, who regarded him as a hero for the dogged, if ineffectual, campaign he had personally waged against the Portuguese. Religion played a role too. Savimbi's father had been an influential Congregationalist part-time preacher (as well as being a stationmaster). The Ovimbundu elite were largely Congregationalist-educated. (Many of the Bakongo leaders were Baptist-educated, and the MPLA leadership tended to be Methodist-trained Mbundu intellectuals.) Savimbi's clandestine relations with Portuguese intelligence resulted in a rapid, formal ceasefire with the colonial army. Thereafter, he made largely successful overtures to the remaining members of the white business community, posing as the "moderate" option for Angolan whites (while promising radical Africanisation when addressing black supporters).

On the initiative of the Kenyan president, Jomo Kenyatta, the OAU tried to reconcile Roberto, Neto and Savimbi at a meeting in Mombasa in January 1975. A pact, the Alvor agreement, was finally signed in the Algarve in Portugal. This stipulated that the three movements would form a coalition government with the Portuguese, then take part in national elections for a constituent assembly in October, and finally achieve independence on 11 November. It was further agreed that Portugal would keep a 24,000-man army until independence, while the three nationalist parties would each contribute 8,000 troops. The FNLA had an estimated 15,000 relatively well-equipped troops, supported by 3,000 guerrillas loyal to Chipenda (who was incensed at being left out of the Alvor pact). The MPLA could perhaps have produced 3,000 trained men, although it was recruiting feverishly in Luanda. Unita, the weakest because most of its armed supporters were isolated in south-central Angola, also launched a big recruitment drive in the Ovimbundu region.

On 31 January 1975 the new transitional government took office. Its most vital task was the integration of the four guerrilla armies (plus other smaller bands fighting in Cabinda and elsewhere in remote areas in Angola) into one national army. Yet, without any hint of genuine political consensus, such a military task was impossible. Proof of this was that on the very next day, FNLA and MPLA soldiers began fighting each other in the capital. The clashes spread throughout the country, despite attempts by the Portuguese army and sometimes Unita to mediate. In March the Russians delivered large quantities of arms to help the MPLA counter the conventional superiority of the Zairean-backed FNLA. Any (slim) hope of reconciliation was destroyed on 23 March at Caxito, a strategic coastal town 35 miles northeast of Luanda. The FNLA took the town and massacred more than 60 MPLA supporters. It looked as if Roberto's men were trying to recreate a climate of fear, as they had done in 1961 on the Zairean border. Neto duly proclaimed the Caxito incident as the formal start of the civil war. In the following six months, 300,000 whites panicked and quit the country, the largest exodus of whites from the continent since the Algerian crisis. The hostilities in Luanda continued unabated. In June Portuguese troops stormed the FNLA and MPLA strongholds in the capital to maintain some semblance of order. In the same month 230 Cuban instructors arrived to set up four military training centres for the MPLA. Freshly equipped with Soviet arms and allied with notoriously bloodthirsty Katangese troops (who had once fought under mercenary leader Mike Hoare and later the Portuguese), the MPLA drove the FNLA and Unita out of the city in July.

The MPLA's seizure of the capital, with some Portuguese connivance, spelt the end of the utterly fragile transitional government. Some elements of the Portuguese security forces, especially in Luanda, helped the MPLA. Elsewhere they huddled in their barracks, sometimes making forays to protect Portuguese refugees, and occasionally to assist the MPLA's rivals. Except for playing bit parts as mercenaries, the Portuguese military role in Angola was over; the great powers were now aggressively entering the fray. With Luanda in the bag, the MPLA concentrated on the capture of the provincial capitals, so that it could exert the maximum diplomatic leverage over the issue of international recognition, especially at the OAU, when Angola attained independence in November. By the end of August, Neto's troops had control of 11 of the 15 provincial capitals, although much of the countryside surrounding these towns was beyond their grasp. Crucially, the MPLA dominated Cabinda, despite French and Zairean support for FLEC (the Front for the Liberation of the Enclave of Cabinda). In September alone, the American Gulf Oil Company paid $116 million in royalties to the MPLA administration. The diamond mines in Lunda province were also held by the MPLA. Their hold on the key ports of Luanda, Lobito and Moçamedes permitted the supply of Cuban and Eastern bloc weaponry and prevented arms reaching FNLA and Unita areas further inland.

On the eve of Angolan independence, Russia and America stepped up their involvement. Like China, each superpower had previously hedged with side-bets on a number of early starters. East-West rivalry and superpower prestige demanded that the favoured horse must win. But the armed intervention of an outsider, South Africa, was greatly to complicate the prestige stakes.

The South African invasion

Once Pretoria intervened, the Angolan stage was set for high drama. Even more than a decade after the invasion, many of the facts are still buried under the weight of massive propaganda and disinformation generated at the time. From one perspective, the events of 1975-76 could easily be presented as a morality play decrying the unholy alliance of South African racism, Western imperialism, CIA recklessness and Chinese revisionism. Alternatively, Russian opportunism and Cuban aggression in the third world could be stressed. A more balanced account might try to eschew the hunt for villains and describe instead an action-reaction cycle, perhaps similar to the manner in which the European powers slithered unintentionally over the brink into the Great War. The prime concern here is with the repercussions for Pretoria: its intervention, an unwitting dress rehearsal for the bigger battles of the 1980s, signified a diplomatic, if not military, debacle. Some observers, with a little exaggeration, depicted this episode as the biggest defeat for Afrikaner power since the Boer War.(9)

During the anti-colonial war in Angola, South Africa had acted cautiously. From 1966-74, the SADF had covertly supplied the Portuguese with intelligence and then later arms, helicopters and pilots. In addition, there was intermittent collusion between Rhodesia, Portugal and South Africa to coordinate moves against a variety of hostile guerrilla movements. Lisbon was always very sensitive about any infringement of its sovereignty: it disliked having to admit that Rhodesian raids against Zimbabwean insurgents in Mozambique or SADF incursions against Namibian bases in southern Angola occurred. Portugal wanted to maintain the fiction that its colonial grip was secure. Nor did she want to add to the political handicaps in world forums by being seen to march under the same banners as apartheid and UDI. The nationalists, on the other hand, overemphasised the tripartite white coalition. An MPLA statement, for example, issued from Lusaka on 25 March 1970, alleged that the SADF presence in eastern Angola consisted of "four commando companies equipped with helicopters, artillery, automatics, bazookas and other types of weapons". The statement also claimed that "the South African military interventionist corps were quartered in their own private barracks" in the Lumega district of Moxico and that "two of these companies took part in many of the October-November 1969 enemy operations in the Luanda region. The remainder carried out criminal acts against population centres, crops and our people's fishing areas, even making incursions into Zambian territory." South Africa did set up joint command posts with the Portuguese at strategic centres, for example, at Cuito Cuanavale, the scene of fierce battles in the 1980s. Pretoria received no direct return on its investment. The purpose, as ever, was to preserve the Angolan link in the white shield.

Mozambique, however, was also a vital segment of this racial bulwark. There, South Africa was sufficiently self-possessed to leave Frelimo—initially—to its own devices. The important Cabora (Cahora) Bassa dam was left undefended by the SADF. And Pretoria scorned the hard-line white Mozambicans who wanted to set up their own UDI republic in the south, adjacent to South African territory. So why didn't South Africa stand back in Angola as it did in Mozambique? Frelimo, after all, was ideologically practically indistinguishable from the MPLA.

In Mozambique, one party inherited the mantle of power, and the country's weak economic infrastructure was largely at the mercy of South African capitalism. No single party had inherited "the political keys to the kingdom" in Angola, potentially a rich country, with few economic ties with Pretoria or Johannesburg. Lacking an economic stranglehold, the military option became more tantalising. Above all, the SADF was extremely anxious to prevent Eastern bloc troops from lining up on the 1,200-mile Namibian/Angolan border, where for ten years the army had been skirmishing with insurgents loyal to SWAPO (the South West Africa People's Organisation). A MPLA victory would inevitably boost the morale and striking power of its SWAPO ally. Angola's excellent ports could also be a strategic bonus for the Russians, who might also manipulate the Benguela rail-link with Zambia and Zaire, countries which were targets of Pretoria's detente policy.

Pretoria had no master plan for its invasion. Nor, apparently, did Washington have a clear strategic framework, although, in retrospect, the FNLA drive from the north and the SADF-led strikes from the south did take on the appearance of a deliberate pincer movement against the MPLA. Constant improvisation marked the "pro-Western" war effort. South Africa's participation was a result of almost inadvertent steps up the ladder of escalation in mid-1975. In August the SADF moved into southwestern Angola, ostensibly to protect the large hydroelectric projects at Calueque and Ruacana. ("Ostensibly" because some analysts have suggested that this move was an excuse to draw off MPLA troops from the north, and thus weaken the capital for a swift sweep south by the FNLA. This theory holds that as the SADF did not send in troops to guard the much more important [and expensive] dam projects in Mozambique, South Africa was participating in a carefully calibrated gesture that might have caught the MPLA completely off-bal-

PLATE 5.1 Eland 90mm armoured cars preparing for the invasion of Angola. *(SADF)*

PLATE 5.2 Elands crossing on motorised pontoon between Rundu and Calai, southern Angola. *(SADF)*

ance.)(10) The Angolan dam projects, largely funded by South African and Portuguese finance, were vital to agricultural development on both sides of the border. Workers on the unfinished schemes had complained of harassment by MPLA soldiers. The South African army also moved into Angola to set up and guard refugee camps at Chitado, Pereira D'Eca, Cuangar and Calai. Many thousands of Portuguese and some black Angolans later were allowed to travel on to South West Africa. Skirmishes occurred between the SADF and the MPLA and SWAPO, and, occasionally, Unita forces.

Although the possibility that these actions were intended to be deliberately provocative cannot be entirely discounted, it seems more likely that the SADF's limited deployment along the southern Angolan border was an attempt to create a localised buffer against possible Cuban/MPLA/SWAPO encroachment into Namibia. Economic factors (the dams) and humanitarian influences (white refugees) were less important considerations. But the fluid situation throughout Angola prompted Pretoria's military planners to consider the wider possibilities. Perhaps South Africa could influence the *national* outcome of the civil war? But not on her own: allies were required; and even then some persuading. In August 1975 South Africa had officially withdrawn its 2,000-strong police contingent from Rhodesia (albeit leaving equipment, pilots and advisers behind—unofficially). After pulling out 2,000 men from one war which Pretoria had thought was lost, why should it commit the same number of men to a much bloodier conflict where South Africa had far fewer traditional ties? That was the dominant train of thought among the doves in the department of foreign affairs. Even the military commanders who were advocating intervention were secretly voicing some concern about the risks of sending their troops thousands of miles from their own borders into largely unfamiliar territory against possibly superior Russian weapons. Actual defeat at the hands of communist-sponsored black troops, perhaps because of vastly superior numbers and modern weapons, and with the UN cheering from the sidelines, was a persistent hidden fear that underlay a racially-conscious arrogance that publicly dismissed the possibilities of a major reversal in the field. There was only one likely scenario that would induce South Africa to take such a risk: an anti-communist alliance with the West, particularly America.

Angola had been largely ignored by America. Secretary of State Henry Kissinger had even admitted to being "bored" by African affairs. But, as the battles shifted in the MPLA's flavour, the competitive juices were aroused, not least in the CIA, and diplomatic priorities were rejigged. Kissinger had previously tried to ride two horses in Portuguese

Africa: he supported officially his NATO ally, while allowing the CIA to sponsor, in a small way, likely allies among the guerrillas. In July 1974 the CIA resumed its financial funding of the FNLA, although requests at the same time from both Savimbi and Roberto for arms were turned down. In January 1975 the CIA donated a lump sum of $300,000 to the FNLA to help promote its position in the transitional government. America's humiliation in Vietnam in April 1975 (coming so soon after the Watergate scandal) encouraged Kissinger to reassert US prestige elsewhere. Soviet intercession in Angola was tilting the global balance, he believed. If the West allowed this to happen then friendly Zambia and Zaire, a client-state of Washington, could slip into the communist net. Malawi and Kenya would be next. As Kissinger later declared to the Senate Africa Sub-Committee in January 1976: "Angola represents the first time since the aftermath of World War II that the Soviets have moved militarily at long distance to impose a regime of their own choice. It is the first time that the US has failed to respond to Soviet military moves outside their immediate orbit." Kissinger was particularly worried about Zaire, which had allowed its regular troops to fight alongside the FNLA since February 1975. After the recent traumas in South East Asia, Kissinger's own experts on Africa in the State Department were hostile to any US intervention in the Angolan conflict. Kissinger ignored them. With the CIA he organised a covert operation, partly to avoid a clash with a highly sceptical Congress, and partly to reduce the risks of an open breach with the Soviet Union. On both counts, "deniability" would be possible. As Kissinger later admitted, it kept American "visibility" to a minimum. On 17 July the "40 Committee" (a four-man sub-committee of the National Security Council) initiated a $30 million programme to provide arms and cash to the FNLA and Unita. More was to follow. Zaire was the main conduit for this subvention. Encouraged by his patron, Mobutu sent armoured car units into Angola in the same month. In August, Zairean paratroopers joined in. Three battalions of regular Zairean soldiers joined Mobutu's expeditionary force in the next few months.

When Kissinger later defended his policies on Angola, he did not admit the possibility that the Russians might have been responding to his own activism. Clearly, the Russians were also influenced by Chinese moves. Because of Angola's mineral wealth, the Soviet Union might have been partly motivated by the then fashionable theory of "resource denial" to the West. The Kremlin must have taken into account also the American mood of isolationism after the fall of Saigon, and the congressional opposition to Kissinger's increasingly aggressive role in Angola.

Although it would be naive to interpret great power diplomacy in Angola purely in terms of knee-jerk rivalry, that such instincts were involved is indicated by CIA Director William Colby's testimony before the House Select Committee on Intelligence on 12 December 1975. Congressman Les Aspin asked Colby why certain countries backed different Angolan parties:

> Aspin: And why are the Chinese backing the moderate group?
> Colby: Because the Soviets are backing the MPLA is the simplest answer.
> Aspin: It sounds like that is why we are doing it.
> Colby: It is.(12)

A great deal of historical debate about Angola has centred on the "who started the build-up of foreign troops and weapons" issue. Some accounts, particularly from South African and American sources, unequivocally blame the Russians and Cubans. After all, Cuban advisers had been involved since 1965; by 1976, 20,000 Cuban troops were operational. Other major questions in the debate are: Did America encourage Pretoria to invade? Was Cuban intervention the cause or effect of the South African invasion?

Slicing through the Byzantine political intrigues that surrounded the events of 1975, it would be possible to construct a strong case for the prosecution against all the great powers, with more or less willing accessories being Cuba, Rumania, Zaire, Zambia, the Congo Republic and South Africa, to name but a few of the culprits. The CIA, for instance, admitted that it had spent in 1975 over $31 million on military equipment, transportation costs and cash payments. Probably, the CIA spent double that sum, which, with the Chinese, Western European and Zairean contributions, is likely to have approximated to the $200 million Kissinger estimated the Russians had spent. According to John Stockwell, the head of the CIA's Angolan task force, who later repented and wrote a scathing account of American involvement, "each major escalation was initiated by our side, by the United States and our allies".(13) A US congressional report on the CIA (the House Select Committee on Intelligence, submitted to the president on 19 January 1976) stated: "Information supplied to the Committee also suggests that the military intervention of the Soviet Union and Cuba is in large part a reaction to US efforts to break a political stalemate, in favour of its clients."(14)

Critics of American policy have argued that Russia stopped its supplies to the MPLA, even though it had recognised it as the sole legitimate liberation movement, and then reactivated its lifeline to Neto only *after* Chinese, Rumanian and Americans arms had reached the FNLA and Unita. Equally, however, it could be maintained that Moscow briefly curtailed (for the second time) its supplies to the MPLA in 1973-74 because of tactical considerations: the party had splintered three ways and Russia did not want the contending factions to use Soviet weapons against each other. Moreover, Rumanian and Cuban subvention could be identified as surrogate Soviet intervention. Soviet assistance in the war was "end-loaded": it rapidly accelerated towards the end of the year. Between November 1975 and March 1976, approximately 20 Soviet ships and 70 flights deposited their contents of arms and Cuban troops in Angola.

America had surrogates too. There is little doubt that Washington (with a little help from France, Zambia and Zaire) gave the green light to Pretoria. Senator Barry Goldwater is reported as saying: "There is no question but that the CIA told the South Africans to move into Angola and that we would help with military equipment."(15) South African recriminations later, both in public and private, strongly suggested American enticement. The then South African defence minister, P W Botha, told parliament that Washington, after encouraging South Africa to invade, then "recklessly left us in the lurch".

Given the superpower incitement of their local allies, Cuba and South Africa, it is also important to note that both the smaller powers had important objectives of their own. For a wide array of reasons, some already alluded to—primarily Pretoria's angst about Soviet expansionism, particularly in Namibia—some key decision-makers in Pretoria were eager to respond to American seduction. Nor can the Cubans be designated as mere puppets of the Kremlin: Castro's Marxism had a tropical flavour all of its own. The Cuban politburo operated with a large measure of discretion within the general framework of Eastern bloc goals. Castro himself often displayed a sense of personal "mission" about revolutions in Africa, despite the high costs in Angola.

For both Pretoria and Havana, the process of Angolan engagement was not the result of a sinister blueprint nor even single decision. More prosaically, it was caused by a gradual escalation: first, military advisers sent into train; then advisers getting sucked into combat; next small specialised support units were required; and, finally, regular army infantry units, with the air force as back-up, were deployed.(16) Thus, there was no single *casus belli*, nor a chief villain of the piece. All the actors in the tragedy became embroiled in a bloody cycle of reaction and counter-reaction, initiative and response, inspired by deliberate opportunism and reluctant parry. To lay the exclusive blame for the Angolan civil war on either Havana's or Pretoria's doorstep is propaganda, not history.

South Africa's chief aim was to prevent, if possible, a MPLA victory. That almost inevitably meant military support for the rival factions. In May 1975 Chipenda, whose headquarters were at Menongue in southern Angola, travelled to Windhoek, the Namibian capital, to consult with SADF military intelligence officials. In July Roberto met a South African delegation in Zaire. In August Savimbi made a rival pilgrimage to South Africa. The outcome was a South African programme to upgrade rapidly the training of Unita and FNLA units in the south (a team of military advisers was later sent to the northern front). The instruction took place at two main camps in southern Angola. One at Calombo trained Unita; another at Mapupa attempted to organise Chipenda's soldiery. Together these two camps were supposed to produce 6,000 "trained" troops within six weeeks. South African instructors were taken aback by the poor quality material they were told to work with. Colonel Jan Breytenbach, one of the SADF's finest combat soldiers, who was largely responsible for the shaping of the FNLA southern forces, commented in his memoirs on the quality of his charges: "They were without a doubt the scruffiest, most underfed, worst armed and most unwarlike troops I had ever seen in my life."(17) Nevertheless, despite this initially unpromising manpower, the SADF led these men into one of the most rapid military advances in history.

The SADF training programme took shape in late August. Independence was set for 11 November. Pretoria asked itself: could the MPLA coalition be weakened enough to prevent its official recognition by the OAU on independence day? It was to be a race against the diplomatic clock. Savimbi, and particularly Roberto, conjured with plans for a triumphal march into Luanda; whereas some of their South African and American advisers privately wondered whether the anti-Neto forces could survive, let alone win.

In August 1975 two opposing armies were lining up for the decisive contest for control of Angola. On the battle fronts the military mosaic was as complex as the political network of alliances. Neto and his MPLA held Luanda as well as most of the towns of central and southern Angola. Crucially, it still retained the Cabinda oil enclave, despite Zairean and French aid to local secessionists. The MPLA could count on the 4,000 Katangese as well as a growing number of Cubans and a burgeoning Soviet arsenal. On the other side, Roberto's FNLA and Zairean regulars occupied parts of the north and the south where Chipenda's wing was active. Roberto had as allies the Chinese, Mobutu, the CIA and a recent recruit, Pretoria. Unita, tribally rooted in central and southern Angola, was supported by the CIA, Zambia and South African arms and instructors. Scattered around the country were units of demoralised Portuguese troops. Most did their best to avoid the war, although small numbers, along with hard-line white settlers, joined the anti-Marxist Portuguese Liberation Army. (In contrast, a small number of white Angolans fought on the side of the MPLA.) Such was the line-up for the next six months of intense and often highly mobile warfare.

The fighting took place on two main fronts, although "fronts" is used loosely to describe advances which often ignored control of much of the countryside. What mattered most was domination of ports, major towns, vital bridges and road and rail links. In the north, Roberto dictated his own strategy, choosing to disregard his American and South African advisers who told him to consolidate the areas he already held. In the south, SADF officers enforced a much more disciplined command and control system on their black allies. In the north they advised from the rear; in the south they commanded and led from the front. The first task was to stop the MPLA advances. South African-led Unita forces first clashed with a MPLA/Cuban unit on 5 October near Nova Lisboa (Huamba). A section of Unita troops was ambushed on a bridge (some four miles from Norton de Matos) and retreated under fire from light artillery, recoilless rifles and mortars, supported by a few ageing T-34 tanks. One of the South African-manned Panhard AML-90s (which the SADF claimed was from Zaire, but was probably the South African version of the same vehicle, known as the Eland-90) managed to knock out a T-34. Another tank was destroyed by a 106mm recoilless rifle mounted on a jeep.(18) The South Africans next fired anti-tank missiles at the enemy position, which was then abandoned.

This encounter with Cuban-manned armoured units prompted the SADF to expand its efforts by forming a number of flying columns. The first column was designated "Zulu". It was led by a somewhat portly, apparently retiring officer, Colonel Koos van Heerden, whose daring campaign was soon to belie his looks and earn him the nickname "Rommel" from his men. Zulu comprised one battalion, largely of Bushmen from the Caprivi, plus 1,000 FNLA troops with a sprinkling of white officers and NCOs in command. Some of these FNLA men had been given a mere three or four days' training. When they came under fire for the first time, especially from artillery, their lack of discipline soon became apparent. The South Africans had no choice but to train their new allies in real combat conditions. Besides Panhards, transport included jeeps and a convoy of "borrowed" Portuguese vegetable trucks (in some cases the drivers were "volunteered" as well; one, at least, stayed with his vegetable truck for the duration of the drive north and back again). Zulu also had on board some 81mm mortars and several old Vickers MMGs.

For the SADF, this was limited war with a vengeance. Although Pretoria went out of its way, after the invasion, to sustain the image of a penny-packet commitment, and deliberately underplayed the numbers of troops committed, domestic political constraints forced the military commanders to restrict the size and fire power of the invading army. "Operation Savannah", the codename for the operation, involved a very small portion of the SADF's potential mobilised force. Various accounts of the war provide conflicting figures for the number of South African combatants. South African official versions admit to 2,000 men initially, rising to 3,000, whereas foreign observers have suggested a higher total (5,000 to 6,000). Besides limitations on manpower, other restrictions were the non-use of tanks and fighter-bombers. The restriction on size was partly to reduce casualties. The authorities had denied even the existence of the invasion and placed a blanket of censorship on the local media. Nonetheless, it would have been impossible to conceal a large number of white fatalities. Too many body bags would have proved politically contentious in the close-knit Afrikaner communities.

The press, parliament and the cabinet were deliberately kept in the dark by the prime minister, John Vorster, and P W Botha, his defence minister. Parliament was not sitting during the height of the crisis. Nor was it recalled, but the leader of the opposition, Sir de Villiers Graaff, was briefed. There might have been rational motivations for disguising the extent of South African involvement so as to avoid embarrassing "friendly" black states such as Zambia and to discourage Soviet escalation, but the clumsy total censorship was an internal disaster. Gradually, the whole world found out what South Africans were not supposed to know: the fact that their country was fighting an (undeclared) war in a neighbouring state. (South African troops, often dressed in green Portuguese uniforms, were told to pretend to be American mercenaries, if they met journalists. Afterwards, South African soldiers started calling their country "the States", army slang which continued in use, especially during future operations in Angola. Some SADF personnel insisted, in the very thick Afrikaans variant of South African English, that they were from England, hardly effective linguistic camouflage against the English journalists who recorded such incidents.)

Soon the extent of the South African advance could not be hidden by any censorship, especially one as ham-fisted as Pretoria's. Setting off on 19 October 1975, the Zulu task force covered just under 2,000 miles in 33 days, sweeping aside all opposition with almost contemptuous ease. A journalist, reporting from the Cuban side, admitted that the South African push had been like a "Sunday drive".

The "drive" began with the capture of Pereira D'Eca, near the Namibian border, on 19 October. Sá da Bandeira, the MPLA administrative headquarters, fell three days later. On 28 October one section of the Zulu column captured the port of Moçamedes. There the South Africans confronted the infamous "Stalin Organs" for the first time. The Russian, truck-mounted, 122mm rocket-launcher has gone through many marks since the days of the Soviet dictator, but the name has stuck. Against inexperienced and undisciplined troops this inaccurate artillery weapon can be very effective, partly because of the tremendous noise the rockets make. The 122mms demoralised FNLA troops during their sally against Luanda from the north. In the south, the South African officers kept a firm grip on their new subordinates. At Moçamedes, according to South African sources, the task force threatened to sink a Portuguese corvette if it did not up anchor and leave before morning. It did. This section of Zulu then raced along the coast road, taking Lucira and advancing on Benguela. Another Zulu element approached Benguela from due south, while a largely Unita force converged from Nova Lisboa in the east. On 4 November Benguela airport was seized, as well as the adjacent MPLA and Cuban bases, which contained much-needed fuel supplies. The next day the three-pronged assault force overran Benguela. Two days later Lobito fell, and Zulu joined up with another task force, Foxbat. Once the South Africans moved forward, they left behind Unita or FNLA "administrations". Thus, a few days before independence, the SADF-led thrust had taken two vital ports and command of the Benguela railway to enable vital supplies to reach Unita and FNLA units in the central highlands.

On 11 November the Portuguese flag flew for the last time above the old fortress of San Miguel in Luanda. The high commissioner, Admiral Leonel Cardosa, held a brief ceremony recognising Angolan independence, and handed over power to the "Angolan people", even though not a single Angolan nationalist was present. Thereafter, the last 2,000 Portuguese troops boarded the ships that were waiting, and they sailed away leaving their 400-year-old colony swamped in violence. The MPLA in Luanda set up a government, which was immediately recognised by a large number of (predominantly socialist) states, but no one

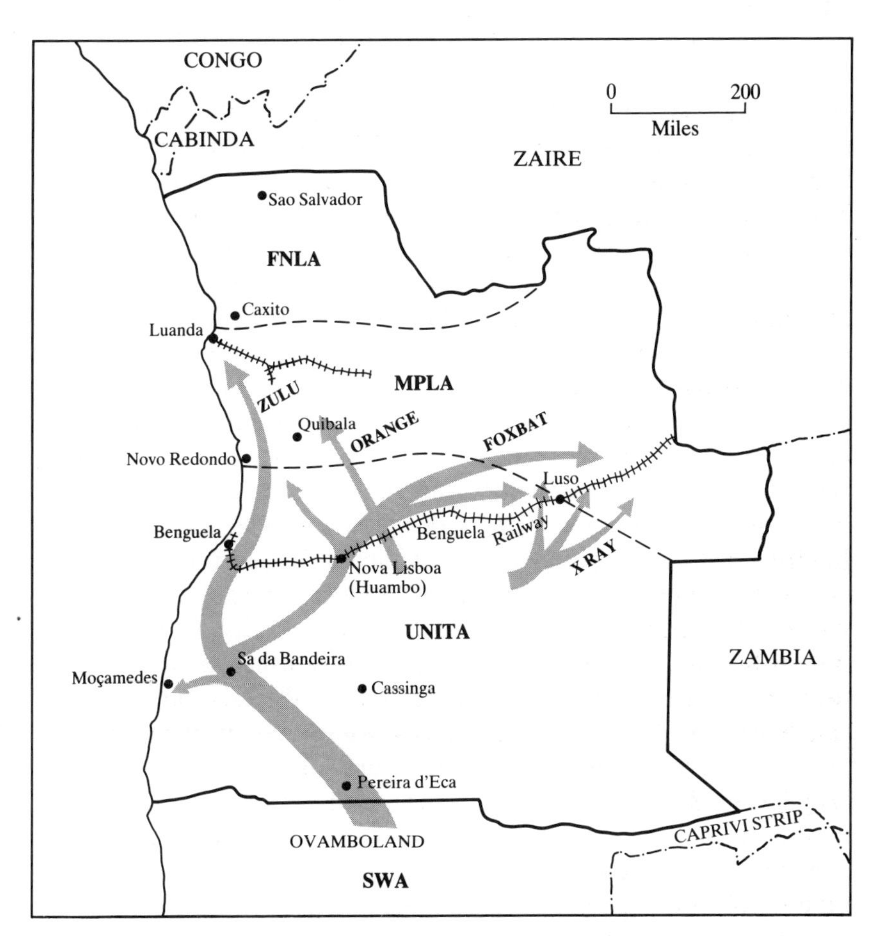

MAP 5 The South African Invasion

recognised the rival FNLA/Unita republic established in Huambo. Despite their diplomatic gains, the MPLA now faced a serious military crisis. The rival coalition threatened water, power and food supplies to the capital. Even the possibility of decamping to Cabinda was mooted by the MPLA leadership.

In the south the MPLA's army (the People's Armed Forces for the Liberation of Angola, FAPLA) was retreating on nearly all fronts. The northern campaign was different. On independence day a FNLA force, supported by two Zairean battalions and 100 Portuguese Angolan commandos, advanced across the wide, flat Quifangondo valley, 12 miles from the outskirts of Luanda. The small army was supported by 12 armoured cars and six 106mm recoilless rifles mounted on jeeps. The South African advisory team, plus four 5.5-inch artillery pieces manned by SADF personnel, positioned themselves on a ridge overlooking the valley. They were accompanied by a contingent of CIA officers. A mile to the rear, two North Korean 130mm cannons, manned by Zaireans, were in place. Roberto felt his hour of destiny had arrived: Luanda was now almost in his grasp. Morale among his 1,500-strong force was high. The foreign advisers were relaxed, even though Roberto had not heeded their military advice to consolidate, not march on the capital.

But this was not to be a northern picnic to match the Sunday drive in the south. The Cubans, some of them in Angola for just a few days, were waiting. They opened up with salvos, 20 at a time, of their 122mm rockets. Caught in open ground, with no cover at all, 2,000 missiles rained down on the FNLA. Roberto's dreams vanished as his men broke and ran. They fled, leaving weapons and wounded alike. The supporting artillery could not help. One North Korean cannon exploded the first time it was fired, killing its crew. The second also misfired, and injured its operators. The vintage South African artillery kept pounding away, but their firepower was very limited compared with the Cubans' 120mms, which had double the range of the 5.5-inch guns. This was an important lesson learnt from the Cubans, which the South African arms industry religiously applied in their later development of their near-revolutionary G5 and G6 artillery systems.

This one action effectively knocked the FNLA and Zaire out of the war. The SADF contingent rapidly exited to the coast, where it was extracted in a risky night operation by the frigate SAS *President Steyn*. As thousands more Cubans arrived in Angola, some were assigned to mop up the FNLA limping northwards. Disciplined troops, such as the Vietcong, could survive heavy bombing and artillery assault by building foxholes, tunnel networks and by orderly withdrawals and counter-attacks. But, as John Stockwell so succintly commented on the retreat: "The FNLA guerrillas and Mobutu's commandos were not diggers."

The CIA tried to stabilise the collapsing northern front by organising French and Portuguese mercenaries, and supplying Roberto with funds to hire British and American soldiers of fortune. The latter included psychopaths, deadbeats with no military experience and even two retrenched dustmen, (apparently) recruited directly from their dustcarts. Their positive military impact was predictably zero, although the atrocities examined at the Luanda trial of some captured mercenaries provided extra ammunition for MPLA propaganda. As the CIA money dried up, the FNLA withdrawal turned into a total rout. Zaire's best troops, humiliated and beaten, conducted an orgy of rape, killing, looting and destruction as they withdrew to their own borders. On 11 February 1976 the last FNLA stronghold, Sao Salvador, fell. Many of the Bakongo tribesmen who had been ardent, long-term supporters of Roberto welcomed the MPLA and Cubans as liberators.

In the north, South Africa had ventured little. In the south the SADF had committed thousands of men along a front hundreds of miles long. Two days after independence the South Africans occupied Novo Redondo. Here the Zulu task force suffered its heaviest casualties since the first days of its lightning advance. From well-placed dug-outs, the Cubans unleashed a barrage of rocket-fire and mortars. One of the mortar-bombs exploded in the middle of the column. Eighteen South Africans were wounded and one was killed, the first South African fatality in the task force. During its 33-day, 1,974-mile incursion Zulu had fought 21 skirmishes and launched 16 rapid-response attacks and 14 more carefully planned assaults. According to South African sources, 210 enemy troops were killed, 96 wounded and 56 captured for the loss of five (including one South African) and 41 (20 South Africans) wounded. But the burgeoning Cuban forces were now dug in for a determined attempt to repulse the SADF/FNLA/Unita onslaught. Battlefield constraints and, more important, international politics now intruded to stem South Africa's push. "Rommel", alias Van Heerden, radioed Pretoria for reinforcements, including a para-drop behind enemy lines. Both were refused. Zulu was told to sit tight at Novo Redondo (after withdrawing from Port Amboim).

Zulu's advance was the most dramatic, but four other task forces were engaged in Operation Savannah. Foxbat had been formed in mid-October; it originally comprised of South African-trained Unita forces and a squadron of vintage Panhard cars. This group, reinforced with 120 Zairean regulars, guarded the FNLA/Unita capital at Huambo. On 25

October Foxbat blocked the Cuban/FAPLA advance on Silva Porto; a Cuban general was killed in the ensuing fighting.

When Foxbat and Zulu joined up in Lobito in mid-November, the South African forces had recaptured virtually all the territory the FNLA and Unita had lost in the preceding months. On independence day FNLA forces held much of the north, although it was soon to be wrested from them; while in the south the SADF commanded a front from Novo Redondo through Santa Comba to Luso in the east.

More Cuban troops were entering the fray. On 27 November three shiploads of combat troops and equipment arrived, despite minor harassment by the US navy en route. (The CIA considered making a feint against Cuba itself in order to distract Castro's new *conquistadores* from their African adventures.) By January approximately 12,000 Cuban troops were operational. Besides Cuban/Russian sea transportation from the Caribbean, five Soviet supply routes have been identified. Soviet An-22 transports flew to Maya Maya, near Brazzaville in the Congo republic, where equipment was forwarded to MPLA strongholds north of Luanda. Some An-22s flew directly from the southern USSR to Luanda or Henrique de Carvalho, only stopping to refuel in Guinea, Mali or Algeria. Soviet cargo vessels delivered small arms to Dar es Salaam in Tanzania, Point Noire in Congo or to Guinea, which were then ferried to MPLA-held areas. In a well-executed and complex logistical exercise, T-34 and T-54 tanks, armoured personnel carriers, MiG-21 fighters, anti-tank missiles, BM-21 rocket launchers, SAM-7s and AK-47 rifles were transported over great distances to Angola.

Initially, the SADF tried to contain this influx. Another combat group, task force Orange, was set up on 12 December. It comprised an Unita battalion, a South African armoured car squadron, and a South African infantry company with artillery. This column occupied the Salazar bridge over the Cuanze river at the northernmost extremity of Unita territory. On 15 December Orange fell upon a large group of Cubans near Quibala. The Cubans deployed MiGs and tanks, while the South Africans had to rely upon old armoured cars, light reconnaissance aircraft and Alouette helicopters. South Africa's "limited" war was bursting at the seams.

While Orange was engaged at Quibala, Foxbat fought perhaps the hardest action of the campaign at the so-called "Bridge 14" north of Santa Comba. Foxbat consisted then of three Unita/FNLA companies, a SADF infantry company, a squadron of Elands, a company of engineers and a mortar platoon supported by eight 5.5-inch (140mm) and 25-pounder guns. A Cuban/FAPLA battle group, armed with several battalions of BM-21 122mm multiple rocket launchers, had blown up the bridge and entrenched in the hills beyond the river. It was the morning of 10 December, exactly a month after a similar Cuban ploy had routed Roberto's advance on Luanda. Time and time again, the Cubans deployed the Stalin Organs to great effect. Each rocket pallet of 40 tubes was usually mounted on a rotating platform. A textbook deployment is a battalion of 18 which can fire 720 rocket rounds in 30 seconds. These can be fired in salvo, "rippled" or selected individually. The vehicle, the Ural 375, has excellent cross-country capability—particularly important in Angola's rough terrain. But the Ural must be parked obliquely to the target to avoid blast damage to the unprotected cab, although this was not always done and occasionally the cab was blown away. Despite the noise and psychological impact of the BM-21s elsewhere, they did not prove to be decisive against the SADF. At Bridge 14 a company of Foxbat sappers, protected by two Elands, examined the remains of the blown bridge. After they had deactivated a number of mines, the engineers started to rebuild the bridge using local material: scrap-iron and bluegum logs. The Cuban/FAPLA force did not react as the engineers constructed a footbridge to secure a bridgehead on the opposite bank. But as soon as an attempt was made to build the main bridge to carry the vehicles, the Cubans opened up with their BM-21s and mortars. Shells exploded all around the engineers, but the bridge was never hit. The bridge-builders withdrew and the SADF replied with their less powerful but more accurate artillery. The next morning the column crossed over the new bridge under heavy but ineffectual fire. Foxbat then stormed the Cuban/FAPLA positions. Pro-communist sources admitted that this battle was a disaster for the Cubans who—according to the South Africans—fled, leaving behind over 200 Cuban and 200 FAPLA troops dead. Four South Africans were killed. Among the equipment captured were ten 76.2mm field guns, 22 120mm mortars and five BM-21s. Crucially, one BM-21 multiple rocket launcher was salvaged intact. It was taken back to South Africa, where Armscor used it as the pattern for the Valkiri. The SADF became absolutely determined to remedy its artillery deficiencies.

In December another task force, X-Ray, was formed at the specific request of Savimbi to guard the Benguela railway. X-Ray split into three roving combat groups, which conducted mopping-up operations east of Bucaco. (The fifth task force was the hastily removed team supporting Roberto.)

Such was the high-water mark of Operation Savannah. Despite the claims of higher numbers, the SADF maintained that it had committed between 2,500 to 3,000 South African troops, with the back-up of a small number of armoured cars, light planes and helicopters. There is no doubt that the SADF performed extremely well. As Stockwell concluded: "The South African armoured columns...teamed with UNITA to make the most effective military strike force ever seen in black Africa, exploding through the MPLA/Cuban ranks in a blitzkrieg, which in November almost won the war." But the SADF was out-gunned and out-numbered. Of particular concern to Pretoria was the presence of the MiG-17s and MiG-21s. The superior fire power enabled the MPLA to go back on the offensive in the south. FAPLA also began to counter with guerrilla harassment behind the overextended lines of their opponents. On 18 December Zulu suffered further losses around Quibala. Elsewhere, four SADF mechanics, who had accidentally strayed into MPLA territory, were captured. The captives were paraded as proof of South African aggression. Pretoria was pilloried internationally. An increasing number of African states which had previously condemned Cuban and Soviet adventurism now switched to the side of the MPLA. On 19 December the US Senate voted to block all additional covert funds, thus forcing the CIA to abandon its allies in Angola. Pretoria, however, was persuaded by Washington and a number of conservative black states to continue fighting until 22 January 1976 when the OAU voted on Angolan recognition. The OAU vote was an inconclusive 22-22 stalemate, but the MPLA was rapidly gaining ground. Then the lachrymose Kenneth Kaunda, who had encouraged Pretoria's gamble, also switched sides and, with a wave of his ever-present white handkerchief, dismissed his racist allies. The South Africans were now left high and dry.

The SADF withdrawal duly began on 22 January 1976. On 11 February the rebel capital of Huambo fell. The FNLA had given up; Unita went back into the bush to fight on with a few thousand guerrillas. As a face-saving device, Pretoria obtained from the MPLA government the promise not to interfere with the southern hydro-electric schemes. South African forces remained in an occupied strip along the southern border until the end of March. Cuban/FAPLA units finally arrived on the Namibian border on 1 April, perhaps a suitably ironic day to confirm the realisation of the nightmare scenario the invasion was intended to forestall.

Results of the South African debacle.

This phase of the Angolan war has been sketched in some detail because it had a profound impact upon the whole subcontinent; most crucially for the West, it diminished the stature of American and South African foreign policies.

Kissinger had tried to win friends in Africa, but his first excursion into the region had been a dramatic failure (although this did not deter him from trying a few months later to solve the Rhodesian imbroglio). The historian-turned-statesman's perceptions of the continent had long been faulty. As discussed earlier, the foundation of US failures had been the acceptance of the Tar Baby option, which discounted the long-term effectiveness of the southern African guerrilla movements. The Lisbon *putsch* caught the CIA completely off-balance. In July 1974 the CIA told the 40 Committee that the $40 million it wanted would be a likely match for any Soviet aid to the MPLA. In the event, Moscow probably spent ten times that amount on the civil war in the 1970s. Ironically, while the CIA accountants haggled over the initial $40 million (more was spent later), the American Gulf Oil Company was making one of its regular $200 million payments to the MPLA. Stockwell admitted that for the CIA "nothing had worked". His account of CIA operations (*In Search of Enemies*) contained a long list of shortcomings. Much of the weaponry sent through Zaire lacked ammunition, instructors, training manuals or simply failed to work, such as the SAM-7s bought from Israel. The Swift patrol craft, he wrote, disintegrated "in short weeks of the Zaireans' pounding misuse". Twenty-four rubber boats were "lost". "Money was wasted on ice plants and fishing boats." French mercenaries ignored their contracts and quit when they were most needed. Much of the CIA cash slipped into Mobutu's pocket. "Most serious of all," concluded Stockwell, "the United States was exposed, dishonoured, and discredited in the eyes of the world."

Like Pretoria, Washington had no clear political aims in Angola. The USA vacillated from a policy of intervention to tacit acceptance of the MPLA to (possible) intervention again (in late 1976) and then veered back to tacit recognition. The last three stages occurred in less than a year. Initially, Washington wanted merely to stalemate the MPLA. But US aid was too small to win, and too large to be kept secret. Thus, a well-disclosed failure resulted. It has been argued that Kissinger, and Pretoria, should have gone for broke. There is some evidence to suggest that in late 1976 Kissinger considered completing the "unfinished revolution" in Angola by injecting Unita with a massive dose of American aid. Congress, however, feared another Vietnam. And Kissinger was like Banquo's ghost at the table of the newly-elected Jimmy Carter. The Carter administration, while not formally recognising the MPLA, moved towards compromise with Neto, in the hope of greater stability in Zaire and Zambia, and, crucially, the removal of Cuban troops which could herald, in turn, the independence of Namibia. But the Cubans remained, so did the stigma of Pretoria's blunder. If Washington suffered a setback, Pretoria had to endure a traumatic political defeat.

The military withdrawal—after nearly reaching Luanda—rankled among some senior SADF officers. As in Israeli messes after the retreat from Egypt after the Yom Kippur War, there were mutterings about "victorious soldiers and defeatist politicians". But the widely accepted view (especially in South Africa) that the SADF retrocession was caused by purely political factors is not accurate. Certainly, the self-imposed limitations on the invasion force were largely political, but the fighting revealed a number of *military* deficiencies, not least the need for longer-range artillery and better armoured vehicles. Command, control and supply problems were also evident. Prime Minister Vorster hinted at some of the military reasons for his decision shortly before the withdrawal. He said that the USSR was sending "sophisticated weapons: tanks, 122mm rockets, mounted in clusters of 50 [*sic*]... infantry-borne SAMs. Only big powers can affect this arsenal. It is certainly beyond our limits."(19) After years of counterinsurgency in Namibia without any SADF deaths in action, the toll in Angola was 43 South Africans killed and approximately 100 wounded. The white electorate's distress at being finally told about such a sacrifice in lives for a war which the government originally said did not exist was compounded by the embarrassment of seeing (in the media) the first-ever SADF prisoners-of-war paraded as MPLA propaganda weapons.

Nevertheless, political factors were paramount: Pretoria had been left in the lurch by its allies. It was a lesson that the South Africans would not forget. As Vorster put it: "When it comes to the worst, South Africa stands alone." Washington had turned its back. Far from cementing US-South African ties, the joint venture had soured relations, soon to be made even worse by the effects of President Carter's substitution of Kissinger's cool *realpolitik* with self-righteous moralising. At least Moscow, Peking and Pretoria could understand the style and content of the modern-day Metternich. No one, allied or hostile, could fathom Carter's patently sincere but ineffectual foreign policy. Kissinger had talked of defeating communism in black Africa, now Carter was talking about majority rule in white South Africa. And Paris had been at its cynical best. After nurturing closer ties with Pretoria, via proxies in Ivory Coast and Gabon, and cheering on the SADF advance, in a sudden *volte face* the French government embargoed vital arms supplies to South Africa. Detente with black southern African states was ruptured, even with those countries which had almost begged Pretoria to move into Angola. Kaunda no longer described Russia and Cuba as "a plundering tiger and her cubs". Tigers, he had no doubt been informed, were not to be found on the African continent.

On the domestic front, the blanket censorship, while foreigners were reading about the invasion in minute detail, caused widespread disillusionment with the government, especially as it came at the same time as the unfolding "Muldergate" scandal. But no heads rolled for the Angolan disaster; no minister resigned. Soon opinion polls began to register support for the government's *post-hoc* rationalisations for the invasion which said, in essence, the republic had struck a mighty blow against Soviet expansionism. White quiescence was not matched in the much more politicised black communities. Many blacks perceived the SADF's withdrawal as the military defeat of Afrikaner racism by African nationalism; whereas some blacks depicted events as the triumph of socialism over Western imperialism. At the nub of these interpretations was the impression that the bubble of apparent white South African invincibility had been pricked. The so-called "awe factor"—the alleged black fear of and respect for white repressive power —had been severely undermined. There is a direct psychological continuum between the SADF's exit from Angola in March and the Soweto uprising in June. Sowetan youngsters knew precious little Portuguese, but they could readily chant *Viva MPLA* and *A Luta Continua*.

A Western diplomat in Lusaka summed up the repercussions of the Angolan fiasco: "I sometimes think that South Africa went into this war to assure an MPLA victory. They went in with a weak force at the wrong time, and they got out on the wrong foot. In between they lied and lied to a world that knew the truth." So much obloquy and for what? Ignoring the Clausewitzian paradigm, Pretoria had no clear political aims for its war effort. Clearly, it wanted to influence the outcome of the war at the expense of the MPLA. But this was woolly ambition, not a precise war aim. Did the South Africans anticipate the possibilities of rapid Cuban and Soviet armed intervention? Probably not. The Americans had not expected it, and presumably their intelligence on Cuban/Soviet intentions was better than Pretoria's. The CIA shared much of its Africa-related information with South Africa's Bureau for State Security. Perhaps both fed off the same misperceptions. Once the Eastern bloc military bridge was operational, did the SADF believe it could defeat the pro-MPLA alliance? Or, more modestly, was Pretoria backing the FNLA and Unita to strengthen their hands should a coalition government with the MPLA finally emerge from the bloody transition? Or, rather, was Pretoria hoping to Balkanise Angola by prompting a Katanga-style secession in, at least, southern Angola? A greater Ovamboland, covering northern Namibia and southern Angola, had always been one of Pretoria's pet schemes to divide and rule. It seems likely that Pretoria had juggled with all these scenarios and, in the end, simply hoped for the best.

Not only was there a lack of precise war aims, but also a distinct deficiency in political leadership. Political direction, such as it was, appeared to have been centred on Vorster and P W Botha. The cabinet and the State Security Council were left out in the cold. The senior military commanders and military intelligence provided the prime input in the Angolan crisis, even though both the influential chief of BOSS, General Hendrik van den Bergh, and the department of foreign affairs preferred a hands-off policy, as in Mozambique. Van den Bergh, who usually had the ear of the prime minister, was personally hostile to the growing influence of military intelligence. (During his regular meetings with his Rhodesian counterpart, Ken Flower, Van den Bergh used to regale him with a multitude of stories about the blunders made by SADF military intelligence. He was, according to Flower, particularly bitter about the Angolan escapade.) Moreover, it appears that a number of American intelligence sources outside the CIA warned Van den Bergh quite early on about the precarious nature of US commitment to the war. And the traditionally dovish department of foreign affairs stressed that South Africa stood to score an own goal if she broke her (purported) golden rule of not interfering in her neighbours' affairs. Direct armed intervention could boomerang, said the doves, and bring intervention against South Africa, not least further economic sanctions. P W Botha had the fullest confidence of the military commanders. The long-serving defence minister had temporarily eclipsed Van den Bergh in the role of primary security adviser to the prime minister. In sum, Vorster sided with the hawks and allowed the operational discretion of his commanders to dictate grand strategy. The military dimensions of this strategy were well-executed, especially as the SADF fought with one hand tied behind its back. The military offensive had been divided into four escalating phases, with phase four being the capture of Luanda. The decision to cross from one phase to the next rested with Vorster. On the ground, however, operational imperatives, with overzealous commanders emphasising local requirements, encouraged a rapid shift through the first three gears, despite Vorster's prevarication. Thus, the tactical tail came to wag the strategic dog, with predictable results.(20)

The invasion of Angola altered the balance of civil-military relations in South Africa, permanently and paradoxically. P W Botha, destined soon for the premiership, became even more determined to forge a comprehensive, politico-military framework for his "total strategy". This implied the dominance of clear-cut political goals. Simultaneously, the SADF began a continuing process of embellishment of their newly acquired status as major, quasi-independent actors in national decision-making. Greater military influence *and* stronger (that is, more authoritarian) political leadership were to be the hallmarks of the dawning Botha era. The two contradictory tendencies could operate in tandem mainly because of Botha's symbiosis with his generals. But this dangerous equilibrium, the elevation of military force to the status of primary political principle, became *the* problem, not an answer to the fundamental dilemmas of white supremacy in South Africa. After the Angolan invasion, the generals said, in effect, to the politicians: give us your full backing and next time we will do much better. Meanwhile, the SADF swiftly applied the practical lessons of its first taste of conventional warfare since Korea. A new generation of armoured vehicles, missiles, artillery and aircraft, skilfully adapted to local conditions, but also suitable for the export market, began to roll out of Armscor factories.

The SADF would be more prepared next time: no more hijacking vegetable trucks! This was the credit side of the balance. The war's local debits were numerous. The MPLA itself, always hostile to Pretoria, became an even more implacable foe. And Savimbi, by supping with the devil, had lost his chance of playing a moderating role in Angolan politics. States throughout the region, particularly Mozambique, grew even more suspicious of Pretoria and more susceptible to Moscow's blandishments. All this made America's role much harder, especially in Rhodesia, where the mounting conflict was about to drain away much more of South Africa's defence budget. The bloodletting in Angola made white Rhodesians even more paranoid about black rule, and even more determined to play upon white racist sympathies "down south". Angola had also boosted the morale of Zimbabwean insurgents, thus further complicating Pretoria's search for a black "moderate" leader to replace the stubborn Ian Smith: better a Muzorewa, than a Neto or Machel.

South Africa's withdrawal in March 1976 was not an end, but the beginning of a different kind of war in Angola. The MPLA became the officially-recognised government (though Washington still held out against recognition). Once it had won—for the time being—its own war, the MPLA proceeded to support the poorly organised guerrilla campaigns of not only SWAPO but also the ANC. ANC bases were established in central Angola, while numerous SWAPO camps were re-established in the south. Over the next decade the SADF attacked these southern insurgent bases repeatedly. The SADF's self-limitations of 1975-76 were whittled away as the levels of manpower and of the sophistication of weaponry on both sides rose. The South Africans often applied their considerable strength in short, sharp strikes as well as later reoccupying swathes of southern Angola. The continued presence of the Cuban army and the upgrading of FAPLA, armed with modern Soviet hardware, dictated a measure of caution. Pretoria always did its best to avoid any hint of a local SADF "defeat" again. The increasing deployment of modern Soviet weaponry, particularly air-defence radar and combat aircraft, made that a real possibility by the mid-1980s. Meanwhile, the entrenchment of the Soviet and Cuban position prompted Pretoria to be all the more reluctant to withdraw from Namibia. The pattern of events in Angola strongly influenced the very distinct but inevitably related bush war in Africa's last colony.

References and notes:

1. According to the 1950 official census, there were 30,089 *assimilados* in a total Angolan population of 4,036,687 (0.75%). The Mozambican leader Eduardo Mondlane described the assimilated status as "at best simply bourgeois social clubs, often called upon to shout their part in the militarized chorus of allegiance to Salazar". John Marcum's two-volume work provides an exhaustive background to the Angolan revolution: *The Angolan Revolution: Vol 1. The Anatomy of an Explosion (1950-1962)*; *Vol 2, Exile and Guerrilla Warfare (1962-1976)*, MIT, Cambridge, 1969, 1978.
2. G. Bender, *Angola under the Portuguese*, Heinemann, London, 1978, p. 28. For a useful summary of the background to the 1961 uprising, consult D Willers, "The Genesis of a Revolution: Angola: 1483 to the Present," *South Africa International*, 12:1, July 1981.
3. A useful insight into Savimbi's character is provided by Fred Bridgland's somewhat uncritical biography, *Jonas Savimbi: A Key to Africa*, Macmillan, Johannesburg, 1986. For a highly critical appraisal of Savimbi, particularly the accusation that he collaborated with the Portuguese, see W Minter, *Operation Timber: Pages from the Savimbi Dossier*, Africa World Press, New Jersey, 1988.
4. For a discussion on the interpretation of the "sides", see G.Bender, "Angola: the Continuing Crisis and Misunderstanding," *Current History*, 82:482, March 1983.
5. Bender, *Angola under the Portuguese, op. cit.*, p. 159.
6. I Beckett, "The Portuguese Army: The Campaign in Mozambique, 1964-1974," in I Beckett and J Pimlott, (eds), *Armed Forces and Modern Counter-insurgency*, Croom Helm, London, 1985, p. 136.
7. For varying assessments of casualties, see A Venter, *Portugal's Guerrilla War*, Malherbe, Cape Town, 1973, p. 75, and B. Davidson, *No Fist is Big Enough to Hide the Sky*, Zed, London, 1981, p. 160.
8. D Porch, *The Portuguese Armed Forces and the Revolution*, Croom Helm, London, 1977, analyses these events with great wit and lucidity.

9. See C Legum and T Hodges, *After Angola: The War Over Southern Africa*, London, 1976, p.35. An Afrikaner professor of law at Potchefstroom, J van der Vyfer, said that "South Africa's escapade in Angola would probably prove to be the blunder of the century". *The Sunday Times*, (Johannesburg), 1 February 1976.
10. For an elaboration, see R Johnson's iconoclastic, but very readable, *How Long Will South Africa Survive*? Macmillan, Johannesburg, 1977, pp. 129-71.
11. For a detailed discussion of Kissinger's policy, see A. Gavshon, *Crisis in Africa*, Penguin, Harmondsworth, 1981, pp. 223-57.
12. Quoted in *ibid*, p.233.
13. Stockwell's account, *In Search of Enemies*, Deutsch, London, 1978, discusses in detail South African-American collaboration, but he insisted that "I saw no evidence that the United States formally encouraged them to join". (p.186).
14. Quoted in Gavshon, *op. cit.*, p. 242.
15. Quoted in M Wolfers and J Bergerol, *Angola; The Frontline*, Zed, London, 1983, p.8.
16. The military style was, however, different. Cuban instructors became involved—integrated—at every level of the FAPLA forces, whereas, perhaps not surprisingly, the SADF instructors retained a distinct identity. The Russian advisers were notorious for their aloofness towards black Angolan troops.
17. Jan Breytenbach, *Forged in Battle*, Saayman and Weber, Cape Town, 1986.
18. A summary of the battles from the official South African perspective can be found in H-R Heitman, *South African War Machine*, CNA, Johannesburg, 1985, pp. 166-75. For the official Cuban version, see Gabriel Garcia Marquez, *Operation Carlotta: Cuba's Role in Angola's Victory*, Centre for Cuban Studies, New York, April 1977. The operation was named after a revolt against Spanish rule led by a female slave. For a vivid account of life in Luanda during the siege, see R Kapuściński, *Another Day of Life*, Picador, London, 1988. For a useful summary of South Africa's involvement in the war, see R Hallett, "The South African Involvement in Angola, 1975-76," *African Affairs*, 77:308, July 1978.
19. For an elaboration of this point, see R. Jaster, *South Africa's Narrowing Security Options*, Adelphi Paper No. 159, International Institute for Strategic Studies, London, 1980, pp. 23-5.
20. For a detailed analysis of South African decision-making, see D Geldenhuys, *The Diplomacy of Isolation*, Macmillan, Johannesburg, 1984, pp. 74-84.

MAP 6 Namibia/South West Africa

6

Namibia (1966-1976)

The last colony

"The land God made in anger"—so Namibia (or South West Africa) is sometimes called. It *is* an angry land, but beautiful too. And very big. With a small population (estimates vary from one to one-and-a-half million), it is the same size as France, Belgium and West Germany combined. It boasts the second lowest population density of any country (Outer Mongolia comes first.) Yet the wild symphony of harsh desert, lunar landscapes, pastoral serenity and almost untouched wildlife formed also the reluctant requiem for the longest and most under-reported guerrilla war. Indeed, never had so few fought so bitterly for so long for so much territory as in this, Africa's last colony. Pretoria intervened in other people's colonial conflicts. In Namibia, South Africa had its very own colony to run, albeit illegally held, in defiance of the world.

Namibia was, arguably, the final unresolved legacy of the German defeat in 1918. If ever a metropolitan country deserved to lose a colony it was Imperial Germany. In the 1880s the German Reich began to colonise the territory. The first commissioner was, almost prophetically, Dr H E Göring, the father of the Nazi leader. When the Herero tribe, and later also the Namas, rebelled, the German authorities issued the infamous extermination proclamation *(Vernichtungsbefehl)*. About 70% of the population in the centre and south of the colony were ruthlessly exterminated. (1) In 1915 South African forces occupied the colony as part of the allied war effort. In 1920 South Africa was mandated the territory as a "sacred trust" by the League of Nations. Trust meant annexation to the Afrikaner leaders. In 1922, during the Bondelswart uprising, the South African air force bombed the rebels into submission. Over 100 men, women and children were killed.

After the demise of the League, Pretoria commenced its long legal wrangle with the UN over the status of the mandate. Regardless of legal debate, South Africa began the process of integration. The territory's whites (about 14% of the population) were granted representation in the South African parliament in 1949. Apartheid was entrenched, particularly after 1964, when the government endorsed the findings of the Odendaal Commission. Much of the best land and all the political power was reserved for whites, while the ten other ethnic groups were offered various degrees of limited autonomy. It was bantustans again, but with a Namibian face.

The UN continued to protest at South Africa's actions in Namibia, but to little avail. In 1958 Andimba (Herman) Toivo ja Toivo, a leading black nationalist, sent a petition to the world body in a recorded message hidden in an old copy of *Treasure Island*. He also wrote to the Pope and to Queen Elizabeth. The letter to the Queen was, however, duly returned with a note saying it should be forwarded through her representative, the governor-general of South Africa. (2) The small (and quarrelsome) group of nationalists, mainly from the Ovambo tribe, decided that should the UN fail to act, then Namibia should become a British protectorate, like Basutoland (now Lesotho), Bechuanaland (Botswana) and Swaziland. There were even demands for the territory to be designated a protectorate of the USA. (3) Clearly, the nationalists were desperate men.

In July 1966, on a technicality, the International Court of Justice delivered a noncommital legal opinion on the status of Namibia. Pretoria interpreted this as a victory. Namibia's 100,000 whites were jubilant. "The bars in Windhoek stayed open all night," wrote one reporter. (4) In October, however, the UN General Assembly revoked the mandate; and in July 1971 the International Court of Justice declared South Africa's presence in Namibia to be "illegal". Bishop Colin Winter, the head of the Anglican Church in the territory, recorded the reaction of the blacks: "The decision at The Hague caused a sensation in Namibia. There was dancing in the African location [the black segregated areas of Windhoek]." (5)

No amount of legal argument was going to lever Pretoria out of what had become *de facto* a fifth province of South Africa. Namibia was set to take the same route as its minder: both black and white nationalists talked past each other and left the diminishing band of "moderates" lost in the middle of nowhere. Many of the Namibian nationalists had worked in South Africa alongside ANC activists. The same pattern emerged: petitions, passive disobedience, strikes and, finally, armed struggle. In both countries, entreaties fell on deaf ears and protest invoked repression. The Afrikaner obsession with ethnicity was rigorously applied to the administration of the new "province". But here the divide-and-rule tactics did prove unusually divisive, for a number of reasons. Firstly, some kind of decentralisation was almost inevitable in such a vast and often arid land where communities, frequently dirt-poor, were widely spread. Decentralisation need not be the same as ethnic segregation, yet Namibians have been very ethnically conscious, no matter how often their politicians substitute "Herero-speaking" or "Ovambo-speaking " for tribal tags. Secondly, there has been real concern among the other ten ethnic groups (ranging from the Herero 7% of the population to the San [Bushmen] who constitute 2.8%) about the numerical dominance of the Ovambo group (50% of the population). (6) The whites, themselves made up of Afrikaners and sometimes rival communities speaking German, English or Portuguese, have been particularly vociferous about any universal franchise system which could be swamped by the Ovambo, which many whites equate with SWAPO (the South West Africa People's Organisation).

Pretoria's propagandists have always played upon ethnic fears of Ovambo population-power, especially after April 1960 when SWAPO, originally largely an Ovambo party, was formed. SWAPO's previous designation, it is true, had been the Ovamboland People's Organisation, but through persistence, and some ruthlessness, SWAPO gradually came to be identified as a major national symbol of independence for all Namibia's ethnic groups.

In 1961 Sam Nujoma and other SWAPO leaders set up their HQ in Dar es Salaam, Africa's revolutionary oasis. Despairing of political change at home and the UN's ability, or will, to oust Pretoria, SWAPO began to prepare for protracted war. Training camps for the initial cadres were established in Tanzania and Zambia, equipped, like all the other alphabet soup of African insurgents, with Chinese and Soviet equipment. Guerrillas began to infiltrate into Namibia during 1965 and they established bases in Ovamboland. The terrain is suitable for partisan warfare. With the exception of a small section in the northwest, along the Cunene river, the Angolan/Namibian border is a straight cartographic line. In the centre, the Ovamboland/Angolan border runs for 280 miles. The line divides, in theory, Angolan Ovambo from their Namibian kinfolk. Ovamboland is exceptionally flat, covered in the west by often dense mopani bush and in the east by forest. In the subtropical climate, the rainy season (usually October to April) provides ample water and luxuriant foliage for guerrilla penetration. Everywhere there are anthills, all for some unknown reason pointing north. And everywhere, too, are the *Cuca* shops, tiny general stores, with very little on sale, but which sport grandiose titles such as "California Inn", "Los Angeles" and "Country Club". The Ovambo are said to be born capitalists, yet this is the same people who have suffered so much because of their support for the Moscow-leaning SWAPO.

The Namibian war began at 7.30 am on 26 August 1966. A South African security police unit of 32 men, led by Major Theunis Swanepoel, attacked the Ongulumbashe SWAPO base inside Ovamboland. The guerrillas were expecting an attack and had decided to stand and fight. In the heliborne assault two insurgents were killed and nine were captured, after a brief resistance lasting two minutes. A sizeable hoard of equipment and documentation was also seized. No South Africans were injured, despite, according to South African accounts, an irregular application of irregular war. One SWAPO warrior, Agapepe Ipangelwa, deployed a bow and arrow tipped with poison, although the other fighters were armed with AK-47s. (7) As with the Sinoia "battle" in the same year, which marked the onset of the Rhodesian war, SWAPO's struggle started with a military fiasco. And, as with many similar African liberation movements, constant military setbacks were nearly always transformed into great victories by glowing propaganda statements issued in faraway capitals. In the case of Ongulumbashe, a SWAPO statement, claiming 15 South Africans had been killed, concluded with a lively sentence: "Rivers of blood have to be crossed, but as night follows day, victory will be ours." (8)

In 1966 SWAPO's prospects of military victory looked decidedly slim. Access to Ovamboland was exceptionally difficult, especially from the first SWAPO bases in Zambia. Guerrillas were forced to make their way on foot via the 250-mile long panhandle of the Caprivi Strip. Carrying heavy equipment for weeks across very sandy soil was arduous. There were dangerous wild animals, South African Police (SAP) patrols and politically hostile locals from rival tribes who would often report sightings of armed strangers to chiefs in the pay of Pretoria. And, until 1974, the Portuguese patrolled parts of southern Angola. Initially, Unita guerrillas helped their kinsmen in SWAPO, but later turned on them because of SWAPO's alliance with the MPLA. It all added up to a political and logistical nightmare for SWAPO.

A SWAPO commander, Rahimisa Kahimise, summed up the difficulties of infiltration in the late 1960s:

> We had to walk a long distance from Zambia through Angola. Some of our people died in Angola and some missions could not reach Namibia, because

> they had to fight through Angola...The battles we were involved in, most of them were in Angola with the Portuguese... but even the South African soldiers were also involved in Angola and really we worked hard because by then we had to train the new recruits and we also had to fight to get food as we had to walk long distances and then we had to try and get transport, also after a battle then you must have more ammunition... I could say by the time we crossed into Namibia we were a bit tired but a bit more experienced. (9)

SWAPO persevered. They sabotaged government installations, killed pro-government blacks, and, occasionally, took on the security forces. Through such "armed propaganda" they persuaded and/or intimidated the increasingly politicised Ovambo population. SWAPO's military forces, PLAN (People's Liberation Army of Namibia), were countered by increasingly sophisticated South African counterinsurgency techniques, supervised initially by the SAP, and, later, by the SADF. The internal political wing of SWAPO, based in the capital Windhoek, remained a legal party, even though it was constantly harassed by the security police. In contrast to the ANC, but similar to London's distinction between *Sinn Fein* and the Irish Republican Army, Pretoria decided not to ban SWAPO's domestic wing. Such limited, and unusual, forbearance was partly a recognition that South Africa could not defeat Namibian nationalism by brute force alone. Hence the policy of "co-optive dominance", enticing "moderate" nationalists with limited power and generous material rewards. Thus, Pretoria developed a two-track policy: of keeping the UN politely at arm's length, while attempting to destroy SWAPO's military wing; and simultaneously encouraging internal black nationalists, including SWAPO members, to accept a domestic settlement engineered by South Africa and its white allies in Namibia (and Europe). Always pretending to juggle with two entirely different balls—a UN settlement or UDI—Pretoria quietly entrenched, in fact, its own power in the 1960s and 1970s. By the late 1970s, Namibia had become almost a SADF fiefdom.

On the purely military level, the SADF conducted a textbook counterinsurgency campaign in the territory. The lessons of Malaya, Vietnam, Algeria, Rhodesia, Angola and Mozambique were skilfully synthesised and applied, often with the assistance of ex-Rhodesian officers and occasionally Israeli experts. (10) Yet, like the Bourbons, on the political level, Pretoria had learnt little...at least as far as Namibia was concerned during the 1970s. South Africa felt no need then to make any political concessions in Namibia. Above all, Pretoria was determined to prevent a military defeat in the field. Until 1976, South Africa was entirely on top of SWAPO. Indeed, the security forces tended to regard SWAPO more as a public nuisance than a military threat.

Nevertheless, SWAPO did tie up thousands of security force members and SWAPO's political activity at home and abroad did tilt South Africa closer towards pariah status. Like Pretoria, SWAPO was running on a dual track: fighting and talking. The volatile Sam Nujoma, SWAPO's external leader, looked around Africa and felt that time was on his side.

For its part, Pretoria was buying time to build up its internal proxies and to destroy SWAPO's domestic political base. During 1966-77, the security police arrested 38 SWAPO leaders, including John Ya Otto, the acting secretary-general, and Ja Toivo. Before their trial, under the so-called Terrorism Act of June 1967, both men claimed they were tortured. Ya Otto described his treatment thus:

> When electricity tears through your body, you cannot think, let alone speak. I discovered that for the [SAP] Special Branch this was the last stage of priming their detainees for cooperation—the last torture before sitting down to 'talk reason'...Each time it felt as if a bomb of thousand sharp needles was exploding inside me, tearing my guts apart, pushing my eyes out from their sockets, bursting my skin open in a dozen places. (11)

When the SWAPO leaders were finally put in the dock in June 1967, Ja Toivo was elected to speak for the group. Addressing the South African judge, he declared:

> We are Namibians and not South Africans. We do not now, and will not in the future, recognise your right to govern us; to make laws for us in which we had no say; to treat our country as if it were your property and us as if you were our masters. We have always regarded South Africa as an intruder in our country...(12)

After the trial, in which the main SWAPO leaders were sentenced to long terms of imprisonment, PLAN stepped up its armed propaganda on the border. Recruitment was increased as was infiltration through the Caprivi. The initial, and successful, counterinsurgency (COIN) operations were conducted by the SAP, for a number of reasons. As in Rhodesia, Pretoria wanted to portray the conflict as policemen versus armed criminals. Secondly, the security police controlled an excellent informer network. Thirdly, the army had little COIN experience at this time and certainly lacked an efficient intelligence-gathering apparatus. The SAP stifled PLAN's first forays. There was little effective insurgency between 1969 and 1970. In 1971, however, PLAN commenced its long love affair with the landmine. Then in December 1971 SWAPO organised a widespread strike. Attacks on "collaborators" with the "Boers" were increased. In the first Ovamboland homeland elections of August 1973, only 2.3% dared to vote in the face of the SWAPO boycott. (In 1975, however, Pretoria claimed a 55% turnout in fresh elections.)

From February 1972 effective martial law operated in Ovamboland. Floggings and torture became commonplace, as the various churches in Namibia increasingly stepped in to denounce excesses by the South Africans (although, often, similar outrages by SWAPO went apparently unnoticed by the anxious clerics). In December 1973 the UN General Assembly voted to recognise SWAPO as the "authentic" representative of the Namibian people, a gesture which was to bedevil the UN's claims, later, to be able impartially to monitor elections in the territory. Pretoria, of course, felt disinclined to recognise the authenticity or the impartiality. By mid-1974, according to South African sources, the security forces had lost 11 men, the majority of them policemen killed by mines.

During 1974 the army took over command of the "operational area" in northern Namibia. The SAP was clearly overstretched. And the army was determined to dominate the COIN programme in a more subtle fashion. Hearts and minds were needed. But, above all, the scene was shifting dramatically in Portuguese Africa. After the Lisbon coup, Portuguese troops started pulling out of southern Angola. Suddenly, SWAPO had an inviting 1000-mile border to move across. The MPLA and Eastern bloc advisers provided arms, bases and training. By mid-1976, PLAN's strength was perhaps 2,000 trained cadres. By 1978 it was approximately 10,000. (13)

SWAPO was shaping up to be a more deadly adversary. The Portuguese scuttle was SWAPO's first real breakthrough in ten years of relatively fruitless campaigning. But, as with the Zimbabwean guerrillas in 1975-76, internal dissension ravaged SWAPO. Dissident leaders, such as Andreas Shipanga, were imprisoned and PLAN insurgents in Zambia mutinied. The usual African cocktail—tribal, ideological and personality clashes, stirred by "imperialist" agents—was blamed. And, on the ground in southern Angola, PLAN and Unita, once on/off allies, now became bitter enemies. This suited the SADF, which enlarged its infrastructure along the entire border. Troop levels were augmented, especially after the South African withdrawal from their Angolan invasion in March 1976. The figures for troop levels varied widely according to the ideological flavour of the writer, but anti-apartheid sources suggested that the number went from 15,000 in June 1974 to

45,000 in 1976 and had reached 100,000 by the early 1980s. (14) This is much too high, especially bearing in mind—unlike the US army in Vietnam—the very lean ratio of combat troops to logistic tail in the SADF. Whatever the precise figures, after the abortive invasion Pretoria's defence planners grew increasingly concerned about the SWAPO-Cuban-MPLA axis.

For ten years after 1976 Pretoria's strategy was constant. Primarily it was to prevent any kind of SWAPO military success against the SADF. The "demonstration effect" would be a dangerous encouragement to the stirring black masses inside South Africa. Thus, the SADF tried hard to destroy SWAPO's military options, by enfeebling PLAN and the MPLA/Cuban infrastructure behind it and, at the same time, to create a viable, "moderate", internal rival to SWAPO's growing political ascendancy inside Namibia. But, like Topsy, the war in Angola just grew and grew, and South Africa's allies in Windhoek looked more and more like puppets. Pretoria failed to keep Namibia on its twin-track route to Pretoria-guided independence. South African policy began to wobble on both international and Namibian fronts, as well as crashing into the black hole of the Angolan conflict. The result? The dirty little war in this last, almost forgotten, colony became South Africa's very own Vietnam.

References and notes:

1. P Katjavivi, *A History of Resistance in Namibia,* Currey, London, 1988, p. 10; A du Pisani, *SWA/Namibia: The Politics of Continuity and Change,* Ball, Johannesburg, 1986, p. 36.
2. Katjavivi, *op. cit.*, p. 22.
3. *Ibid.*, p. 38.
4. Quoted in UN, *A Principle in Torment,* New York, UN, 1971, p. 36.
5. C Winter, *Namibia: The Story of a Bishop's Exile,* Butterworth, London, 1977, pp. 110-11.
6. Population estimates are: Ovambo: 526,385 (50.1%); Kavango: 97,808 (9.3%); Herero: 77,826 (7.4%); Dama: 76,774 (7.3%); whites: 75,722 (7.2%); Nama: 49,430 (4.7%); coloured (mixed race): 43,120 (4.1%); Caprivians: 39,965 (3.8%); San (Bushmen): 29,448 (2.8%); Basters (Rehobothers): 26,293 (2.5%); Tswana: 6,310 (0. 6%); others (including Himba and Tjimba): 11,569 (1.1%). Total: 1,150,650. (Figures based on 1983 population *estimates* provided by the Department of Manpower, Windhoek; see Pisani, *op. cit,* p. 11.) Other estimates suggest that the figure is much higher, especially if Ovambo refugees in Angola and elsewhere are included.
7. R Shay and C Vermaak, *The Silent War,* Galaxie, Salisbury, 1971, pp. 171-7; M Morris, *Armed Conflict in Southern Africa,* Spence, Cape Town, 1974, pp. 3-5.
8. Quoted in Morris, *op. cit.*, p. 5.
9. *Verbatim* interview, quoted in Katjavivi, *op. cit.*, p. 85.

10. The influence of Israeli strategy and weapons supplies is discussed elsewhere. Israeli observers and instructors have been active in southern Angola in connection with Unita. The specific role of Israeli instructors in Namibia was difficult to probe. When this writer met Israeli army personnel in Namibia, they usually claimed to be journalists, or on academic study leave, etc. Israeli instructors were allegedly involved with the use of sophisticated devices for tracking humans on the border.
11. J Ya Otto, *Battlefront Namibia,* Heinemann, London, 1982, p. 42.
12. Quoted in UN, *Trial and Sentencing of Namibians,* New York, UN, 1969, quoted in Katjavivi, *op. cit.,* p. 63.
13. See figures in J Serfontein, *Namibia?,* Rex Collings, London, 1976, p. 324; C Legum, *The Western Crisis and Southern Africa,* Africana Publishing, London, 1979, p. 184.
14. See G Cawthra, *Brutal Force,* International Defence and Aid Fund, London, 1986, p. 178, and F Toase, "The South African Army: The Campaign in South West Africa/Namibia since 1966," in I Beckett and J Pimlott, (eds), *Armed Forces and Modern Counter-insurgency,* Croom Helm, London, 1985, p. 207.

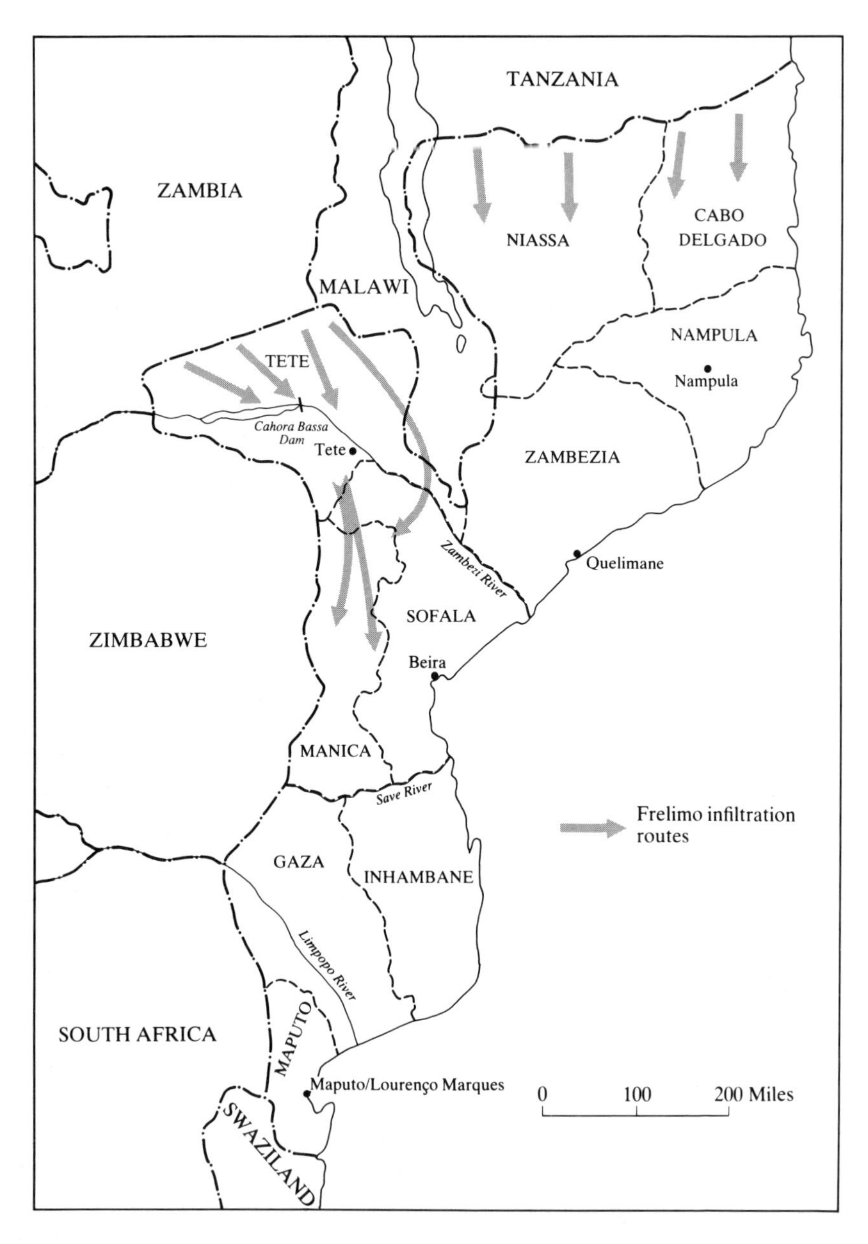

MAP 7 Mozambique: guerrilla infiltration.

7

Mozambique (1964–1975)

The search for Namibia's sovereignty had been a long odyssey into the mirages of the desert. By comparison, Mozambique's march to freedom was short and not particularly sharp. But peace did not follow independence. As in Angola, civil war was to accompany the hasty imperial scuttle. Unlike Angola, however, only one nationalist movement, Frelimo, inherited power.

Frelimo emerged in 1962 from three groups which were themselves influenced by a kaleidoscope of tribal, religious and ideological sentiments: Makonde traditionalists argued with Marxists while Coremo *(Comite Revolucionário de Moçambique)* supported guerrillas separately from Frelimo. Even within the core of Frelimo intense rivalries surfaced between the military and political wings. Small groups of Frelimo cadres were trained in Algeria from 1963. In 1964 some of these men set up training camps in southern Tanzania. Soon instructors arrived from Cuba, China and Eastern Europe. A few of the most industrious trainees were sent to study political warfare at the Komsomol school in Moscow and the guerrilla warfare centre at Simferopol in the Ukraine. At the opening of hostilities Frelimo had 250 trained and equipped insurgents.

On the night of 25 September 1964, Frelimo launched its first major assault, on a Portuguese administrative post at Chai in Cabo Delgado. During the early years of the war Frelimo found it very hard to break out of its ethnic bases in the northern provinces of Cabo Delgado and Niassa, even though Portugal's grip had always been weak away from the coastal towns. Major tribal rebellions inland had been common as late as the 1920s. The entire European population, concentrated largely in Beira and the capital Lourenço Marques, numbered only 27,000 in 1940, although subsidised waves of poor white immigrants pushed the total to 200,000 by 1970. A few settled in military-style *kibbutzim* in the rural areas, but most preferred the sheltered employment and racial privileges of the urban fleshpots on the coast. This sudden surge of settlers made Mozambique the fourth largest white "tribe" in sub-Saharan Africa, after South Africa, Angola and Rhodesia.

Yet it was different from the Afrikaner and Anglo-Saxon racial oligarchies, mainly because Mozambique had precious little autonomy. Lisbon's rule was rigid. The neo-fascist Portuguese dictatorship brooked very few reformist experiments in Mozambique. And the feared secret police, with its extensive urban informer networks, made sure Lisbon was obeyed. The secret police were sometimes dubbed "animals officered by intellectuals". Forced labour continued in various forms until the 1960s and, on road works, until 1973. Most crucially, the Mozambican economy was run for the benefit of the mother country. The settlers, therefore, did not have an effective political, economic or moral basis when, later, they tried their own half-hearted (and half-baked) UDI.

Mozambique was one of the poorest colonies of the poorest state in Europe (after Albania). Frelimo recognised the superficiality of the settler economy by dubbing it "shopkeeper colonialism". (1) As the colonists did not exert economic control, they served or managed foreign and metropolitan enterprises. The settlers were usually poor and unskilled, often illiterate peasants or shopkeepers. The colony survived largely by servicing its richer and more powerful neighbours, Rhodesia and South Africa. Trade, transport fees, tourism and black miners working in South Africa made Mozambique tick...albeit with typically Iberian *mañana*. Two years before independence South Africa took over from Portugal as the main supplier of goods to Mozambique. Although Pretoria watched the growing Frelimo insurgency with alarm, it knew that, ultimately, Mozambique was criticially dependent upon South Africa whatever the pigmentation of the rulers in Lourenço Marques.

In 1964, the Frelimo president, Dr Eduardo Mondlane, predicted that the war would last "maybe ten or maybe 20 years, even then it will be a negotiated settlement like Algeria". It was to be a long haul, but by the end Frelimo claimed to have 10,000 men under arms. The insurgency did grow slowly partly because of the isolation of the first in-country bases in the far north and the multiplicity of tribes and clans. Mozambique comprised a population of seven million, made up of 19 tribes from nine major ethnic groups speaking 17 different languages. The Portuguese successfully manipulated this demographic hotchpotch: the Muslim Yao tribe, for example, was susceptible to colonial blandishments because it feared a guerrilla ban on its faith. The insurgents' military operations consisted largely of mine-laying and hit-and-run attacks known as *flagelaçao* (whipping bursts). Frelimo's tactics were undermined by divisions over strategy. Three approaches were debated: firstly, risings in the main cities; secondly, emulating the Cuban/Guevara line by deploying small groups of guerrillas in the countryside as a "focus" to trigger off mass insurrection; and, thirdly, a Maoist protracted war. The military wing, later dominated by Samora Machel, a former hospital orderly, got its way when the last option was adopted. Various factions still wrangled over such issues as the correct roles of female cadres, chiefs, the churches, and socialism. These disputes, never fully resolved, resurfaced as causes of the post-independence civil war.

In February 1969 Mondlane was assassinated in his Dar es Salaam office by a letter bomb, planted probably by internal rivals, but with a little help from the Portuguese secret police. (2) Mondlane was not only the country's first PhD, but also the first Mozambican recipient, in 1963, of a CIA donation of $10,000. (3) It was briefly, and bizarrely, mooted that his white American wife, Janet, could take over as interim leader. A white American female guerrilla leader might have done wonders for Frelimo's image in the salons of the West, but little to induce conservative black peasants to join the cause. Instead, the diminutive Machel succeeded Mondlane.

When Machel took command, Frelimo claimed to control 20% to 25% of northern Mozambique, nominally liberated zones with a crude infrastructure. A new front was opened in the strategically more important Tete province, adjacent to the Zambian border. Frelimo could rely upon sanctuaries in, and aid from, Zambia and Tanzania. Zambia, however, was vulnerable to counter-sanctions because of Portuguese control of rail transit routes.

The Portuguese tried to contain Frelimo activity in the north, which had little economic significance and where, by 1960, fewer than 2,500 whites had settled. Approximately 50% of the black inhabitants of the area, 160,000 peasants in Niassa and 270,000 in Cabo Delgado, were herded into *aldeamentos,* the Portuguese version of strategic hamlets. To counter landmines placed on dirt roads, 870 miles per annum of tarmac roads were being constructed by 1972. Major offensives, such as Operation Gordian Knot in 1970, commanded by General Kaulza de Arriaga, tried to sweep away the guerrillas' main bases. Up to 50% of Arriaga's troops were assigned to the social aspects of containment, such as building schools and clinics. The number of blacks educated in primary schools rose from 427,000 in 1964 to 603,000 by 1972, for example. The Portuguese offered few significant political reforms, but they did try hard with propaganda. In one year, 1972, planes dropped over five million pro-government pamphlets. (4) Persuasion and bribery often worked. And, as in Rhodesia, a large number of captured guerrillas were "turned" and used in elite units such as the *Flechas*. Many Africans volunteered for military service: 60% of the 60,000 troops in the country were black. Dramatic high-level defections from Frelimo to the Portuguese also boosted white morale. Racism in Mozambique was never as rigid as in its white neighbours. Class was often as significant. A well-to-do black was usually more acceptable in polite European society than a down-at-heel white. The Portuguese army worked hard at disseminating the various icons of the pro-Western, pro-Christian, anti-Marxist crusade. This was particularly true of elite black units where sometimes up to an hour a day was dedicated to politicisation. General de Arriaga, who encouraged his own personality cult and his nickname, the "Pink Panther", also introduced a political programme (called "mentalisation") for his white troops.

Nevertheless, outside the elite black and white units, army morale was low, especially among white conscripts, who had to serve for at least four years. In 1973 one Portuguese noted sadly: "The impression grows that the wars are a surrealism, and that the troops are protecting something which grows less and less Portuguese daily." A Portuguese officer, who had defected, added: "The soldiers don't know what they are defending. Before they are sent off to Africa they don't even know where Mozambique is. They are also victims of the war..." (5) Except for unusually strong-minded commanders, such as Spinola (in Guinea-Bissau), military strategy was dictated in faraway Lisbon. But Caetano's dictatorship was out of touch. There was little coordination with, and between, the African colonies. In particular, the intense hostility between the regular army and the secret police was allowed to fester.

No one in Lisbon wanted to admit that the imperial wars made no sense; the police clamped down hard on dissidents, even in the armed forces. Lisbon was equally prickly about criticism from Salisbury and Pretoria. On an *ad hoc* basis the Rhodesian security forces, with and without Portuguese permission, had been operating deep into Mozambique during the late 1960s. An unofficial "council of three" representatives from Mozambique, Rhodesia and South Africa began to meet regularly after February 1971 to coordinate military policies. In 1973 the commander-in-chief of Mozambique, Kaulza de Arriaga, disclosed a gentleman's agreement which allowed the Rhodesians to operate up to

60 miles inside the Portuguese colony. The Rhodesians, particularly the deep-penetration units such as the SAS, were often loath to work with the Portuguese army, not least because of its reluctance to engage the enemy. On patrols, Portuguese soldiers, particularly conscripts, would often make as much noise as possible to warn off Frelimo. The Rhodesians, however, often soldiered effectively with the much more aggressive elite units in both the police and army. Cooperation with the *Flechas* often bagged Zimbabwean and Frelimo insurgents working in tandem. Such successes paved the way later for the Rhodesian creation of the Mozambique National Resistance Movement, the nemesis of Frelimo's rise to power.

One important symbol of South Africa's involvement was the giant Cahora Bassa dam in Tete province. It turned out to be the biggest white elephant in southern African economic history. It only made sense to sell the electricity to South Africa, but constant sabotage was to make the supply lines inoperative for over a decade. As the dam was being built in the early 1970s, it was reportedly guarded by over 15,000 troops. Frelimo kept up a nominal pressure on the dam and then moved southwards to the Umtali-Beira rail and road line and the beginning of the white commercial heartlands. By 1973 Frelimo was deploying 122mm rockets for stand-off bombardments and, by 1974, SAM-7 missiles. Frelimo's penetration into white farming areas shook the confidence of the settlers, who complained bitterly about the army's failure to protect them. As in Algeria, the relationship between the army and the settlers was often poor. In particular, white civilians accused the officer corps of fighting a comfortable "air-conditioned war". When De Arriaga left Mozambique in August 1973 he tried to bolster white confidence by asserting that what Frelimo could do to the army was "what a mosquito could do to an elephant". Yet by 1974 morale and efficiency had waned dramatically in the security forces. In May General Costa Gomes admitted in the Mozambican capital that the army had "reached the limits of neuro-psychological exhaustion". Tired and dispirited, yes, but not defeated. Frelimo was winning almost by default.

Something was in the air. The generals did not want to be blamed for another defeat like the 1961 fiasco, when India marched into the Portuguese enclave of Goa. In fact, the colonial wars, not yet lost, were not the primary cause of the April coup in Lisbon. The "discreet dictatorship" had simply run out of steam, as had the Falangists next door. The administration and the economy, with an inflation rate of 72% in February 1974, were beginning to fall apart, as Portugal struggled to catch up with the rest of Community Europe. There had been at least nine failed coups against Salazar and three attempts already against Caetano. The dissident Armed Forces Movement (MFA) was going to try again.

An accelerated promotion scheme for graduate officers *(miliçianos)* had enraged the traditionalists, even though there was a chronic shortage of young officers. The new scheme helped to radicalise and proletarianise the junior officer ranks. To political rigidity, social backwardness and economic decline was added the explosive mixture of bruised national pride and wounded professional vanity in the armed forces. One of the sparks was Spinola's famous book, *Portugal and the Future.* In it he wrote: "We must begin by divesting ourselves of the notion that we are defending the West and the Western way of life." As with France in Algeria, Portugal was not making an economic profit by holding on to its African obsession, especially as the wars expanded. Mozambique, for example, contributed only 20% towards the local war effort. The colonies were an anachronism of Europe's oldest Empire led by its oldest dictatorship. They had to go.

And so, after so many years, in so few hours and with very little bloodshed, the dictatorship and Empire collapsed as the MFA moved on Lisbon. Spinola played the revolution's Neguib, but no Nasser emerged. The MFA set about democratising Portugal and its African "provinces" (called "states" after 1972). The army had not been tainted by Gestapo tactics, unlike the French paras in Algiers or the Portuguese secret police. Nor had there been the bitterness spawned by urban terrorism. Flowers and optimism filled Lisbon. (6)

The MFA ordered the forces to fight on in Africa. Since most troops refused to do so, an undeclared ceasefire prevailed in many areas. On 7 September 1974 the new Portuguese government signed an accord with Samora Machel, paving the way for a provisional multiracial government in Lourenço Marques. Independence was set for June 1975. On 8 September die-hard whites attempted a counter-coup. This feeble but bitter UDI lasted about as long as the generals' *putsch* in Algeria. In Mozambique the Portuguese army, with Frelimo assistance, quelled the rebellion. A white exodus began. In October a spate of racial bloodletting erupted again. By June 1975 more than half the whites had fled; within a year only 10% remained. The towns were full of scavenging stray dogs, once pampered pets now abandoned. Farmers killed their cattle rather than leave them. Mechanics sabotaged their machinery. The few whites who stayed did so for a number of reasons. Some were financial prisoners; others were ideologically committed to socialism. The latter often rose to senior positions in government. Frelimo had always insisted that it had been fighting to rid the country of colonialism not whites. The remaining skilled whites were desperately needed. Few blacks had been trained to take over the reins, at any level. As Joseph Hanlon noted, at independence, of the 350 train drivers, only one was black. (7)

So what did Pretoria make of Frelimo's victory by default? During the war, South Africa had provided material and financial support for the Portuguese, but had carefully avoided getting too involved (although claims were made that up to 1,000 SADF troops had fought inside Mozambique).(8) There were some discussions in intelligence and military circles about backing the white die-hards and propping up a white-ruled southern Mozambique. After all, at the beginning of 1975, the whites still numbered about 200,000. Frelimo influence had hardly touched the south, a region of considerable importance for Pretoria's transport routes, and which stood right alongside South African territory. The Mozambican capital, renamed Maputo, was just an hour's drive from the eastern Transvaal. But the idea was dropped as Mozambique slid into anarchy. Some Portuguese hard-liners who fled to South Africa indulged in a number of OAS-style activities against Frelimo and its white sympathisers.(9) It is possible that Pretoria turned a blind eye to these ultras, for a while.

In essence, however, the South African military option was ruled out. No pretext could be manufactured such as intervention in a civil war, as in Angola in 1975. And it bears repeating that Mozambique, unlike Angola, was very dependent economically upon Pretoria's goodwill. Even with the Portuguese gone the giant Cahora Bassa dam still only made sense by dealing with Pretoria. Over 100,000 Mozambican miners worked in South Africa. They were paid in gold at the official price which Mozambique could resell at the free market rate. This deal had originally been maintained as a kind of subsidy to the Portuguese war effort, but by 1974 the gold price was three times the official level. So this became a vital component of Mozambique's foreign exchange earnings. Frelimo could not afford to bring home the miners. Massive unemployment already wracked the economy. And most of the miners came from the south, where Frelimo had little popularity initially. The economic ties cut both ways of course: Maputo was the most convenient port for the bustling Witwatersrand. The mine-labour and transport arrangements, codified in the Mozambique Convention, suited both countries. After a decade of war and the massive dislocation caused by the flight of nearly all the skilled personnel, Frelimo was desperate for peace, and for time to rebuild and to consolidate its hold on power. Pretoria, initially helpful, sent technical advisers to keep operational the port and rail facilities in the south.

So a *modus vivendi* was possible between "fascism", as Machel termed apartheid, and the newly-triumphant revolutionaries. The economic leverage gave Pretoria the self-confidence to act with military restraint. Economic self-interest transcended, it seemed, ideological rivalry. Yet it was not quite that simple. Pretoria was worried that Machel might be pushed into the waiting arms of the Russians. Both China and Russia had supplied Frelimo's army, the FPLM *(Forças Populares de Libertação de Moçambique),* during the war and after. Some Chinese instructors remained. Moscow was angling for naval facilities, although Machel was politely aloof. Soviet naval bases in the Mozambique Channel was the last thing Pretoria wanted. Better, then, to play along with Maputo for the time being, especially as Machel had not yet closed his borders with Rhodesia.

The softly-softly approach could not mask the psychological damage. Angola was so far away. Geographically, Moscow is nearer to London than Luanda is to Cape Town. Few South Africans had ever visited Angola, but Mozambique was a place for regular holidays. "LM" radio was a youth cult for whites. LM played the Beatles when the ultra-conservative South African Broadcasting Corporation banned their records. Cheap prawns, wine and sex, especially the multiracial variety banned in South Africa, as well as gambling, attracted many whites, including all the conservatives who needed to taste sin before they could adequately condemn it at home. Suddenly the Rolling Stones and the Beatles were replaced by martial music, then African voices attacking neo-colonialism. The glorious Mozambican beaches were soon deserted by South Africans, whose youngsters reluctantly turned back to the SABC.

Another domino had fallen, but Pretoria tried to grin and bear it. One writer described the Kafkaesque situation: "On the south bank of the Limpopo Frelimo was faced with the energetic friendliness of the Transvaal, on the northern bank by armoured cars and Hawker Hunters hurtling in with guns ablaze. But somehow—because both countries wanted it to—the compromise held." (10) For a while. Almost overnight, though, the lucrative Mozambican tourist trade evaporated: 30,000 prostitutes in Maputo were suddenly out of work. To the chagrin of Johannesburg business magnates, Pretoria impetuously reduced the number of Mozambican mine workers and started to divert trade from Maputo to South African ports further south, despite the extra costs. In Rhodesia, the Central Intelligence Organisation was busy creating a Frankenstein's monster: the Mozambican National Resistance Movement. With Pretoria's help it was soon to ravage Frelimo's dominion. In

March 1976 Machel closed the border with Rhodesia. Direct Rhodesian raids and sabotage via the MNR were about to bring Mozambique to its knees. This agony was only the beginning. Mozambique was now entering the very heart of darkness.

References and notes:

1. J Hanlon, *Mozambique: The Revolution Under Fire,* Zed, London, 1984, pp. 15-23.
2. A and B Isaacman, *Mozambique: From Colonialism to Revolution,* Zimbabwe Publishing, Harare, 1983, p. 98.
3. M Meredith, *The First Dance of Freedom: Black Africa in the Postwar Era,* Abacus, London, 1984, p. 251.
4. For a useful summary of the military details of the war, see I Beckett, "The Portuguese Army: The Campaign in Mozambique," in I Beckett and J Pimlott, (eds), *Armed Forces and Modern Counter-insurgency,* London, Croom Helm, 1985.
5. Quoted in M Morris, *Armed Conflict in Southern Africa,* Spence, Cape Town, 1974, p. 205. For a summary of the disintegration of the Portuguese army in Mozambique, see B Munslow, *Mozambique: The Revolution and its Origins,* Longman, London, 1983, pp. 125-9.
6. For an account of the coup, see D Porch, *The Portuguese Armed Forces and the Revolution,* Croom Helm, London, 1977.
7. J Hanlon, *Beggar Your Neighbours,* Catholic Institute for International Relations, London, 1986, p. 38.
8. See R Jaster, *South Africa's Narrowing Security Options,* Adelphi paper No. 151, International Institute for Strategic Studies, London, 1980, p. 19 quoting *The Economist,* 6 March 1969. For a summary of the military ties between Portugal, South Africa and Rhodesia, see Munslow, *op. cit.,* pp. 115-6.
9. The OAS *(Organisation Armée Secrète)* was the ultra-right wing group which refused to accept decolonisation in Algeria. For a discussion of the OAS and the fascinating parallels between the end of white rule in northern and southern Africa, see A Horne, *A Savage War of Peace: Algeria, 1954-1962,* Penguin, Harmondsworth, 1985.
10. R Johnson, *How Long Will South Africa Survive?,* Macmillan, Johannesburg, 1977. p. 132.

8

Rhodesia (1965-1980)

Kith and kin

The collapse of white power in Rhodesia had a tremendous impact on the Afrikaner psyche. As with the Portuguese colonies, the loss of Rhodesia diminished the defence perimeter of the white-ruled laager. But the defeat of Ian Smith's rebellion meant much more psychologically to white South Africa. Afrikaner racism, in particular, extended to the Portuguese, who were seen as idle, incompetent and poorly disciplined. Many Portuguese soldiers were from the metropole; they could pack up and go home. Rhodesia was supposed to be different. In Rhodesia, it was claimed, a new white nation had been formed, although Rhodesia was in truth merely a white suburb masquerading as a country. If pressed, white Anglo-Saxons would fight black savages, and win. Such was the mood of white popular opinion in South Africa until the very late 1970s.

Nonetheless, in government circles in Pretoria, a deep-seated ambiguity about the Unilateral Declaration of Independence (UDI) was pervasive. In 1965, the republic's premier, the dour Hendrik Verwoerd, cautioned Smith against revolt. (1) Pretoria, like the rest of the world, refused to recognise officially the Rhodesian regime. On the other hand, the South African government had a vested interest in proving that sanctions did not work. After the fall of Lisbon's empire, South Africa became the heart machine for the rebels' survival. South African businessmen made huge profits from their captive market, although generous voluntary support was also provided by various South African bodies, such as the Friends of Rhodesia. Historically, there had often been bad blood between the two white supremacist states: the infamous Jameson Raid had been launched with help from Rhodesia, which had also fought on the "wrong side" in the Boer War; and then, in 1922, the colony disdained the offer of union with South Africa. Some 20%, however, of Rhodesia's whites had Afrikaner roots. Many nationalists in Pretoria looked upon these Afrikaners "as Hitler regarded the Ausland deutsche" *[sic]*. (2) This kith and kin factor, plus the South African origins of many English-speaking Rhodesians, forged a strong emotional bond, which was augmented by the large annual influx of South African tourists. Ultra-rightists within the Afrikaner secret society, the Broederbond, and Herstigte Nasionale Party, which had broken from the ruling National Party in 1969, insisted that the Zambezi and not the Limpopo was the natural northern military boundary. Military cooperation between the two states had preceded the rebellion: joint exercises between their air forces, for example, had taken place as early as 1961.

Despite the historical antagonisms, after UDI, Rhodesia's white supremacist policies shifted ever closer to the apartheid model. Both white communities were deluged by a massive tidal wave of internal propaganda. Both gloried in verbose rhetoric about defending their Christian civilisations against godless communism, the convenient depository for all claims by blacks for equal rights. In Rhodesia, however, a quarter of a million whites were outnumbered by blacks by 25:1; in South Africa the ratio is 4 or 5: 1 (depending on how "blacks" are calculated and designated). The historian Robert Blake commented during UDI: "Apartheid south of the Limpopo is a religion, north of it a dubious and impracticable expedient."(3) Despite the racist ties, Pretoria understood that, in the long term, white rule in Rhodesia was impracticable—not least for South African interests. The best solution for her was the peaceful transition to a pro-Western "moderate" black ruler, preferably one that was beholden to South Africa.

Hence the greatest paradox of the Rhodesian war. Rhodesia broke away from Britain to avoid black rule and then, with the onset of the guerrilla war, became completely dependent upon a South African regime which was even more determined than Britain to establish a black premier in Salisbury. Above all, Pretoria dreaded the possibility of a victorious Marxist army marching through the streets of Salisbury and Bulawayo, a precedent which it feared might be repeated in Pretoria and Johannesburg. Rhodesia transformed itself from a self-governing British colony into an occasionally truculent but inevitably subservient sector of Afrikaner imperium. Ian Smith became, in effect, the leader of another South African homeland. Pretoria cynically manipulated its Rhodesian satrapy by providing just enough military support to allow Smith time to reach the elusive "settlement" with black "moderates". The policy totally backfired and, by extending the duration of the war, boosted the tally to 30,000 lives lost.

Ian Smith and the leading acolytes of his Rhodesian Front (RF) issued their illegal declaration on the eleventh hour of the eleventh month of 1965. Couched in the language of the American declaration two centuries earlier, and timed to coincide with Armistice Day to stress Rhodesia's contributions to Britain's wars, the RF insisted that it was an act of justified defiance against a Labour government, not the Crown. UDI was gross folly because it prompted international involvement in a previously bilateral tussle. Without it, London, under Tory or Labour rule, would have left the whites in Rhodesia to their own devices, provided some kind of polite constitutional verbiage about eventual majority rule was agreed upon. That was the purpose of the series of Anglo-Rhodesian talks from 1966-71.

In 1965, however, the whites in Southern Rhodesia (to give the colony its official designation) were in an obstinate and beleaguered mood. Their confidence had been shaken by the recent savagery in the former Belgian Congo, the break-up of the Central African Federation because of the rise of black nationalism, the British refusal to grant them independence along with the other members of the federation (Zambia and Malawi) and the depletion of their armed forces and white community by emigration. The RF believed that a dramatic move could stop the rot.

UDI was a huge military bluff. "Except for one or two senior members of the British South Africa Police (BSAP) and a few South African hotheads in the depleted Rhodesian Light Infantry (RLI)", white Rhodesians would not have resisted a rapid British show of force. (4) "A pipe band and a detachment of Royal Marines marching through Salisbury would have done the trick", admitted one senior Rhodesian defence official after the war.(5) The bluff was never called, partly because of a parallel reticence within the British armed forces, especially in the air force, to resort to force.(6) Despite this reluctance, if Prime Minister Harold Wilson had decided to send in his troops, no doubt the British armed forces would have complied... after a few resignations. But Wilson threw away his best cards by renouncing force at the outset. He opted for sanctions instead. Threatening "to throw the book" at the RF, he simply flicked a few pages one at a time. Sanctions were a gesture, never a concerted policy. Until 1974 they boosted rather than undermined the rebel economy.

Wilson was torn by what he termed his four "constituencies": the Tories, the Commonwealth, the UN and South Africa.(7) The inevitable compromises that ensued gave Wilson's policies "that madcap flair", in the words of the American ambassador to Zambia.(8) The end result was an impasse: no force, no confrontation with South Africa and no "sell-out". Wilson described his dilemma in a famous mixed metaphor: "What we are trying to do is to go straight down the middle of the road in a four-dimensional situation." The inherent contradictions meant a gradual imposition of half-hearted, leaky sanctions and growing RF resistance. Thus ensued a long diplomatic melodrama punctuated by angry encounters on ships, foolish estimates and silly superlatives. These negotiations gave Smith credibility at home and respectability abroad. Wilson boasted that UDI would last "months, if not weeks", while Smith offered his supporters a thousand years of white rule. As the same US ambassador noted at the time, UDI "was to be a middle-of-the-road revolution led by businessmen, a double contradiction and a shockingly bad estimate". (9) In contrast, Pretoria kept a cool head. South Africa played a subtle game until 1978, when Prime Minister Botha risked nearly all to back the internal settlement, with Bishop Muzorewa as the chief "useful idiot".

But few of the key players in the Rhodesian saga foresaw the main elements of the unfolding Greek tragedy. Not only was black rule inevitable, but it was almost inevitable that once they were allowed to get away with UDI, Rhodesian whites were unlikely to accept their fate without a considerable struggle. That struggle was bound to be prolonged, if, firstly, the black nationalist movement were to become divided, and, secondly, international pressures, especially sanctions, were not comprehensively applied. Pretoria circumvented easily the feeble sanctions, and the black nationalists spent as much time fighting each other as combating Smith's troops. So the war dragged on for 14 years.

The course of the war

The war can be divided into three stages: from UDI to 1972, the small Rhodesian security forces were engaged in a winning war; from 1972-76, it can be described as a no-win war; and from 1976-80 the Rhodesians became engulfed in a losing war. If the Lancaster House talks had not intervened, military defeat was around the corner for white Rhodesia.

Politically motivated strikes and isolated attacks on whites had predated UDI. After 1965 the main nationalist movements, the Zimbabwe African National Union (ZANU) and the Zimbabwe African People's Union (ZAPU), hoped that their dramatic, if forlorn, military gestures would, firstly, encourage a general African insurrection and, secondly, prompt British armed intervention. From 1966-68 both nationalist movements launched guerrilla forays. In April 1966 a small group of

ZANU insurgents infiltrated from Zambia into Rhodesia and split up into three teams. They planned to cut power lines and attack white farms. A white farmer and his wife were murdered near Hartley in May, but the most significant contact took place earlier near Sinoia on 28 April. A seven-man ZANU squad, some of whom were originally trained at Nanking military college, was wiped out by the security forces, who suffered no casualties. The current Zimbabwe government has apotheosized this military fiasco as the central event of the liberation war. The date is commemorated as Chimurenga Day.(10) The ruling party in Zimbabwe, now called ZANU-PF, wanted to emphasise that it began the war before its old rival, ZAPU.

In fact, all seven ZANU "heroes of the revolution" involved in the debacle were being fed by police special branch (SB), and the political commissar of the group was allegedly an agent of the Rhodesian Central Intelligence Organisation (CIO).(11) They were supposed to lead the security forces to arms caches and nationalist sympathisers. Instead, because of an administrative foul-up, they were all killed, inefficiently. An air force gunner in an Alouette expended 168 rounds, from a hastily rigged MAG 7.62mm, to shoot dead one guerrilla running across open ground in daylight. The regular and reserve policemen involved in the hunt were mostly armed with World War One vintage rifles and Second World War revolvers. According to one eyewitness, "It was nothing more than a baboon shoot, the police reservists congregating like farmers (which most of them were) around every kill and exposing themselves unbelievably to enemy fire."(12) A history of the Rhodesian air force commented thus: "It was a very unconvincing and unprofessional action...Fortunately for the police, the guerrillas were too confused to take advantage of the inexperience of the hunters."(13) Racially arrogant, the Rhodesians always overplayed guerrilla incompetence, terming it disparagingly the "K factor" (kaffir factor). Indeed, the military performance of the guerrillas, particularly in the early part of the war, was appalling; "the worst this century", according to one British expert.(14) Both sides, however, learnt from their mistakes. In the end, the Rhodesians often met fierce resistance and came to repent underestimating their enemy.

In 1967 and 1968 the nationalists dabbled in urban warfare. A number of armchair revolutionaries, white intellectuals at the country's single university, helped to plant bombs. They were soon rounded up and deported, or imprisoned. Throughout the war, because of excellent police work based on a large network of black informers, urban terrorism rarely posed a major threat. More serious, in August 1967, a combined force of 90 guerrillas from ZAPU and the South African ANC entered Rhodesia near Victoria Falls. They tried to set up large Viet Cong-style base camps inside Rhodesia. Later the ANC cadres planned to infiltrate through Botswana to head for Soweto township in Johannesburg. But the guerrillas were on a suicide mission. They had been told they would be welcomed by the local people, but the tribesmen in the sparsely populated shrubland of northwestern Rhodesia were suspicious of strangers. Soon the bush telegraph brought the news to Rhodesian intelligence. In the first large-scale operations of the war, 47 of the insurgents were killed by the army in three weeks. In 1968 two more tandem forces of ZAPU/ANC guerrillas, one 123-strong and another 91 in number, tried again. Despite some determined resistance, these infiltrators were routed. By the end of 1968 more than 160 insurgents and 12 security force members had been killed.

From 1969 to 1972 the war wound right down. The slackening tempo lulled the government into a false sense of complacency and lazy assumptions of inevitable military supremacy. Indeed, some Rhodesians thought that the war was over. The economy had more than recovered from the initial setbacks caused by sanctions, and white immigration was increasing to reach a peak white population of 275,000.

The disastrous large-scale incursions by ZAPU and the ANC had two main repercussions. Firstly, they encouraged ZANU, which called the attacks a "gross blunder", to revamp its strategy. ZANU argued that ZAPU tactics had ignored the first two stages of classic Maoist insurgency. By jumping to the third conventional stage ZAPU had handed inevitably the operational advantages to the better-equipped security forces. Instead, the military wing of ZANU, the Zimbabwe African National Liberation Army (ZANLA), prepared for a protracted war based upon the full-scale politicisation of the peasantry. As Portuguese sway over Mozambique evaporated, ZANLA, with logistic support from Frelimo, began to infiltrate across the border, especially in the northeast where government administration had always been poor.

The second repercussion was that South Africa was prompted to send police units to aid Rhodesian counterinsurgency operations in the Zambezi valley. Later, army and air force personnel were added. The "police" label was used to discourage international accusations that Pretoria had intervened militarily in a British colony. The initial South African contingent numbered about 2,000 men, although, according to one writer: "By 1969 the number of South African troops at the front reached 2,700, only a thousand short of the Rhodesian regular army."(15) The official rationale for the South African presence was the pretext of preventing ANC penetration of the Transvaal via Rhodesia. In the beginning Rhodesian troops regarded their South African allies with near contempt and disparagingly dubbed them "clumpies" because of their clumsy bushcraft. Rhodesian units were forced to operate behind the South Africans to fill in the gaps created by their allies' inexperience. When senior Rhodesian officers protested that their allies were more of a liability than a help, they were informed that the presence of South African forces was a *political* necessity.(16) The South Africans gradually improved for they were in Rhodesia to gain much-needed operational experience as much as to help their white brethren. John Vorster, the South African premier after 1966, explained that he had sent his men in order "to pull our own chestnuts out of the fire". Vorster included his own 18-year-old son in the contingent. Later on in the war Salisbury was to become totally dependent upon South African military largesse, particularly the loan of helicopters and their air crews. Equally vital was South African economic subvention, which eventually amounted to perhaps as much as 50% of the annual Rhodesian defence budget.

The South African expeditionary force held a northern line from Victoria Falls to the end of Kariba, but ZANU's political programme was advancing apace along the eastern border with Mozambique. The Rhodesian intelligence organisation, the CIO, was aware of the politicisation, but not its extent. The Rhodesian Front hardliners, particularly in the Department of Internal (formerly Native) Affairs, complained, however, about security lectures that were "all doom and gloom which never materialised".(17) The Salisbury government was, nevertheless, very concerned about Portugal's weakening grip on its colonies.

Late 1972 marked round two of war. ZANLA had built up an extensive political underground in the northeast. Crucially, the spirit mediums had been won over. The superstitious peasantry, the "masses" in ZANLA parlance, then came over in droves. (Salisbury also tried to enlist the aid of mediums. The government issued leaflets proclaiming that the spirits were on the side of the RF. Few tribesmen were convinced; they reckoned that in the past the spirits had not had access to printing presses.) In December Salisbury announced that national service would be increased from nine months to one year. On 21 December the first wave of ZANLA offensives struck. Guerrillas attacked the isolated Altena farm in the Centenary district. Casualties were minor—an eight-year-old white girl was wounded in the foot—but this was the beginning of seven years of protracted struggle. Other attacks on farms followed as the guerrillas infiltrated a wide arc from Sipolilo, west of

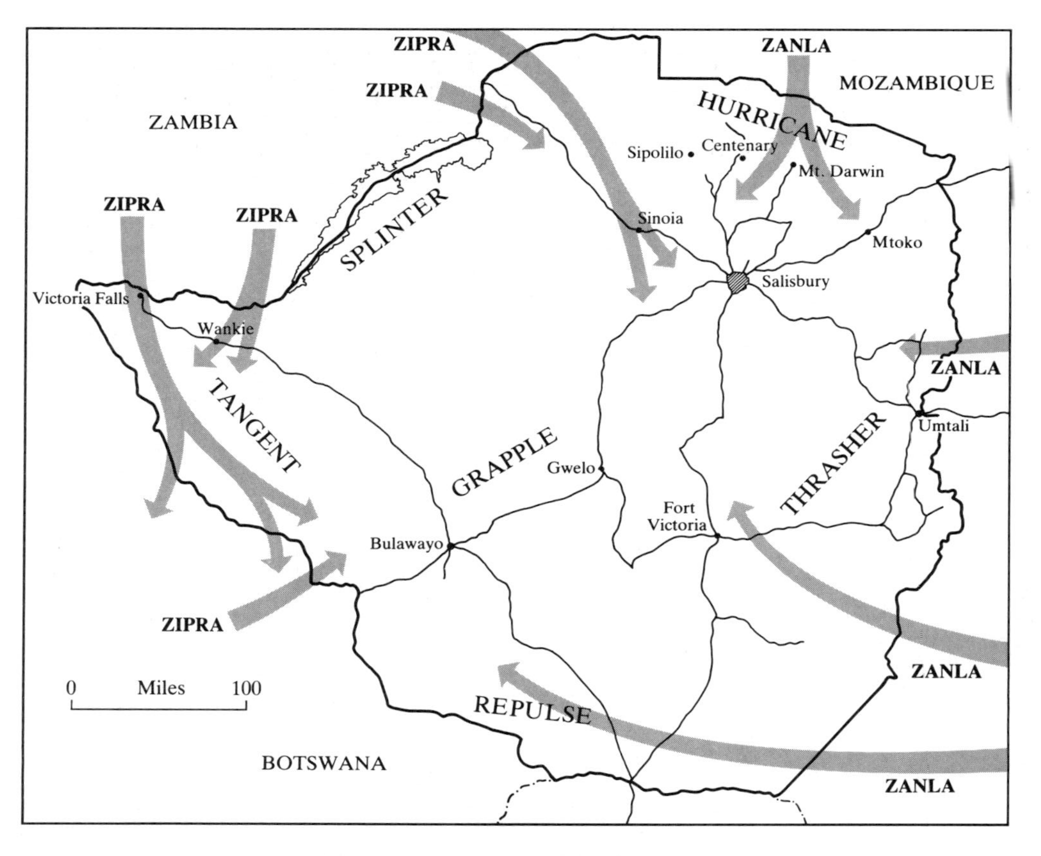

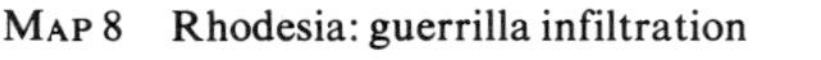
Map 8 Rhodesia: guerrilla infiltration

Centenary, to Mtoko, and southwards towards the Chiweshe and Madziwa Tribal Trust Lands (TTLs). Operation Hurricane was set up to repulse the guerrilla drive, but the response was slow and unsure. In January 1973 Smith ordered the border with Zambia to be closed to pressurise Kenneth Kaunda into dropping his support for ZAPU bases there. Collective fines were imposed by the government in the affected areas. Cattle were impounded. Shops and clinics were closed in the Chiweshe TTL. Although intelligence improved, the collective measures also embittered many peasant farmers. Protected villages (PVs) were established: whole communities were uprooted and put "behind the wire". Although initially effective in military terms, they were a propaganda gift to the guerrilla recruiters, as were the "free-fire zones" along the Mozambique border.

Call-ups were extended for whites. Eventually, even men in their fifties were scooped up to serve in "Dad's army" police units. Inevitably the drain of white skilled labour and the accelerating pace of emigration diluted the efficacy of the war-strained economy. Some RF MPs and businessmen argued that a large standing army, blacks officered by whites, would be more cost-effective, but the government still asserted publicly that the insurgency was a "temporary emergency". From 1974, however, the regular army was expanded. A second battalion of the Rhodesian African Rifles (RAR) was formed. Manpower deployment was improved and a halting start was made to wage a psychological counter-offensive. The Ministry of Internal Affairs rushed through a programme of rural development schemes. Tribespeople were offered large rewards for pointing out guerrilla arms caches. But the stick was always bigger than the carrot. In the two years from mid-1974, 240,000 Africans were put into protected and "consolidated" villages. Some PVs did provide excellent facilities, but many were primitive and disease-ridden. By the end of 1974, however, government measures seemed to have worked: Rhodesian intelligence reported that only 70-100 hardcore guerrillas remained operative in the country. Salisbury was temporarily on top. Then came an international upset which went by the name of detente.

Pretoria's alliance with Salisbury was undermining Vorster's "outward policy" of trying to improve relations with black Africa. The Portuguese collapse was bound to intensify the Rhodesian war. So a compromise was planned by Kaunda and Vorster. Hendrik van den Bergh, the powerful head of South Africa's Bureau for State Security, and Mark Chona, Kaunda's top aide, had been busy organising the outlines of a ceasefire. The Rhodesian war was destroying Zambia's economy, and Kaunda was heartily sick of rival Zimbabwean nationalists feuding in his country. After some hefty arm-twisting by both Vorster and Kaunda, backed by Julius Nyerere, a ceasefire was agreed in December 1974. Some senior Rhodesian nationalists were released, including Joshua Nkomo and Robert Mugabe. As a *quid pro quo* for Kaunda's cooperation, Vorster promised to remove his forces from Rhodesia.

The ceasefire did not work. The guerrillas continued to infiltrate, and the Rhodesians did not release all the expected political detainees. On 1 August 1975 Pretoria officially withdrew all its "policemen". In fact, under the codename Operation Polo, helicopters, pilots, and ground support crews remained. Later, training facilities were extended in South Africa, and South African elite forces joined the Rhodesians in cross-border raids. The public withdrawal was a prelude in the same month to a constitutional conference between the Rhodesian antagonists, held imaginatively on a coach standing in the middle of the Victoria Falls bridge. Previous peace talks had been staged on ships in a storm. Now it was above a chasm with the roaring Zambezi below. Neither proved to be stable environments for compromise. The talks were aborted.

The ceasefire had been a major psychological setback for Salisbury. The nationalists spread the word that the whites had been defeated and were surrendering. But the liberation movements were in no position to take advantage of this propaganda bonus; for ZANLA spent most of 1975 ripping itself apart. The feuds were based upon a wide variety of factors ranging from ideological rifts and ZANU-ZAPU tribal animosity to serious complaints about inadequate logistics, training and weapons. One bloody firefight in a joint ZANLA-ZIPRA camp in Tanzania was caused by a row over poor food. A number of revolts, such as the Nhari rebellion, were quelled with great loss of life. The most serious incident was caused by the assassination of the ZANU leader, Herbert Chitepo, in Lusaka in March 1975. A high-powered Zambian enquiry blamed rivals in ZANU. A large number of ZANLA officials were tortured and imprisoned, including the highly competent (and innocent) military commander, Josiah Tongogara. Zambia ejected ZANU altogether, and bequeathed all the Zambian bases to Kaunda's protégé, Nkomo, the burly supremo of ZAPU. ZANU survivors fled to Mozambique, but the military infrastructure had been emasculated. Inexperienced ZANLA commanders were pushed into Rhodesia and the security force kill-rates rocketed. According to Rhodesian intelligence: "In December 1975 there were only three groups of 10 terrorists each operating in Rhodesia." (18)

Chitepo's death had led to a chain of events which set back the guerrilla advance by a year or two. The head of the CIO, Ken Flower, a short, enigmatic Cornishman, was well-pleased. Two ex-British SAS men, working for the CIO, had planted a car-bomb built by a South African working in Rhodesian special forces, Captain Rob Warracker. The Chitepo assassination team was headed by a man from Cardiff, codenamed Taffy, who was later tasked to kill Mugabe at Lancaster House.(19) Rhodesia fought a very effective dirty war, which sometimes backfired. The CIO killed J Z Moyo, the ZAPU vice-president, on 22 January 1977 with a bomb hidden in a Reader's Digest book. This was an own goal of World Cup standards because Moyo was allegedly special branch's top agent. On the "need to know" principle, SB had not told CIO.(20) Flower also terminated one of his own agents deliberately. In his memoirs, Flower related how the Reverend Arthur Kanodareka, a top aide to Bishop Muzorewa, had supplied poisoned uniforms to guerrillas for years. The CIO shot Kanodareka and blamed nationalist rivals. The contact poison scheme became "so diabolically successful that exposure seemed inevitable and so the principal perpetrators had to be eliminated—rather as a hunter will finish off a wounded animal to stop further suffering".(21)

At the beginning of 1976 ZANLA began to recover and launched fresh offensives. In February the Rhodesians set up Operation Thrasher, based at Umtali, to monitor the eastern border. In May 1976, as the war seeped into the white heartlands, Operation Repulse, with its HQ at Fort Victoria, was established to counter infiltration into the southeastern lowveld. To most whites the war still seemed restricted to the border areas. In the towns and cities, where the vast majority of whites relaxed in their comfortable suburban cocoons, life seemed reasonably normal. The police informer network was intact. The black majority in the regular armed forces stayed loyal in the fight against what the RF termed "international communism". In March Ian Smith conducted a series of cosy talks with Nkomo about a settlement—a settlement which as far as Smith was concerned would never include black majority rule.

But again international pressures were about to lead to Pretoria's heavy-handed intervention. Pretoria was itself in a diplomatic corner. The SADF had just retreated from Angola, Soweto was soon in flames and the UN was calling for a mandatory arms embargo against the apartheid regime. Smith was a big liability. On 3 March 1976 the new Frelimo government closed its border. One-sixth of Rhodesia's rolling stock was trapped, as well as massive amounts of sanctions-busting exports. The rebels were now completely dependent upon the two rail lines to South Africa. This was a leverage Pretoria would soon exert.

From mid-1976 ZIPRA forces began to infiltrate from Zambia and Botswana. In August Operation Tangent was opened to counter the new front. Smith's generals wanted to launch big cross-border raids, "externals" in Rhodesian parlance, to wipe out the guerrilla troop concentrations, partly for military reasons and partly to bolster sagging white morale. Vorster had cautioned against such action and warned Smith that an escalation could risk the entry of Cuban combat troops. The guerrillas stepped up the war. Convoys were introduced on the main roads. On 5 August a group of 60 insurgents attacked a security force base near Umtali. Three days later four territorial soldiers were killed in a mortar attack in the same area. Salisbury decided it was time for action.

The target would be Nyadzonya, about 25 miles northeast of Umtali. On 9 August a convoy of vehicles containing 84 Selous Scouts crossed the Mozambique border. The column was made up of seven armoured Unimogs and four Ferret armoured cars (pre-UDI donations from Britain). Two of the Unimogs were armed with Hispano 20mm cannons scavenged from retired Vampire aircraft. The Selous Scouts, including many blacks and an attached SAS soldier who spoke Portuguese, were dressed as Frelimo troops. The vehicles, too, were disguised as Mozambican. After deploying some of the force along the route, 72 men, led by the same Captain Warracker who had devised the Chitepo bomb, drove coolly into the major ZANLA base containing over 5,000 personnel. In abusive Portuguese, the SAS man ordered the gate to be opened. It was 8.25 am. Dropping off a mortar unit at the entrance, the Scouts drove on to the parade ground, where excellent intelligence had accurately predicted that the inhabitants would be assembled. While the SAS soldier and a Shona-speaking Scout harangued the assembly with revolutionary clichés, the ZANLA cadres began to swarm around the Rhodesian vehicles. Eventually, as those pressed right against the vehicles realised that whites were huddled inside, Warracker gave the order to fire. Carnage ensued. Hundreds were shot, burnt or drowned while trying to escape in the nearby Nyadzonya river. The commanding officer of the Selous Scouts later wrote that the raid was "the classic operation of the whole war... carried out by only seventy-two soldiers... without air support... and without reserves of any kind".(22) ZANLA insisted, however, that Nyadzonya was a refugee camp and later held up the raid as the worst atrocity of the war. It seems that although nearly all the personnel in the camp were unarmed, many were trained guerrillas or undergoing instruction. According to ZANLA documents captured later, 1,026 were killed (without a single security force fatality). ZANU had been totally surprised.(23)

So was Vorster. When he heard about the raid, he promptly terminated Operation Polo. Despite some attempts at foot-dragging by the SADF, the remaining South African military personnel were pulled out. The Rhodesian air force's strike capacity was cut in half. Suddenly "congestion" problems on the two rail links cut off ammunition and oil to the rebels. As one writer put it: "South Africa, as frontline troops were only too aware, was withholding arms supplies; only twelve days' ammunition was available."(24) And there was more. On Vorster's instructions, Dr Hilgard Muller, the foreign minister, declared that Pretoria supported the principle of majority rule in Rhodesia. The unsayable had been said. Politically, Vorster had pulled the rug from under Smith.

Then Henry Kissinger, the US secretary of state, strolled on to the African stage. He understood that the key to compromise on Rhodesia (and Namibia) lay in Vorster's hand. The wily ex-professor promised Vorster concessions on American anti-apartheid policies if Vorster would deliver Smith's head on a platter. During a series of talks in Pretoria in September 1976 Vorster did just that. He read the riot act to Smith: publicly agree to majority rule or we will cut off your supplies totally. Kissinger had shown to Smith three US intelligence reports which indicated that the rebels' war effort would collapse within three months without further supplies. Vorster's arrogant diktat was described as "meat-axe diplomacy" by the Americans. A Damoclean sword, wielded by a fellow white supremacist, doomed the rebels (or saved them from themselves). Vorster, as much as the liberation struggle and sanctions, undermined Rhodesia. The Rhodesians present at the Vorster-Smith-Kissinger summit were shocked by Vorster's neo-Stalinist style. It paralleled the way Hitler dictated to President Schuschnigg the terms of the *Anschluss* with Austria or the harsh *realpolitik* when Chamberlain forced Benes to surrender Czechoslovakia. Pretoria had shown itself a master of how to apply sanctions: short,sharp, and comprehensive measures aimed at a precise goal. Smith described himself as the "sacrifical lamb". The lamb duly went to the slaughter. On 24 September, on Rhodesian television, Smith conceded the principle of majority rule as part of the Kissinger package to end the war and sanctions. In a single speech, Smith had reversed the original war aim of the whites. Morale in the army slumped.

The Rhodesian Front tried to put a brave face on the climbdown. The

Kissinger package, whispered nervous RF parliamentarians to their constituents, would buy time. Even if the proposed two-year transition to "majority rule", which was never defined, was implemented, the whites would still control the security apparatus. And if things did not work out during those two years, then after that period of grace from sanctions and war, Rhodesia would be in a much stronger position to finish off the guerrillas for good—with Pretoria's backing and perhaps even a wink from the West.

Kissinger had been dancing on air. His conjuring tricks had finessed Smith and Vorster, but not the black frontline states. The Kissinger "deal" fell apart at the ensuing Geneva conference. In 1977 the new Carter administration in Washington tried a different, more hostile, tack, while Smith insisted that the Kissinger package was not negotiable. When the Geneva conference ended without any result, Pretoria loosed its stranglehold on Rhodesia. Salisbury would get enough arms to hold off the guerrillas until a settlement could be reached, but not enough to obliterate them, which might have sucked in the Russians and their East German and Cuban proxies. Smith decided to dispense with international diplomacy and move towards a so-called "internal settlement".

When the chairman of the Geneva conference, Ivor Richard, tried to resuscitate the international talks in early 1977, the proposal to involve the guerrillas in the transitional security arrangements shocked Smith and outraged his commanders. To them the internal route to (qualified) black rule looked much safer. Rhodesian suspicions grew intense when Dr David Owen, the British foreign secretary—perhaps one man Rhodesians grew to hate more than Harold Wilson—teamed up with the flamboyant American diplomat, Andrew Young, to solve the imbroglio with UN intervention. Field Marshal Lord Carver was designated to supervise the political and military integration process, aided by a UN-appointed military supremo, General Prem Chand. After the bestial treatment of whites in the Congo, the UN was equated with the anti-Christ by white Rhodesians. This phobia, shared by most white South Africans, may be hard to comprehend by those who have not witnessed at first-hand white primaeval fears of black disorder. Rhodesians dreaded the possibility of the UN holding the ring between rival black factions once whites had lost their grip on power. Such primordial fears may or may not have been realistic, but they help to explain much of the instinctive security reflexes in southern Africa.

The majority of white voters backed Smith's rejection of the British modifications of the Kissinger deal: the RF again won all the 50 white seats in the 66-member parliament in the August 1977 general election. As the (fortunately) inimitable Rhodesian foreign minister, P K van der Byl, said so dramatically: "If this new proposal was to be imposed on us, it is better to fight to the last man and the last cartridge and die with some honour than die in front of one of Mugabe's people's courts." The easing of the South African pressure had ensured that the security forces were not down to their last cartridge, but nonetheless the full-scale war was about to begin.

By April 1977 the Rhodesian government conceded that about 2,350 guerrillas were active in the four existing operational areas. ZANLA and ZIPRA troops were breaking down the government infrastructure in the countryside. Schools, clinics and mission stations were forcibly closed. African councils could not function. Stock theft and attacks on white farms mounted. The most publicised attack in 1977 took place on 7 August when a bomb exploded at a Woolworths store in downtown Salisbury: 11 people were killed and more than 70 injured. Most of the casualties were black. New operational areas were opened in central Rhodesia (Grapple), the Salisbury area (Salops) and Lake Kariba (Splinter).

The ultra-right wing of the RF (which hived off to form the Rhodesia Action Party) demanded a full mobilisation, while a large regular army was being created, to destroy all the insurgent bases in the frontline states. There were also numerous complaints of poor coordination of the war effort. In response in March a Combined Operations HQ (ComOps) was set up under Lieutenant General Peter Walls. Walls, the former officer commanding the Rhodesian army, who had been trained at Sandhurst and commissioned into the Black Watch in 1946, maintained, after the war, that he had never been given enough authority to coordinate the war properly. Many administrative snarl-ups continued; the SAS, for example, used to call ComOps "the Muppet Show", until a formal ComOps directive ordered the SAS to desist.

Conscription was extended to the 38-50 age group and exemptions severely reduced. Those older than 50 were asked to volunteer for the police reserve. Very few blacks were conscripted (only doctors and some apprentices) partly because so many volunteers flocked to join the RAR. Some enlisted for ideological reasons or because they had relatives in the RAR, but most signed up for secure employment. The two battalions of the RAR were augmented with a third. Later the nucleus of a fourth was set up, but the high standards of the original 1 RAR were never matched. The PV programme was also extended. By August 1977 the anti-government Roman Catholic Justice and Peace Commission asserted that 203 PVs had been erected and 580,832 people were living behind "the wire", often in squalor. (25). Severe curfews were imposed in many TTLs and the "no-go" areas along the Mozambique and Botswana borders were extended. The external raids continued. One unsuccessful raid against Mapai in Mozambique, near the South African border, again antagonised Pretoria. Vorster advised Smith not to bomb his way to an internal settlement.

Smith had targeted the diminutive Bishop Abel Muzorewa, the head of the United African National Council (UANC), as a suitably pliant and moderate protagonist. Ndabaningi Sithole's breakaway faction of ZANU also looked set to try the internal route. In September Smith flew secretly to Lusaka to persuade the old warrior, Nkomo, to join the internal parties. Nkomo was evasive. Salisbury decided on a show of force before entering real negotiations. This time, Pretoria nodded its assent. (On most occasions, until the very last months of the war, the Rhodesians avoided consulting the South Africans, if they could, in case they disapproved. Dependent as they were on SADF supplies, Salisbury tried not to openly disregard Pretoria's advice.)(26)

On 23 November 1977 the Rhodesians launched their biggest operation to date. The army, with a crucial SAS core, hit the ZANLA HQ near Chimoio, about 60 miles inside Mozambique, opposite Umtali. Three days later, a second wave overcame Tembue in Tete province (140 miles from the Rhodesian border). The two assaults, codenamed Operation Dingo, were classic examples of vertical envelopments. At Chimoio, 97 SAS and 48 RLI parachutists landed on two sides of the base, while 40 heliborne RLI troops were dropped on the third side. The fourth side of the trap was, in theory, to be sealed by fire from Alouettes armed with 20mm cannons, after the inital bombing strikes. Chimoio was estimated to hold at least 9,000 ZANLA and Tembue 4,000. Practically the entire air force (42 helicopters, eight Hunters, six Vampires, three Canberras, six Dakotas and 12 Lynx [Cessna] aircraft) was deployed for air strikes and to transport the 185 troops. Without modern troop-carrying helicopters—12 decrepit Bell Hueys were later smuggled in to the rebels—the air force found it difficult to air-transport more than 200 troops at one time. Normally, a 3:1 superiority is required for attacking an entrenched enemy. In this case the Rhodesians were massively outnumbered. The elements of surprise and air power were supposed to fill the gap. ComOps claimed that the Rhodesians killed more than 1,200 guerrillas for the loss of one Rhodesian soldier and eight injured in Operation Dingo. According to ZANU, the figures were much higher, probably nearer 2,000, many of them women and

SOWETO
Is your conversation KILLING?
ZIMBABWE RHODESIA
We are all going to Vote
That is what the people want
MAKE A TERRORIST HAPPY. TALK BIG
be a dumb blonde
Think about national security — don't talk about it.
GOD
AWB
AWB
BEER TALK is DEAR TALK
ZIMBABWE RHODESIA
I am staying to help make it work.
That is what the people want

children. The Chimoio complex contained schools and hospitals, as well as military training facilities.

Chimoio caused Muzorewa to break off his negotiations with Smith, but they were resumed after a week. Eventually, in March 1978, Smith reached an agreement with Muzorewa, Sithole and a docile Shona chief, Jeremiah Chirau. These four men, nicknamed the "gang of four", hoped to bring about a kind of majority rule which would end the war and pre-empt a military victory by the Patriotic Front (PF), as the loose coalition of their guerrilla opponents was called. The Patriotic Front denounced the March agreement as a sham, another UDI, and escalated the war. Keeping back 8,000-10,000 men, Nkomo never deployed more than 2,000 troops inside Rhodesia. With Cuban and Russian backing, he was preparing for a conventional assault on Rhodesia. He hoped that ZANLA and the security forces would exhaust themselves and then his forces would march in over the bones of his black and white rivals. The conventional invasion was scheduled for 1981 or 1982. Nkomo, as usual, got his timing wrong and lost out.(27) By June 1978 ZANLA had pushed in 13,000 troops who were assisted by up to 50,000 locally trained cadres and young scouts called *mujibas*.

The internal settlement failed. Instead of ending the war, it expanded it. Smith sidestepped his black allies to establish a private war council made up of his white commanders. Lacking real power, the three black leaders looked like stooges. Not surprisingly, the government's amnesty campaign failed to attract more than a few hundred genuine guerrilla opponents. Smith seemed to regard the removal of racial discrimination as an exchange for the internal blacks' ability to wind down the war, while the black leaders argued that white intransigence over race laws had undermined their efforts to persuade the guerrillas to come home. Some PVs, however, were closed.

Many white officers regarded the settlement as an opportunity to Africanise the war under effective white leadership. With blacks in a semblance of power, a tougher policy against the frontline states might be more acceptable to the world. Whites also agitated for more black conscription. Muzorewa and Sithole built up their own private armies, known as auxiliaries, which eventually numbered about 20,000, most of them loyal to the UANC. Many of these auxiliaries (known as *Pfumo reVahnu*) were unemployed thugs from the cities, spiced here and there with a small number of genuine insurgents who had "come onsides" to join the government. The stage was being set for the whites' worst fear: civil war. Warlordism became rampant as five different armies—ZANLA, ZIPRA, the security forces, and two separate armies loyal to

Sithole and Muzorewa—plus roving bandit gangs, ravaged the land. Atrocities and excesses resulted from all sides. In May 1978 in the Gutu district, the security forces opened fire at a night-time *pungwe* (a ZANU political meeting) and killed 50 black civilians and one guerrilla. In June regular ZANLA forces variously raped, mutilated and finally killed 12 whites, eight adults and four children, at the Elim Pentecostal mission near Umtali.(28) By mid-1978 fatalities within the country were running at 100 a week, compared with an average of three a week in the first five years of the war. White emigration was edging up to 1,500 a month. On 20 July the government announced a compulsory national defence levy of 12.5% extra income tax to help cover a record budget deficit.

White Rhodesia was sinking. In July the US Senate voted against lifting sanctions. Rhodesia under a black-white coalition was still the same outcast. Smith tried again to get Nkomo to play ball. On 14 August he flew secretly to State House, Lusaka, in a Lonrho company jet.(29) But

PLATE 8.1 Rhodesian troops at the scene of the Elim massacre, 1978. (*Rhodesian Ministry of Information*)

any hope of a deal with Nkomo exploded, along with the unarmed Air Rhodesia Viscount which ZIPRA shot down with a SAM-7 missile on 3 September 1978. Of the 53 people on board, 18 survived the crash, but ten of them, including six women, were massacred by ZIPRA guerrillas. During a BBC interview the ZAPU leader incensed white Rhodesians by chuckling over the tragedy.

Salisbury launched a series of massive retaliatory raids into Mozambique and later Zambia. By December 1978, 75% of the country was under martial law. The figure reached 90% later. While the civilians squabbled in Salisbury, the generals were left to counter the rapid growth of ZANLA and ZIPRA control in the countryside. Despite the regular armed clashes between both sections of the Patriotic Front, in disputes over territory, they cooperated in other areas. ZANLA was preparing to establish formal liberated zones and defend them with a locally trained people's militia. The groundwork for the initial, crude structure of administration was being laid. The war edged closer to the cities. On 11 December ZANLA guerrillas fired rockets and tracers at the central oil storage depot in Salisbury and destroyed 25 million gallons of precious fuel. The fire raged for six days. Literally, a black pall hung over the last white Christmas for Rhodesians.

The Rhodesian government entered 1979 in dire straits. The only improvement in the war effort had been the increase in Pretoria's backing, after P W Botha, always sympathetic to Salisbury, became prime minister in September 1978. The SADF chief, General Magnus Malan, was now "responsible for putting South African steel behind the Rhodesian defense effort".(30) Daily flights of arms arrived at New Sarum airport, Salisbury, in South African Lockheed C-130 transports. When the Rhodesian air force launched a retaliatory bombing raid deep into Angola on 26 February, as revenge for ZIPRA's shooting down of a second civilian airliner, the South African air force was on standby in case Russian and Cuban-piloted MiGs tried to intercept the four Rhodesian Canberras, which were operating at the extremes of their maximum range.(31) The ZIPRA base at Luso was over 625 miles from the Rhodesian border.

The Luso raid was a temporary morale-booster. Rhodesian strategy had always relied upon sound morale. But now the prospect of black rule, even by the internal leaders, sapped white resilience. Courage was transformed into weary resignation. No one wanted to be the last white man to die for Zimbabwe, or Zimbabwe-Rhodesia, as the country was called after June 1979. The political leaders were at loggerheads, as were the top commanders. Colonel Ron Reid-Daly, the head of the elite

Selous Scouts, had a blazing public row with the army commander, Lieutenant General John Hickman, after Reid-Daly found a bugging device in his office, planted by military intelligence. There followed a welter of allegations of gun-running and poaching. Some Selous Scouts were busy lining their pockets from ivory sales. It was even mooted that the SAS would have to be used to curtail some of the Selous Scouts units which were getting out of hand. Then Hickman was sacked because the puritanical co-defence minister, Hilary Squires, decided that Hickman's extravagant personal lifestyle amounted to conduct unbecoming a senior officer. Hickman sued and won, on a technicality, his case for wrongful dismissal. After a reprimand, Reid-Daly also resigned and later sued Hickman and Muzorewa, *inter alia.* The scandals surrounding the departure of two of Rhodesia's best-known soldiers came just before the major trial of political strength: the April elections, the first one man, one vote poll. Daring and highly efficient raids continued, however. The SAS, for example, led an Entebbe-style assault on ZIPRA HQ in Lusaka, but failed to assassinate Nkomo. Rhodesian troops also hit targets in Botswana.

ComOps regarded the April election as its crowning success. Never had a ruling minority done so much to hand over (apparent) power to a dominated majority. Few Rhodesians expected the elections to work at all. They thought it would be like a British league soccer match: enjoyed only by the foolhardy, the fanatical and the well-armed. In a 64% poll (if the population estimates were correct) 1,859,077 voters took part, with little Patriotic Front disruption of the polling which they told their followers to boycott. Muzorewa won 51 of the 72 seats reserved for blacks in the new 100-seat parliament. He became, for a while, premier. The election was a success comparable to that in 1966 in war-torn South Vietnam. It proved that the PF was nowhere near "imminent victory" and the security forces were still capable of a massive logistic exercise, involving at least 70,000 troops and policemen.

Rhodesians believed implicity in Margaret Thatcher's promise, when in opposition, that she would recognise the April poll if the Tory group of observers in Rhodesia said the election was fair. They did, and she did not. This was a catastrophic setback for Muzorewa. Many Africans (accurately) interpreted this as lack of faith. If a Conservative British administration would not go along with the internal settlement, who would? The South Africans were incensed by the British attitude. Pik Botha, the foreign minister, said angrily: "The Zimbabwe-Rhodesia settlement issue is beginning to look like a rugby match where the game was played until the winners lost." The internal settlement's goals had been peace, recognition and the removal of sanctions. The only tangible result was all-out war. Muzorewa launched another amnesty campaign, but no one was listening. For behind the facade of black power, the whites were still in control. But their grip was tenuous. Emigration was destroying the crucial skilled manpower core of the army and the economy. As South African units, in Rhodesian uniforms, filled some of the gaps and the Cubans, Frelimo and Tanzanian troops entered the fray, the war was becoming dangerously internationalised.

At the Commonwealth conference in Lusaka in August 1979, Thatcher secured agreement to try one more time to cut the Gordian knot of the Rhodesian impasse. Muzorewa was bitterly disappointed, and the main Rhodesian newspaper, the *Herald,* thundered: "Is Mrs Thatcher really a Labour Prime Minister in drag?" The Lancaster House conference opened on 10 September. As during the Geneva conference, three years earlier, the guerrillas talked and fought, but this time there were four times as many guerrillas in the country. The Rhodesians launched a fresh offensive to improve their diplomatic position. Instead of just hitting the now well-defended PF bases, Salisbury aimed to destroy the economic infrastructure of Zambia and Mozambique. Flower, in his memoirs, dubbed the strategy "Total War—to please our South African allies".(32) ComOps, minus Flower and Walls, who were tied up at Lancaster House, set about annihilating the transport systems of the guerrillas' hosts.

The Rhodesian raids were no longer walkovers. Two particular battles confirmed this. In the three-day Operation Uric against Mapai, the 360 men from the RLI, SAS and the Engineers met very fierce opposition. Two helicopters were shot down. In the second, the three-man crew and 11 Rhodesian soldiers were killed when an RPG-7 rocket hit the chopper. This was the worst single military disaster of the war. As a history of the Rhodesian SAS noted: "For the first time in the history of the war, the Rhodesians had been stopped dead in their tracks." (33) The RLI and the SAS were forced to make an uncharacteristic and hasty retreat.

The Rhodesians had underestimated their enemy. They were outgunned. Their air support had proved unable to winkle out well-entrenched troops and they were even more vulnerable when the aircraft—even when the whole air force was on call—returned to base to refuel and rearm. ComOps decided to use more fire power in the battles that followed, particularly on the raid on New Chimoio. Surveillance from the air was provided by a Dakota bristling with antennae, nicknamed the Warthog. The South African air force became heavily embroiled in these last months, both in the fighting and as standby reserves, as they had done during Operation Uric. Super Frelons and Puma helicopters were difficult to pass off as Rhodesian equipment, but the Canberras and Alouettes also on loan were practically indistinguishable from their Rhodesian counterparts. At least one of the South African Pumas, with a South African crew, was shot down in this period. But Pretoria's cornucopia could not tip the balance. At the end of the climactic raid on the ZANLA HQ at New Chimoio, one Selous Scout admitted: "We knew then that we could never beat them. They had so much equipment and there were so many of them. They would just keep coming with more and more."

The political warfare at Lancaster House was almost as intense. The British had bugged the PF's hotel suites and knew how far to push the guerrillas. The frontline states, especially Mozambique, added their pressure. Zambia and Mozambique were reeling from Rhodesia's "Total War". There had been too much suffering for too long in the whole region. On 12 December Lord Carrington, the British foreign secretary who had chaired the Lancaster House marathon, took a gamble and sent Lord Soames to Salisbury as the new British governor. This was the first time in colonial history that a white governor had replaced an elected black president. As soon as the portly governor stepped on Rhodesian soil, the rebellion against the Crown was over. On 28 December a ceasefire creaked uncertainly into life. By 4 January 1980 more than 18,000 guerrillas had entered the designated assembly points monitored by a British-led Commonwealth force of 1,300 men. Many trained guerrillas, especially ZANLA troops, remained outside the assembly points, as reserves, should the Rhodesians try to obliterate the assembly points, and as armed educationalists to teach the masses to vote the right way. Their charismatic commander, Josiah Tongogara, who was committed to reconciliation with ZIPRA, had just been killed in a "car crash" in Mozambique, though there are some indications that he might have been assassinated by rivals within ZANLA.(34)

Soames was sitting on a powder keg. One writer summed up Rhodesia at the end of the war as "a country the size of France; ravaged by war; where contending armies represented political allegiance; in which civil administration beyond the main urban centres was little more than the gallant endeavours of exhausted survivors".(34) Thirty thousand had been killed, although less than 1,000 were white civilians and servicemen. This was a high figure for a small, close-knit community, although the tally constituted less than 0.5% of the total white population, far less proportionately than the literal decimation during the first *Chimurenga* of the 1890s. But the whites were bitter, particularly the officer corps. Soames had to rely upon the very distrustful Rhodesian armed forces and civil service to run the country until independence. Frelimo troops, ANC cadres and a large contingent of South Africans in the south of the country compounded his problems.(36) The country teetered on the edge of a resumption of civil war. Would the ceasefire hold until the elections?

A number of factors held the country together. The courage of the monitoring force was one. So was Soames's larger-than-life personality. As one Nkomo aide put it: "We Africans get on with old-fashioned Tories better than modern Labour politicians." But the key figure was Peter Walls. Soames was at the mercy of the Rhodesian high command in a country which was 95% under martial law. Another important factor was the belief in each main camp that their man could become prime minister. The Rhodesians believed that the British had opted for the ABM option—"Anybody but Mugabe". Pretoria was convinced the British wanted to patch together a Nkomo-Muzorewa-Smith coalition to keep out the Marxist Mugabe. South Africa had poured in money for Muzorewa's campaigns in both the 1979 and 1980 elections. They went along with the CIO's prediction that the mild Bishop would garner at least 30 of the 80 seats reserved for blacks.

PLATE 8.2 Lieutenant General Peter Walls before a para-drop. *(Rhodesian Ministry of Information)*

PLATE 8.3 Rhodesian Alouettes on fire force operation. *(Rhodesian Ministry of Information)*

And so it was that 2,702,275 men and women, under the watchful eye of 570 British "bobbies" standing next to the polls, voted in the middle of African rainstorms. The February 1980 election brought a 93% turnout. Muzorewa won only three seats, fewer seats than the campaign helicopters Pretoria had paid for. Mugabe won a stunning overall victory of 57 seats. Nkomo got the 20 everyone outside ZAPU had predicted. ZAPU was shattered. As a top Nkomo aide lamented: "You give them one man, one vote and look what they do with it." Rhodesian whites and Pretoria went into a state of almost catatonic shock. There was consternation in Moscow too. Even the foreign press got it wrong; very few had anticipated an outright victory for ZANU-PF. As one correspondent noted sagaciously after the event: "It was yet another classic example of the way the logic of white outsiders was shown to have little relevance to African experience, and not least because few whites possessed either the capacity to identify or the ability to communicate with the blacks."(37) Nyerere, however, had stuck his neck out. Just before the election results he had called the exercise a fraud "concocted for the purpose of satisfying a bunch of racists in Rhodesia, South Africa and Britain". Unlike the massed array of foreign journalists in Rhodesia, he had the grace to retract: "This is not the first time I have been wrong." He added: "This is not the first time I am very pleased I was wrong."

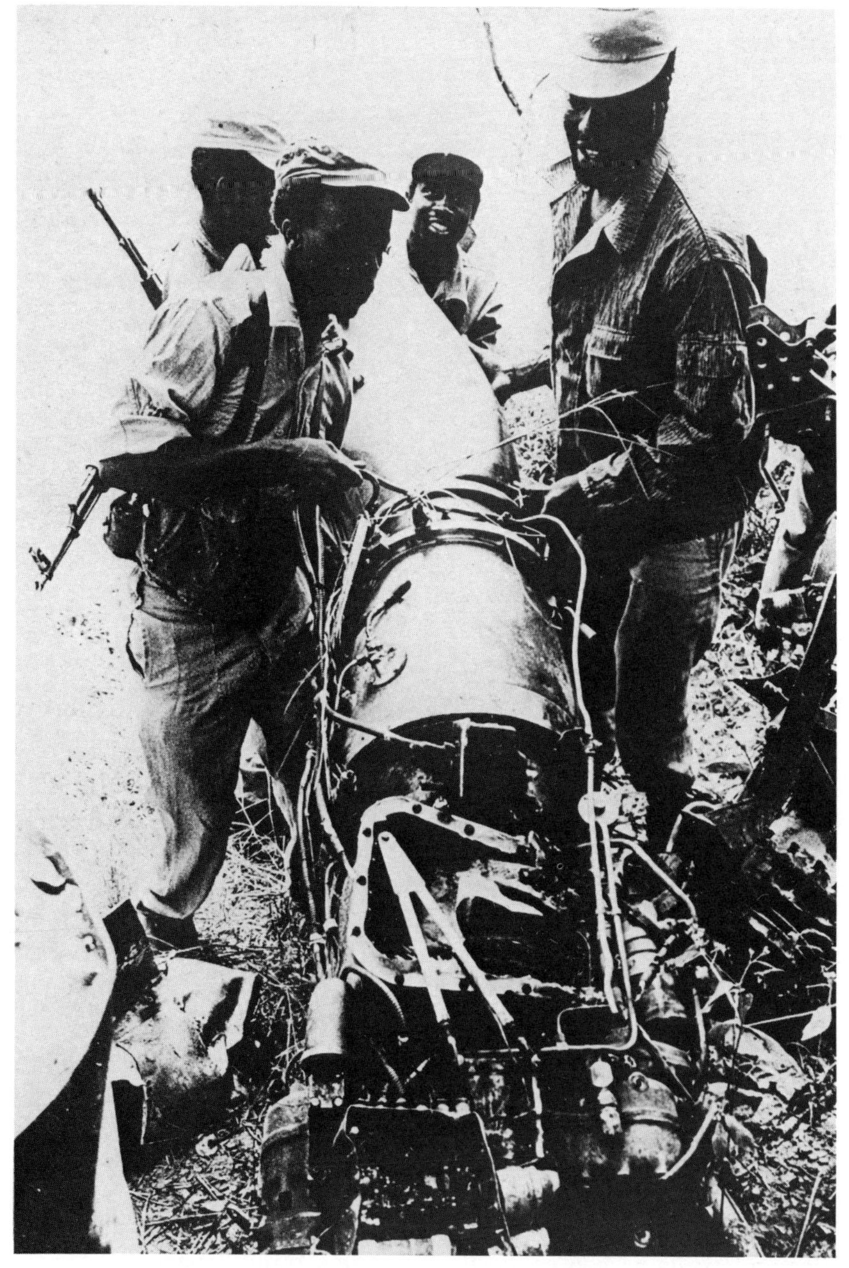

PLATE 8.4 ZIPRA guerrillas examine a Rhodesian helicopter shot down during a raid on Victory camp, Zambia, in 1979. (*National Archives, Zimbabwe*)

PLATE 8.5 Bishop Abel Muzorewa electioneering, 1979. (*Allen Pizzey*)

Meanwhile, heavily-armed Rhodesian troops had taken up positions around the main communications points in the capital. Rhodesian-manned T-55 Russian tanks (seized by the South Africans from a ship in Durban en route to Amin's Uganda and donated to Salisbury late in the war) were on standby. A coup seemed imminent. In fact, this was an elaborate contingency plan to prevent a pre-emptive move by ZANLA should it have decided to act before, or after, what it might have perceived as a rigged ballot. (ZIPRA was specifically excluded from the plans on the assumption that its forces would stay neutral or even help the Rhodesian security forces.) The Rhodesian SAS had indeed arranged for "favourable results" bogus ballot boxes to be available. They were not used. The CIO, SAS and Selous Scouts had been involved in early 1980 in a number of dirty tricks to prevent a Mugabe victory, including two failed assassination attempts. There was even an unauthorised SAS plan to shoot down, with a captured SAM-7, a plane carrying the ZANU-PF central committee. It was called off at the last minute. But once the results were announced, it was too late. Walls, in fact, scotched all talk of a coup to prevent Mugabe taking over. He told his ComOps staff that Rhodesia "will not copy the rest of Africa".(38)

Massive intimidation had plagued the election. ZANLA cadres were the main culprits, although the Bishop's auxiliaries had indulged in some vicious canvassing too. But Mugabe was clearly the favourite son of the masses. Only he could stop the war. The Rhodesian military disbelievingly and very reluctantly accepted the verdict. A rapid exodus of South African troops and equipment followed. Special Branch shredded its files and the Central Statistical Office destroyed its sensitive information, particularly the details of Rhodesia's trade with the Eastern bloc, (which was larger than commerce with Western sanctions-busters). The CIO destroyed its files on its links in the Vatican, with British and French intelligence and on its extensive network of allies throughout black Africa.(39) Cabinet papers were spirited away to South Africa along with the mess silver from Rhodesia's regiments.

On 18 April 1980 Zimbabwe became independent. A right-wing Tory prime minster had caused, probably by accident, the first electoral triumph of a Marxist in Africa. To Rhodesians, Lancaster House was a betrayal, another Munich. Carrington was a second Chamberlain.(40) One very senior Rhodesian defence official claimed that he had heard Carrington separately and definitively promise both Muzorewa and Mugabe that London unofficially supported each man. "In Carrington's view," he added, "the only way to stop the fighting was to hand over to Mugabe. It was a convenient way of getting rid of the problem. It

PLATE 8.7 Rhodesian T-55. A number of these tanks, destined for Idi Amin, were seized by the South Africans and sent to Rhodesia in 1979.

was dishonest, immoral...but effective."(41) It was ironic that a namesake, Major General Sir Frederick Carrington, had presided over the consolidation of white power in Rhodesia in 1896 after the first *Chimurenga*. Symbolically, what one Carrington gave, another took away.

Why Rhodesia lost the war

The Rhodesians were losing in the field, despite their operational ingenuity. Indeed, the history of the armed forces is one of tactical brilliance and strategic ineptitude. Rarely in military chronicles have such thinly-stretched troops, hampered by chronic manpower, training, equipment and financial constraints, achieved such consistent successes against enemy forces which enjoyed the tactical and strategic initiative for most of the war, and often reached numerical parity in the field. On a technical level, the achievements of the security forces will be studied in military colleges for a long time to come. There were failures, for example the PV programme, and projects, such as the auxiliaries, which could have been either very successful or disastrous if the war had continued. Some of the covert operations, such as the pseudo-guerrilla activities of the Selous Scouts, and the sheer bravado of the external raids, will continue to interest military specialists. The most notable development was the rapid deployment of heliborne troops, usually consisting of RLI and RAR soldiers, to hunt guerrillas. This "fire force" concept contributed to most (approximately 12,000 guerrillas) of the kill-rate inside Rhodesia.(42) But the Rhodesian obsession with successful operational techniques created a fatal blindness to the strategic political imperatives required to counter a protracted insurgency. The Rhodesian government for long insisted that it was waging a campaign against violent criminals rather than a civil war. External communism, not internal nationalism, was blamed. Van der Byl appeared convinced that: "This is not a racial war, but black terrorists and white-skinned Communists on one side and a multiracial army of black and white soldiers fighting shoulder-to-shoulder on the other." But politicans proved more adept at explaining why Africans should not support the guerrillas than at explaining why they did.

The initial aim of the war, however, was to prevent the passing of power to any black government, no matter how moderate. An admission of racism, if only within the high command and cabinet, might have produced a more coherent grand strategy, but no clear political programme—beyond a vague preservation of the status quo—was ever articulated. Indeed, Rhodesian officers prided themselves on being *apolitical.* In starkest contrast with the guerrillas, there was very little or no political indoctrination in the Rhodesian armed forces; no school of political warfare was established. Rhodesian grand strategy, such as it was, was shot through with a fatal negativism. There was litle faith in far-reaching reform as a war-winner. Such a recognition, of course, would have undermined the very reasons for the war ever being fought at all. White Rhodesians struggled long and hard against the only thing which could have avoided a war—African participation in national politics. To change horses in mid-stream was extremely difficult, but the Rhodesians did try it. The war shifted from a confrontation with the principle of black majority rule to a war for the sort of black government white Rhodesians were prepared to live under. But once the principle of having any kind of majority rule government at all was conceded, the Rhodesians' war aims became increasingly confused and their strategy consequently weaker.

Faced with the inner weaknesses of their strategies, the Rhodesians resorted to more and more desperate measures. The policy of winning hearts and minds was largely abandoned in the field just as the first moves towards a political strategy of a moderate black government were coming to fruition. Perversely, it was considered that black participation in the political process would permit tougher, war-winning operations. Martial law was introduced, the punitive destruction of villages and livestock of those who were accused of aiding the guerrilllas became routine, and a more aggressive external strategy was adopted. As one senior officer at ComOps admitted: "We relied 90% on force and 10% on psychology and half of that went off half-cock. The guerrillas relied 90% on psychology and only 10% on force."

The insurgents, on the other hand, had a clear vision of their purpose: to break the back of white supremacy and establish a black majority government. This gave the guerrillas remarkable stamina and their cause the strength to weather numerous political crises and consistent military defeat in the field. The apparent simplicity of the guerrilla objectives, of course, masked enormous confusion and conflict as to how to achieve them. At times, dissension among the nationalists was far more potent than the fire power of the Rhodesians in delaying majority rule. The divergences in ideology, tribe, training and deployment contributed to the divisions within the Patriotic Front. For ZANLA, the works of Mao, Marx and Lenin were the staple fare of political education. Nkomo's army paid little attention to Maoist doctrine, but did in practice use Chinese revolutionary tactics. The Soviet connections

TO ALL ZANLA FORCES

In order that all the people of Zimbabwe/Rhodesia can take part in the one-man, one-vote Majority Rule Elections in April, we, the Executive Council, in a unanimous decision, have instructed the Commander of Combined Operations, Lieutenant General G. P. Walls, G.L.M., D.C.D., M.B.E., as follows:

"That any member of the ZANLA Forces who returns home in peace before the election will be well treated. They will be fed, clothed and given proper medical treatment. They will be integrated with the Interim Government Auxilliaries (Pfumo reVanhu) under the command of Combined Operations, and will be armed for this purpose. On no account will those returning members of the Zanla Forces be stopped from voting in the elections in April, should they wish to do so."

BISHOP THE HON. A. T. MUZOREWA **REV. THE HON. N. SITHOLE**

SENATOR CHIEF THE HON. J. S. CHIRAU **THE HON. I. D. SMITH**

A GUARANTEE FROM THE COMMANDER OF COMBINED OPERATIONS

In accordance with the instructions I have received from the Executive Council:

I guarantee the safety of all Zanla Forces who wish to return home before the Elections. You will come to no harm at the hands of the Security Forces. You will be fed and clothed and given proper medical treatment. If you so wish, arrangements will be made for your transfer to the Interim Government Auxilliaries (Pfumo reVanhu) under the command of Combined Operations. The Pfumo reVanhu already have many ex-Zanla Forces working with them. You will be supplied with your own weapon and will be allowed to choose your area of operation. If you wish to be reunited with your family and operate in their area, this can be arranged. You will be allowed to participate with no restriction in the April Elections. This will enable you to play an important part in the establishment of the first black Majority Rule Government in Zimbabwe/Rhodesia.

Come home before the Elections in April 1979 and I guarantee you a safe return.

LT. GEN. G. P. WALLS, G.L.M., D.C.D., M.B.E.

PLATE 8.8 An amnesty poster.

meant that Castro's Cuban experience was more important to them. ZANLA was dominated by Chinese theory diluted by Frelimo experience. Despite these important influences, nationalist objectives tended to dominate all political thinking. ZANLA recruits were educated in the "national grievances". Issues such as land alienation, education, health and welfare discrimination, political oppression, low wages and social inequalities were the fundamentals of the recruits' political diet. Nkomo's cadres were steeped in the history of the chicanery used by the British South Africa Company to destroy the Ndebele state in the 1890s, while the Shonas in ZANLA were taught the history of their first *Chimurenga*.

While such nationalist propaganda was heavily laced with the jargon of scientific socialism, some bizarre contradictions intruded. A most glaring example was the guerrillas' embrace of traditional religion, charms against Rhodesian bullets and the reliance on spirit mediums. While the PF talked of modernising a society the whites were trying to freeze, its military wings in the TTLs were destroying nearly every vestige of modern advance such as animal dip tanks, schools and clinics. Marxist doctrine had a strong emotional appeal for the guerrilla leaders in that it offered them a straightforward explanation of what had happened in Rhodesia and a model for the solution to their struggle. Yet, despite the presence of some convinced Marxists in the ZANLA leadership, the adherence of both wings of the PF to anti-capitalist and anti-Western dogma was largely pragmatic: despairing of their efforts to involve Britain in the 1960s, they felt obliged to look to the communist bloc for guiding principles in the same way as they begged for arms. Despite being clothed in the ferocious Asian garb of a people's war, the guerrillas accomplished what Marxists would term a "bourgeois nationalist revolution".(43)

The guerrillas waged a far more effective psychological war than their opponents.(44) The vast majority of whites made the cardinal error of believing their own mindlessly optimistic propaganda, proof of the old adage that people will usually believe what they want to hear. Blacks tended to ridicule RF propaganda aimed at them. While the Rhodesians viewed hearts and minds as adjuncts to the more important business of killing guerrillas, the nationalists placed a major emphasis on psycho-military campaigning. Guerrilla propaganda was simple and effective. White Rhodesians were generally contemptuous of African culture and, although there were training courses on "African customs" for most soldiers and policemen, there was still an unbridgeable gulf of misunderstanding. The guerrillas, however, were in close touch with the aspirations of Africans and they used skilfully in their propaganda their intimate involvement with the civilian population. Although guerrillas disseminated printed material, including dramatic posters of the socialist realist school, the major medium was the spoken word. On the international front, the insurgents gained the support not only of the Eastern bloc and the third world, but much of the Western press. In particular, the guerrillas managed to create the impression that atrocities, especially against "refugee" camps, were a Rhodesian monopoly. Ultimately, it was on the propaganda fronts, both internally and internationally, that the guerrillas created the political conditions for victory.

The Rhodesians lacked a political programme to (try to) win over the blacks who outnumbered them 25:1. As one Rhodesian officer said bluntly at the end of the war: "How on earth did the generals think they could contain seven million houts?" (45) After the war some Rhodesians insisted that the war had been winnable. They asserted that detente in the mid-1970s was mere appeasement, that the nationalists released from detention should have been indefinitely imprisoned or shot, and that the guerrilla bases in the frontline states should have been obliterated in the early 1970s. "War is war," argued the die-hards, "so why didn't we bomb Lusaka or do a 'dam-buster' on the Cahora Bassa dam and knock out Mozambique in one single blow?" Such an escalation depended upon the wholehearted support of Pretoria which was never forthcoming. Any successful long-term containment of the guerrillas would have been dependent upon diplomatic recognition and military aid from the West. Yet that would never have been given to a white-dominated government. If a plausible political solution—perhaps an assertive Muzorewa administration in 1976—had been gracefully conceded by the RF then Anglo-American military backing might have led to a defeat of the PF, if the guerrillas had fought on. But the RF always gave far too little, far too late.

Sanctions too played a role in the rebels' defeat, albeit a secondary one to the pressures of guerrilla war.(46) For some years economic constraints were merely nuisances: shortages of razor blades, ladies' stockings and good whisky resulted and, as Flower points out in his memoirs, the Salisbury Club ran out of port for the first time since 1896. By the late 1970s, sanctions were biting. They did play a part in winding down the morale of the whites and prompting emigration, a key factor in undermining military strength. Most of the consequences of sanctions, half-hearted and hypocritically applied as they were, were unintended. While privileged whites suffered a loss of perhaps ten Rhodesian dollars a year, most of the hardships were shifted on to the poorest blacks, particularly in the TTLs and frontline states.(47) Sanctions polarised the political spectrum: whites became more intransigent; but similarly black peasants became radicalised as they slipped deeper into poverty. The incomplete sanctions against Rhodesia generated international credibility and legimitacy for the liberation movements, and far more radicalised peasants, a far cry from making the whites bend the knee in a few months as Wilson had predicted.

Pretoria, particularly in 1976, played a vital role in bringing Smith to heel. Getting Smith to agree to a firm commitment to reform was like nailing jelly to a wall. Only Vorster managed that. The war, sanctions, propaganda and Pretoria crushed the rebellion, but its repercussions still reverberate throughout southern Africa.

The impact on South Africa

Rhodesians fought not only an unwinnable war, but, politically, they fought it in a most unwinnable way. Applying the implicit lesson for his homeland, a South African writer aptly summarised the war:

> Shades of Vietnam. Side A has overwhelming firepower, radio communications, a monopoly of air support, and all the access to public propaganda. Side B has nothing but rifles and boots, and even operational commands are conveyed by handwritten scraps foot-slogged through the bush. Side A's propaganda machine makes much of "winning the hearts and minds of the people". But its soldiers in the field think this is a lot of pious nonsense and place their faith instead in the Nixonian amendment: "When you've got them by their balls, their hearts and minds will follow". Side B is perceived by the majority of the population as its liberators... And it all comes to its inevitable end. Side B in the seat of government struggling desperately to restore a shattered economy. Side A writing books in the past tense from distant places, its former officers all blaming each other for their failure.(48)

Would the Rhodesian domino topple the next ones, Namibia and South Africa? Pretoria had now to man a defence perimeter on the Limpopo, not the faraway Zambezi. A new front for ANC infiltration was to open in the northern Transvaal. Zimbabwe had the strongest economy and army in the region, after South Africa. And it was led by a highly competent and pragmatic Marxist who was the dedicated enemy of apartheid. Mugabe became a hero to black youths in South Africa. White political power looked even more fragile. So did its economic leverage. A Muzorewa-led Zimbabwe was to be the central satellite in P W Botha's proposed "Constellation of States". Mugabe, instead, helped to set up a rejectionist front.

Mugabe's accession to power emphasised the basic tenet of pan-Africanism: that Africa could not be truly free until the whole continent was purged of white supremacy. The searchlight was now on Pretoria. The battlelines were drawn.

References and notes:

1. M Meredith, *The Past is Another Country: Rhodesia, UDI to Zimbabwe,* Pan, London, 1980, p. 145.
2. J. Sprack, *Rhodesia: South Africa's Sixth Province,* International Defence and Aid Fund, London, 1974, p. 26.
3. R Blake, *A History of Rhodesia,* Methuen, London, 1977, p. 390.
4. K Flower, the Director-General of the Central Intelligence Organisation, series of interviews with author, 1979-87.
5. Assistant Secretary, Rhodesian Ministry of Defence, interview, 1981. This theme was repeated in a number of interviews with Rhodesian intelligence sources.
6. Discussions with a variety of British army officers when the author was a senior instructor at the Royal Military Academy, Sandhurst, 1973-75. The writer conducted a series of informal polls with classes of officer cadets. An average of between 75% and 9O% said that they would not be prepared to take action against white soldiers in Rhodesia, although they had no qualms about shooting (white) soldiers in the IRA.
7. H Wilson, *A Personal Record: The Labour Government, 1964-1970,* Weidenfeld and Nicolson, London, 1971, p. 164. A Verrier (*The Road to Zimbabwe,* Cape, London, 1986) offers the idiosyncratic view that Britain placated Pretoria throughout the Rhodesian crisis because London relied on gold and uranium from South Africa.
8. R Good, *UDI: The International Politics of the Rhodesian Rebellion,* Faber, London, 1973, p. 294.
9. *Ibid.*, p. 293.
10. *Chimurenga* is a Shona word which implies "resistance". It was also applied to the uprisings against the settlers in the 1890s. Some historians have stressed the continuity of both wars. See, for example, T Ranger, *Revolt in Southern Rhodesia,* Heinemann, London, 1967.
11. Interviews with Flower, *op. cit.*; K Flower, *Serving Secretly,* Murray, London, 1987, p. 106. For an alternative view of the incident, see D Martin and P Johnson, *The Struggle for Zimbabwe,* Faber, London, 1981, pp. 9-12. Flower told Martin about the CIO connection with the Sinoia seven but, according to Flower, the journalist chose to ignore the crucial information.
12. D Cowderoy and R Nesbit, *War in the Air*, Galago, Alberton, 1987. pp. 47-8.
13. *Loc. cit.*
14. N Downie, "Rhodesia: A Study in Incompetence," *Defence,* May, 1979. Interviews with author, 1984.
15. C Coker, "South Africa: A New Military Role in Southern Africa," *Survival*, March/April, 1983.
16. Interviews, Flower.
17. *Ibid.*
18. According to Rhodesian intelligence papers in author's possession.
19. See P Stiff, *See You in November*, Galago, Alberton, 1985, and D Martin and P Johnson, *The Chitepo Assassination*, Zimbabwe Publishing, Harare, 1985.
20. Stiff, *ibid.*, pp. 145-8.
21. Flower, *op. cit.*, p. 137.

22. For full details of special forces' raids, consult R Reid-Daly as told to P Stiff, *Selous Scouts:Top Secret War,* Galago, Alberton, 1982, and B Cole, *The Elite: The Story of the Rhodesian Special Air Service,* Three Knights, Amanzimtoti, 1984.
23. For an alternative perspective on the Nyadzonya raid, see Martin and Johnson, *The Struggle for Zimbabwe, op. cit.*, pp. 240-2.
24. Meredith, *op. cit.*, p. 260.
25. For details on the role of the Commission and the Catholic Church in general, see I Linden, *The Catholic Church and the Struggle for Zimbabwe,* Longman, London, 1980.
26. Interviews, Flower.
27. For details of the planned invasion (Operation Cuba), see Martin and Johnson, *The Struggle for Zimbabwe, op. cit.*, pp. 305-8.
28. ZANU blamed the atrocity on the Selous Scouts, but the author's researches, based upon interviews with the BSAP investigating officers and notebooks of the guerrillas involved, indicate that ZANLA was responsible.
29. See J Nkomo, *Nkomo: The Story of My Life*, Methuen, London, 1984, pp. 189-90.
30. R Leonard, *South Africa at War,* Hill, Westport, 1983, pp. 84-5, quoting the *New York Times,* 23 December 1979.
31. For details of the raid, see Cowderoy and Nesbit, *op. cit.*, pp. 149-52.
32. Flower, *op. cit.*, p. 245.
33. See Cole, *op. cit.*, and Reid-Daly, op. cit.
34. Author's interviews with Rhodesian, South African and Frelimo sources suggested that Tongogara was murdered, although Flower, for one, was always sceptical about the assassination theory.
35. Verrier, *op. cit.*,pp. 252-3.
36. The size of South Africa's involvement has been extensively debated. Mugabe claimed 6,000 troops in late 1979; Flower suggested that 600 was closer to the mark. Excluding Rhodesians of South African extraction and genuine volunteers from the south, the author would hazard a figure of perhaps 3,000 in late 1979. The number of Frelimo regulars inside the country was about 500; 300 ANC cadres were active in the Gwanda region during the ceasefire.
37. A Gavshon, *Crisis in Africa,* Penguin, Harmondsworth, 1981, p. 186.
38. Author's interviews with SAS officers involved with the operations. For a discussion of the "coup", see P Moorcraft and P McLaughlin, *Chimurenga: The War in Rhodesia,* Sygma/Collins, Marshalltown, 1982, pp. 235-6. There is very little material on civil-military relations in Rhodesia. For a analysis of the political power of the Rhodesian military, see P Moorcraft, "The Fall of the Republic: The Collapse of White Power in Rhodesia," unpublished doctoral thesis, University of South Africa, 1987.
39. Flower in his memoirs cited many examples of sanctions hypocrisy. See also M Bailey, *Oilgate: The Sanctions Scandal,* Coronet, London, 1979.
40. A revisionist school has recently suggested that Chamberlain's policy was necessary to provide time for British rearmament; in the short and long term it would be possible to argue that Carrington prevented a savage escalation of the war.
41. The official had been the Acting Secretary, Rhodesian Ministry of Defence. Interview, 1981.
42. For a remarkable first-hand account of fire force operations, see C Cocks, *Fireforce,* Galago, Alberton, 1988.
43. Mugabe has been criticised for selling out the revolution: see A Astrow, *Zimbabwe: A Revolution that Lost its Way?,* Zed, London, 1983.
44. The best account of the psychological war from both sides is J Frederikse, *None But Ourselves: Masses vs the Media in the Making of Zimbabwe,* Ravan, Johannesburg, 1982.

45. *Hout* is a derogatory Afrikaans term applied to Africans. A word used to denote guerrilla, "gook", borrowed from Vietnam, was also very common.
46. A most useful survey of sanctions can be found in H Strack, *Sanctions: The Case of Rhodesia,* Syracuse UP, Syracuse, 1978.
47. E Cross, "Economic Sanctions as an Instrument of Policy," *World Economy,* March, 1981.
48. D Beckett, "The Tough Guys Lost—Despite the Lies," *Frontline,* February, 1983.

DESTABILISATION

MAP 9 SADCC versus the Constellation (until 1989)

9

Battlelines Drawn

As the white-ruled colonies collapsed, the black-controlled successor states formed a frontline alliance against apartheid: the friendly buffers became deadly enemies. The *cordon sanitaire* was transformed into guerrilla sanctuaries and mini-Ho Chi Minh trails. The previous section was concerned with Pretoria's attempts to *stabilise* colonial rule; the following chapters detail South Africa's determination to *destabilise* her neighbours.

Mugabe was the central figure in the redrawing of the new battlelines, which extended along the Cunene and Limpopo rivers. After April 1980 an anti-apartheid curtain fell, dividing black- and white-ruled Africa. To be sure, this was a flimsy, transparent curtain, riddled with SADF bullet holes and the unctuous hypocrisy of black presidents-for-life spewing forth praise for democracy and demands for sanctions while begging for food and petrol from the pariah. It was not an ideological curtain. Unlike the two blocs in Europe, socialist and capitalist leaders were camped on both sides. Yet, even though this was primarily a racial divide, there were valid comparisons with Europe's Cold War. Two rival military coalitions, the black frontline states versus the SADF and its Namibian and homeland cohorts, were partnered by two economic alliances, the Southern African Development Coordination Conference (SADCC) and Pretoria's co-prosperity sphere, the Constellation of Southern African States (CONSAS). Both blocs were much looser than the NATO/EEC and the Warsaw Pact/Comecon groupings, but the parallel did extend to the fact that, like the Warsaw Pact, the frontline states' and the SADF's armies performed dual functions: external deterrence and internal control. Both southern African variants operated more or less sophisticated protection rackets as well as carrying aloft the national flags.

The European analogy should not be stretched. The SADCC was, for example, not intended to emulate the EEC (or even the failed federations of central and east Africa). But the Manichean passions and paranoia of the Cold War were more than replicated in southern Africa. From the north the black Armageddon was striding down to devour Christian capitalist civilisation; from the south racist Boers rained destruction on the dignity of man in the whole subcontinent in order to stall the inevitable liberation of the enslaved majority. The frontline states accused South Africa of destabilising the region by military, economic and political measures, a charge which Pretoria vehemently denied, despite the mountain of contrary evidence. The plans for white hegemony, they said, were, at worst, a corruption of the Brezhnev doctrine of limited sovereignty and, at best, a transplant of America's Monroe doctrine. Pretoria, in turn, accused the frontline states of harbouring SWAPO, ANC and PAC terrorists dedicated to the destruction of law and order. The frontline states were, therefore, guilty of the primary destabilisation, according to South Africa. Moreover, the same frontline states, while decrying imperialism and colonialism, had invited in Cuban, East German and Russian forces to threaten South African borders. This was the new socialist imperialism. And the harsh rhetoric and calls for sanctions imperilled the granary and industrial powerhouse of a region beset by drought and man-made disasters. Both sides cried justice in a noble cause. The trouble was nobody was listening to Pretoria's special pleading.

Pretoria's relationship with its neighbours was important because it had long been a tenet of South African diplomacy that the road to the West ran through Africa. Membership of the "West" and the "Free World" depended upon at least some kind of rapprochement with the southern members of the OAU. In the 1960s Vorster promulgated his "outward policy" and later, in the mid-1970s, his "detente" initiatives, centred on resolving the Rhodesian impasse. But these moves, intended to form a "commonwealth" of economically interdependent states regardless of ideological differences, produced very few diplomatic results. Only the eccentric, right-wing dictator, Dr Hastings Banda, endorsed full diplomatic ties with Pretoria. Vorster's diplomacy crashed in the aftermath of Portuguese collapse, Soweto 1976, and the Information scandal. The late 1970s were dedicated to internal diplomacy: the bantustans and the "internal settlements" in Namibia and Rhodesia.

From 1980 to 1984 the sword and economic blackmail largely replaced polite diplomacy. *Machtpolitik* took over from summitry.

Anxieties about the deepening wars in Angola and Mozambique did, however, prompt a brief respite in 1984. A non-aggression pact was signed with Machel and a limited agreement on troop withdrawal was reached with Luanda. Both agreements were hailed as diplomatic breakthroughs by South Africa, but the practical effects were short-lived. The temperature soon plummeted. The wars raged on in Mozambique and Angola. Pretoria's relations with its neighbours slipped below zero in October 1986 when Machel died in a plane crash just inside the South African border. Pretoria was accused (probably unfairly) of engineering the incident. The South African government, distracted by internal crises, did not return with gusto to its diplomatic offensives until late 1988. The optimism radiating from the initiatives to secure Namibian independence made the rejectionist front in southern Africa totter, as P W Botha sallied forth on tours of Malawi, Mozambique and Zaire. Mugabe, as ever, was unmoved. In his view the Botha peace gesture was a temporising sham, a breathing space before renewed bouts of military destabilisation. The basic problem was apartheid. As Joseph Hanlon, an authority on destabilisation, put it: "The South African government will continue to sjambok its neighbours as long as it sjamboks its own people."(1)

The frontline states

The concept of the frontline alliance goes back to the 1969 Lusaka Manifesto, drafted largely by Nyerere and Kaunda, which supported the liberation wars against colonial rule in the south. In 1971 the Mogadishu Declaration advocated an intensified armed struggle.(2) During the mid-1970s Angola, Botswana, Mozambique, Tanzania and Zambia formed a loose coalition to coordinate their policies on Rhodesia. (Nigeria, as one of the most powerful black states, became an honorary member.) Practical military aid was provided by Zambia, Tanzania and Algeria, and funds were coordinated in the OAU's African Liberation Committee based in Dar es Salaam.

Ideological cohesion was impossible, except for a catch-all commitment to anti-colonialism, because the Commonwealth states, particularly Botswana and Zambia, shared—paradoxically—Pretoria's concern about a "Marxist saddle" (Angola, Mozambique and potentially Zimbabwe) straddling southern Africa. Hence Kaunda and Vorster worked together in 1974 and 1975 to try to prevent the Rhodesian war spiralling into a major East-West confrontation. Neither man wanted a repetition of the calamitous great power and UN intervention in the

Congo during the 1960s. This was partly the reason why the frontline states forced Mugabe and Nkomo to form the Patriotic Front. It was bound to be an unworkable, short-term shotgun marriage, especially as Zambia, Angola and (reluctantly) Botswana backed Nkomo's ZIPRA forces while Tanzania and Mozambique aided ZANLA. Russian and Chinese involvement, especially in the form of arms supplies and training, compounded the problem. Moscow sponsored the "charmed circle" of so-called "authentic" liberation movements (ANC, ZAPU, SWAPO and earlier the MPLA) while China assisted, in the Russian view, the "splinter" groups (ZANU, the PAC and earlier the FNLA and Unita). Crudely, the formula—for those with a taste for alphabet soup—was China/PAC/ZANU/Mozambique/Tanzania and USSR/ZAPU/ANC/Zambia/Angola. This was, very approximately, the position in the late 1970s, although the divisions were never watertight partly because Russia supplied weapons, directly or indirectly, to all the movements.

Rhodesia wonderfully concentrated the minds of the frontline presidents because the war threatened the very survival of the regimes in Zambia, Mozambique and perhaps Botswana. Namibia was different. The SWAPO war affected only Angola immediately. And Namibia did not directly involve the black Commonwealth states and Britain in the way Rhodesia did. Moreover, the Patriotic Front deployed much more impressive guerrilla forces than SWAPO, whose poor leadership was frequently derided by the frontline presidents. After Nujoma spoke at one frontline summit, Machel is said to have ridiculed SWAPO's war efforts: "Don't tell me how many white farmers you ambushed. How many South African soldiers have you killed?" (3)

The frontline states, however, were in no position to criticise SWAPO's military endeavours. The Zambian army's reactions, for example, to the major Rhodesian raids of 1978 were uniformly farcical. The Zambian air force had apparently no idea how to operate or maintain the Rapier air defence system provided by the British Aircraft Corporation. When they were helped to get it working, they managed only to shoot down their own planes. Further, Kaunda found himself in the same invidious position as King Hussein when he hosted the Palestine Liberation Organisation. In 1970 the King bloodily asserted his sovereignty, but Kaunda's Fred Karno army, of less than 9,000 men, was no match for the better-trained (by Cubans and Russians) and better-armed ZIPRA forces of 12,000-15,000 troops. It was rumoured (in Salisbury) that there was Zambian complicity in the devastating October 1978 attacks on ZIPRA bases. But it has never been proved that Rhodesia "did a Hussein" on behalf of Kaunda. Certainly, ZIPRA soldiers often acted in Zambia as if they were a state within a state, and Kaunda's police and army dared not act. Not until ZIPRA left the country in 1980-81 could Kaunda even pretend to be master in his own house.(4)

Despite the military deficiencies, political fissures and daunting economic problems, the frontline alliance did notch up some successes. As outriders for the OAU, the frontline states did act as a buffer to discourage direct Soviet penetration and US meddling. Both superpowers were forced to defer on occasions to frontline decisions on Rhodesia and Namibia. No formal bureaucratic machinery cemented the alliance: a group of (sometimes) like-minded dictators conducted their own personal foreign policies, a little like the Concert of Europe in the early nineteenth century. But they took risks which would have made Metternich balk. Their alleged backing of the hare-brained Cuban plan to invade Rhodesia in 1979 was very dangerous. That could have provoked a massive, overt SADF entry into the war and chronic superpower tension. And in mid-1979 they were apparently prepared to blast the Commonwealth out of the water. At the very least they might have tried to eject Britain from its own creation. It did not quite come to that. Instead they prompted the Lancaster House settlement, in which Kaunda, Machel and Nyerere acted out the roles of honest brokers. Machel, especially, played a vital, last-minute role in dictating to Mugabe: the Mozambican leader threatened to cut off support to ZANLA if Mugabe did not compromise. Machel knew that Mozambique was falling apart under the impact of Rhodesia's last, desperate, all-out blows.

Rhodesia had been "the hole in the doughnut". In 1980 independent Zimbabwe was the most developed country with the best economy and battle-hardened armed forces in the region, after South Africa. Zimbabwe became the core state of the SADCC, established at Arusha, Tanzania, in 1979 and then formally enlarged, inauspiciously perhaps, on 1 April 1980. The SADCC's purpose was to reduce the frontline states' reliance on Pretoria's economic muscle. It was not seen as a common market because, compared with their joint trade with South Africa, their inter-bloc commerce was minimal. The SADCC was primarily an attempt to coordinate transport, food production and general commerce. Because the South African Transport Services (SATS) dominated the regional rail network and access to the best ports, SADCC's rival (if barely functioning) transport links were the keys to liberation or domination. SADCC grew to embrace nine member states: the original frontliners, Angola, Tanzania, Zambia, Mozambique and

Botswana, the new boy Zimbabwe, and the latecomers, Malawi, Swaziland and Lesotho.

SADCC was immediately, and correctly, perceived as an enemy by Pretoria, a direct rival to its plan to erect a constellation dominated by South African capital. P W Botha specifically called it a "counter-constellation". Could SADCC work? Lesotho was surrounded by South African territory and all its foreign trade went via its giant, literally all-embracing neighbour. Sanctions and war had locked Zimbabwe into South Africa's grip. Malawi was heavily dependent upon South African trade and development loans. Botswana, Lesotho and Swaziland were tied into a customs union and the rand monetary zone. South African personnel kept Maputo's power, port and railways access functioning. The Zambian economy was in shambles. Most of its mines, like many in the frontline states, were run by Anglo American. As one SADCC official noted laconically: "SADCC does not have to worry about regional coordination of mining; Anglo American already does it."(5) Admittedly, Angola and Tanzania remained relatively aloof from South African economic tentacles, but Angola's dwindling resources were committed almost entirely to the civil war and Nyerere had reduced Tanzania to an economic basket case. Moreover, their rail and road routes were closed by war or disrupted by poor maintenance. More insidiously, both black and white businessmen throughout the frontline region were used to dealing with Johannesburg. Better goods came from there, often more cheaply and certainly more quickly than from Europe. The old habits of the colonial period died hard. Frelimo authorities often found it more convenient to chat in Portuguese to white exiled Mozambican or Madeiran businessmen in the Transvaal in order to get supplies for the party elite. The patterns of kickbacks and bribes were well-established. Hence much of the foreign aid donated to the SADCC ended up in the vaults of Johannesburg banks. Sweden actually had to ban Mozambique from using its aid to buy goods in South Africa.(6) SADCC's chances looked slim. Nonetheless, it did survive, despite Pretoria's best attempts to destroy it.

Unless SADCC worked, neither could sanctions against apartheid. As long as the frontline states traded with or via South Africa, Pretoria could manipulate its rivals. The opportunities were limitless. South African goods could be relabelled in Swaziland and exported. Dummy companies could be set up. False destinations could be put on export licences. And they were. It was almost bound to be a re-run of the Rhodesian sanctions farce. Transport, it bears repeating, was the linchpin; and, in particular, the Benguela railway through central Angola to

Zambia and Zaire, and the road-rail-oil pipeline from Umtali (Mutare) through Mozambique to the port of Beira. If the SADF kept these access routes to the Atlantic and Indian Oceans cut, and they usually were, courtesy of Renamo and Unita, then Pretoria could survive, probably, even the most comprehensive sanctions, short of naval blockade. That was the bottom line.

At this point, Pretoria had to ask itself a fundamental question. Should the SADF destroy these routes or should South Africa revive the frontline economies, these routes in particular, and thus entice SADCC states into an unofficial constellation? (Indeed some South African optimists even talked of merging SADCC and CONSAS.) (7) Was it to be military destabilisation or trade leverage? Pretoria tried both, often simultaneously. And how would the frontline states react, especially the hardliners? With cool economic pragmatism or a passionate ideological martyrdom? They, too, tried both.

The Constellation strikes back

In one of the first authoritative official statements on a Constellation of Southern African States, in March 1979, Pik Botha envisaged between seven and ten states south of the Zambezi and Cunene rivers comprising 40 million people, joining hands to form a pro-capitalist alliance.(8) The scheme was formalised in November 1979 at the Carlton Conference in Johannesburg. Named after the hotel in central Johannesburg in which the conference was held, the event was heralded by the South African press as the marriage between big business and a National Party newly committed to the free enterprise ethic. A constellation would do very nicely for both the hawks in the party and the "liberal" multinationals based in the country.

There were two potential hiccups: Namibia and Rhodesia (or Zimbabwe-Rhodesia, as it was called then). A DTA administration in Windhoek and Muzorewa sitting uneasily in Salisbury were billed as the up-and-coming stars in the constellation. Again, the optimists ranged farther: maybe Zaire and Zambia might join too. Mugabe's membership of SADCC pricked the balloon. Instead the constellation became a mere rump of South Africa and its homelands. Nonetheless, the *idea* behind the constellation, economic hegemony, but now by more indirect means, continued to animate the Afrikaner leadership.

Mugabe's victory, this too bears repeating, initially astounded Pretoria's planners and then his anti-apartheid rhetoric continued to incense the South African government. From April 1980 a markedly more aggressive policy towards the frontline states developed. Pretoria launched its own version of a total onslaught. Initially, Pretoria teased with primarily economic tactics, such as slowing down fuel supplies, aimed at trying to keep Mugabe in line. But simultaneous commando raids on the Lesotho capital on 9 December 1982 (in which 42 people were killed) and on a fuel depot in Beira, causing damage worth £15 million, marked—according to some specialists—a new military phase of the destabilisation onslaught.(9)

"Destabilisation", despite its convenience as shorthand for Pretoria's misdeeds, is something of a misnomer because elements of *re*-stabilisation, for example economic aid to Mozambique, no matter how self-interested, were part and parcel of the process. The policy has also been termed "destructive engagement" because Washington's "constructive engagement", to some critics, was a mischievous endorsement of SADF aggression.(10) Hanlon was more blunt: he termed this second front of apartheid a "beggar your neighbours" plan.(11) Amid the welter of debate on the precise nature of destabilisation, certain strategic goals were clear. Obviously, first and foremost, the survival of the white regime has been a self-evident goal; as were the territorial imperatives of regional hegemony and the psychological demands for status, particularly after the rebuffs of SADCC and Mugabe, the personification of cold, calculating evil for white conservatives. More general aims included a desire to replace the colonial *glacis* with a cordon of instability so that the frontline states would be too weak not only to succour ANC and SWAPO guerrillas but also to impose or even urge sanctions. The resulting chaos induced by military operations and economic blackmail, on top of drought, famine, floods, bureaucratic bungling and endemic corruption, would convince South African blacks that "black rule doesn't work", especially the Marxist variety. The mailed fist would confirm the "invincibility" of the security forces. This would not only show local blacks that the government had not gone soft—that Mugabe-ism would be stopped at the Limpopo—but would also demonstrate to the West that Pretoria was willing and able to act as an independent regional superpower, with or without a nod and a wink from Washington.

There were specific goals as well. The most important were military. Crucially, the ANC and SWAPO had to be pushed as far north as possible. Guerrilla sanctuaries would not be tolerated in contiguous states. Later, this operational goal turned, perhaps haphazardly, into the strategic ambition of foisting non-aggression pacts on those adjoining states from which the ANC infiltrated. Other operational goals, such as the initial need for combat experience and the capture of massive amounts of communist weaponry as well as, occasionally, real live Cubans and Russians—which was used to justify to the white electorate the propaganda claims of a total onslaught by the Reds—were of secondary importance. As were plans to persuade the neighbouring states to allow SADF personnel to enter their territory to assist in regional security (for example, to protect the Cahora Bassa powerlines) or provide civil aid during natural calamities such as mine disasters (South African *civilians* had frequently assisted in such cases). Except for a projected deal to protect the Cahora Bassa lines with SADF men working in Mozambique, in uniform or dressed as private security officials, the possibility of SADF troops being *officially* invited into the frontline states was unlikely.(12)

Political goals included attempts to persuade the frontline states to recognise the nominally-independent homelands. And, even more forlornly, Pretoria hoped that more governments would follow Malawi's example by exchanging ambassadors. (Four states, Mozambique, Swaziland, Zimbabwe and Lesotho, did exchange trade representatives.) Like the desperate hunt for diplomatic recognition, Pretoria's attempts to lean over the fence to persuade the neighbours to tone down the volume of their anti-apartheid rhetoric largely failed, except in the case of Lesotho, when a South African blockade helped topple the noisy and erratic regime of Chief Leabua Jonathan. Explicit economic aims included manipulation of the captive markets to secure less crucial needs, such as water and elcctricity supplies, and the macro-requirements of wiping out competition by the exploitation of the transport and trade dominance of South Africa's relatively small, inefficient (compared with Western norms), monopolistic industrial base.

But why spread chaos, South African businessmen would ask. It would spill over into South Africa. Moreover, the long-term cost benefit of a captive market required more trade not scorched earth. Beggaring your neighbours was not only bad for local business, but it also discouraged much-needed foreign investment in South Africa. Who would want to risk capital in the middle of a battle-zone? Here economic pragmatism collided with Afrikaner pride, especially that of the soldier-imperialists in the State Security Council. To some hawks military means became an end in themselves. (Foreign critics tended to single out senior officers such as Major General N van Tonder and Major General Pieter van der Westhuizen, military intelligence specialists who were [allegedly] tasked with the military destabilisation programme, particularly the control/liaison with the allied forces such as Renamo.) The military option became holy writ, and opponents, the "cocktail diplomats" in foreign affairs, were sometimes detested as much as the communist enemy. Clausewitz was again turned on his head.

Militarisation of policy-formulation could be one straightforward explanation for the contradictions of destabilisation. But, as more and more analysts disagreed on how to decipher Pretoria's signals, it became clear that militarisation was not a sufficient explanation. Nor could it be in a complex matrix where "aggressor and victims are linked by direct-dial telephone, railways and extensive trade".(13)

There is little dispute that conflict in the region has caused massive losses. Hanlon suggested in 1986 that South African destabilisation, directly or indirectly, had cost 100,000 lives, £10,000 millions worth of damage and one million homeless.(14) Another source put the figure for 1980-86 at $25-30 billion in the SADCC countries—$400 for every man, women and child in the whole region of southern Africa.(15) Everybody was suffering, from the profit-mongers in Johannesburg to the starving Mozambican peasant reduced to wearing bark to hide his nakedness. Why?

Deon Geldenhuys, a young professor of political science at the Rand Afrikaans University in Johannesburg, has been accused (inaccurately) of being the architect (in some versions, the Kissinger/Metternich) of destabilisation. Geldenhuys's thorough and prolific analyses of the phenomenon were, however, not intended as a blueprint for military action. He was not the Svengali whispering in the ears of the State Security Council. In fact, he was summoned before council members and pilloried for his views. He was also frozen out from government contacts. Some military leaders, it is true, have used Geldenhuys's academic studies as an *ex post facto* rationalisation. And, certainly, South African government leaders are unusual in the way they pay so much attention to the work of academics—to utilise or ban their theories—but Geldenhuys is simply the wrong target for the many critics of destabilisation.(16)

Geldenhuys suggested, initially, that destabilisation was an end in itself. The British writer, Simon Jenkins, also commented: "South Africa's policy towards its northern neighbours seems governed not by consistency but by some arcane Afrikaner intuition. From time to time, an incipient black nation needs to be taught a lesson to emphasise who is regional boss."(17) Crude racism and instinctive reactions to perceived threats and actual anti-Boer rhetoric may well have been significant factors. Prime Minister Botha was, reportedly, so angry when Mugabe, in a bitter speech, called the Afrikaner leader a "racist" that Botha

PLATE 9.1 A hospital in Caia, Sofala province, Mozambique, devastated by the fighting between Renamo and Frelimo.

PLATE 9.2 SADF troops searching for SWAPO guerrillas, northern Namibia.

ordered immediate punishment: locomotives borrowed from South Africa and desperately needed to shift Zimbabwe's record 1981 harvest were abruptly recalled.(18)

Whether it was motivated by pique or racism, some opponents within the Afrikaner establishment criticised the militarisation of South African foreign policy. They argued that economic cooperation, restabilisation, worked better than retaliation. It has become a popular academic pastime to dissect the dichotomies: dove/hawk or foreign affairs versus SADF/police or State Security Council hardliners versus *verligtes* in the National Party and cabinet. In particular, the debate is characterised by comments on the swings of the power pendulum between "forward" and "laager" strategic schools within the military elite, as well doubts as to whether the argument about the economic versus military options within the political establishment in general were as straightforward as the South African press implied. Thus, for example, the politicians might decide upon peace with Mozambique, as in 1984, while the military, or elements within it, would disagree and quietly continue to arm Renamo. Phyllis Johnson and David Martin, however, insisted that: "Given the authoritarian nature of the South African regime, such an argument is, at the most charitable, ill-informed. At another level, it may be disinformation."(19) Yet the same study considers in detail the splits between the government and the SADF over military aid for Renamo, as revealed in the Gorongosa documents.(20) The authors clearly accept the damning documents as fact, although Pretoria insisted that some or all (according to various statements) of the papers were forgeries. Unless one assumes that the damaging revelations were intended to be found, which is highly unlikely, then these documents suggest, *prima facie*, that on the important issue of support for Renamo there were indeed major differences of opinion on the destabilisation programme. In Johnson and Martin's view the alternation of carrot and stick were not the result of domestic friction, but rather a calculated oscillation, an explicit variant of the "good-guy/bad-guy" method of interrogation.

This thesis assumes a consistency and mastery of political and military strategy over a long period in numerous operations which few governments have ever displayed. Over such vital issues as intervention in the Angolan war in 1975 and in Rhodesia in the 1970s (before the formal theories of destabilisation were developed) and, later, the abortive Seychelles coup in 1981 and the debate over Renamo, there has been well-documented evidence of major disputes within not only the intelligence and military elites but also within the cabinet. Has all this been for show, clever disinformation for a decade to fool apartheid's enemies? If this is true, the Afrikaner leaders deserve a collection of Oscars. In the 1980s the style of the Botha regime was predominantly reactive. Circumstance and chance, not Machiavellian prescience, were the real dictators in southern Africa. Hanlon commented on the Nkomati pact thus: "While the formal verdict must be left to historians, it seems that the State Security Council went into Nkomati not so much intending to violate it, but simply with no commitment as to how to abide by it." And this pact was the main political achievement of the programme (unless the Namibian/Angolan settlement results in real peace in the 1990s).(21)

We return, therefore, to the same paradox. Peter Vale summarised it: "At one and the same time, Pretoria appeared to be involved in waging war and building structures for peaceful co-existence."(22) A Marxist would at this point emphasise the inevitable (and terminal) contradictions of capitalism at bay in southern Africa. The problems of comprehending this duality of economic dependency and race war (or class war, *pace* the Marxist analysis) was aptly summarised in *Destructive Engagement*:

> The question arises as to whether South Africa's strategy and tactics for regional hegemony form a seamless web of diabolically clever Machiavellian (or Kissingeresque) cunning, a wandering minstrel show lurching from one piece of crisis management to another, or a mass of internal contradictions and insoluble conflicts among South African objectives. The answer is probably none of the above by itself, but some of each combined.(23)

A combination of reasons, then, may be the most accurate, if tamest, explanation. It is also important to remember that the pace of destabilisation varied from time to time and from country to country during the 1980s. The military instruments—raids, assassinations, sabotage and support for (arguably) "proxy" forces such as Unita and Renamo—were interlaced with economic actions both positive, such as South African Transport Service's on/off but often helpful "transport diplomacy", and negative, the withdrawal of locomotives at the Botha whim, for example. Sometimes the hectic business of wielding the carrot and stick taxed the memory of the rider: beating and bribing took on a mechanistic logic of its own, forgetting that moving the beast was the purpose of it all. At other times, though, military adventures were timed and aimed precisely: for example, the May 1986 raids on three Commonwealth frontline states were intended to scuttle the peace plans proposed by the Eminent Persons' Group. Covert destabilisation, as opposed to open war in Angola, was most intense in the period 1980-84, particularly in late 1982 and early 1983. Indeed, it has been suggested that the SADF, never slow to emulate their Israeli mentors, were directly encouraged by the Israeli Defence Force's aggressive forward policy and, in particular, the invasion of Lebanon in late 1982.

Although it is convenient to assume that destabilisation was the work of prescient devils in Pretoria with a perfectly concocted hell-brew, the truth is both much more mundane and complex. Through the fogs of war, angry telegrams, racist bigotry, patriotism, ignorance and doubt, a competing group of frequently highly competent Afrikaners, all committed to white survival and/or supremacy, plotted, prayed, won some points and lost sometimes, depending upon a combination of timing, skill and chance. It was like wars everywhere and in all times, with the important exception that many Afrikaners felt that, unlike their black opponents, they could only lose once. Unlike the period after the war of 1899-1902, they could not hope to live and fight another day. There could be no conditional surrender. That fear fuelled a ruthlessness and a determination that made destabilisation a word almost as dreaded in the region as apartheid.

Those Afrikaners who believed that survival depended upon compromise knew that. The "compromisers" (to a point) and the militarist "supremacists" were to be found in all sections of the security elite. This tended to confound those who pigeon-holed Pretoria's actions into simplistic either/or categories. For example, some senior police chiefs, although usually dubbed extreme reactionaries, supported Nkomati because they appreciated that it was aimed at ejecting the ANC from Mozambique, while some senior SADF officers opposed the accord because it implied the betrayal of Renamo.(24) And, as the debates on Angola confirm, even the most dovish allies of Pik Botha, himself a staunch convert of the carrot school, were as concerned as the generals about the dangers posed by the Cubans. Even the flag-bearer of the forward military school, P W Botha, was also a powerful advocate of the economic drive, epitomised by CONSAS. He was also, apparently, well aware of the risks of repeating the Portuguese experience when over-extension on the colonial periphery led to the collapse of the centre.(25)

And, yet, it would be folly to assume that the leaders of Afrikanerdom were mere feathers blown hither and thither by the the harsh winds of change. Yes, there was much impulsive reaction and ham-fisted crisis-management. On the other hand, many of the short-term, mid-term and long-term goals were shrewdly calculated.(26) The use of the Cuban threat, for example, kept Washington on-side in Pretoria's campaign to portray itself as a crusader-in-arms in the war on the Evil Empire, and thus limited congressional sanctions in the short-term. Some of the mid-term goals, such as pushing back the ANC from forward bases in the frontline states, have been largely successful. The need to curb the ANC (and SWAPO) has been stressed by some analysts as the prime purpose of destabilisation.(27) But it should be noted that when the destructive stabilisation began in earnest in 1980 the ANC was considered by Pretoria to be largely a spent force. The arming of Unita and the regeneration of Renamo also preceded the invigorated SWAPO and ANC campaigns. Nor is it possible to believe that such audaciously provocative raids as the bungled Cabinda escapade in 1985 were aimed at the ANC, as Pretoria claimed at the time. Moreover, assistance to Renamo continued after the ANC was thrown out of Mozambique following the Nkomati accord. Other mid-term goals, such as keeping the frontline economies dependent, have been achieved. But, crucially, the political orientation of the enemy-neighbours has not been altered, except in Lesotho. On the long-term aims, the preservation of white supremacy, the participants, or contestants, within the security elite are in agreement. They share the same values and ideology. They accept that the factor common to all the external pressures is the perceived challenge to the very survival of the white regime.(28) In this important sense the hawk-dove classification misses the point. As one writer has perceptively observed:

> This division, however, relates to means rather than ends. Both the SADF 'hawks' (military coercion) and the DFA [Department of Foreign Affairs] 'doves' (economic coercion/diplomatic pressure) have similar, if not identical, foreign policy objectives. Therefore, if one insists on bird imagery it would be more accurate to describe the inhabitants of the competing foreign policy nests as eagles (military) and hawks (DFA) for the difference is one of degree rather than kind.(29)

The formulation and the execution of the destabilisation war was a much more complex phenomenon than the simplistic notion of the evil of apartheid overflowing its borders. It is that, of course, but it so much more as well.

Destabilisation after Nkomati

The TV cameras caught, before the massive press censorship, the drama of the war in the South African townships. The second front, destabilisation, has been much more savage, but this has been a series of almost secret wars. The cameras could not usually get to the war zones to record the extent of the misery. This was not true of the well-publicised jewel of South African policy, the Nkomati accord. This was signed amid the glare of world publicity. "The irony of a smiling Machel, the victim, in a London-tailored marshal's uniform and a dour Botha, the destabiliser, in a rumpled civilian suit, could have hardly been lost on a more sophisticated TV audience. Each side could believe it had upstaged the other." (30) Both men were losers, although, at the time, Botha looked, for once, like an emperor with clothes on. The Afrikaner leaders craved respectability. (If they had believed their own propaganda about communist treachery, a pact with Marxists would be worthless.) According to an Israeli authority on pariah states, Pretoria acted like a rejected lover. "Thus, South African policy-makers are not satisfied with tacit, informal arrangements, with lover-mistress type of relations; they rather strive for open, formal arrangements, for regional solutions involving the recognition of South Africa's legitimacy by its black neighbours."(31) This was not always true: Pretoria had already signed a secret pact with Swaziland in 1982, but it was evident that Pretoria had an outcast's passion for status. Nkomati bestowed it. Destabilisation had proved its point: that even the most anti-apartheid frontline president loved power more than he hated Pretoria. As Simon Jenkins noted, "Pretoria had stopped pleading with the world to love South Africa despite apartheid. Instead it has gone on the regional offensive, bluntly assuming that the enemy must at least shake your hand if your gun is in his back." (32) Economic blackmail and Renamo had helped bring Machel to heel. Machel's socialist economy was forced to beg from the racist capitalist, the ultimate humiliation for African socialism. This was surely intended as a classic lesson in "de-Marxification" for the restless masses in South Africa.(33) And it was one mighty punch in the solar plexus for SADCC and the Western sanctions campaign.

Prancing as a regional peacemaker almost immediately after Nkomati, P W Botha set out on a rare official visit to Western Europe. He was received with a coolness bordering on disdain, but the South African media hailed his "grand tour" as the best diplomatic days since Jan Smuts strode the Western stage. From being a political leper, the regime strutted as though its status as a regional superpower was finally formalised. No longer was South Africa a gazelle among a world of lions, or like Israel besieged by enemies. No, the fashionable comparison circulating in the establishment was that South Africa in its region was like the USA in the Caribbean. Didn't Washington restore order in Grenada by invading it? Force brought peace there as well, purred South Africa's diplomats smugly. And Washington sought advantage from its "proxy's" invasion of Lebanon. So what was the difference between Israel being allowed, even encouraged, to arm the Christian militias there and South Africa sending weapons to the anti-Marxist Renamo? Pretoria even pressurised Washington to help ease the arms embargo on South Africa so that the government could reinsure its new status as a now respectable ally of the Reagan doctrine. So P W Botha had got his way with the new constitution at home and seized the high ground in regional diplomacy.

Hubris preceded a fall. Suddenly everything began to come apart at the seams. The war in Angola began to take off while South Africa's continued backing of Renamo was revealed by an understandably irate Machel. Most dramatically, from August 1984 the domestic "unrest" erupted into continuous insurrection. As Hanlon observed: "The diplomatic gains of Nkomati were lost on the streets of the townships." Then it was downhill fast: the states of emergency, sanctions, the Rubicon rand, set-backs in the conventional war in Angola, and an almost total collapse of Nkomati as Renamo grew into a monster.

The West was caught in a dilemma largely of its own making. The bigger states tried to balance their South African trade with aid to the frontline states. Vacillation and inconsistency characterised Western policy. Washington armed Unita, while trying to pose as an honest broker in Namibia and Angola. The US imposed tougher sanctions on Pretoria, but cut aid to Zimbabwe, while initially refusing it altogether to Mozambique. The European Community helped all the SADCC states, especially Mozambique, while applying politely mild sanctions on Pretoria with no clear objectives. Scandinavia piously demanded mandatory sanctions, while Margaret Thatcher denounced the very principle of sanctions. Thus, she and her foreign secretary, Sir Geoffrey Howe, were regularly insulted by Mugabe and Kaunda, yet Britain was the only Western country which trained the Zimbabwe and Mozambique armies to fight Renamo.(34)

Destabilisation had travelled to the West. Confusion over policy reigned there almost as much as in the frontline states. No one knew how to handle the rogue elephant on the rampage. The frontline alliance was nowhere nearer coordinating its military forces or strategies.(35) The involvement of Tanzanian and Zimbabwean troops in Mozambique had not crushed Renamo. Often the military cooperation backfired, as Frelimo resentment of Zimbabwean "imperialism" grew apace. There was little practical basis for a frontline joint military high command. Some of the states were ambiguous about military support for the ANC.

Angola, Tanzania and Zambia, those conveniently farthest removed from the SADF's reach, risked allowing ANC military bases. The others—officially—permitted only diplomatic or humanitarian representation. And trade, of course, continued almost unabated: loans and credits were doled out from South Africa, which carried on overt or secret trade with at least 40 African states.

As the fires of insurrection died down in the townships after 1986, Pretoria began slowly to reassert its regional status. The desire of nearly all the southern African states to wind down the Angolan war provided the opportunity for P W Botha to play the peacemaker again. The roles of Presidents Mobutu of Zaire and Denis Sassou-Nguesso of the Congo were important. Although ideologically at odds, neither wanted the Angolan conflict to spill over again into their own countries. A number of francophone conservatives also pushed for peace, and specifically talks between Unita and the MPLA. In September 1988 President Botha leaped on board the peace train. Pik Botha secretly shuttled around a number of African capitals while his party leader paid official visits to Malawi, Mozambique and Zaire. Mugabe, as ever, remained aloof to Pretoria's overtures, but elsewhere the hardline unity of the frontline states wobbled noticeably.(36)

Conclusion

For the eight years following Zimbabwe's independence, South Africa had bribed, seduced and thumped (and fair-traded with) her neighbours. Despite the long "unrest" crisis of 1984-86 and the bruising economic pressures, the apartheid regime was still, in regional terms, a colossus. Destabilisation, for all its contradictions, had kept the growing ANC infiltration largely at bay. The formal political attitude of the frontline states was that the civil war in South Africa was not an anti-colonial struggle, but rather a campaign for majority rule where whites, as Africans, would have a permanent place in the sun. During Nkomati, Frelimo officials had explicitly stated that the ANC was involved in a civil-rights struggle not a classic guerrilla war to overwhelm a colonial regime.(37)

Pretoria had taken up the cudgels of the Reagan doctrine with a vengeance. The South African-backed Unita and Renamo had given the socialist-trained MPLA and Frelimo more than a run for their Eastern bloc money. Russian, Cuban and East German advisers found it difficult to cope with the new breed of guerrillas fighting established pro-socialist regimes with the techniques of classical revolutionary warfare.

The Russian scuttle from Afghanistan was perhaps a pointer to the future in southern Africa. As with the *Mujahedin*, South Africa's guerrilla allies had become instructive tools of counter-revolution. Up to a point. Neither Unita nor Renamo looked like making it all the way to power in Luanda or Maputo. The thought of trying to keep Savimbi or Afonso Dhlakama, the Renamo chief, in power—if they ever won—was daunting. The MPLA and Frelimo would no doubt go back to the bush, and the Soviets would find themselves in the happier position of once again trying to subvert governments, not fight insurgents. The South African leadership was trying to shed direct rule of black territories by its homelands policy. Pretoria wanted economic, not actual, *Lebensraum*. By the late 1980s the military planners had probably given up all hope of replacing Frelimo and the MPLA with their friends in the bush. The guerrilla allies were still important to the hardliners in the SADF, but politically they had become an embarrassment to the settlement process in Namibia and to a restoration of the spirit of Nkomati with Maputo.

Here a double distortion enters the picture. Pretoria had always assumed, or at least said, that the ANC and SWAPO were mere puppets of Moscow. Apartheid's critics said that Unita and Renamo were mere pawns of South Africa. It would be totally inaccurate, of course, to draw an exact parallel between the long history of a nationalist movement like the ANC and a bastard organisation such as Renamo, born in double original sin from Rhodesian and South African parentage. Nevertheless, whatever the debate about the nature of their birth, in maturity these movements developed an independence of their mentors. Unilateral actions by SWAPO or the ANC could, for example, have derailed the Namibian settlement. And certainly, like Frankenstein's monster, Renamo outgrew its handler's leash and threatened to act against Pretoria's interests in a Nkomati Mark II. In short, neither the superpowers nor the regional states can simply shut down completely the guerrilla players in the drama, although they could severely curtail their activities. This raises the question of whether Pretoria could stop the destabilisation process, even if it wanted to.

Irretrievable damage has been done in all sorts of ways, even if Pretoria's leaders all underwent immediate moral conversions. Destabilisation was intended to establish and maintain a critical leverage over the behaviour of the frontline states. It tried to do so by a ruthless and sometimes foolhardy display of naked power. It did confirm South Africa's status as a regional superpower, although its political achievements, the Nkomati and Angolan/Namibian agreements, were brokered by the influence of a real superpower, the US.(38) The frontline states were forced to modify their behaviour towards South Africa but not, with very limited exceptions, their political attitudes. Pretoria had not managed to install a ring of conservative client-states as substitutes for the bygone colonial regimes. The destabilisation battles on all the economic, military and political fronts could prove to be Pyrrhic victories. Instability is infectious, not least for white South Africans. Famine, death, roving bands of desperate refugees, destruction and, above all, bitterness and hatred stalked the region. Mugabe's view was that comprehensive sanctions, despite the increased suffering, were worth it to end more quickly the agony caused by the root cause: apartheid. The carrot and the stick began to look the same to the masses of numbed victims. As Sam Nolutshungu put it so aptly: "For those within its range, there is no more safety in submission than in resistance." (39) *Pax Pretoria* had bloodily stored up the anger of an entire subcontinent.

References and notes:

1. J Hanlon, *Apartheid's Second Front*, Penguin, Harmondsworth, 1986, p. 2.
2. For an excellent analysis of the frontline states, see R Jaster, *A Regional Security Role for Africa's Front-Line States: Experience and Prospects,* Adelphi Paper No. 180, International Institute for Strategic Studies, London, 1983.
3. Quoted in *ibid.*, p. 24.
4. For details, see P. Moorcraft, *A Short Thousand Years*, Galaxie, Salisbury, 1980, pp. 116-20.
5. Quoted in R Green and C Thompson, "Political Economies in Conflict: SADCC, South Africa and Sanctions," in P. Johnson and D Martin, (eds), *Destructive Engagement*, Zimbabwe Publishing, Harare, 1986, p. 265.
6. Hanlon, *Apartheid's Second Front, op. cit.*, p. 25.
7. For example, J Shaw, "The Southern African Development Co-ordination Conference (SADCC) and the South African Response," *International Affairs Bulletin,* (Johannesburg),5:3, 1981. Shaw was a counsellor at the South African embassy in Malawi.
8. For details of the early period, see D Geldenhuys, *The Constellation of Southern African States and the Southern African Development Co-ordination Council [sic]: Towards a New Regional Stalemate,* The South African Institute of International Affairs, Johannesburg, 1981.
9. For example, Hanlon, *Apartheid's Second Front,* pp. 5-12.
10. A seminal text was Johnson and Martin, (eds), *Destructive Engagement, op. cit.* Updated material is contained in their *Apartheid Terrorism: The Destabilization Report*, Commonwealth Secretatiat/Currey, London, 1989.
11. J Hanlon, *Beggar Your Neighbours,* Catholic Institute for International Relations, London, 1986.
12. Author's interviews, 1984, with senior officials from ESCOM, the South African Electricity Supply Commission. What ESCOM planned and what Frelimo might have agreed to were two different matters, but the South African protection of the Cahora Bassa lines inside Mozambique was discussed in some detail with Maputo.

13. Hanlon, *Apartheid's Second Front,* p. 2. For an excellent summary of the history and debate about militarisation in South Africa, see K Grundy, *The Militarisation of South African Politics,* Oxford University Press, Oxford, 1988.
14. Hanlon, *loc. cit.*
15. V Brittain, *Hidden Lives, Hidden Death,* Faber, London, 1988, p. 140. Brittain is quoting from UNICEF and SADCC estimates.
16. Hanlon and Johnson and Martin, for example, emphasise Geldenhuys's influence. Hanlon, however, does say that Geldenhuys "articulates *verligte* policy on regional issues better than any other academic". This is almost certainly true, but there is frequently the inference or direct accusation by critics of apartheid that somehow Geldenhuys was the *éminence grise* who supplied the deadly logic behind tens of thousands of deaths. This writer believes that Geldenhuys began his analysis as a purely academic exercise. It is important to note that there is a dearth of competent strategic studies specialists in South Africa, unlike Israel, for example. This might explain why the local generals might have seized on his work. Foreign critics certainly did. Author's interview with Geldenhuys, September 1988.

    Some of Geldenhuys's relevant works are: "Some Strategic Implications of Regional Economic Relations for the Republic of South Africa," *Strategic Review,* Institute for Strategic Studies, University of Pretoria, Pretoria, January 1981. (This work is often cited, because the institute allegedly has ties with military intelligence, as one of the seminal blueprints for detabilisation); *Destabilisation Controversy in Southern Africa,* SA Forum Position Paper, Johannesburg, September, 1982; and *The Diplomacy of Isolation*, Macmillan, Johannesburg, 1984.
17. S Jenkins, "Destabilisation," *The Economist*, 16 July 1983, p. 24.
18. *Ibid.*, p. 23.
19. Johnson and Martin, xxi.
20. For a discussion of this important document, see the section on Mozambique in Chapter 12 of this book.
21. Hanlon, *Beggar Your Neighbours,* p. 50.
22. P. Vale, "Regional Policy: The Compulsion to Incorporate," in J Blumenfeld, (ed), *South Africa in Crisis,* Royal Institute for International Affairs, London, 1987, p. 177.
23. Green and Thompson, *op. cit.*, p. 257.
24. See, for example, H Adam and S Uys, "From Destabilisation to Neocolonial Control: South Africa's Post-Nkomati Regional Environment," *International Affairs Bulletin*, 9:1, 1985, p. 18.
25. Green and Thompson, p. 258.
26. See R Price, "Pretoria's Southern African Strategy," *African Affairs*, 83:330, January 1984, and the illuminating synthesis of the debate by J Spence, "South Africa's Military Relations with its Neighbours," in S Baynham, (ed), *Military Power and Politics in Black Africa*, Croom Helm, London, 1986. See also J Spence, "The Military in South African Politics," in S Johnson, (ed), *South Africa: No Turning Back*, Macmillan, London, 1988.
27. See Spence, "South Africa's Military Relations with its Neighbours," *ibid,* especially for his comments on Price's thesis (Fn 26) about the ANC threat.
28. For an attempt at quantifying South Africa's threat perceptions, see K van Wyk, "South Africa's Foreign Policy Behaviour 1977-1987: An Event Analysis," *International Affairs Bulletin*, 12:2, 1988.
29. G Sheldon, "Theoretical Perspectives on South African Foreign Policy Making," *Politikon*, Pretoria, 13:1, June 1986, p. 9.
30. Adam and Uys, "From Destabilisation to Neocolonial Control...", *op. cit.*, p. 10.
31. M Tamarkin, "South Africa's Regional Options: Policy-Making and Conceptual Environment," *International Affairs Bulletin*, 7:3, 1983, p. 66.

32. Quoted in Hanlon, *Beggar Your Neighbours*, p. 42.
33. For a discussion of the "De-Marxification" theme see Adam and Uys, *op. cit.*
34. R Martin, "Regional Security in Southern Africa," *Survival*, September/October 1987.
35. M Evans, *The Front-Line States: South Africa and Southern African Security*, University of Zimbabwe, Harare, 1986.
36. M Hornsby, "Why Botha Wants Peace," *The Times*, 8 October 1988; B Nelan, "The Frontline Begins to Wobble," *Time*, 17 October 1988.
37. See Adam and Uys, *op. cit.* for a discussion of this important issue.
38. See R Jaster, *South Africa and its Neighbours: The Dynamics of Regional Conflict*, Adelphi Paper No. 209, IISS, London, 1986, pp. 62-68.
39. S Nolutshungu, "South Africa and its Neighbours," in S Johnson, (ed), *South Africa: No Turning Back, op. cit.*, p. 342.

10

Angola (1976-1989)

The key war

Destabilisation in Angola was different. Because Pretoria lacked economic leverage, blunt military force was the chosen instrument. Subtle railway diplomacy elsewhere gave way here to a series of major incursions and, later, large conventional battles.

Angola was considered a serious threat because oil makes the country relatively wealthy by local standards. Her potential could not only have fuelled Angolan development, but also the regeneration of the frontline states, especially once the Benguela railway was functioning. Left alone, an oil-rich Angola might (perhaps) have matured into an alluring multiracial model for South Africa's blacks. But, for Pretoria, the military challenge loomed largest. Angola played host to the entire range of Afrikaner demons: the ANC, SWAPO, Cubans, East Germans and Russians. Often, they were convenient demons, however. The presence of external communist troops, especially Cubans, was used partly to justify Pretoria's Namibian filibuster; not least to the Americans, for whom Castro was the apex of their own demonology. Although legally distinct issues, the removal of Cuban troops became "linked" to Namibian independence. This had suited Pretoria and Washington (and, arguably, Moscow).

Castro's latter-day *conquistadores* allowed South Africa to square the circle: continual SADF operations in Angola ensured that the Cubans stayed, but Castro's men made it impossible for the South Africans to quit Namibia, argued Pretoria; the Reagan administration went along with this self-serving rationale, and indeed went further by arming Unita, thus forming an implicit alliance with the apartheid state. Seemingly, it took nearly eight years for the Reagan administration to come around to the realisation that the fundamental obstacle to peace in the region was not winkling out the Cubans from Angola, but cajoling the SADF out of Namibia. Meanwhile, the diplomatic impasse and the spiralling conflict had enabled Moscow to demonstrate its commitment to the cause of African liberation. At the same time, Angola's red armies were providing real-live evidence of the total communist onslaught to the increasingly paranoid Afrikaner leadership. It was more difficult to gauge the benefits for America of her military dalliance with Savimbi and P W Botha while simultaneously carrying on a half-hearted sanctions war on South Africa's economy.

While it had been abundantly clear that Pretoria's policy in Namibia was to hang on to the territory for as long as possible, mainly for its military advantages, South African grand strategy in Angola was less discernible. The options ranged across a wide spectrum, including:

— replacing the MPLA with Unita;
— forcing both into a coalition government;
— establishing a secessionist state in southern Angola;
— forming a greater Ovamboland in southern Angola and northern Namibia;
— and simply keeping the MPLA government on the defensive.

The specific military strategy was more apparent. To prevent a Marxist axis in Luanda and Windhoek the SADF tried to ensure:

— widespread destruction of Angola's infrastructure;
— the containment of the ANC and SWAPO by destroying their bases and pushing them ever northwards;
— and the subvention of Unita. If Unita could not win, then at least it could constitute a military buffer against the Cuban/Russian/FAPLA/SWAPO socialist alliance.

Officially, the SADF stated that its "hot pursuit" and "pre-emptive" raids against SWAPO bases in Angola were intended to deter guerrilla infiltration into Namibia. For years, military aid to Unita was hushed up. SADF action was always characterised as anti-SWAPO sweeps. But, as the Unita versus SWAPO war grew after 1983, it became increasingly difficult to maintain this fiction. Technically, the SADF was fighting two distinct wars: a largely successful counterinsurgency campaign against SWAPO over the fate of Namibia, and the conventional war of attrition in southeastern Angola to project and, later, protect Unita. Politics fused these conflicts, but for the purposes of military analysis the concern here is with Unita, the most sophisticated of Pretoria's agents of destabilisation.

An Invisible Unita

Just before Savimbi led his tattered remnants into the bush in March 1976, Unita issued a final communiqué from Gago Coutinho. It said that 17 Cuban prisoners had been executed by an all-woman firing squad. Five of the soldiers had been accused of rape.(1) It might have been a touching feminist gesture, but it was poor PR for the guerrilla leader who was later to excel in the art of media manipulation. Indeed, for seven months after this, Savimbi disappeared. According to his (sympathetic) biographer, Fred Bridgland, Savimbi led 1,000 followers on a 3,000-kilometre trek through central Angola. At the end of his own version of Mao's long march, 79 supporters, including nine women, were still with him.(2) At the nadir of his fortunes, Unita strength tottered at around 200 armed guerrillas (according to Marcum) (3), although Savimbi claimed over 2,000. Nonetheless, Unita still retained sizable popular tribal support. Even the MPLA admitted that at least 350,000 peasants, and possibly as many as a million, in Bie and Huambo provinces, fled into the bush, encouraged no doubt by MPLA revenge for earlier Unita atrocities.(4)

Savimbi had not thrown in the towel: low-level insurgency continued. Attacks on the Benguela railway particularly distracted FAPLA resources in the period 1976-78 when 20 out of 25 diesel locomotives were destroyed.(5) The line was virtually closed. Unita, however, was on its own; SADF supplies had petered out. By the end of 1978, from Luanda's perspective, the civil war, it seemed, was effectively over. It was merely a case of mopping up stray Unita bands. Some Cuban troops were sent home. The remaining combat soldiers assumed largely guard and training functions. There was still the South African war against SWAPO, it was true. But Luanda hoped that increasing international support for the MPLA would deter the Afrikaner hawks. Relations with Zambia were thawing, for example. Kaunda, deeply immersed in the Rhodesian war, was desperate to secure supplies via the eastern Benguela route. The Luanda government also reached out a neighbourly hand to the ever-mercurial Mobutu, but only after a few sharp blows. In 1977 and 1978, the Katangese gendarmes had been unleashed from their Angolan bases. They committed unspeakable atrocities in the Shaba province, particularly during a massacre of white civilians in Kolwezi. French and Moroccan troops restored order and tried to entice back the Zairean troops who had fled into the forests. Thereafter, a somewhat chastened Zairean president made a reluctant peace with the MPLA...for a while.

The MPLA leaders grew overconfident and, in some cases, corrupt, as they sat back a little to taste the spoils of power. The ruling central committee took incautious steps. In particular, revolutionary zealots tried to construct, almost overnight, a by-the-book Marxist state, even though the concept of class struggle had very little relevance to Angola in the late 1970s. Marcum summed up the MPLA's follies thus:

> Lacking the educated cadres that would in any case have been essential to realise their vision, MPLA leadership embarked upon programmes of economic centralization and agricultural collectivization. They imposed restrictions on organized religion and rejected the legitimacy of such issues as the under-representation of rural sectors and ethnic groups (notably the Ovimbundu) in positions of political influence. The result was ambitious, maladministered, alienating governance by a largely Luanda-centred *mestiço* and ethnically Mbundu elite propped up by an influx of thousands of Cuban, Soviet, East German and other East European advisers and technicians.(6)

An alien ideology backed by foreign troops: this was perfect propaganda fodder for a slowly recuperating Unita, and Pretoria. Savimbi could claim that the MPLA had substituted one white imperialism for another. To win over the Angolan peasantry in any hearts-and-minds contest, the MPLA needed peace, organisational skills and funds on top of political moderation. Luanda could counter, with some justice, that it was Unita and SADF depredations which prevented reconstruction. The MPLA leadership did not win over the bulk of the disaffected peasantry, particularly the Ovimbundu, Unita's natural constituency, and, more dangerously, it provoked Pretoria by establishing ANC training camps in the north and a large military infrastructure for SWAPO in the south.

A vengeful SADF was preparing to move back in force. Cross-border raids had never ceased, but the army was gearing up to do the job properly, not as in 1975 when politicians, it felt, had hogtied its offensive capability. The decision to go to war with independent Angola was (apparently) taken in December 1977 in surprisingly peaceful surroundings: an unpretentious seaside cottage at Oubos, near Port Elizabeth.(7) It belonged to the prime minister, John Vorster. To this unlikely war conference he had summoned his top brass. His generals advocated a large-scale operation against the reinforced SWAPO bases in southern Angola. But Vorster, it was reported, was "not too enthusiastic".(8) After all, the recent invasion had destroyed his detente policy in Africa and undermined his own government. Despite, later, the opposition of the department of foreign affairs, the ailing Vorster succumbed to the hardline option. It was a decisive step in the rise of the South African military.(9) The immediate outcome was Operation Reindeer in May 1978. This incursion and the others that followed dwarfed the 1975-76 intervention.*

Despite the renewed tempo of SADF activity that continued through 1979, the MPLA remained confident. The Luanda politicians felt they were getting on top of their military and economic problems. In August 1979 the Benguela line was opened for the first time since 1975. The MPLA-PT (in line with its new ideological thrust it had added "-PT", *Partido de Trabalho*,or Workers' Party) held its first (one-party) parliamentary elections, albeit in only a few regions of the country. The party predicted rapid social transformation.

Such optimism was naive. Unita was expanding. Despite all the pious denials from Pretoria and Jamba, Savimbi's provisional "capital", SADF aid was also expanding. According to Savimbi's biographer, at the end of 1979, "South Africa's support for Savimbi, which since early 1976 had varied from the non-existent to the unpredictable, had become a substantial commitment".(10) At this time, support included weapons and military instructors. Nor was Pretoria the sole donor. During 1979, 500 Unita officers were trained secretly in Morocco. (Savimbi maintained an external base in Rabat.) Senegal provided more open political backing. Money came from Saudi Arabia and the Gulf states. And Mobutu, as usual, was playing a double game. Despite the official rapprochement with Luanda, he was giving covert aid to Unita.(11) Savimbi now publicly proclaimed that he *controlled* one-third of Angola. In 1979 that was an exaggeration, although his *range of operations* probably extended to at least a third of the country.

The high-water mark of the MPLA's tide of success was probably 1980. Military and diplomatic pressures began to mount against the new socialist leader, Eduardo dos Santos, who had taken over after the death of President Neto in September 1979. Most especially, Mugabe's victory in the February 1980 elections in Zimbabwe had shaken the ruling Afrikaners to the core. Pretoria was now even more adamant about preventing a similar outcome in Namibia. In June 1980 South Africa unleashed Operation Sceptic (more commonly called Operation Smokeshell) against SWAPO bases in southern Angola. One British military historian dubbed this South Africa's "biggest combined land and air operation since the Second World War".(12) This was merely the

---

* (These operations are discussed in more detail in the section on Namibia, as initially they were aimed primarily at Namibian insurgents not Angolan regular forces.)

PLATE 10.1 Jonas Savimbi with a commander, 1979. (*To The Point* Magazine)

beginning. The SADF's confidence and boldness grew apace once Ronald Reagan had replaced Jimmy Carter in the White House. Savimbi was soon welcomed in Washington. Unita joined the Nicaraguan "Contras" and the Afghan *Mujahedin* as "freedom fighters" sponsored by a new administration dedicated to clawing away at the peripheries of the Soviet empire.

Savimbi's resurrection

From 1980 onwards South African military strategy fused the anti-SWAPO and pro-Unita wars. Simultaneously, the Reagan administration's diplomacy transformed the "Namibian problem" into the "Angolan problem". Gradually, Pretoria shifted from insisting that the SADF would withdraw its troops from *Namibia* only if the Cubans went home, to the much more ambitious demand that South Africa would quit *Angola* when Castro's men left, too. Thus, the stakes were dramatically raised, both "problems" became much more intractable and, at the centre of the conundrum, Savimbi rose Houdini-like from his political grave.

Almost without exception, military experts who have closely observed Unita guerrillas in action confirm that Savimbi's soldiers are of excellent calibre. They are competently led by their officers, well-trained and disciplined under fire.(13) Yet Unita's renaissance was only partly due to its fighting qualities; Pretoria's helping hand was crucial. South African aid came in various packages. Training, supplies and intelligence were provided first. Also, South African and Portuguese businessmen traded with Unita: smuggled diamonds, poached ivory and rare wood were some of the contraband.

Communications aid was also vital in a sprawling, rugged country like Angola, which is five times the size of Britain. Savimbi's main base, Jamba, hugged the southeastern border with Namibia. The Portuguese used to call this area "the end of the world". Savimbi's well-camouflaged, 50-miles-wide capital was thus very isolated. Savimbi had to rely upon two supply routes: via Zaire, courtesy of the CIA, and via Namibia, thanks to the SADF. Most visitors, especially journalists, chose the easy route: from Wonderboom airport near Pretoria, flying in an old Dakota which dropped to tree-top level in the final stages of the journey to avoid stray SAM-7s. Guests would be met by extremely well turned-out Unita officers, searched and then offered the unique opportunity to have their passports stamped with "Free Angola". Most declined, as it would have invalidated their passports for travel elsewhere in Africa.

Driving in a captured Russian truck along empty dirt roads, signalled forward at deserted intersections by immaculate military policemen wearing spotless white gloves, guests reached an officers' mess, where they were regaled with South African wines and beers. This, then, was a comfortable war to cover for the majority of newsmen who avoided, or were kept away from, the front. Savimbi, a self-publicist of genius, garnered acres of favourable news coverage. The message, though, eventually palled. It was always the same: "next year in Luanda".

Such ambitions rested upon South African military assistance in two fields: sabotage and invasion. Frequently, highly professional SADF Reconnaissance Commandos ("Recces"), the premier army unit composed of blacks and whites, would enter Angola to destroy installations, leaving behind false evidence of Unita complicity. Many of these operations were skilfully accomplished by "4 Recce" based at Langebaan in Cape Province. This unit specialised in seaborne assaults. It is probable that this elite group raided the Lobito oil terminal (12 August 1980), Luanda oil refinery (30 November 1981) and destroyed road and rail bridges over the Giraul river near the port of Namibe (7 November 1982). Limpet mines were attached to Angolan and Eastern bloc ships in harbour. Cabinda, the oil lifeline for the MPLA, was an obvious target. It was here that the SADF's daring covert operations were later to backfire dramatically. Inland, particularly in the north, much of the sabotage was the work of genuine Unita special forces.

More important for Unita's expansion were the continuous minor raids and occasional full-blown conventional assaults from the SADF-occupied zones in the centre of southern Angola. These sorties hammered SWAPO and, increasingly, FAPLA as well. SWAPO units tended to hug Angolan bases and sometimes wore identical uniforms. Such raids distracted FAPLA's attempts to crush Savimbi's resurgence. Enmeshed in the south, FAPLA could not prevent Unita cadres pushing ever northwards, across the Benguela line and then to threaten communications both to Luanda and the important diamond-mining centres to the northeast.

The SADF raids continuously strained FAPLA's resources. According to the MPLA's president, in the first 11 months of 1981, there were 53 SADF troop operations, more than 100 bombing raids and 1,600 reconnaissance flights.(14) FAPLA could not counter the big conventional air and ground attacks. After the three-week incursion of June 1980 (Sceptic) there followed Operation Protea in August/September 1981. During Protea, several Soviet military personnel were killed and one warrant officer was taken prisoner. Over 10,000 South African troops occupied a 44-mile-deep strip of Cunene province, including Ngiva, the provincial capital. The SADF was to sit tight there for over three years. FAPLA, not SWAPO, became the main antagonists. Unita troops were very thin on the ground in Cunene province, but the SADF christened its occupied zone "Unita-liberated territory". Operation Daisy came next, in November 1981. A mechanised ground force, backed by strikes from Mirages, Canberras and Buccaneers, made the deepest penetration north since the 1975 adventure. During 1982 the SADF kept piling on the pressure in the south, as Unita troops moved into northern provinces such as Malanje and Cuanza Sul. In December 1982 FAPLA launched a counteroffensive against Unita's southern strongpoint at Mavinga.

Unita not only claimed SADF successes as its own, it also seized hostages for its propaganda machine. In March 1983, for example, Unita captured 84 Czechs and Portuguese working on a construction project in central Angola. Savimbi sought indirect international recognition by insisting that official representatives of the foreign governments concerned should personally receive back their nationals in Jamba. It was ironic that President Reagan was sliding towards military sponsorship of Savimbi at a time when Unita was regularly bagging foreign hostages; the taking of hostages was one of the prime definitions of terrorism in the Reagan lexicon.

PLATE 10.2 Operation Smokeshell, 1980. (*SADF*)

PLATE 10.3 Young Unita soldier (see page 3)

Southern Angola, however, had sunk even deeper into anarchy than southern Lebanon. Various rival armies marched across the flat wastelands. The innocent man-in-the-middle, as usual, suffered most. In three weeks Operation Protea alone generated 80,000 peasant refugees. In 1983 President Dos Santos estimated that the total cost of South African "aggression" was US$10 billion. The Luanda government was spending perhaps as much as 50% of its overall budget on the war.(15)

An overstretched FAPLA and a rampant SADF boosted the resurgent Unita's expansion into central and northern Angola. The crunch came at Cangamba in August 1983. This was the first major conventional assault by Unita in the history of the civil war, and it went all wrong. Savimbi's forces had performed well as guerrillas, but even conventionally-trained Unita troops could not then match FAPLA . . . without the SADF's intercession. Accounts of the battle vary, but it seems that only the SADF's air strikes saved Savimbi from a total rout. FAPLA alleged that over 1,000 Unita soldiers were killed, including a large proportion who were blown up in their own minefields as they retreated in panic.(16) Despite Pretoria's self-righteous denials, it was, apparently, the first example of the SADF openly intervening to save its protégés.

Cangamba was a significant escalation for the SADF. There were some indications that this precisely suited the hawks in Pretoria. The generals had clearly adapted to the military lessons of the 1975-76 debacle (even if South Africa's political goals in Angola remained elusive). The SADF had jettisoned the previous penny-packet commitments: the size of troop deployment, fire power on the ground and concentrated air strikes were rapidly increased. But that pushed up costs in treasure and in young conscripts' lives. In August 1982, for example, a SAM-7 missile brought down a Puma helicopter ferrying 12 soldiers during fighting in Cunene province. The 12, none older than 22, were killed along with the three-man crew. That was the highest SADF death toll in a single incident in more than 16 years of fighting in Namibia and Angola. Angolan troops now more than stood their ground against the SADF: battle-trained and well-stocked by the Russians, FAPLA grew more aggressive. The cross-border war was no longer a pushover for the marauding South Africans. And defence planners worried that Cuban combat troops and Soviet advisers would step up their frontline involvement. The SADF had killed or captured a handful of Soviet soldiers, but it was not proven that they had been performing combat duties.

Some defence hardliners still thought that the war could be won in one short, sharp blow. It seemed as though South African military intelligence was once again trying to outdo the Israelis in flamboyant tactics. This plan entailed a second grab at Luanda. In 1983—allegedly—hawks in the State Security Council backed a military intelligence proposal for a a rapid thrust towards the capital to instal Savimbi. According to reports, a number of hardliners, including the defence minister, General Magnus Malan, were determined to reverse the verdict of 1976: the next time, with enough force, the SADF could seize Luanda.(17) The cover, as usual, would be a big drive against SWAPO. The FAPLA HQ at Lubango was the immediate target. Then, if all went well, would come the quick thrust to Luanda. It is not clear what SADF military intelligence had to say about the Russian SAM-9 sites and the elite Cuban tank squadrons defending the road to the capital. There was, however, a contingency plan in case the Cubans shifted troops to Mozambique to open up a diversionary second front. The SADF might have combined with Renamo to make a real or feint assault on Maputo, the capital.

Threatening to invade the capitals of *both* South Africa's Marxist neighbours was too much even for some hawks in the SSC. According to one well-informed account:

> A furious running argument is known to have broken out in the SSC between the hawks and the chief of the army, General Jannie Geldenhuys, over the operational feasibility (indeed the sanity) of this plan. General Geldenhuys, a

> cautious veteran of the Namibian wars and now [1985] emerging as dominant in South African security policy, is believed to have threatened to resign and take the political platform against his colleagues. The prime minister, Mr P W Botha, normally sides with hawks in security matters. This time he opted for General Geldenhuys and caution.(18)

The Russians also warned Pretoria to be cautious. In November 1983 Russian diplomats at the UN met secretly with the South African UN ambassador. He was told bluntly that the Russian missile systems, Cuban-piloted MiG-23s and Cuban-manned tanks, plus all the Soviet reinforcements required, would be deployed if the SADF tried to move on Luanda.

Nonetheless, on 6 December 1983 Operation Askari was launched with 10,000 troops. SWAPO vanished into the bush, and the SADF was confronted with Cuban and FAPLA forces. In a fiercely contested encounter three miles northeast of Cuvelai, the SADF suffered 21 dead. The biggest single losses occurred when a Ratel-20 was cornered in a minefield and then knocked out by a T-54 tank.(19) Although Cuban and Angolan losses were, as usual, much higher than South Africa's, the very stiff resistance had surprised Pretoria and thus vindicated Geldenhuys's caution. Bad weather and the Soviet missile systems had challenged the SADF's accustomed superiority in the air: one Impala Mk2 was reported as returning from a reconnaissance mission with a SAM-9 warhead stuck in its tail. (20).

Enough was enough. Askari had been a major disappointment for the SADF. Their conventional opponents had stuck in their heels. SWAPO guerrillas were still a nuisance and Savimbi was just as far from Luanda. The Russians were levering up the costs of South Africa's war, already running at an estimated $4 million a day.(21) Perhaps it was time for diplomacy. The Americans, certainly, were eager for a foreign policy success in Angola and Namibia: in 1984 Reagan was trying for a second term of office. So far, years of constructive engagement with South Africa had produced nothing but frustration.

The Lusaka Accord

Both FAPLA and the SADF needed a breathing space. The South Africans, fighting on a 250-mile "front", were overextended. The Angolan forces were straining to contain the SADF; Unita had taken the opportunity to consolidate its operations in the north. Thus, American diplomatic pressure on South Africa coincided with battlefront incentives. Pik Botha's department of foreign affairs, for once, was given its head to try a diplomatic assault on Angola (and Mozambique). Pretoria needed to break out of its isolation, especially when it was introducing its new constitution at home and P W Botha was planning a major tour of Western Europe, a rare event for the pariah state. Some of P W Botha's generals, however, opposed any deals with Marxists merely to placate what they dubbed "Pik Botha's cocktail party friends".

Nevertheless, in February 1984, an agreement was signed in Lusaka between Pretoria and Luanda. The SADF was to withdraw in stages from its three-year occupation of Cunene province. Angola promised to end SWAPO's incursions from this zone. A joint monitoring commission (JMC), comprised of SADF soldiers with FAPLA in tow, supervised the withdrawal. Unita was not involved in this local ceasefire. Surprisingly, the Angolans and their white enemies on the JMC got on well. It was the not unusual phenomenon of professional soldiers' natural empathy surfacing in the absence of politicians. On a few occasions, they even fought together against stray bands of SWAPO and Unita who opened fire on JMC units.

The Lusaka accord was a temporary truce, not a non-aggression pact (such as the ensuing Nkomati agreement between Mozambique and South Africa). The SADF's withdrawal slowed down and then stopped after the exit from Ngiva. It was to take over a year for a (temporary) total exodus from a 25-mile-wide strip between Ngiva and the Namibian border to be completed. The Lusaka agreement, optimists prayed, would lead not only to peace in Angola, but also a settlement in Namibia. It was not to be. Separate talks between SWAPO and South Africa broke down in May 1984, probably because of a Russian veto. Pretoria, once more, upped the stakes. It insisted that there could be no peace in Namibia unless Unita was included in a settlement in Angola. The war in southern Angola was recharged.

A single incident now mightily embarrassed Pretoria and laid bare the sinews of destabilisation. On 21/22 May 1985, in the Cabinda enclave, a FAPLA patrol clashed with a 4 Recce Commando sabotage unit. Six of the nine-man team escaped, two were killed and one, Captain Wynand Petrus du Toit, was shot and taken prisoner. After interrogation, he revealed details of the raid at a press conference a week later. Du Toit said that he had spent four months preparing for the operation. The unit left Saldanha Bay, in Cape Province, in an "Israeli-built" ship (presumably a Minister class strike craft) and landed in inflatable boats near Malembo. Their targets were oil storage tanks of the US-operated Gulf Oil complex, which was also intermittently patrolled by Cubans. The South African commandos intended to put two limpet mines on each tank. In addition, the saboteurs carried Unita propaganda material and a small tin of paint to daub "Viva Unita" on the road. The luckless captain also admitted that he had taken part in previous raids in Angola, including the sabotage of the Giraul bridge for which Unita claimed responsibility. Pretoria lamely tried to argue that that its commandos had been on a reconnaissance mission to gather intelligence on SWAPO and ANC bases in Cabinda. The army's crack unit would hardly have carried such an interesting array of sabotage and deception material merely to gather information on non-existent insurgent bases. The very best of the SADF's soldiery had been caught out and had confessed. A writer, sympathetic to the MPLA, summed up the impact of the du Toit escapade:

> That one incident shattered the credibility of 'constructive engagement', destroyed the peacemaking image the apartheid regime was trying to create for itself, and called into question all the Unita claims over the years. Had it not been for the action of that FAPLA patrol, the Angolan economy would have been deprived of its main foreign exchange earner and of the fuel needed to keep everything going, including the armed forces. Headlines would have declared that Unita was in control of Cabinda province and about to make its long-announced but continually postponed assault on the capital. One can only speculate as to what the reaction of foreign oil companies operating in Angola would have been, or the reactions of their governments.(22)

The American government's response was, however, to propose the repeal of the Clark Amendment, which had previously prevented official US military aid to Savimbi. At the same time, the US was buying $600 millions-worth of Cabinda oil every year. Ironically, then, Gulf Oil was effectively financing the MPLA to pay the Cubans to protect its installations against capitalist-backed Unita guerrillas (and South African imposters). Nevertheless, Washington claimed to be the "honest broker" in Angola. The US refused to recognise Angola even though Luanda was a valuable and reliable trading partner. US trade with Angola was the fourth biggest in black Africa. The American commercial connection was much larger with South Africa, however.

The diplomatic web was complex. Israel, for example, in the early 1980s, had assisted in the training and equipping of the Zairean army with CIA approval. Some of this support went, allegedly, to Unita as well as to attempts to revive the moribund FNLA (without Roberto) and insurgent secessionist movements in Cabinda. In 1983 a (temporarily) revived FNLA launched a short-lived offensive in the north. It soon collapsed. In 1985 Unita absorbed some of the FNLA remnants and began a more substantial northern campaign. A Unita Kimbundu officer, Colonel Antonio Dembo, apparently established an effective force in the Dembos forests, northeast of Luanda. (23) This was a psychological blow to the MPLA, for it was in this region that the Marxist party had founded its ideological and military "focus" for the start of its war against the Portuguese.

The northern campaigns by Unita and the SADF were, however, diversions from the main killing fields of the south. From mid-1985 onwards the SADF and Unita were sucked into a series of conventional battles, the largest in Africa since the Second World War.

Conventional wars

The Soviet Union and its allies had gone to great lengths to build up FAPLA. The East Germans had installed the SAM systems. Air force training had been carefully supervised. Iko Carreira, commander of the Angolan air force, had received several years' advanced instruction in Russia. Cubans and (perhaps) Russians were flying the more advanced aircraft, but Unita reports about the presence of a Soviet infantry battalion were fanciful. In 1983 Moscow delivered approximately $800 millions worth of military equipment.(24) General Secretary Chernenko declared forcibly in March 1984 that "no one has the right to turn back the pages of history in southern Africa".(25) Soviet resolve was hardening.

In late August 1985, the Angolan army launched Operation Party Congress against Unita strongholds around Mavinga and Cuito Cuanavale. Soviet officers, probably serving at regimental level, assisted.(26) South African military intelligence, which had intercepted cockpit conversations in Russian, declared that Soviet pilots were flying Angolan MiG-23s and helicopter gunships.(27) FAPLA recaptured Cazombo, and Unita fell back towards Mavinga. Jamba was also threatened. In mid-September (a few days after finally pulling out entirely from southern central Angola, according to the Lusaka deal) the SADF decisively intervened with air strikes and a mechanised battalion (the 32nd Buffalo Battalion). The South African Air Force (SAAF) also transported Unita reinforcements in its C-130 Hercules aircraft. Savimbi's men had been wrong-footed, and so found themselves badly positioned to withstand the main assault. Defence Minister Malan even stated publicly that South Africa was helping Unita (albeit with "humanitarian aid"). For three consecutive days in late September, with its almost complete mastery of the air, the SAAF bombed and strafed advancing

FAPLA units. The SADF eventually stopped and then turned the offensive. Unita had been saved to fight another day. The 1985 offensive had almost succeeded in overwhelming Unita. Luanda was bound to try again.

On 24 October the battle lines were further demarcated in Angola with the declaration of the "Reagan doctrine" to counter Soviet imperialism in the third world. Unita officially joined the list of protected species in Afghanistan, Cambodia, Ethiopia and Nicaragua. In November Reagan approved a covert aid package of $13 million to the Angolan "contras".(28) In January 1986 Savimbi was received in Washington amid a blaze of publicity. Within two months Stinger ground-to-air missiles and TOW anti-armour weapons were passing through Kamina air base in Zaire into Savimbi's (and, no doubt, Pretoria's) hands. (29) As in Afghanistan, the Stingers were to prove lethal to low-flying aircraft. Savimbi now had the capacity to deter the MPLA's helicopter gunships and the MiG-23s which had caused so much damage to Unita in the 1985 offensive.

The first six months of 1986 witnessed a major arms build-up on both sides and a strengthening of the rival patrons' commitment to their Angolan surrogates. A general feeling permeated both camps that the make-or-break battles would come in that year's *cacimbo* (dry season). Castro pledged that his support for the MPLA would continue, if necessary, until apartheid had been dismantled. In February Angola, Cuba and the USSR signed a joint communiqué on solidarity. In June, after South Africa's sabotage of two Soviet cargo ships in the port of Namibe, Moscow issued a strong warning that "actions of this kind cannot be left unpunished".(30) At the same time America, South Africa and Unita intelligence sources vied with one another to disclose details of the Soviet arms shipments. The Soviets were determined not to repeat the fatal mistakes of 1985. What was required above all was air defence for FAPLA air and ground forces. For six months, via a sea and air bridge, Moscow poured in arms. According to Bridgland, "New SA-6, SA-8 and SA-13 air defence missile batteries and anti-aircraft radar systems were ... lifted in on a scale far in excess of anything the South African Air Force could hope to master."(31) South African sources talked about the Russians importing "virtually the entire range of Soviet-made SAM missiles". The main radar stations were sited at Lubango, Menongue, Luena and Cuito Cuanavale. The Russians planned to dominate all of southern Angolan air space. According to Bridgland, "by the beginning of 1986 Western intelligence agencies estimated there were 27 MiG-25s, 23 MiG-23s, 70 MiG-21s and 10 Sukhoi 22s in

Angola". This could have been an exaggerated tally. A range of combat and transport helicopters were also imported, including the Mi-25, Mi-8, Mi-16 and Mi-17. Angolans flew the helicopters and the MiG-21s, although the more advanced aircraft were probably still being flown by the "internationalists", foreign communists. (32) Large numbers of T-62, T-55 and PT-76 tanks were airlifted in, as well as BTR-60 and BRDM-2 armoured vehicles.

Unita intelligence put the total balance of manpower as follows:

80,000 FAPLA
45,000 Cubans (35,000 combat troops)
7,000 SWAPO
4,000 Russian and East German personnel
2,500 Portuguese
1,200 ANC
Plus remnants of Katangese gendarmes.(33)

This estimate was probably exaggerated. FAPLA would probably have numbered around 50,000 (including 24,000 conscripts and 10,000 members of the ODP militia serving at any one time with the regular army). Not all the total pro-MPLA forces would be in action, of course, against Unita. SWAPO in 1986 would have probably committed about 3,000 troops to fighting alongside the MPLA against Unita as a form of "rent" for FAPLA support of the war in Namibia. In short, perhaps 20,000 pro-Marxist troops were directly involved in the 1986 offensive in the south.

On the rival side, Unita claimed to field 28,000 "regulars" and 30,000 militia/part-timers. In 1986 the number of SADF troops in the frontline alongside Unita was probably very small. For all its skills in irregular warfare, Unita had little with which to counter a large-scale conventional assault. It boasted an array of captured T-34s and T-55s as well as various armoured personnel carriers, but they were not generally in use. Unita's main bases, highly organised with well-camouflaged schools, hospitals and clinics, bristled with a variety of anti-aircraft weapons (such as the ZU-23-2 23mm guns). But in 1986 the key defensive weapon was the Stinger. Man-portable, weighing 15.7 kilogrammes and slightly longer than 1.5 metres, it is an ideal guerrilla weapon. It can reach 1,500 metres altitude and it is equipped with a highly accurate infra-red guidance system that permits it to be fired at a target from any angle. Here was a weapon which could counter the awesome Hinds, the Mi-24 flying tanks. The Stinger has an eight-kilometre range compared with the three-kilometre range of Unita's then existing stock of (often unpredictable) SAM-7s. By July 1986, Unita officers were claiming a strike rate of eight in ten with their new Stingers, against one in ten with the SAM-7s. In addition, there were the US TOW anti-tank missiles and, apparently, some Redeye ground-to-air missiles. (34) Besides this sophisticated arsenal, the SADF had donated a cornucopia of small arms, mortars and logistical material, especially fuel. The total amount of South African largesse has been estimated at between $200 million and $1 billion, although it would be difficult to evaluate precisely the large amount of equipment captured from SWAPO and FAPLA by the SADF, and then handed over to Savimbi.(35)

By African standards this was a monumental accretion of hardware. No wonder intelligence experts expected 1986 to be decisive. It was not, however; 1987 was much bloodier. Nonetheless, the Soviet advisers still hoped to capture Jamba and destroy Unita as a credible opposition to the MPLA. According to Unita sources, the Russians wanted to open the 1986 offensive in March, but the Cubans advised that FAPLA had not fully recovered from the previous year's battles. Fighting erupted on 27 May. Two columns left Luena, one heading towards Munhango, Unita's last salient across the Benguela line, and another towards Lumbala (Gago Coutinho). Unita intelligence termed this a "deception movement". In the 1985 campaign Unita had fallen for a similar feint at Cazombo. The bulk of Savimbi's regular forces were tied up there when the main attack was unleashed at Mavinga. Caught off-guard, it was only the SAAF's air bridge that enabled Savimbi to transfer his troops for the defence of Mavinga, the gateway to his capital.

In June 1986, the main FAPLA thrust was accurately predicted as emanating from Cuito Cuanavale to the south of the feint. According to a briefing, during the fighting, by Brigadier Perigrino Chindondo, Unita's chief of military intelligence, the FAPLA thrust developed along two axes: a cautious advance by FAPLA from the south of Cuito Cuanavale to engage Unita's anticipated main counterattack, while a rapid Cuban push from the northwest would fall on Mavinga. The Russians, according to Chindondo, had augmented their air power in nearby Menongue, the main Soviet/Cuban airbase in the region: 12 extra MiG-21/23s had been added to 11 already stationed there. Four extra Sukhoi-22s complemented the existing four. (36)

On 9 August 4,000 Unita regulars foiled the planned FAPLA/Cuban pincer by a pre-emptive assault on Cuito Cuanavale. On the next day Unita cut, temporarily, the road to Menongue. On 11 August Unita claimed to have destroyed Cuito's air base. Savimbi's troops withdrew from the town after damaging the surrounding military installations.

FAPLA sources maintained that the battle for Cuito Cuanavale was against South African forces, although Savimbi insisted it was a Unita success. Unita also claimed to have brought down 22 aircraft including MiG-21s, MiG-23s, and Mi-8 and Mi-25 choppers. Interestingly, Chindondo said that French-built Dauphin helicopters, flown by Cubans, had been observed for the first time during the battle.

Unita officials also claimed that their enemies had deployed chemical weapons. They spoke of "quick death" after the use of "grenades and aerial bombardment" in three separate engagements. One officer gave an eyewitness account: "The leaves of some trees became totally dark, the sand became very, very dark as well...The smoke was yellow and green." Savimbi, who said he had personally directed the Cuito Cuanavale battle, explained: "They threw grenades which didn't explode in the normal way. They gave out smoke and the soldiers felt dizzy. They couldn't fight so they dropped their weapons. Some of them became blind."(37) In the absence, however, of concrete scientific evidence, these reports must be treated with some scepticism. Observers of other wars, such as Afghanistan, will have noted how often guerrilla spokesmen harp on the theme of the enemy's use of chemical weapons. They perhaps think it is the kind of information Western journalists want, or ought, to hear.(38)

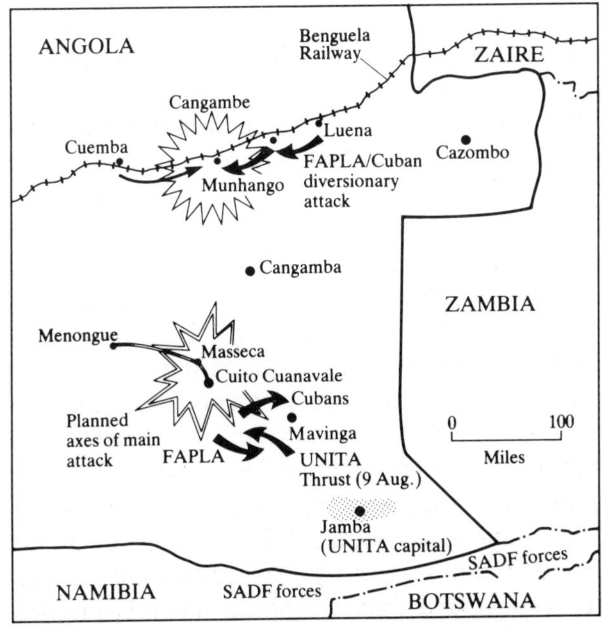

MAP 10 The 1986 thrust against Jamba. (Fighting in the first week of August)

At a press conference in Jamba on 21 August 1986, Savimbi was ebullient about containing the offensive which experts had predicted would overwhelm his forces. There was an extra Patton-like swagger to the bearded warlord, who also carried a pearl-handled colt revolver slung low over one hip. Savimbi did not openly admit that the American Stingers had turned the tide of battle for him, but he hinted to the same effect very broadly: "We have got all we asked President Reagan to give us and it has arrived in a very quick manner." Artistic appreciation of that generosity was displayed in the massive mural of Savimbi and Reagan which dominated the central parade ground of his HQ. The Unita president said that the offensive was as good as over: "The Russians have only a month left...September. After September, it is the rainy season again. Their tanks will be dead, useless." He admitted that in the 1985 campaign three factors had threatened Unita's survival: "Air power, armour and Soviet advisers. But we are in a position of challenging their airpower and armour." Thank you, Stinger and TOW, was left unsaid but understood.

FAPLA had not won the 1986 season. The feint attack from Luena had made some progress by recapturing Cangamba. But, further south, the more important conflict around Cuito Cuanavale had proved inconclusive for FAPLA. Mavinga, the key target, had not fallen. Unita not only lived to fight again, but it had reopened the war (once more) in the northern provinces of Zaire, Uige, Luanda and Cuanza Norte. The war had also threatened to spill over into Zambia. The MPLA was negotiating with Zaire and Zambia to open the Benguela railway. Paradoxically, Washington showed great interest in this project, while simultaneously arming Unita which kept it closed. Perhaps, as a prelude to the diplomatic dance to resuscitate the railway, there were hints that Kaunda, Savimbi's old friend, would allow FAPLA to open up a new front in the northeast from Zambian territory. Savimbi, with characteristic rhetoric, dismissed this threat: "There is a difference in having soldiers for parade and having soldiers for fighting. Mine are seasoned soldiers for fighting, those in Zambia are for parade."

The precise numbers of fighting soldiers in the SADF and in the Russian contingent during the 1986 campaign are not known, although the official communiqués from both FAPLA and FALA (technically Unita's military wing, the Armed Forces for the Liberation of Angola) played up their respective indigenous prowess, not that of their white allies. As soon as the rains brought the conventional war season to an end, the Soviets patiently set about rebuilding FAPLA's offensive capabilities. The 1987 campaign was planned largely by General Konstantin

Shaganovitch, who was reportedly the highest-ranking Soviet officer ever to be posted outside Europe or Afghanistan.(39) He arrived in Angola in December 1985. He was assisted by another Soviet officer, General Mikhail Petrov, a counterinsurgency specialist. As in Afghanistan, Russian officers found it hard to adapt their conventional, often hidebound, experience to the dictates of guerrilla warfare; the revolutionary arteries of the Red Army had grown sclerotic. In Mozambique and Angola the guerrilla victors of the independence wars became ossified conventional forces. In Angola the set-piece Warsaw Pact-style offensives compounded this tendency. In contrast, it could be said that the SADF has shown not only how to contain communist tactics of insurgency (especially in Namibia), but also how to wage a potent counter-revolution. In one sense Pretoria's generals became the true exponents of the Reagan doctrine, especially in the destabilised states. Hence, discomfited Soviet generals were forced to witness their Marxist counterinsurgency tactics being emasculated, and their clients besieged, by new guerrilla "liberators" backed by the SADF.

But this argument can only be taken so far: so far as Pretoria's white supremacists could afford the high costs of their military counter-revolution. The money spent in Angola might have been better used for more effective containment (or reform) at home. It could be argued that every gun, truck and military radio given to Unita was one less weapon to repress the domestic black struggle. The massive destabilisation efforts ranging from Luanda to the Seychelles, and further afield, distracted a great deal of the apartheid government's intelligence in both senses of the word. From this (narrow) perspective, Pretoria's forward military policy nicely dovetailed with the goals of the South African Communist Party. Counter-revolution can, therefore, also play into the hands of the revolutionaries.

The FAPLA campaign in 1987 was a case in point. That year's fighting pushed up the ante for South Africa and, more dangerously, raised the spectre of the great powers imposing a settlement in Angola and Namibia which was inimical to Pretoria's interests. The South African government, however, believed that an escalation in Angola would cause East-West collision not collusion. Once again, it was wrong. Pretoria's analysis of the MPLA's strategy was often simplistic and contradictory. On the one hand, the MPLA was portrayed as a willing tool or dupe of the Cubans, who were themselves puppets of the Kremlin. (In 1988, however, Pretoria tried a different tack: the "radical" Cubans were said to be preventing the "moderate" Russians and MPLA from settling the conflict.) On the other hand, the MPLA was sometimes depicted as an independent actor. In this version, Pretoria's analysts liked to stress the so-called "peace party" within the MPLA which wanted negotiations with Unita (minus, usually, Savimbi) and which was in contention with the hawks who wanted each year one more chance to win on the field of battle. Although there clearly were disputatious factions in the much-purged and coup-ridden party, there appeared to be a general consensus about hostility to Unita. Whatever was actually discussed in the central committee of the MPLA, the knock-out option triumphed once more.

In July 1987 the offensive of 1986 was repeated on a grander scale. Two thrusts, one from the north at Lucusse and another from Cuito Cuanavale, moved on Mavinga. The battle groups advanced very cautiously, sometimes at the speed of two to three miles a day, under extensive air cover and heavy armoured support. Unita initially avoided direct contact; instead the guerrillas severely harassed the supply and communications lines of this ponderously mobile Siegfried line. Preliminary encounters developed along the Lomba river north of Mavinga. By September perhaps as many as 15,000 FAPLA troops were engaged in a fierce conventional battle with approximately the same number of Unita regulars.

Both sides banned battlefield press coverage by independent journalists and tried to dramatise their enemy's losses while minimising their own. Casualties were very high on both sides. Estimates of FAPLA dead varied from 1,000 to 4,000.(40) Unita's were far less. Savimbi also claimed four Russians and 20 Cubans killed.(41) At the end of September, Unita asserted that it had destroyed 52 tanks, 111 vehicles, 21 armoured vehicles, three MiG fighters, 11 helicopters and a Sukhoi-22. Although this claim had to be treated with scepticism, Unita's new weaponry had exacted a heavy toll. Also, both the SADF's G5 and G6 howitzers were reported to have been involved—at some financial cost to Savimbi, according to a disputed interview with the Unita leader:

> During the offensive and at the battle of Lomba, when they [the SADF] were showering shells and bombs on the enemy—2,000 to 3,000 shells in the course of one night—they listed everything we owed them. And at the end of the offensive they presented it to us. And it was a lot. We need our friends to help us settle the account.(42)

In the air, advanced Israeli electronic countermeasures were deployed in SAAF Mirages. Israeli-developed Seeker drones were also said to have been used to jam Angolan radar connected with anti-aircraft missile batteries.(43) Repeating the techniques by which the Israeli air force destroyed the advanced Soviet air defence system deployed in 1982 in Lebanon's Bekaa valley, a SAAF-converted Boeing airliner was used as an airborne electronic warfare centre to direct air strikes into Angola within range of FAPLA's missile screens. In this way, the Soviet mobile SAM-8 launchers and one SAM-13 launcher were wiped out. The SAAF did not have it all its own way. Pretoria admitted that at least one plane, a Mirage hit by a SAM-8 missile, later crashed.

On the ground, SADF casualties were more serious. The South Africans fought on two fronts. In what Pretoria denied was a move to distract the enemy flank during the Unita/FAPLA battles, its army attacked a SWAPO complex near Cuvelai in south/central Angola. The SADF insisted that it was merely pre-empting the annual SWAPO rainy season offensive. In October, 12 SADF soldiers and one SWATF soldier were killed. At the same time, on the eastern battlefront, another 11 SADF members died. Such high white casualty figures could not be hidden. Defence Minister Malan admitted for the first time that the SADF was actually fighting alongside Unita, although Savimbi conceded only that the SADF was running a field hospital near the Mavinga front. Malan said that direct Russian and Cuban intervention had forced South Africa either to accept "the defeat of Dr Jonas Savimbi or halt Soviet aggression". The very last thing Savimbi needed was the SADF trumpeting that it had saved him. After years of subtly trying to build up Unita's credibility, it was strange of Pretoria to upstage Savimbi, especially at a time when his forces were performing creditably. One explanation could be that Pretoria was anxious to emphasise the dramatic confrontation with professional white communist troops to justify and explain the high October casualties to a concerned white electorate. It would have been politically difficult to explain away all the deaths at the hands of black insurgents such as SWAPO in the Namibian war, which Pretoria had claimed was as good as won.

It was also mooted that Pretoria had lied about white fatalities. Were they in fact much more serious? The SADF denied this strongly. It was, after all, difficult to hide so many deaths in the relatively small white society, which still had tattered remnants of a free press. The number of whites seriously wounded was impossible to assess. Even more difficult to obtain were full details of the blacks killed and wounded in both the South African and South West African armies. Reports about "rebellions" and a "mutiny" in the 101 and 102 SWATF Battalions filtered out. Soldiers from these battalions, some containing "turned" SWAPO insurgents, fought alongside Unita during the climactic battles around Cuito Cuanavale. A large number of these black Namibians refused to continue fighting in Angola. They objected, it was reported, to wearing Unita uniforms and acting as cannon fodder to reduce white SADF casualties.(44)

For FAPLA, the knock-out had degenerated into a slogging match. The socialist alliance had not totally mastered South African air power, so crucial to a FAPLA victory in the south. Pretoria's enemies could lose and fight again; the SADF could not risk one major reverse. The Russians could easily re-equip their allies, but it was much more difficult for the SAAF to replenish its ageing inventory. (Although it was alleged that Pretoria bought some Mirages from Argentina to replace its losses in Angola.)(45) Pretoria admitted to having lost three planes during this FAPLA offensive, but the real losses could have been higher. On the ground, white casualties were mounting and so was the cost of the electronic cat-and-mouse games in the sky. Previously, the rains had brought a respite from conventional war, when mud became the real enemy. Then getting to a battle was often more difficult than winning it. The SADF could half-relax and deal with the rainy season infiltration of their weakest opponents, SWAPO. But, this time, there was to be no let-up.

A town too far?

Precise details of the 1988 battles are still shrouded in the mists of disinformation. But it is clear that the nature of the Angolan war had changed. Despite its severe mauling, FAPLA decided to dig in. The centrepiece of the fighting was Cuito Cuanavale. Castro described the fighting there as "the turning point of African history" and the Angolans called the town "the Stalingrad of the South African army". Both are exaggerations. It is possible that the SADF did not intend to take the town, but rather to contain it. Certainly the fighting in the area was very bitter. What remained of the civilian population fled, and, it seems, the airport outside the town was captured. Cuito, at one stage, looked as though it might fall. But it became a symbol of socialist resolve. FAPLA and Cuban reinforcements fought their way into the town from the north. In mid-January Colonel Alberto Neto, the FAPLA air force chief of staff, announced that the South African-led advance on the town had been halted. He said that 6,000 South African troops were besieging Cuito Cuanavale, supported by G-5 artillery which was lobbing 200 shells a day into the town.(46) Probably, the self-propelled G6 also saw action. This 46-ton gun can accurately fire at ranges up to 25 miles, six miles further than NATO's 155mm artillery. The mobility of the G-6 to "shoot and scoot" was perhaps vital, not only because of the difficult terrain in bad weather, but also to avoid retaliatory air strikes.

The Russians had continuously upgraded their air defence network. Mobile radar systems (of seven different types) based upon 23 sites formed a series of overlapping arcs which covered nearly the whole country. The offensive arm consisted of the fighters (MiG-21s, MiG-23s and Su-22s) with the defensive punch provided by six anti-aircraft missile systems and four calibres of anti-aircraft guns. As back-up, field units deployed up to three forms of shoulder-launched weapons.(47) This system usually worked, as the SAAF found out regularly. In February Pretoria admitted that another one of its Mirages had been shot down. Cuban pilots, once extremely reluctant to (and sometimes under orders not to) engage the highly-skilled South African pilots, now became anxious to do so. Faced with the massive air defence network, superior Russian aircraft and bolder aviators, an unaccustomed wariness was detectable among SAAF pilots. From 1986 Stingers had given a new technological edge to Unita. Low-flying attacks were deterred. But Soviet electronic countermeasures at local level and the national air defence systems eventually swung the war in the air back in Luanda's favour. Cuito Cuanavale was the operating centre of the most south-eastern arc of the radar defence. To regain air superiority, particularly over Unita territory, the SADF wanted to smash a hole in the FAPLA cordon and eliminate that key component of the air defence system.

The Angolan air force intervened more confidently in its defence of the "African Stalingrad". The contested skies prompted the SADF to switch to artillery rather than aerial bombardment of the besieged town, sometimes from extreme range. There was some anxiety, too, that Russian Frog ground-to-ground missiles, with a range of 40 miles, might have been introduced to deal with South Africa's superior artillery. (48) The SADF's other alternative, a full-scale infantry offensive, was ruled out because of the high casualty risks. Hundreds of white soldiers might have been killed.

In March 1988 there were reports of an audacious SADF operation 400 miles inside Angola, far to the north of the main battleground.(49) But it did not undermine FAPLA's dogged resistance in Cuito Cuanavale. At the beginning of April Pretoria admitted that it was using tanks in the battle. It was a response to FAPLA's claim that Angolan troops had captured an unspecified number of South African tanks. Pretoria conceded that one tank had been damaged by a mine. In April the SADF began to pull back its reported 8,000-9,000 troops from the FAPLA front. The Cubans were jubilant: "a disaster" had been inflicted on the racists.(50) The SADF, however, had not been defeated, but it could no longer afford the costs of trying to win. It had lost over 40 soldiers, mainly young white conscripts, in the battlefields around Cuito Cuanavale. It had also lost a handful of planes and tanks. But, much more important, it had lost the game of technological leapfrog with the Russians, as it was bound to do if Moscow persisted in resupplying the MPLA. For so long the SADF had strutted with arrogant impunity, deploying its superior forces whenever and wherever Pretoria had so chosen. At Cuito Cuanavale, the SADF had bogged down in the mud and trenches; 1988 was Flanders briefly revisited or, more prophetically perhaps, an echo of the German retreat from Stalingrad. It was certainly a long way from the heady days of the 1975 blitzkrieg.

It was time to talk again. And it was General Malan who publicly suggested a possible opening to Moscow. The Afrikaner leaders must have reckoned: after Afghanistan, why not a Russian exit from Angola too? (51) The arch-enemy of Russia's (supposed) total onslaught on Afrikanerdom, in effect, gave the first formal recognition of not only Moscow's power and influence, but also its legitimate stake in the region. From Pretoria's perspective, Reagan was on the way out; even that old-time conservative crusader had let South Africa down. Sanctions had already removed much of the US moral and economic leverage. Indeed, anti-Americanism was much more virulent in Afrikaner circles than any Russophobia. (In late 1987 the foreign affairs ministry had established a full-scale Soviet desk, after realising that the Russians had 53 diplomats busy full-time on Pretoria-watching.)(52)

The bitter conventional battles between 1985 and 1988 had altered the military balance in the region. Despite the relative decline of SADF power, the attrition on both sides dictated prudence. Could either side ever win militarily? And at what cost? These were questions the superpowers were not prepared to answer publicly. Their thinking, however, converged at the Reagan-Gorbachev Moscow summit in June 1988: they agreed that the war should end soon. So it was that in London, Brazzaville, Cairo and New York, with superpower prodding, the Angolans, Cubans and South Africans met face-to-face. SWAPO and Unita were excluded, although, as the egregious deputy director-general of Pretoria's foreign affairs department, Glen Babb, put it: "The presence of Unita will be there, just like Banquo's ghost was present at Hamlet's feast."(53)

The burst of diplomacy was supposed to stop the Angolan war escalating and dragging in the superpowers any further. Few diplomats anticipated that South Africa could be persuaded to get out of its colony soon.

But there was a gleam of hope that the Angolan war might be wound down a ratchet or two. Even the most stubborn Afrikaner leaders could see the sense in negotiating a deal before Reagan left office. Yet, in June 1988, even a formal ceasefire seemed elusive as a force of Cuban troops 3,000-5,000-strong (Pretoria said 10,000) erected a 300-mile-wide new front right along the edge of the southwestern border of Namibia. The SADF called up extra citizen force reserves. On 27 June a combined FAPLA-Cuban air and ground attack near the Calueque water scheme resulted in the death of 12 SADF troops (and much higher Cuban and Angolan casualties). Was Castro posturing to gain advantage during the itinerant peace conferences, trying to stall the peace process until a Democrat might win the US presidential race, or spoiling to inflict a final bloody nose on the SADF before bringing his men home as heroes? Whatever his motives, a powerful force of confident Cuban troops stood along the Namibian border. This was April 1976 all over again. Thirteen years of fighting in Angola and what had South Africa gained?

The US-USSR convergence of interests, the costs to South Africa in lives and rand, the loss of SAAF air superiority, and war-weariness on all sides prompted a ceasefire in August 1989. Thanks mainly to superpower midwifery, the main contestants, after ten rounds of talks, signed a final agreement in New York in December 1988. The South African foreign ministry had been given a new lease of life. The energetic director-general, Neil van Heerden, played a prominent role abroad and at home in his attempts to soothe the worries of the hawks. The New York accord meant the end of two of the three wars in the region. The SADF's COIN war with SWAPO and the conventional war with FAPLA and the Cubans were over, or so the agreements stipulated. The accord did not cover the Unita-MPLA conflict. But it was implicity assumed that the New York accord would lead to a Savimbi-Luanda deal. In exchange for dumping Unita, Pretoria got its pound of flesh: the ejection of the estimated 6,000 ANC guerrillas from Angola. That understanding was a crucial demand of the South African hawks. The hardliners were in a similar position to that of Iran at the same time. "Like Ayatollah Khomeini, failure on the battlefield has compelled them to drink the 'poison of peace'".(54)

The December 1988 agreement was potentially a turning point equivalent to the Lancaster House settlement. Above all, it established a timetable for Namibian independence. On 1 April 1989 the UN transition began. On 1 July the SADF was supposed to reduce its troops in Namibia from 50,000 to 1,500. Elections were scheduled for November 1989. The last 25,000 Cuban troops, monitored by the UN, were set to quit Angola on 1 July 1991. Cuba's *Afrika Korps* had helped to curtail the SADF's power, but some estimates put Cuban losses as high as 10,000 men.(55) Castro had vowed to stay until apartheid was crushed. He had failed: the Afrikaner generals lived to fight another day. Yet the loss of Namibia might prove eventually to be a mortal blow to Pretoria's hawks.

It might also be a mortal blow to Savimbi. The civil war in Angola continued, but Unita was cut off from its southern sources. The CIA stepped up its supplies to Unita through Zaire and encouraged Savimbi to move his main base to Quimbele in the north, a long way from his tribal base. The Americans thus tried to compensate for the removal of the SADF lifeline. Not only were Savimbi's arms supplies in jeopardy , so was his image. In 1989 a spate of reports about his ruthlessly dictatorial rule surfaced. Even the warlord's faithful biographer, Fred Bridgland, gave credence to the reports of Savimbi burning some of his rivals as witches.(56) Savimbi was clearly in trouble.

Since both the MPLA and Unita were losing the military support of their immediate allies, the Cubans and the SADF, and OAU members, particularly in francophone Africa, put pressure on both sides to negotiate an end to the 15-year civil war. Savimbi was encouraged to go into exile in Morocco, but he refused. In June 1989 Mobutu brokered a ceasefire agreement at his Gbadolite palace, the "Versailles in the jungle". It was the first time that the MPLA president, Eduardo Dos Santos, had met Savimbi since 1975. The ceasefire was broken almost immediately, but a start with reconciliation had been made. Unita (minus Savimbi) could "merge" with its mortal enemy, the MPLA. The elections promised in 1975 might even be held. Or the war could drag on.

The Angolan agreement had certainly helped to derail the war train, but talk of a "peace epidemic" was an overstatement. True, the precedent of Angola was applied with vigour in Mozambique, where the OAU tried to broker a Renamo-Frelimo settlement. But the core issue of apartheid power remained. This applied particularly to Namibia as it struggled to grasp its independence.

References and notes:

1. F Bridgland, *Jonas Savimbi: A Key to Africa,* Macmillan, Johannesburg, 1986, p.192.
2. *Ibid.*, pp. 194-218.
3. J Marcum, "Regional Security in Southern Africa—Angola," *Survival,* January/February, 1988, p. 5.
4. J Hanlon, *Beggar Your Neighbours,* Catholic Institute for International Relations, London, 1986, p. 157.

5. *Ibid.*, p. 158.
6. Marcum, *op. cit.*, p. 6.
7. W Steenkamp, *Borderstrike: South Africa into Angola,* Butterworth, Durban, 1983, p. 5.
8. *Loc. cit.*
9. For a detailed discussion of military influence in this period, see D. Geldenhuys, *The Diplomacy of Isolation,* Macmillan, Johannesburg, 1984, p.83.
10. Bridgland, p. 276.
11. *Loc. cit.*
12. F. Toase, "The South African Army: The Campaign in South West Africa/ Namibia since 1966," in I. Beckett and J. Pimlott, (eds), *Armed Forces and Modern Counter-Insurgency,* Croom Helm, London, 1985, p. 214.
13. One of Britain's foremost experts on guerrilla warfare, Nick Downie, formerly in the British SAS and now a war correspondent who has either fought in, or covered, numerous insurgencies, maintained that Unita and Polisario were the two most competent guerrilla organisations he has experienced. The worst, he said, were ZANLA and the *Mujahedin.* Conversations with the author, 1985, after Downie had returned from making a film on Unita.
14. Hanlon, *op. cit.*, p. 159, quoting from Dos Santos's 1982 New Year message.
15. M Holness, "Angola: the Struggle Continues," in P Johnson and D Martin, (eds), *Destructive Engagement,* Zimbabwe Publishing, Harare, 1986, p. 100.
16. *Ibid.*, p. 101.
17. For an account of this alleged plan from a well-informed source, see S Jenkins, "America and South Africa," *The Economist,* 30 March 1985, pp. 18-22.
18. *Ibid.*, pp. 20-21.
19. H-R Heitman, *South African War Machine*, Central News Agency, Johannesburg, 1985, p. 152. Heitman, a SADF citizen force officer, generally reflects the official South African viewpoint.
20. *Ibid.*, p. 151.
21. Holness, *op. cit.*, p. 102, quoting the *Financial Mail*, Johannesburg, 13 January 1984.
22. *Ibid.*, p. 105. For a South African version of the raid, see A Soule, G Dixon and R Richards, *The Wynand du Toit Story,* Strydom, Melville, 1987.
23. Bridgland, p. 470.
24. K Campbell, *Southern Africa in Soviet Foreign Policy,* Adelphi Paper No. 227, International Institute for Strategic Studies (IISS), London, 1987/8, p. 11.
25. *Loc. cit.*
26. *Ibid.*, p. 10.
27. Holness, p. 106.
28. Bridgland, pp. 462-63.
29. Marcum, pp. 8-9.
30. Campbell, *op. cit.*, p. 15.
31. Bridgland, p. 468.
32. See *Strategic Survey 1986-1987,* IISS, London, 1987, p. 189.
33. Intelligence briefing, Jamba, 21 August 1986.
34. Bridgland, p. 468.
35. Campbell, p. 61; Marcum, p.6. Campbell offers the lower figure.
36. See Fn 33. Also, P. Moorcraft, "A New Heart for the UNITA Army," *Jane's Defence Weekly,* 13 September 1986.
37. Author's interviews with Unita officers, Jamba, August 1986.
38. For example, during a three-month period in the northeastern and southeastern parts of Afghanistan and the adjoining tribal areas of Pakistan in 1984, the author was repeatedly told about the Russian use of chemical weapons, but no evidence was ever produced.

39. Campbell, p. 10.
40. Campbell, *loc. cit.*, suggests the first figure while Marcum, p. 11, indicates the second estimate.
41. South African sources emphasised that a large number of Cubans were involved on the ground during the bitter fighting around Cuito Cuanavale, but US intelligence experts denied this. See *Strategic Survey*, 1987-1988, IISS, London, 1988, p. 193.
42. The original version of this controversial article appeared in the *Paris-Match* and a translation was reprinted in the Johannesburg *Star*, see *The Star* (weekly edition), 18 March 1988. Savimbi later said the interview was distorted, and General Malan cut off *The Star* and and its sister newspapers from all contact with his department.
43. S O'Dwyer-Russell, "South Africans turn to Israel over 'Hidden War' in Angola," *The Sunday Telegraph*, 11 November 1987.
44. M Urban, "Namibian Mutiny over Orders to Join UNITA," *The Independent*, 20 November 1987. The SADF denied reports of mutinies, but acknowledged that 47 members of one battalion had been discharged, and that 27 members of the other had protested about the way they were being utilised.
45. R Dowden, "Argentina Sells Mirage Aircraft to South Africa," *The Independent*, 9 June 1988.
46. The official Angolan News Agency, quoted in R Dowden, "UNITA Claims Capture of Vital Angolan Town," *The Independent*, 27 January 1988.
47. *Jane's Defence Weekly*, 19 March 1988.
48. P Godwin, "Secret Talks on the Angolan War," *The Sunday Times*, 13 March 1988.
49. T Allen-Mills, "South Africa Moves Deep into Angola," *The Independent*, 23 March 1988; "The War Continies Despite Peace Talks," *Southscan*, 27 March 1988.
50. V Brittain, "Cuban Steps up Role in Angolan Fighting," *The Guardian*, 6 June 1988.
51. For an interesting background to the negotiations, see P. Vale, "The Lesson of Cuito: SADF Can't just Shoot their Way to Luanda," *Weekly Mail*, Johannesburg, 22 April 1988; and A. Robinson, "South Africa in a Political Whirlpool," *Financial Times*, 15 March 1988.
52. Godwin, *op. cit.*
53. As quoted in *The Independent*, 6 May 1988.
54. J Spence, *The Soviet Union, the Third World and Southern Africa*, the South African Institute of International Affairs, Johannesburg, 1988, p.28.
55. C Toomey, "Hard Labour Awaits Cuba's War Veterans," *The Sunday Times*, 22 January 1989.
56. F Bridgland, "Savimbi: Fallen Idol of Angola," *The Sunday Telegraph*, 12 March 1989.

11

Namibia (1976-1989)

Ambiguous colony

Namibia was not, of course, formally an Afrikaner colony, but rather a territory illegally occupied by South Africa. Pretoria not only kept a large army there, in contravention of the original mandate, but also used the vassal state as a forward base to send its legions into Angola, Zambia and Botswana. If Namibia fitted a little awkwardly into the mould of "colonial" war, it also differed from the destabilisation programme imposed upon the frontline states. And yet it was an important component of destabilisation for two reasons: firstly, it was a base for regional destabilisation, and, secondly, at least according to some critics, Pretoria had scheduled the independent Namibia for neo-colonial dependency. Whatever the future holds, from 1976-89 Namibia was a crucial element of Pretoria's defensive *glacis*. Indeed, as far as many Afrikaner conservatives in both Namibia and South Africa were concerned, SADF power in the territory was *the* key to survival of the entire white laager.

It had been a cliché of southern African politics to assume that, when the thumbscrews came, to stave off real sanctions, Pretoria would have had to free either Namibia or Nelson Mandela. Major constraints in 1988-89—the war in Angola, international diplomacy and the ailing condition of both prisoners—forced Pretoria to make concessions on both.

The bush war burgeons

After the 1976 retreat, Pretoria desperately tried to consolidate its position on the Angolan/Namibian border. Economically, South Africa struggled to keep the Cunene river hydro-electric project alive. And, on the military front, she attempted to sanitise the border. Politically, the internal Namibian anti-SWAPO front had to be built up.

The northern section of Namibia was fortified during 1976. White Namibian reservists in the citizen force and commando units were activated. Small towns such as Ruacana and Ondangwa were transformed into sprawling stockaded garrisons. A string of new military bases was established, and airfields were constructed for the expanding fleet of helicopters and fighters sent from South Africa. Thousands of Ovambo villagers were moved as a kilometre-wide, free-fire zone was instituted along the defoliated "cutline", the Angolan/Namibian border.(1)

Despite its messy internecine fighting, SWAPO did its best to exploit its alliance with the Cuban and MPLA forces. During 1976 the number of guerrilla attacks and skirmishes were more than three times the total for the previous ten years.(2) PLAN insurgents began to probe the white farming areas south of the Ovambo homeland. On 30 June 1976 defence headquarters in Pretoria claimed that 26 guerrillas had been killed in the previous 20 days. At the same time, South Africa proclaimed martial law in the "operational area" of Ovamboland. Zambia, meanwhile, complained to the UN that SADF forces based in the Caprivi were repeatedly violating Zambian territory in their operations against PLAN.

By August 1976, the SADF's strength in Namibia stood, it was claimed, at 50,000.(3) The UN Council for Namibia put the figure at 45,000. The total was said to consist of a combat force of 12,800 (one motorised infantry brigade, one specialist army COIN brigade, a police COIN unit and a field artillery squadron); 5,000 men in support, including three light anti-aircraft batteries and a paratroop battalion; and a logistical tail of 26,300 men and 3,000 air force personnel maintaining two squadrons of Impala 11 and Mirage jets. In addition, there were an unspecified number of helicopter squadrons.(4)

That was the SADF shield. Behind it, Pretoria tried to sharpen its blunt political sword: the internal option. That had two edges. Firstly, the Namibianisation of the indigenous forces. Ethnic units had already been established: the "Bushman battalion" (1974) and units from the Ovambo, Kavango and East Caprivi peoples (1975). White reserve units were beefed up. From 1977 onwards multi-ethnic units were formed. The goal was to establish a Namibian army loyal to Pretoria. But there had to be local politicians up front. That was more important than the cutting edge. So, secondly, during 1975 a gaggle of politicians had been meeting at the old German Gymnasium (Turnhalle) in Windhoek. From the Turnhalle conference evolved the bones of the internal political "settlement". It was decided that South West Africa—Namibia was not a popular name with many of the Turnhalle delegates—should become an independent, unitary state, but the old apartheid system of the three-tier government would remain. Some of the more obvious and obnoxious aspects of discrimination, such as bans on mixed marriages and petty apartheid in restaurants, would have to go, and soon. But shibboleths, such as separate schools, would not. This the three-tier government would ensure. The tiers, local government, black homelands and white areas, and on top a national administrative tier comprising a National Assembly and a Ministerial Council, would depend upon consensus in this council. The council would represent all the 11 ethnic groups, but each group, and most crucially the whites, would have a veto. And behind the clumsy, complex, bureaucratic facade Pretoria and the SADF ruled.

In the real world outside, two UN Resolutions, 385 and 435, provided the bases for an international settlement. Resolution 385 was adopted with Western support on 30 January 1976. This insisted that South Africa should withdraw its administration and that UN-supervised elections should lead to Namibian independence. Further details, enshrined in Resolution 435, about the timing, the size and deployment of UN monitoring forces, and the electoral and constitutional processes, became the grist for a decade of haggling. There was one massive obstacle: until Pretoria had little other economic or military alternative, it would stall, with every trick in the diplomatic book, on a UN-style transfer to independence because SWAPO would probably win. Hence followed ten years of chicanery, of Namibianisation as futile as America's Vietnamisation, because Pretoria adamantly rejected what it called "the red flag in Windhoek".

Washington did not want any more red flags flying either. During Henry Kissinger's whirlwind safaris to Africa in 1976, he embroiled Pretoria in his plans to set up pro-Western black moderates in Salisbury and Windhoek before it was too late. The internal settlements in both states were carefully manipulated by Pretoria once Kissinger left office. By March 1977, the dominant figure in the Turnhalle conference was not a pliant black, but a tough white, the former deputy leader of the National Party in Namibia, Dirk Mudge. Was Mudge to be a second Ian Smith? Pretoria provocatively dangled the possibility of another UDI in the air. In the same month, the five Western members, at that time, of the UN Security Council—Britain, Canada, France, West Germany and the US—formed an ambassadorial "contact group". These important trading partners of South Africa, despite their economic clout, were to be strung along for years. As long as Pretoria was seen to be talking to the contact group about the UN route, sanctions could be put on the back-burner. That suited both sides perfectly.

Meanwhile, South Africa dug in. In August 1977 military activity in the whole of the territory was centralised in Windhoek. Previously operations had been decentralised, first to the SAP, then to the regional control of the SADF in the large military base at Grootfontein. Some writers maintained that this marked a new phase of more aggressive "break-their-bones" operations in Angola and Namibia and a down-playing of the hearts-and-mind approach.(5) More likely, it was an organisational preparation for the establishment of the South West African Territory Force (SWATF) and the enhancement of the Windhoek politicians' image as leaders with their own army, just like Nujoma and PLAN. Later (theoretical) control of the local police (SWAP) was also devolved to Windhoek, as were various administrative functions previously transferred to Pretoria. In fact, the (South African) general officer commanding the SWATF (when it was formally inaugurated in 1980) doubled as the commander of all SADF forces in Namibia. Pretoria's generals still ran the show, although Namibianisation of the army did mean that more black and white locals became cannon fodder in the Angolan frontline. And centralisation of command and control of all elements of the burgeoning security apparatus did improve efficiency.

A prime political component of the entrenchment of South African power was the appointment of Judge Marthinus Steyn as administrator-general on 1 September 1978. While the Turnhalle politicians continued to squabble, Steyn repealed some apartheid legislation, such as the hated pass laws. Also, he relaxed some of the draconian security provisions of the 1972 emergency proclamation in Ovamboland and its extension throughout northern Namibia in May 1976, although the Terrorism Act and the sections on solitary confinement remained intact.

Namibian nationalists were not appeased. Middle-of-the-road political parties such as the Namibia National Front and the influential black Lutheran Church leadership edged further away from the Turnhalle politicians grouped in the Democratic Turnhalle Alliance (DTA) and sidled towards SWAPO's position. During the latter part of 1977 larger combat units of PLAN fighters infiltrated Ovamboland. The SADF admitted that the security forces were involved in an average of 100 clashes a month. PLAN's strength then stood at an estimated 2,000 guerrillas in Angola, 1,400 in Zambia and 300 operational inside Namibia.(6)

For all the patent weaknesses of the internal option, it did confirm a

U-turn in Pretoria's strategy. Integration with South Africa, permanent direct rule and bantustan Balkanisation had all been tacitly dropped. The skeleton of Namibian independence had taken on real flesh, even in the cold corridors of power in Pretoria. Yes, the ever-changing blueprint still implied indirect South African rule of a putative independent, confederal, white-dominated Namibia, and, yes, *de facto* SADF control was intended, but the idea of some kind of independence greater than, say, the Transkei—and that automatically meant excluding SWAPO rule—began to percolate through the white South African Establishment.

Throughout 1978 Pretoria bargained with the contact group about a transition deal. Now was added the issue of Walvis Bay. SWAPO insisted that the area, the only deep-water port on the 1,000-mile coastline, was an integral part of Namibia. A former British enclave, it had been annexed to the old Cape Colony in 1884, and hence, with some legal justification, was claimed as South African territory. Like Gibraltar, Hong Kong and the Falklands, it was a small colonial legacy which was destined to divert much diplomatic energy.

Both Pretoria and SWAPO tended to talk and fight at the same time: the more summitry, the more bloodshed. PLAN was very active in 1978. Hit-and-run attacks were stepped up in Ovamboland. In one incident, 119 mission school students were abducted across the Angolan border. Such abductees (and volunteers) were usually offered the same bait—university scholarships abroad which often ended up as military conscription "for the duration". In February 1978 the Ovambo minister of health was assassinated. A month later Clemens Kapuuo, a Herero chief who was a founder of the DTA and a prominent non-SWAPO contender for leadership of the country, was gunned down. South Africa claimed that SWAPO was about to set off a wave of such assassinations and economic sabotage. Administrator-General Steyn was now given sweeping new powers of arrest and detention. Much more was to come.

In May the SADF launched the first major planned incursion into Angola to destroy SWAPO bases: Operation Reindeer. There was, apparently, great debate in the cabinet about the risks.(7) The doves warned of the danger of sanctions, but the generals persuaded a vacillating Vorster. Reindeer consisted of three sub-operations: an airborne force, roughly a battalion, struck a PLAN base codenamed "Moscow", near Cassinga, some 160 miles inside Angola; a mechanised force attacked the "Vietnam" camp, some 18 miles north of the border, near Chetequera; and a heliborne force swept through a series of small bases east of Chetequera.

The military had invested considerable political capital in the success of Operation Reindeer. Although it was commanded by Major General Ian Gleeson, the army chief, Lieutenant General Constand Viljoen, flew into the thick of the fighting, in the tradition of the Boer war chieftains. The SADF's toughest commander, Colonel Jan Breytenbach, known to his men as the "Brown Man" because of his deep tan, commanded the Cassinga attack. Amid frequent bouts of chaos on both sides, PLAN put up fierce resistance. During the fighting at Cassinga on 4 May—which involved female guerrillas in combat—an action described by a South African journalist, who was also a citizen force officer, detailed the fate of a male insurgent who had stationed himself under a bus. The South African paratroopers had trouble dislodging him:

> After offering a spirited resistance he solved the problem himself by running out of ammunition, after which Swart [a SADF paratrooper] says, 'he threw his rifle out and said: "You can't shoot me, I'm a prisoner!"' Legal niceties tend to blur in a fighting situation, however, and an exasperated paratrooper shot him dead in the same instant.(8)

The belated intervention of FAPLA and Cuban forces almost turned the operation into a disaster. According to a semi-official South African account: "Had the opposing armour been handled less ineptly, the operation could well have turned into a costly and embarrassing disaster. As it was, enemy tanks were actually on the landing zones as the last of the force was lifted out by Pumas." (9)

The almost unchallenged South African air power was crucial. Canberra and Buccaneer aircraft had bombed the main bases before the infantry and armour went in, and helicopters were on standby for evacuation. Considerable amounts of equipment were captured as well as valuable intelligence documents. Pretoria claimed that 1,000 PLAN insurgents were killed and 200 captured. SWAPO counter-claimed that most of the dead were noncombatant refugees. In SWAPO and some UN chronicles, Cassinga is rated as a massacre, the moral equivalent of My Lai.

Certainly, Operation Reindeer was a severe military setback for PLAN. Previously SWAPO had thought that its bases deep inside Angola were safe from SADF depredations because of the political and military cover provided by their hosts. From now on PLAN, literally, went underground. The classic Soviet-style bases with parade grounds, formal buildings and elaborate trench systems, all too visible from the air, were transformed into the Vietnamese style of heavily camouflaged base areas.

The SADF changed its operational techniques too. Invaluable lessons had been learnt. The line separating disaster from victory had been thin, even though only six South Africans had been killed. It was, for example, the first real parachute attack (consisting almost entirely of reservists) carried out by the SADF and "probably the largest of its kind in Africa since World War Two".(10) And perhaps the last large SADF paradrop. Dropping troops into the thick of battle from lumbering transport aircraft needed reappraisal as the Angolan-based forces developed their missile screens.

Reindeer was significant because it marked the SADF's entry into large-scale semi-conventional warfare. It was a precedent for the expansion of the war into Angola with sophisticated conventional incursions. New weapons were tested, notably in the field of artillery and armoured personnel carriers. Penetrations grew deeper and contacts with Angolan and Cuban forces became commonplace. Reindeer confirmed the shift from a small COIN war against insurgents in the 1970s to the big conventional battles, backed by superpower arsenals, of the 1980s. Reindeer also had important political ramifications in Pretoria. The "wets", to borrow a Thatcherite phrase, had lost. Despite the preachifying by the foreign ministry about sanctions devils, no hell-fire descended. The SADF thus won the political and military battles. So did the defence minister, P W Botha, who needed a fillip after the failures in Angola in 1976.

SWAPO regrouped. An attack was planned on the Caprivi's capital, Katima Mulilo. The Caprivi, named after General Count Georg Leo von Caprivi di Caprara di Montecuccoli, Chancellor of Germany when the territory was acquired from Britain, was a finger of land which the Second Reich tried to stretch out to touch German East Africa (Tanganyika). This strategic crossroads borders on Angola and Zambia in the north and Botswana in the south, while Kasangula, at its extreme eastern tip, is the point where Zambia, Botswana and Zimbabwe intersect. Here is perhaps the shortest border in the world: Botswana and Zambia touch for just 45 metres. Katima was, therefore, a handy international flashpoint to retaliate for Cassinga. At precisely 1.15 am on 23 August 1978 a single 122mm Redeye rocket landed on Katima's military base. More than 20 others followed in quick succession. Then the Zambian army joined in PLAN's rocket attack with a few 82mm mortar shells. One of PLAN's rockets smashed into a SADF barracks. Ten South African soldiers were killed and ten were wounded, more than had died in Operation Reindeer.

Reindeer had been a bombshell which landed smack in the middle of the contact group's credibility. The Western diplomats regrouped too. On 30 August Secretary-General Kurt Waldheim presented the official UN peace plan. It called for a UN force of 7,500 troops, with civilian back-up, to ensure free elections, which were to be held within one year. The UN would monitor a sequence of events: end of hostilities, repeal of apartheid laws, release of detainees and a return of refugees; then "free and fair" elections; adoption of a new constitution; and, finally, independence as the constitution came into force. This was later formalised as UN Security Council Resolution 435.

Then came the big shake-out in the South African government. On 20 September 1978 John Vorster announced his retirement and the cabinet's decision to go it alone in Namibia. An internal election would be held before the end of 1978. A week later a hawk on Namibia, P W Botha, became prime minister. The arch-dove on Namibia, Pik Botha, despite his tremendous popularity with the white electorate, came third in the premier stakes. (11)

The internal settlement plan, a slap in the face for both the UN and the contact group, caused a serious problem for the Western powers: the African states now bayed for a sanctions showdown. Pik Botha signalled the cabinet's hard line in mid-October when the foreign ministers of the Western contact group travelled to Pretoria for urgent talks. With the SADF chief of staff next to him, Pik Botha stated: "If it comes to a choice between the friendship of the world and internal stability [especially in Namibia] then we shall have to choose internal stability." The internal option was rammed into top gear.

In the December 1978 poll, the DTA, led by Mudge, won 80% of the poll in a 75% turnout. The DTA took 41 of the 50 seats, with the Afrikaner-dominated AKTUR (Action Front for the Retention of Turnhalle Principles) group taking six. Critics alleged the result was rigged as part of Pretoria's master plan, which included a Rhodesian carbon copy the following year.(12) SWAPO and the Patriotic Front boycotted both elections. In both cases lavish election rallies, with free food, drink and T-shirts, were funded by South Africa. In both cases the voting turnout was exaggerated. The Pretoria-flavoured internal parties both won landslides, although neither result was recognised by any government except the one which manipulated the exercises. So say the critics, although both elections and, in particular, the Rhodesian poll, approximated to the Western models more closely than 90% of other, internationally-recognised elections in Africa. Whether either election was "free and fair", even in the context of civil war, was, however, irrelevant. Without SWAPO (and the PF) neither made diplomatic sense.

Pretoria knew that. South Africa had gone a long way towards accepting the UN position. So had SWAPO in giving up its claim to power without first competing in an election, and by making concessions over the status of Walvis Bay. Pretoria wanted to "buy time" for the DTA to build up credibility as a rival to SWAPO when the day of reckoning, UN elections, finally came. But was Pretoria buying or losing time? South Africa's international position was weakening. The sanctions bandwagon was starting to roll. And South Africa's oil supplies were as shaky as its main supplier, the Shah's Iran. Nevertheless, in Pretoria's blinkered eyes, the December poll was a triumph. Now it was time to do the Namibian waltz again with the Western Five, while trying to bring off another internal coup in Rhodesia.

Anti-apartheid critics continued to accuse South Africa of total insincerity in its negotiations. In this perspective, the hawks versus doves split on such issues as destabilisation in general, and Namibia in particular, was merely a device to confuse and mislead foreign opponents, especially the hopeful right-wingers who were always looking for "change" in Pretoria's hard line. But such divisions did exist, as revelations about Renamo, for example, were later to confirm. Most Afrikaner leaders intensely disliked being treated as pariahs, whether it was by being denied visits by rugby teams or diplomatic status. Pretoria desperately wanted to be accepted by the Western world, to which it believed it naturally belonged. So there was always a genuine base to the Namibian negotiations. Nor did Pretoria want sanctions, even though in the 1970s they were not considered a major threat. But the government also did not want to leave Namibia, for political and military reasons, as well as the fact that Namibia's large deposits of uranium, diamonds, phosphates and other minerals made a substantial contribution to South Africa's economy. Time was needed to denude these deposits. In short, a balance of genuine desire for rapprochement was always mixed with cynical filibuster. South African diplomats, often the clumsiest representatives of an unsaleable regime, became Machiavellian princes over Namibia. It was partly a matter of longevity and local knowledge. Foreign diplomats changed jobs and foreign ministers came and went according to whim and electoral fortune, but Pik Botha, the longest-serving foreign minister in the "Western" world, was always there. So were a group of his able lieutenants.

Given, then, a background of genuine desire for an improved entente with the contact group, the hawks and doves typology must be understood as a crude generalisation. A kaleidoscope of sometimes changing views rattled around the Afrikaner leadership. They only *looked* as if their ideas and personalities were frozen in stone. And there were contradictions. For example, a hawk on defence issues, such as P W Botha, was also considered to be a relative liberal on the question of restoring the franchise to the coloured community. Even the wets, traditionally associated with foreign affairs, would give an instinctive, hard-line response when basic security issues were threatened.

The doves who were pushing for an international settlement in Namibia were forced on the defensive by the prime minister's angry condemnation in February 1979 of both Waldheim and the Western Five. P W Botha accused them of duplicity because, he said, they had agreed, behind South Africa's back, to allow SWAPO to have its own bases inside Namibia during the projected ceasefire period. He said also that the military component of the UN Transition Assistance Group (UNTAG) would not now, as previously agreed, be required to monitor the restriction of SWAPO troops in bases outside Namibia. Negotiations were to be put on ice for five months. In March 1979 Pik Botha, in a major speech, developed his chief's favourite theme: a constellation of southern African states. Pretoria would solve its regional disputes without meddling foreigners. This "sub-continental solidarity" would include seven to ten African states south of the Cunene/Zambezi line. It would be a military alliance as much as a political and economic pact. Pretoria's new Maginot line would include Namibia and Rhodesia, but ruled by moderates. As if to enforce this defence perimeter, the SADF launched a series of raids into Angola and Zambia in the same month. And SADF troop levels in Namibia were reportedly boosted from 20,000 to 30,000.(13)

Again, the internal option was fired up. The DTA-dominated National Assembly was given extra power over fiscal affairs. As a sop to the right, there was yet another crackdown on SWAPO's internal representatives. Over half the territory and 80% of the population were placed under some form of martial law.(14) Nevertheless, a rash of right-wing extremism broke out. Neo-fascist white supremacists compiled a death-list that targeted black church leaders.(15) The Afrikaner-led AKTUR was also up in arms because Mudge's DTA wanted to whittle away the powers of the AKTUR-controlled old legislative assembly, which ran white affairs. Mudge made it clear that the retention of apartheid laws and the constant intervention of Pretoria undermined his credibility. The puppets were roaring. Mudge was to prove too independent for Pretoria's liking. Administrator-General Steyn appeared to go along with Mudge on the necessity for curbing exclusive white control of the best amenities. And the military were—apparently—averse to Steyn.(16) In August, Professor Gerrit Viljoen, a "super-Afrikaner" and head of the Broederbond, replaced Steyn. He could sort out the right-wing. P W Botha, in a typical authoritarian flourish, did not consult his own department of foreign affairs on such a sensitive appointment.(17)

Viljoen had a tough job: he would need "the balance of a ballerina, the diplomacy of Solomon, the stamina of a long-distance runner and the hide of an ox".(18) The new administrator-general seemed over-anxious to placate the conservatives. He revived the notion of the three-tier government which would allow whites to hang on to their segregationist selfishness. Namibia's numerous internal parties, forever changing, coalescing and splitting, were once again in disarray. The multiethnic DTA wanted a strong central government, increasingly free of apartheid, so as to outbid SWAPO. Viljoen, as viceroy, represented both the iron (and dead) hand of Pretoria and a return to the old local white domination of the ethnic hotchpotch. Did he want the bantustans again or rule by the administrator-general: one man, one government (almost) or one-man government?

In August 1979 South Africa and the Western Five resumed talks. President Neto of Angola had proposed a demilitarised zone (DMZ) extending for 30 miles on both sides of the border as part of the transition. This was taken up by the important Commonwealth conference held in Lusaka in the same month. SWAPO was pressurised to drop its demands for bases inside Namibia, while the frontline states, not the UN, would offer to monitor SWAPO's bases in Angola and Zambia. Pretoria gave a cautious nod to the DMZ idea.

The war in Namibia ground on. PLAN, now with an estimated 8,000 men, but losing 90 a month in battle (according to Pretoria), kept up the pressure. In one dramatic raid, PLAN knocked out the Ruacana power station. Large parts of Namibia were blacked out.

From the August Commonwealth conference through the Lancaster House talkathon to the February 1980 elections, attention in southern Africa was focused on Rhodesia. Britain was concerned above all to throw off the UDI albatross; the US was absorbed in presidential elections. The sanctions threat wound down. Pretoria, buoyed up by a gold price of $600 a fine ounce, egged on the DTA, and further Namibianised the war effort, while confidently expecting that Muzorewa would score a victory in the second round of the Rhodesian elections.

Mugabe won. Pretoria was shattered. So how could Mudge, a white former National Party leader, do what Muzorewa, once an internationally accepted black nationalist, could not? The ghost of the luckless bishop was destined to haunt Windhoek for years. So Pretoria resumed negotiations with the West, particularly on the minutiae of the DMZ. In a 60-mile wide, 700-mile long DMZ, 7,500 UN troops would be insufficient, argued the South African government, which also wanted to retain 40 SADF bases in the Namibian section of the DMZ.

SWAPO was cock-a-hoop over Mugabe's ascendancy. PLAN geared up its campaign. In May 1980 a SWAPO mortar attack destroyed several military planes at Ondangwa. White civilian and military casualties mounted. Armed convoys were needed on the northern roads. The operational zone edged closer to the capital. Anti-apartheid sources claimed that the 75,000-strong "occupation" force, because "it was hard-pressed to retain control", fell back on "terrorist tactics". "Evidence of indiscriminate brutality, including barbarous torture and mutilation, was coming to light."(19)

There was no mistaking the ferocity of Operation Sceptic (Smokeshell) launched on 9 June 1980. SWAPO leaders had declared 1980 to be a "year of action". They got it with Sceptic, the South Africans' biggest ground and air operation since 1945. The target was a well-entrenched, sprawling (65-square-kilometre) PLAN base in southern Angola, codenamed "Smokeshell". A South African officer described a section of the task force as it prepared to cross the border:

> Early on the morning of June 8 Battle Group 61 began to form up in order of march. It was an awesome sight to the young troops. Drawn up in lines were scores of huge Ratels, homely high-reaching Buffels, Eland 'Noddy cars' (as the mechanised force infantrymen had taken to calling the little vehicles) with their long 90mm guns, 140mm artillery-pieces hooked on to massive tractors, Unimog ambulances, ungainly recovery vehicles festooned with cranes and cables, fuel-bowsers grunting along like pregnant elephants; there had been few such concentrations of war machines on the border in anyone's experience.(20)

Apparently, Sceptic was originally intended as a short raid, but it grew into a massive three-week operation. SWAPO was well dug in. PLAN deployed its light anti-aircraft (AA) guns, especially 14.5mm single and 23mm twin guns, in a ground defence role. One ZU-23-2 knocked out several Ratel infantry combat vehicles. After a brief artillery barrage, three mechanised groups swept in. The infantry normally remained in their Ratels, de-bussing only to deal with stubborn opposition. Close air support was provided by Impalas firing cannon and rockets. Helicopters were used as additional transport and for casevacs (casualty evacuations). The SADF, according to the South African version, clashed with two semi-mechanised PLAN columns. Ground armour and air strikes destroyed several BRDM-2 scout cars and BTR-152 armoured personnel carriers (APCs). A FAPLA mechanised force was also drawn in. The Angolans brought down at least one SADF chopper.(21) The South Africans claimed to have blown up 50 tons of enemy equipment and captured approximately 250 tons, including SAM missiles, AA guns and APCs. For the loss of 17 men, the SADF also claimed 360 PLAN fighters killed.(22) Pretoria insisted that it had wiped out PLAN's nerve centre. Whatever the exact truth, Sceptic, the first real armoured infantry operation for the SADF, was certainly a serious military setback for SWAPO.

It was time to pump up the DTA again. On 1 July 1980 a Council of Ministers, with Mudge in the chair, was sworn in. Now Mudge & Co. had the authority to administer 20 government departments, including a department of defence whose first act was to promulgate a law establishing compulsory military service from 1981. On 1 August the South West African Territory Force was formally inaugurated. Mudge now had his own army. On 1 September control of the police (SWAP) passed to the National Assembly.

The monotonous rhythm of South African diplomacy in the territory jangled the nerves: bash SWAPO, boost Mudge, and then talk to the UN. Pretoria, however, continued to make the (not unreasonable) point that so long as SWAPO activities were funded by the UN and SWAPO was recognised as the sole authentic representative of the Namibian people, how on earth could the UN claim to be impartial monitors of an election? South Africa raised the ante: the government began to insist that in future talks the DTA should be represented, and separately from the Pretoria delegation. This proposal made little headway. At home also the DTA fared badly. In mid-November, in second-tier elections, AKTUR won 56% of the white vote. The DTA ended up with seven seats to AKTUR's 11, exactly what it had before. These elections were seen as a test of white opinion. If the multiethnic DTA won, it would show that the whites were ready for the principle of one man, one vote in a unitary state. They were not.

Pretoria also raised the stakes by hinting that it wanted Unita involved in any international settlement. This gambit was possibly part of a rumoured "separate deal" with Luanda. Mudge had called the Lancaster House agreement a "fiasco". Pretoria heartily agreed. So why not an "international" deal that excluded the troublesome Commonwealth, UN and Western Five? A bargain with Angola? Pretoria would drop Unita if the MPLA withdrew support for SWAPO. Unita

PLATE 11.1 Soldier with rifle/grenade-launcher; Bushmen troops patrolling in Caprivi; SADF patrol searching for SWAPO guerillas in northern Namibia; mounted unit, Ovamboland.

would be afforded some regional autonomy in central and southern Angola, the Cubans could be progressively removed, and Pretoria would help with rebuilding the economy, the Benguela railway in particular. And somehow the Angolans were led to believe that the Thatcher government backed this bilateral bargain.(23)

Namibia has always been an imbroglio. With at least 40 competing Namibian political parties and eight different armies involved in the fighting, plus a host of international bodies and concerned, but usually self-serving, foreign governments, it was bound to be. Behind the web of international intrigue, what was the real nature of the conflict in the heartland of the struggle, northern Namibia?

The nature of the war

SWAPO's war has varied according to the terrain and ethnic affiliation. The SADF throughout most of the 1980s had restabilised the Caprivi. Kaokoland, because of its barren deserts and minimal population, was used as an occasional infiltration route, and for mining the main (gravel) roads. Kavango, partly because of its relative economic development and tribal factors, was less politicised by SWAPO than Ovamboland, PLAN's natural stamping ground.

The SADF always claimed that SWAPO had remained stuck in the initial "terrorist" stage of insurgency, but large groups of trained guerrillas regularly infiltrated into the white farming areas, often displaying great military skill, particularly in anti-tracking procedures. Tactics included regular ambushes of SADF patrols, frequent attacks on bantustan officials, sabotage of installations and railways, and occasional bombings in urban areas. Despite the difficulties of carrying mines long distances, PLAN specialised in mine warfare, including the techniques of tunnelling under or lifting sections of tarred roads. Anti-personnel mines were often laid alongside anti-vehicle mines to hamper mine-clearance. The SADF, with its panoply of sophisticated mine-proofed vehicles, usually escaped heavy casualties. The civilians suffered. In 1980, for example, 220 Ovambos were killed and 256 injured by mines.(24).

SWAPO often avoided direct assaults on the SADF: stand-off bombardments with mortars and rockets became another speciality. PLAN's arsenal comprised the usual Eastern bloc medley of AK-47s and RPG-7s. The SKS carbine was deployed because it could fire rifle grenades. Besides 60mm and 80mm mortars, and 122mm rocket launchers, some insurgents, especially in PLAN's special forces, carried

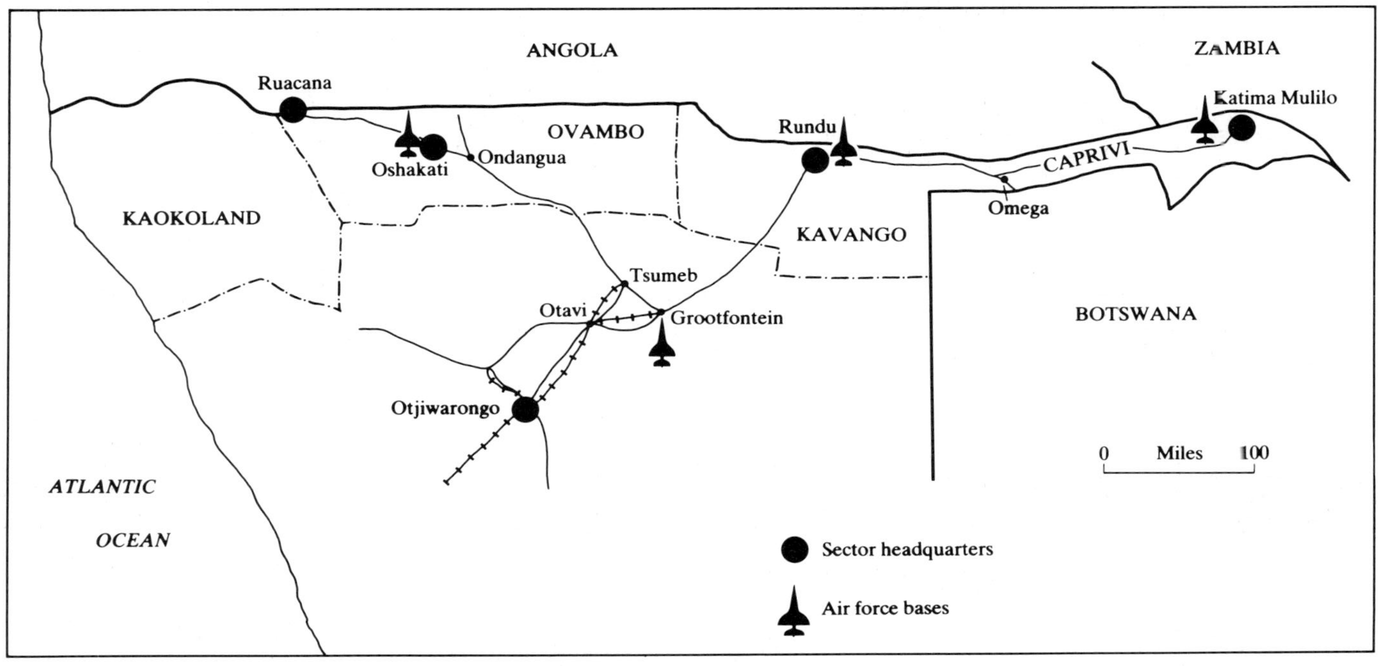

MAP 11 Namibia/South West Africa: "The Operational Area"

PLATE 11.2 Hearts and Minds: SADF brings water and tobacco to remote Ovahimba people in Kaokoland.

SAM-7 AA missile launchers. From the mid-1980s the Dragunov sniping rifle made an appearance. (25)

In response, the SADF's COIN strategy was extensive and expensive. In the 1980s, the cost of the war reached perhaps R4 million a day.(26) As noted earlier, estimates of troop levels varied immensely. On average, the complement was approximately 20,000 to 30,000 SADF personnel plus 22,000 SWATF by the mid-1980s, when Namibian forces were said by Pretoria to have taken over 50% of the SADF's manpower deployment. With logistic back-up and police forces, especially during preparations for big "ops" in Angola, the tally of "occupation" forces could have reached 100,000, a ratio of one man in uniform for every 14 Namibians.(27) By 1988, Pretoria claimed over 11,000 PLAN killed for the loss of approximately 700 members of the security forces.(28) Both sides claimed that their enemy cooked the figures. The SADF tended to discount the very high "accident" figures in the operational area as well as black SWATF casualties. One study, putting white casualties at 2,500 (by the mid-1980s), claimed that as a proportion of the white population the SADF and SWATF lost more than three times the proportionate losses of the Americans in Vietnam.(29) This is an exaggerated view, but so may be the estimates of SWAPO dead: 11,000 deaths in a guerrilla army which has deployed a standing force of between 9,000 and 16,000 is a very high figure. Either SWAPO was able to maintain morale and troop levels to a remarkable degree or Pretoria overestimated the body counts. In total, the war cost at least 20,000 Namibian lives, directly or indirectly. And perhaps 10% of the population went into exile. (30) So, at great cost in lives and treasure, Pretoria erected a massive COIN edifice, which many generals were loath to jettison in order to rebuild another Siegfried line a thousand miles to the south along the Orange river.

The SADF recreated a mirror image of itself in the SWATF—with minor changes in insignia—except that in Namibia the army had far more blacks. A black officer corps was trained at the military college in Okahandja. The same command and control systems operated in the seven military sectors which paralleled the commands in South Africa. The militia-based area force was similar to the South African commando system. The mobile conventional forces, composed of motorised infantry and a parachute battalion, comprised a reaction force similar to the SADF citizen force. And there was a standing force which included six infantry battalions and special forces.(31) The SWATF was supposed to be a unified, multiethnic army, but white elitism and the residual tribalism of the original ethnic battalions undermined, to some extent, efforts to totally integrate the Namibian army. The selective conscription also tended to reinforce ethnicity. In theory, after 1981 all males between 16-25 were liable for call-up (as well as men aged 17-54 for commando duties, although this was not extensively applied). In practice, conscription was not enforced in Ovamboland. Many Namibians, however, were prepared to volunteer for military service because of the pay and privileges. Often the security forces provided the only form of paid employment in the Caprivi and parts of Kavango. One study estimated that as much as 44% of the total buying power of Kavango was generated by the resident SWATF 202 battalion.(32) Some SWAPO supporters crossed the border to avoid conscription, while others apparently attempted to join the SWATF in order to infiltrate it and to gain military experience for later use with PLAN. SADF instructors, however, claimed that their security screening weeded out nearly all these fifth columnists.(33)

Besides ethnic and ideological tensions, traditional inter-service rivalry also intruded, not least between the army and the police. Except for some specialist units, the police and army did not usually share bases. The role of the police became increasingly important, partly because the UN proposals for demilitarisation excluded police forces. Their size and functions, therefore, were increased by Pretoria. Besides a conventional SWAP COIN unit, various other police units were active. A Task Force was set up to counter guerrillas outside the operational area, particularly insurgents who came via Botswana. Two units, the Home Guards (Special Police) and *Koevoet* (Crowbar) became notorious because of their alleged atrocities against civilians. Some army officers tended to be hostile towards *Koevoet* because they felt its activities undermined the SADF's hearts-and-minds programmes.

South African COIN took many forms, from high-tech to terror. Pretoria's intelligence services did everything possible to divide the SWAPO leadership. Agents in Lusaka probably played a role in the mutinies and faction-fighting during the 1970s. Dissidents such as Shipanga and leaders of CANU (the Caprivi African National Union), which had merged with and then left SWAPO, were wooed into the internal fold. Pretoria had hoped to split SWAPO by releasing Toivo ja Toivo in 1984. They anticipated serious friction between him and Nujoma. Amnesties were offered to guerrillas. They were never very successful: in 1985, for example, four PLAN members took up the offer. Captured insurgents, however, were sometimes "turned" and took part in "pseudo" operations, often under the aegis of *Koevoet*. (34) The security police were often successful in buying their way into the pockets, if not the hearts, of a large number of Ovambo informers. Some of these agents became wealthy by local standards. The foolish ones became conspicuous consumers who bought *Cuca* shops and new cars in Ovamboland and were then eliminated by PLAN, while the wiser informers invested discreetly in real estate in Windhoek.(35)

A more direct strategy was counter-terrorism. *Koevoet's* pseudo operations, like those of the Selous Scouts, aroused a great deal of media criticism. Both Namibian and South African churchmen regularly condemned their exploits and accused them of indiscriminately murdering civilians for bounty money (*kopgeld*, literally "head money").(36) The Namibian Bar Council complained that few cases of alleged *Koevoet* crimes reached the courts. When they did, sentences were often derisory. The activities of 32 (Buffalo) Battalion, a special infantry unit largely made up of former FNLA guerrillas led by white Portuguese, South African and Rhodesian officers, were condemned as much as *Koevoet*. Deserters from the battalion offered journalists lurid accounts of atrocities against Ovambo civilians, particularly in southern Angola.(37) A South African military expert, however, commented:

"Among those who know the business, 32 Bn is widely regarded as the premier light infantry unit in the world today."(38) In providing intelligence and reconnaissance for the major operations in Angola, as well as constant search-and-destroy missions against PLAN forward bases and camps, the Buffalo Battalion was a key element in countering SWAPO. *Koevoet* and 32 Battalion accounted for thousands of kills; whether they were all PLAN insurgents is a moot point.

The SADF, often with great efficiency, also conducted the more traditional COIN operations. Its small-unit ground patrols and high-speed, cordon-and-search operations with helicopters, sometimes called "Hawk Ops", were often models of military precision. The topography of Ovamboland, particularly its flatness, discouraged the use of standard measures such as observation points, although imaginative use was made of patrols on horseback and motorbikes. For both political and sound agricultural reasons, the concept of strategic hamlets was not applied as it was in Rhodesia and Portuguese Africa.

Like their colonial counterparts, the SADF emphasised psychological action (PsyAc) or civic action. Besides obvious functions such as protection of convoys and administrative infrastructure, the SADF became a mini-welfare state in the north. Sometimes idealistic, young national servicemen, especially graduates, went into the schools, hospitals and local civil service, (although SWAPO accused the SADF of attacks on mission hospitals and schools). The SADF's PsyAc mixture of genuine idealism and cynical manipulation largely backfired, however. Often, local blacks resented job competition from paternalistic whites in uniform. The PsyAc showcase, the Omega Bushman base in the Caprivi, for example, provided employment for Bushmen, many of whom suffered a great deal from rival ethnic groups in Angola, but the Bushman culture, critics maintained, was being destroyed by the militarisation and racism of their South African mentors. The bogus cultural and nationalist tribal movements, such as Etango in Ovamboland, largely comprised members of the security forces and their relatives. Often civic action, or "social upliftment", as the SADF liked to call it, was simply a means of propping up crumbling bantustan structures. The SADF largely took over the running of the health services in the north and made genuine improvements, but the major reason for the collapse of the medical services (besides SWAPO sabotage) was the inefficiency and the corruption of the ethnic administrations and their ten separate health services. Like all COIN it came back in the end to the political strategy, or lack of it.

Constructive relations: 1981-1984

The political strategy for Namibia grew much tougher at the beginning of 1981 for two reasons. Firstly, Prime Minister P W Botha called an election for April 1981. Election time always meant banging on the military drum. Secondly, Ronald Reagan entered the White House. In Reagan's words, South Africa was a "friendly country", "a country that strategically is essential to the free world in its production of minerals that we must all have". This was sweet music to Pretoria's ears. Dr Chester Crocker, assistant secretary of state for Africa, dealt a new set of cards—the "linkage" of Cuban troop withdrawal to Namibian independence—much to the chagrin of other members of the contact group. Resolution 435 was to be sidestepped or rejigged. In the dying days of the Carter administration, from 7-14 January, all the Namibian poker-players—including for the first time the DTA—met face-to-face. Mudge demanded the removal of the UN's pro-SWAPO bias, an end to the funding of its activities and its observer status at the world body. SWAPO made concessions, and the Western Five asked Mudge whether he would go along with 435 if his objections about the UN bias were resolved. Mudge and Pretoria now backed off; their bluff had been called. But South Africa had manoeuvred its pipsqueak ally to the international conference table. By its lights, the DTA had been transformed into a legitimate and credible player.

In March senior SADF officers, including intelligence officials, visited the US, the first such trip in years. In the same month two other allied delegations pitched up in Washington: Savimbi plus entourage and the DTA. The polecat was tacitly becoming a partner in Reagan's goal of "rolling back" Soviet influence in Africa. Major General Charles Lloyd, the SADF commander in Namibia, started to warn of a build-up of Soviet weaponry in Angola, especially the recent introduction of an early warning radar and a ground-to-air missile system. That threatened air support for SADF incursions into southern Angola. It was a measure of South African arrogance that the installation of an air *defence* system protecting a foreign country after a decade of raids and interventions should be considered a provocative act. Lloyd warned that South Africa had to prepare itself for conventional war against Cuban and Angolan regulars. It soon came.

On 24 August 1981 the SADF launched a massive attack 120 miles into southern Angola. Operation Protea involved a series of incursions by mechanised columns, moving from bases at Ruacana and Ondangwa. The targets were the new radar installations, AA sites and

PLAN strongholds. Serious encounters with FAPLA ensued. Two T-34/85 tanks were knocked out by Ratel-90s in one engagement. In another, a large FAPLA column was destroyed by air strikes. Two Russians were killed and one captured. Pretoria jubilantly held up the captive as proof that SWAPO was being directed by Russians, although it was just as possible that the Soviets were attached to FAPLA. It was, however, frequently impossible to distinguish between FAPLA and PLAN forces as they were often integrated, wearing the same uniforms and carrying similar weapons. The SADF claimed 1,000 FAPLA/PLAN kills, including a number of senior enemy officers, plus the capture of nearly 4,000 tons of modern equipment, including eight T-34 tanks. The raid cost the SADF one helicopter and ten men. In November, another smaller operation, Daisy, penetrated further than any incursion since the 1975-76 invasion. The army pushed forward more than 150 miles north. A mechanised force hit a PLAN regional HQ at Chetequera. During Daisy, FAPLA avoided general contact, but the Angolan air force clashed with South African Mirages. A MiG-21 was shot down. (A second MiG-21 was brought down by two Mirage F-1s in October 1982.)

Protea had justified once more the hawks. Angola's Cunene province remained under SADF occupation. And, although Luanda threatened to invoke its defence treaties with Cuba and the USSR, nothing happened. Protea had inflicted serious reverses on the enemy; now it was convenient to parley again. By the end of 1981 the South African government was hinting that it was prepared to take the 435 route again, without a prior constitutional conference, and to accept the UN peace-keeping role. Pretoria had to make some kind of diplomatic obeisance to Washington's constructive engagement. After the military engagements came the political constructiveness. The US argued that only by working with Pretoria could the SADF be reined in, and the Cubans would then leave. But it was always the proverbial chicken and the egg. Linkage could never work as long the SADF's occupation of southern Angola forced Luanda to turn to Cuban protectors. Washington could never answer the fundamental question: who would protect Luanda if Castro's men left? The French, increasingly out of step with the contact group, suggested that their troops, perhaps with some Portuguese help, could replace the Cubans.

Pretoria made polite noises and no substantive concessions. Nevertheless, off-centre-stage, the right-wing Conservative Party, a breakaway from the National Party, was accusing P W Botha of being a "liberal", a swear-word in conservative Afrikanerdom, and of selling out the whites in Namibia. To make matters worse, the DTA looked as if it was on its final legs. The alliance had suffered defections to the right and, more important, to the left, when its Ovambo president, Peter Kalangula, quit. The National Party had to sell its internal option to the West, the Namibians and to the South African electorate. But nobody wanted to buy the DTA. Meanwhile, via "proximity talks", that is, without the antagonists actually meeting, the contact group tried to deal with Pretoria's attempts to rig the future Namibian constitution. South Africa wanted a system of proportional representation which would give the whites and moderates enough seats in the planned parliament to form a blocking third, which would prevent an alteration of the system by a SWAPO administration.(39) But would Pretoria's allies grab a third of the representation, even in a lop-sided system?

In January 1983 the DTA administration gave up the ghost. Mudge resigned as chairman of the Council of Ministers. Willie van Niekerk, a gynaecologist whose previous claim to fame was a treatise on hermaphrodites, took over direct rule as the new administrator-general. He tried to revive the internal option. The first go, a "state council", was still-born. Eventually, the Multi-Party Conference (MPC), a disparate group of eight fractious parties, including the Afrikaner nationalists and remnants of the DTA, was coaxed into administrative life. Later, three major elements of the MPC walked out, saying that the MPC was merely an anti-SWAPO front funded by Pretoria and right-wing West Germans.(40) The Thirion Commission's report of September 1983 further lambasted the three-tier structure in Namibia for its corrupt and bungling management.

SWAPO, encouraged by the mess in the Augean stables that Windhoek had become, pressed on with the war. In February 1983, as part of the annual rainy season offensive, 1,600 PLAN combatants infiltrated into Namibia.(41) Pik Botha, knowing that the Namibian policy was on the ropes, had met Angolan government leaders in unprecedented direct talks in the Cape Verde islands the previous month. The talks were complicated by Unita's resurgence. The anti-SWAPO war was being sucked into the vortex of the general conflagration in Angola.(42)

Washington pestered Pretoria to pull back its troops from southern Angola and to arrange a 30-day ceasefire. A few days after Pretoria offered a ceasefire, the SADF began a massive operation (Askari) inside Angola (on 6 December 1983). PLAN's and FAPLA's offensive capability was to be weakened before a ceasefire was implemented. Operation Askari led to serious engagements with FAPLA and Cuban armoured units in which the SADF lost 21 men, the highest total for a single operation since the beginning of the war.

On 30 January 1984 a delegation from the SADF's military intelligence directorate, led by its head, Major General Piet van der Westhuizen, met the SWAPO leadership in Lusaka at a discreet meeting convened by Kaunda.(43) The Zambian president had recently asked P W Botha to give Namibia its independence as a "Christmas present". The next day in parliament Botha announced that the SADF had begun its withdrawal from Angola as a first step towards a formal ceasefire. Namibia, the prime minister conceded publicly, was costing too much in blood and rands. On 16 February the ceasefire was formalised with Luanda. Pretoria showed further flexibility by releasing Andimba Toivo ja Toivo in March, as well as other political prisoners and guerrillas captured at Cassinga in 1978. Kaunda also organised a three-day meeting between the MPC and SWAPO. The talks collapsed, however. SWAPO maintained that Pretoria was trying to get around Resolution 435 and to seduce it into joining the internal fold; just as Ian Smith had tried to entice Joshua Nkomo and ZAPU.

Pretoria, meanwhile, had cracked down on opposition in Ovamboland, alleging that 800 PLAN fighters were moving south through Kaokoland. Approximately 1,000 SWAPO supporters were rounded up. And the already strict press censorship was tightened in the territory.(44) It was the carrot and stick again. Talk and thump.

Pretoria, it seemed, was now taking linkage to its logical extreme: a straight MPC-SWAPO deal tagged on to a Unita-MPLA settlement, cutting out all the non-African troublemakers. In June 1984 the South African government offered SWAPO a token rule in the interim government in Windhoek. "We are being offered nice cars and and nice apartments and asked to play the part of South African puppets," replied a SWAPO spokesman. In July the administrator-general met Nujoma face-to-face in the Cape Verde islands. Pretoria wanted PLAN to stop fighting while the Cuban issue was sorted out, but Nujoma was prepared to agree to a ceasefire only if South Africa went ahead immediately with the UN settlement plan.(45) It was deadlock once more.

Steps to a settlement: 1985-1988

The Angolan war and the internal insurrection consumed the attention of the SADF and Pretoria from 1985. Namibian independence took even more of a backseat as conventional battles raged in southeast

Angola and the South African townships went up in flames. To some extent the internal politicians in Windhoek were left alone to ponder their predicament. Leaders such as Mudge evinced a certain smug self-confidence: Namibia, certainly south of the operational area, was a haven of peace compared with Big Brother's troubles. Perhaps Windhoek's experiments in social engineering could act as a guide for the South Africa of the future?

The ruling Multi-Party Conference looked back at the mistakes of the DTA. It had failed because of its collaborationist ethic, its obvious dependence on Pretoria. It had never been a decolonisation or nationalist movement but, at most, a "civil rights" movement: "Odendaal with a human face", as one specialist dubbed it.(46) The internal option had repeated the pattern of Northern Ireland: attempts at self-government would fail and the territory would revert to direct rule from outside.(47) The MPC, therefore, tried to take a more nationalistic approach, a more robust stance towards Pretoria, and it concerned itself with social reforms in the areas of health and education. Yet it still lacked credibility. For, unlike the DTA, it was an appointed, not an elected, administration.

In June 1985 the MPC became the Government of National Unity. Of course it squabbled from the start. Ministers started suing each other and arguing in public. It was like a three-legged race where right and left legs had different ideas of where the finishing line was. Some of the ministers were determined to shake off the stultifying hand of Pretoria. But they knew that they owed their careers, if not their heads, to the protection of the SADF. And the war went on.

Inside Namibia: October 1985

Namibia at war was a strange, beautiful, almost surreal place: images flashed by of Vietnam, Rhodesia and, occasionally, the savagery of the Congo. Yet, for the casual foreign visitor, it was a place that worked: unusually for Africa, for example, the roads were as good as the beer. The game parks were well run, so were the hotels, with their odd mixture of German efficiency, Afrikaner hospitality and African good manners. The clarity of the light made it a photographer's dream. The overwhelming sense of grandeur and space harmonised with the champagne quality of the air. Because of the war and its isolation, it was almost untouched by the greatest scourge of the twentieth century: packaged tourists. Out of the northern war zones Namibia was usually the quintessence of primeval tranquility. Enchanting classical German buildings, relics of the Second Reich, looked as though they had been plucked from Rhenish forests and planted in the desert. Brechtian characters strolled along the sand-scoured, melancholic streets of picturesque little towns such as Lüderitz and Swakopmund. Life was very pleasant for a visitor, especially if he were white.

There were so many lyrical paradoxes and brutal contradictions—much deeper than the simplistic political picture of illegal, repressive South African occupation. It was that too, but Namibia was so much more. The essence of Namibia needs to be understood not only for its own sake, but as a paradigm perhaps for South Africa's future. Snatches of the territory, word-pictures with Namibians speaking out loud, gathered together during one random month, October 1985, might be able to provide a more realistic impression.(48)

> First, a cramped Hercules transport aircraft, full of national servicemen reading comics, travels from Pretoria to Windhoek. Then that old war-horse, the Dakota, comes in flying low over the flat scrubland just in case a SAM-7 missile is waiting. The Dak touches down near the Omega base. It is hot, very hot, in the Caprivi strip. The Bushman troops (201 Battalion) at Omega are unerring trackers. Their white South African officers confirm they are also very reliable under fire. Off-duty, however, they can be erratic, explains the camp doctor, as he points to a corporal nursing a wound in his rear. "He was shot with an arrow by a Bushman who refused to work after drinking too much." A discussion follows on the San's cultural survival. A white officer, who can speak one of the 17 highly complex local Bushman dialects, is defensive: "The army is not turning the Bushman into a war machine; it is preventing their extinction." Another officer adds: "We are not trying to Westernise the vulnerable Bushman culture. We just want to make him a better Bushman." The army, he says, encourages Bushman troops to spend a day a week with their children teaching them the old customs and fieldcraft.
>
> Travel to Oshivello, and then Ondangwa, where the white civilians and soldiers' families live in stockaded areas, each with a trim, little, sandbagged bomb-shelter in front of their bungalows. At the air bases, artists are evident. An Alouette gunship has "I'm Noddy" painted on its Browning. On a Buffel APC someone has carefully painted "Boswell Wilkie Circus" on the sides, but "Road Runner" tops the logo-list. Oshakati has the best collection of propaganda posters to inspire bored troopies: "Think: it might be a new experience"; "Winners Never Quit". Warnings about mines abound. And always the unofficial scrawl, *Min dae* [a few days left of national service]. This is not *Apocalypse Now,* though. There is no "fragging". Morale is generally high. And, despite the posters warning of the dangers of drugs, this army is not "dropping out".
>
> Ovamboland, utterly flat. The rains are beginning: the sandy soil smells rich and fecund. The ubiquitous *Cuca* shops, always grandly named, often apparently selling nothing, except maybe information. A BMW might be

parked outside. The huts and villages are often very poor and scruffy, a sharp contrast with the regimented tidiness of the army bases. The ordinary soldiers are suspicious of foreigners; some are told not to talk to writers and journalists. After a few hours, relaxed, they talk like young soldiers anywhere. "Ag, man, the army is all hurry up and wait." They admit to boredom, that the army doesn't give them jobs that match their skills, a comment that is echoed by the many graduate conscripts.

The officers, particularly the regulars in the PF, permanent force, are also suspicious. Justifiably. The SADF is castigated in the media throughout the planet. The drinks flow in the mess, so does the frank talk, usually in Afrikaans. English is often the language of formality, of reserve. The SADF is bilingual, but Afrikaans is the dominant language. Slangy Afrikaans is the language of combat, fear, orders, prayer, and laughter for the troops. The talk is of war, sex and sport. Universal clichés of men-at-war. Firstly, always the war. "SWAPO is good, so we have to be too," says a keen citizen force "camper" [reservist]. More beers. A graduate officer admits: "We might be winning the war here, but we might also be losing it at home." A *Koevoet* T-shirt emblazoned with "Our business is killing and business is good". An army captain comments on the reputedly poor relations between the army and the police: "We have the odd punch-up, especially with *Koevoet,* but here it [the relationship] works, because the police do what the army tells them to do. In South Africa, the townships are in a mess, because the police do their own thing, and cock it up. The army must bring them under control."

Along the Ovambo/Angolan border by road, in Buffels, then patrolling in a Puma helicpoter. Always dust, the real enemy of the chopper, not SAM-7s. Then patrols with SWATF units on motorbikes and horses. "PLAN doesn't hear us coming until it's too late," is the theme. "The terrorists are dead scared of the horses, you know." The motor-cyclists act as outriders for the convoy. The enemy here is camel thorn—punctures—not mines.

Foot patrol, searching kraals. Later, capture of four PLAN insurgents. They are not terrified. They are not mistreated. They know they are destined for a long captivity, unless they join the SWATF. Better training, food, money, medical attention, entertainment. Why not? Two of the captives, however, quietly explain that they are committed to SWAPO ideology and they would never fight for "the puppets in Windhoek".

Ruacana, overlooking the big hydro-electric project. Because of the war less than 10% of the potential electricity power is produced in the region, despite the chronic underdevelopment. The base commander plays Elvis Presley tapes in his civilian pick-up truck, chews on a pipe and calls his wife "Corporal". "Corporal" is proud of the new "tourist wing" at the base, right next to the mess. Very few tourists can enter the area, but the small wooden building, a mile from the border, is used for official visitors. The commander complains about the new restraints on fighting in Angola [following the Lusaka accord]. He says plaintively: "Now we are supposed to wait for the bastards to come and hit us first." The next night SWAPO obliges with a stand-off bombardment. The Ruacana base is hit by 122mm rockets, mortars and a recoilless rifle. The new hotel/hut is partially destroyed. Two SADF officers are slightly wounded. The commander is angry and embarrassed. He tries to hide the damage. An angry reaction force caught up with the attackers and, reportedly, killed eight PLAN fighters a few miles inside Angola. In the mess afterwards, one of the officers admits: "I'm here in the operational area because this is the one place I can kill kaffirs legally."

The atmosphere is more relaxed at Opuwa, the midget capital of Kaokoland. During a patrol in Buffels, the soldiers provide water and tobacco to the primitive, handsome Ovahimba people. Only a few thousands of these "cattle people" are left in the deserts of Kaokoland. They daub themselves in fat and ochre. The women plait their hair and look like red Bo Dereks. Most are almost untouched by civilisation, although a few less noble savage ladies are to be found drinking and smoking pipes outside a tiny store next to the SADF base. A black SWATF major takes some drinking friends to his girlfriend's hut. It is a corrugated iron square. Although the inside is immaculately tidy, the tiny hut has no windows at all. The major's lady, Dorcas, explains why: "I want no windows," she says slowly in broken Afrikaans, "SWAPO come and shoot me otherwise."

The discussion in the Opuwa mess is hearty and sophisticated. A graduate in law from Stellenbosch university, doing his two-year army stint, explains why he no longer believes in a political strategy for the SADF. "When I was at Stellenbosch, a student asked P W [Botha], during his speech there, about the political future for the blacks in South Africa. He replied in as many words: 'Shut up and concentrate on your job, studying, and leave me to my job, politics.' We all felt insulted by that." The more conservative officers disagreed with the law graduate. They spouted the "Africans-are-generally-happy-here-we-only-need-to-kill-the-small-amount-of-communist-trouble-makers" philosophy. They were talking specifically about Namibia."Same applies to South Africa," they said. "If they are so happy, why not give them the franchise and let them vote happily for the National Party?" responded the law man. "Ag, man. Be serious." The variety of opinions, often openly expressed, ranging from brutal racism to liberal concern, suggests that this is not a brainwashed war machine. Moreover, standards of military professionalism are high. And, so, generally is morale. There are exceptions. For example, some coloured troops refused home leave because they fear reprisals in their own communities in South Africa because they are serving in the army.

Away now from the operational area. Okahandja, the training school for the SWATF. Namibia is not a polite word here among the officer instructors. "We are fighting for South West Africa. We are not prepared to die for Namibia." This is the fundamental paradox of this war: why should young South African conscripts fight and die to *defend* one sort of black majority rule in Namibia while they are fighting and sometimes dying in South Africa to *prevent* the same principle being applied at home? One SWATF officer from the local German community admits: "I'm HNP [Herstigte Nasionale Party] in my heart, but I know in my head there has to be change." A change, for example, to a professional regular army in Namibia, er, South West Africa? To avoid the political problems of conscripting Ovambos and other SWAPO supporters? He replies coolly: "A regular army? And what if it turns against us?"

Windhoek. The airport is named after J G Strydom. You can usually characterise a developing country by its main airport. This is clean, efficient and ultra-modern with all the international signs awaiting independence. Yet it is named after the Afrikaner apostle of apartheid. Typical South African ham-fisted PR. A local official says: "That's a little thing. You know, this independence takes time." A masterly understatement. Another misnomer is the grandiloquently titled Government of National Unity, which can't even agree on the name of the country. The new administration reeks of Muzorewa's defeat. The rationale is to buy the time that the bishop never had. The same white Rhodesian clichés: "preservation of standards" and "respect for different cultures" permeate the conversations. The new black ministers have a taste for blonde secretaries and black Mercedes. One, Moses Katjiuongua, 43, a former Maoist with an American accent, and now the SWANU leader, admits: "If things go wrong this time, we should blame ourselves, not Pretoria." But Andreas Shipanga, the head of SWAPO-D [Democrats] and minister of nature conservation, mining, commerce and tourism, wants to pass the buck: "This country has become a pawn of superpower rivalries." The ever-affable Shipanga has the shakes. The tough-talking Mudge emphasises the major reforms made despite the fact that A-G 8 [residual segregation laws which can only be repealed by Pretoria's diktat] blocked other necessary changes. There's a multiracial cabinet and one man, one vote. The hated Group Areas Act is gone, he says. Windhoek is 15 years ahead of South Africa. In a somewhat set-piece tone, he insists: "As a result of these reforms, we have relative peace. We have a war on our border, but no women and children protesting in the streets."

Many Namibian whites indeed feel that their country is being used as a social laboratory, as a litmus test for the faint-hearted in the south. A Windhoek restaurant-owner, who still refuses, illegally, to allow blacks into his establishment, says very bluntly: "The *huigelaar* [two-faced] Botha clan is using South West as a playground to see if it [multiracialism] works. If it doesn't, they will shoot the kaffirs." Social engineering clearly has its limits in Windhoek. Squabbles about what race can use what facilities still abound. Not least among the ministers. As one very senior, and also very exasperated, white civil servant puts it: "Instead of fighting over the rules, we should be playing the game." Competing with SWAPO not with each other, he explains.

> Intelligence briefing, defence HQ, Windhoek. Just before the rainy season offensive, "only 40 SWAPO terrorists are active in the operational area," explains a senior SADF intelligence officer. (He concedes that the rains would make the number grow considerably.)
>
> Question: "Is it cost-effective to have such a massive and expensive military machine running around after 40 guerrillas on the border here when South Africa itself is said to be infiltrated by hundreds of ANC insurgents?"
>
> Answer: "No comment. I was not briefed to reply to such a question." End of briefing.
>
> Windhoek is seductive, with its dusty, small-town charm and graceful buildings. Afternoon tea with the administrator-general, Louis Pienaar and his wife, an ultra-courteous couple. Pienaar suggests that South Africa could leave suddenly: "like a thief in the night". Pretoria is sick of the shenanigans of the Windhoek politicans. The feeling is reciprocated. Yet Windhoek's most famous character, Johannes Martin Smith (Smitty to his admirers) says fiercely: "The Boers will never leave in the twentieth century." Smith, who runs the *Windhoek Observer* almost single-handedly, is the local Cassandra, the scourge of the Establishment. People avidly read his paper, sometimes banned for carrying nudes on the back page, for his political and social column, "The People Hear", "one of the most libellous gossip columns of modern times".(48) Smitty is what might be called a South West African nationalist in his dislike of Pretoria. A highly articulate white lawyer, Anton Lubowski, is a more conventional, pro-SWAPO Namibian nationalist. He is concerned with human rights. He politely and patiently explains that SWAPO has already accepted that the constitution for the future Namibia would be based upon the International Declaration of Human Rights. He claims that the internal government's "bill of fundamental human rights" is flawed as it specifically excludes the existing "inhumane" security legislation.
>
> There are lighter moments. It is the *Oktoberfest,* full of Germans, some in *Lederhosen,* guzzling quarts of lager. Then a desert journey to Lüderitz, where quaint *hoch Deutsch* is still spoken by some whites and blacks. Apparently, the Kaiser's birthday is still celebrated here. Finally, Windhoek to Keetmanshoop, 13 hours by train. One goat joins the train and some AWOL soldiers, accompanied by military policemen, leave. In the compartment is a scholarly SADF colonel who is researching ethnology. He tries, unsuccessfully, to explain what makes up Namibia. (49)

What made Namibia tick economically was mineral wealth, particularly the uranium and diamonds. Described as a "political timebomb" for the Government of National Unity, the Thirion Commission, which had previously revealed the worms in the administrative woodwork, in 1986 published its report on the mining industry, concentrated in the monopoly held by Consolidated Diamond Mines, a subsidiary of De

Beers. It was alleged that a systematic "scorched earth" policy had been stripping the territory of its diamond wealth before independence and illegally stockpiling diamonds outside the country.(50)

The SADF had better news for the embattled internal leaders in the Windhoek Tintenpalast (Ink Palace), the seat of government. The commander of the SWATF, Major General George Meiring, insisted that SWAPO's war effort had been ground down. It was partly because of the Angolan war. Both the SADF and PLAN had been diverted by the manpower demands of the Unita-FAPLA battles. Meiring claimed that 3,400 PLAN combatants were fighting alongside their Angolan hosts as part of their "rent" for their bases in Angola. Besides this factor, attrition had worn down PLAN from 16,000 in 1978 to 8,000 in 1986. A maximum of 1,200 PLAN insurgents were available for deployment inside Namibia. The SADF, he said, had killed 10,000 guerrillas. "SWAPO losses over the last 20 years are unparalleled in the history of modern revolutionary warfare." There were over one-third less incidents in 1986 than 1985, it was claimed. "Instead of blowing up power stations, they are blowing up telephone poles."(51) The SADF tried to give a "strong man" image in the mistaken racist belief that "blacks respond to a strong hand". It was mistaken, for the SADF, and certainly the police, were widely hated. The "beaten" SWAPO was often hero-worshipped, especially among the young. In the first legal SWAPO rallies inside Namibia during 1986 crowds of up to 10,000 were reported.

SWAPO was far from beaten. During early 1987 PLAN slipped through the security forces' net into the white farming areas around Etosha, about 120 miles south of the border. The last time they had managed this, in 1983, they created havoc, killing a number of white farmers and soldiers in fierce contacts.(52)

Like the DTA, the Government of National Unity was slipping into a rapid decline. Pretoria stamped on its attempts to wrest real power, and its nominal army, the SWATF, was rocked by disaffection among its black troops, who were reluctant, in some cases, to fight alongside Unita.(53) The crunch came in 1988. South Africa had power in Namibia and SWAPO the popular support. Neither could come to terms with the other...until the escalation of the Angolan war forced the great powers to step in.

The endgame

The internal parties had always faced an obstacle race of horrifying complexity with the odds heavily in favour of the obstacles. The men in the Tintenpalast—and some of the black ministers had shown great spirit in trying to beat Pretoria by working within the system—might have gained some credibility if the war had been stifled. But, as in Rhodesia in 1979, only the guerrillas could guarantee peace. In February 1988, a massive 25kg bomb exploded in a packed First National Bank in Oshakati killing 18 people and injuring 31. SWAPO denied responsibility for this tragedy, the bloodiest, if not the biggest, blast in the history of the war. The previous highest death toll in a single bomb incident had been the explosives planted in a butchery in Walvis Bay in 1986, when six people died.(54)

Exhaustion had set in. The Angolan wars had begun in 1961 and the SWAPO campaign in 1966. By 1988, the SADF found itself fighting on three fronts: a PLAN insurgency inside Namibia, a series of direct clashes with the Cubans on the Namibian border and the conventional battles in support of Unita in the south east. The MPLA and its allies claimed to have snatched air superiority from the SADF, even though in air-to-air battles the South African air force claimed a 9-1 superiority in aircraft shot down.(55) And on the ground the Cubans were giving the SADF a good run for its money. With a strangled economy, Pretoria could no longer afford the military, political and economic costs of the Namibian millstone. And the internal option had reached a dead end. South Africa's Namibian policy was in tatters. But so was the entire Angolan infrastructure. Washington had effectively vetoed Angola's access to the World Bank and the International Monetary Fund. Angola's economic crisis, incomparably more critical than Pretoria's, grew even more desperate as the government, which got 90% of its export earnings from oil, watched the world oil prices fall.(56) And, most important, Moscow was cutting back on its foreign adventures, most notably in Afghanistan and Angola.

Battlefield attrition and the convergence of superpower self-interest in Angola provided the proverbial window of opportunity for Chester Crocker's eight-year campaign of constructive engagement. Starting in London in May 1988, representatives from Angola, South Africa and Cuba huddled together to look for a way out. Crocker was usually in the chair, and the Russians nudged the Cubans when they became too revolutionary for the new apostles of *glasnost*.(57) For seven months they haggled in Cairo, New York, Geneva and most frequently Brazzaville to implement Resolution 435, the 1978 proposals upon which they had all in principle agreed. The target was obvious: how to stop the Angolan war before it sucked in the superpowers, now eager for cosy entente. That meant getting the 52,000 Cuban troops back home and the SADF out of

Namibia. In the end, despite years of scorn from left and right, Crocker's linkage had—apparently—worked. Through sheer ruthless determination, the Georgetown professor now had the Holy Grail—Namibian independence—within his grasp, and before Reagan handed over to George Bush.(58)

A ceasefire came into effect in Angola on 1 September 1988—although Unita forces were excluded from the negotiations.(59) The core of the settlement process was a *de facto* non-aggression pact between Angola and South Africa. The finer details of the transition process for Namibia were agreed at a meeting at Geneva on 15 November. Cuba would withdraw 3,000 troops almost immediately, the balance over 27 months. The SADF would reduce its strength to 1,500 confined to two bases in Namibia. UN-monitored elections would ensue within seven months and independence would be achieved before the end of 1989. Pretoria stalled for a while on the methods of third-party verification of the Cuban exodus, apparently after senior officers had raised serious objections to the SADF's troop reductions.(60) Because of the dramatic delays, the Cuban deputy foreign minister accused Pik Botha of behaving as if he were in a "second-rate movie show". Sceptics forecast that Pretoria would once more draw back from surrendering Namibia. Kaunda, though, finally received his belated "Christmas present". In late December Pretoria ratified. As Pik Botha put it: "The hard nut has been cracked."

After a 100 years of colonial rule, this looked like the real thing, even though jaded Namibians, after so many false dawns, were cynical. *The Times,* however, editorialised: "The agreement if implemented deserves to be hailed as the most important diplomatic breakthrough in Africa since the colonies first began to emerge into independence some 30 years ago." (61) Despite the SADF's blatant reluctance to quit its fiefdom, P W Botha, who had carefully consulted his defence and intelligence leaders at nearly every stage, seemed unlikely to derail the peace train after travelling so far. (62) Reagan, his protector against further US sanctions, was gone.

All the main antagonists could make plausible claims to success. Cuban troops could return with honour. Pretoria had kept its promise to prise out Castro's intruders and would soon extricate itself from a painful war. The Russians could shed an imperial burden. SWAPO looked set to win the elections. Washington could wave a diplomatic triumph. And Angola could begin the mammoth task of rebuilding. But at this stage the whole pack of cards could have fallen down because Angolan reconstruction depended upon a deal with Unita. Savimbi was not party to the negotiations. As noted earlier, Morocco had offered him a comfortable exile. If he continued to refuse the offer and he tried to fight on, would the South African generals really allow their man to be thrown to the wolves?

The future

The core issue, the Angolan civil war, could not be resolved without a compromise between Savimbi and Luanda. That was the tacit assumption of the deal brokered by Crocker. Savimbi, as ever, was the wild card. Besides the Unita factor, many other diplomatic landmines were waiting to explode; for example: the pace and verification of Cuban withdrawal; the deployment and behaviour of the SADF/SWATF/police forces during the election; the impartiality of the UN troops and civilian advisers; white Namibian extremists; and the antics of the internal leaders. The byways to disaster were numerous.

The very first day of the UN transition, ominously 1 April 1989, justified the fears of the pessimists. The Cubans had pulled back and the South African troops had returned to their bases in preparation for demobilisation and the move south. In direct contravention of the UN agreements, over 1,000 SWAPO troops poured over the borders. Despite Pretoria's often-repeated warnings, UNTAG (the United Nations Transition Advisory Group) had been reduced from 7,500 men to 4,650. Less than 1,000 were in position on Day One (1 April) and no UN infantry units were on the northern border where SWAPO poured in. SWAPO's flagrant breach of the agreement seemed inexplicable. It stood to win the election. All it had to do was sit back and wait. Instead it handed a wonderful excuse to Pretoria to renege on the whole deal. It might have been another example of Nujoma's arrogant and impetuous folly, a result of divisions between the military and political wings of SWAPO, a case of local commanders seizing the initiative or simply poor communications with the troops on the ground, who misunderstood the transitional arrangements. Whatever the reasons, with UN blessing, and after the intercession of Mrs Thatcher who flew into Windhoek on 1 April (the "African Queen", as she was dubbed, was touring southern Africa), the SADF remobilised. This was a replay of Lord Soames's use of Rhodesian troops in January 1980 to counter ZANLA excesses. It was a bizarre twist of fate: SADF troops were hunting SWAPO guerrillas with UN consent. "It feels strange to be in the right for once," said a senior South African officer. "I'm not sure we can handle it." In a week of savage fighting, over 260 guerrillas were killed for the loss of 26 South African dead and 120 wounded. SWAPO's catastrophic diplomacy and UNTAG's belated and inadequate deployment had achieved the impossible: they had put South Africa in a good light. The poor performance of UNTAG—not the fault of the disparate hotchpotch of UN units on the ground—convinced Pretoria, if it needed further convincing, that the UN was a bad bet to hold the ring in any "settlement" of Africa's civil wars.

A handful of SWAPO guerrillas turned themselves into UN-supervised assembly points, but most of the survivors scrambled back over the border. Unarmed refugees and exiles could return to take part in the forthcoming election, but not SWAPO guerrillas festooned with weapons and claiming victory. The UN's unique honeymoon with Pretoria did not last longer than the invasion crisis. The South African government threatened, with some justification, to pull out of the exercise. It stalled for while, but kept the transitional process going. But soon angry encounters ensued with the UN troops (who translated UNTAG as UN "Touch and Go"). The same troops, however, needed mine-proofed vehicles to protect them from SWAPO landmines. UNTAG was forced to lease SADF Buffels and Casspirs, built by Armscor in defiance of the UN bans. This was a further irony: the UN was forced to shop for equipment it had prevented others from buying. Soon more deep-seated problems arose. The UN accused the local paramilitary police, especially elements of *Koevoet*, of intimidating the population. Indeed, the entire internal structure of the old regime was accused of trying to manipulate the voters. But if they were anyway largely pro-SWAPO, did it really matter, as long as the secret ballot was fair?

There were bound to be many bitter recriminations, some deaths and shouts of betrayal, but the intensity of the diplomatic effort, the happy congruence of international interests, and war-weariness were combining to set Namibia free. Then what? Could Namibia afford independence? There has been much debate about South Africa's economic exploitation. In 1984 two experts noted: "Namibia is a fiscal and military personnel drain. The gross cost of holding down Namibia is already 10 per cent of South Africa's state budget, about half of its external borrowing, and over R500 per white South African."(63) It was, allegedly, private companies, especially multinationals such as De Beers, a part of the Anglo American group, which made the big profits from the illegal occupation.(64) Independent Namibia will also be burdened by a large external debt and, perhaps, some of the costs of the UN transition machinery. Drought, war and recession have also enfeebled this potentially rich economy. So too has the bureaucratic monstrosity bequeathed by apartheid. If the homeland and security apparatus is entirely dismantled will Nujoma find them all jobs? Will disgruntled former professional killers from *Koevoet,* or for that matter PLAN, finding themselves unemployable, become dissidents or agents for Pretoria?

Pretoria will hold the whip hand. Nearly all the economic systems, especially the transport infrastructure, are interlocked. A SWAPO government will have to tread carefully to avoid the exodus of white skills and capital. Its foreign policy will be severely constrained. The SADF, fortifying new lines along the Orange river, will be able to range freely across the empty, arid terrain of southern Namibia, if it is provoked. And Walvis Bay, Namibia's main port and a large SADF base, will remain as a Trojan Horse under South African control.

SWAPO rule portends changes greater than even Mugabe's victory. Like the ANC, SWAPO had long been portrayed by Pretoria as the embodiment of Satan. Pretoria was now forced to change tack and depict the negotiations over Namibia as a diplomatic victory, not a military withdrawal. Many white conservatives would not agree, especially if the "social laboratory" aspects of Namibia collapse in the dust of a white exodus. The right wing will then cry treachery, and demand military intervention, especially if the remaining Namibian whites are physically endangered.

Pretoria, however, could pluck some rabbits from the hat. The money wasted in Namibia could be redeployed to satisfy domestic social, and security, demands. A dignified retreat from Namibia will enhance Pretoria's regional diplomacy. Moreover, Crocker's constructive engagement might have confirmed the Thatcherite line that persuasion, not sanctions, secures change in southern Africa. And the very positive Russian contributions to the peace process could inhibit some of the paranoia in South Africa about the total communist onslaught.

Much more than Angola, Mozambique and Zimbabwe, Pretoria is intimately tied to the fate of Namibia. South Africa took over in 1915. After 1966, at great cost in young Afrikaner lives, the SADF created a military empire in northern Namibia and southern Angola. Will the SADF pull back, with rancour, as the Israelis did from Sinai? At least then the Americans paid for much of the reconstruction of new bases. Who will pay for the immense SADF base at Grootfontein to be relocated in the Cape Province? The temptation to intervene in Namibia directly and to destabilise it by more subtle means will grow in direct proportion to the nature of the SWAPO regime and the extent its supports the ANC. Will Namibian independence mean a new period of detente in southern Africa or will the SADF raise an underground army in Namibia, another Unita, or, more savagely, the Renamo insurgents in Mozambique?

References and notes:

1. G Cawthra, *Brutal Force*, International Defence and Aid Fund, London, 1986, p. 182.
2. *Loc. cit.*
3. *Ibid.*, p.181.
4. *Strategic Survey, 1976*, International Institute for Strategic Studies (IISS), London, 1977, p. 50.
5. Cawthra, *op. cit.*, p. 194. See also F Toase, "The South African Army: The Campaign in South West Africa/Namibia since 1966," in I Beckett and J Pimlott, (eds), *Armed Forces and Modern Counter-Insurgency*, Croom Helm, London, 1985, pp. 208-9.
6. Figures quoted in *Strategic Survey, 1977*, IISS, London, 1978, p. 39.
7. D Geldenhuys, *The Diplomacy of Isolation*, Macmillan, Johannesburg, 1984, p. 83.
8. W Steenkamp, *Borderstrike: South Africa into Angola*, Butterworth, Durban, 1983, p. 62. Most military accounts by South African writers, especially serving officers, tend to be couched in the heroic mould or are bland because of official censorship. Steenkamp, the military correspondent for the liberal *Cape Times*, although he writes from a SADF perspective, provides a refreshingly open account of the difficulties faced by the SADF from the frontline vantage-point of combat troops.
9. H-R Heitman, *South African War Machine*, Central News Agency, Johannesburg, 1985, p. 144.
10. Steenkamp, *op. cit.*, p. 15.
11. The premiership was decided by a vote of National Party MPs. Pik Botha's strength in the party caucus was small compared with his two main rivals, P W Botha and "Connie" Mulder. In the final round of voting Pik Botha gave his support to his namesake. This writer stood outside the parliament building in Cape Town on 28 September 1978 while the caucus was making its final decision. Despite looking rather like a slightly seedy, second-hand car salesman, with his slicked-back hair and pencil moustache, the large crowd outside kept chanting "Pik, Pik", even after P W Botha's victory had been announced.
12. For example, P Manning and R Green, "Namibia: Preparations for Destabilisation," in P Johnson and D Martin, (eds), *Destructive Engagement*, Zimbabwe Publishing, Harare, 1986, pp. 118-9.
13. *Strategic Survey*, 1979, IISS, London, 1980, p. 91.
14. Cawthra, p. 183.
15. R Leonard, *South Africa at War*, Lawrence Hill, Westport, 1983, p. 68.
16. A du Pisani, *SWA/Namibia: The Politics of Continuity and Change*, Ball, Johannesburg, 1985, p. 436.
17. *Loc. cit.*
18. W Nussey, "A Taxing Task of Viljoen," *The Star*, 28 August 1979.
19. Cawthra, p. 183.
20. Steenkamp, *op cit.*, p. 185.
21. Heitman, *op. cit.*, pp. 144-6; Toase, *op. cit.*, p. 214.
22. *Strategic Survey, 1980-1*, IISS, London, 1981, p. 90.; Toase, *loc. cit.*
23. For further details of this alleged "separate deal", see du Pisani, *op. cit.*, pp. 452-3.
24. For an analysis of mine warfare and the range of South African anti-mine warfare equipment, see P Stiff, *Taming the Landmine*, Galago, Alberton, 1986, pp. 86-125.

25. Heitman, p. 158
26. B Seery, "'Dirty Little War' in the Bush Turns 20," *The Sunday Star,* 31 August 1986; Cawthra, p. 176.
27. Cawthra, p. 178.
28. *The Sunday Star,* 1 June 1986; figures provided by SADF sources to author.
29. *The Star,* 2 November 1985; the study was by Professor R Green of the Institute for Development Studies in Sussex, UK For a discussion of Green's work, see Cawthra, pp. 178-9.
30. Cawthra, p. 179.
31. See Appendix 2 for details of SWATF structure.
32. G Tötemeyer, *Detente or Aggression?: South Africa's Namibian Policy,* South African Institute of International Affairs, Johannesburg, 1985, p. 13.
33. Author's interviews with SADF and SWATF instructors at Okahandja, 1985.
34. Interviews with captured PLAN guerrillas, 1985.
35. Interviews with South African intelligence sources.
36. For a summary of the allegations, see Cawthra, p. 36.
37. For details, see Cawthra, p. 150; Leonard, *op. cit.,* p. 80.
38. Heitman, p. 153.
39. For an illuminating discussion of the constitutional and other issues, see M Sinclair, "Namibian Constitutional Proposals: The Fleeting Options and Implications for South Africa," *South Africa International,* April 1982.
40. Manning and Green, *op. cit.,* p. 122.
41. Figures quoted in *Strategic Survey 1983-1984,* IISS, London, 1984, p. 110.
42. The growing inter-relationship between the two wars is discussed in more detail in Chapter 10.
43. Manning and Green, *loc. cit.*
44. For details of the crackdown, see Cawthra, p. 178.
45. *Strategic Survey 1984-1985,* IISS, London, 1985, p. 109.
46. See A du Pisani, "Namibia: The Quest for Legitimacy," *Politeia,* UNISA, 2:1, 1983, and "South Africa in Namibia," *International Affairs Bulletin,* South African Institute of International Affairs, 10:3, 1986. For a commentary on the Odendaal Comission, see Chapter 6.
47. For an interesting extension of the analogy, see A Guelke, "The Political Impasse in South Africa and Northern Ireland," unpublished paper presented to the Special Meeting on "Pre-Post-Apartheid Politics in South Africa: Getting from Here to There," at the IPSA World Congress, August 1986, Washington DC.
48. See D Beckett, "The One-Man Sideshow who is South West's Conscience," *Frontline,* February 1983, and also Beckett's colourful and incisive three-part article: "Namibia: The Tragedy Behind the Land of Comic Opera," *Frontline,* May, June, July, 1983.
49. This writer has visited Namibia on a number of occasions. October 1985 was chosen because he travelled throughout the territory for the entire month and gained unusual access to the military zones, travelling the entire length of the frontline from Caprivi to Ruacana. All the interviews were conducted by the author. See also, P Moorcraft, "Namibia/Angola: Africa's Yo-Yo War," *Jane's Defence Weekly,* 12 April 1986, "War in a 'Surreal Place,'" *Army,* July 1986; and also Moorcraft, "Suidwes Afrika: Onvoorspelbare, Ongetemde Land," *Die Ekonoom,* 1:2, 1986.
50. B Seery, "Corruption Report Set to Explode in Namibia," *The Star,* 9 February 1986. For details of the CDM's activities, see D Pallister, S Stewart and I Lepper, *South Africa Inc: The Oppenheimer Empire,* Simon and Schuster, London, 1987, pp. 102-121.
51. See B Seery, "'Dirty Little War' up in the Bush Turns 20," *op. cit.,* and "Namibia's Season of Infiltration," *The Star,* 5 December 1985; also "Swapo has to Change its Strategy," *The Sunday Star,* 1 June 1986

52. *The Star,* 20 April 1987.
53. M Verbaan, "Namibians Mutiny over Orders to Join Unita," *The Independent,* 20 November 1987.
54. C Kotze and B Seery, "Namibia Bush War Explodes," *The Star* (weekly edition), 23 February 1988.
55. Editorial in *Ad Astra,* the SAAF magazine, quoted in *The Star* (weekly edition), 14 December 1988.
56. M Holman, "A Long War Draws to a Close," *Financial Times,* 16 November 1988.
57. A McEwan, "Soviet Role Vital in Angola and Namibia Talks," *The Times,* 28 November 1988.
58. R Dowden, "Crocker's Patience Leads him to Africa's Holy Grail," *The Independent,* 17 November 1988.
59. For the Angolan perspectives on the 1988 settlement, see Chapter 10.
60. S Robinson, "Peace, What Peace?" *The Daily Telegraph,* 17 November 1988. For a detailed, South African perspective on the military aspects of the transition, especially the SWAPO invasion, see P Stiff, *Nine Days of War*, Lemur, Alberton, 1989.
61. *The Times,* 26 December 1988.
62. R Dowden, "Pretoria Keeps the World Guessing," *The Independent,* 6 December 1988.
63. Green and Manning, *op. cit.,* p. 135.
64. Pallister, Stewart and Lepper, *op. cit.*

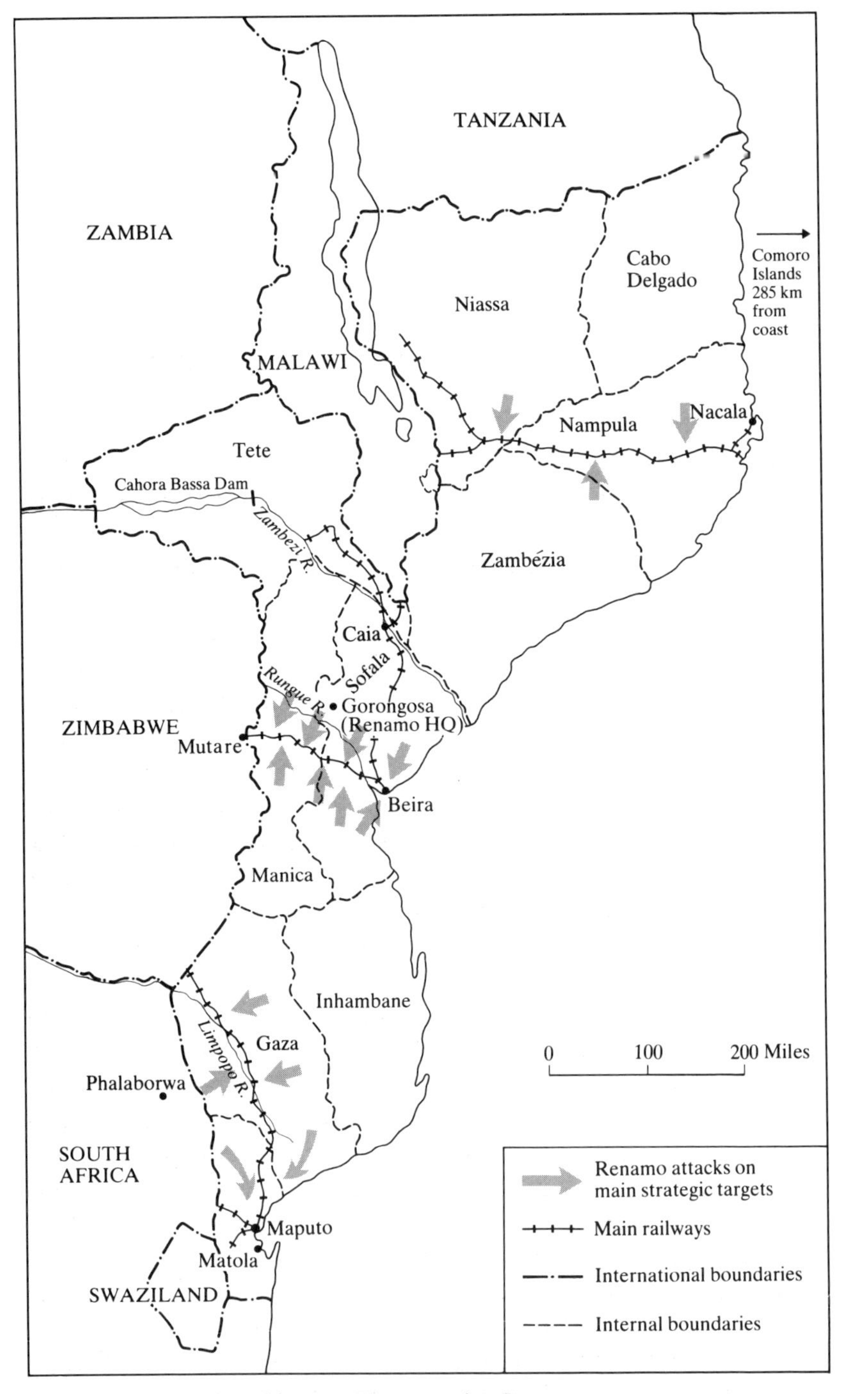

Map 12 The war against Renamo

12

Mozambique (1976-1989)

Frelimo might have inherited the political kingdom at independence in 1975, but unfortunately the departing whites took nearly all the keys of that kingdom: the money, the expertise and, in some cases, even the machinery. Frelimo had initially to quash an attempted white coup, encouraged by Rhodesia,(1) and a series of military revolts within Frelimo, caused partly by friction between a sometimes envious military wing and the pork-barrelling politicians.(2) Amid the economic, political and military chaos, President Machel insisted that he would build on a Marxist, not colonial, model. Unlike the MPLA, Machel had assumed power without massive Soviet and Cuban military assistance because Frelimo had not been challenged by any significant rival liberation movement. Nonetheless, his first state visit outside Africa, in May 1976, was to the USSR. In Moscow, he declared his intention to transform his country into the "first fully Marxist state in Africa". Frelimo was soon fashioned into a Russian-inspired, Marxist-Leninist "vanguard party"—despite the fact that Frelimo had fought a largely Maoist-style war, with limited support from the peasantry and the tiny, urban working class. Under a 20-year treaty with the USSR, Mozambique received a variety of tanks, armoured vehicles, SAM-missiles and, later, combat aircraft and helicopters (which, except for the aircraft, were largely obsolete). The initial influx of 200 Soviet instructors helped to transform the guerrilla force into a conventional army. Other Eastern bloc allies, notably the East Germans, shaped the internal political system, especially the propaganda and security organs.(3)

Thirty days after independence, Machel proclaimed the immediate nationalisation—with little or no compensation—of all private educational institutions, hospitals, clinics, funeral parlours and legal practices. In the countryside, although Mozambique did not possess a single agronomist, a Marxist "villagisation" scheme, similar to the disastrous Tanzanian plan, was set in motion, despite the opposition of much of the peasantry. The secret police, SNASP, rounded up thousands of opponents and placed them in gulags for "re-education".(4) Some were executed. The rapid nationalisation of nearly all facets of life created chaos, all of which was blamed on the departure and sabotage of the whites. The white exiles, however, said that they left *because* of the massive upheavals. As one refugee lamented: "This excuse reminds me of the apocryphal child who murders his parents, then demands leniency from the court on the grounds that he is an orphan." (5) Everybody was blamed by Frelimo except itself: the Portuguese, then the Rhodesians, and, finally, the *bête blanche*, South Africa, although, as the disorder became endemic, Machel had the grace, later, to blame also the rushed implementation of his socialist policies.(6).

Frelimo's hasty revolution was perpetually under fire. The party had to fight three wars in succession: an anti-colonial war against the Portuguese army, then a bitter struggle against the UDI rebels, and, most savagely, after 1980 a double-barrelled war against Renamo and the SADF.

At independence in June 1975 there were some hopes for peace, although the new regime believed, with some justification, that the South Africans were weighing up the option of an invasion to topple the Marxist regime. There were rumours in intelligence circles that the defence minister, P W Botha's rival, Hendrik van den Bergh, had scuttled a secret Botha plan to send in South African military support to aid the white coup attempt in 1975, with the aim of setting up a UDI republic in the south. Vorster, however, seemed committed to a wait-and-see position.(7) There were various alternatives which could be tried later: namely, the direct overthrow of Frelimo, keeping Mozambique in chaos, or co-opting Machel by economic inducements.(8) Evidence of all three options was to surface in the following decade. Because of the fear of SADF intervention, the Mozambican foreign minister, Joaquim Chissano, stressed as early as 1974 that Mozambique would become "a base for revolutionary change in Africa", but qualified his statement by adding that he meant a "revolutionary base in ideas". The masses of South Africa would have to act as their own saviours, he explained.(9) Nevertheless, Frelimo had to prepare its armed forces for a possible conventional thrust from South Africa, and, more immediately, to resist the large-scale Rhodesian offensives which began in August 1976.

The war against Rhodesia

Machel closed his borders with Rhodesia on 3 March 1976. Although a *modus vivendi* was perhaps possible with Pretoria, the new president was committed to support ZANLA's insurgency because it was the same kind of war against colonialism that Frelimo had waged. ZANLA had fought side-by-side in contacts with the Rhodesians and Portuguese. There was a personal bond between Mugabe and Machel, although the down-to-earth, ill-educated Machel found it much easier to communicate with a fellow soldier, the ZANLA commander, Josiah Tongogara, than the aloof, austere and intellectual Mugabe.(10) The tightening of the sanctions noose and the ZANLA-Frelimo military alliance led in early 1977 to the eastern front's domination of the course of the Rhodesian war. Salisbury responded in two ways: pre-emptive and retaliatory raids on joint Frelimo-ZANLA forces and the "creation" of a secret anti-government army, Renamo. But did the Rhodesians create Renamo? Mountains of disinformation have obfuscated the heated debate about the movement's origins and development. The central question, however, is clear: is Renamo simply a puppet, originally set up by the Rhodesian Central Intelligence Organisation (CIO) and then stage-managed by Pretoria or has it become a genuine symbol of an indigenous popular revolt by the Mozambique people against the excesses of Marxist rule? Nearly all the writers on the subject assume the former, but the truth, as usual, may—somewhat prosaically—lie somewhere between the two extremes: Renamo appears to be both.

An understanding of the genesis of Renamo is critical to a clear appreciation of the long years of savage, hidden warfare in Mozambique. Yet for every "fact" about Renamo, there is often an opposite one, depending upon the source. Unita was different. Savimbi has nearly always been portrayed, even by his detractors, as a genuine nationalist leader. But, depending upon on the version, he fell by the wayside when he, allegedly, collaborated with the Portuguese in the early 1970s or the Afrikaners, unquestionably, after 1975. Renamo, however, scratched around to find even a crumb of international credibility as a genuine nationalist movement. When it comes to guerrilla warfare, Renamo's PR must rate even lower than the Khmer Rouge's. So what is the nature of this beast?

The godfather of Renamo was Ken Flower, the wily Cornishman who ran the CIO for two decades.(11) From the early 1970s he had tried to persuade his Portuguese counterparts of the need to establish a pseudo-guerrilla force in Mozambique. Flower, who had an excellent personal rapport with the BOSS chief, Hendrik van den Bergh, kept Pretoria informed of his plans, but the South Africans played no part in setting up Renamo.(12) After the Portuguese collapse, the CIO and the Rhodesian special branch collected together a number of black and white Mozambican soldiers and policemen of varying degrees of professionalism and thuggery. A small band of about 40 ex-*Flechas*, led by the Angolan-born Colonel Oscar Cardoso, joined the Rhodesians, who already had a nucleus of disgruntled white Mozambicans who were trying to form an anti-Frelimo political front. What the CIO wanted was a black leader. During 1976 disaffected ex-Frelimo soldiers crossed the border. One potential leader, André Matsangaisse, arrived in mid-1976.(13) He was a Frelimo junior officer who had become disillusioned with the party. (That is the Renamo version; Frelimo insists he was cashiered for the theft of a Mercedes car and other goods. Thereafter, he was sent to, and then escaped from, the Sacuze "re-education centre", a concentration camp in Sofala province.)(14) In June 1976, a radio station called *Voz de Africa Livre*, Voice of Free Africa, started broadcasting from Gwelo in Rhodesia. It used a huge, old-fashioned, 400-kilowatt transmitter nicknamed "Big Bertha". The station, broadcasting in Portuguese, attacked the "communist tyranny" in Mozambique. The station was directed by Orlando Cristina, a colourful character who imagined himself to be Mozambique's answer to Lawrence of Arabia. He advocated a "pure", non-communist Mozambican nationalism. His line was that the democratic nationalism of the first Frelimo leader, Eduardo Mondlane, had been corrupted by the "Algerian gang" around Machel. Because of their communist indoctrination in Algeria they betrayed the revolution and handed it over to Moscow. (Frelimo says that Cristina was a straightforward agent of the Portuguese secret police who had been sent to infiltrate Frelimo.) Cristina had worked for Jorge Jardim, a wealthy Portuguese businessman utterly addicted to intrigue. Jardim had close ties with both Salazar and Banda. Jardim was said to have donated some of his personal fortune to help run the radio station and to arm the anti-Frelimo force.

This force became known as the Mozambique National Resistance (MNR) or, more commonly, Renamo (*Resistência Nacional Moçambicana*). Its first base was at an old tobacco farm outside Odzi, not far from Umtali. Other camps were established in Rhodesia, as the propaganda beamed from Gwelo and the conditions inside Mozambique generated a flow of anti-Frelimo refugees. The Odzi camp was controlled by an officer from the CIO's Mozambique desk, Eric "Ricky" May. He brought in former SAS personnel to train the embryonic army. In April

PLATE 12.1 A early Soviet BTR-152 used by Frelimo until a Rhodesian raid destroyed it. (*Rhodesian Army*)

1977, Matsangaissa led a daring raid on his former prison at Sacuze and released 500 prisoners. More than half agreed to follow him back to Odzi to join Renamo. In June Afonso Dhlakama arrived in Odzi, after being imprisoned by the Rhodesian special branch and interrogated for a month in Umtali. He became second-in-command to Matsangaisse. The SAS thought highly of the commander, whom even Frelimo concede was a natural fighting soldier, but the CIO felt that Dhlakama lacked fighting spirit and charisma. Dhlakama had been conscripted into the Portuguese colonial forces, but had defected to join Frelimo in the closing stages of the war. He, too, claimed that he quit Frelimo because he believed in Mondlane's views on nationalism, although Frelimo counter-claims that he had been thrown out of Frelimo because he was a "petty criminal", an epithet frequently used to describe ideological opponents.(15) Much of Renamo's simplistic "philosophy"—Mondlane's Frelimo was described as "good", "real" and "nationalist", while Machel's was "evil", "communist" and "totalitarian"—seems to have been concocted by CIO case officers and, by the style of it, late at night after too many whiskies. The white Mozambican dissidents associated with Cristina also were involved in creating a makeshift political platform for the radio station.(16) Right from the start the Rhodesians kept the political elements separate from the fighters in Odzi: to this day, Renamo officials blame the Rhodesians as the original cause of the continuous tensions in the 1980s between the (mainly white) external leadership and the black military command inside Mozambique. The CIO was suspicious of Cristina's ties with Jardim, whom Salisbury accused of betraying sanctions secrets. With gradually increasing support from the SAS, the CIO concentrated on building up Renamo's military potential. Flower implied that Renamo was designed primarily as a unit to spy on and disrupt ZANLA operations, "the eyes and ears of our intelligence in Mozambique". In a secret CIO document, he wrote:

> The undoubted success of the [Renamo] movement also signified that FRELIMO in Mozambique (as between MPLA and UNITA in Angola) lacked that essential measure of support that they needed from the population: or the Portuguese had acted too hastily in transferring power to a liberation movement which could not establish popular support through free elections. (17)

This passage raises a number of questions. The first is about the initial aim of Renamo. Was it merely to disrupt ZANLA or was it intended actually to topple Machel? The SAS apparently assumed that they were helping Renamo to overthrow Frelimo. The history of the Rhodesian SAS noted: "When [the Rhodesian Combined Operations] suggested the MNR attack ZANLA, the CIO pointed out that as the resistance's main objective was to overthrow Machel; the very last thing they wanted at that stage was to become involved with ZANLA."(18) The SAS account states that Renamo spontaneously engaged ZANLA forces. Frelimo, however, claims that nearly all the "350" Renamo and SAS attacks between 1976 and 1979 were led and organised by white Rhodesians.(19) Although the CIO was surprised at the rapid successes of its protégé, the Rhodesian war ended before Frelimo's grip on the reins of power was severely challenged. Some CIO officials, after the war, maintained that if more money had been pumped into what had been a shoestring operation, then Frelimo might have been toppled and, therefore, the war on the eastern front *might* have been won.

The second, more important, question is the extent of the Mozambican dissidents' independence. Renamo apologists insist that the Rhodesian role was limited to finance and training. According to a history of the movement:

> An accepted necessary condition of successful guerrilla war is a sanctuary in a neighbouring country. The Afghan Mujahedin use Pakistan. The Eritreans use Sudan. The Nicaraguan Contras use Honduras. But the Pakistanis did not "create" the Mujahedin... and neither did the Rhodesians create RENAMO. Internal oppression and political tyranny with the grossest violation of human rights, supported by an imperialist foreign power, created an indigenous resistance... whether in Afghanistan, Eritrea, Nicaragua, Angola, or in Mozambique.
>
> The Rhodesian government had every reason to provide a sanctuary for RENAMO, as the Mozambican government was providing a sanctuary for Marxist guerrillas trying to overthrow it. But the fact remains that the Mozambican National Resistance was created, and its activities were conducted, by Mozambicans. (20)

Renamo has tried to play down considerably the contribution of the SAS. It concedes, however, that the spectacular destruction of the Beira oil storage depot in March 1979 was organised by an SAS captain, Bob McKenzie, an American Vietnam veteran. "But for the most part, joint SAS/RENAMO activities inside Mozambique were limited to RENAMO providing guides every so often for SAS attacks on ZANLA sanctuary camps." (21) In fact, the SAS involvement was much greater. As was the case with the CIO and special branch, who decided on most of the targets for Renamo actions.

But an acceptance of Rhodesia's crucial role does not mean that the orthodox view—that the CIO recruited mercenaries and criminals to spread random terror and disorder in Mozambique—is correct. Whatever their unholy origins, the guerrillas did come to represent a ground swell of popular hostility to Frelimo rule. The Renamo "bandits", as Frelimo termed them, were in some cases motivated by a political antipathy to the doctrinaire excesses of Marxist rule. And Renamo's early forays did encounter widespread sympathy from the peasantry in central Mozambique. That support might have been offered for a wide number of reasons, from clan loyalties to ideological convictions, from resentment against Frelimo by sacked chiefs, to peasant dislike of villagisation, and because of old religious affilations among Catholics and Muslims. In short, the inchoate Mozambican resistance was undoubtedly cynically fostered by the CIO, but it also fed upon very real discontent among blacks inside the country. But any Renamo claims to have developed an organised internal resistance inside Mozambique and to have established an effective external political network *before* the CIO set up the Odzi base are not credible.(22)

By 1978 Renamo guerrillas numbered about 500 trained men. Initially they operated in the Manica province of Mozambique. Their targets were Frelimo bases and convoys, the capture of weapons, and attacks on "re-education" centres to gain recruits. There were attempts also to set up an infrastructure among the peasantry in Manica and Sofala provinces. Renamo's military strength doubled in 1979. A central internal HQ was built in the Gorongosa mountains, an area where Matsangaissa had operated as a Frelimo guerrilla. The Renamo commander, along with 200 Mozambican insurgents and a dozen SAS men, consolidated their position on the Gorongosa plateau. Another 200 guerrillas, led by Lucas Mushlangu, with no SAS back-up, set up another permanent base at Gogoi in the Sitatonga mountains of southern Manica. The remainder stayed at Odzi. From January 1979 the SAS had augmented its initially small contribution. In particular, in the last three months of the war, in Operation Bumper, the SAS escalated its commitment as part of Rhodesia's all-out final offensive against Mozambique (and Zambia). The CIO and Combined Operations grew optimistic about their little counter-revolution, or "the second war of liberation" as Renamo dubbed it.

Then Renamo came unstuck. On 17 October 1979 Matsangaissa was killed while personally leading a foolhardy frontal assault—against his SAS companions' advice—on the Frelimo garrison in Gorongosa town at the base of the mountains. Dhlakama was apparently flown to the Gorongosa base the next day in a Rhodesian helicopter to take command. The CIO had their doubts about Dhlakama, a short, bespectacled man then aged 26. Mushlangu was, apparently, preferred by some CIO officers. Anti-Renamo sources say that the matter was settled "in a gun battle" between the two men and their immediate supporters. This may not be true. (Renamo says that 600 guerrillas later voted for Dhlakama at the Sitatonga base. In June 1980 Dhlakama took on the title of "President and Supreme Military Commander".) But in late 1979 Dhlakama inherited a small army that was about to face annihilation. The Lancaster House settlement caught Renamo in a vice between Mugabe and Machel. The Rhodesian sanctuary, so vital for guerrilla operations, was about to disappear. Who would back Renamo now? Enter, centre stage, South Africa.

The Pretoria connection

Mozambique's war against Rhodesia had caused massive dislocation in the central provinces, the loss of thousands of Mozambican lives, and, according to UN estimates, the sanctions blockade had cost Maputo £250 million. After nearly two decades of conflict and with his ally, Mugabe, in power, Machel looked forward to peace and social reconstruction. He assumed, in particular, that Renamo "banditry" would wither away. He was quite wrong.

Flower had been trying to get Pretoria to contribute towards a larger Renamo force since 1976. BOSS was said to be sympathetic, but Vorster apparently refused to back the insurgents because of the harm it might do to his detente policy.(23) But P W Botha was more interested. From 1978 he opened the coffers wide to supply Rhodesia's military needs. South African weapons and vehicles were also provided to Renamo in 1979. A frequent visitor to the Odzi base was Colonel Charles van Niekerk, of South African military intelligence—SAMI or "Sammy" as the Rhodesians sometimes called it. Cornelius (Charles) van Niekerk had been a military attaché in Nampula in the early 1970s. His job had been to monitor the limited involvement of the SADF in Portugal's counterinsurgency campaign. Apparently he spoke both Portuguese and Macua. He became a central figure in the Renamo story. His first role was as the liaison officer with the Rhodesian operation, and later as the contact man between Dhlakama and Pretoria. Flower and General Peter Walls had arranged directly with the SADF chief, Magnus Malan, that "compromised" units of the Rhodesian army, such as the Selous Scouts and some of Muzorewa's auxiliaries, could be transferred to South Africa to avoid possible reprisals. Flower ensured that Renamo was included. There has been much debate about the details of the transfer, but there is no doubt Pretoria took over Rhodesia's functions, lock, stock and barrel. The Renamo leadership was quite happy to adopt its new benefactor.

Some estimates put Renamo at 2,000 men in March 1980, but Flower suggested it was lower, perhaps 1,000 trained insurgents.(24) Some were sent directly from Odzi back into Mozambique. Cristina moved the radio station initially to the SADF's special forces' base near Phalaborwa, in the eastern Transvaal, and started broadcasting with the claim that the Voice of Free Africa was now operating *inside* Mozambique. SADF transport planes also moved Renamo personnel and equipment to Phalaborwa, from where (according to Martin and Johnson) Dhlakama and his HQ staff shifted to a new base on the edge of Lutabo river, one kilometre from the Kruger National Park. Renamo, however, insists that Dhlakama's HQ remained inside Mozambique during the transfer.(25) (Indeed Renamo sources maintain that Dhlakama, far from sitting comfortably in South Africa, stayed in the Mozambique bush throughout the 1980s, except for rare diplomatic forays to Europe and Pretoria.) Members of the Rhodesian SAS simply drove Renamo's South African-supplied vehicles in a convoy through the main Zimbabwe/South African borderpost at Beitbridge. The SAS commander, Lieutenant Colonel Garth Barrett, had asked General Pieter van der Westhuizen, the director of South African military intelligence, to allow his men to stay together to form a new regiment of the South African Reconnaissance Commandos. Eighty per cent of the SAS, 127 men, including Barrett and Captain Bob McKenzie, a fervent advocate of Renamo, joined the "Recces", although only a handful stayed on after their year's contract expired.(26)

All this activity took place with the knowledge and tacit acquiescence of the British colonial authorities. Flower made a point of informing the governor's staff of the transfer. It has been suggested that this was a churlish repayment for Machel's assistance to the British at Lancaster House, but in practical terms there was very little the British could do. Rhodesia was a powder keg in March and April 1980. If Lord Soames had insisted on handing over Renamo to a possibly grisly fate at the hands of Frelimo, it could have been a repeat of the controversy over the alleged betrayal of the pro-German Russian forces by the British army in 1945. The British were glad to turn a blind eye. No one in 1980 foresaw the consequences of saving Renamo.

Flower remained at the head of Mugabe's CIO. Although he informed the new premier of the broad outlines of Renamo operations, the intelligence chief did not, he said, hand over *details* of bases and the new South African administration. Pretoria, however, later accused the spymaster of betraying Renamo operations when the insurgents suffered serious reverses in 1980 and 1981. South African intelligence retaliated by deliberately leaking stories that Flower was a British agent who had sold out both Renamo *and* Rhodesia. Flower vehemently denied both allegations and suggested that the SADF had incompetently managed both Renamo and their SAS advisers, a view held by some of the SAS personnel involved. Also, the shake-up of the three main South African intelligence services, initiated by P W Botha after the Information scandal, demoralised many of the former BOSS agents, who had been highly successful. BOSS (renamed DONS, later NIS) had previously been the dominant agency working in the neighbouring states. The ascendency of military intelligence, under P W Botha, disturbed the spy network throughout southern Africa.(27)

While the SADF was rebuilding Renamo at bases inside South Africa, Machel's forces attacked the scattered insurgents inside Mozambique. Rebel bases near Gorongosa were overrun and, in Operation Leopard in June and July 1980, the stronghold at Sitatonga was captured, along with supplies of South African ammunition and parachutes. Hundreds of Renamo guerrillas were killed, captured or deserted. Dhlakama fled with a few hundred followers 90 miles south to a small base, Garagua, on the Save river. This was the nadir of Renamo's fortunes. Without South African help, the movement might have been obliterated.

In October 1980 Pretoria went all-out to resuscitate its secret ally. According to Martin and Johnson, Dhlakama and a SADF military intelligence delegation, led by the ubiquitous Van Niekerk, hammered out a new strategy.(28) Pro-Frelimo sources say that while the Rhodesians encouraged Renamo to adopt a hearts-and-minds approach so as to gather intelligence from a supportive peasantry, now the SADF ordered a scorched earth policy of straightforward destruction and destabilisation.(29) There were certainly differences of emphasis between the two white supremacist strategies, but it would be inaccurate to entirely dismiss the attempts by the revived Renamo to politicise the *povo*, the peasant masses. Externally, too, Pretoria tried to improve Renamo's almost invisible image. Cristina became secretary-general of the political wing, and a third-generation Mozambican of Goan ancestry, Evo Fernandes, opened up Renamo's first European mission outside Lisbon. Fernandes had been connected with Jorge Jardim as well. When Jardim died in 1982, Fernandes apparently obtained funds from his former employer, the millionaire industrialist, Manuel Bulhosa, whose oil refinery in Maputo and other assets had been nationalised by Frelimo. Dhlakama is reported to have undertaken, in November 1980, a secret tour of right-wing groups in Portugal, West Germany and France.(30)

The second prong of the new strategy was military. According to Renamo, the relocated radio station had caused a big upswing in recruitment. They now claimed 10,000 men under arms.(31) This tally was boosted by the infiltration of newly trained (and retrained) men from the South African bases. Renamo had fresh objectives. In Gaza they tried, it seemed, to create a buffer to prevent the reinvigorated ANC thrust into South Africa. Renamo also tried to establish control in parts of Inhambane, so that it could be resupplied by sea rather than expensive airdrops. The South Africans might also have played a part in

PLATE 12.2 Renamo guerrillas on the march in Zambézia province

encouraging the rebels to wage an urban terror campaign in Beira and Maputo. Crucially, Renamo began to concentrate on the road and rail routes which crossed the country, as shots across SADCC's bow.

As Renamo fanned out across the countryside, they found a welcome in some areas. Although much of Renamo's political programme was a flimsy concoction of Rhodesian and South African propaganda, the simple message of Mozambican nationalism versus Soviet colonialism did strike a chord. The guerrillas attracted dissident and disillusioned Frelimo officials, villagers exasperated by the excesses of Marxist collectivisation, youngsters seeking adventure and, more often, food, Muslims and Catholics who were alienated by the government's anti-religion crusade, as well as traditionalists for whom Renamo's restoration of *régulos* (chiefs) meant a welcome return to the old ways. In central Mozambique, the guerrillas often shared the same Shona culture, with its emphasis on spirit mediums and ancestor worship. When the guerrillas were not destroying or mutilating, which they clearly did, they could choose to show a reforming front, by being all things to all men. They often looted Frelimo stores and cooperatives and distributed some of the goods to the peasants. These Robin Hood tactics worked well in the short-term, but the peasants soon realised that Renamo could not restock the pillaged shops. As in all bush wars, perhaps the majority of the *povo* cursed the military outrages of both sides and tried to keep their heads down. Although some Mozambicans joined Renamo willingly, many of the rank-and-file soldiery appear to have been press-ganged into military service. Desertion was often punished by execution.

Frelimo reacted slowly to the Renamo resurgence. The ruling party seemed to believe its own propaganda about isolated bands of criminal bandits. It was not until late 1981 that Frelimo began to realise the extent of Pretoria's connivance and that the SADF-Renamo axis posed a serious threat to the Marxist regime. Frelimo had, in effect, a civil war on its hands. Machel appointed experienced ex-guerrilla commanders as regional governors, not the Soviet-trained heavy weapons specialists. Frelimo tried to construct a lightly armed, highly mobile COIN force without dismantling its conventional deterrence against the SADF repeating a Mozambican rerun of its invasion of Angola.(32)

Besiding arming Renamo, the SADF itself stormed into Mozambique. On the 30 January 1981, in the first direct SADF raid on Mozambique, "Recce" Commandos crossed the border in vehicles painted in Mozambican army colours and drove 50 miles to Matola, a suburb of Maputo. They set up road blocks on the main Matola-Maputo road. With pinpoint accuracy the raiders destroyed three houses on the tree-lined streets of the quiet neighbourhood. Thirteen ANC members were killed (the SADF claimed 30) and one innocent passer-by. Frelimo reported that at one house the ANC fought back and killed two of the attackers, both permanent force sergeants. In fact, one ex-British soldier, Robert Lewis Hutchinson, threw a grenade into the window of the house, while he was lying beneath the sill and pressed against the wall. Unfortunately for him—and contrary to the detailed intelligence report on the house—the window had a metal grill. The grenade bounced back and exploded, catching the ammunition in his chest webbing. After another raider was killed, the Commandos cut short their raid and escaped, leaving—unusually—at least one SADF body. Frelimo blamed the audacious raid on information supplied by CIA agents in the

Frelimo general staff. Actually, the raid had all the hallmarks of the daring Rhodesian incursions, which also deployed Mozambican vehicles in the 1976-77 period. This was not surprising. Hutchinson was a former member of the Rhodesian SAS. So were most of his companions. According to Colonel Garth Barrett, the unit's former commanding officer, the SAS taught the Recces "all they knew" about Israeli-style "externals" (cross-border raids). The ex-SAS comprised the spearhead of this first Israeli-type raid on Mozambique. The Rhodesian connection extended further: information about Zimbabwean troop movements in Mozambique and Frelimo intelligence in general was leaked via South African agents in Zimbabwe's special branch and the CIO, which retained much of the personnel from the UDI period. Most of the white experts in Zimbabwe were loyal to the Mugabe government. But such were the snakes and ladders of southern African sabotage that ex-Rhodesians on one side of the fence were able to provide intelligence for their ex-countrymen in the service of the SADF. This was particularly true of Renamo intelligence and counter-intelligence.(33)

Other SADF raids followed. Three were launched before the second SADCC annual conference on 19-20 November 1981 in Blantyre, Malawi. All were aimed at railways and port facilities servicing Malawi. This was a general warning to the SADCC and Malawi's membership especially.(34) One of the raids was a failure. On 14 October, a Mozambican patrol came across a group laying mines on the Beira-Umtali (Mutare) railway. During the shooting a mine exploded, killing the saboteurs. One of them was later identified as Alan Gingles, a Sandhurst-trained soldier who had joined the Selous Scouts and subsequently enlisted with the SADF.(35) Two weeks later two vital bridges over the Pungwe river were blown up. The bridge carrying the road and oil pipeline was destroyed, and the one carrying the railway was damaged. All traffic between Zimbabwe and Beira was cut, and the Recce Commandos were blamed. The bridges were expertly sabotaged, so it probably was the work of the SADF. The rule of thumb in such matters in intelligence circles was that if the job was botched, it was Renamo; if it was done properly, it was the Recces.

The SAS/Recce backing for Renamo could not prevent, on 7 December 1981, Frelimo forces overrunning the Garagua HQ. But it was almost deserted as informers inside Frelimo had tipped off the Renamo leadership.(36) Frelimo denied this and produced documents captured there which contained details of Dhlakama and South African meetings in late 1980.(37) Nevertheless, Renamo activity expanded. In

February 1982 Machel toured Inhambane and Gaza provinces to try to raise morale, and to encourage the peasantry to oppose the rebels. But within weeks some of the areas were inaccessible to Frelimo. In the early 1980s much of the territory held by Renamo was in relatively uninhabited parts of the country, but the rebels could interdict road and rail traffic to the main population centres. Authorities on Mozambique such as Hanlon insist that there were no attempts to set up classic "liberated zones".(38) This is true of the early 1980s, but gradually, as rebel influence spread, a crude infrastructure of sorts, with primitive schools, clinics and barter-trade, emerged.

Nonetheless, Renamo's emphasis, no doubt with SADF prodding, was on military action. Some of the targets appeared to contradict South African interests, however. The rebels destroyed electricity pylons from the Cahora Bassa project, which caused supply problems in the Transvaal, even though Mozambique contributed less than 12% of South Africa's supply. Renamo claimed that this demonstrated its independence of Pretoria, although it may have been a SADF miscalculation: the South African electricity supplier, ESCOM, might have informed the military that Cahora Bassa's input was irrelevant. It usually was, except that freak conditions, including especially cold weather, caused an unexpected shortfall in electricity supply, and some blackouts.

The second contradiction was Malawi's entanglement with Renamo. During the 1980s there is little doubt that at various periods elements in the Malawian army and intelligence supported Renamo, although the extent of that support, including allegations of large rebel military bases inside Malawi, has been grossly exaggerated. How much Banda knew is a moot point. Like Pinochet in Chile, Banda was a dictator who claimed to know where every leaf fell. Renamo was hitting rail and road routes to landlocked Malawi, which had good diplomatic relations with Pretoria. It just did not add up. Various rationalisations have been offered. The simplest is that Pretoria used Renamo attacks to remind Banda that his membership of SADCC would carry penalties, but that would not explain why some Malawians helped the rebels. There were, however, strong cultural/tribal ties between the rebels in Zambézia and Tete provinces and southern Malawian communities. Another rationalisation might be that Pretoria manipulated its economic leverage over Malawi to force Banda to provide sanctuary to Renamo guerrillas in southern Malawi. A more complex explanation is that Banda supported the idea of a separate "Rombezia", the area from the Ruvuma river, the northern Mozambique border with Tanzania, to the Zambezi. Jorge

Jardim, formerly the Mozambican consul in Malawi, apparently encouraged Banda in this scheme. In the early 1960s Banda tried to persuade Nyerere that much of the Rombezia area was historically part of greater Malawi (with a slice for Tanzania). Elements in Renamo had originally advocated such separatist tribal designs. Banda's quirky territorial ambitions might well partially explain the paradox. The Malawian connection probably played a part in Renamo's August 1982 offensive. The insurgents consolidated their position in Zambézia and Gaza provinces. Renamo sources stressed the agreement on 15 August with Jimo Phiri, the leader of a small anti-Frelimo guerrilla movement called *Africa Livre*, which had ties with Malawi.(39)

Renamo claimed over 1,500 military engagements in 1982, including a spectacular assault on Beira harbour on 9 December. Renamo further claimed that, although the SADF had trained the saboteurs in Gorongosa, the movement had accomplished the task on its own. It seems much more likely, however, that the Reconnaissance Commandos blew up the 34 oil storage tanks with limpet mines after landing by sea. (It was probably the same Commando unit which attempted to repeat the same operation during the disastrous Cabinda escapade in May 1985.) Damage was estimated to be at least £10 million. An immediate fuel crisis hit Zimbabwe. The South African state-controlled TV service revelled in showing long lines of frustrated Zimbabwean motorists pushing their cars in miles-long queues at petrol stations. Hanlon reported that South African agents working for Manica Freight Services (then owned by Anglo American and Safmarine) were responsible for the intelligence behind the operation. Manica Freight Services office in Beira "was effectively a MNR office".(40) Earlier in the year, on 17 August, South African agents were blamed for the assassination of the anti-apartheid author and academic, Ruth First, the wife of Joe Slovo, the ANC and South African Communist Party leader. She was killed by a parcel bomb in her office at Eduardo Mondlane University.

On 23 May 1983, in retaliation for the devastating ANC car-bomb explosion in central Pretoria, South African jets bombed Matola and Liberdade suburbs of Maputo. Frelimo asserted that the victims were three workers in an innocent jam factory, a soldier guarding a bridge, a child playing and an ANC man washing his car. The SADF counter-claimed that 41 ANC, 17 Mozambican soldiers and six civilians had been killed. The SADF was embarrassed by reports from Western journalists who had inspected the destroyed jam factory. The SADF's version was that, except for a Mozambican SA-3 missile site, the jets hit carefully chosen ANC facilities. The timing, 7.25 am on a Monday, and the weapons used, were carefully selected to restrict civilian casualties. The SADF limited the strike to rockets and cannon fire because bombs were felt to be too inaccurate. Impala Mk11s were deployed because, being slower, they would be more accurate than the more advanced Mirages. (41)

While the SADF, almost unopposed, exercised its military superiority in the skies above Mozambique, on the ground Frelimo launched a number of successful counter-offensives against Renamo, particularly in the southern Gaza and Maputo provinces. Captured rebels were regularly paraded and publicly executed. In late 1983 Renamo conducted its own series of offensives. One, codenamed "Black September", led to the capture of 24 Soviet technicians in Morrua in Zambézia. By the end of 1983, Renamo claimed that its "zone of active operations"—not control —extended throughout Mozambique, except for the two northernmost provinces (Niassa and Cabo Delgado), western Tete and southern Maputo.

SADF air raids, captive Soviet personnel and Renamo's creeping domination of the rural areas left the Russians in an awkward position as guardians of Frelimo's revolution. Pretoria's destabilisation posed a serious test for Soviet prestige and resolve. It was a test they had manifestly failed, despite the grandiose fraternal rhetoric. In May 1982, the Mozambican chief of staff, General Sebastião Mabote, went to Moscow to discuss Maputo's deteriorating position with Marshal Dmitri Ustinov, the defence minister, as well as Marshal Nikolai Ogarkov and Admiral Sergei Gorshkov. Almost immediately, General Alexei Yepishev, the chief of the main political directorate of the Soviet army, toured military facilities in Mozambique and analysed in detail the Renamo advance.(42) And Soviet warships docked at Maputo to wave the flag. After the Matola commando raid, the Soviet ambassador to Mozambique directly warned Pretoria that the USSR would come to the aid of Frelimo if the SADF interventions continued. The introduction of Cuban combat troops was mooted, a suggestion which drew a counter-warning to Maputo from the US State Department. But nobody wanted the "Angolanisation" of the Mozambique war, especially the Russians. Moscow was bluffing. Its interests in Mozambique were limited. Soviet weaponry there, except for the MiG-21s, Mi-24 gunships and SAM-7s, was out-of-date and costly. And there was a growing local dissatisfaction with the quality of the socialist bloc advisers. The East Germans were good at tapping phones, but they could not stop Renamo. Soviet economic aid, especially during the calamitous 1983 famine, was deemed by Frelimo to be totally inadequate.

To survive, Machel needed better allies. In April 1982, Mozambique signed a treaty of military cooperation with Portugal. The old enemy returned to help train elite sections of the Mozambican army. Zimbabwe, and later the UK, agreed to provide officer training for the army. In a direct slight to the East Germans, Maputo recognised West Germany's rights in West Berlin as part of a food aid agreement. This opened the door to additional EEC aid. In 1984 Mozambique renewed links with China, and joined the IMF and the World Bank. All these steps seemed to justify the US State Department's "weaning theory": Western aid would seduce Machel from the Soviet embrace. The Western press started to reprint—possibly apocryphal—stories of Machel's growing distaste for the Russians. During a tour of development projects in Mozambique, Machel was told that one section was being built by the Russians, another by the East Germans and Romanians. "But the only trouble is," Machel is reported as saying, "they all want to be paid in US dollars."(43) Renamo's right-wing adherents in the US, most notably in the Heritage Foundation, argued that the weaning theory was nonsense; that Frelimo was irredeemably Marxist. Aid should be given to the anti-Marxist rebels, as part of the Reagan doctrine, they said. Neverthless, Mozambique did take steps to dismantle the most negative aspects of its Soviet-inspired economy, allowing a measure of decentralisation in agriculture and economic planning. Foreign investment was encouraged, although there were few takers because of the war and Frelimo's bureaucratic inertia.

In October 1983 Machel toured Western Europe. He was hungry for Western investment. In London he reportedly had a secret meeting with Anglo American's chairman, Harry Oppenheimer. Later, he had a highly publicised meeeting with Lonrho's Tiny Rowland. Rowland agreed to fund various projects, some of which required the protection of private British security firms which were not unconnected with British intelligence. Washington boosted its famine relief, although military aid was blocked by congressional conservatives. Machel indeed looked like changing horses in mid-gallop.

It was Pretoria's sword, not Western food, which had made Machel put on the mantle of a born-again capitalist. His economy was in absolute chaos. On top of war, drought and floods, Pretoria had tightened its economic blockade. Foreign exchange earnings dwindled partly because South African trade through Maputo in 1983 was down to 16% of its 1973 levels. This was partly because of the derelict state of the harbour and partly because of economic blackmail. Legal migrant workers had been reduced from 118,000 in 1975 to 45,000.(44) In short, no amount of Western or Eastern charity or trade could compare with the benefits of the release from Pretoria's stranglehold.

It all depended upon what Pretoria really wanted. The complex debate within the security elite boiled down to the "minimalists", who thought that destabilisation could change Mozambique's political behaviour, and the "maximalists", who believed that the time was right to overthrow the Frelimo government.(45) In support of the maximalist view, Zimbabwean intelligence had presented a secret report to Mugabe which argued that Pretoria was capable of toppling Machel in 48 hours.(46) Magnus Malan had explicitly warned that South Africa might find it necessary to initiate a "Lebanese-style" invasion of Mozambique to rid it of "ANC terrorists".(47) Yet the minimalists on the State Security Council asked what would Renamo do in Maputo if Machel fell. The minimalists, led as ever by Pik Botha, doubted whether Renamo "had the capacity to run anything more than a Mercedes and a few atrocities".(48). The foreign minister was attempting to draw Frelimo into a formal pact with Pretoria, but he complained that "the South African military intelligence was a trickier negotiating opponent than the Frelimo Marxists".(49) The debate within the SSC grew red hot. Perhaps not unrelated was the assassination of the Renamo secretary-general, Orlando Cristina, in April 1983 at "a farm" (possibly a Renamo training —centre) near Pretoria by "an unknown gunman"/enemies within Renamo/Frelimo secret police/SADF agents, according to rival versions. Evo Fernandes, who took over, was said to be hostile to a pact with Frelimo. Washington was not. Chester Crocker became directly involved in the SSC debate. When Magnus Malan was presented in the SSC with the American-sponsored outline of a Maputo-Pretoria pact, he is reported to have said: "This piece of paper is not worth my signature."(50) The final decision on a treaty with Machel was apparently clinched when the Americans persuaded the chief of police, Johan Coetzee, the former head of the security police, that Frelimo would stick to an agreement to eject the ANC. Coetzee's conversion reportedly swayed a sceptical P W Botha.(51)

After some haggling with Maputo, the two heads of state met in a circus atmosphere alongside the Nkomati river on 16 March 1984. With cameras whirring, 1,500 guests lunched sumptiously alongside the white VIP railway carriages that had been used for the abortive Rhodesian conference at Victoria Falls nine years earlier. Behind the polite, if bizarre, *coup de théâtre* lay the the simple truth: Pretoria had put a gun to the desperate Machel's temple, and said, "Kick out the ANC, or else". Or, as Hanlon put it, "Frelimo was screaming, 'Of course, I love you, just don't hit me again' ".(52)

Both sides pledged to curtail the activities of their protégés, the ANC and Renamo—without naming them. A joint security commission was established to monitor the agreement. Nkomati was a victory for Pretoria, and a clear defeat for the frontline states, as well as for the legion of anti-apartheid groupies in the salons of the West. The apartheid chieftain had sat down over lunch with the Marxist Machel, so surely now it was OK to play rugby, cricket...Pretoria had broken out of its dangerous diplomatic quarantine, and the ANC was unceremoniously turfed out of Mozambique, except for a small political representation. The ANC leadership was shattered at the abrupt, almost brutal way, its comrades had been booted out. Oliver Tambo, the ANC president, managed, however, to sound a conciliatory note at a press conference in London: "...the South African regime had decided to destroy Mozambique, to kill it as a state, and the [FRELIMO] leadership was forced to decide betweeen life and death. So if it meant hugging the hyena, they had to do it."(53) Moscow reacted very coolly to the hyena's triumph. The frontline states, while sympathising with Machel's dilemma, were outraged by the blatant success of Pretoria's blackmail. Machel put on a brave face, and prayed, no doubt, that Nkomati would buy him a breathing space.

It all depended whether the Afrikaners kept their word. Some did and some did not.

The old divisions resurfaced after the temporary facade of Nkomati bonhomie. According to Renamo sources, the head of military intelligence, Van der Westhuizen, against the express wishes of both Pik Botha and Chester Crocker, had ordered a massive resupply of military equipment for the rebels, just before Nkomati. Much of it was Soviet weaponry captured in SADF raids on SWAPO camps in Angola. Some of it was dropped by air near the Gorongosa base. This assistance was supposed to keep Renamo self-sufficient for at least six months' fighting. After Nkomati, however, Renamo maintains that all aid from South Africa ceased, except that Colonel van Niekerk still faithfully remained at his liaison post. The Voice of Free Africa was stilled. Renamo spokesmen tried to a put on a bold face after Nkomati. They said that it would prove conclusively that the movement could wage war without holding hands with the SADF. Privately, Dhlakama was incensed about the way Pretoria had behaved. He said he was told about Nkomati less than a week before it was signed.(54) Was the Renamo chief being disingenuous? For it became clear that the SADF continued to supply Renamo *after* Nkomati. But on whose orders?

Important documents, captured by Frelimo at the rebel Gorongosa HQ in August 1985, indicated a serious rift within the South African security establishment. Although Renamo protested that the documents were forged, there is little doubt that they are essentially genuine, albeit with some Frelimo gloss perhaps. Van der Westhuizen is quoted in the Gorongosa documents as saying: "We, the military, will continue to give them [Renamo] support without the consent of our politicians in a massive way so that they can win the war." The whole South African cast appears in the documents (three diaries and military papers), but most frequently mentioned is Van Niekerk, ("friend Commander Charlie"). The documents indicate that the SADF bugged private conversations between the "treacherous" Pik Botha and Frelimo officials. Obviously the foreign ministry was totally at odds with the hardliners in military intelligence. Where did P W Botha stand? When the documents were made public, the president's responses were highly ambiguous.

The Gorongosa documents indicate that at a very high level, despite political opposition and/or knowledge, the SADF secretly kept the supply lifeline open long after the 1984 pact. Frelimo appears to have kept its side of the bargain. The ANC's military wing, *Umkhonto we Sizwe*, did shut up shop in Mozambique. But, like Renamo, the ANC suffered only a temporary setback. By 1985 both insurgencies were more active than before Nkomati. Pretoria alleged that although the ANC had sought new infiltration routes, Mozambique was still being used. Both signatories breached the agreement, although Pretoria's transgressions were undoubtedly greater and far more calculated.

Boosted by the continuous logistical support, Renamo went on the offensive again. The rebels blew up Maputo's power station, one month after Nkomati. The capital was without electricity for a week. Renamo pushed into the north of the country for the first time, where cordial ties were established with the largely Muslim tribe, the Macondes. They had once formed the bulk of Frelimo's guerrilla force before independence, but they had become alienated by the government's religious intolerance. The Muslim factor was to prove invaluable later in building up Renamo's international links. At the end of 1984 Renamo claimed that its "zone of active operations" had spread through all ten provinces, while the movement also said it held "consolidated control" over the entire rural area of seven provinces in Nampula, Niassa, Zambézia, Tete, Manica, Sofala and Inhambane. Their army, they claimed, numbered 15,000.

With South African help, Renamo started to build up an international network of right-wing allies. Besides its military constituency and revanchist sympathy among the 600,000 to 700,000 members of South Africa's Portuguese community (amounting to perhaps 15% of the registered white electorate), sections of both the government and military in Portugal had links with the rebels. Renamo had friends in high places in

Bavarian politics, and allegedly the CIA. There were even rumours that some of the Irangate money had trickled into both Unita and Renamo war chests. Intelligence information, in some cases deliberately leaked by Pretoria, indicated that Saudi Arabia and probably other moderate Islamic states, such as Oman and the United Arab Emirates, plus other members of the so-called "Safari Club", originally put together by King Hassan of Morocco to help Savimbi, provided money for Renamo. The Muslim money, channelled by ex-Rhodesian sanctions-busting firms and ex-CIO executives in Holland, bought weapons (and other supplies) on the European arms market and passed them down the ancient Arab trade route from Oman, Somalia and Zanzibar to the Mozambique coast. The Comores, just 190 miles off the northern coast of Mozambique, had close ties with Pretoria after mercenaries, with Rhodesian help, overthrew the government in 1978 and restored a pliant conservative, Ahmed Abdallah, as president. Many of Renamo air supplies were said to come from these islands. And, elsewhere in Africa, Zaire was not unfriendly and a Renamo representative was established in Kenya.(55)

Renamo was stronger inside Mozambique and it had made its first tentative steps towards international recognition. For the rebels' allies in Pretoria it was time to take the next logical step: to get Frelimo to recognise Renamo. Frelimo officials met secretly with Fernandes in May 1984 in Frankfurt. In June and July Pik Botha and Van der Westhuizen talked with Frelimo officials in Maputo. From 1-3 October the Mozambique government delegation met face-to-face with Renamo, led by Fernandes. (Dhlakama was also in Pretoria, but apparently took a back seat.) The "Pretoria Declaration" called for a ceasefire and a tripartite commission, with the SADF, to monitor it. Pretoria had secured, in its view, a second, albeit minor, diplomatic victory by forcing Frelimo to implicity recognise the rebels by meeting them around a conference table. The ceasefire was supposed to lead to a political settlement. But neither materialised. Fernandes, possibly manipulated by hardline revanchists in the Portuguese government, adopted a tough, arrogant stance towards Frelimo. The rebels demanded a power-sharing arrangement with Maputo, while Frelimo conceded only an amnesty to those who surrendered.(56) But why accept an amnesty, if Renamo was increasingly more confident of actually *winning* the war?

Pik Botha was bitter at the failure of the Pretoria summit. In particular, he blamed the revanchists in the Portuguese government and intelligence community who were hostile to Frelimo because of the seizure of Portuguese property, as well as ideological motivations. The foreign minister was stone-walled by Lisbon when he complained, but a clampdown on Portuguese activists inside South Africa was ordered. In December 1984 Pik Botha flew secretly to Malawi, Somalia and the Comores in an attempt to stamp out pro-Renamo sentiments. President Botha, meanwhile, had made the SADF chief, Constand Viljoen, personally responsible for clamping down on the dissident pro-Renamo groups within the army, and especially in military intelligence. Viljoen acted quickly. Although none of the senior officers implicated were touched, some of the lower ranks were shifted sideways, posted away from Phalaborwa or dismissed. Renamo's liaison officer in Pretoria was literally locked out of his office. The Americans applauded these gestures, but they wanted more: for Pretoria not only to rein in Renamo, but actually provide military aid to Frelimo. Was Crocker suggesting, in particular, that SADF regular troops should assist Machel? That, as Jenkins put it, Crocker wanted to make the SADF "his Cubans"?(57) With some scorn, the military pointed out that while America was maintaining an arms embargo, the SADF was unlikely to act as a cat's paw for Washington. Operations in Mozambique would require, especially, the deployment of large helicopters. And South Africa was desperately short of these. In the end, the SADF was prevailed upon to provide about £1 million in vehicles and radio equipment to Frelimo.

Thus, Pretoria found itself aiding both sides in the civil war. Cynically, that could maximise chaos, yet there was also genuine assistance when South African experts regularly repaired communications infrastructure ravaged by Renamo action. The radio donations to Frelimo also made sense: it could facilitate a ceasefire and, if that meant a political advance for Renamo, it was a bonus for Pretoria. Playing both sides against the centre was not the deal struck at Nkomati, however. By early 1985 Machel realised that the Afrikaners were acting in bad faith. The resurgent Renamo was, to quote a senior Frelimo official, "unpicking the social fabric".(58) Frelimo held the cities, but—throughout the country—Renamo owned the night.

Machel turned to his neighbours. The Tanzanians offered to send troops. In July Britain granted funds to enlarge the officer training scheme at Nyanga, Zimbabwe, to include Mozambicans. The Zimbabwean expeditionary force had mushroomed from 1,500 in mid-1984 to 12,000 in 1985.(59) That figure soared to perhaps 18,000 during major offensives. Even to some of its supporters in Pretoria, the Renamo war was getting out of hand. The tame beast had become viciously uncontrollable. In March 1985 it was announced that a "Mafia-style syndicate" had been unearthed in the Portuguese community in Johannesburg. It had been smuggling money and supplies to the rebels. Acting on Mozambican information, the SADF found "a dozen" members of the SADF who were "purged". At least that was the official version.

The whitewash did not help. On 28 August 1985 Zimbabwean paratroopers, backed by Mozambican troops, stormed the Renamo main HQ, "Casa Banana", at Gorongosa. Renamo sources said that, facing a heliborne assault by 12,000 Zimbabwe National Army (ZNA) troops and 8,000 Frelimo, they retreated in good order, with small losses. Two of the Soviet officers, who coordinated the assault, were killed, it was claimed. Left behind, however, apparently thrown in a latrine, were the diaries of Major Joaquim Vaz, secretary to Dhlakama. On 16 September Machel told Pik Botha in Maputo about the diaries. The Afrikaner was reported to be furious when he found out that he had been called "treacherous" by General Viljoen and that the SADF had bugged his conversations.(60) Two weeks later, to coincide with Machel's surprisingly warm welcome by President Reagan in the White House, some of the captured documents were made public by Colonel Sergio Vieira, the minister of security, at a press conference in Maputo. It was all there in telling detail: weapons supplies, Pretoria's targeting of economic infrastructure in Mozambique, the SADF's construction of an air strip at Casa Banana, submarines picking up Renamo VIPs, and the record of three visits by the deputy foreign minister, Louis Nel, without the knowledge of his boss, Pik Botha. That really set the cat among the pigeons in Pretoria. As Hanlon observed: "There can be no stronger indication of continued high-level support for a surrogate army than for a deputy foreign minister to illegally enter a foreign country to talk to that army's leader."(61) The strains between foreign affairs and the SADF and their respective supporters in the cabinet and SSC reached breaking point. Viljoen and Pik Botha gave contradictory press conferences. (62) Eventually, as the entire Afrikaner leadership started shooting itself in both feet (in a fashion similar to the French government's handling of the Greenpeace *Rainbow Warrior* affair), a compromise line was formulated: yes, there had been "technical violations" of Nkomati, but, no, destabilisation was not intended. What Louis Nel had been trying to do was to set up a "Camp David-style" settlement, but the army did not want to tell Pik Botha in case the foreign minister would not let Nel go to the Renamo HQ as it would be too dangerous. That took some swallowing, even in Pretoria.

And, once again, where did the president stand? He was without question an authoritarian figure, and the military was his main constituency. Could he really have been unaware of the military's shenanigans? Yet he had committed himself publicly to Nkomati, the touchstone of his foreign policy initiatives in 1984. Some of the hawks who had conspired to continue Renamo's alliance were promoted, not punished. Van der Westhuizen, for example, was moved up to the powerful position of secretary of the SSC.

The Gorongosa documents had brought the in-house Afrikaner squabbles about destabilisation into the glaring light of day. As Martin and Johnson noted: "Gorongosa had given the diplomatic initiative back to Mozambique, leaving South Africa in the dock."(63)

That might have been the moral position. The military position was different. Despite the regular presence of 12,000 ZNA troops and 2,000 Tanzanians (and the promise of 5,000 Nigerians), the Frelimo armed forces in the countryside started to disintegrate. Some were Frelimo by day and Renamo by night. Renamo held, or ran riot in, vast swathes of territory, while Frelimo dug in in the cities. And even the few major cities were more scrapheaps than modern conurbations. Alistair Sparks, a not unsympathetic observer, noted in 1986 that Beira was a "city of 300,000 people with no electricity, water, telephones, food or goods in the shops".(64) Jenkins commented that the capital was like Luanda, "a city under siege from its hinterland, rationed, curfewed, black marketed and miserable". (65) Renamo, adopting classic Maoist tenets, hoped that once the rural areas were fully consolidated, the Frelimo-held cities would fall like ripe plums. Such was the economic collapse and Frelimo's military performance that by 1986 Mozambique could hardly be called a state any more.

However, 1986 was a good year for Renamo. On 14 February the Gorongosa HQ was recaptured. In October the movement launched its biggest offensive to date. For the first time it seized and held towns in Zambézia, Tete and Sofala provinces. Renamo, it seemed, planned to dominate the central provinces in order to divide the country in two, and to gain permanent access to the sea. In one of the larger captured towns, such as Caia in Sofala province, Renamo could have proclaimed a provisional government. If the town did not fall, this would have boosted the rebels' drive for international recognition.

Pretoria also applied the usual economic medicine. In early October, in the same week that the American Senate overrode Reagan's veto of a new sanctions bill, Pretoria announced that all the estimated 70,000 legal Mozambican workers (nearly all miners) would be forced to leave when their current labour contracts expired. The ejection of these legals (and perhaps as many as 140,000 illegal workers) would have cost Maputo at least £25 million per annum in lost foreign exchange. This indicated South Africa's determination to retaliate against Western sanctions by punishing its neighbours—even those, like Mozambique, who were too weak to vote for them.(66) The move was also intended as a warning to Maputo about ANC activity in the country. Six SADF personnel had just been injured in a landmine explosion next to the Mozambique border. This time it was economic jabs, not jets.

At the same time Mugabe and Machel exerted pressure on Banda to cut his links with Renamo. The international press, all fed by one source, the official Mozambican news agency, was full of largely inaccurate or, at best, simplistic stories that Banda had caved in to frontline diktat and had pushed 10,000 Renamo insurgents out of the southern Malawian bases, which had been staffed by South African (and even Israeli) advisers. And—*voilà*—the October offensive.(67) Renamo, however, had secure bases aplenty in Mozambique: they simply did not need such military sanctuaries in Malawi. Nor was Banda a man to be dictated to. It seems more likely that Banda refused "the offer he could not refuse". On 19 October a Soviet-crewed Tu-134 jet, with Machel and other Frelimo VIPs aboard, crashed on South African territory. In the wreckage, the police found evidence, they said, that proved that Machel and Mugabe were planning to support an internal coup against Banda.(68) So Renamo hung on to its Malawian connection.

Joaquim Chissano, the 47-year-old foreign minister, was elected to replace Machel in Frelimo's darkest hour since independence. The tall, slim, elegantly-dressed Chissano was a sharp physical contrast to the short, rough-and-ready Machel. He was as collected as Machel was turbulent. He needed to be. As Chissano took up office, the war was lapping around the edges of the capital. More than 40% of the national budget was soaked up by the fighting. The recent Renamo advances had further demoralised government forces. And there were reports that 1,500 soldiers had just crossed into Malawi to offer Renamo their weapons and equipment.(69) Malan had once talked about a Lebanese-style invasion. The parallel in late 1986 was more that of Uganda.

November 1986: a cameo

The Mozambican civil war was not a media event, such as Lebanon. The Frelimo government did not allow much freedom to report from its side, and the sheer inaccessibility of the guerrillas, poor international connections and their bloodthirsty image discouraged reportage from their perspective. Unlike Pakistan for the *Mujahedin* or Honduras for the *Contras*, there has been no convenient sanctuary for easy access. Nevertheless, this writer, and one companion, an ex-soldier who spoke Shona, in November 1986 travelled hundreds of miles, on foot, in dug-out canoes and on captured Frelimo motorbikes through Renamo-controlled territory. The main purpose was to interview Afonso Dhlakama, the self-styled president, at a remote bush camp near his Gorongosa HQ. What was Renamo's Mozambique like then?

> The entry: dug-out canoes wobbling through swamps. Hippos grunt. Then a long march, sometimes waist-deep in water. A kingfisher darts down to seize a fish and lily-trotters hop dementedly. Drier land. Eventually contact with a Renamo agent. Expectations of Khmer Rouge. Instead a genial figure in blue jeans, a purple tea-cosy hat, and a clean check shirt. His jeans are tucked into his socks, as he is pushing a bicycle along the bush path, while carrying the ubiquitous symbol of Renamo rank, a transistor radio in a gaudy bag, made of curtain material. Unlike the smartly-dressed officers in Savimbi's "Free Angola", the man in the tea-cosy does not want to stamp any passports.
>
> A small transit camp. Our communication is in basic Portuguese and broken Shona. Fed ground corn and chicken, three times a day, the same food precisely for weeks, except for captured Frelimo tinned food, usually Russian fish and canned Australian cheese. The insurgents operate a hand-cranked generator for their communications, probably an old Mortley-Sprague, but difficult to get near radio hut. The defensive lay-out of the base is exactly the same as the ZANLA camps of the 1970s.
>
> A signal is sent to the main Renamo base in Zambézia province. It is 40 miles away, well-hidden among mountains and forest. It holds about 500 ragged troops and perhaps two to three thousand camp followers (as well as a much bigger army of rats). The camp is made of wood and thatch, with bits of looted furniture indecorously adorning the primitive style. We had just visited Unita's Jamba HQ, the Las Vegas of guerrilla bases. But this is very crude, with one generator occasionally providing power. The base has a small clinic with virtually no medicines; the top motor-bike mechanic doubles as the doctor. Nearby there is a school, where the teacher has one book, a Frelimo textbook, with the pages containing Marxist propaganda torn out. The camp commandant and rebel governor of the province is Commander General Calistu Matade Meque, a dangerous eccentric. His whimsically autocratic manners are reminiscent of Shaka Zulu's not-so-gentle court. We are told about the reasons for Renamo's fight. There are complaints about harassment of religion and traditional chiefs, and forced communisation of the land. There is talk of free elections and the end of Marxist tyranny. But this is also Shona territory. The old ways, the spirit mediums, the need for polygamy, and *lobola* (bride price), are also discussed.
>
> The insurgents are clearly under formal discipline. The worst infringement of the code is to intimidate the *povo*, the peasantry. Most guerrilla armies have similar codes. This one is similar to ZANLA's and that was breached as much as it was observed. Male soldiers are not supposed to smoke or frater-

nise with the large number of female cadres in the camp. Both sexes volunteer, or are press-ganged, for the "duration". Morale appears high, but military standards are decidely low. The rebels wear rags; the officers wear a bizarre array of Rhodesian, East German, Tanzanian, Zimbabwean, Portuguese and Frelimo camouflage dress. Weapons are in a terrible condition, never cleaned (except with soap and water!). There is Malawian or home-made beer for the officers, but no oil for weapons. Some of the officers keep their AKs in good condition. These are second-generation guerrillas: Frelimo perhaps absorbed, say, 30% of the expertise of their Eastern bloc instructors during the 1960s. In turn, Renamo soldiers, many of whose officers are ex-Frelimo, have adapted a percentage of that original training, which has been beefed up by Rhodesian and South African advisers. During the whole journey of hundreds of miles we see, however, no direct evidence of South African involvement, except the radio network, which had been donated, apparently, before Nkomati. We see no white or black South African troops. Indeed many of the villagers seem to be astounded at the sight of our white faces.

The zany general puts on a weapons and training exhibition. The rebels on parade are hardly the brigade of guards, but nor do they behave like unruly bandits. Renamo rolls out for its guests a galaxy of ill-assorted hardware, ranging from old German Mausers to Russian AGS-17 grenade-launchers, which are rare in Africa. They have some SAM-7s, but they don't know how to operate them. They ask us to demonstrate. Half-guests, half-hostages we manage to politely refuse. Thus, the Zimbabwean gunships and the Frelimo air force, when it manages to fly, are a major problem for the rebels, who have no effective defence against air attacks. Otherwise, boasts General Calistu, "Zimbabwean troops run away just like Frelimo when we attack them. They always call up air support." Renamo claims that it captures all its weapons. Frelimo says that the rebels' arsenal is largely comprised of SADF donations of Russian weapons seized in Angola.

Two hundred miles travelling south, cross-country, in a convoy of three small Japanese motorbikes. The rebels drive with great speed and little skill. Usually villagers rush out to greet us. They bring corn and water. There is a religious college: people wave Bibles at us. There seems little starvation, although the peasants are dressed in rags, sometimes even in bark. Long columns of porters pass, going north. They are carrying bags of ground corn on their heads for sale or barter in Malawi. This is no PR fix: we stop and go where we want. The peasants do not appear cowed. In this raw, primitive, regressive society, there appear—on the surface—to be few local problems with hearts and minds.

We hop from base to base in what Renamo calls liberated zones. We pass abandoned Portuguese stores, farms and once pretty little colonial towns, painted in light pastel shades. Everything now is utterly deserted. A beautiful, isolated, desecrated cathedral arches towards the heavens. Blasphemous graffiti despoil the walls. On the road a bright red tractor stands gutted. A train is strewn across an embankment. All the carriages are overgrown by fast-encroaching bush. Once this part of Mozambique teamed with wildlife. We see only four deer, a few monkeys and many tree-snakes during the entire trip. Then the majestic Zambezi river. A half-finished bridge stands to attention on either side. A large sub-station for the Cahora Bassa hydro-electric scheme mourns its crippled and useless state. Bits of the transformers decorate the roofs of the villagers' huts, although hardly any part of Mozambique has regular electricity. Petrol is king here. For the Renamo elite's motorbikes and for boats to cross the wide, surging Zambezi. Everything is cannibalised to keep the few machines and motors running. "This is something out of Mad Max," comments my companion. On the other side of the fast-running river, crossed in a captured Frelimo inflatable, bikes and all, are millions of pounds worth of heavy plant. Massive cranes bend, as if, in pain, they are marooned like the Martian machines from Wells's *War of the Worlds*.

Caia, a largish small town in Sofala province. It has a big air strip, but no sign of air activity at all. The town was recently captured from Frelimo. Caia is absolutely empty, as though vultures had picked clean its carcass. A child's tin rocking horse and a 1930s typewriter are the only artifacts left behind after the flight or pillage. It is as if a neutron bomb had been dropped. Indeed, the whole of Mozambique seems to have that dread feeling of a post-apocalypse film. Renamo camps outside the town. Is this a Khmer Rouge addiction to the ideological purity of the countryside or prudent fear of Zimbabwean airforce gunships? Hundreds of Frelimo prisoners are also camped outside the town. They look hungry and miserable. Renamo says they would be freed, after a time. Those who wanted to enlist could. None would be kept against their wishes. That seemed dubious. As did the Renamo officers' explanation that the town had been ravaged by retreating Frelimo troops, not the advancing Renamo.

The motorbikes race along now on tarmac roads in broad daylight to reach the edge of the Gorongosa forest. We camp at a satellite of the main HQ, from where Renamo sends out its forces to disrupt the Beira Corridor. We are to meet Mozambique's Scarlet Pimpernel, Afonso Dhlakama. Is he a nationalist committed to an African variant of, say, Dr David Owen's brand of social democracy, as Renamo propagandists imply, or the most vicious mass-murderer since Hitler, as Frelimo insists? Is he a patriot, or a puppet of Pretoria? These thoughts pass through our minds as we are introduced to an unprepossessing, chubby young man dressed simply, in a blue shirt and dark slacks. There is no Savimbi-style posturing with fancy six-guns. He is sitting quietly and alone at a plain table in a grass hut.

He is 33, and looks like a younger version of his arch enemy, Mugabe. Dhlakama, too, is Catholic-trained. He is a family man with three children. He is confident, quietly-spoken and relaxed. Obviously intelligent, he speaks a very precise Portuguese, although he understands English. Unlike most politicians and generals he is prepared to listen. He discusses international

PLATE 12.3 Afonso Dhlakama, the Renamo leader.

PLATE 12.4 Renamo arsenal: captured from Frelimo or donated by the SADF?

affairs and questions why everybody rates his movement as the most cut-throat of the world mafia of insurgencies. He offers us a "Coke", the most ubiquitous capitalist symbol in Africa (although not in Mozambique) and a suitable rival accompaniment to the Russian AKs that surround us.

The conversation goes on for two whole days. He vehemently denies that he receives military support from Malawi or South Africa. He emphasises in almost Maoist terms his self-sufficiency. "We have no complex theory. Our strategy is simple. It is based upon the support of the people." He claims to control 85% of the country. He laughs at the idea that Renamo needs bases in Malawi. "When we launch an offensive near Malawi, they say we have bases there. But when we take towns near the Zimbabwe border, they do not say we get support from bases in Zimbabwe." He denies any part in a grand scheme to destabilise southern Africa. He has had no contact with Unita, he says, and proceeds to criticise Savimbi's current overtures to Frelimo, which followed the condolences Savimbi sent after the death of Machel. And the plane crash? "It looks like an accident to me," says the unlikely-looking warlord.

The West, he maintains, particularly America, has no idea of what is really happening in Mozambique. "The people of Mozambique are now independent, but they are not free. Here in Mozambique everything is done by force. People are taken by force to live in communal villages, their children are sent to Cuba without their parents' consent. We believe independence has nothing to do with this sort of thing. The ideals which drove us to take up arms against the Portuguese rule haven't yet been fulfilled." He launches into a tirade against Chester Crocker and the State Department, "who have been doing a good job of promoting the cause of the Marxist Frelimo". He also accuses Pretoria of betraying him.

And what of the Vaz diaries, which said Pretoria was still helping? He insists they are forgeries. The president changes the subject.

Renamo is winning, he insists. "We are not the *desperadoes*, it's Frelimo that's desperate...All the aid money is used to buy weapons to keep them in power, not to those who are dying of hunger...They spend their days watching the ports along the coast, hiding and waiting in Maputo for the arrival of a boat from the US bringing food and everything else that's necessary for the survival of Frelimo which is surrounded in the city of Maputo. In fact, Frelimo survives only in the big cities." The war can be won militarily, he asserts, but, paradoxically, he concedes that negotiation is possible, especially if there were to be a military coup—a favourite theme of Dhlakama's—by some Frelimo generals who are tired of fighting a no-win war.

The "president" claims that he has 22,000 trained regulars, while he is also building up a part-time force which currently stands at 7,000. So Renamo is doing well on the ground, but what about its atrocious external image? "The Marxists have traditionally been brilliant at propaganda," he admits. He also admits to the fact that he needs to jack up Renamo's external political representation. He adds quickly that he doesn't get money or supplies from external sources.

> We leave Dhlakama. His off-the-record remarks seem to confirm his naivety if not his integrity. We are utterly cynical about some of his claims. But the fact remains that we saw no evidence of South African involvement and no evidence in Malawi of bases, although there were refugee camps for over 80,000 Mozambicans. After travelling for hundreds of miles, we did see basic organisation and an infrastructure. We saw food being grown. We witnessed no cruelty to the peasantry, although Renamo is hardly likely to stage a quick atrocity for the benefit of Western journalists and their cameras.
>
> On the harsh return journey, we stay at camps where no sentries are posted. The camps lack basic defence perimeters, which even a lowly SADF corporal would insist upon. The Viet Cong would have made mincemeat of this lot, we think. We conclude that Renamo guerrillas are doing so well militarily, not because they are any good, but because Frelimo is so bad. The journey to "Free Mozambique" had been instructive, but we left as cynics, still wondering about the amazingly coincidental congruence of Renamo's and Pretoria's strategies.(70)

The Chissano era

Joaquim Chissano, a popular choice with the party, swore that he would continue on Machel's path. Given the deteriorating military situation and limited political options, the new leader had precious little room to manoeuvre. Almost immediately, he was impelled to devalue the currency by 420% to secure World Bank and IMF loans. On the military front, Chissano tried to improve the chronic relations with Malawi. In December 1986, both countries signed a security agreement. Malawi promised to stop Renamo using its territory as a sanctuary, and to allow Frelimo troops the right of hot pursuit inside the country. And Malawian troops—about 500 by June 1987—were sent to guard the Malawi-Nacala railway.(71) Mugabe also obtained permission from Banda for ZNA troops to cross Malawi's territory to get at Renamo bases in Zambézia.

The neighbourhood fences mended, Chissano ordered an immediate offensive against the rebels, despite and because of growing pressure within the military high command that talks, brokered by the Catholic Church, should be held with the rebels.(72) In February and March 1987, Zimbabwean and Tanzanian forces recaptured the towns that Renamo had seized in Zambézia in 1986. Frelimo believed that Renamo could no longer use the province as a base to declare a provisional government of "Free Mozambique". Maputo claimed that 2,200 rebels were wiped out in this counter-offensive.(73) Many of the significant military rebel gains of 1986 were eliminated by the surprisingly successful Frelimo-ZNA counter-blow.

Gleams of hope punctured the dark gloom in Maputo. Western aid increased too. The US provided over £40 million worth of food and economic assistance, although the pro-Renamo right-wing forces in Washington, led by Senators Jesse Helms and Bob Dole, tried to cut all aid to Chissano. British aid was more precisely targeted at military efficiency. At the official level, 480 field-grade Mozambican officers had so far been trained by the British army in Zimbabwe. The UK also gave £750,000 to Malawi to buy non-lethal equipment for its troops guarding the Nacala railway. Mozambican units, trained by ex-British SAS personnel at Manica, also protected the line. That was the public British connection. Various small private armies were also set up and, allegedly, paid by Lonrho and the UK government, and then supplied by Hall and Watts (Defence Sales) and trained in some cases by Defence Systems Ltd, a polite job employment agency for ex-SAS soldiers. Foreign projects such as Lonrho's cotton plantations at Montechoeria and the ESSO scheme at Cabo Delgado needed to be protected against Renamo, otherwise foreign investment would have withered away completely.(74) Yet it was an unflattering commentary on Frelimo's military performance that ex-SAS men were needed to help secure these projects, alongside thousands of Malawian, Tanzanian and Zimbabwean troops, plus all the hundreds of Eastern bloc advisers still in place. These various armies did manage to keep the main routes open, most of the time, especially the Beira corridor. Renamo hit the corridor, but less often, and it was rapidly repaired, usually by Zimbabwean staff. In particular, the Lonrho-owned oil pipeline was promptly and expertly patched up after Renamo sabotage. Nevertheless, the protection of the corridor cost much in lives and money. Fortified bunkers were built all along the route; convoys were hit frequently. Between 1981 and 1986 over 200 Zimbabwean railway workers were killed and 600 injured trying to run the Renamo gauntlet. And, at the end of the line, Beira was still a scrapheap, not a modern port.

What was Pretoria doing about Renamo's reverses? In May 1987 the SADF was reported to have provided a "heavy" resupply to its secret ally.(75) Pretoria might also have had a hand in helping Renamo forge an alliance with a so-called guerrilla army led by that professional political victim, Ndabaningi Sithole.(76) Partly because of the 1987 Frelimo offensives, Renamo forces had taken refuge in the mountains along the Zimbabwean border. And earlier, in 1986, Dhlakama had declared war on Mugabe. Foraging, as much as political, raids blighted the eastern Zimbabwean highlands. Sithole did have a tribal base in southern Manicaland among the small Ndau group, a tribe that was over-represented in the Renamo military command. The Sithole alliance was, however, almost entirely restricted to newspaper articles. Even Sithole's wife dismissed the pact as "absolute nonsense".(77) Much more practical assistance was still being given by the South African police, which continued to entice unemployed Mozambicans into signing up for Dhlakama. By late 1986 South African statistics showed that 73,146 Mozambicans were registered as migrant workers (63,705 were miners), but an estimated 250,000 Mozambicans had entered South Africa illegally in search of food, security and work.(78) The desperate illegals were wonderful recruitment fodder. Arrested, usually in the eastern Transvaal, because they did not have correct papers and, faced with the alternative of starving to death if they were forced to return home, they would be given small amounts of cash and offered an interesting job. Renamo would not be mentioned until the luckless migrants were in a rebel training camp. Then they were threatened with death if they tried to desert.

On 19 July 1987 the massacre of nearly 400 peasants at Homoine in Inhambane province provoked another crisis in the uneasy Pretoria-Maputo detente.(79) Renamo was blamed, but the rebels insisted that the atrocity was the work of mutinous government militiamen. Renamo also alleged that the ZNA had established a special pseudo unit, from the 6th Brigade and under the command of Colonel Lionel Dyke, which was raping, pillaging and murdering in the name of Dhlakama.(80) Other atrocities ensued in quick succession, sometimes in the same locations. Maputo continued to damn Pretoria. It looked like the final nail in the Nkomati coffin. But neither side wanted the pact to die. Surprisingly, the agreement was revived and even the joint security commission, defunct since 1985, was resuscitated. Lisbon was actively involved. The Portuguese government, largely bearing the burden of debt on the construction costs of the huge Cahora Bassa scheme, hinted that South Africa's sanction-busting centres in Madeira and other facilities in the Azores might be in jeopardy.

Chissano's moves had been adroit. Within a few months he had stopped Renamo's advance and repaired some of the broken fences with Malawi, South Africa and the West. He now felt confident enough to purge his armed forces of the veterans of the liberation war, some of whom were talking to Renamo about a negotiated settlement. He appointed younger officers, loyal to himself, who were committed to defeating the rebels.(81)

Despite the formidable array of opponents, Renamo refused to accept Maputo's continuous amnesty offers and fought on for a victory, or at least a power-sharing arrangment. Externally, its position had not improved: Renamo still depended not only upon "a South African father who wavers on his alimonies, but a Portuguese mother who continues to nourish the unacknowledged offspring".(82) Renamo enthusiasts in the US and UK kept sniping at Reagan's and Thatcher's diplomatic dance with Chissano. An American conservative, writing in *The Sunday Telegraph*, observed: "Renamo is in fact the world's fastest-growing anti-Communist insurgency. A mere 2,000 guerrillas eight years ago, it now numbers 20,000, an increase that makes it twice the size of Marxist-Leninist Frelimo when the Portuguese packed their bags in 1975."(83)

Yet no matter how well Renamo performed militarily, it was plagued by the South African alliance and its poor external representation. These plagues were not unrelated. Elements within Renamo wanted to ditch Pretoria, but this was opposed by Evo Fernandes. And, in Washington, there was almost a mirror-image of the SADF-foreign affairs antagonism; there it was the CIA versus the State Department. Elements in the CIA wanted to "wean" Renamo away from Pretoria, whereas Crocker's men desired a more straightforward, clean-hands relationship with Maputo. Fernandes wanted to continue the Pretoria nexus. In 1986 he was removed from his post as secretary-general, but he remained as head of the "research department". Besides the question of allegiance to Pretoria, much of the debate centred on communications. In 1980, the SADF had set up a communications network in Mozambique, but allegedly doctored it so that all lines went through Pretoria, making it difficult for the regional commanders to deal with each other and Renamo HQ. Some elements of the external leadership wanted to set up a new communications system independent of the SADF, although there were also disputes about where the nerve-centre should be: Washington or Lisbon. In December 1987 two Renamo activists opposed to Pretoria's involvement were killed in a "car crash" in southern Malawi. Then in April 1988 Fernandes was assassinated in Lisbon. As usual, rival explanations abounded: Fernandes was killed by the CIA or SNASP or the Portuguese or Renamo opponents. One theory has them *all* conspiring against the unfortunate man. (84) (Later reports suggested it was the work of Frelimo agents.) The fratricide within Renamo was destroying the determined efforts of the ultra-right wing in both the US and the UK, largely coordinated by an energetic young American, Tom Schaaf, to present a credible international front organisation.(85)

In April 1988 the Gersony report, a damning indictment of Renamo, compounded the external activists' problems. Robert Gersony, an independent consultant, prepared the report for the US State Department's Bureau for Refugee Programs. Taking evidence from Mozambican refugees in six countries, including the 500,000 in Malawi and 225,000 in South Africa, Gersony concluded that 100,000 innocent people had died and that 90% of the attacks had been caused by Renamo.(86) The report's methodology was suspect, but the political damage done to Renamo in the US was beyond question. Renamo called for an independent enquiry into Homoine, and offered to prove that Zimbabwean gunships had strafed Red Cross centres, but no one was listening. Roy Stacy, the former US deputy assistant secretary of state for Africa, accused Renamo of committing "one of the worst holocausts since World War Two"; another Western diplomat described the rebels as "starving wolf-packs, who kill, first and foremost, to eat".(87) Other reports emphasised the "instrumentalised" children, who had been kidnapped and programmed to kill by Renamo.(88) This would add to the future misery: Mozambique had one trained psychiatrist for a population of 14 million. Who would help to heal a traumatised generation?

Renamo always argued that the rebels were not assassins without faith or law. A British journalist, Nicholas della Casa, freed by the guerrillas in December 1988, after being held captive for 18 months, said that, in his view, "the population of Renamo-held areas regarded the guerrillas in much the same way as the population of Dorset regards Nato soldiers: occasional grumblings, but no real resentment".(89) To most other observers—and very few commentators, admittedly, had ever been in Renamo territory—that could be the understatement of the year. Renamo said that Frelimo's murderous incompetence and ZNA pseudo-gangs were largely responsible for outrages against civilians. Renamo's protests went unrecorded in the world press. British foreign correspondents were fascinated instead by the trivia: by the visit, for example, of Neil Kinnock, the Labour leader, to Zimbabwe, partly to acquaint himself with the British army's role in training Mozambicans. He managed to get himself and his party arrested. That did hit the headlines.

In June 1988 the defence ministers of Mozambique, Tanzania and Zimbabwe met at Quelimane to coordinate a massive offensive against the rebels. In August four combat groups, of about 2,000 allied troops each, launched a combined onslaught in central Mozambique. Renamo melted into the bush and lived to fight again. The central purpose of this attack was to completely clear the main communications routes, especially the Beira corridor, which had been annexed *de facto* by Zimbabwe.

PLATE 12.6 Some of the Renamo soldiers are early teenagers

PLATE 12.5 Frelimo prisoners, captured in Sofala province, 1985-86

No armed solution, however, was possible without Pretoria's nod. In mid-1988 and early 1989 Pretoria made overtures to Maputo, to coincide with P W Botha's diplomatic campaign in September, when the South African president met Chissano. Pretoria began to deliver £15 million-worth of equipment, including vehicles, radios, medicines, mine-detectors and uniforms, to help protect the Cahora Bassa power-lines and to repair the 520 sabotaged pylons. In early 1989, as a sequence to the Angolan agreement, South Africa offered to extend the peace process to a settlement in Mozambique.(90) Yet ANC sources indicated that the original "Operation Mila", involving a company called Frama International, based near Johannesburg, which shipped SADF supplies, was still providing a military lifeline.(91) By 1989, however, it seemed as though the SADF's hawks were finally listening to their master's voice. Renamo support had become a taboo subject. Then the master fell ill. P W Botha was a sorcerer who had conjured up a semblance of unity in the SSC and cabinet. With his departure, would the sorcerer's apprentices run riot, especially in Mozambique?

The mood of Angolan/Namibian settlement, however, did spill over into Mozambique. Evidence accumulated that Pretoria had indeed backed Renamo, if more secretly and less consistently, from 1984-88.(92) But mid-1989 appeared to mark a fresh approach by Pretoria to bring the two sides together. Behind the scenes were Portugal and Britain, which used its connections in Kenya. The Kenyan government in June and July tried to organise a Renamo-Frelimo face-to-face meeting. Maputo offered to intensify its amnesty campaign, which had brought in hundreds of ex-Renamo soldiers in 1988. But Chissano refused to discuss constitutional changes. Renamo, however, demanded to be taken more seriously. After its first national congress, held in June 1989 in Mozambique, Dhlakama insisted that a government of national unity be set up and then an election be held. At the time of writing, Dhlakama and Chissano had not shaken hands as Dos Santos and Savimbi had done (very reluctantly), but hopes of some kind of settlement looked better than at any time in the 1980s. Meanwhile, with Chissano's approval, various Mozambican churchmen were meeting with assorted Renamo spokesmen in Nairobi.(93) Perhaps a joint superpower shove, as in Angola, was all that was needed to get the two warring sides to talk seriously.

Future prospects

Perhaps half Mozambique's population was starving. Besides the one million refugees in neighbouring countries, millions had become internal refugees. In this very real sense, everyone had lost the war. Mozambique was prostrate. The only winner—in the short-term—was Pretoria. In different measures, the SADF had backed both sides, thus earning Mozambique an unusual accolade: "a South African-backed, Soviet surrogate state", as Renamo dubbed it. There were numerous other ironies. The right wing in the US camp often supported Renamo, yet it had been omitted from the Reagan doctrine's laundry list. The "weaning" theorists in the State Department had a point. In the aid game, the West could always outdo the Soviets. Thus, economic largesse (or neo-colonialism) played to America's strong suit, just as weapons supplies, as in Angola, played to Russian strengths. Another paradox involved Zimbabwe. Cecil Rhodes had dreamed of providing Rhodesia with a corridor to the sea. Hence his sponsorship of the railway to Beira in 1899. Mugabe made the colonial dream a reality: the Zimbabwe National Army (ZNA) became master, albeit disputed by Renamo, of the Beira corridor. Frelimo troops were considered more of a hindrance than a help. ZNA senior officers made it clear that they wanted to place all local Frelimo units under their command, restrict them to base or disarm them. The ZNA was convinced of Renamo penetration of Frelimo at all levels, and therefore tended to mount operations without informing Frelimo.(94) The disdain was epitomised by the frequently told, if possibly apocryphal, story of the same ZNA officer capturing the same Renamo prisoner on two successive days. The disconcerted Zimbabwean was told that the Frelimo officer to whom prisoners were handed was the captive's uncle. Zimbabwean businessmen developed a similar disrespect for Frelimo's curious management techniques, a compound of the worst of Portuguese bureaucracy and East German central planning. In turn, the Mozambicans, not unnaturally, grew to resent what they saw as Zimbabwean imperialism. Rhodes could rest comfortably in his grave.

Despite all the foreign entanglements, Mozambique appeared to be in the grip of an indigenous and massive peasant revolt. It would be incorrect, however, to overemphasise the clash of a Marxist revolution versus a pro-Western counter-revolution. The melange of ethnic, cultural, religious, racial, linguistic and ideological differences would be too complex to allow for such a trite generalisation. Widespread disaffection with Frelimo rule has been evident, but Renamo has been just one major manifestation. On the other hand, Renamo's flimsy rhetoric about social democracy, elections *et al*, has not proved to a be a convincing explanation as the motor of revolt.

The war seems unwinnable in the foreseeable future. Even if Renamo's infrastructure were to be smashed, local warlordism could become endemic. Even if Renamo won, and Frelimo crawled back into the bush to fight on, Pretoria would be unlikely to risk being transformed from a backseat fairy godmother to sitting in the driving seat with Dhlakama on its lap. That could be Vietnam revisited. Or at least Angola. Pretoria had managed to extricate itself from that quagmire. Once was enough. So, for the time being, the Mozambican mayhem distracts the frontline states from their *Jihad* against apartheid, precisely what Pretoria intended. Thus, no matter what indigenous or foreign backing Renamo motivates, its role in scuttling the frontline crusade against Pretoria must deny the rebels any real chance of international credibility.

References and notes:

1. See K Flower, *Serving Secretly*, Murray, London, 1987, p. 260.
2. A Seegers, "Revolutionary Armies of Africa: Mozambique and Zimbabwe," in S Baynham, (ed), *Military Power and Politics in Black Africa*, Croom Helm, London, 1986, p. 145.
3. K Campbell, *Southern Africa in Soviet Foreign Policy*, Adelphi Paper No. 227, International Institute for Strategic Studies, London, 1987, p. 15.
4. SNASP is the *Serviço Nacional de Segurança Popular* (the People's National Security Police).
5. Lucinda Pires, an emigré quoted in J Wheeler, *RENAMO: The Mozambique National Resistance*, mimeo, report prepared for the Foreign Policy Research Institute, California, June 1988, p. 8.
6. Machel warned Mugabe in 1980 not to repeat the Mozambique experience. The key was keeping white expertise in the country, he said.
7. A Isaacman, "Mozambique," in *Survival*, 30:1, January/February 1988, pp. 18-19.
8. J Hanlon, *Beggar Your Neighbours*, Catholic Institute for International Relations, London, 1986, p. 148.
9. R Johnson, *How Long Will South Africa Survive*? Macmillan, Johannesburg, 1977, p. 130.
10. Author's interviews with Frelimo officials. The bond did not prevent Machel from putting both men under virtual house arrest during a period of ZANLA infighting in the mid-1970s.
11. Flower was in some ways proud of his unruly step-child. After he retired as director-general of the CIO in June 1981, he worked as a part-time consultant for the organisation. On a number of occasions Mugabe told Flower that Machel had a great deal of respect for the spymaster. Just before he died in the plane crash, Machel had asked whether Flower would spend some time in Maputo as his personal guest, presumably to discuss Renamo. Author's interview with Flower, 1987.
12. The South African journalist-spy Gordon Winter claimed in his sensational (and inaccurate) book, *Inside BOSS*, that BOSS helped to create Renamo. See J Hanlon, *Mozambique: The Revolution Under Fire*, Zed, London, 1984, p. 220. For an excellent account of the CIO's connections with Renamo, see D Martin and P Johnson, "Mozambique: To Nkomati and Beyond," in P Johnson and D Martin, (eds), *Destructive Engagement*, Zimbabwe Publishing, Harare, 1986, especially pp. 1-14.

13. There are various transliterations of the Renamo chief's name. This text follows the usage of Renamo officials.
14. Martin and Johnson, *op. cit.*, p. 5.
15. Author's interview with Dhlakama in a bush camp near Gorongosa HQ, November 1986.
16. Martin and Johnson, p.10.
17. Quoted in Flower, *Serving Secretly*, op. cit., p. 302. There is some ambiguity here (as there is in much of the book). The document is dated April 1974. In the previous paragraph, Flower talks of the previous five years of Renamo activity. "1974" could be a misprint on the original memorandum. Elsewhere in his memoirs, there are contradictory statements about Renamo's genesis. Flower traces back his involvement with pseudo-forces to the 1940s during his war service in Somalia. There were, apparently, discussions about a Mozambican counter-force in the mid-1960s, when Rhodesia's own first pseudos were formed, later to become the Selous Scouts. In the early 1970s there were various discussions with the Portuguese. But, for practical purposes, 1976 may be taken as the date of Renamo's birth.
18. B Cole, *The Elite: The Story of the Rhodesian Special Air Service*, Three Knights, Amanzimtoti, 1984, p. 245.
19. The "350" estimate is given by Isaacman, *op. cit.*, p. 22. Depending upon the definition of "attack"—would that mean an ambush or a large engagement?—350 seems too low. Isaacman is presumably quoting Frelimo sources.
20. Wheeler, *op cit.*, p. 19.
21. *Ibid.*, p. 20.
22. For a well-informed analysis of the origins of Renamo's external structure, see Martin and Johnson, pp. 7-10.
23. *Ibid.*, p. 13.
24. Author's conversations with Flower; Martin and Johnson, p. 12.
25. Wheeler, p. 23, Fn. 46.
26. Martin and Johnson, p. 15, say that the SAS formed the 5th Reconnaissance Regiment; Renamo sources refer to the 2nd Regiment and *Africa Confidential* refers to the 1st Regiment. Most of the SAS men disliked the excessive regimentation of the SADF with its Afrikaans orientation and they disagreed with SADF tactics, especially when the SAS was used as cannon fodder. Author's informal interviews with various SAS officers and Colonel Barrett.
27. Various author's interviews with Flower, 1980-87. See also Fn 26. During the Rhodesian war there was a gentleman's agreement between the Rhodesian and South African intelligence services on a number of operational matters. For example, both had agreed not to run agents in each other's territories without prior arrangement, nor should either ally poach agents. This understanding broke down after 1978. At the end of the war Pretoria recruited a large number of high-ranking agents in the police, army and intelligence services, for activation in the post-independence period. Flower felt that this was not on. Many were weeded out after Flower left the CIO, and they were imprisoned or fled to South Africa. For those who remained, see Chapter 13.

    An example of South Africa's leaking disinformation/propaganda about Flower can be found in A Parker, "How Lord C [Carrington] Sold Out Rhodesia," *The Citizen*, 24 February 1982, and R Lange, "The Rebel Road—It's a 30km Hell-Route," *The Sunday Express*, (Johannesburg), 28 February 1982. Aida Parker, an eccentric if well-informed journalist, had a fixation that Flower was a British mole. This charming old lady pursued her quarry almost as obsessively as Peter Wright dogged Roger Hollis in *Spycatcher*.

    DONS = Department of National Security and NIS = National Intelligence Service.
28. Martin and Johnson, p. 19.

29. See, for example, Hanlon, *Mozambique: The Revolution Under Fire, op. cit.*, p. 227.
30. Martin and Johnson, p. 19.
31. Wheeler, p. 25. This late 1980 figure is almost certainly an exaggeration, bearing in mind the disastrous events of June/July 1980.
32. For a discussion of Renamo and Frelimo strategies, see Hanlon, *Mozambique: The Revolution Under Fire*, pp. 219-33.
33. See *ibid*, p. 224.
34. Hanlon, *Beggar Your Neighbours*, p. 136.
35. Martin and Johnson, p. 22. See also *The Observer*, 20 February 1983.
36. According to Wheeler, p. 26.
37. Hanlon, *Mozambique: The Revolution Under Fire*, p. 222.
38. *Ibid*, p. 227.
39. Wheeler, p. 27.
40. Hanlon, *Beggar Your Neighbours*, pp. 138-9.
41. H-R Heitman, *South African War Machine*, Central News Agency, Johannesburg, 1985, pp. 180-1.
42. Campbell, *op. cit.*, p. 15.
43. The South African press loved to reprint such stories. This incident was quoted in J D'Oliveira, "Africa Has Lost a Shining Son," *The Sunday Star*, 26 October 1986. The same article quoted the occasion when Machel and the Soviet ambassador visited the Soviet pavilion at the Maputo industrial and agricultural fair. Machel was reported as taking a ride in a Russian limousine which was on display. The smiling ambassador asked him how he liked the car. "Very nice," responded Machel, " a very comfortable car indeed. But I am afraid I have the same tastes as you and I prefer a Mercedes-Benz."
44. Martin and Johnson, pp. 27-31 for details of the squeeze.
45. The terms are fully explored in R Davies, "Mozambique: What is South Africa's Strategy?" *Southern African Report*, 2, 1986, pp. 13-17.
46. S Jenkins, "Destabilisation in Southern Africa," *The Economist*, 16 July 1983, p. 20.
47. Isaacman, p. 24.
48. S Jenkins, "America and South Africa," *The Economist*, 30 March 1985, p 23.
49. *Loc. cit.*
50. Author's interview with a South African diplomat.
51. Jenkins, "America and South Africa," *op cit.*, p. 23.
52. Hanlon, *Mozambique: The Revolution Under Fire*, p. 259.
53. Quoted in Martin and Johnson, p. 28.
54. In conversation with the author, November 1986.
55. Hanlon, *Beggar Your Neighbours*, p. 147; Jenkins, "America and South Africa", p. 24; Wheeler, p. 42.
56. Jenkins, "America and South Africa," p. 24; Martin and Johnson, p. 33; G Cawthra, *Brutal Force*, International Defence and Aid Fund, London, 1986, p. 166.
57. Jenkins, "America and South Africa," p. 24.
58. V Brittan, *Hidden Lives, Hidden Deaths*, Faber, London, 1988, p.60.
59. J Grest, "Mozambique Since the Nkomati Accord," in *South African Review 4*, Ravan, Johannesburg, 1987, p. 357.
60. Martin and Johnson, p. 38.
61. Hanlon, *Apartheid's Second Front*, Penguin, Harmondsworth, 1986, p. 109.
62. For South African analyses of the Viljoen-Botha tussle, see K Owen, "Keeping an Eye on the Colonels," *The Sunday Times*, (Johannesburg), 13 October 1985, and "Heart of Darkness," *Financial Mail*, 11 October 1985.
63. Martin and Johnson, p. 40.

64. A Sparks, "The Beira Prospect," *The Star*, 3 December 1986. Sparks was the former editor of the liberal *Rand Daily Mail*.
65. Jenkins, "America and South Africa," p. 24.
66. See "The Ruins of Nkomati," *Financial Mail*, 17 October 1986.
67. For example, G L'Ange, "Knife in Maputo's Back Given a Twist," *The Sunday Star*, 19 October 1986; see also Isaacman, p. 27.
68. *Strategic Survey 1986-1987*, International Institute for Strategic Studies, London, 1987, p. 192.
69. M Bole-Richard, "Rebels at Turning Point," (translated), *Le Monde*, 5 November 1986.
70. This account is extracted from the author's diary of his three-week trip through Renamo territory in November 1986. See also P Moorcraft, "Mozambique's Long Civil War—RENAMO, puppets or patriots?" *International Defense Review*, 20, October 1987; and *idem*, "The Savage, Silent Civil War," *Army*, 37:4, April 1987.
71. Isaacman, p. 31.
72. "Mozambican Officers Call for Peace Talks," *The Star*, 30 January 1987. The churches risked much criticism by calling for a settlement. For the churches' role, see "All Condemn Renamo. Except the Bishops," *Weekly Mail*, (Johannesburg), 15 September 1988.
73. Isaacman, p. 32.
74. *Ibid*., p. 33; G L'Ange, "Private Armies on the March as Machel's Men Fail," *The Sunday Star*, 19 October 1986.
75. *Strategic Survey 1987-1988*, IISS, London, 1988, p. 197.
76. K Kattzin, "MNR and Sithole Sign Pact to Topple Two Governments," *The Star* (weekly edition), 4 July 1987.
77. According to author's interviews with Renamo officials, 1988.
78. Figures quoted in *South African Digest*, 8 January 1987, p. 2.
79. M Hornsby, "Massacre at Homoine," *The Times*, 25 July 1987.
80. Wheeler, p. 47, Fn. 96; see also the debate in the Australian parliament: *Hansard* 35151, House of Representatives, 18 April 1988.
81. Isaacman, pp. 33-4.
82. H Adam and S Uys, "From Destabilisation to Neocolonial Control: South Africa's Post-Nkomati Regional Environment," *International Affairs Bulletin*, (Johannesburg), 9:1, 1985, p. 13.
83. R Grenier, "Why Do We Let Down the Rebels with a Real Cause?" *The Sunday Telegraph*, 20 September 1987.
84. "Death of MNR Leader is Big Blow to Rebels and S Africa," *The Star*, (weekly edition), 4 May 1988; K Maier, "Defector Reveals Power Struggle within Renamo," *The Independent*, 25 May 1988. For details of the attempt to modernise its communications, see J Battersby, "Pariahs Abroad, Mozambique Rebels Fight on," *New York Times*, 31 July 1988, "Pretoria has the Key," *Africa Confidential*, 4 March 1988; and "Mozambique: Marketing RENAMO," *Africa Confidential*, 9 September 1988.
85. For an analysis of the rightwing alliance, see D Leigh and P Lashmar, "Terrorist Supporters Woo Tories," *The Observer*, 9 October 1988.
86. For a South African perspective on the report, see N Lurssen, "Shock Report on MNR...," *The Star*, (weekly edition), 4 May 1988.
87. Both quoted in A Louyot, "A Journey to the Extremes of Horror," *L'Express*, no date, translated in *World Press Review*, September 1988.
88. F Douglas, "The Children of Death," *Sydney Morning Herald*, no date, in *World Press Review*, September 1988.
89. Quoted in B Anderson, "Ambushed—on the Malawi Border," *The Sunday Telegraph*, 18 December 1988; author's conversation with Della Casa, December 1988.

90. K Maier, "Pretoria Offers to Help in the War against Renamo," *The Independent*, 3 May 1988; see also "SA Provides Non-lethal Military Equipment," *Windhoek Advertiser*, 19 November 1988.
91. "Renamo Supply Trail Begins in South Africa," *The Independent*, 24 February 1988.
92. W Minter, *The Minter Report*, Holland Committee on Southern Africa, Amsterdam, 1989.
93. "Mozambique: Bad Timing," *The Economist*, 22 July 1989.
94. R Martin, "Regional Security in Southern Africa," *Survival*, September/October, 1987, p. 396. Author's interviews with Zimbabwean officials, February 1987.

13

Zimbabwe (1980-1989)

Supping with the devil

"We've got to sup with the devil or starve, but if we starve many other African countries starve with us. And that's where South Africa knows it's got us cornered for a long time." That was the judgement of one of Robert Mugabe's top aides more than a year after independence.(1) The UDI war had locked Zimbabwe into the South African economy. In 1980 about 40% of Zimbabwe's manufactured exports went to South Africa, while 90% of its exports passed through its transport system (although this latter figure was reduced throughout the 1980s). About 40,000 Zimbabweans worked legally in the racist republic.(2)

South Africa and Rhodesia had quarrelled from the time of the Jameson raid until the late 1970s, when Salisbury strongly resented Pretoria's on-off blackmail tactics. After 1980 Pretoria's hatred of Mugabe was more than reciprocated by Zimbabwe's new rulers. Despite the avowed policy of reconciliation, many of the ZANU(PF) bosses were understandably bitter men. Educated in hate during exile and war, the top echelon of ZANU(PF) became a "hothouse of restless paranoia, hostility and conspiracy".(3) Some had been killed at the hands of Smith's agents and soldiers, others on the long knives of their comrades. Many had spent more than a decade in prison. They felt betrayed by the British and the West in general for the half-hearted sanctions farce *and* by the Russians for backing Nkomo. Much of this bitterness was played out in the arcane clan politics of the ZANU(PF) central committee, which continued to rule as if it were still running a liberation movement, not a government. The one thing they could all agree on was their hostility to apartheid. The anti-South African rhetoric was nearly always intemperate. The harsh facts of economic life, however, dictated a

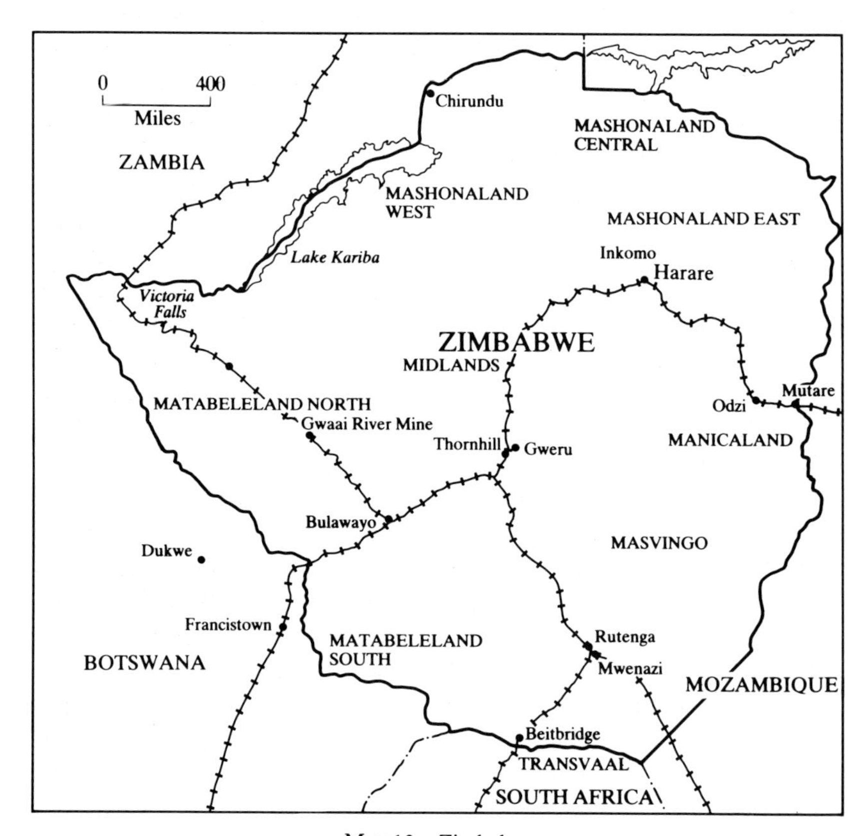

Map 13 Zimbabwe

modus vivendi. Harare would not provide bases for the ANC, only moral support; there would be trade with the pariah, but no formal diplomatic relations. Harare refused to allow any ministers to negotiate with Pretoria. Business was done openly via the respective trade representatives, while diplomacy was usually conducted secretly between the security officials on both sides.

Pretoria served up its spiciest and most varied destabilisation menu: economic pressures, particularly in 1981 and 1982, support for its dissidents, selective assassinations, sabotage and propaganda, but it generally stopped short of direct military intervention. Zimbabwe was not like Angola or Mozambique. It was a Commonwealth state where British army instructors trained its security forces. Washington would not countenance direct SADF entanglement, as it had in Angola. Moreover the economic nexus worked both ways: Zimbabwe was a main route for South African trade with Zaire, Zambia and Malawi. South African capital, especially the Anglo American Corporation, was heavily involved in the Marxist state. Such business interests often allied with the doves in Pretoria, who believed in the more positive aspects of transport diplomacy. In addition, the large and battle-hardened Zimbabwean armed forces were a partly effective deterrent against major incursions. And the historical intelligence links—Jenkins called it a "jigsaw of fiendish complexity" (4)—cut both ways too. South African military intelligence was often embarrassed by the extent of Harare's inside knowledge of Pretoria's destabilisation plans for Zimbabwe.(5)

Nevertheless, Pretoria had the best cards: economic dominance, a large potential fifth column of white agents and sympathetic white businessmen in Zimbabwe, a big reservoir of revanchist Rhodesians attached to, or incorporated in, the SADF, and, most important, the glowing embers of tribal passions in Matabeleland. Mugabe was said to have "a core of controlled, cold rage...that never forgives and never forgets".(6) The Jesuit-trained prime minister, with firm notions of good and evil, managed to implement a policy of live-and-let-live towards his former white enemies, but he found it much harder to reconcile himself to sharing real power with his erstwhile ally, Nkomo. Throughout the 1980s, Pretoria played nearly all its cards, especially the ace of spades in Matabeleland. Destabilisation fanned the inherent paranoia in the ruling ZANU(PF), which tended to characterise even indigenous political opponents as "enemies of the state". Thus, the state of emergency was retained, with all the same abuses of human rights inherited from the days of Ian Smith. Smith's self-fulfilling prophecies were thereby partly realised: after the fall of white rule, the black tribes would fall on each others' throats, a Marxist one-party state would wind down the economy, and the country would be at war with South Africa. Drought, corruption, excessive bureaucracy and doctrinaire socialism played a part in Zimbabwe's economic woes, but destabilisation was equally to blame. Pretoria's stop-start blockades and stirring up of the Ndebele pot tugged at the old wounds of the UDI war, which Mugabe's government, for all its faults, tried to heal. Pretoria was determined that Mugabe's pragmatic Marxism should fail. It survived, despite the barrage of anti-Zimbabwean sentiment in the South African press. Once it was clear that Mugabe had consolidated his position, Pretoria's "main goal seemed simply to show Prime Minister Mugabe who was boss in the region and to cause as much disruption as possible, without overt military intervention".(7)

Piling on the pressure

It was in the nature of the Lancaster House agreement that all the major black antagonists expected to win the 1980 elections. Bishop Muzorewa's and Reverend Sithole's auxiliaries felt as cheated as their leaders and as angry as their white allies. The white professional soldiers had the option of joining the SADF; some of the more embittered or desperate black troops, both from the auxiliaries and regular army, were retrained in the northern Transvaal. According to Harare, there were 5,000 such irregulars waiting to stage a southern African replay of the Bay of Pigs. Mugabe, however, behaved circumspectly. Initially, his authority in the country and the ruling party was not unchallenged. Pretoria demanded that about 300 ANC insurgents inside Zimbabwe be ejected. They had moved south with ZIPRA forces in late 1979. Some were holed up in ceasefire assembly points and others had taken refuge in the sprawling black townships of Bulawayo. They were quietly rounded up and dumped back in Zambia.

Then the economic squeeze began. It started in low gear. Pretoria stalled on renewing the pre-independence tariff arrangements. In July 1980 South African Railways began to withdraw its technicians and engineers loaned to the *ancien régime*. Then it was "inexplicable" bottlenecks in the ports and especially on the railways. The "notoriously drunken stationmaster at Messina" (the small railway town near Zimbabwe's main borderpost at Beitbridge) became a legendary figure in this blackmail scenario.(8) Next, force was exerted. In December 1980 white raiders stole $Z250,000-worth of arms from Cranborne Barracks in Harare. Pretoria later tried to explain away some of these clandestine operations—those that came to light—as "freelance" ventures, unauthorised by the SADF command. As it happened, the Cranborne raid was possibly one of the few genuine freelance Rhodesian escapades.(9) In the same month incendiary devices were discovered at the King George V1 Barracks.

The most important development for Pretoria was the series of mutinies in the half-integrated Zimbabwe National Army (ZNA). ZIPRA officers objected to the increasing dominance of ZANU(PF) in the civil service and army. Party loyalty, not merit, became the criterion. The anti-Nkomo propaganda in the government-controlled media exacerbated tensions. In November 1980 three of the "integrated" ZIPRA-ZANLA battalions of the ZNA ran amok. The skirmishes erupted into full-scale fighting around Bulawayo, the Ndebele "capital". More than 50 people (mainly civilians) were killed and 400 were injured. In February 1981 more than 10,000 ZNA troops were involved in faction-fighting. Both rebellions were quelled by loyal ZNA troops, consisting mainly of the still white-officered Rhodesian African Rifles. Mugabe had wanted to disband the RAR, but General Walls and senior civil servants had dissuaded the premier. Without the RAR's intercession, and the intimidatory role of helicopters and Hawker Hunters, the ZIPRA mutineers, armed with BTR-152 armoured cars and with tanks in reserve, might not have been contained. The whites in Zimbabwe discreetly cheered on "their" RAR and air force as they once again went into combat against guerrillas, but this time on the orders of Robert Mugabe.(10)

Even though a ZIPRA coup was rumoured to have been planned for Christmas 1980, the tribal animosities did not explode into all-out civil war. With British army help, the ZNA was re-integrated, as most of the whites and many of the Ndebele soldiers quit. ZANU(PF) consolidated its control of the national administration, but it could not win over the disgruntled Ndebele minority. Nkomo, though, had shot his bolt: his "second coming" seemed very remote. It had been mooted, in South Africa, that Nkomo might have tried to repeat the experience of Katanga and declare his own UDI. That could have survived only with Pretoria's connivance, perhaps in exchange for a promise to prevent ANC fighters infiltrating through Ndebele territory. Apparently, South African intelligence had been in touch with Nkomo for years, although ZAPU's links with the ANC and Moscow obstructed a closer relationship. ZAPU officials were alleged to have approached Pretoria, but it was clear that, in 1980, a Unita-style campaign was just not on. And, in contrast with Nkomo, Pretoria shared Mugabe's contempt for the Russians.(11)

PLATE 13.1 Robert Mugabe. *(IDAF)*

Mugabe's bloody assertion of his authority over ZIPRA was the local equivalent of Kennedy's Cuban missile crisis. Mugabe looked like a more decisive leader. Pretoria interpreted it rather differently: Zimbabwe was now ripe for further destabilisation.(12) In April 1981 South Africa withdrew 25 locomotives previously loaned to Rhodesia. On 3 August Joe Gqabi, the ANC representative in Harare, was assassinated outside his home. Mugabe blamed Pretoria. The South African government retaliated by stating that all Zimbabweans working legally in the republic would be repatriated when their contracts expired. This was a warning shot before more serious measures. As a senior SADF officer said: "If it came to a showdown, we could wring Zimbabwe's neck like a chicken."(13) It was alleged in Harare that South African agents had twice attempted to kill Mugabe.(14) On 16 August explosions at the armoury at Inkomo Barracks near Harare destroyed $Z50 million-worth of weapons and ammunition. The CIO blamed Captain Frank Gericke, who was in charge of the armoury. He was arrested, but was sprung from prison by the police investigating officer, Fred Varkevisser.

The policeman's wife and two children, said Harare, had been kidnapped to encourage his compliance. Both men were then spirited away to South Africa. Such was the official Zimbabwean version.(15) But sources within the Zimbabwean ministry of defence, who had actually conducted the departmental enquiry into the explosions, said it was an accident.(16) That still left the cloak-and-dagger extraction of Gericke, who later joined the SADF, unexplained. The mastermind behind some of the early sabotage, according to Harare, was Geoffrey Price, the head of Mugabe's own close security unit. He was accused of recruiting agents in the CIO for South Africa, especially two men, Colin Evans and Philip Hartlebury. Evans and Hartlebury were charged with espionage, but the charge was dismissed by a High Court judge, and the pair were detained under emergency legislation. Price escaped to South Africa via England.(17) On 18 December a blast ripped through the Harare ZANU(PF) HQ. The blast blew the roof off the five-storey building and hurled masonry and shards into the crowd of lunchtime Christmas shoppers in the street below. Seven bystanders were killed and 124 were injured. The party's central committee was to have met at the building that day, but the meeting had been postponed. Meanwhile, the railway blockade continued. By the end of 1981 it had cost $Z100 million in delayed exports of maize, asbestos, sugar and coal. (18)

Pretoria was planning something more sinister than rail stoppages: "Super-ZAPU". Super-ZAPU was made up of Ndebele dissidents trained in the Transvaal. Some were genuine ex-ZIPRA guerrillas, although the majority of ZIPRA dissidents operating in Matabeleland were hostile to ties with Pretoria. In February 1982 large arms caches were "discovered" on property, especially farms, owned by ZAPU. Nkomo and three of his cabinet colleagues were kicked out of the government by a highly irate Mugabe. ZAPU property was confiscated by the state. Many of the demobilised ZIPRA troops had put all their army severance pay into the confiscated farm cooperatives. Hundreds of serving ZNA troops joined their demobilised compatriots who took to the bush in revolt. The former ZIPRA senior commanders, Dumiso Dabengwa and General Lookout Masuku, were charged with treason and were detained at Chikurubi maximum security prison, after they were acquitted. This crisis fuelled the barely repressed rebellion in Matabeleland. Large parts of the area became ungovernable. Three sometimes rival groups ranged across vast swathes of rugged bush: Ndebele bandits feeding on the anarchy; genuine ZIPRA dissidents held together by a disciplined command structure, with support from sanctuaries in Botswana, and loyal to Dabengwa and Masuku, with perhaps only titular allegiance to Nkomo; and Super-ZAPU, supplied by South Africa. Harare lumped them all together as disorganised "bandits" contaminated by Pretoria's agents.

Matt Calloway, ex-CIO and Rhodesian special branch, was a key liaison man between Super-ZAPU and SADF military intelligence. Much of the planning and weapons supply was organised in Francistown, Botswana. Later, in March 1983, a propaganda station, disseminating very simplistic material, was supposed to have started operating from Matabeleland. In fact, it emanated from SABC studios near Johannesburg. Although Pretoria denied any connection with the station, on 25 November 1983 the tapes of the theme music of Renamo's *Voz de Africa Livre* and that of Super-ZAPU's Radio Truth were inadvertently switched. Now Zimbabwe had taped evidence that its guerrilla opponents were broadcasting from one place, Johannesburg, not from Mozambique or Matabeleland.(19) Pretoria supplied ZIPRA and Super-ZAPU with equipment, especially ammunition, once the pre-independence caches were exhausted. Old ZAPU loyalists resented the connection with South Africa, but often there was no alternative supply source. Sometimes ZIPRA engaged in fire fights with Super-ZAPU because of the apartheid ties. Mugabe's strident rhetoric against Nkomo, and especially the anti-ZAPU diatribes of one of his ministers, Enos Nkala, himself a Ndebele, fanned the flames of ethnic rivalry. And then Super-ZAPU, never more than a few hundred men, stirred up the explosive mixture.

Pretoria's Ndebele strategy was based upon a number of factors. Firstly, the troubles in Matabeleland undermined the policy of conciliation, and thus hastened the white exodus, especially of white farmers. More than 60 members of the white farming families in Matabeleland were killed by dissidents, far more than during the liberation war. Some remaining white farmers resuscitated their old Rhodesian PATU (Police Anti-Terrorist Unit) sticks and the former Agric-Alert radio network, with the encouragement of the Zimbabwean police. Whether the whites were killed by ZIPRA, bandits or Super-ZAPU is a moot point. But this further undermined the economy and discouraged foreign investment. Secondly, it drew off ZNA forces from the Mozambique front. Thirdly, it encouraged Mugabe to overreact. The ZNA, especially the ruthless, North Korean-trained 5th Brigade, exacted ferocious reprisals, killing hundreds if not thousands of Ndebele peasants. The massacres and mutilations provoked an international outcry, and strong domestic pressure from the churches. Mugabe took Smith's place in the moral pillory, and relieved some of the pressure on Pretoria. And, as a bonus, the saturation of ZNA forces in southern Matabeleland discouraged ANC penetration of the northern Transvaal.

Incitement to overreact, against the Ndebele, Shona political opponents, such as Muzorewa, and the whites, was a persistent South African theme which harmonised well with ZANU's inbuilt paranoia about ubiquitous enemies of the revolution. It has been suggested that South African agents in the CIO might have encouraged ZIPRA's illegal stockpiling of weapons in 1980 and then chosen a convenient time, February 1982, to tip off Mugabe, thus precipitating a full-blooded crisis in the government and a near-civil war in Matabeleland and the Midlands.(20)

On 25 July world attention was drawn to the abduction of six foreign tourists on the road south from the famous Victoria Falls. Their bodies were not found for two years. ZIPRA was accused of the crime, but South African sources (perhaps as disinformation) alleged that a secret ZNA unit, which later formed the 6th Brigade pseudo-gangs in Mozambique, was implicated in the murders. ZIPRA spokesmen also pleaded innocence. Thus, in addition to the three groups of rebels already in the field, a fourth, a ZNA pseudo operation, could perhaps be added.(21) The plot thickened two days later when a quarter of Zimbabwe's air force was sabotaged at Thornhill base near Gweru (Gwelo). Thirteen fighters and trainers, including Hawk Mk60s recently purchased from Britain, were blown up. Six white air force officers, including an Air Vice Marshal, were detained, tortured, tried, acquitted, redetained and, eventually, released and expelled from the country. The six men were, almost incidentally it seemed, innocent. John Cox, one of the officers, called the trial "one of Africa's finest examples of a comedy of errors —incompetence compounded by greater incompetence...that was to make the Goon Show look serious". Cox, a Briton, said all this only after he had safely returned to Winterbourne, near Bristol.(22) The sabotage, perhaps with some inside cooperation, but not from the six accused, was probably perpetrated by ex-SAS personnel serving with the SADF. The audacious raid virtually eliminated the jet strike capability of the air force and propelled a mass exodus of the remaining white pilots and technicians. As some of the six accused had British passports, Mugabe's request for further British officers to be sent to assist in the training of his forces fell upon deaf ears (at least until the six men were freed). Already damning reports from the British army instructors about the 5th Brigade's atrocities had been suppressed in Whitehall.(23) Was the Thornhill raid intended to wreck the air force's offensive capability and prompt a witch-hunt that would devastate the morale of white Zimbabwean officers? Was the latter an accidental bonus, or Machiavellian planning by Pretoria? South African sources suggested that Pretoria was not that subtle and countered with the view that pro-Moscow elements in the Zimbabwean hierarchy wanted to clear out pro-Western white military influence. That sounded even more convoluted. (Other theories suggested that it was the work of North Korean instructors working in the country or disaffected ex-ZIPRA.)

In August relations with Pretoria were further strained when three white soldiers from a larger SADF raiding party were killed on the wrong side of the Limpopo river. The three, ex-Rhodesians who had served in the Rhodesian Light Infantry and SAS, were said by General Constand Viljoen, the chief of the SADF, to have been on an "unauthorised raid", a freelance operation to rescue political prisoners held in southeastern Zimbabwe. As a South African newspaper noted, the explanation "was greeted with frank incredulity in Western embassies in Harare".(24) Viljoen added, almost limp-wristedly, that the SADF would stop posting its ex-Rhodesian soldiers anywhere near the Zimbabwe border.

This embarrassing incident did not deter Pretoria's hawks. Former SAS soldiers continued to attack Zimbabwe's oil lifeline through Mozambique. By December 1982 Zimbabwe was down to two weeks' supply of petrol. To cap it all, Pretoria asserted that an "industrial dispute" had delayed alternative oil routes through South Africa. Chaos hit Mugabe's administration. Cars were abandoned, factories closed, power cuts became frequent. Eventually Washington told Pretoria to desist. The pipelines were repaired and South African trains ran again, but Pretoria had made its point. It could turn off the tap precisely when it wanted.(25)

For reinsurance, Harare started to improve its slender ties with Moscow. In 1983 relations were warmed up with extra trade and political agreements. A visit by the Bolshoi Ballet added a cultural dimension, although the audiences were nearly all white, and many of the balletomanes came from South Africa. The Kremlin had apparently finally cut its losses with Nkomo, and in 1986 Zimbabwe formally opened its embassy in Moscow. Mugabe also sidled up more closely to another former Nkomo ally, Botswana. In February 1984 Emmerson Munangagwa, the security minister, announced that some of the top ZIPRA dissidents had been rounded up in Botswana and handed over to Harare. The (mainly white) Commercial Farmers Union had been lobbying the government incessantly about its members' predicament in Matabeleland. Two white farmers had been killed in 1981. In 1983 the numbers had risen to 33. The CIO also gave a very detailed dossier of Pretoria's complicity in dissident activity to South African military intelligence. The implicit, and embarrassing, question was: why was the SADF helping to kill so many whites?(26)

In May, two months after the Nkomati agreement, General van der Westhuizen travelled discreetly to Harare for talks with the ZNA chief of staff, Sheba Gava. Neil Barnard, the youthful head of the National Intelligence Service, also made a secret trip to Zimbabwe.(27) Both sides set up a liaison system to prevent what one Zimbabwean minister termed "nuclear war by accident".(28) An informal, uneasy truce was to last about 15 months, although Harare insisted on publicising evidence of past SADF misdemeanours.(29)

Pretoria appeared to put on the brakes, and at the same time the ZNA swamped the dissidents, particularly during the run-up to the general election of June 1985. Nkomo, who had fled and then returned from exile in Britain, called the elections a "fraud before they started". He had said the same thing about Smith's election in 1979. Any election he did not win was bound to be a fraud. He said that the Mugabe government was "led by fascists, not even comparable to Herr Hitler...We stand a cursed people. Independence has meant nothing to us." Muzorewa, however, was released, after 10 months detention, to compete in the "fraud". The whites still were blinkered enough to argue that Mugabe was unpopular and that the Bishop and Nkomo would make a comeback, if the polling was fair. Not a single white liberal had been elected for the 20 seats reserved for whites (out of 100) in the lower house of parliament. Some of Smith's 20 MPs had defected to form an independent group, leaving the former premier with a rump of seven members. The repackaged RF managed to secure 15 seats in the 1985 poll; the independents, all conservatives, got the rest.

Mugabe interpreted Smith's surprising comeback as a rejection of his conciliation policy. Many whites, however, saw the 1985 election as their very last political chance to show their disapproval of Mugabe's march to a one-party state. After the results were announced—ZANU(PF) had increased from 57 to 64 of the 80 black seats—Mugabe made it clear that he intended to revise the British-engineered constitution: the white seats would go and ZAPU would be merged with ZANU(PF) to form one ruling party with himself as executive president. This was the traditional African way. White politics now reversed the UDI pattern: white liberals—at least those who had chosen actually to live under the black rule they had so long advocated—embraced the idea of one-party rule as the "last best hope of stability"; the faithful followers of Smith juggled with unaccustomed theories of pluralism and tolerance as devices to stall a one-party Zimbabwe. The Zimbabwean whites, however, were now finished as a political force. Mugabe's enemy was Pretoria. A month after the election, dissidence flared up again in Matabeleland and, in the east, ZNA troops poured into Mozambique for a major offensive against Renamo.

In May 1986 the SADF openly raided Harare, as part of its assault on three Commonwealth states to sink the Eminent Persons Group's peace drive. An ANC house and office were hit. Harare's *Herald* responded with banner headlines: "Racists Bomb Frontline Capital" and "PM Accuses Pretoria of State Terrorism". Editorials lambasted the "Boer Vampires" and Mugabe seemed to have lost his temper publicly when he talked of "killing Boers".(30) Three times Mugabe went to the brink of declaring all-out (and suicidal) sanctions against South Africa, only to be restrained by his more pragmatic cabinet colleagues at the last moment.(31) Kaunda, too, shouted for sanctions, but the economic chaos in Zambia crowded out dreams of kamikaze heroism in Lusaka.

By 1987 Ndebele dissidence had waned. Pretoria seemed to have lost interest in Super-ZAPU perhaps because the Mozambican war was fully occupying the ZNA. Defence spending was 14% of the 1987-88 budget. On the roads to Malawi through Tete province, the local ZNA commanders seemed to have reached a *modus vivendi* with Renamo. Renamo controlled the countryside and left the ZNA to run the convoys, with just the occasional harassment of traffic.(32) Elsewhere in Mozambique the ZNA dug in. After major ground and air offensives in 1985 and 1986, with some half-baked support from Frelimo, Zimbabwean troops began to limit their role to defensive patrolling. For political reasons they held on to the area around the Casa Banana Renamo HQ in Gorongosa. But they hardly moved beyond their defensive perimeters because of the bad (and mined) roads. Renamo shifted its main bases away from the ZNA. Military observers likened ZNA tactics to an admiral leaving a flotilla to guard the patch of ocean from which the enemy fleet had recently been driven away.(33) In the Beira Corridor the ZNA manned the bunkers on the railway and concentrated on trying to keep the convoys protected. Supplies got through, but nowhere near enough to replace the South African routes. Renamo was left to roam around outside these defended areas.

During 1986 Renamo had started to hit targets in Zimbabwe. In August 1987, in a skirmish near the Jersey tea estate, about 300 miles southeast of Harare, Renamo killed four ZNA soldiers. This was the first (recorded) incident of Renamo killing Zimbabwean troops on their own soil. Renamo depredations in eastern Zimbabwe became so bad that the ZNA had to resort to recreating the war-time protected villages to defend some of the more isolated peasant settlements. Nevertheless, Mugabe vowed to fight "to the last man" in Mozambique: "We have decided it is wiser to fight the war now rather than later on, when the situation had grown worse and much more unfavourable to us."(34)

Mugabe again edged towards sanctions, but was pulled back following vigorous private sector representation.(35) The prime minister was in a corner. Diplomatic rumours circulated of a new defence pact with Russia which would include Zimbabwe's purchase of Mig-29s, which Moscow had never sold to any African state (not even Angola or Ethiopia). The West showed its concern when Britain offered instead to supply Harriers and new Hawk aircraft.(36) Britain was not only Zimbabwe's largest aid donor, but also its major Western military backer. British military advisers had played a key role in overseeing the integration of the three main armies after independence. Thereafter, the British Military Advisory Training Team (BMATT) had participated in various major projects. BMATT had retrained the notorious 5th brigade, originally trained by the North Koreans. The training team was also closely involved in the running of the ZNA staff college in Harare and the Zimbabwe Military Academy in Gweru, as well as instructing Mozambican officers at the Nyanga battle school. British cash and military experts also assisted in reopening the Limpopo rail line through Mozambique.

At home, Mugabe offered Nkomo a final chance to merge his party with ZANU(PF). This time the exhausted "father of Zimbabwean nationalism" took the bait. The second shotgun marriage (the Patriotic Front was the first) resulted in a successful amnesty campaign. In June 1988 *The Times* correspondent described how 43 ZIPRA dissidents arrogantly surrendered in the Nkayi area: "Some looked like extras from the film Mad Max: lean men with intense eyes, adorned with dreadlocks, pink scarves, necklaces, bangles, jeans and heavy military boots with puttees. Others, in overalls and floppy hats, could have been farm labourers."(37) The government had portrayed the dissidents as disorganised gangs of bandits, but the cocky interviews they gave during the amnesty period demonstrated that they had a strong command structure, that they were well-equipped and that they propounded a Marxist philosophy.

Some dissidents remained at large, but the low-level civil war in Matabeleland looked as it had burnt out. Tensions on the southern border with South Africa remained, however. The SADF blamed ANC infiltration from Matabeleland for a spate of landmine explosions in the northern Transvaal, while Harare continued to point the finger at Pretoria when bombs exploded in the Zimbabwean capital. At the beginning of 1988, the CIO rounded up a sabotage ring of (initially) five whites, all ex-Rhodesian security force members. At the trial, one of them, Kevin Woods, a former CIO man himself, suggested that the CIO was hostile to the ANC because of its still-existing ties with ZIPRA dissidents. The tale became more confused when a group of raiders tried, in June 1988, to rescue the five men as they travelled from Chikurubi jail to court in central Harare. The attempt was bungled, although two of the would-be rescuers, a white Zimbabwean air force helicopter pilot and a "female commando", managed to escape with a Bell helicopter, and then flew by Dakota to South Africa. The remaining rescue "commandos" dispersed, each man for himself. At the same time, the SADF suffered a number of abortive missions in Botswana. Via the Johannesburg *Sunday Times*, military intelligence repudiated the Zimbabwean fiasco with the old disclaimer: the rescue operation was attempted by a "renegade group" of former Rhodesian soldiers who "once had links with the South African authorities". This "crazy gang" had tried to rescue "friends and relatives off their own bat". It seemed strange that, eight years after their defeat, ex-Rhodesians were still so bitter and so well-organised and well-financed that they could attempt such a complicated mission, without the knowledge of the highly efficient South African intelligence services. The "unauthorised" raid excuse was wearing more than thin. (38)

As Zimbabwe entered its 24th year under a state of emergency, relations with Pretoria appeared as acrimonious as ever. Just as the Rhodesian war engulfed the whites who chose to stay on in Zambia after independence, so the remaining whites in Zimbabwe risked being dragged into the anti-apartheid war. One white farmer's wife, a veteran of the UDI bush war, said simply: "We had a paradise here once, now we must adapt to joining the real world." Despite all its homemade problems and Pretoria's troublemaking, Zimbabwe has survived as a multiracial society. During the "unrest" of 1984-86 in South Africa, hundreds of ex-Rhodesians, disillusioned with life in the apartheid republic, and afflicted by a sense of *déjà vu*, made a reverse trek back to their former homeland. The future of Zimbabwe is important. Because, despite all the differences, it is the closest paradigm, for both hope and despair, for South African whites as they struggle to unscramble sheer survival from racist domination.

References and notes:

1. J Barber, "Supping with the Devil—Zimbabwe-South Africa Relations," *International Affairs Bulletin*, 6:1, 1982, p. 4.
2. S Jenkins, "Destabilisation in Southern Africa," *The Economist*, 16 July 1983, p. 23.
3. G Frankel, "Zimbabwe: Repression and Progress," *Guardian Weekly*, 20 July 1986.
4. Jenkins, *loc. cit.*
5. *Ibid.*
6. Frankel, *op. cit.*
7. J Hanlon, *Beggar Your Neighbours*, Catholic Institute for International Relations, London, 1986, p. 173.
8. R Martin, "Regional Security in Southern Africa," *Survival*, September/October 1987, p. 399.
9. The raid was apparently performed by ex-RLI soldiers (Cranborne was the RLI barracks) who had joined the SADF. The venture had been sanctioned by their immediate South African superiors, but not the army command in Pretoria. The SADF did not need the weapons, but it has been suggested that this was a piece of "private enterprise" to embarrass the new Zimbabwean army. Author's interviews with ex-Rhodesian intelligence sources.
10. For an analysis of the ZIPRA revolt, see P Moorcraft, "Will there be a Civil War in Zimbabwe?" *South Africa International*, April 1981.
11. See P Moorcraft and P McLaughlin, *Chimurenga: The War in Rhodesia*, Sygma/Collins, Johannesburg, 1982, pp.234-43. Also, P Moorcraft, "Zimbabwe: Reality vs Utopia," *The Star*, 16 February 1982, and "The War Drums Begin to Sound," *The Star*, 17 February 1982.
12. H Patel, "Zimbabwe," *Survival*, January/February 1988, p. 48.
13. Quoted in "Pressure from Pretoria," *Newsweek*, 24 August 1981.
14. In December 1981, according to Hanlon, *op. cit.*, p. 174, and July 1982, according to Patel, *op. cit.*, p. 51.
15. See Patel, pp. 48-9, Hanlon, p. 175 and D Martin and P Johnson, "Zimbabwe: Apartheid's Dilemma," in P Johnson and D Martin, (eds), *Destructive Engagement*, Zimbabwe Publishing, Harare, 1986, pp. 48-9.
16. Author's interviews with white ministry of defence officials after they had left Zimbabwe.
17. Patel, p. 49; Martin and Johnson, *op. cit.*, pp. 47-8.
18. Patel, p. 45.
19. Martin and Johnson, p. 64.
20. Hanlon, p. 183.
21. Author's interviews with Super-ZAPU sources; see also "New ZIPRA has Ditched Nkomo," *The Aida Parker Newsletter*, 3 April 1983.
22. J Cox, "Life with 'Live Wires' and a Bucket En Suite," *The Star*, 18 August 1984. "Live Wires" refers to the police who used electric shock torture. Some of the officers were sadistically tortured and sexually abused, according to author's interview with the physician who examined them in prison. For full details of the treatment of the officers, see B Cole, *Sabotage and Torture*, Three Knights, Amanzimtoti, 1988.
23. See "Tortured Officers Block Aid to Mugabe," *The Sunday Times*, (Johannesburg), 24 October 1982.
24. S Taylor, "Disbelief Greets the SA Statement on Incursion," *The Sunday Express*, (Johannesburg), 29 August 1982.
25. For an analysis of the oil squeeze, see Jenkins, *op. cit.*, pp. 23-4.
26. Martin and Johnson, p. 61.
27. Hanlon, p. 181; R Drew, "Where Pragmatism Rules," *The Star*, 29 December 1984.
28. Martin, *op. cit*, p. 400.

29. G Frankel, "Zimbabwe Spells Out its Case on South African Support of Rebels," *The Washington Post*, 23 June 1984.
30. *The Herald*, 20 May 1986.
31. Martin, p. 393.
32. *Loc. cit.* Author's interviews with various Zimbabwean road hauliers.
33. Martin, p. 393.
34. K Maier, "Zimbabwe's Fighting Elite," *The Independent*, 15 September 1987.
35. T Hawkins, "Zimbabwe Rejects Call for S. Africa Trade Sanctions," *Financial Times*, 1 August 1987. (The Zimbabwean business community defined a pessimist as an optimist who had tried to trade through Beira.)
36. K Campbell, *Southern Africa in Soviet Foreign Policy*, Adelphi Paper No. 227, IISS, London, 1987/8, p. 21. R Drew, "Britain Offers War Planes to Zimbabwe," *The Star*, (weekly edition), 11 July 1987.
37. J Raath, "Zimbabwe's Dissidents Unbowed as They Lay Down their Arms," *The Times*, 1 June 1988.
38. For background on the raid, see "Ex-Rhodesians behind SA Bid to Free Suspects," *The Herald*, 22 July 1988, "S. Africa's Zimbabwe Debacle," *Southscan*, 6 June 1988, K Maier, "Murder Hearing Reveals Covert SA Role in Zimbabwe," *The Independent*, 18 October 1988.

14

Fellow frontliners

Lesotho

Lesotho, the size of Belgium, boasts, or laments, some unusual claims to fame. For example, it is the only country in the world where the entire area is more than 1,000 metres above sea level. Its dramatic mountain scenery and usually friendly 1.4 million inhabitants attract a little tourism and a lot of foreign aid. Besides being one of the three remaining independent African kingdoms, it also has the shortest railway line on the continent, 1.5 km to be precise. Its most distinctive feature, however, is that it is one of only three countries completely surrounded by another state. Unfortunately for Lesotho it is the often hostile South Africa. (The other two, the Vatican and San Marino, have not been recently threatened by their big brother, Italy.) Its coat of arms proudly proclaims its aspirations: *Khotso, Pula and Nala* (peace, rain and prosperity.) Sadly, it has missed out on all three in recent years.

In 1868 King Moshoeshoe asked to become "like a flea in the blanket of Queen Victoria". It was not quite a 100-year itch, for the Basutoland protectorate became independent in 1966, when London set a precedent for Pretoria's bantustans. The country's ruler, Chief Leabua Jonathan, established a pattern for the Matanzimas and Sebes, including a penchant for bowler hats. The difference was that Lesotho joined the UN and the Commonwealth, and so received aid when Pretoria turned on Jonathan. Initially, Pretoria funded the chief, a former herdboy who had worked as a compound clerk in the New Modderfontein gold mine in South Africa. Like the tinpot dictators in the Transkei and Ciskei, he was particularly averse to free elections. He aborted the 1970 elections when he looked like losing them to his rivals, the Basotho Congress Party, led by Ntsu Mokhehle. Jonathan thereupon declared a "holiday

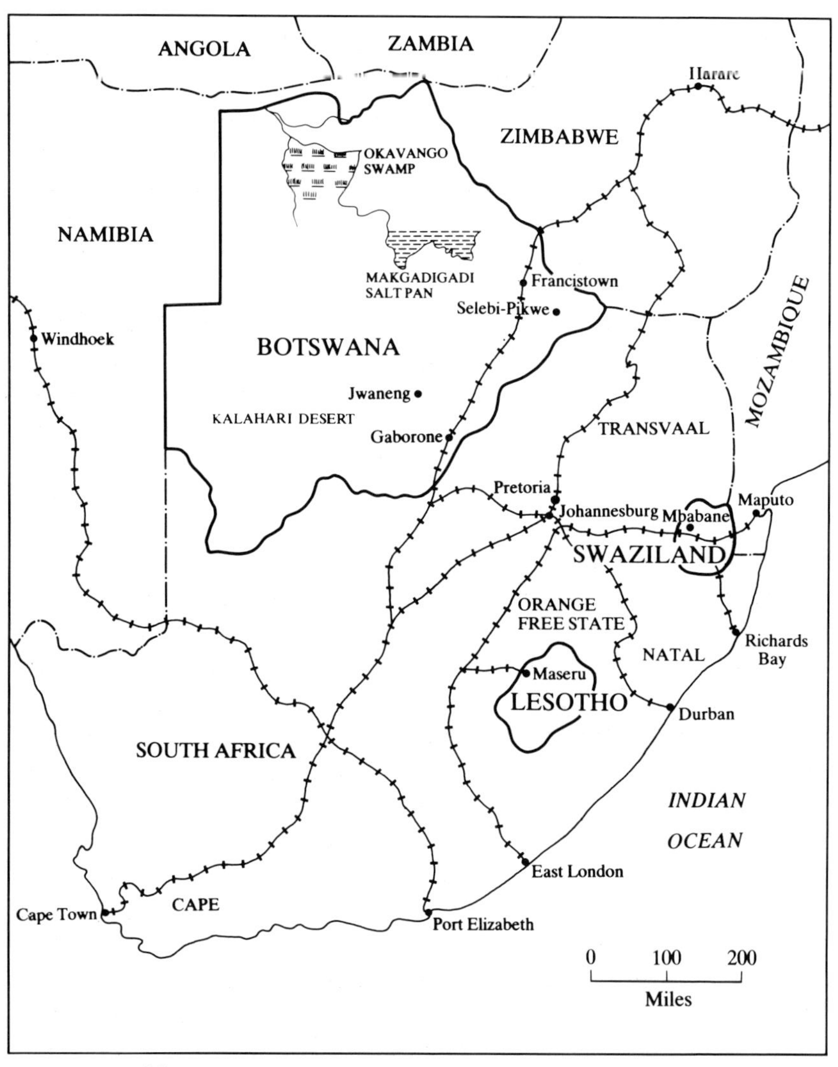

MAP 14 Hostage states: Botswana, Lesotho and Swaziland

from politics", perhaps one of the more imaginative and honest dictatorial phrases to emerge from Africa. Pretoria went along with this quite happily because the Congress Party was deemed to be dangerously socialistic.

In 1971 Jonathan started to distance himself from Pretoria, partly because of his growing domestic unpopularity and partly because his anti-apartheid tirades brought in aid money. Initially, he adopted a stance somewhat akin to Malawi, then, in 1972, he started to become more outspoken, like Zambia. But his independence was entirely rhetorical. More than half of the kingdom's able-bodied men worked in South Africa, and the economy and transport routes were run by South Africans. Moreover, Jonathan's small security forces were controlled initially by Englishmen sympathetic to Pretoria. In 1974, after a bloody rebellion, some members of the Congress Party went into exile, including Mokhehle. Despite his earlier affiliations to the PAC, Mokhehle decided "to ride on the back of the devil", Pretoria. In 1979 the Lesotho Liberation Army (LLA) was founded and funded by South Africa. The attacks began in May 1979 and increased in 1981, as Jonathan became more outspoken. What really incensed Pretoria was Jonathan's invitation to communist states, particularly Russia, China, North Korea and, finally, Cuba to open embassies in Maseru, the capital, and the use of Lesotho as a sanctuary for ANC refugees and guerrillas. Just as Jonathan was first a protégé of Pretoria and then an antagonist, so Mokhehle switched from being an opponent of South Africa to being head of a SADF-SAP surrogate force, which killed and sabotaged from 1979 to 1986. The raids, launched from South African territory, with the knowledge if not always the connivance of the South African police, did not lead to a popular uprising against Jonathan. Even though the Congress Party would have won the aborted 1970 elections, and Mokhehle retained his personal following in Lesotho, Jonathan manipulated historical Basotho enmity towards the "Boers" to tar the LLA with the pro-apartheid brush. Also, Jonathan used the LLA as an excuse to ruthlessly repress all his domestic political opponents. Pretoria kept up a campaign of intermittent economic harassment (even though the Lesotho economy was essentially controlled by South African capital) and the LLA and the SADF attacked the homes of ANC members.

Then came the big raid, the first large-scale direct attack by the SADF on one of the former British Protectorates. On the eve of Human Rights Day, 9 December 1982, at one o' clock in the morning, more than 100 SADF commandos (probably drawn from 1 Reconnaissance Commando based in Durban) landed from five helicopters. They hit a dozen flats and houses simultaneously, some in the middle of Maseru, and killed 40 people, 28 South Africans and 12 Mosothos. The SADF warned the Lesotho army (the Lesotho Paramilitary Force) by phone not to intervene, as some of the raiders got lost on the way out. The LPF deputy commander, Brigadier B M Ramotsekhoana, agreed, after "some agonised consideration".(1) Pretoria claimed that the ANC was about to launch attacks on targets in South Africa and the Ciskei and Transkei homelands.

While Jonathan turned up the international volume of his moral condemnation of apartheid, domestically his rule became more autocratic. The younger technocrats in the ruling Basotho National Party moved to the left, while the right wing in the army grew concerned at the increasing confrontation with Pretoria and the interference of the Eastern bloc embassies, especially the North Koreans. The Catholic Church, royalists who suppported the rusticated King Moshoeshoe II, and opposition parties, including the internal wing of the LLA-Congress Party, plotted to undermine Jonathan. Pretoria naturally encouraged them. The South African government wanted Lesotho both to recognise the homelands, particularly the adjacent Transkei, and to sign a similar pact to the Nkomati agreement: an end to the LLA in exchange for the ejection of the ANC. The information minister, Desmond Sixishe, mocked the idea of a security pact. "There is no need for a non-aggression pact between an elephant and an ant," he said.(2)

Jonathan was still vulnerable on his domestic front, although he tried to bring disaffected members of the internal wing of the Congress Party into his government. The foreign aid donors also pressurised Jonathan to hold elections. In 1985 he went through the motions, although all the opposition parties were effectively disbarred. The suave Sixishe would counter criticisms of a one-party state by saying, "If people choose to vote for one party..." (3) Nevertheless, splits within his own ruling party continued to undermine Jonathan's position. In particular, his North Korean-trained Youth League began acting like Maoist Red Guards, much to the disgust of the more conservative elements in the army, whose prestige was already dented by the failure to curb the sporadic excesses of the LLA.

In late 1985 Jonathan's 20-year dictatorship was approaching its final crisis. Pretoria continued to fund an alliance of Basotho opposition parties and to manipulate payments from the customs union. Pik Botha dangled funding of the massive Highlands water project in front of Maseru if it played ball. Jonathan did try to mend his fences with Pretoria and King Moshoeshoe, but it was too late. Events were getting out of hand. On 19 December 1985 the SADF attacked several houses in Maseru and killed six ANC members and three Lesotho citizens. Pretoria then gave a list to Lesotho and demanded that all the ANC members on that list be expelled or handed over. On 1 January 1986 Pretoria imposed a severe but not total blockade of the landlocked country. Cars and trucks were subjected to intensive searches and some took three or four days to get through the border posts. The blockade was a catalyst for the simmering conflicts inside Lesotho, particularly between (and within) the army and the Youth League, which was supported by the more radical members of Jonathan's party such as Sixishe. After a complicated series of domestic manoeuvres, the army commander, Major General Justin Lekhanya, toppled Jonathan in a near-bloodless coup on 20 January. Lekhanya pushed the king back into the political limelight to give the new regime local credibility. The general had already made a pilgrimage to Pretoria to explain his conservative views on the ANC. So the South Africans were happy. After the coup there were scenes of wild jubiliation in the streets of Maseru to welcome the end of the blockade, the Youth League's rampages and Jonathan.

The coup was interesting for a number of reasons. It was the first full-flown military coup in a southern African state. More significantly, it was a classic demonstration of the utility of sanctions. By direct, almost comprehensive, sanctions Pretoria had forced a state to rapidly change its political stance. An apt lesson for the UN. Nevertheless, the coup was very much a family affair: Jonathan's executive power passed nominally from Jonathan to his uncle, the king. "While South African footprints can be seen all around the coup, it will be a mistake to conclude that Pretoria engineered the military takeover."(4) Nevertheless, Pretoria pressed home its advantage.

The new military government included a number of civilian ministers, some of whom had been linked to the ANC. And the Oxford-educated king was known to have liberal views. Nonetheless, Lekhanya and his ruling military council tipped their hats politely in Pretoria's direction. ANC members were periodically rounded up and expelled at short notice (though not usually to South Africa). The influence of the remaining Eastern bloc embassies was curtailed. Some of the radicals, such as Sixishe, were murdered. Maseru opposed sanctions and disinvestment. In return, the LLA was wound down and Mokhehle returned home. The Highland water scheme was set in motion.

During the Pope's visit to southern Africa in September 1988, the escorting convoy of South African vehicles from Jan Smuts airport, Johannesburg, where the Pope's plane had been forced to land because of poor weather, ignored the Maseru border controls and the waiting posse of local security officials and VIPs, and ploughed on to the Pope's first rendezvous, a Catholic mission at Roma, 40 miles inside the country. During a simultaneous hijacking in the country, SADF commandos stormed in and ended it. As a British correspondent noted: "The message from both the hijacking and the Pope's travels was clear—South Africa does what it likes in Lesotho."(5) Lesotho, the so-called kingdom in the sky, had been brought down to earth. It was back in Pretoria's fold.

Swaziland: the conservative kingdom

Swaziland is the second smallest country in Africa: it can fit at least 70 times into South Africa, which surrounds it on three sides. After independence from Britain in 1968, King Sobhuza became not only the longest-reigning but also the most absolute monarch in the world. With a skilful mixture of modern and feudal statecraft he beat the white settlers, imperial bureaucrats and black radicals at their own games. His initial alliance with Swazi whites against the African socialists was tactically astute. The king compensated for his kingdom's vulnerability—a country small in size and few in numbers defending so coveted a location—by reasserting traditional values. Tradition meant conservatism in land tenure, in resource husbandry and, above all, government. The survival of the monarchy and country became fused in the public mind. The monarchy brought stability to the country, despite its sensitive position locked between the apartheid republic and revolutionary Mozambique.

When the king died in August 1982, after ruling for 61 years, both Swaziland and the monarchy looked vulnerable. The ANC "presence" in the country became a live issue as the SADF pounded piously into Botswana, Lesotho and Mozambique. Despite the cordial relations between the Swazi police and the SAP, Sobhuza had limited the crackdowns on the ANC. He did this for a number of reasons, but mainly because he was trying to maintain Swazi credibility in the OAU and Commonwealth. That meant some distancing of the kingdom from Pretoria. As Sobhuza's personal grip on power began to wane in his final years, his technocrats encouraged him to join the SADCC. But in the same month that Swaziland signed up, a South African trade mission, a *de facto* embassy, was opened in Mbabane, the capital. Swazi foreign policy was always a balancing act between its anti-communism and the need to publicly oppose apartheid. When Swaziland became a SADCC

PLATE 14.1 A study in contrasts: Swazi troops on parade for Prince Michael of Kent and wearing traditional war dress during the 1986 coronation

member, Pretoria felt that it had to woo back the kingdom, which it considered, like Malawi, to be a natural conservative ally. In February 1982, not long before the king's death, Pretoria had signed a secret security agreement with Swaziland. Although it was eventually made public in 1984, after the Nkomati pact, the Swazi arrangement was somewhat different. Swaziland did not need the kind of military pressure, such as Renamo, that had induced Mozambique to come to heel. There was often a meeting of minds between the security elites in both Mbabane and Pretoria. So, unlike Nkomati, the 1982 agreement allowed the SADF and SAP to operate against "international terrorists" inside Swaziland. (6)

After Sobhuza's demise, Swazi politics fell into total confusion. Would the security pact hold, especially if radical socialists came to power as a reaction to the long autocracy? Unlike Lesotho, there were no political parties for Pretoria to manipulate. And not even the most subtle Africanist in the South African foreign ministry could fathom all the nuances of the ever-changing feudal cabals that controlled the interregnum. For, technically, Swaziland is not a monarchy, but a dyarchy. A Queen Regent reigned after Sobhuza, but she was deposed and another one of Sobhuza's very many wives took her place. The regency was riddled by Byzantine intrigue, tales of witchcraft, massive corruption, and various assassination attempts. Personality clashes within the remarkable ruling clan, the Dlamini, as well as ideological rivalry between the modernising technocrats and the traditionalists inside the royal council, the Liqoqo, threatened the survival of the conservative monarchy. Eventually the traditionalists triumphed and in April 1986 a 19-year-old boy became King Mswati III.

Thereupon most of the domestic bickering ended. The world's youngest ruling monarch inherited much of the nation's awe of his late father. Nor was the young king troubled by the complex array of formal opposition forces which delayed the king of Lesotho's return to grace. The elaborate coronation marked the official confirmation of the traditionalists' emphasis on absolute monarchy. P W Botha and Pik Botha sat alongside Samora Machel and Prince and Princess Michael of Kent, representing the British Queen. Maureen Reagan stood in for her father, a hereditary representative from the most elective of institutions, the American presidency. The Americans got it right, quite by accident: sending a favoured daughter is a mark of respect in the local Nguni culture. The vulnerable Swazi monarchy was back in the saddle, but no-one knew which advisers in the king's coterie now called the shots.(7)

One of South Africa's main concerns, as ever, was to keep out the ANC. Pretoria had been active on this score during the regency. In 1982 Sobhuza had been offered a straightforward swop: South African land in exchange for keeping out the ANC. This had been the sweetener for the security agreement. Regaining foreign-owned land in Swaziland had been the leitmotif of his long rule (even though the economy had ended up largely in South African hands). But large Swazi irredentas still existed in South Africa. The king had always talked of "bringing all his children together". Although ethnically related to the Swazis, these territories, KaNgwane and Ingwavuma, had become parts of existing South African homelands. The chief minister of KaNgwane, Enos Mabuza, one of the more progressive bantustan leaders, wanted none of it. "We have no wish," he said,"to be part of a medieval monarchy that rules by decree." The KwaZulu leader, the mercurial Gatsha Buthelezi, was also extremely hostile to the deal and he took the issue to the supreme court. Although the proposal would have given the landlocked kingdom direct access to the sea, it would have also more than doubled the existing Swazi population. The country's social and employment structures could not have coped. Such a transfer would have legitimised the bantustans and reinforced the apartheid doctrine of stripping blacks of their South African nationality. Moreover, the deal would have contradicted a basic OAU tenet that sanctifies colonial borders.

Pretoria had got what it wanted, a security agreement, and, once the king was dead, the land deal was quietly dropped. Swaziland continued to cooperate with the SAP's monitoring of ANC activities, especially after the Nkomati accord forced some ANC personnel to take refuge in the kingdom. In 1984 over 300 ANC members were deported from Swaziland. Also, the SADF entered the country on a number of overt hot-pursuits and secret operations. A complicating factor was Renamo which had reportedly set up bases in the mountainous border area. Occasionally, during actions to root out the ANC, the Swazi security forces fought with Renamo by mistake.(8)

Another important South African propaganda aim was to encourage Swaziland to publicly oppose sanctions, which it did. The cheerfully eclectic Swazi economy has been almost totally dependent upon its big white neighbour. The kingdom's trade faced both ways: to South Africa via the customs union and to Europe via the Lomé agreement. In the mid-1980s it began to benefit enormously from sanctions evasion, particularly the relocation of firms such as Coca-Cola, which had divested from South Africa, and from the relabelling of South African products. The Israeli embassy's flag fluttered proudly in Mbabane, and the most arresting new building was the Pagoda-style Taiwanese embassy. Swaziland pragmatically paid lip-service to the radical OAU creeds, while heartily trading with the three main pariahs of the world.

Occasional attempts to delink from the South African connection met with the usual mix of economic harassment, including border "delays". As with Lesotho's Highland water scheme, attempts to improve the domestic economy often involved South African capital. Swazi railways, which until 1986 was the only all-steam system in the world, opened up in February 1986 a new southern link which was plugged in at both ends to the South African rail network. It made economic sense, but it also meant that the SADCC rail route through Maputo, sometimes sabotaged by Renamo, became less important.

If Lesotho returned to the fold in 1986, Swaziland had never really left. It did flirt briefly with a more rebellious stance at the end of the 1970s, when it rejected membership of South Africa's constellation plan. Like the other royal mini-state, Lesotho, its economic options were always few. Politically, the alternatives to its current balancing act appear sombre, narrowing to the stark choice between clienthood as a quasi-bantustan or becoming another Mozambique, torn apart by SADF adventurism. Swazi policy, therefore, has always been pragmatic. Because of its feudal, royalist structure the conservative members of the ruling elite would be directly threatened by the rapid advance of African socialism at home or in South Africa. Probably, the Swazi monarchy needs Pretoria in order to survive.

Botswana: an African success story

Botswana is big: the same size as France and, if Texans will forgive the comparison, the same size also as the Lone Star state. It is, however, 80% desert or semi-desert. Like Lesotho and Swaziland, it is essentially ethnically homogenous. About one million people, and three times as many cattle, inhabit Botswana. It is a country of stark, often unspoilt beauty. In the centre lie the exquisite Okavango swamps, in the north the nature reserves teaming with wild life, and to the south and east large cattle ranches. Most of the inhabitants live in the south along the South African border. Botswana, independent from Britain since 1966, is surrounded on three sides by South Africa and (formerly) SADF-controlled Namibia. And yet, for all the poor examples set by its black and white neighbours, Botswana has survived as one of the handful of functioning democracies on the continent.

Despite its domination by the South African economy—85% of imports originated or passed through its white neighbour—Botswana attempted to distance itself from apartheid. During the 1970s President Sir Seretse Khama tried to prevent the fighting in the Caprivi, southern Zambia and Rhodesia from spilling over his borders. Botswana did suffer from minor SADF incursions in the northwest and from Rhodesian raids in the east. Nevertheless, Sir Seretse became a prominent member of the frontline states, although his economic and geographical position forced him to mute some of his criticisms of his white neighbours. After Zimbabwe's independence, the main refugee camp at Dukwe continued to serve as a recruiting ground for both ZIPRA and Super-ZAPU dissidents. Botswana joined the SADCC and, in 1983, the organisation's HQ was defiantly established in the capital, Gaborone, a few miles from the South African border.

In the 1980s Pretoria's concern, as ever, was to deter the infiltration of ANC insurgents. Sir Seretse's successor, Quett Masire, continued to honour the "open door" policy for South African political refugees, but he refused to allow guerrillas to operate from the country. The ANC, however, did use Botswana as an entry point for operations in the Transvaal. Botswana argued: if the SADF, with all its resources, cannot monitor and prevent all ANC infiltration, how can the tiny Botswana Defence Force (BDF), especially across such vast ranges of bush? Pretoria replied that Botswana was not trying, or not hard enough. Every year Pretoria would present Gaborone with a list of ANC suspects which it wanted expelled or handed over. Botswana would ask for proof that ANC refugees were involved in military operations. Pretoria also wanted Botswana to sign the usual non-aggression pact, as well as to recognise the homelands, especially the Tswana bantustan, Bophuthatswana. Botswana always refused

Botswana was in a much stronger position than either Lesotho or Swaziland to resist Pretoria's untender traps. For besides owning vast herds of cattle, it found lots of diamonds. Like South Africa and its diamond partner, the USSR, Botswana produced 30% of the world's supply. Jwaneng, in the southern Kalahari, became the world's most valuable diamond mine. This piece of nature's bounty generated Botswana's amazing 11% growth rate in the first half of the 1980s. By 1989, Botswana's foreign reserves ($2.26 billion: R5.6 billion) had overtaken South Africa's gold and foreign exchange reserves (R4.93 billion), according to South African estimates. There were two problems, however. Firstly, this new-found wealth, as in the oil-rich states, was not spread evenly. The resulting disparities and discontent were not, however, manifested in a strong opposition party. Rival political groups did challenge the dominant Botswana Democratic Party, which had been in power since independence, making Botswana a *de facto* one-party state. But the rival parties secured only a few seats in parliament. Nevertheless, Pretoria did meddle in internal party politics by encouraging elements in the Botswana National Front to advocate a non-aggression pact. (Pretoria also had good connections with senior members of the defence force.) None of this led anywhere, partly because Masire's ruling party appeared to be genuinely popular, not least in the way it played David to the apartheid Goliath. In the 1984 election, for example, a white cabinet minister won the highest popular vote. And although Botswana was not entirely free of political thuggery and corruption, there were no political prisoners. The second problem was the manipulation by South African capitalists of Botswana's mineral windfall. De Beers, the diamond arm of Anglo American, effectively controlled the sale of Botswana's precious stones. De Beers, however, needed Botswana—to preserve its marketing monopoly—as much as Botswana needed South African investment and industrial expertise. Yet, like the Highland water scheme and the Swazi railway extensions, Pretoria was quite happy to use major projects, such as the development capital required for the extraction of soda ash in the huge Sua Pan salt lake, to force the Botswana government to make political concessions.

Botswana tried hard to delink. In 1976, for example, it left the rand monetary zone, but its trade and transport dependence kept it a hostage, albeit not a helpless one, of Pretoria's volatile goodwill. And the wealth that accrued to the grasping black middle classes meant that the consumer goods that festooned their suburban lifestyles were purchased on regular shopping sprees in nearby Pretoria or Johannesburg. Moreover, European and American international companies implicitly reinforced this dependency by treating southern Africa as one commercial, colour-blind entity. Often, when the Botswana government tried to work directly with companies in the West, it was told to deal with the local agency or subsidiary which was almost inevitably based in Johannesburg. Even the most radical relief agencies in black southern Africa found themselves shopping in the pariah state.

Pretoria found it almost as easy to handle Botswana as the tiny royal kingdoms. The same old siege machines were wheeled out: border "delays", withholding of customs dues and manipulation of capital investment. "The best managed economy in Africa," as the Johannesburg *Financial Mail* put it, was lightweight armour against Pretoria. But, until 1985, both countries practised peaceful coexistence, to their mutual economic benefit. The SADF raid on 14 June 1985 ruptured the cosy pattern. Three weeks after the highly publicised military fiasco in Cabinda, South African commandos fired rifles, mortars and grenades for just under an hour in the capital city. Twelve people were killed, five with identifiable ANC links. As in Lesotho, local security forces kept their heads down. The Cabinda raid had already embarrassed the US government. Now the American ambassador in Pretoria, the ex-journalist Herman Nickel, was recalled. In Washington, the State Department summoned the South African ambassador-designate to warn him: "If you want to bring down the wrath of God on your head, I couldn't think of a better way of doing it."(9) The British Foreign Office, deploying more diplomatic language of course, called the attack on a fellow Commonwealth state "indefensible". In May 1986 the indefensible was repeated when SADF attacked Gaborone again during their triple assault on Commonwealth states to destroy the EPG peace initiative.

Botswana had always been one of the most easy-going countries in Africa. The sense of friendliness and lack of tension was almost palpable. As the confrontation intensified, roadblocks and security checks spread throughout southern Botswana, as they had elsewhere along the racial fault-line in southern Africa. ANC activity increased as did overt SADF incursions and dirty tricks. Tourism, an important money-spinner, suffered as Pretoria issued a number of warnings about the potential dangers in Botswana for South African holiday-makers.

On 28 March 1988 the SADF once again atacked the outskirts of Gaborone, destroying an alleged ANC base and killing four people. Botswana officials insisted that the victims were genuine refugees and innocent Batswana. General Magnus Malan, however, congratulated the SADF for "a surgeon's incision against the ANC, with minimum force to achieve maximum advantage".(10) This time there was an investigation as to why the security forces did not react. A scapegoat was of course found: a corporal who failed to order his patrol to fight the invaders was sentenced to 15 years in prison for cowardice. (11) Botswana now felt obliged to join the local arms race. The 3,150 members of its armed forces were to be better equipped and trained. (Already, in 1981, Botswana had purchased armoured personnel carriers and surface-to-air missiles from Moscow.) In April 1988 Botswana announced that it would spend more than $130 million on modernising its forces in the next two years. This was a big jump. The defence budget had already risen fron $8 million (1986-87) to $27.29 million (1987-88).(12) Britain agreed to sell nine second-hand Strikemasters to boost the air force's almost non-existent combat role.(13) British military advisers also assisted the BDF.

Botswana's economic success story, due to mineral resources and sound conservative fiscal policies, is almost unique in Africa. It is literally a diamond in a continental desert of mismanagement. For long it has prudently avoided entanglement in the wars that encircled it. And it has made arrangements to act as an entrepôt for South African external trade should sanctions really bite. But whether it can avoid being sucked into the simmering civil war in the south is an open question.

Zambia: an economic wreck

Besides being an economic wreck, Zambia is a political paradox. President Kaunda has been a public scourge of apartheid, yet in private he has often been the main black interlocutor with Pretoria. He took over as chairman of the frontline states from Nyerere in 1985 and he plays host to the ANC HQ and (formerly) to the large SWAPO facilities in Lusaka; yet his mining-based economy is largely run by Anglo American. A South African defence white paper termed Zambia "a Marxist satellite", yet Pretoria's doves regard him as a useful "moderate".

Zambia's political dilemmas stem primarily from the vast chasm between Kaunda's emotive rhetoric and the country's desperate economic performance. The economic woes have various causes, including: gross corruption and mismanagement, harassment of the small but vital Indian business community, the effects of the UDI war and sanctions, the closure of the Benguela railway, and, most important, the collapse of the world price of copper. So bad has been the economic deterioration—inflation touched 300% in 1986—that Zambia has considered demoting itself to apply for the UN status of a "least developed country". Kaunda has blamed much of his misfortune on Rhodesia and South Africa, which is a politically useful but not entirely accurate expedient.

The Rhodesian war did a great deal of damage, particularly in 1978 and 1979, when the Soviet Union supplied a squadron of MiG-21s, as well as military advisers and equipment for the lacklustre Zambian army. But military aid did not translate into political influence: "Kaunda has followed a strict policy of non-alignment in the superpower competition and, while he does not oppose an active role for the USSR in regional politics, neither is he a champion of Soviet desires and ambition."(14) With the political defeat of the Soviet-backed Nkomo, an ally of Kaunda's, the Russian connection diminished. South African military forays into Zambia had been limited mainly to operations in southwestern Zambia adjacent to the Caprivi strip. From 1975 the SADF trained and assisted a dissident group led by Adamson Mushala. The rebels operated for seven years, waging a low-level bandit war partly in the name of Barotse tribal separatism.(15) During the last Rhodesian offensives into Zambia, the SADF simultaneously moved into the Western province in some strength. The spillovers from both the SADF's pro-Unita and anti-SWAPO campaigns disrupted the area throughout the early 1980s.(16)

The SADF was held in check for a number of reasons: the amount of South African mining involvement, and trade with and through Zambia, and Kaunda's diplomatic usefulness. On a number of important public occasions Kaunda provided a means for Pretoria to break out of its diplomatic cocoon: in 1975 during the Victoria Falls conference, in 1982 during the P W Botha-Kaunda summit and during the separate South African talks in Lusaka with Angola and SWAPO in 1984. And, often, Kaunda has worked secretly behind the scenes as a mediator. Less to Pretoria's liking, perhaps, was series of meetings in Zambia between South African business and opposition leaders and the ANC, fixed up by Kaunda. Meanwhile, Lusaka was also the venue for a major ANC conference, as well as frontline and SADCC summits. These were often gala occasions. Despite the shabby surroundings, the fleets of new Mercedes and flowing wine would have added some tone, except for the fact that all these luxuries were provided by South Africa. When Zambian shops have goods for sale, they are often from the despised republic, but nobody bothers to disguise the "made in South Africa" labels.

By 1986 Kaunda seemed to have despaired of his role as regional mediator and his ability to persuade Pretoria to see reason. The SADF raid on alleged ANC bases in Lusaka in May 1986 may have been the last straw. His position hardened dramatically at the Commonwealth summit in London in August where he committed Zambia to applying sanctions, without any contingency plans or discussions with his ministers. (17) Anti-white paranoia about "foreign agents" resulted in numerous cases of arrest and maltreatment of tourists and visiting businessmen, which further strained relations with Zambia's major aid donors. This was made worse by Zambia's repudiation of its IMF agreements. The repudiation was precipitated by widespread food riots in December 1986 after the government had been forced to drop food subsidies as a precondition for the desperately needed IMF loan. The riots, mainly in the northern Copperbelt, were eventually put down by the army, with some loss of life. Zambia was in no position to feed itself properly, let alone impose comprehensive sanctions on the regional superpower. But Kaunda felt obliged to honour his promise to Maputo by sending a token force of troops to help anti-Renamo operations in Tete province.

Besides the economic malaise, Kaunda—who has ruled since independence in 1964—is faced with active discontent among the Zambian technocrats, unions and the professional class as well as a more passive hostility from the peasantry. The sacrifices demanded by the Rhodesian war against the enemy nextdoor were often met with some sense of national purpose. Smith is long gone and things have got worse, not better. On a number of occasions, in 1980 and 1986 at least, it was rumoured that coups had been planned against Kaunda's misrule.(18) Zaire, Nigeria and Tanzania may have neglected essentials such as transport and agriculture, but they were never foolish enough to run out of beer. Yet Zambia managed to run out of that politically sensitive commodity in the 1980s. The Zambian army, however, was supplied with cheap and plentiful beer, but in October 1988 there were rumblings of a military coup even in the army.(19) For all his lachrymose bluster, Kaunda poses no real military threat to Pretoria. Without South Africa's economic props, what remains of Zambia's economy could collapse completely. Direct and sustained military destabilisation or economic blackmail could topple the president, a man Pretoria might well need again as a regional referee.

Malawi: the odd man out

Like the biblical description, Malawi is in the frontline but not of the frontline. It is a conservative state with formal diplomatic relations with South Africa, even though it is separated from the outcast by more than 440 miles of Mozambican territory. Malawi is conservative because His Excellency The Life President Ngwazi Dr Hastings Kamuzu Banda is ultra-conservative. Malawi is Banda squared: small, disciplined and notably intolerant. He rules as a modern African monarch, dressed in black homburg, three-piece suit and thick spectacles. Pictures of the *Ngwazi,* or conqueror, are everywhere. The highly eccentric and very aged president (estimates vary but he could be in his 90s) lived away from his homeland for over 30 years, mainly in England where he worked as a general practitioner. He was also an elder of the Church of Scotland. Banda often harked back to the colonial era and appeared to believe that, in non-political positions, whites are often more qualified than blacks to hold key positions. This anachronistic viewpoint was epitomised in the founding of the well-known Kamuzu Academy.The academy is an Eton in the bush, complete with white teachers. Banda argued that an educated man should know European history and Latin and Greek—he gives speeches in English which are rendered into the vernacular by a translator.

Malawi's relations with South Africa, although basically sound, have vacillated. During the 1960s and 1970s, Malawi was the darling of hardnosed economists. The growth rate was 6% per annum and the country exported food. South African aid and loans had helped, although Pretoria predictably dangled funds for big projects in return for political concessions. Pretoria provided soft loans for the building of a new capital at Lilongwe and for a railway to Nacala, the Mozambican port. Banda was always grateful, in particular, for his new capital, as Western donors had refused to assist in the grandiose scheme. In 1967 Malawi and South Africa exchanged ambassadors. Malawi was the only African country ever to do so. In 1970 John Vorster paid a state visit and Banda reciprocated the following year. The life president also established diplomatic relations with Taiwan and Israel. All three pariahs, but especially South Africa, helped train Malawi's four security-related services: the army, police, special branch and the Young Pioneers. The heads of each service were handpicked by Banda, who ruled with an iron fist. He maintained his autocracy by keeping his opponents divided, in jail or exile. But he also dished out favours, money and properties judiciously, especially to the active women's section of the sole legal political group, the Congress Party. In this he was astute, for women are the backbone of African society and agriculture, a fact which is politically ignored by nearly all the leaders in male-dominated African politics. In 1981, for example, he simply appointed 13 extra women to parliament, making the total number 34. In a 128-member parliament, this probably gave Malawi the highest percentage of female parliamentarians in the world. (20)

Although South African companies were well-represented in the economy, as were South African and Rhodesian managers, the financial structure was never dominated by apartheid capital, partly because a small number of parastatals, directly controlled by Banda, supervised most of the economy. Malawi, sometimes dubbed "capitalism without capitalists", initially prospered because of the retention of white expertise and, a rarity in modern Africa, an efficient and honest civil service modelled on the British system. By the mid-1970s the rigidity of parastatal control and poor weather conditions caused a rapid decline in agricultural production. In 1976 a coup attempt, led by the head of special branch, Focus Gwende, was ruthlessly crushed. As special branch had close ties with Pretoria, this might have been a factor in the cooling of relations with South Africa.(21) When Malawi joined the SADCC, Pretoria tried to woo back its fellow conservative with more loans. The stick was also applied. The SADF used Renamo to cut Malawi's transport links through Mozambique. Strangely, Malawi also had ties with the rebels. So, as Hanlon noted, Malawi was "an agent for its own destabilisation".(22) One of the reasons might have been the jockeying for position to succeed Banda, rumoured to be losing some of his mental faculties. Some conservative elements might have wanted to back Renamo, while the more radical technocrats leaned towards Maputo and Harare. In this context, Zimbabwe's alleged support for the small and outlawed Malawi Freedom Movement made some sense. In 1987 Malawi's position shifted, both in its own interest and under pressure from Mozambique and Zimbabwe. Malawi's tiny but competent army sent troops into Mozambique to protect the Nacala line. During Margaret Thatcher's visit to Malawi in March 1989, she offered £720,000 to equip Malawian forces operating in Mozambique and a team of Royal Engineers to help with mine clearance on the Nacala line.(23)

The future of Malawi, the so-called "heart of Africa", depends upon the kind of political animal who takes over from Banda. Whoever it is, he (or she) is unlikely to favour such cosy relations with Pretoria.

Adventures elsewhere

Pretoria's destabilisation was primarily aimed at the frontline states. All suffered in varying degrees from the cutting edge of South Africa's military and economic power. Mozambique was torn apart by the Renamo war, while Tanzania was relatively unscathed because of its geographical distance and minimal trade with South Africa. The blockade of SADCC southern routes actually benefited Tanzania because it forced Zambia and Zimbabwe to make more use of facilities at Dar es Salaam.

Pretoria's military adventurism extended far beyond the frontline states, and even beyond Africa. The long arm of the SADF and its agents could reach out to London, where, for example, Pretoria was accused of bombing an ANC office on 14 March 1982, or to Paris, where an ANC representative was assassinated. But Africa was the main battleground. Pretoria, with its French and Rhodesian allies, meddled in many African wars. South Africa provided clandestine military and diplomatic backing for both the Biafran and Katangese secession movements. White South Africans were prominent among the mercenaries who fought for Moise Tshombe as leader of Katanga in 1960-63 and as Congolese prime minister in 1964-65. The Congo wars spawned a hard core of mercenaries who were employed on and off by Pretoria for 20 years. Some were used in Zaire, where Pretoria and the CIA cultivated ties with the venal Mobutu, particularly for the supply routes to Unita. One of the best-known Congo veterans, "Mad" Mike Hoare, came out of retirement in Durban to lead the November 1981 coup attempt in the Seychelles. Hoare was past his prime and, although his 50-odd-member team included experienced ex-Rhodesian and serving SADF soldiers, the coup was poorly planned and financed. The precise extent of Pretoria's involvement is unclear. Military intelligence knew all about it and middle-ranking SADF officers provided small-arms. There was some opposition, and cautious distancing, at senior military and political levels, but that might have been about the mechanism of "deniability", if the plan backfired. If it had worked the top brass would, no doubt, have taken all the credit.(24) In parliament, Magnus Malan dismissed the opposition's outrage at the government's handling of the aftermath of the bungled coup, when Hoare's men were jailed for hijacking an Air India Jumbo jet to get back to Durban, by saying: "If the government wanted to take over the Seychelles government or cause its downfall, it could have used the best army in Africa to do the little job in a jiffy."

A successful coup, engineered partly by Rhodesia and South Africa, did take place in a jiffy in the Comores. In the early morning light of 13 May 1978, another ageing ex-Congo mercenary, Bob Denard, accompanied by a pet German shepherd and 30 other dogs of war, waded ashore at Itsandra beach to claim possession of the republic of Comores on behalf of the deposed ex-president, Ahmed Abdallah Abdermane. The inhabitants of the islands, a former French protectorate, greeted Denard as a liberator from the repressive and manic rule of Ali Soilih. Ali Soilih was shot "trying to escape" two days later. Soilih once had a vision of being assassinated by a man with a dog, so he ordered all the dogs on the islands to be killed. Hence the reason for Denard taking his pet to war. More than ten years later Denard still ruled the islands behind the powerless facade of President Abdallah.*

One of the four main islands in the archipelago had opted to stay French: Mayote (Mahore) kept a battalion of the French Foreign

*After the death of the president in highly questionable circumstances, French pressure forced Denard to quit the island in late 1989. He took refuge in South Africa.

Legion. The islands were considered to be of strategic importance because they sit astride the main sea lanes of the Indian Ocean. South Africa is reputed to have established a powerful communications listening post on the main island Njazidja (Grande Comore) which monitors not only shipping but also eavesdrops on radio traffic throughout much of east Africa.(25) There were persistent reports that Pretoria used the Comores as a staging post for supplying Renamo and for selling arms to Iran during the Gulf war. With some reservations, the French cooperated with South Africa in funding Denard's "presidential guard". The cost, about £2 million, was part of a wider operation, agreed between King Fahd and CIA chief William Casey, to support anti-communist movements worldwide. The French, and their friends in Morocco and Gabon, were also involved in not only the Comores gambit, but other ventures in Equatorial Guinea, São Tomé and Principe, as well as in Unita territory, all with South African connections. French influence in the Comores was embodied in the former deputy commander of the guard, Commander Charles (alias Rogér Ghys, a French protégé, despite his Belgian origins). After a protracted struggle with Denard, Charles was pushed out of the islands in October 1987, leaving Pretoria, for the moment, as the main influence.(26) Besides its military and sanctions-busting utility, South Africa expanded the tourist infrastructure of the islands. South African aircraft, painted in Comores' livery, as well as South African Airways, established regular flight schedules to the new apartheid dependency.

Destabilisation: what next?

South Africa's muscular foreign policy has been both crude and subtle. It will give ground, when necessary, as in Namibia, but will then consolidate, as in Mozambique, or go on the offensive as in Lesotho or the Comores. Whatever the internal disagreements within Pretoria's governing elite about the means, the desired end is the same: the creation of a circle of compliant states in southern Africa. These states are simultaneously meant to be military and political buffers, and conductors of economic domination. For, as Hanlon noted, South Africa is defending "not merely a set of racial taboos but an economic system". Further Western economic sanctions will invite more counter-sanctions which could further weaken the frontline states and, therefore, increase their dependency upon apartheid. And this in turn could create a sanctions-busting co-prosperity sphere. According to the SADCC, the key to solving this dilemma is massive Western support for the frontline alliance. So far,

SADCC has survived, but delinking from Pretoria has not made much progress. Indeed, the technocratic elites in the frontline sometimes oppose sanctions, despite the flood of idle rhetoric from the presidential palaces. And some of the pro-sanctioners are selfish pragmatists hoping to make a fast buck out of setting up sanctions-busting fronts.

Nevertheless, despite the general triumph of economic greed (or commonsense), destabilisation has not achieved many of its political goals. True, two states have signed non-aggression pacts, but no homelands have been recognised. And South African political refugees are rarely handed back to Pretoria. No one sends diplomatic representatives to Pretoria, except for wayward Malawi. Domestically, the SADF's raids have bolstered the National Party's tough-guy image, despite the opposition Conservative Party's criticisms that the government is too soft on its neighbours. At the same time, the *Pax Pretoria* has reinforced the tendency in South Africa to solve political problems with military "solutions". But, for all the frenetic military activity, the ANC has grown in stature during the 1980s. The settlements in Angola and Namibia, however, resulted in its military bases being pushed ever further away from the heartland of white power. In this sense, destabilisation, as an Afrikaner "counter-revolution", has rolled back the externally based ANC guerrillas. But it is a military counter-revolution without a political content. It has depended largely upon tanks and blockades, not ideas.

Meanwhile, the train-loads of food, soap, and cooking oil for the masses as well as expensive consumer goods for the elites continue to roll north. The more Marxist-oriented frontliners have confirmed the old cliché: the misery of being exploited by capitalists is nothing to the misery of not being exploited. Pretoria makes the valid point: ironically, just as southern African countries increasingly start embracing private enterprise, private capital is fleeing the continent. It cries to the West: help our capitalist counter-revolution by boosting, not stopping, trade with us. The SADCC replies that aid and private investment must be channelled to the frontline so as to make sanctions work. But this money should be a complement to, not a substitute for, economic war on apartheid. SADCC is doing its best, it says. The Beira corridor is working better, and the Limpopo corridor started creaking back to life in late 1988. The security issue is paramount. The 331-mile Limpopo line was estimated to need at least 10,000 troops to defend it.(27) The only available force is the Zimbabwean army. For most of the line's length it passes within 36 miles of the South African border. So, like the Beira run, the Limpopo corridor "will likely remain a hostage of South Africa's facade of detente towards Mozambique".(28) Eddie Cross, the Zimbabwean moving force behind the resuscitation of both links, said frankly that if Pretoria intends to attack the lines, "we are wasting our time and money".(29)

After years of being punch-drunk with pessimism, glimmers of hope breached the gloom of the region after the 1988 Angolan-Namibian settlement and the revival of the Nkomati accord. Zimbabwe, the crucial component of real detente, still led the rejectionist front. Pretoria still wanted to include Zimbabwe, Botswana and Zambia in its "multiple Nkomati" design. So, Pretoria might well ask itself: why release the hostages of destabilisation too early? Let the axe of military action hang over the corridors until Zimbabwe signs a non-aggression pact. For Pretoria holds most of the cards in the dour poker game with Mugabe. If Zimbabwe plays roughly, Pretoria could apply the "Lesotho option", a full-scale blockade. It is possible that some South African hawks *want* Mugabe to go for sanctions so that they can teach him a lesson in *realpolitik,* and perhaps even topple their arch-enemy. The most likely policy, however, is the continuation of the "flexible squeeze", an on-off tourniquet when required.(30) A permanent blockade of any or all the SADCC states is clearly not in Pretoria's interests.

Destabilisation, then, has been an effective sword in the hands of Pretoria's hawks. But there has hardly been any public debate about the strategy inside the republic. Few South African whites have any real awareness of the scale of the damage. Few South African whites, cocooned in their cosy, censored little world, realise that, on the other side of the frontline, "destabilisation" is a venomous hate-word. The red blood of the massacres in Mozambique or Angola has taken on a hideous monochrome. Harvey Tyson, the editor of *The Star,* Johannesburg's main English daily, in his weekly columns, has often tried to make his complacent white readers aware of regional realities. What if destabilisation was reversed, he asked his readers.

> What if Botswana sent an army unit to Pretoria to blow up a building; Swaziland sent in secret police to grab some AWB [the neo-Nazi Afrikaner Weerstandbeweging] plotters; Zimbabwe landed troops at Port Elizabeth where they blew up the petrol tanks, and Mozambique dropped military equipment and equipped mercenaries to capture White River, Nelspruit and Middelburg?...And what would you call Captain Wynand du Toit's excursion into northern Angola? If it were Cuban troops scouting around Saldanha, we'd call it more than destabilisation—we'd cry invasion.(31)

Hanlon tried to do the same thing for a British audience:

> ...suppose a foreign power trained Welsh guerrillas, aeroplanes dropped arms and other supplies into the Welsh mountains, submarines came close to the coast to land instructors and pick up men for training, commandos came ashore and blew up British Rail bridges, and a pirate radio station broadcasting in Welsh called for an uprising. All this and more has been done in Mozambique. This example is, of course, hypothetical; there is no war in Wales. But because the Welsh nationalists have more support in Wales than the MNR has in Mozambique, it is perhaps reasonable to ask what would would happen if a foreign power were to support them. In this case Britain is rich and powerful and would be able to quell a substantial guerrilla insurgency in the Welsh hills, were one to be organised; by comparison, Mozambique is poor and weak and hasn't much chance against the South African-backed MNR.(32)

Hanlon continued his analogy by noting that Britain and Spain have "indigenous dissidents". He asked what would happen if substantial international support were given to the IRA or the Basque ETA organisations. Hanlon's comparisons are interesting, but he undermines his case against South Africa by arguing: "It is necessary and important to understand the weaknesses South Africa plays on, but it is equally important to realise how vulnerable our own countries would be to similar actions, and to appreciate that dissident movements are not just 'African' or 'tribal' problems."(33)

It is true that any nation will support dissent in a rival country during war. The great European conflicts are full of such examples. But the engine for destabilisation in southern Africa is different: the preservation of a uniquely racist system. In this important respect, South Africa is not like other great regional powers. It is to the core of the subject that we must now turn: the war against the apartheid homeland. Destabilisation in the frontline states and the war against white supremacy are two sides of the same coin. Destabilisation is apartheid exported. The fundamental question is: how do 30 million blacks get majority rule? So far, the implicit question has been: how do their (at least) 30 million neighbours survive the process? Destabilisation will end only when the conflict inside South Africa is resolved. Will South Africa take the same road as Zimbabwe? The ruling Afrikaners might hope for another Botswana. But their great evasion of history might, in the end, lead to a second Mozambique. It would be an irony, indeed, if the clinical dispensers of destabilisation were visited with the same agonies as their victims.

References and notes:

1. H-R Heitman, *South African War Machine,* Central News Agency, Johannesburg, 1985, p. 179. See also, *Massacre at Maseru,* International Defence and Aid Fund, London, 1985.
2. J Hanlon, *Beggar Your Neighbours,* Catholic Institute for International Relations, London, 1986.
3. Author's interview with Sixishe, 1985. See also, P Moorcraft, "Lesotho: A Strange Case of Disappearing Elections," *Frontline,* October 1985.
4. R Edgar, "The Lesotho Coup of 1986," *South African Review 4,* Ravan, Johannesburg, 1987, p. 380.
5. T. Allen-Mills, "Lesotho police 'Beat and Stab Hijacker to Death,'" *The Independent,* 17 September 1988.
6. R Ajulu and D Cammack, "Lesotho, Botswana, Swaziland: Captive States," in P Johnson and D Martin, (eds), *Destructive Engagement,* Zimbabwe Publishing, Harare, 1986, p. 161.
7. G L'Ange, "Swazi Power Firmly back with the Monarchy," *The Star,* 27 June 1986, and J Ryan, "All Eyes on the Boy King, 20 Years on," *The Star,* 6 September 1988.
8. Hanlon, *op. cit.,* p. 97.
9. Ajulu and Cammack, *op. cit.,* p. 152.
10. S Robinson, "S Africans Kill 4 in Botswana Commando Raid," *The Daily Telegraph,* 29 March 1988.
11. "Botswana Soldier Gaoled for Failing to Fight South African Raiders," *The Times,* 14 May 1988.
12. "Botswana's $130m Forces Upgrade," *Jane's Defence Weekly,* 9 April 1988.
13. I Mather, "Britain Arms Botswana," *The Observer,* 1 May 1988.
14. K Campbell, *Southern Africa in Soviet Foreign Policy,* Adelphi Paper No. 227, International Institute for Strategic Studies, London, 1987/8, p. 25.
15. Hanlon, *op. cit.,* p. 244.
16. G Cawthra, *Brutal Force,* International Defence and Aid Fund, London 1986, pp. 173-4.
17. R Martin, "Regional Security in southern Africa," *Survival,* September/October 1987, p. 393.
18. C Allen, "The Politics of Apathy," *Africa Report,* May/June 1988.
19. V Mallet, "Zambians near Dying for a Pint," *Financial Times,* 16 September 1988; N Woodsworth, "Embattled Kaunda takes Few Chances at the Polls," *Financial Times,* 21 October 1988.
20. P Vale, "Malawi: Its Feet and its Heart are a Long Way Apart," *Frontline,* May 1982.
21. Hanlon, *op. cit.,* p. 237.
22. *Ibid.,* p. 240. For further details, see Chapter 12.
23. R Oakley, "Thatcher Aid Boost after a Sight of the Real Africa," *The Times,* 1 April 1989.
24. Author's interviews with some of the soldiers who took part in the attempted coup. See also M Hoare, *The Seychelles Affair,* Corgi, London, 1987.
25. K Vernon, "Our Man on the Perfume Islands," *The Star,* (weekly edition), 18 March 1988.
26. "Comoros: Under New Management," *Africa Confidential,* 22 January 1988.
27. J Raath, "Harare Pledges Forces to Defend Limpopo Rail Link," *The Times,* 4 August 1988.
28. N Jones, "Limpopo Rail Reopens," *The Guardian,* 3 August 1988.
29. *Ibid.*

30. R Martin, "Regional Security in southern Africa," *Survival,* September/October 1987.
31. H Tyson, "Were You in the War, Dad?" *The Star,* (weekly edition), 17 November 1987.
32. J Hanlon, *Apartheid's Second Front,* Penguin, Harmondsworth, 1986, p. 83.
33. *Loc. cit.*

WAR IN SOUTH AFRICA
(1945-2010)

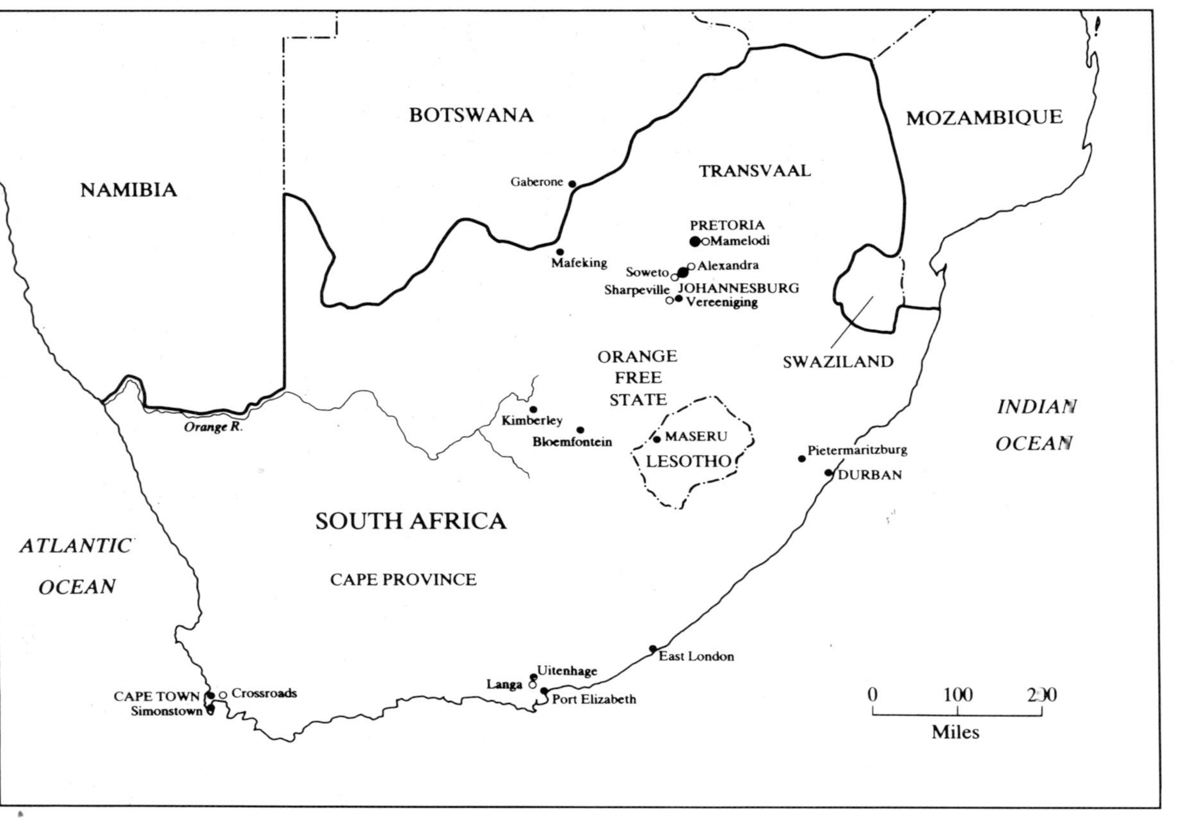

Map 15 South Africa

15

Black resistance

The African National Congress is the continent's oldest black nationalist party. It was founded in 1912, nine years before the Chinese communist party and two years before the Afrikaner National Party. Its longevity is both an asset and a liability. Although the ANC stands head and shoulders above its rival liberation movements, it is still a long way from "seizing" power. Its political clout among the black "masses" inside South Africa is not in doubt, but its military campaigns have been largely ineffective. The ANC has often been called the most unsuccessful guerrilla army in the world, but guerrilla wars are not necessarily won on the battlefield.

The ANC has suffered from periodic crises of survival, but each time it metamorphosed into a more militant force. One of the most contentious issues has been its relationship with the South African Communist Party, founded in 1921. The SACP has provided a vital organisational core and a crucial arms and training link with Moscow, but this nexus also alienated black nationalists inside and outside the party, as well as potential allies in the West. Joe Slovo, a Jew of Lithuanian origins, whom Pretoria says is a colonel in the KGB, has been a leading figure in both the ANC and communist party. As chief of staff of the ANC's guerrilla army, he was responsible for much of the military strategy. The SACP espoused a two-stage theory of revolution. The party theoreticians argued that Pretoria represented an internal colonial force which oppressed the black as well as the white working class, despite the latter's privileges. The first stage of democratisation would be accomplished by an anti-colonial, multiracial, nationalist revolution. The communist party would then act as the vanguard for real change, the second stage: a socialist government via a socialist revolution. (The "new thinking" of the Gorbachev era was, however, to dilute the party's revolutionary aspirations, as we shall see later.) As there is considerable overlap in the membership of both the ANC and communist party, does the ANC subscribe essentially to the first "nationalist" revolution, while eschewing its ally's final goal? The important question still remains: to what extent is the ANC influenced by Moscow?

Petitions and pleas

The first of the ANC's many battles was the opposition to the 1913 Native Land Act, which consolidated white possession of most of South Africa's land. Sol Plaatje's great classic, *Native Life in South Africa*, published in 1916, vividly captured the suffering of the black peasantry. Black rights were further eroded by the 1936 Land Act. Land hunger was always a prime ingredient of early ANC militancy. The ANC flag is striped green for the stolen land, as well as black for the people and yellow for the gold.

The ANC was originally led by conservative, black, middle-class figures. They supported, more or less, the Union's war efforts in both world conflagrations in the hope that the British government and the emerging Commonwealth would intervene eventually on their behalf. But, as with the Rhodesian nationalists, their faith was misplaced. Neither petitions to London nor Pretoria worked. A younger, angrier generation formed the ANC Youth League in 1943-44. Its leaders included the eventual pantheon of ANC heroes: Nelson Mandela, Oliver Tambo and Walter Sisulu. In 1948 the advent of full-blooded white supremacy helped to push the ANC towards further organised defiance. Spontaneous peasant revolts in the rural areas had long been a feature of black anger. In 1950 tribespeople rose in rebellion in Witzieshoek; in February 1960 a peasant insurrection erupted in Pondoland. Rural resistance met with brutal police action. In the cities the ANC launched better publicised and more organised defiance campaigns, based largely upon Gandhi's model of passive resistance.

The ANC became an omnibus national movement, not a party, which encompassed supporters from a variety of classes, tribes and races. But "Africanists" within the movement were hostile to an alliance with whites, especially those in the communist party. On 26 June 1955 the ANC helped to organise a "Congress of the People" at Kliptown, near Johannesburg. The ANC later adopted the Freedom Charter which emerged from the Kliptown congress. This vaguely-worded, Utopian document became the moral constitution of the ANC and its political vision of a multiracial society. In 1958-59 the Africanists broke away

PLATE 15.1 Oliver Tambo, President of the ANC. *(IDAF)*

PLATE 15.2 Nelson Mandela, before his 27 years in jail. *(IDAF)*

from the ANC to form the Pan-Africanist Congress. They advocated direct action against apartheid without, they said, the patronising support of white liberals and communists. Even within the ANC there was still opposition to the "pleading, cowardly and *hambe-kahle* [go slow/well]" attitude of the conservative, often middle-class, leadership.(1) The PAC-ANC split reflected a continuing debate within nationalist movements throughout Africa. Fundamentally, it revolved around the issue of a "pure" African nationalist response versus the concept of a class, race and ideological alliance to overturn the coloniser/racial oppressor. This divergence was to widen dramatically in South Africa in the 1980s. The ANC has even been accused of multiracial collaboration with Pretoria, while the PAC and its allies were damned for reverse racism. Accusations of crude black racism were interspersed with the arcane, incestuous lexicon of Marxist and neo-Marxist debates.

The ANC-PAC competition came to a head in 1960. The ANC had decided to hold, on 31 March, massive demonstrations against the hated pass laws, linked with a national campaign for a minimum wage of £1 a day. But on 18 March the PAC, led by Robert Sobukwe, pre-empted the ANC by announcing that an anti-pass campaign would begin on 21 March, linked to a demand for a slightly higher minimum wage. In most places the demonstrations passed off peacefully. But in Sharpeville in the Transvaal the police panicked, opened fire and killed 69 protesters and injured 180. On 30 March, in Cape Town, 30,000 Africans marched on parliament. Troops and armoured cars were deployed around the legislature to deter them. (One of these units was led by a young captain called Magnus Malan.) After police promises to negotiate (which were reneged upon), the protesters were persuaded to disperse peacefully. This march, not Sharpeville, was the immediate pretext for the government's declaration of a temporary state of emergency. The ANC and PAC were banned; their leaders went underground or into exile.

The genesis of the armed struggle

For nearly 50 years, from 1912 to 1961, the ANC had pleaded and protested, totally in vain. Black rights had been whittled away, not improved. The days of passive resistance were over. On 16 December 1961 *Umkhonto we Sizwe* (Spear of the Nation) was set up as the military wing of the ANC. It was a symbolic day: the Afrikaners commemorate the battle of Blood River on that date. Ironically, too, the armed struggle officially began five days after Chief Albert Lutuli, the president of the ANC, received the Nobel Peace Prize. Could peaceful methods ever have worked against such an obdurate regime? Lutuli warned in 1957 that the road to freedom "was sanctified with the blood of martyrs—in other words, no cross, no crown".(2)

Black politics was to produce numerous martyrs but no original military tacticians: no local Giap or Guevara emerged to lead the armed struggle. In January 1962 Nelson Mandela did leave South Africa secretly and visited a number of African countries, where he received some rudimentary military training. Few of the ANC or PAC leaders had enjoyed the benefits of formal military instruction and it showed.

The decision to wage civil war was not taken lightly, despite the sustained fury inspired by Pretoria's legalised tyranny. It took decades for the ANC to become a revolutionary party. It was always, as Anthony Sampson described it, "a baffling mixture of purpose and muddle, radicalism and conservatism, Christianity and communism".(3) Some leaders welcomed the armed confrontation; others lamented and hoped that this necessary evil would be brief, and that the Boers would soon come to their senses and negotiate. In the first phase of the ANC insurgency (1961-65) operations were limited almost entirely to sabotage attacks avoiding the loss of life. In retrospect, the decision to opt for a sabotage campaign, which developed eventually into a people's war, seems an almost inevitable progression. At the time the more militant leaders were influenced by the recently successful guerrilla campaigns in Cuba and Algeria. The ANC debated four possible forms of military action: sabotage, guerrilla warfare, terrorism and open revolution. Sabotage was chosen because, in Mandela's words, "It did not involve loss of life and it offered the most hope for future race relations."(4) Nonetheless, other peaceful stratagems *might* have worked, even in the 1960s, if they had been properly applied. As it was, the first phase of ANC's warfare was a fiasco. A much better organised and sustained nationwide campaign of civil disobedience might have been more effective, especially if it had been accompanied by a "populist" strategy of strikes. Gandhi's *satyagraha* campaigns, first developed when he lived in South Africa, did eventually work in India. Both the British Raj and the Afrikaner pigmentocracy rested upon the same risky political levitation act. Awe, more than military power, kept the ruling minority suspended above the masses. The population ratio of underclass to rulers, it is true, was much greater in India than in South Africa. And Gandhi's peaceful resistance targeted the British overlords precisely: he made them feel uncomfortable in their cherished field of moral rectitude. The Afrikaners defended their status quo in a different moral universe. Moreover, the demands for self-rule in India were much better organised; the

ANC could not design a mass mobilisation properly nor even the small-scale sabotage campaign. *Umkhonto* gradually improved. Nonetheless, the decision to opt for an armed struggle meant that the resistance movements were attacking the government at its strongest point: the means and the will to deploy the mailed fist.

The PAC attempted an even more apocalyptic approach. Unlike the ANC, it wanted to kill whites from the beginning. It set up a military wing, *Poqo*, meaning, like Ireland's Sinn Fein, "ourselves alone". With little overall political direction, *Poqo* tried to inspire a spontaneous grass-roots insurrection against white rule, a Mau-Mau-style night of the long knives, which was nearly every white African's secret fear. But spontaneity presumably includes an element of surprise. Potlake Leballo, the mercurial PAC leader, spoiled the effect by announcing the 1962 uprising in advance at a press conference in Maseru.(5) No nation-wide rebellion ensued, although a number of pro-government chiefs were murdered in the Transkei and, notoriously, on 22 November 1962, 250 blacks carrying axes, pangas and homemade weaponry went on a rampage in Paarl, in Cape Province. Two whites were killed there, and five others in the Transkei. A police crackdown, however, soon crushed *Poqo*. The PAC has been criticised, not least by the ANC, for its theory of spontaneous combustion, on tactical and moral grounds. Although effective insurgency usually demands thorough political preparation, the PAC's early strategy was perhaps, in some ways, justified by the spontaneous aspects of the Soweto rebellion of 1976 and the 1984 unrest, which caught the ANC almost unawares. Because of *Poqo's* failures in the early 1960s and, later, the chronic infighting within its exiled leadership, it has become fashionable to write off the PAC's future role in the liberation struggle. This could be a mistake.(6)

The initial phase of both the PAC's and ANC's armed struggle was emasculated by police action. Some of the leaders set about rebuilding their banned parties in exile. The ANC turned to Moscow for more help; while the PAC received funds from China and, for a while, the CIA.(7) The PAC made unhelpful friends: FNLA, Unita and Coremo. The ANC made better progress on the cocktail circuits abroad and in their choice of allies. In the internal underground the small, disciplined, largely white communist party proved itself to be a true heir of Lenin in its clandestine activities. In contrast, the ANC leaders blundered around in the twilight world of illegal politics. Their amateurishness was exhibited by the Rivonia fiasco. Mandela had been operating underground for 17 months, despite some close shaves. On one occasion a black security policeman recognised him, but the policeman winked, gave the ANC thumbs-up salute and passed by.(8) He spent some of his time at Lilliesleaf farm in Rivonia, a white middle-class suburb on the outskirts of Johannesburg.(9) He read a great deal during this period, especially Clausewitz. On 5 August 1962 he was captured, possibly after a tip-off from British and American intelligence sources. While Mandela was in prison, on 12 July 1963 the security police pulled off the most spectacular coup: the leaders of *Umkhonto*, including Walter Sisulu, Denis Goldberg, a white civil engineer, and Govan Mbeki, were all caught in one place, the Rivonia farm, with a mass of incriminating documents. One of Clausewitz's truisms, never underestimate your enemy, had been studiously ignored. As Mandela's biographer commented:

> ...undoubtedly some men in the political collective at Rivonia had become over-confident of their security as, disguised, they functioned from the unreal world of 'underground'. Always referring to the government as 'fascist', they never operated as though it was; a failing that would continue to weaken the liberation movement.(10)

The ensuing lengthy trial of the Rivonia men and Mandela, all charged in essence with treason, allowed the ANC a political platform. Mandela, who had set up a legal practice in Johannesburg with Oliver Tambo, spoke with great power from the dock. Facing possible capital punishment, he said:

> During my lifetime I have dedicated myself to this struggle of the African people. I have fought against white domination, and I have fought against black domination. I have cherished the ideal of a democratic and free society in which all persons live together in harmony and with equal opportunities. It is an ideal which I hope to live for and to achieve. But if needs be it is an ideal for which I am prepared to die.(11)

No-one was hanged then, but the life imprisonment of Mandela (then aged 44) and his colleagues, plus the police round-up of many other underground ANC personnel, decapitated the movement. The *Umkhonto* leaders were taken away to the bleak Robben Island, off Cape Town. The prison acquired a romantic notoriety like Alcatraz and Devil's Island, although Mandela might not have found his labouring in a quarry so romantic. His speeches in court and the 27 years spent behind bars transformed him from a partisan prophet into a national saint. But *Umkhonto*, or MK, as its members call it, needed generals in the field, not martyrs in jail. The armed struggle collapsed into a decade of torpor.

Poqo advocated an explicitly murderous policy, while the ANC's sabotage concentrated on destroying property not people. Both had failed to elicit a mass response. Both were crushed by state power. Isolated acts of resistance, sometimes involving white radicals, continued. A member of the tiny African Resistance Movement, John Harris, placed a bomb in the concourse of Johannesburg station, despite the ARM's commitment to damaging only property. One of the 15 injured in the explosion later died. Harris was duly hanged, the only white insurgent ever to be executed in South Africa.(12) One of the best known whites to take part in the liberation struggle was the communist leader, Bram Fischer, a QC and scion of a distinguished Free State Afrikaner family. He had helped to defend Mandela. After a period underground, he was caught and sentenced to life imprisonment in 1965. Fischer was treated particularly badly by his Afrikaner captors.(13). He was released from prison in 1975 shortly before his death from cancer. Fischer's politics incensed conservative Afrikaners: even his ashes were denied to his family.(14) The continued involvement of whites in the resistance, from revolutionaries such as Fischer to liberals like Helen Suzman, did much to prevent the South African struggle descending into a stark black versus white cataclysm. These whites were reviled by large sections of the white community but, in the long run, perhaps all whites in the future South Africa will owe a large debt to the courage and stoicism of these individuals. In the short term, the ANC's multiracial approach helped in its restructuring after the Rivonia fiasco. The first phase of the armed resistance had stalled because of "lack of bases, inadequate organisation and discipline, logistical deficiencies, insufficient international support, poor political mobilisation, shortage of funds, vulnerability to the regime's counterespionage and counterinsurgency tactics..." (15)

ANC

The second phase

The second phase of the resistance, essentially from the Rivonia period to the Soweto uprising in 1976, was spent regrouping ANC forces and strategy. The long exile in the frontline states often proved demoralising. Although both the ANC and PAC were recognised equally by the OAU, the PAC's bloody internecine feuds almost led to the OAU stripping the movement of its funds and recognition. To a lesser extent the ANC was also prone to internal wrangling. One of the causes was the disastrous ANC participation, alongside Zimbabwean insurgents, in the incursions into Matabeleland in 1967-68. They were wiped out by the Rhodesian army. In 1968 Portuguese troops ambushed and killed a small PAC raiding party trying to infiltrate through Mozambique.

The ANC tried to expand in four directions: its underground inside the republic; the preparation for mass mobilisation; the armed struggle; and international diplomacy. Until 1976, the ANC made better progress in the final aim, especially in procuring contacts in Africa and in the Eastern bloc. At the Morogoro conference in Tanzania in 1969, the ANC streamlined its military structure and dedicated itself to mobilising its domestic constituency, especially among the youth.

The ANC remained a broad church of resistance politics, despite its increasing dependence on the Soviet arsenal and the South African Communist Party. Although there were revolts by, and purges of, Africanist and Trotskyite elements in the movement, the ANC tried to keep to the middle of the road. Despite Pretoria's barrage of accusations that the ANC was a mere tool of the KGB, "under the guidance of the Rivonia generation, the political culture of the ANC remained characterized by military moderation, multiracialism and nationalism".(16) One aspect of this was ANC President Oliver Tambo's signature on the protocol of the Geneva convention, which legally bound the ANC to avoid attacks on civilian targets and to "humanitarian conduct of the war", the first time a guerrilla group had ever done so. Pretoria, meanwhile, treated all captured ANC insurgents as common criminals, sometimes hanging them.

The ANC's successes, getting guns and training in Eastern Europe and with cocktail diplomacy in the West, did not threaten white supremacy at all in this period. The ANC leaders seemed to sit back and let other people's battles create a more favourable environment for their war. Frelimo's victory allowed the ANC to shift its operational base to Maputo, and the SADF's withdrawal from the Angolan civil war in 1976 inspired a mood of expectancy among South Africa's restless majority. But it was a majority whose intellectuals seemed more in tune with a creed of "black consciousness" which owed few debts to the ANC. In 1976 the ANC was "out of touch, a resistance movement in waiting".(17)

In the aftermath of Soweto, the Johannesburg *Sunday Times*, described the situation as "riots looking for a place to happen". It did happen on 16 June in Vilakazi Street, about a mile from the Soweto stadium where thousands of schoolchildren were set to congregate to protest against the use of Afrikaans as a medium of instruction in their schools. The children in Vilakazi Street never reached the stadium. They were confronted by a small group of armed white policemen. Tear gas was fired, rocks were thrown, and then shots rang out. The first to die was Hector Petersen, aged 13, and shot in the back. That was the start of it. Within the first week 176 people had been killed; within a year at least

PLATE 15.3 Protest: Johannesburg 1976. *(Beeld*, Johannesburg).

600. For 18 months the country was rocked by strikes and riots. The catalyst was the blandly named but formidable Soweto Students' Representative Council, and the various imitations which spread across the country. This was a children's crusade: the young puritans closed down the illegal shebeens, smashed the township official liquor outlets and ordered a boycott of Christmas, even Christmas cards.

The ostensible cause of the uprising was instruction in Afrikaans. That in itself was a considerable historical irony. The secret and powerful Afrikaner Broederbond had been born out of the frustration caused by Lord Milner's colonial policy of Anglicisation. Decades later the arrogance of power had dispelled the lessons of these old injustices created anew. Now Afrikaans was being forced on blacks who regarded it as the language of apartheid. Relatively few teachers were qualified to teach in the language. The youth wanted better education via the medium of a universal tongue, English. But the language question was the detonator, not the cause of the explosion. Behind the riots was the bitter rage at the inferiority of the children's segregated education and anger at their parents for not doing something about it. Besides the general and specific hostility towards apartheid, poverty also fuelled the rebellion. A survey in 1976 indicated that 43% of the householders of

Soweto, a few miles from the richest city in Africa, were living below the Poverty Datum Line.(18)

Soweto shattered the complacency of the white rulers and the docility of the black majority. It would never be the same again: the iron certainty of apartheid began to bend. Anxious pragmatism began to replace ideological conviction. Nonetheless, the intellectual motivation behind the organisers of the revolt, the black consciousness movement, was apparently crushed by late 1977. Its chief symbol was Steve Biko. Without being anti-white, he argued that blacks must be responsible for their own liberation and rejected direct white involvement in the anti-apartheid movement. No matter how well-meaning white tutelage of the struggle might be, liberals all too easily assumed that blacks merely wanted to become incorporated into a social system hog-tied by white cultural and economic values. Biko wanted first for blacks to secure their own psychological emancipation after hundreds of years of conditioning to see themselves as inferior. Biko's charisma, intelligence and contacts with the white media made him an international figure after his murder by the police in September 1977. The callous manner of his treatment by the security police was exacerbated by the fact that South African politicians, most notoriously the police minister, Jimmy Kruger, were seen to dance on his grave. That was a serious error of judgement. Biko's death would haunt Pretoria for years to come, not least because of the *Cry Freedom* film on the young martyr.

The core organisations of the black consciousness movement were SASO (the South African Students' Organisation) and BPC (Black People's Convention). Despite their attachment to Frantz Fanon's radical philosophy, especially as articulated in *The Wretched of the Earth*, the black consciousness organisations tried to stay within the bounds of the law. In the beginning, Pretoria seemed to have encouraged the movement, as it appeared to tie in with its own ethnic ambitions to divide and rule. Moreover, Biko's outlook, despite the historical ties with Africanists in the PAC, distanced itself from both the PAC and ANC. Again this suited Pretoria. After the Soweto rebellion continued to spread, the security police had fewer reservations about clamping down on Biko and other black consciousness leaders. Thousands of black youngsters fled the country. Perhaps 75% joined the ANC. Logically, the black consciousness activists should have enlisted with the PAC. The ANC, however, was the only liberation movement capable of absorbing and training the enraged new Soweto generation.

The third phase

The third phase of black rebellion emerged in the years 1977-83. This so-called period of "armed propaganda" was intended to mobilise domestic political support while continuing to hit dramatic targets from time to time. Rioting and strikes, particularly in the Western Cape in 1980, were supported by the demonstration effect of military raids. One of the most spectacular raids took place on 2 June 1980. Three skilled ANC teams hit the showcase SASOL oil-from-coal plants. These vital strategic installations were guarded by the most highly-rated commando reservists in the country. The ANC magazine, *Sechaba*, exalted the "sea of flames, the fires of freedom, the most beautiful fire which symbolised the largest act of sabotage in South Africa".(19) In August 1981 the ANC launched a 127mm rocket attack on the SADF complex at Voortrekkerhoogte, a little like the IRA mortaring Sandhurst. In December 1982 *Umkhonto* hit South Africa's only nuclear power station, at Koeberg, causing $22 million-worth of damage. In May 1983 an ANC bomb exploded (prematurely) near the air force HQ in Pretoria, killing 18 people and injuring nearly 200.

The ANC conducted numerous smaller operations. According to Gavin Cawthra, between January 1977 and October 1982 there were, *inter alia*, 33 attacks on railways, 25 on industrial and power installations, 14 on administrative buildings, 13 on police stations, three on military bases and 19 clashes between guerrillas and army units.(20) Many of the operations were linked to particular local issues: an attack on a railway installation during a rail strike or the bombing of a township administration building during a rent boycott, for example. Between 1976 and 1986 the frequency of bombings, raids and political assassinations rose by 62-fold.(21)

By the mid-1980s the ANC was beginning to look more like a government-in-waiting: it had its HQ in Lusaka, military training and educational centres in Tanzania and Angola and diplomatic missions throughout the world. The senior officials of the so-called "external mission" of the ANC tended to shun PLO-style camouflage uniforms; executive suits were the norm. It was still a coalition of differing viewpoints trying to influence millions of blacks in a country a thousand miles to the south. About 60% of the manpower was taken up by the fighting wing, *Umkhonto*; the rest worked in agriculture, education and political activities. By the mid-1980s the various estimates averaged out at a figure of 10,000 externally-trained guerrillas, based outside the country, mainly in northern Angola, and perhaps 500-2,000 externally-trained men active inside South Africa. (The PAC had perhaps 500

PLATE 15.4 ANC attack on SASOL plant, 1980.

insurgents in training in various African states.) Increasingly, the external guerrillas were considered to be an officer corps, both as instructors for internally-based cadres and as the nucleus of a post-apartheid army. The annual *Umkhonto* budget was estimated to be $50 million.(22)

The breakdown of the ANC's arsenal commonly used inside South Africa was hand grenades, explosives and small-arms, although in 1985-86 limpet mines and landmines also were deployed regularly. The most common weapons found in caches by the SAP were the Czech Skorpion 7.65mm machine pistol and the Russian Tokarev 7.62mm and the Makarov 9mm pistols, as well as the ubiquitous AK-47. Later RPG-7s and SAM-7s were introduced.

In his excellent study of the ANC, Stephen Davis summed up *Umkhonto's* military predicament:

> Few national liberation movements in Africa have waged guerrilla wars under conditions as difficult as those with which the ANC grapples. Pushed by South African power to command posts five hundred to a thousand miles from the target frontier, the Congress attempts to control a nationwide anti-apartheid rebellion with limited resources, outdated weaponry, restless soldiers, and perilous channels into and out of the Republic. Yet its exile bureaucracy has imperfectly but doggedly adapted to the hostile strategic environment of the subcontinent.(23)

ANC

One of the most important ANC assets was its sanctuary status in the frontline states. It was especially dependent upon the formal goodwill of the outer arc of sanctuary states, Tanzania, Zambia and Angola, and the unofficial collaboration of the transit states, particularly Botswana, Mozambique and Zimbabwe, to enable the various Ho Chi Minh trails to function. Sometimes the frontline states would intercept *Umkhonto* guerrillas and send them back to Zambia. Botswana was especially vulnerable to SADF pressure to do so. Even when the neighbouring states tried to bend to Pretoria's diktats, few of them possessed the security infrastructure to stop all the infiltrators, often disguised as ordinary travellers. "It's very easy to cross from Zimbabwe to South Africa," confirmed Eddison Zvogbo, Zimbabwe's minister of legal and parliamentary affairs. "We're not paid by South Africa to be their policemen."(24) Mozambique could not afford to take such a cavalier attitude. After the Nkomati agreement *Umkhonto* was unceremoniously ejected. Sometimes, the squabbling of the ANC politicians and the behaviour of the occasionally mutinous guerrillas antagonised their hosts. Generally, however, they displayed a political and often personal commitment to the ANC leadership which transcended these problems. When a drunken ANC driver (reportedly) killed by accident the Tanzanian vice-president, Edward Sokoine, in April 1984, Dar es Salaam hushed it up.(25)

Other guerrilla organisations had suffered from similar problems while in exile. And they had become the government in the end. The ANC leadership, however, recognised that South Africa was different; not least in that it is industrialised and devoid of large areas of jungle or thick bush and so is not suited to classical African insurgency. Nor had the other insurgencies encountered such a resolute and well-armed incumbent power. Thus, the ANC tried to redefine the traditional notion of a people's war. It wanted to encourage a "gathering of forces" for a *cumulative* destruction of the Afrikaner edifice. The military campaign, coordinated by the exiled movement, was only one element of the struggle. Equally important were the underground cadres working permanently inside South Africa and the legal but severely harassed internal allies in the churches, schools, unions, "civic" associations and political groups opposed to apartheid.

Political allies

The exiled ANC, PAC and black consciousness movements were related to a complex array of domestic forces. The two most important have been, firstly, the United Democratic Front (UDF), founded in 1983, and a supporter of the Freedom Charter, and, secondly, the Azanian People's Organisation (AZAPO), founded in 1977, which subscribed to the more radical Azanian Manifesto drawn up by the National Forum. The black consciousness, Africanist viewpoint is expressed primarily via AZAPO and the National Forum, whose target is "racial capitalism". Its declared means of change is a workers' struggle. Although much of its rhetoric is socialist and "workerist", critics allege that AZAPO is a worker organisation in name only.(26) In black township politics ideological disputes are sometimes a matter of political etiquette rather than a formal difference of belief systems. Nevertheless, AZAPO and UDF rivalry has often seemed to match that of their mutual hostility to the apartheid regime.(27) Both black groups waged their private civil war in the black ghettos. But the UDF, often viewed as the overground of the ANC, has tended to catch the imagination of the media and, perhaps, the majority in the townships.

The UDF was fashioned deliberately as a loose coalition of anti-apartheid groups. Some of its 600-odd affiliates sported such intriguing titles as the Deepawali Cheer Society, the Seventh Avenue Social Organisation and the Johannesburg Scooter Drivers' Association. Some of the affiliates were large union or student bodies; some were mere dial-a-quote groups which did not extend far beyond an executive committee, but were always good for a punchy quote for journalists with pressing deadlines. The bizarre battery of organisations should be understood in terms of the abnormal politics of South Africa. Because democratic politicking is so circumscribed, nearly every aspect of township life, including areas not normally associated with political affairs, becomes politicised. These would especially include religious sects, burial societies and gangs, including prison gangs.(28). The loose and hydra-headed UDF was deliberately designed to allow the front to survive the constant culling of its top echelons by the police. Others would spring up to replace them. The UDF, which struggled to stay legal, despite the banning and imprisonment of its leaders and the curtailment of its foreign funds, acted as a "strategic transmission belt", to cross-fertilise nationwide the successful tactics adopted at local level.

The UDF and the smaller AZAPO, besides their links with the banned external resistance, functioned through their own domestic networks and via sympathetic bodies in the various legal student, church and union movements. All these groups were founded on the politics of refusal: no collaboration with the regime. On the other hand, a number of black organisations were tactically committed to working *within* the apartheid system. The most prominent of these has been Chief Gatsha Buthelezi, the leader of Inkatha and the jigsaw-puzzle empire of the KwaZulu homeland. He assumed the colours and sometimes the rhetoric of the ANC, of which he was once a member. The ANC mocked his "loyal resistance" and accused him of trying to hijack the revolution. "He has left the nation and joined the tribe," asserted Dr Nthato Motlana, the highly respected Sowetan leader.

Buthelezi has built up his largely Zulu power base in Natal and he claims an Inkatha membership of 1½ million. If true, this membership has been founded on force and intimidation as much as on his charisma and tribalist rhetoric. An Inkatha card is sometimes the only means for a black to secure employment, a house or scholarship in the region. Partly because he has been lionised by the white business community and the SABC, because of his anti-sanctions stance, the chief became the black man that the ANC, UDF and AZAPO could all agree to hate. A man criticised from so many quarters could not be all bad perhaps. Although the Zulu leader called for Mandela's release, Pretoria hinted that any political settlement must include the chief of six million Zulus. When the chips were down, it was felt, the two strongest tribes, the Afrikaners and their old black foes, could unite to surprise the rest of the world. Yet Buthelezi was well aware that the white embrace could turn him into a Muzorewa Mark II. The banned external movements insisted that it was impossible to work within the system. How could reform work "within" a system which is based upon the principle of exclusion? Only the armed struggle, they argued, would force the government to surrender, or at least to the negotiating table. Buthelezi, along with the Indian and coloured leaders who co-operated in the tricameral parliament, maintained that apartheid could be destroyed from the innards of the beast. But was this merely playing Pretoria's game, being co-opted as junior allies in an up-market form of racial domination? Had Buthelezi become a Gucci freedom-fighter? "Although he [Buthelezi] is just ambitious and independent enough to be an occasional embarrassment to it, the government has nevertheless found that, given a long leash, Buthelezi serves the basic game plan of divide and rule very well indeed."(29)

So black resistance had taken many forms: from the most servile and pro-capitalist toady in the homelands, those sophisticated tribal concentration camps, to the most radical PAC spokesman who might claim that only guerrilla warfare in all its forms could usher in the dawn of a socialist Azania. (30) All pretended to occupy the vanguard position in the crusade against white supremacy. The black spectrum stretched from "*Ja-Baas*" collaboration with Pretoria to pathological rejection of all whites. Even the most dedicated and moral opponents of racial injustice disagreed enormously as to how far the armed struggle should go. Some felt that eventually Pretoria would have to settle for a "transfer of power" in a national convention; others shouted for total victory on the battlefield.

By 1984, the Orwellian nightmare began to assume a tangible form in South Africa: from the blasphemy of the "necklace" (a burning, petrol-filled tyre placed around the neck of an alleged collaborator) to the doublespeak of frenzied government propaganda. At the beginning of that ominous year the armed struggle was just over 22 years old, and white power looked more firmly entrenched than ever. The first phase of the civil war had ended in the debacle at Rivonia. From the Sharpeville massacre to the June Soweto uprising 16 years had elapsed. On the cusp of each crisis capital and whites had fled. They had panicked, but the security forces had not. Each wave of resistance was absorbed, diluted, pushed back, pumped underground. Each time that "dreadful calm"—to use Nadine Gordimer's phrase—returned to white society. The second phase of revolt, from the Rivonia aftermath to 1976, had helped to mobilise and polarise blacks. After Soweto, the third phase lasted until 1984; the cycle of revolt had been reduced to eight years. But there was no ANC masterplan: the leadership in Lusaka was always slow in keeping up with, let alone controlling, the events forged in the crucible of volcanic anger in the townships. From 1984-86 blacks in the urban areas, and in the countryside this time, would rise up once more. During those heady days, the radicals liked to suggest that Soweto 1976-77 was like Russia's failed but preliminary revolution of 1905. Hyped up by the foreign media, the events of 1984-86 took on the appearance of the beginnings of another 1917. It was not to be. 1984, however, did mark the genesis of an important fourth phase of South Africa's deepening civil war.

References and notes:

1. G Carter and T Karis, *From Protest to Challenge*, Vol 2, Hoover, Stanford, 1973, p. 338.
2. Albert Lutuli, "What June 26th Means to African People," *New Age*, 27 June 1957, quoted in T. Lodge, *Black Politics in South Africa since 1945*, Ravan, Johannesburg, 1983, p. 202.
3. A Sampson, *Black and Gold*, Hodder and Stoughton, London, 1987, p. 149.
4. Quoted in M Benson, *Nelson Mandela*, Penguin, Harmondsworth, 1986, p. 108. For further information on Mandela's views, see N Mandela, *No Easy Walk to Freedom*, Zimbabwe Publishing, Harare, 1983, and W. Mandela, *Part of My Soul*, Penguin, London, 1988.

5. A Stadler, *The Political Economy of Modern South Africa*, Croom Helm, London, 1987, p. 159.
6. See G van Staden, "Return of the Prodigal Son: Prospects for a Revival of the Pan-Africanist Congress," *International Affairs Bulletin*, Johannesburg, 12:3, 1988.
7. Stadler, *op. cit.*, p. 158.
8. Benson, *op. cit.*, p. 110.
9. Al J Venter, a colourful South African journalist, who is frequently castigated for being a propagandist for the SADF, bought the Lilliesleaf farm. He liked to show visitors the bedroom where Mandela slept.
10. Benson, p. 134.
11. *Ibid.*, p. 159.
12. Lodge, *op. cit.*, p. 241. In 1973 *Okhela*, a "white consciousness" resistance group was set up in Paris. Its best known member was the Afrikaner poet, Breyten Breytenbach. Apparently Oliver Tambo encouraged this short-lived affiliate of the ANC as a possible counter-balance to the influence of the SACP. After some quixotic adventures, which included the jailing of Breytenbach and the revelation that its chief spokesman had been a police informer, *Okhela* collapsed in 1979.
13. See H Lewin, *Bandiet*, Heinemann, London, 1981, for a fascinating account of the life of a white political prisoner. Lewin describes how the guards tried to humiliate Fischer by making him do the most menial jobs like cleaning the latrines.
14. F Meli, *South Africa Belongs to Us*, Zimbabwe Publishing, Harare, 1988, p. 158. According to Fischer's daughter, however, a security police colonel, who was monitoring the lawyer's final days outside prison, described the communist leader as "a noble Afrikaner". Author's interview with one of Fischer's two daughters, 1977.
15. S Davis, *Apartheid's Rebels*, Yale University Press, London, 1987, p. 19.
16. *Ibid*, p. 75.
17. *Ibid*, p. 28. Davis probably offers the best military account of the ANC; for a useful, recent popular study, consult, H Holland, *The Struggle: A History of the African National Congress,* Grafton, London, 1989.
18. M Meredith, *In the Name of Apartheid*, Hamish Hamilton, London, 1988, p. 143.
19. Quoted in Meli, *op. cit.*, p. 191. Meli was editor of *Sechaba*, the official organ of the ANC.
20. G Cawthra, *Brutal Force*, International Defence and Aid Fund, London, 1986, p. 218.
21. Davis, p. 156.
22. *Ibid.*, p. 72.
23. *Ibid.*, p. 74.
24. Quoted in *ibid*, p. 47.
25. *Ibid.*, p. 45.
26. For a summary of the various parties, see A Harber, "Who'll Talk to PW?" *Weekly Mail*, 30 August 1985.
27. See editorial (by Denis Beckett), "Civil Wars," *Frontline*, February 1987, and N Mathiane, "The Deadly Duel of the Wararas and the Zim-Zims," *Frontline*, February 1987. "Wararas" is a nickname for Charterists, those who support the Freedom Charter, such as the UDF and ANC. It means people with no clear policy, the waars-waars, the "what-wheres".) "Zim-Zim" stands for AZASM, the Azanian Students' Movement, founded in 1983, and affiliated to AZAPO.
28. For a brief overview of the role of gangs, see P Moorcraft, "Close Encounters with the Gangs," *Frontline*, October 1982.
29. J Saul and S Gelb, *The Crisis in South Africa*, Zed, London, 1986, p. 238. For a general background on Buthelezi and Inkatha, see W de Kock, *Usuthu! Cry Peace*! Open Hand, Cape Town, 1986, for a sympathetic treatment, and G Maré and G. Hamilton, *An Appetite for Power*, Ravan, Johanesburg, 1987, for a hostile appraisal.

30. The ANC rejects the term "Azania", derived from an Arabic term of abuse for the peoples of east/southern Africa. The PAC, which favours the name, apparently wrote a polite letter to a bemused Evelyn Waugh, the author of *Black Mischief*, for enlightenment, as he called his imaginary country "Azania" in the book.

16

States of emergency

For the first half of 1984 P W Botha's imperial presidency was riding the crest of a wave. He had toured Europe after the signing of the Nkomati pact. At home his victory in the 1983 referendum enabled him to proceed with his new "dispensation", the tricameral parliament for whites, Indians and coloureds. New local authorities had also been set up for blacks. Black councillors were supposed to handle the complex township administrations with neither a popular base nor adequate funds. On the other hand, the UDF, AZAPO, civic and student organisations as well as black labour unions had formed a popular front, of sorts, to ensure a boycott of both the national tricameral and black municipal elections. The turnout for the Indian and coloured polls was poor and for the earlier black councils disastrous. Political conviction and intimidation both contributed to the electoral boycotts.

The politics of refusal grew apace, for cooperation meant stark collaboration to the resistance movements. Instead of repressive domination, Pretoria was offering "co-optive domination", as Frederik van Zyl Slabbert put it. The Progressive Federal Party summarised its opposition to the new system thus:

> It was one party's solution imposed on the rest of the country; it excluded blacks from its workings and therefore would polarize black/white and promote conflict and dissatisfaction; it entrenched racial laws which lay at the heart of apartheid as we and the rest of the world came to know it; and it gave too much power to the new executive President. (1)

There was precious little wrong with the old Westminster system perhaps: all it needed was the extension of the franchise, equally, to blacks. But, no, P W Botha had insisted on taking the Gaullist route, although the "Mussolini option" was a more common description.(2) As with

Hitler in 1933, Botha tried to gather up the business community in his drive against the Bolshevik menace. Most senior businessmen agreed to hold hands with P W. After all, this was "a step in the right direction", wasn't it? The tricameral parliament, however, was not a step in the right direction: it was a declaration of war on the black majority. Approximately 75% of the population was officially excluded from the new system.

This arrogant exclusion was a major cause of the revolt of 1984-86. Also, the new black councils, with Pretoria's typical short-sighted parsimony, were left to raise most of their finance from rents and service charges. Rent increases for a hard-pressed underclass led almost inexorably to more rent boycotts. The economy was not in good shape: inflation was then 12%, drought ravaged the countryside and Pretoria was forced to import grain from Zimbabwe for the second year running. In addition to economic conditions and political anger at the national and local political changes introduced by diktat, there was the widespread disaffection with the low standards of education. Expenditure on African education per head was still only a seventh of that spent on white education. This "gutter" education led nowhere except to unemployment lines, menial labour, or, for the more spirited, the guerrilla bases abroad. This was the argument of the Congress of South African Students, who helped to organise school boycotts throughout 1984.

The revolt of 1984 was not, however, merely a children's crusade. Entire communities were sucked into the maelstrom of rebellion: parents, teachers, unionists and churchmen. But as the turmoil grew a cumulative, but definitive, objective emerged: the overthrow of apartheid.

The proverbial spark came on 3 September, the very day on which the new constitution came into effect and Botha was sworn in as the "state president". Residents in Sharpeville, Bophelong, Boipatong, Sebokeng and Evaton townships in the Vaal Triangle (the industrial area on the Rand which included Johannesburg, Pretoria and Vereeniging) protested about rent increases and other charges. Protest turned to riot. Mobs attacked local authority buildings and homes of black councillors and policemen. The deputy mayor of Sharpeville was hacked to death on his own front doorstep. Shops were looted. Police action resulted in 26 killed. Their funerals were transformed into venues for mass protest. In September black labour flexed its muscles too. Over 40,000 mineworkers went on strike (their first legal one). The violence spread rapidly throughout the Transvaal.

In October Pretoria sent the army into the townships. The SADF had often worked with the police, for example, in providing manpower for extensive roadblocks, and the police had fought alongside the army in Namibia. But this was different. The troops went into the townships in large numbers like an alien occupying force. The first major incursion was Operation Palmiet. On 23 October a combined force of 7,000 police and troops poured into Sebokeng, searching all 19,800 houses. Most of those arrested were charged with very minor offences; none were charged under security laws. The increasing use of the SADF, and accusations of police brutality, raised the temperature of the revolt.

In November students and unions organised a mass two-day general strike or "stay-away". Perhaps as many as 500,000 workers struck and 250,000 students boycotted classes. They demanded a withdrawal of the SADF and police from the townships, the resignation of black councillors, a freeze on township rents and bus fares, and the release of political prisoners.

Vicious attacks on black officials, some corrupt, some genuinely committed to community service, escalated in the townships. Many officials fled to the rural areas; others, such as policemen, gave up their gutted homes and moved with their families into tents in fortified army or police bases. The black radicals, the "young lions" of the revolt, echoed the ANC line: the townships were to be made "ungovernable". They talked romantically, and unrealistically, of establishing "liberated zones". Pretoria reacted predictably with more strong-arm measures, locking up union, student and community leaders. The years of carefully developed labour relations looked like collapsing in ruins. In an unprecedented rebuff to Pretoria, the major business organisations, including the *Afrikaanse Handelsinstituut* (the Afrikaner chambers of commerce), issued a manifesto condemning detention without trial and calling for political rights for blacks, open trading areas, the abolition of influx control and an end to forced removals. They wanted industrial peace, but the price was a political settlement. Anti-apartheid groups, especially in America, took up the local businessmen's (admittedly self-interested) call. The disinvestment lobby expanded rapidly: more and more US municipal authorities, colleges and churches decided to sell their holdings in companies with South African stock. In December a number of prominent Americans, including 23 congressmen, were arrested in Washington for staging protests inside the South African embassy.

Then the "unrest", in Pretoria's parlance, began to snowball. The focus of insurrection kept shifting. For the first few weeks the action was in the Vaal Triangle, then it moved outwards to the East Rand. Beginning in 1985, the turmoil switched to the Western and Eastern Cape; then it slid into Natal and then back once more to the Transvaal. There appeared to be a subconscious realisation that each region should take it in turn to keep the momentum up and thus prevent a repeat of the early burn-out of the attempted national effort of 1976-77.

The cycle of insurrection fed on itself, as one area emulated the tactics of another. It was all recorded, faithfully and otherwise, on TV, thus stimulating further pressure, especially from the USA. There Bishop Desmond Tutu, the winner of the 1984 Nobel Peace Prize, whipped up the sometimes prefabricated moral fervour of the chattering classes. American pressures on South Africa duly encouraged the radicals in the townships. TV cameras, ravenous for blood and guts, also fed this cycle. The South African government believed that TV sometimes created rather than merely recorded the grim events. Pretoria's almost total ban on non-SABC coverage of the unrest was not, therefore, surprising; although the year or so it took to implement the ban was. It was a cynical gesture which seemed to work. Perhaps Pretoria had adequately sized up the attention span of Joe Public in America. But in 1985 apartheid

PLATE 16.1 The Johannesburg *Star's* comment on censorship during the state of emergency, (1986).

was the moral fad of the year in the USA. The clamour even influenced the re-elected Ronald Reagan. At the end of 1984, America had joined an unanimous summons by the UN Security Council for a voluntary embargo on the *purchase* of South African arms.

Opposition in Washington and other world capitals was energised by the Uitenhage massacre of 21 March 1985. Police in two armoured vehicles, without warning, shot dead 20 and wounded 25 blacks among an unarmed crowd, many of whom were attempting to flee. They had been marching to a funeral for earlier victims of police action. An official enquiry found that the police had acted without provocation. This shooting at Langa township, outside Uitenhage, on the exact 25th anniversary of the Sharpeville massacre, was a turning point in the domestic rebellion and world condemnation of apartheid.

Perhaps, just perhaps, until Langa, Botha's reforms, if far-reaching enough, might have made some immediate political impact. In January 1985 some "concessions" had been granted. Laws which banned interracial sex and multiracial political parties were repealed. Black and white could now share a bed and a political party, but not a house, because the Group Areas Act forbad that. (A black woman could not live with her white husband in a white area, but a white man was generally allowed to "move down" to live with his black, Indian or coloured wife in her respective group area. The real problem came with schools and hospitals.) Nelson Mandela made the same point when President Botha offered to release him, provided he (Mandela) renounced violence. In February 1985, via his daughter Zindzi, the ANC leader, *inter alia,* said:

> What freedom am I being offered when I must ask for permission to live in an urban area? What freedom am I being offered when I need a stamp in my pass to seek work? What freedom am I being offered when my very own South African citizenship is not respected?
> Only free men can negotiate. Prisoners cannot enter into contracts.

After Langa, any "contract", any deal in the near future between the ANC and Pretoria seemed unlikely. P W Botha's strategy had always been a Jekyll and Hyde concoction. From now on repression took command of the milder persona of reform.

The UDF perservered with its boycotts, stay-aways, rent-strikes, marches and other peaceful, if often illegal, demonstrations. At funeral services, one of the few legal outlets for the outpouring of political grief (before they were generally restricted), ANC and Russian flags were openly displayed, along with wooden replicas of AKs. The cutting edge of the insurrection was arson and murder of suspected informers and black councillors and policemen, perceived to be the main, and available, local representatives of apartheid. The "necklace" became a trademark of the young "comrades" in their war on collaborators. After Langa, 46 councillors in the Eastern Cape resigned. By June, some 240 councillors had quit, leaving only five out of the 38 new town councils functioning. Not all the violence was directed against apartheid officials. Often UDF and AZAPO supporters became embroiled in their own bloody feuds. Naturally, Pretoria made much of the black-on-black violence, touted as a visible symbol that blacks were not fit to rule. Much of the inter-black rivalry was entirely spontaneous, but the police later fuelled the indigenous animosities by encouraging conservative vigilantes in the Cape and Buthelezi's Inkatha in Natal to take on the comrades at their own game.

Meanwhile, South Africa was going up in flames. That at least was the image sometimes conveyed in the compressed, often breathless, reportage on TV screens in Europe and America. In contrast, little of the violence, except the occasional necklacing to emphasise black barbarity, was show on SATV. (Helen Suzman often made the point that if only the locals could see just a little of the barbarous police behaviour shown on foreign networks, then "tens of thousands of decent white South Africans" would raise their voices in angry protest. Maybe.) If the media sometimes exaggerated the revolutionary violence, the government had to err in the other direction to show that it was entirely in control, especially to an electorate tempted by the hard-line solutions advocated by the increasingly assertive far-right Conservative Party. On 21 July the president declared a state of emergency, the first in 25 years, in 36 magisterial districts in the Eastern Cape and in the industrial areas of the Witwatersrand. The security forces already possessed extensive powers of arrest and detention, which exempted them from potential prosecution for any act carried out in "good faith". To the comrades, this appeared to be a licence to kill. By the end of the year over 1,000 blacks had indeed been killed, many by police action. Over 7,000 people had been detained, usually without trial.

In America the demands for a harsh sanctions bill became irresistible. Far more serious was the action of private bankers. In the 1960 emergency Chase Manhattan had been Pretoria's ally. On 31 July 1985, however, William Butcher, the conservative chairman of the bank, refused to roll over further loans to South African borrowers. The "Butcher of the Rand", as he was called in desperate business circles in Johannesburg, well knew that his decision would start a chain reaction akin to a classic run on the banks. Nearly all the American bank loans were short-term; $14 billion was due over the next 12 months. South Africa's most serious financial crisis ever followed Butcher's knifing. Despite its fundamentally sound economy (in spite of the recession) Pretoria's credit rating was now lower than even the chronically mismanaged economy of Zaire.

To restore confidence, Pik Botha and other government officials hinted strongly that the president was set to deliver an epoch-making speech at the National Party congress in Durban on 15 August. As the crisis in the country mounted, so did the expectation that P W Botha would finally break the political deadlock. The least that was expected was the freeing of Mandela. Instead, P W dug in his Achilles' heel. During a bleak performance watched on TV around the world, the president wagged his finger and contemptuously dismissed his critics in a much-revised (and, reportedly, much-diluted) speech. He offered little, beyond threats.

It was billed as the Rubicon speech. In one unintentional sense it was. When Caesar crossed the Rubicon it led to three years of civil war which eventually destroyed the republic. Botha's posturing might, just, have impressed some of his backwoods Afrikaner faithful, but it alienated the vast majority of South Africans and the rest of the watching world. If Langa had finally destroyed any hope of winning over "moderate" blacks, the Rubicon fiasco finally switched off the English-speaking business magnates in South Africa. The influential *Business Day* described the president as a "hick politician". Not only was the content diabolical, but so was the exaggerated and bellicose presentation. The mannerisms were like Botha's renowed impersonator, Pieter-Dirk Uys. The president stuck out his jaw, like Mussolini, while uttering the tired clichés of the eternal irreconcilable himself, Ian Smith. There was the occasional flash of lunacy in his eyes as he shot out the arrogant words. It was obvious that the president was totally oblivious to the PR disaster he was inflicting on his country.

Money talks loudest: the rand fell to an all-time low against the dollar of $0.38. Foreign investors deserted in droves. The government suspended trading on the foreign exchange markets and closed the Johannesburg stock exchange for five days. Pretoria then announced a four-month freeze on repayments of principal on foreign debts and introduced new exchange control regulations. With a performance like Botha's Rubicon, market-led sanctions became much more important than official government-sponsored strictures. Once again, Pretoria had shot itself in both feet. Amid growing stagflation, Pretoria had stood its avowed financial policy on its head. A government so (apparently) committed to freeing the financial markets and exchange mechanisms from state interference, suddenly interfered on an unheard-of scale. It was not, of course, well-received in the banking centres of America and Europe. When, in September, Gerhard de Kock, the governor of the Reserve Bank, visited his erstwhile capitalist allies, cap and cup in hand, he was treated like a leper.

On 9 September, to sidestep a tough sanctions bill from Congress, President Reagan announced a somewhat milder package which restricted Krugerrand sales in the US, new loans to the South African government and exports of computers and nuclear-related goods. Eleven of the European Community states introduced measures of their own on the next day. The exception was Margaret Thatcher. But even she modified her stand somewhat at the October Commonwealth conference, which tightened up existing measures, and demanded an end to apartheid, and the state of emergency, the release of Mandela and the lifting of the ban on the ANC. The Commonwealth also agreed to appoint an Eminent Persons Group (EPG) to secure these demands via dialogue with Pretoria and the main black political movements.

In South Africa dialogue seemed improbable while Botha squatted on the throne. The important business magazine, the *Financial Mail,* called for his resignation in September. Under the headline "Leave Now" the newspaper said bluntly:

> It's like a watching a bad magician at work—the kind who embarrasses even the children at birthday parties. See him talk about the "creation of structures to give effect to the foregoing principle..." and see the rand plunge. Hear him growl "Don't push us too far," and hear the applause from the ANC. See him pledge R1 billion to improve conditions in black areas, and watch the flames over Guguletu...
>
> That's how the world perceives us—on the skids.
>
> The world is also frightened of the Nationalists' *götterdämmerung* stance: "Don't push us too far..." Or what? Or we'll impose martial law, wreck the economies of our neighbouring states, nuke Lusaka? What did the man mean? We, too, are disturbed by this bully-boy posturing, since the Nationalists have always shown themselves as people of their harshest words...
>
> He played a gauleiter instead of statesman—and the deathliness inspired by him and his waving hands is with us still. So all we have to say is: do it and go. And if you can't bring yourself to do it, go anyway. (3)

P W didn't go anywhere, but the despairing businessmen did: to Lusaka. A small group of senior South African businessmen and journalists, led by the chairman of Anglo American, Gavin Relly, flew to Zambia in

September for talks with the ANC. Critics of South Africa's unique marriage of "economic exploitation and racial oppression", racial capitalism, argued that "for once the apartheid government and its paymasters were running scared and in different directions".(4) Whether Anglo was really a friend or foe of apartheid, no sensible businessman could stand by and do nothing to try to break what was seemingly an unending cycle of township unrest, government repression, disinvestment and sanctions.

Pretoria blamed nearly all the violence on the ANC and more particularly the South African Communist Party which was said to control it. Pretoria was wrong on both counts. The ANC was taken by surprise by the outbreak and the enduring scale of the revolt that began in 1984. It had not instigated it. And the SACP was an important restraint on the hotheads in *Umkhonto* who wanted to hit white soft targets. In June 1985, however, at its Kabwe conference, the ANC had adopted a strategy of "people's war" which was intended to take the struggle into the comfortable and almost untouched white suburbs, at precisely the same time as the ANC was gaining ground, and respectability, in Washington and London. This was unfortunate timing, too, for the arrival of the white business leaders three months later.

On 13 September, at Kaunda's Luangwa Lodge, Relly, wearing a white floppy hat and an open-necked shirt, amiably discussed the rival virtues of socialism and capitalism with the ANC leadership, dressed impeccably in suits and ties. "What we are concerned with," Relly told the ANC leader, Oliver Tambo, "is not so much whether the following generation will be governed by white or black people, but that it will be a viable country and that it will not be destroyed by violence and strife." Tambo argued that he hated violence, but that without the dismantling of apartheid the civil war would inevitably escalate. Despite their disagreement over the need for nationalisation, Relly confessed that "it was one of the nicest days I've ever spent. A picnic among South Africans talking about the future together."(5)

Despite Pretoria's temper tantrums about Relly's safari, capitalism's very own journey to Canossa prompted a stream of prominent whites to make the same pilgrimage. P W Botha fulminated and promised to confiscate their passports. Nevertheless, Pretoria's propaganda obsessions and the visits to Lusaka by desperate (and curious) white liberals, churchmen, academics and businessmen had promoted the ANC to a government-in-waiting.

If the business community wanted to talk to some of the real representatives of South Africa's peoples, Botha was determined to annihilate the liberation movement. Then the president could beckon those elusive moderates. These shadowy personages—never named, although Buthelezi, the surviving black councillors and the homelands leaders were implied—were scheduled to participate in a national statutory council. No-one stepped forward, not even Buthelezi, who insisted that Mandela's freedom was a precondition for serious talks. The roller coaster of often savage repression and the occasional wilted carrot of reform had become mutually exclusive. As veteran journalist Stanley Uys noted: "Botha's reformism in South Africa today is like a lift going up in a building that is coming down." (6) Every gesture of friendship by Pretoria was usually accompanied by a sharp kick in the groin. As Denis Healey, the British Labour politician, acidly observed: "In the week before Christmas, Mr Botha has invaded Angola yet again, sent his death squads into Lesotho to murder his opponents, has moved a great stride towards martial law itself and, finally, has arrested Mrs Mandela for the crime of living in her own house." (7) All this at a time when the president was trying to use seasonal goodwill to preach conciliation.

Yet Pretoria continued with its switchback strategy. The major reform of 1986 was the scrapping of the hated pass laws and influx controls. Since 1916 more than 18 million Africans had been arrested for infringing these laws.(8) More than any other law, Africans loathed having to carry this "badge of inferiority". In the 1960s such a reform would have inspired black jubilation. In the very different climate of 1986 it looked like a grudging concession to the liberation struggle, a quarter of a loaf. There were a few more crumbs. Despite the opposition of the hawks, in March 1986 the partial state of emergency was lifted. The harsh security laws on the statute book were still intact, so was the endemic violence. The lifting was a tactical move to appease foreign bankers and the conservative Western governments.

Appearances mattered. Keep the violence off their TVs, tell them apartheid is dead often enough, play with doublespeak at home, rule by loud semantics and the quiet sword. That'll do the trick.

The end, far too late, of the pass laws was a real reform, but the central issue of political power was totally obfuscated. Chris Heunis, the minister in charge of constitutional change, looked as though he had been appointed because of his ability to talk at great length in a meaningless babble. Right from the start Pretoria had decided to emulate Humpty Dumpty when he said to Alice: "When I use a word, it means just what I choose it to mean—neither more nor less." The act in question had been passed into legislation as "The *Abolition* of Passes and Coordination of Documents Act (1952)". That *tightened* up pass laws by changing the name of "passbooks" to "reference books", but blacks kept to the old name. Then came a classic: "The *Extension* of University Education Act (1959)". This forced established South African universities to kick out blacks. Another well-known example of doublespeak was "The Prohibition of Political Interference Act (1968)". This allowed only the National Party to interfere in black politics. Multiracial white opposition parties such as the Liberal Party had to eject their black members or disband. All this was in the name of "grand apartheid" (placing unwanted blacks in the homelands where a Sowetan had probably never been) and those who were privileged enough to work in "white South Africa" (populated by a vast majority of non-whites) had to obey the rules of "petty apartheid" (which kept blacks out of white beds, cinemas and, most of all, toilets). And so the babblespeak went on. There was much talk of "self-determination" for blacks. That was Pretoria's code for the denial of their political rights.

After 1984, P W Botha introduced his much-vaunted "new dispensation" (translated as "apartheid under a new name"). Unfortunately, this new vocabulary, intended to confuse the world and the local blacks, did not confuse the white right wing at all. Hence Heunis. He made incoherency into an art form that not even General Alexander Haig could touch. Now the reformist language had to fool left and right, at home and abroad. That meant jettisoning English and relying on the subtleties of Afrikaans. Any problems could be brushed off as a mistranslation. Black and white affairs were now divided into "own", (an awkward translation of *"eie"*) affairs and "general" affairs; that meant Pretoria could interfere in everything, although coloureds and Indians could look after a small amount of issues which were culturally specific. When dealing with the conservatives, Heunis-speak became really esoteric. Power-sharing, in the tricameral dispensation, was paraded as nothing but a "division" of power with a clever play on the Afrikaans word *magsdeling* (power-sharing) and *magsverdeling* (division of power). It didn't work: the right wing knew it meant "giving kaffirs the vote", just as much as blacks realised the whole thing was a wordy edifice to keep them from getting at real power. In short, reformism meant sharing power without giving up white control.

No wonder the leader of the opposition, Van Zyl Slabbert, cut through Pretoria's verbose Malice in Blunderland by resigning from parliament. For him it had become a pointless talking shop. (Not all liberal parliamentarians agreed; they pointed, for example, to Helen Suzman's public role, with parliamentary privilege, as an heroic scourge of apartheid's evils.) Many of his fellow MPs were, said Van Zyl Slabbert, "sinecured cowards" on a "safe route to a retirement gratuity and a pension". He decided to cooperate with extra-parliamentary forces among the black majority.

Meanwhile, the more militant members of that majority were trying to finish off the remnants of civil administration in the townships. In its place the comrades started to construct their own area and street committees. This counter-system was a descendant of the embryonic "M" plan, designed by Mandela in the early 1950s. His plan for "cells" as the basis of an underground resistance was itself founded on the structure of the Zionist Irgun insurgents. Street committees were first set up in the Eastern Cape townships and in Soweto. "People's courts" were also established to enforce the comrades' often arbitrary rule. The levels of voluntary compliance and intimidation, backed by kangaroo courts, varied from township to township. Sometimes adults were terrorised by bands of feral youngsters, especially if they dared to break consumer boycotts. Often their victims were forced to consume all their "illegal" purchases on the spot, sometimes fatal if they were everyday items such as cooking oil, washing powder, soap and paraffin. Parents also grew frustrated with the long school boycotts, and the self-defeating demand for "liberation before education". Nonetheless, despite the fear and war-weariness, the "alternative structures" garnered a great deal of support across the social spectrum. But effective organisation and discipline of these tenuously self-administered zones were difficult because of constant security force harassment and the arrest of each layer of leadership as it rose to the top.

The ANC in Lusaka was battling to feed trained men into the townships. The ANC designated 1986 as the "Year of *Umkhonto we Sizwe*". If this was more than a propaganda gambit, it was a misnomer. During 1986 the liberation mania began to dissipate. The severity of the repression, sheer physical exhaustion and frustration with the excesses of both disciplined comrades as well as roving bands of *tsotsis* (criminal thugs) and psychopathic Pol Pot-type elements, over two years, had taken their toll. A particular point of contention was the school boycott. Eventually, after due consultation with the leadership in Lusaka, the Soweto Parents' Crisis Committee urged a return to school. Sacrificing the education of a generation was not the best tool of liberation. As Zwelakhe Sisulu, a prominent newspaper editor, and son of Walter Sisulu, warned: "We are not poised for the immediate transfer of power to the people. The belief that this is so could lead to serious errors and defeats." In short, chaos in the townships was not the same as people's power.

Yet the mood of weariness and questioning in the townships was not reflected in the international media's coverage of the "imminent revolution" in South Africa. P W Botha was sometimes characterised as a second Shah, Baby Doc revisited, or like Marcos, dead on his feet. The ANC still talked of "turning every corner of our country into a battlefield". And Winnie Mandela (literally) fuelled the sense of holocaust with her infamous statement: "Together, hand-in-hand with our boxes of matches and our necklaces, we shall liberate this country." In fact, the revolt, not the president, was dying on its feet.

The overexaggerated sense of crisis—as journalists (including this one) ran out of extreme ephitets to describe another extra turn of the screw applied by Pretoria—helped, however, to set up the conditions for the Commonwealth intervention. For the first five months of 1986 the EPG scurried around southern Africa trying to erect a bridge of compromise between Lusaka and Pretoria.

Despite Pretoria's hostility, the EPG reached the edge of perhaps the most important breakthrough of the 1980s. In exchange for a commitment from the ANC to suspend, not renounce, violence, the South African government would have to release Mandela and the other political prisoners and detainees, end the military occupation of the townships, lift the ban on the ANC and PAC and allow normal political activity. The alternative was more sanctions and further isolation.

In military terms, at least, Pretoria in 1986 was not Smith's Salisbury in 1976. On 15 May the president accused outsiders of "meddling" in South Africa's affairs. Four days later he ordered SADF raids on purported ANC targets in Harare, Lusaka and Gaborone. Apparently, military intelligence was dubious about the accuracy of its information on current ANC positions in the Zimbabwean and Zambian cities. It offered Botha instead precise and ripe targets in Mozambique but, it seems, the president was insistent upon lashing out at the three capitals of the Commonwealth states. The raids deliberately obliterated the EPG peace mission which was still in South Africa at the time of the attacks. The military action severely embarrassed not only the EPG members, but also Pik Botha who, it is said, first heard about the attacks on his car radio while travelling to work. The raids were entirely political. (9) Militarily they made no sense. The field intelligence was out of date and nothing was gained. Perhaps this was deliberate. It is possible that the Zimbabwean Central Intelligence Organisation was tipped off by SADF military intelligence just to make sure ANC officials got out of the way. (10)

After the raids, Sir Geoffrey Howe went to southern Africa to try to rescue something from the Commonwealth mission. The British foreign secretary was treated very frostily by P W Botha, who told him bluntly that South Africa's problems would not be solved by *uitlanders*. (Sir Geoffrey was even more humiliated by Kaunda, who gave the diplomat a public dressing down for his government's attitudes towards sanctions.) As Helen Suzman bluntly summed up the aborted peace mission: "EPG got the raids; Sir Geoffrey got the finger." (11)

There was endless speculation about the precise motives for the raids, although the main reason seemed to have been what the press dubbed "Rambothaism", a tough policy to satisfy the clamour of the right wing (especially at a time when the ultra-right Herstigte Nasionale Party won its first seat in 17 years, in a by-election.) There was no doubt, however, about the repercussions of the raids: renewed isolation and more dollops of the sanctions brew. Yet Pretoria pretended to look surprised at the international reaction. As Stanley Uys commented: "Are the Pretoria politicians and the military chiefs trying to tell us they had not anticipated the consequences? A corporal with a lobotomy could have told them that the raids would wreck the mission." (12) It was a raid against reason.

Black-white polarisation escalated. The right wing praised the military operations, while the EPG left and issued a damning indictment of Pretoria. The EPG report, published as *Mission to South Africa,* stated that Commonwealth intervention "may offer the last alternative to avert what could be the worst bloodbath since the Second World War". (13) A smaller scale bloodbath was taking place at the same time the EPG book was launched: at the KTC squatter camp in the Crossroads area near Cape Town. For years the government had been trying to move squatters out of the area to a resettlement camp many miles away. Pretoria's new allies, black conservative vigilantes called *witdoeke* locally (because of the white scarves worn to identify themselves from the comrades), forced out, with machetes and fire, 70,000 people. Not only had the most stubborn squatters in the Cape been moved but, more crucially, the support base for the UDF groups too. In June George De'Ath, a freelance cameraman working for the BBC, died from head wounds received from axes and pangas deployed in the fighting between the *witdoeke,* the SAP and the comrades. He was the first journalist to be killed while covering the South African civil war. The Cape *Argus* newspaper described the mood in the black communities in the area: "You can reach out in front of you... clench your fist and squeeze fear out of the air." (14)

On 12 June 1986 the state of emergency, lifted in March, was reimposed. Four days before the 10th anniversary of the Soweto uprising, the security forces arrested the remnants of the leadership of the internal resistance still at large. By the end of the year more than 23,000 people, including about 9,000 children, had been jailed for varying periods under the June decrees. The SADF smashed the pretensions of the liberated zones in the townships. Pretoria was back in charge. The details of the crackdown could not be analysed because of the total ban on all but official reporting of black unrest. The ludicrous, but powerful, Bureau of Information handed out leaden lumps of Orwellian newspeak. During this period, at daily briefings in Pretoria, Brigadier Leon Mellet told the press what the government thought they should know about the unrest. The SAP brigadier insisted upon being called "Mr" Mellet in case anyone should think that the police were running the country.(15)

The new state of emergency, destined to run for years, totally swamped the internal resistance. The UDF, though allowed, just, to continue to exist, was reduced to a shadow of its former self. By early 1987 even the radical college students and schoolchildren had heeded Lusaka and gone back to their desks under the compromise slogan of "education for liberation". As the domestic turmoil began to subside, the festering resentment of the Commonwealth leaders about the treatment meted out to the EPG crystallised into a fresh round of efforts to punish and isolate Pretoria.

In June the British government first met the ANC at ministerial level, and thus ended the paradox where Margaret Thatcher was urging Pretoria to talk to the ANC, something she refused to do herself. In October, after overriding the presidential veto, Congress imposed fresh sanctions. They barred new corporate investment in South Africa and fresh loans to the government. South Africa's iron, steel, coal, uranium, textiles and some foods were off-limits. Landing rights for South African Airways were ended. In September the EC had adopted a diluted version of the new US measures. Japan also prohibited imports of South African iron and steel products. South Africa's main trading partners were beginning to line up against her. The logical, economic arguments against sanctions, and there were many, no longer mattered. Imposing sanctions was a question of standing on the side of the angels; it meant you were either for or against apartheid. It had become an almost purely emotional issue. The tide of opinion swept up even the stonewallers like Reagan and Thatcher. The South African economy could survive all this in the short-term but, to take one aspect, the exodus of major companies implied a permanent withdrawal, and permanent long-term damage.

The fourth phase of the resistance (1984-86): a summary

More than 2,000 South Africans had been killed in the unrest by the end of 1986; only a handful were white. The gentle rhythm of the sprinklers on the luxuriant lawns of the comfortable white suburbs had scarcely missed a beat. Pretoria's security forces had, once again, overwhelmed the passionate, but inchoate, black resistance.

The centralised National Security Management System (NSMS) had erected a parallel, shadow government throughout the country, run mainly by the military. The NSMS had played a major part in defeating the fourth phase of the resistance. It had picked up the original crude and vague total strategy doctrine, refashioned it into a subtle, workable form and then applied it at local level, often with great ingenuity. This more sophisticated approach to counterinsurgency was generally associated with the army's domination of the urban containment strategy by 1986, although there were sympathetic elements within the SAP, notably the scholarly General Johan Coetzee. Originally, the somewhat simplistic 80%:20% ratio of political to military input had been the received wisdom. That became refined operationally as 30:20:50. This formula assessed black attitudes. About 30% were reckoned to be moderates, who would go along with the status quo, provided they were left alone to mind their own business. About 20% were considered to be comrades and their supporters, who were resolved to overthrow white rule. The remaining 50% were adjudged to be fence-sitters, waiting to see who would win.

The strategy could be summarised as coercion, co-option, divide-and-rule and WHAM (winning hearts and minds). After the putative 20% of radicals had been stamped on hard, the NSMS set about wooing the supposed uncommitted and moderate/conservative 80% of township dwellers. WHAM/civic action, in particular, was taken very seriously. Lieutenant General Charles Lloyd, who had developed the Namibian psychological operations, championed this approach when he took over as secretary to the State Security Council in 1987. Major General Bert Wandrag, the head of the police anti-riot units, summarised this strategy: "Drastic action must be taken to eliminate the underlying social and economic factors which have caused unhappiness in the population. The only way to render the enemy powerless is to nip the revolution in the bud by ensuring there is no fertile soil in which the seeds of revolution can germinate."(16)

Whether Pretoria's "psyops", in fact a refined version of the French civic action in Algeria, can work in the long run is dubious. It did not work in Rhodesia or Namibia. True, there did seem to be a general sense of relief in the townships chosen for development (most notably Alexandra, in the centre of the plush northern white suburbs of Johannesburg), not only about new roads, schools, shops and houses, but that the reign of the comrades was over. Nevertheless, it was unlikely that good sewers could act as a substitute for the vote.

That was the acceptable face of the NSMS. The localisation of the total strategy also had a much more sinister, and effective, manifestation: the rise of the vigilantes. The vigilantes' names varied according to the region and local popularity of (American) TV programmes: they were called, for example, "A Teams", "Fathers", "Green Berets", *"Amabutho"* and so on. In sum, they represented a privatisation of state repression. The *witdoeke* and A-Teams became the internal equivalent of external destabilisation: the vigilantes in Crossroads could be just as ruthless as Renamo. (17) Vigilante forces played a deadly role in demoralising the UDF-ANC resisters in 1986. They were especially disruptive because they came from the *within* the community. There were constant allegations that the SAP supported, or at least turned a blind eye to, Inkatha's impis in the wars with the UDF; evidence mounted also of police complicity with the vigilantes in the Cape and the Transvaal. Nevertheless, some of the vigilante action reflected a genuine conservative backlash against the comrades; a backlash based upon ideological, tribal and generational factors. In the rural areas and the homelands, the vigilantes were often organised under the traditional patronage of the chiefs.

Since 1986 the use of vigilante violence has been further refined. Local, professional hit-teams (sometimes called "Z squads") have bombed the buildings of anti-apartheid organisations and assassinated both black and white activists. One victim was David Webster, who was, in a bizarre twist of fate, a leading academic authority on death squads. He was shot outside his Johannesburg home in May 1989, the 61st anti-apartheid campaigner to be assassinated since 1977. (A Natal university lecturer, Rick Turner, was shot in his home in 1977. Since then, in only one case was a suspected murderer charged.) Hit-teams also operated in the frontline states and Europe, although local nationals were often paid to do the dirty work. The South African Z squads' Latin American-style operations caused great anxiety in both black and white liberal communities. The phantom squads became increasingly busy. In 1988, again no one was prosecuted for any of the 48 attacks on anti-apartheid individuals, organisations and property.(18) This caused a crisis not only for the (low) credibility of the SAP, but also for the (once high) reputation of the legal system. The state had imposed draconian legislation, but even then it chose to act outside its own sweeping laws —if the extensive evidence that the government was behind the death squads is accurate.

It was alleged that some of the Z squad members were off-duty policemen and on-duty members of a dirty-trick group within the SAP. There was also rumoured to be a highly secret death squad entirely outside the SAP, SADF and NIS. Nonetheless, not all the clandestine activities should be blamed upon the security forces, whether offically sanctioned or freelance. Some of the assassinations, both inside South Africa and outside, appeared to be either internal feuding within and between the ANC and PAC or, occasionally, foreign intelligence and mercenary operations, which had a side-effect of discrediting the South African government.(19)

By 1987 the security forces had gained an undoubted ascendancy over the domestic resistance. The reform ingredients had been ladled out at the national level, with the repeal of certain apartheid laws and, at the local level, with the souped-up civic action. The townships sank back into a mood of sullen, resigned anger. The young lions had been beaten on the streets in their uneven battles, but the ANC had won the propaganda war. Mandela had become much more famous internationally than the finger-wagging Mussolini strutting around Libertas or his home in the Cape, complete with a bugler who trumpeted the emperor's each arrival and departure.

Yet largely random violence and pious poses at the UN were not likely to change the government in Pretoria. That required from the resistance movements a coherent strategy. How did the ANC match up to that demand?

ANC strategy had four prongs: mass action, the political underground, international diplomacy and the armed struggle. Taking mass action first, it could be argued that "*kragdadigheid* (hardline attitudes) by intractable bureaucrats", not revolutionary conspiracy, had precipitated the major phases of rebellion. (20) The classic examples were the Bantu education bureaucracy's insistence upon the use of Afrikaans in 1976 and the insensitive way the bureaucracy urged the black councils to raise rents in 1984. Once the mass revolts had been triggered, the ANC in Lusaka could not keep up with events. As Van Zyl Slabbert said in parliament: "It is not the external ANC that is radicalizing the internal situation. It is the internal situation that is radicalizing the ANC." The ANC leadership might optimistically term rampaging mobs of schoolkids "mass combat units", but very few ANC officers were involved in leading or organising them. The largely spontaneous mass mobilisation was of course useful in itself for the revolutionaries. The children, for example, turned the group areas to advantage: the ghettos became, in some cases, temporary no-go areas. And the younger generation were being "conscientised" (politicised) and educated by the struggle:

> The 1985 school boycotts afforded thousands of children the opportunity to learn the practical science of making petrol bombs; the street sociology of taunting armed soldiers; the pavement politics of pamphlet distribution and slogan painting; the geography of safe houses and escape routes; and the grammar and dialectics of undercover operations. (21)

The second aspect of the ANC strategy was the expansion of its underground structures inside the country. Ironically, it was constructed along not dissimilar lines to Pretoria's NSMS. (22). But the underground lacked sufficient trained manpower and weapons. The security police constantly eviscerated the internal wing of the ANC, despite its tight cell structure. So, during the years of township turmoil, there were never enough leaders or hardware to match the ardour of the local comrades. "Our aim of arming the people had a long way to go," admitted Ronnie Kasrils, the senior *Umkhonto* strategist. "Every stone-thrower wants a gun. We have to put guns in their hands."(23) A strange kind of urban warfare emerged, therefore, where the rioters outpaced the radical organisations, where the masses led the supposed vanguard.

The third prong, the international front, was largely successful. Talks with senior US and UK representatives undermined Pretoria's (and Inkatha's) tarnished legitimacy as well as boosting black morale inside South Africa. Yet an obvious contradiction surfaced between the craving for international respectability in the West and the terrorism of the armed struggle, the fourth prong. Success in the one arena tended to weaken the other. Advances on the cocktail circuit boosted the ANC doves who argued for a negotiated settlement. The hawks preferred Molotov cocktails. As with the rise of the SADF in Pretoria, so too in Lusaka hints about a "creeping military coup" were dropped, associated in particular with the rise of Chris Hani, officially number two in *Umkhonto.* Men like Hani wanted to strike at soft targets inside the republic to shake the whites out of their awesome complacency. As Hani put it: "We are prepared to see a wasteland if that is the price of freedom." (24) The ANC was clearly divided on the issue of white civilian targets. The divisions were not only along the lines of older conservatives versus young hotheads, but also they were inspired by ideological and, possibly, regional differences between the "Jo'burgers" and "Kaapies" (similar to the liberal Cape/class clashes with the blue-collar/ hardliners in the Transvaal within the National Party). Black and white politics have exhibited strong regional nuances, sometimes cutting across race, in that sprawling country. Typically, Pretoria explained away the ANC divisions purely in terms of African nationalists versus communists and tribal splits, especially hostility to alleged Xhosa dominance.

After the important Kabwe conference in 1985, when the ANC formally launched its "people's war", *Umkhonto* tried to step up its campaign. Landmines were first introduced in November 1985. In 1976, according to Pretoria's figures, two MK incidents were recorded every six months. In 1986 five bombings, raids and assassinations occurred every week, although there were far fewer "spectaculars", like the attacks on the SASOL plants, Koeberg and the air force HQ. (25) Yet the Lusaka hierarchy displayed a continuous ambiguity towards bombs which claimed civilian victims, such as the incidents in the Amanzimtoti shopping mall and outside the Ellis Park rugby stadium. Sometimes the leadership claimed that their units had acted without orders: the Nkomati agreement had overextended and disrupted the guerrillas' chain of command and communications. This made wildcat attacks more likely. Nonetheless, within the MK's high command, elements were agitating for more strikes on white civilians, partly to maintain the battered morale in the townships, especially after 1987. Yet taking the war into the white areas, making whites specific racial targets, contradicted not only the basic tenet of a multiracial struggle, a philosophy enshrined in the SACP's ideology, but also the fact that a growing number of whites were joining the ANC and climbing its hierarchy. White veterans were to be found in the national executive committee. Targeting whites specifically was also impolitic, to say the least, at a time when visits to the ANC in Lusaka by white businessmen, politicians and, increasingly, sports chiefs had become so fashionable. A race war was the last thing the ANC's doves wanted. At times, though, the ANC spoke with two tongues. In its radio broadcasts directed at a popular black audience the language could be very strident:

> The regime's police and soldiers who have been massacring our people in millions over the years still return to their homes and spend comfortable nights in the warmth of their beds...They must be haunted by the mass offensive. We must attack them at their homes and their holiday resorts just as we have been attacking their bootlickers at their homes. This must now happen to their white colleagues. All along it has only been the black mothers who

> have been mourning. Now the time has come that all of us must mourn. White families must also wear black costumes. [Domestic servants must play] a leading role. They know where their employers keep their weapons and they are the ones who can devise plans of transferring the ownership of these weapons.(26)

That was in 1985. Yet in America the ANC could be described as "a community of love and justice on a pilgrim's road to freedom".(27) Joe Slovo, the SACP leader, had tried to fudge the contradictions: he termed white civilian casualties "diversions and blemishes". Slovo, demonised by Pretoria, explained that the government needed to blame all the bomb attacks on him, a white man, because they could not admit that blacks were sophisticated enough to organise a sustained bombing campaign. "Botha and Botha have done for me what Saatchi and Saatchi have done for Mrs Thatcher," he said. As the ANC stepped into the diplomatic limelight (and perhaps because of Moscow's revisionist initiatives in southern Africa) Slovo dropped his Stalinist mantle and went public, after decades in the shadows.(28) "We have moved a long way from being an agitational opposition to presenting an alternative government...Before the [South African] government wouldn't talk to us at all. Now they say they will talk to us if we stop violence. That shows it has been effective."(29)

In the 1960s the violence was almost a form of "political graffiti"; then came the period of armed propaganda in the 1970s. By the end of 1986, the ANC and SACP perceived three essential pre-revolutionary factors: a crisis in the enemy ranks; a clear demonstration that the masses were prepared to pay the ultimate sacrifice; and the widespread recognition that the ANC was the alternative source of authority. In the early phases of the 1984-86 uprising there was a general feeling that an apocalyptic moment of change was at hand. In a novel interpretation of Revelation Chapter 21, Pretoria's men would, as in a vision, sign a surrender document, no doubt in a railway carriage. By 1987, that mood had vanished. The ANC had ordered the townships to be made ungovernable. That invited chaos, as we have seen, not people's power. The security forces smashed the comrades and restored Pretoria's writ throughout the land.

Nevertheless, a comparison of the two insurrections, 1976-77 and 1984-86, is instructive. Soweto was quelled, with the death of hundreds of blacks, fairly rapidly by the police, on its own, with existing legislation. From 1985 the military was required in large numbers to back the police, deployed under a state of emergency. 1976 was largely a children's war which marshalled the support of an elite group of established community leaders. In 1984 working class adults joined in, more or less willingly. 1976 was an urban revolt; by 1986 even the most remote *platteland* towns had become inflamed. The revolutionary and political climate in the 1980s was much more intense. The organisation, which was often poor, was at least better than in 1976-77. Belatedly, the ANC tried to manipulate the internal and international dimensions of the revolt, although bodies such as the UDF and the powerful labour unions (not all of whom toed the ANC line), were, arguably, more influential. The sustained, better organised unrest created embryonic alternative structures which, although eventually destroyed, gave the masses a taste of people's power. (This could boomerang on the potentially dictatorial ANC as much as the current dictatorship in Pretoria.) The flamboyant and extensive political exploitation of funerals was a new weapon used by the liberation movements to publicise their cause. Finally, marginally better weapons, especially limpet mines and landmines, and more AKs, were smuggled into the frontline. In 1976 the resistance sported few guns. According to Peter Magubane, a well-know photographer who was raised in Soweto and who has covered the conflict since the 1960s:

> Things are getting tougher, more clinical. If there is a protest march or a funeral procession, you will find buckets of water placed at every house along the way. That's in case there is tear gas, so the marchers can wash it from their eyes and from their faces. That was not true at the time of the Soweto riots in 1976. The children have become more politicized. They have left the adults behind. (30)

The persistent assault on black collaborators with the government reflected a total rejection of apartheid. The system was not to be reformed, but destroyed. In the heady days of 1984-86, the black majority smelt victory. The rulers had lost confidence in their ideology and the ruled were convinced they could win. The balance of confidence, if not the immediate balance of power, changed during the rebellion of the mid-1980s.

But the triumphalism of this period was soon blown away. "Battle fatigue" among the young militants, harsher and more sophisticated police tactics, the detention of thousands of their leaders, a genuine backlash from moderate blacks, as well as vigilante activity, and the end of the school boycotts, which took thousands of combatants off the streets, all helped to persuade the radicals that the revolution was not around the corner. You could almost touch the collective political hangover in the townships. After two years of pumping adrenalin around the black body politic, a sullen cloud descended. It was like Pinochet's Chile in the late 1970s or Poland in 1982 after martial law had been declared and Solidarity was, for the time being, crushed. As a correspondent for *The Times* observed in mid-1987: "South Africa is a sadder but perhaps wiser place. There are no illusions that the struggle for power is over. At best the emergency and tough security force action has created a truce —a breathing space in which both sides can prepare for the long haul." (31)

And on this long march there would be many strange twists and turns. Pretoria's decapitation of the Black Consciousness movement in 1977 had promoted the fortunes of the ANC. After 1986 the ANC had made substantial diplomatic gains, but it may also have suffered setbacks in the townships. The ANC had been quick to grab the credit (largely unjustifiably) for the uprising, but, when it failed, it also had to take the blame. The post-1986 frustration was a good breeding ground for the revival of the Africanists, especially the PAC.

Yet, despite the military defeat of the comrades, a psychological corner had been turned. It might take a generation, but the belief in ultimate victory had been firmly planted in the popular psyche. As Tom Lodge, an eminent analyst of the ANC, concluded: "In South Africa, therefore, the role of guerrilla warfare is likely to remain chiefly inspirational and psychological, important mainly to the extent that it can help the ANC exercise political leadership over constitutencies it is unable to organise directly."(32)

The twilight of the imperial presidency

The "great crocodile", as the president was nicknamed in the National Party, led his followers into the May 1987 election with all his customary Teutonic charm. The campaign soon degenerated into a plebiscite on which party had the best security policy. As John Barratt, the astute head of the South African Institute of International Affairs, observed: "The *swart gevaar,* the *rooi gevaar,* the *buitelandse gevaar* were all combined into one really big *gevaar.*" (33) The National Party took 54% of the vote and increased its seats from 118 to 123. Some observers interpreted this result as a vote for reform. The emasculation of the liberal opposition and the 22 seats won by the the Conservative Party (up from 17)—the first time since 1948 that the official opposition had been on the right— indicated rather that the voters, especially English-speakers, had moved to the right, attracted by the security ticket. With its new reliance on the English-speaker, the NP probably no longer represented even the majority of Afrikaners. Botha now led a minority of a minority tribe.

As expected, Pretoria launched a raid on the ANC just before the election. Five people were killed in Livingstone in April, although Kaunda claimed that none of the victims had ANC connections. This was the only cross-border raid to be officially acknowledged by the SADF in 1987.

The electoral triumph of the NP, despite a disastrous economic and political performance which would have caused it to be immediately thrown out of office in any Western state, plus the wind-down of the unrest, brought a renewed confidence to the whites. Except for the liberal minority, South African whites seem to be naturally (or is it desperately?) inclined to be optimistic. Their peculiar political environment demands constant psychological reassurance. They like to feel good about themselves: "There's nothing wrong with us, the world just doesn't *understand* us." Hence the importance of international sports tours and the massive attention given to the visit of a most minor starlet. Few people watch them, but that doesn't matter. The important thing is that foreigners "come to see for themselves". We are not alone.(34) Township violence was off the world's TVs; therefore, out-of-sight, out-of-mind. Even tourists were coming back, so were some of the whites who had panicked and taken the "chicken run" to Australia and Britain. Even the economy began to pick up a little. In short, by late 1987 the whites had relaxed into their cyclical post-crisis complacency.

Of course, all was not well. In August 300,000 miners went on strike, the biggest and costliest mine strike South Africa had ever faced. Although the miners returned in the end with few gains, it was intended as a political challenge as much as an economic one. The savage feuding between the UDF and Inkatha intensified, claiming hundreds of lives in 1987. Then Allan Hendrickse, the leader of the majority Labour Party in the coloured House of Representatives, blocked the mechanisms of the clumsy tricameral system to demand the repeal of the Group Areas Act. This was a challenge to a fundamental pillar of the apartheid temple. Pretoria buzzed with talk that the president, no friend to Hendrickse, would suspend parliament and rule by decree rather than let the Labour leader block his path. Botha went to extremes: the president used his tame television service to spend 22 minutes on the main half-hour news broadcast to humiliate Hendrickse. Botha had brought the two Indian and coloured parliamentary majority leaders into his cabinet, but both were forced out.

Dissatisfied with the mild truculence of his junior allies in the constipated tricameral show, Pretoria made tentative gestures towards the ANC. In November Govan Mbeki, the frail 73-year-old former chairman of the ANC, was freed, without conditions, after 23 years in jail. This was seen as a trial run for Mandela's release. Mbeki, however, at a press conference, refused to renounce the armed struggle or the ANC. The government confined him to Port Elizabeth and banned him from making public statements. Mandela's release did not look imminent.

Meanwhile, *Umkhonto* tried to keep up the momentum, even though the townships were relatively quiet. Pretoria claimed that 220 ANC insurgents had been killed or arrested during 1987. The one spectacular occurred in July when the ANC detonated a bomb outside a military HQ in downtown Johannesburg; 68 people were injured. As long as the ANC kept up its campaign and the Conservative Party bayed for tougher action, the president found it difficult to move ahead with his stalled, if not moribund, reform programme. The rise of the right and the antics of the pathological Afrikaner fundamentalists in the Afrikaner Resistance Movement (the *Afrikaner Weerstandsbeweging,* the AWB) mesmerised Pretoria. Afrikaner interests, especially regarding security matters, always came first, reform and the rest of the world very much second. In February 1988 Pretoria banned 17 black organisations affiliated to the UDF and detained many of their leaders.

In a token balancing gesture later in the year, a small fanatical *white* right-wing group, the White Liberation Movement, was also banned—a very rare action against a white group—after an ex-policeman, Barend Strydom, had massacred seven blacks and wounded 17 in the centre of Pretoria. The AWB was not touched. Pretoria did not want to drive the neo-Nazis underground and provide them with a mystique that could boost their support as well as make them more difficult to monitor. Pretoria hoped that given enough rope, the AWB leader, Eugene Terreblanche, a spell-binding orator, might hang himself. After a series of antics, most notoriously his well-publicised, alleged dalliance with a liberal, English-speaking, ex-beauty-queen-turned-journalist, he did become something of a music hall Hitler. Nevertheless, he did have a large following, including a hard-core of armed die-hards. In the future the AWB or its successor may not be such a laughing matter. The AWB's military wing, Aquila, could form the basis of a deadly underground movement.

There was an international outcry over the banning of the 17 organisations. If Pretoria crushed legal groups, what choice was there but to join the armed struggle? The government was unmoved. West German and British pressure did, however, manage to restrain further reactionary legislation. In the first case, the Foreign Funding Bill, which would have cut off all foreign aid to anti-apartheid organisations, was amended. In Germany, in particular, the bill was seen to threaten the inflow of humanitarian aid. This caused offence to German public opinion at a time when the film *Cry Freedom* had captured the imagination of West German youth. Secondly, both London and Bonn demanded the stay of execution for the Sharpeville Six, six blacks accused of being members of a large lynch mob. The case of the condemned six prompted a general campaign against the "judicial carnage" in the republic: only China had a busier official hangman. (Presumably states such as Iran were executing far more of their own countrymen, but they did not bother with elaborate court cases.) Pretoria was inclined to listen to both foreign governments, as they had their fingers in the dyke against further EC sanctions. Another issue was the threat to *tighten* up some aspects of the Group Areas Act, while allowing a few "grey areas" for mixed racial habitation. The Germans threatened to withdraw their ambassador and more if the Sharpeville Six were hanged. As the *Daily Telegraph* correspondent tartly observed: "Suddenly, white South Africans were contemplating the prospects of no more air filters for their Mercedes."(35) The Foreign Office, apparently, made it clear to Pretoria that Mrs Thatcher had read the supreme court judgement on the six as a trained lawyer and not as just another foreign meddler, "and that in her opinion, the convictions against at least two of the accused were redolent, and that the death penalty against all six of them positively stank".(36)

Pretoria backed down on the Group Areas Bill, the execution of the Sharpeville Six and the banning of foreign funds. That might have proved that international pressures worked, or the contrary: Pretoria listened to Bonn and London only because both governments had argued against sanctions. Pretoria also showed some flexibility regarding imprisoned nationalist leaders. The aged and sick Zeph Mothopeng, the PAC leader, was released on humanitarian grounds. But what terrified Pretoria was Mandela dying in prison. That could have triggered off a cataclysm. But so could his release. Mandela had been moved to a Cape Town clinic for medical treatment and it was made clear that he would not be going back to Pollsmoor prison. A critic suggested that the incremental release of Mandela was "a brilliantly conceived exercise in ruthlessly marginalising the ANC leader, while appearing to be scrupulously compassionate...It is difficult to make allegations against the 'racist regime' if the running dogs of racial exploitation are accommodating Public Enemy Number One in a five-star private clinic." (37) Mandela was then moved to a bungalow in the gardens of Paarl prison. The ANC leader had dedicated much time to horticulture in his long years of being entombed in grey concrete. He had been proud of his pot plants. Now he was living in a rose garden. But it was not freedom.

All these signs of tractability, however, had had to wait for the October 1988 municipal election results. As usual, the pace of reform was chained to possible advances by the National Party's arch rivals, the Conservative Party. The October poll, however, suggested that perhaps the CP's rapid growth had reached a plateau. The NP's electoral reprieve and the neanderthal politics of the CP-controlled towns in the Transvaal (most notoriously Boksburg, where the council regressed to the segregationist policies of the 1960s) made P W Botha more inclined to proceed with his strange hop-step forward and jump-back strategy of reform. (38) All depended upon getting blacks into the government. Not one single African, 75% of the population, was in central government: no MP, no Cabinet minister, let alone a general. This was the Fabianism of a tortoise. Some black faces were desperately needed. Buthelezi was the obvious choice, perhaps the only one. And he did have a modicum of credibility. But he still refused to accomodate Pretoria while Mandela was in prison and the ANC was banned. Besides, he was seriously distracted by the UDF-Inkatha war which had caused more than 1,800 deaths by the end of 1988. The proposed national council, without Buthelezi, was dead in the water. Even at the local level, the turnout for the black municipal elections in October was once again poor. The government claimed 25% of the registered voters, but that meant only 2%, about 500,000, of the black population had voted. (39) The government had spent a small fortune promoting these elections and had criminalised any boycott activity. The pro-voting propaganda campaign, which included cartoons of two civic-minded squirrels solemnly debating the electoral process, failed to persuade the vast majority of blacks to join the squirrels. They had no intention of collaborating in their own oppression.

Despite the muted factionalism in Lusaka and the rampant version in the townships at home, the insurgency continued. According to Pretoria, 300 guerrillas were killed or captured in 1988, but the ANC bombings, often of soft targets, claimed 49 lives. The SADF retaliated with a raid on Gaborone in March 1988. The ANC claimed that Pretoria was responsible for a covert operation in Paris in April when Dulcie September was assassinated, the first ANC official to be killed outside Africa. In the same month Albie Sachs, another ANC activist, was severely wounded in a car bomb in Maputo. In an apparent response, 100kgs of explosive, packed in a stolen BMW and probably set off by remote control, exploded outside Ellis Park rugby stadium. This Beirut-style attack killed two white men and injured 35 other people, minutes after the final whistle of a top league rugby match. This was a blow to the very core of the Afrikaner male psyche: rugby. And it was the biggest bomb explosion in the history of the insurgency. Two months before, the SAP had seized the largest quantity of arms yet found by the police in South Africa, on a smallholding at Broederstroom, north of Johannesburg. The haul included a SAM-7 missile-launcher and one missile. Four of the five ANC operatives were arrested. All were white. Four of the men involved were South Africans and the woman was reported to be a Swazi who had taken out British citizenship.(40)

The increasing attacks on soft targets coincided with not only the internal debate in Lusaka, but also a shift in the stance of the SACP towards the inevitability of successful revolution. Moscow's experts on Africa began to stress the possibility of a political settlement and the need to preserve the South African economy intact. Via public exchanges between journalists and academics and private meetings of officials, relations between Pretoria and Moscow thawed, even though there had been no formal diplomatic contacts since the mid-1950s. Relations between the foreign ministries improved markedly during the lengthy talks to secure an Angolan settlement. *Glasnost,* it seemed, was even reaching into the dusty corners of Union Building.

The new direction of Soviet foreign policy was likely to help mould South Africa's future. For its part, Moscow clearly no longer felt that history was inevitably on its side. There were more national liberation struggles directed against Soviet-backed regimes than US ones. Moscow wanted to divest itself of the costly commitments to Angola and Ethiopia, let alone the enormous handouts to Cuba and Nicaragua. Gorbachev emphasised that the USSR was tied into the global economy: East-West competition was not a zero-sum game. As Anatoli Gromyko, director of Moscow's Institute of African Studies, admitted: "We should not export revolution. The idea that socialist revolution would spread around the world was a romantic view."(41) In South Africa, revolution might also harm Moscow's cosy arrangement with Pretoria to sell diamonds and gold. Here Soviet policies began to coalesce with Washington's. Reagan's major foreign legacy had been his rapprochement with Moscow. That rapprochement, whether founded on Reagan's defence build-up or Gorbachev's internal agenda, or both, suggested a possible convergence of interests on South Africa. This could result eventually in joint superpower initiatives to ensure a less bloody transition to black rule.

By 1989 President Botha had reached a political dead end. After a stroke in January he announced, eventually, his resignation as NP leader, although not as president. During his more than ten years in power he had become an authoritarian bully, who terrified members of his own cabinet. His predecessors, such as Malan and Verwoerd, were essentially modest, unpretentious prime ministers, even if they were also racial bigots. Botha, however, had taken on the trappings of the great dictator. He assumed an increasingly imperial manner, as he grew remote from his immediate colleagues and his party. Like all tyrants, he tended to disdain criticism or advice. English-speakers often found his finger-wagging bellicosity embarrassing, and even the white South Africans, "who shivered with wicked delight" every time he told the rest of the world to get lost, eventually deserted him to join right-wing parties. (42) Yet he had displayed bravery in splitting his tribe when he rid himself of the CP prophet, Andries Treurnicht. He had shown courage, too, in insisting that his countrymen must "adapt or die". But, temperamentally and intellectually, he lacked the will and the ability to proceed along the reform path he sometimes pointed to. After the whirlwind of protest raced through the republic in 1984 he lost his way completely. He thrashed and blundered around in the dark. Then followed the catastrophes: the Rubicon speech, the curt dismissal of the EPG peace mission and the public humiliation of Allan Hendrickse, which lit up the tricameral parliament as a ship of fools.

As he recovered from his stroke in early 1989 he tried to use the SABC-TV to resurrect his position in the party. This time on TV the hand that had jabbed defiance at the world shook visibly. The great crocodile had lost his teeth. Yet like any other African leader he was mighty reluctant to give up his throne. In the face of a major constitutional crisis, the emperor with no clothes on conceded that he would finally go, after the general election scheduled for September 1989. Political pressure from F W de Klerk forced him to quit in August, before the elections. The old man left gracelessly, cursing de Klerk and providing much ammunition for the rival white parties. Botha had served the National Party his whole life. It was sadly ironic that the manner of his departure from power severely damaged the party he had served so faithfully.

Despite Botha's awesomely self-important public speeches, the departing president left no intellectual legacy. As his old rival, Van Zyl Slabbert, put it:

> His political philosophy is remarkably uncomplicated: if things go wrong, there must be an enemy responsible, and if they go right it is because of 'good Government'. The simplicity of the total onslaught philosophy appealed to him as Minister of Defence and he carried its logic into his office as Prime Minister and State President. If all else fails, Moscow must be responsible for what goes wrong, whether it be regional instability or domestic unrest, and those who do not accept this are the witting or unwitting tools of it. (43)

P W Botha's successor as leader of the NP was F W de Klerk, a brighter and more sophisticated figure. But how would the military react to F W replacing P W? The constitutional structure and the total strategy in South Africa had rested on Botha's power and his personal relationship with his generals. F W de Klerk was not a part of the charmed circle of securocrats. Nor did he appear to want to be. Civil-military relations looked set for a sea-change. The constitution had been designed to fit one man. But so had its part-model, the Gaullist constitution. And that had survived the demise of its mentor.

As the chief icon of white rule crumbled, so to did the major black symbol of resistance at large in the country: Winnie Mandela. The "Black Evita" was also rejected by her own people because of the scandals associated with her bodyguards, the tip of the iceberg of a long series of incidents in which Mrs Mandela had more than overplayed her position as a stand-in for her husband. She had become a local heroine because not even Pretoria could suppress her; nor could the ANC. The Indian leader Amichand Rajbansi fell from grace too. In the last days of this *"Raj"* not even his NP allies could tolerate his mafia style of politics.

As South Africa geared up for another election—in which yet again blacks could not vote—parties across the political spectrum were in a state of flux. There were constants too. Disinvestment continued, although more slowly in the beginning of 1989. Mobil was the latest to decamp. High inflation, low business confidence, the government's mounting deficit and the inability to raise major foreign loans all contributed to the erosion of the formal economy. The political log-jam remained: no credible black leader could talk to Pretoria until the ANC was unbanned. The state of emergency was renewed again in June 1989. Only a handful of dissidents remained in detention, but many of those freed had been severely restricted and were under virtual house arrest. Thirty-two organisations, from civic groups to student bodies and the UDF, were banned from carrying out any political activities. The refined National Security Management System continued its careful scrutiny of political dissent throughout the country. And the shooting war went on. According to figures released in June 1989, in 1986 there were 231 guerrilla attacks, in 1987, 235, and 245 in 1988. The emergency had not deterred an escalation in the number of MK assaults. (44)

The security forces had driven the black internal opposition deep underground. That was the short-term success of the states of emergency. But if such repression were to became a permanent feature of South African life, that would guarantee that whites would continue to live in an ominously precarious garrison state.

References and notes:

1. F van Zyl Slabbert, *The Last White Parliament,* Sidgwick and Jackson, London, 1985, p. 117. For details of the new political structure, see Figure 2, Appendix 2.
2. K Owen, "Like Mussolini, Il Duce gets what he wants," *Business Day,* 29 August 1988.
3. *Financial Mail,* 6 September 1985.
4. D. Pallister, S Stewart and I Lepper, *South Africa Inc.: The Oppenheimer Empire,* Simon and Schuster, London, 1987, p. 185.
5. M Meredith, *In the Name of Apartheid,* Hamish Hamilton, London, 1988, pp. 205-6.
6. Quoted in the *Financial Mail,* 8 November 1985.
7. Quoted in *The Star,* 24 December 1985.
8. Meredith, *op. cit.,* p. 210.
9. The information for the above is a synthesis of discussions with various South African government officials. Originally, it was rumoured that the SADF had attacked the capitals *without* the president's say-so. This is almost certainly untrue. (See, for example, J Spence, "Botha's Slap in the Face for the West," *The Times,* 20 May 1986.) The target data was discussed between Botha and Chief of the SADF Viljoen, according to the author's sources. The car radio incident was confirmed by a number of officials in the foreign affairs department.
10. See H Adam, "Exile and Resistance: The African National Congress, the South African Communist Party and the Pan Africanist Congress," in P Berger and B Godsell, (eds), *A Future South Africa,* Human and Rousseau/Tafelberg, Cape Town, 1988, p. 107.
11. Speech in Johannesburg city hall, 5 August 1986. The writer sat in the audience, by chance, next to Harry Oppenheimer, one of the richest and most powerful businessman in the world, let alone South Africa. The author engaged him in casual conversation. He sat on his own without aides or, apparently, any bodyguards. That would have been unlikely in America, let alone in many other societies enduring a low-intensity war.
12. S Uys, "Why did Pretoria see the EPG as Foe instead of Friend?" *Business Day,* 10 June 1986.
13. *Mission to South Africa,* Penguin, Harmondsworth, 1986, p. 141.
14. *The Argus,* 10 June 1986. See also J Cole, *Crossroads,* Ravan, Johannesburg, 1987.
15. Mellet should have known better: he had been a professional journalist on an Afrikaans newspaper.
16. Quoted in M Swilling, "WHAMMING the Radicals," *Weekly Mail,* 26 May 1988.
17. See N Haysom, "Order without Law," *Southern African Review of Books,* December 1988/January 1989, and *The Rise of Right-wing Vigilantes in South Africa,* Centre for Applied Legal Studies, University of the Witwatersrand, 1986. In

a later study, Haysom developed his views. He argued that the vigilante phenomenon represented "a Reaganomic tendency in one of South Africa's 'growth industry'—the privatisation of repression." Haysom attacked the constant press description of all vigilante violence as "black-on-black" conflict. "This label has as much heuristic value as describing the Second World War as white-on-white violence." A nice analogy. See N Haysom, "Vigilantes and the Militarisation of South Africa," in J Cock and L Nathan, (eds), *War and Society: The Militarisation of South Africa,* Philip, Cape Town, 1989.

18. *Ibid.*
19. G L'Ange, "Who are these Silent Killers?" *The Star* (weekly edition), 13 June 1987. See also: D Beresford, "Botha's Black Warriors," *Weekly Guardian,* 8 June 1986; J-A Bekker, "Those Violent Men of Peace," *Weekly Mail,* 7 February 1986; A Robinson, "Pretoria Accused of Secret War against ANC," *Financial Times,* 18 July 1987; T Allen-Mills, "Informers for Apartheid," *The Independent,* 20 March 1987; A Hadland, "A Diary lost at Kidnap Site leads Trail to Army HQ," *Weekly Mail,* 17 February 1988; and P Laurence, "Why are few Political Murder Cases Solved?" *The Star,* (weekly edition), 10 May 1989.
20. See K Gottschalk, "State Strategy and the Limits of Counter-Revolution," in *South African Review 4,* Ravan, Johannesburg, 1987.
21. H van Dyk, *A Look at South Africa's Youth Politics,* SA Forum, 10:7, 1987.
22. For a sketch of the ANC structure, see "South Africa: Hani's Rise," *Africa Confidential,* 12 August 1988.
23. Quoted in *Sechaba,* May 1986, p. 4.
24. Quoted in A Harber, "The Two Pillars of ANC Strategy Keep Falling over one another," *Weekly Mail,* 14 July 1988.
25. See T Lodge, "The African National Congress after the Kabwe Conference," in *South African Review 4, op. cit.*
26. Quoted in T Lodge, "State of Exile: The African National Congress of South Africa, 1976-86," in P Frankel, N Pines, and M Swilling, (eds), *State, Resistance and Change in South Africa,* Croom Helm, London, 1988, p. 246.
27. Quoted in *ibid,* p. 247.
28. There was also a great deal of publicity about the film of his tragic family life, *A World Apart,* written by his daughter.
29. The quotations by Slovo in this paragraph are taken from R Dowden, "Slovo Emerges to Dismantle the Myth about Slovo," *The Independent,* 4 November 1988.
30. Quoted in P Hawthorne and B Nelan, "Black Rage, White Fist," *Time,* 5 August 1985.
31. A Robinson, "Preparing for the Long Haul," *Financial Times* Survey, 10 July 1987.
32. Lodge, "The African National Congress after the Kabwe Conference," *op. cit.*
33. Literally, black, red and foreign dangers. For a detailed analysis of this period, see D van Vuuren, J Latakgomo, H Marais and L Schlemmer, *South African Election 1987,* Burgess, Pinetown, 1987. For a useful summary, see E Lourens and H Kotzé, "The South African White General Election of 1987: Shifting Deckchairs or Burning Boats?" *International Affairs Bulletin,* Johannesburg, 11:2, 1987.
34. A Robinson, "Why White South Africa has lost its Sense of Panic," *The Daily Telegraph,* 13 October 1987.
35. S Robinson, "Botha responds to Thatcher's Carrot," *The Sunday Telegraph,* 27 November 1988.
36. *Ibid.*
37. S Robinson, "The Outflanking of the Mandela Crusaders," *The Daily Telegraph,* 6 September 1988.
38. N Mathiane and D Beckett, "The Battle for Boksburg," *Frontline,* April 1989.
39. J Spence, "Pretoria's Image is no Better off," *Sunday Tribune,* 30 October 1988.

40. D Braun, "White ANC Cell Smashed after Betrayal from Within Movement," *The Star,* (weekly edition), 18 May 1988.
41. Quoted in S Talbott, "Credit Where Credit is Due," *Time,* 23 January 1989.
42. S Robinson, "Pretoria's Great Crocodile defies the Wind of Change," *The Daily Telegraph,* 7 March 1989.
43. Van Zyl Slabbert, *The Last White Parliament, op. cit.,* p. 147.
44. P Godwin, "Pretoria Keeps the Lid on Protest," *The Sunday Times,* 11 June 1989.

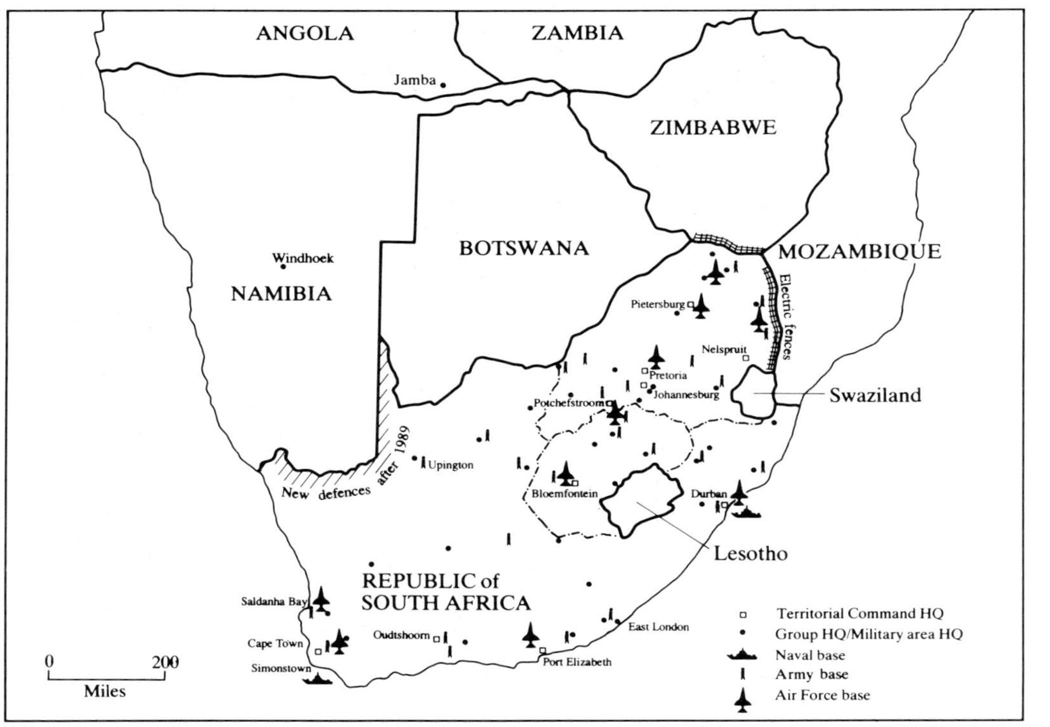

SADF deployment 1989. (The map does not include SADF deployment in Namibia, as the SADF was withdrawn in late 1989/early 1990 as part of the Namibian independence process. New defence structures were implemented in the northern Cape, along the southern Namibian border.

MAP 16 SADF deployment, 1989

17

The garrison state

South Africa has frequently been termed a "garrison state", in which the military have become increasingly dominant and white society, including the business community, is engulfed in a siege mentality, largely of its own making.(1) Until F W de Klerk's presidency there was indeed mounting evidence of the republic's militarisation, although, theoretically, there appears to be no inevitable, positive correlation between a continuing military crisis and the increasing likelihood of military intervention: Britain in 1940-41 is one example of this caveat.

South Africa's civil-military tradition absorbed much of the British ideal of apolitical armed forces, as well as the entrenched Boer/Afrikaner dislike of an independently-minded standing army. Professional armies, in the Western model, are supposed to be the subservient instrument of the political will of the state. Yet the politicisation inherent in effective counterinsurgency, especially in the third world, has tended to reverse this orthodoxy. Hence the term "new professionalism" has been applied to the *deliberate* politicisation of armies fighting long insurgencies, especially in coup-ridden Latin America.(2) According to the views of two prominent academics, "In Latin America the armed forces are usually politicized; in the beleaguered ethnic state, however, the policy becomes militarized. The political power of the State Security Council, in which military influence is strong, epitomizes this trend." (3)

Although it has been suggested that the military actually considered a takeover in 1976, this seems most unlikely.(4) Other writers suggest that the militarisation began in earnest in 1978 with the premiership of P W Botha. Since then, it was often argued, the parliamentary system, including the power of the National Party, had declined. In particular, the liberalisation of apartheid's economic strategies has "as a necessary corollary the limitation of the political rights of whites most vulnerable to the changes it is likely to usher in".(5) To summarise a complex debate, the State Security Council and its nationwide shadow government, the National Security Management System, was said to operate a sham democracy (even for whites) as the inner cabal of securocrats (military and civilian) undermined the privileges of poor whites to grant economic rights to blacks, as part of a limited "reform by stealth". Meanwhile, real political power was kept in the hands of a civil-military elite.

This may indeed be part of Pretoria's repressive reform strategy. The two sides of this equation have been described, in shorthand as it were, as hawks versus doves. But the SADF and SAP have contained elements of both these styles of domination. Since the crushing of the 1984-86 revolt a fierce debate has raged within the security elite. Until 1984 the grand reformist programme rested upon measures to stabilise urban blacks (after the earlier Riekert Commission, attempts were made to establish a conservative black "insider" middle and working class in the cities), the unions (via the Wiehahn Commission which had legalised black unions) and the political system (by "extending democracy" by means of the tricameral parliament, with a national council for blacks tagged on as an afterthought). Low-level protest action and township organisations would be tolerated to an extent, but anything more than blowing off a little steam would be controlled by immediate repression: banning, detention and infiltration. During the 1984-86 period the hawks appeared to be in the ascendancy; probably the annihilation of the EPG mission was a high watermark of the hardline position.

The National Security Management System (NSMS)

After 1987 the reformists were resuscitated, but they came back with a more subtle approach. Yes, grand gestures were still necessary. Talks with a declawed ANC were mooted. But, more importantly, instead of a "top-down" strategic emphasis, there would be a re-emphasis of the "bottom-up", grassroots approach developed during the unrest. The top tier of the government's carrots, the national council, was not enticing anyone. Instead, there would be intense manipulation at the third and second tiers. This was economic determinism. Through the NSMS, whose network began to parallel the nine areas of regional economic development, a type of economic federalism would be built. Later, the homelands, urban areas (perhaps as city states), the national council, and the tricameral parliament could be tied up in a "consociational"/ federal political system.

The lesson of 1984-86 was that a total strategy dictated from above just did not work; a dynamic, grassroots civic action programme might. Under the NSMS a national counterinsurgency system was erected. A government manual, *The Art of Counter-Revolutionary Warfare*, outlined this grassroots campaign. It was almost as if the famous "M" plan was written large and then put in reverse. The first step was the elimination of what remained of the comrades' alternative structures. That was done. The second stage, according to the manual, was the restoration of "effective administration...An effective and well-motivated administration will deny revolutionaries the initiative". The next step was to pump millions of rand into the townships, particularly the 34 most rebellious ones such as Alexandra, Mamelodi, New Brighton and Bonteheuwel. It was not just a question of new houses, post offices and pavements. The counter-revolution required better educational facilities, social clubs, sports grounds, clinics, career advice and the involvement of religious organisations. All this was to be done on a person-to-person basis. The aim was social control and a restoration of the informer network. The new "loyal" infrastructure would have to be able to defend itself. "Self-defence" is the "most important part of counter-organisation of the masses". Hence the recruitment of what the British in Malaya called "special constables", in South Africa "*kitskonstabels*". These "instant police" would supplement the local black municipal police and the SAP as the first line of containment in an emergency. (See Appendix 2 for a summary of the various police forces.) These pacified areas would transform "hotspots" into what the manual defines as "oilspots" which would gradually seep outwards to join other "loyal" local areas to form swathes of satisfied customers, grateful for Pretoria's largesse.(6)

That was the plan. In many ways it was the direct application of the homelands principle to the cities: shift the burden of control on to allies in the black community—policemen, councillors, businessmen and vigilante groups. Local black defence structures were vital to destroy the radical opposition. At the same time material advances would, it was hoped, create a stable, property-owning, middle-class nucleus with a stake in the system and opportunities for political advancement at municipal and regional levels. If this worked, then the homelands and semi-autonomous "city-states", such as Soweto, could be represented in the national council, with a few token blacks in the cabinet as well. Perhaps even some "nationalists" from the ANC might be enticed too. This was Pretoria's version of the Namibian and Rhodesian internal settlements. At the end of the day, of course, this upmarket version of apartheid would still leave the whites in control.

This turbo-charged version of racial domination was designed with almost the same missionary zeal and determination as the 1950s vintage model. The apex of the system was the SSC, which in turn controlled the NSMS, set up originally in 1979. It came into its own in the 1984-86 period. Later, officials tended coyly to drop the "Security" part of the title: "National Management System" sounded much more benign.

How did the NSMS work? The SSC had a secretariat and various committees which plugged into the conventional governnment bureaucracy. Indeed, at every level, from cabinet to local councils, there was a parallel NSMS organ (see diagram in Appendix 2). At the main regional levels there were Joint Management Centres (JMCs). Originally the JMCs corresponded to the (then) 11 SADF area commands, although the system was rejigged to tie in with the nine economic development regions. Lower down the hierarchy were 82 sub-JMCs, which were supposed to cooperate with the Regional Services Councils being set up. These councils were to raise, from business levies, much of the finance for the "upliftment" of the townships. At the bottom level there were about 320 mini-JMCs which worked with the local black, coloured and Indian councils and other local bodies. Each JMC, sub-JMC and mini-JMC had three major committees dealing with firstly, intelligence, secondly, political economic amd social matters and, thirdly, communications.(7)

Political engineering on such a vast scale was much more sophisticated than anything the British in Malaya or French in Algeria attempted. It would have to be. After all, General Magnus Malan had experienced first-hand the French operations in Algeria. He had not only been on the losing side, but he must also have seen how the war ripped French society apart. And, of course, De Gaulle sat in Paris, not Algiers. The Afrikaner securocrats only had to travel a few miles from the citadel in Pretoria to the surrounding townships to sample the revolutionary turmoil. In short, the whole NSMS strategy was an elaborate ploy to steal the thunder of the radicals. The ANC targeted the masses' main grievances as: the lack of freedom of movement, health, education and housing. So Pretoria scrapped influx control and passes (while tightening up on movement into the cities by rigorous squatter and health regulations). Next it poured money into building new houses, clinics and schools. Nearly $2 billion was spent in 1988 on such measures in the 34 "difficult" townships. A further $8 billion was earmarked for 200 other townships in the following five years. Some of the money came from central government; the rest was to be raised by the Regional Services Councils (often unpopular, especially with white businessmen because of the levies raised from them) and directly from private enterprise. The Urban Foundation has been active in providing new houses, for example.

The resistance organisations have refused to collaborate with this vast Pecksniffian programme. Reform is a dirty word. Fair enough. But who will say "no" to better roads, houses and libraries? As one senior officer attached to the SSC argued: "These people have their aspirations, of course, but they are really concerned about bread-and-butter issues—housing, schools, motor cars, 'the good life'. And if you want their support, you can *buy* it."(8)

But can you? One researcher has pointed out the main weaknesses in the NSMS plan to buy off the revolution.(9) First of all there was the cost. "Upgrading a deprived township is as expensive an operation as the development of a new generation of armoured cars."(10) Could Pretoria afford new tanks for its border wars and tens of thousands of new houses for a black middle class, which is just as likely to lead a revolution as stop it? And can and would the small white tax base continue to support guns and butter? Especially butter for blacks? The right wing constantly advocates the cheaper, cruder (if ultimately less effective) forms of repression. International sanctions could continue to shrink the economy. This will create more unemployment, the real time-bomb ticking under any hearts-and-minds programme. How can so many blacks be bought off?

In the short term, the project may have had some successes, especially in the aftermath of the black disillusionment with the 1984-86 unrest. In that period it was essentially a military operation. The main JMCs were staffed by SADF generals and brigadiers with a sprinkling of senior policemen. The SSC staff was perhaps 75% SADF/SAP, with the remainder coming from the NIS and the department of foreign affairs. After 1987 the system "civilianised" itself a little, especially at the lower levels, by bringing in civil servants, white businessmen, MPs from the Indian and coloured chambers of parliament and black councillors. Yet, in essence, the system was a policy of short-term military containment, not a long-term political solution. That appeared to be F W de Klerk's appraisal when he took over from President Botha. First, he shored up his own position in the party and then he reasserted political control over the military. He ordered cut-backs in defence spending and reduced national service to one year. More significantly, he relegated the SSC and demililitarised the whole NSMS system, by trying to turn it into a series of regional coordinating committees to maintain the task of upgrading black facilities. There was opposition in military and police circles, partly for political reasons. De Klerk's changes were interpreted as an assault on right-wing, especially Conservative Party, influence in the old system. This opposition was fuelled by the president's determination to release political prisoners. But could the new broom really make a clean sweep in a white community which had been heavily indoctrinated by apartheid ideology for over 40 years and which, for a decade at least, had revelled in the glorification of the military?

White society

Conscription. One of the most important aspects of the militarisation of white society was the growing length of time more and more whites served in the SADF and police. Conscription is the one case where apartheid falls more heavily on whites rather than on blacks. Unlike the Rhodesian army, the SADF expends a great deal of effort to (further) indoctrinate its conscripts in the fundamentals of the total onslaught. Originally, the doctrine may have been a cynical instrument to obtain a bigger defence budget for the generals. And by the late 1980s Pretoria had distanced itself from the total red threat thesis, partly because it was proving counter-productive. Yet since the 1970s a military generation of true believers may have been cloned in its image. Certainly, the white population at large seems to have swallowed the dogmas hook, line and sinker after a decade of SABC propaganda; and many conscripts seem to have imbibed it, as have many middle-ranking officers.(11) Whether the top brass are believers or cynics is difficult to estimate, particularly after some of the generals seemed to have struck up a degree of bonhomie with their Soviet counterparts during the Angolan settlement negotiations.

A major critique of the doctrine surfaced in the anti-conscription movement, centred in the late 1980s on the End Conscription Campaign (ECC). This small, mainly middle-class, English-speaking group raised objections on political, moral and religious grounds. In 1988 the minister of law and order, Adriaan Vlok, silenced the ECC. But that did not end a thriving South African export industry: the exodus of white graduates. Many left, not for idealistic reasons, but because they regarded call-ups as a hindrance to their career prospects. When the SADF started tapping the manpower resource of young male foreign residents, that doubled the exodus. (Perhaps as much as one-third of the SADF conscript force was reckoned by one source to hold dual citizenship of one of the 12 European Community states.) (12) Others try to get deferments, just do not turn up or go underground in South Africa. Nevertheless, draft-dodging is a minority taste, because young South African whites are programmed throughout their education to accept national service as a duty.

Besides the moral arguments against defending apartheid, there are a number of practical reasons why a professional volunteer army would be a more efficient one than a conscript force. Pretoria has regularly rejected this option, however. Afrikaners, like Americans, have displayed an historical antipathy towards large standing armies, not least because of their experiences in the respective wars of independence against the British. Both Afrikaners and Americans have tended to prefer the concept of temporary militia forces. Paradoxically, most Afrikaners opposed conscription during the two world wars. Now they insist it is a national duty (for whites). Moreover, a volunteer, well-paid army would probably be largely black. Afrikaners have always been reluctant to arm too many "natives". Since the 1960s Pretoria has argued that national service is cheaper and safer politically. A more recent twist to the worries about the army's political stability is the deliberate infiltration of the police and SADF by the right wing. A smaller professional army is probably more susceptible to political control by the neo-fascists than a large conscript force, infused each year by thousands of young English-speakers who are often imbued with impeccable liberal values from their university education. It may be much harder to organise a coup with a broad-based, part-time force. (13)

The arguments, however, for a larger volunteer army might well become compelling. The Rhodesians had toyed with the idea of creating a large, white-officered, Askari-type army on the model of their successful Rhodesian African Rifles. Even the most patriotic Rhodesian whites became more and more annoyed when they found blacks taking "their" places in the civilian economy because constant call-ups made cheaper black labour more attractive. In this sense, conscription allowed blacks to win the war without weapons. In South Africa there is usually no shortage of black volunteers, because of economic factors, but many whites go into the SADF very reluctantly, partly because of the financial sacrifices. There is nothing worse for a regular soldier than to serve next to a reluctant conscript. A dominant topic of conversation in the operational area was always "how much longer do you have to do?". The "*min dae*" attitude ("only a few days left") was very common, and demoralising, on the border. Also, there is the beginning of a tendency for unhappy ex-conscripts, especially those on the ashheap of unemployment, to reflect the Vietnam veteran syndrome: a feeling of alienation sometimes resulting in anti-social behaviour, such as the misuse of firearms.*

The alternative, a professional army, has been debated: the old United Party and the New Republic Party put forward a number of interesting schemes. There are a variety of forms such an army could take. The SADF says that it needs a large conventional force to dissuade an external invasion threat. Taking Pretoria's perspective, and despite the historical fears, a large, predominantly black professional army could fit this bill. Generals in modern armies with ultra-sophisticated weaponry have often had to face the fact that the most effective way to kill a guerrilla with a rifle is to use another man with a rifle. Blacks would provide the numbers that whites cannot (economically or demographically). They are the "right" colour, and possess the language skills, for conventional ground coverage, and they provide vast scope for pseudo operations in South Africa, as well as deployment in the destabilisation forces alongside Renamo, Unita, etc. Even in the last days of colonialism the Askari regiments in Portuguese Africa, Kenya and, classically, Rhodesia proved efficient and loyal. Even in the savage war in Algeria tens of thousands of Arab *harkis* remained loyal to the French right to the end, even though perhaps up to 150,000 met a most grisly fate at the hands of their victorious compatriots.(14) With good pay and promotion prospects, regimental loyalty can outface guerrilla blandishments, even in extreme circumstances. Given Pretoria's insistence on white supremacy, this new army would have a core of highly-skilled white soldiers. Conscription in the long run is inefficient and expensive; the money saved could ensure that the crucial white core of technicans and NCOs would not be tempted into the civilian economy. The elite units of the army and the air force would remain essentially white, which would help counter Pretoria's fears of a black palace revolution. An essentially black standing army could launch a large-scale, cross-border attack almost at will, without all the preparations for mobilisation of reservists which always tip off foreign powers. A large black army would also make good PR sense. Blacks bashing township dwellers, if they have to, or invading Lesotho or Gaborone, might make for less provocative TV pictures. Today the SADF is seen to defend not South Africa, but merely the whites, or perhaps just the National Party.

---

*The technical term is "post-traumatic stress disorder". See D Sandler, "The Psychological Experiences of White Conscripts in the Black Townships," in J Cook and L Nathan, (eds) *War and Society: The Militarisation of South Africa*, Philip, Cape Town, 1989.

From the liberal perspective, a fully multiracial army could aid the process of transition and integration. War, after all, is a great leveller: there are no apartheid signs in foxholes. Most white soldiers who have served closely with well-trained black combat troops end up far less racialistic than when they started soldiering. A multiracial SADF could be the first step in teaching the futility of the civil war itself.

From the last-ditchers' perspective, the argument could run in the opposite direction: "If the blacks want to storm their way into Pretoria, let the ANC fight a largely black SADF. Use the black troops as cannon fodder. Let us run the economy and let the blacks kill each other on the borders, or better still, on our neighbours' plots."

In short, the country's armed forces will not disappear, even if apartheid vanished overnight. Ending conscription and forming a professional, fully multiracial force may be one way of satisfying the current demands of all shades of white opinion, while also assisting in the transition process. The present need to keep up conscription involves a great deal of indoctrination, as well as economic damage. This encourages a militarisation of white society which is entirely counter-productive.

In the end, of course, no amount of military reorganisation is going to keep blacks away from the ballot box, at best, or barricades in central Pretoria at worst. A *post-bellum* republic will have an army, presumably a smaller one. Better that it be professional and multiracial. Maybe then *white* township dwellers can look to the army for national protection, not local oppression. (15)

Education. As in most societies, schools play a vital part in socialisation. "Christian National Education" is the fundamental basis of all white state schools. This tends to create a susceptibility to NP (or CP) ideologies. Such intrinsic indoctrination is reinforced by cadet training programmes throughout the state educational system for boys and, sometimes, girls. Many school-children, particularly in the Afrikaans-medium institutions, attend special camps, or *veld* (field) schools, during the school vacations. As part of the "youth preparedness" courses in schools, children are taught about "terrorism". Two young English-speaking, high-school students from Johannesburg defined what they had been taught about the subject:

> Marie: It's like communism, you know. Russia's trying to take over South Africa for the strategic position, and the gold and all that and the blacks don't know any better because they're not properly educated, and if a communist is going to come to them and say, do this and that and the other and we'll give

> you a black government—well, they just don't know any better, the blacks don't, and they'll believe the communists...
>
> We build them schools and they just burn them down...
>
> Michelle: ...you just have to go slowly and, listen, all our taxes go to their houses. Okay, Soweto's nothing fantastic, but at least they've got a roof over their heads. They want all the facilities that we've got, but you can't all of a sudden just give them everything. They're not prepared to take it in stages.(16)

Those comments encapsulate many white adults' views as well.

Propaganda. The military ethos is propagated extensively in the media. The most faithful voice of official orthodoxy is found, not surprisingly, in the SADF's monthly magazine, *Paratus*, which is distributed widely for sale to the general public. In 1977 the SADF established its own public relations department on a full-time basis. Unlike in NATO armies, where PR posts are often dumped on reluctant "passed-over" captains and majors, some excellent regular officers serve in PR in South Africa (although there are also some failed journalists who like to parade in colonel's regalia).(17) Because of a panoply of censorship (including a veritable minefield of legislation such as the Defence Act, Prisons Act, Internal Security Act and the Publications Act) it is often impossible to report on the security situation. Normally, only a select handful of military correspondents can get close, with the SADF, to any combat in Angola or Namibia. Those that do, such as Al J Venter, Willem Steenkamp (of the *Cape Times*) and Helmoed-Römer Heitman (a correspondent for *Jane's Defence Weekly*), have very close relations with the military. Indeed Heitman and Steenkamp are both citizen force officers. (Even affiliated correspondents, who, like Steenkamp, have produced incisive reports, have complained about the ludicrous extent of military censorship.)

Via the obedient state-controlled electronic media and pro-government newspapers, the SADF and SAP encourage an emphasis on "positive" and "balanced" (that is, pro-Pretoria) aspects of the news. The SABC not only plays down internal problems, but also plays up other nations' troubles, especially in countries which attract white emigrants. This message is echoed ubiquitously in private conversation: "It's happening all over the world. Look at Northern Ireland. It's *worse* there. I'd rather stay here, thank you." This type of propaganda is paradoxical: the government wants it both ways. On the one hand, Pretoria claims its troubles are not unique: "We are a microcosm of the first and third world issues everywhere." Yet on the other hand, the official diplomatic line is: "Our problems are uniquely complex, and we require time for a uniquely South African solution."

The end result for most whites is the conditioning of Huxley's *Brave New World*. For blacks the aim, if not the result, is intimidation along the lines, though not extent, of Orwell's *1984*. It is ironic that the government's propaganda is internalised by the whites, but usually scoffed at by the blacks, presumably the most important target. Whites seem generally to give credence to the communist onslaught which blacks often regard as probable liberation (if they believe in the theory).(18) The Angolan war, with real-live Russians and Cubans involved, and captured, added flesh to the abstraction. But for years Pretoria had whipped up a less tangible, groundless paranoia, a little like the rockets fired by the authorities of Oceania on their own people in *1984*. But if the Angolan wars disappear entirely from the paranoia list and if Pretoria's flirtation with Moscow continues, then the total onslaught must be literally internalised. (Compared with the red peril, international sanctions, in the near future at least, may not be a sufficiently total nor tangible threat as a means of white mobilisation.) As Van Zyl Slabbert observed:

> Inevitably, as the external onslaught subsides, the internal onslaught will come under sharper focus—the enemy without will become the enemy within. I fear that the government has in any case managed to militarize the white population to such an extent that it won't matter much to the ordinary person who the "enemy" is, as long as he is ready to fight. There, I believe, lies one of the greatest obstacles to evolutionary and negotiated change.(19)

One of Pretoria's prime weapons against its own electorate is ignorance. Blacks in the more closely-knit townships rely upon a very effective news grapevine; whites have to resort to a less effective gossip-machine which, in the twilight world of censorship, produces epidemics of alarmist rumour-mongering. The media is not totally shackled, however; Pretoria's claims that it has the freest press in Africa is not far off the mark, although Africa is hardly a good yardstick. South Africa's "alternative" press, such as the *Weekly Mail*, and sometimes the more establishment-oriented English-language papers, such as *The Star*, the *Cape Times*, the *Financial Mail* and Ken Owen's blistering editorials and columns in the *Business Day*, and even, occasionally, Afrikaans papers such as *Die Beeld*, attack the government with some ferocity. But if they want to report in any detail on security matters, they have to play Russian roulette with the censorship laws. According to opinion polls, most whites rely upon (and trust) TV for their news information. But the SABC-TV wages a "scorched air" policy on truth. This produces a breast-beating angst in the liberal community, or emigration, and increasingly *verkrampte* views on security among the silenced majority of whites. *Bittereinder* statements have become common parlance. As one Afrikaner farmer's wife said stoically: "We will never give up. We will fight to the last Afrikaner. We did not accept English rule and we will never accept Bantu rule. We don't mind sanctions. We will go back to oxwagons, if they cut off our petrol."(20) Even the *verligte* Afrikaners are said to be prepared to compromise only a little on security: "They'll put headlamps on their oxwagons." Another white woman, this time from a liberal business background, was ruthlessly candid: "Let's be completely logical. We can hand over peacefully now, fight and lose, or we kill the lot of them [blacks]."(21)

Social trends. Many overt signs of militarisation are evident in white society. The SADF encourages support groups such as the Southern Cross Fund to raise money for the "boys on the border". It also sponsors such campaigns as "Ride Safe", a national scheme to give lifts to servicemen. And some of the radio request programmes are very reminiscent of wartime Britain. Yet there is not the general sense of a "white nation" at war, as in Britain in the 1940s or, yet, Rhodesia in the late 1970s.

An unobservant American visitor, say, could travel to South Africa, exchange his dollars at a bounteous rate, stay in excellent five-star hotels in Johannesburg, visit the well-managed game parks in the eastern Transvaal, tour the exquisite wine farms of the Cape, swim on the Durban beaches and not notice a sign of warfare in "your beautiful country". He would be unlikely to visit a township or the Namibian border. Nor would our hypothetical visitor know (or perhaps care) that one million whites possess (legally) 2.5 million privately-owned firearms, often hand-guns kept in the glove compartment of cars. He would probably be unaware of the bizarre wave of Afrikaner working-class fathers and mothers who shoot their own families, the so-called "wipe-out" phenomenon. The rates for white suicides, divorces, alcoholism, drug abuse and even road accidents are unusually high.(22) (On the other hand, the homicide rate of blacks in Soweto is ten times higher, proportionately, than in New York city.) It is not all doom and gloom: many whites revel in the Californian shopping habits and life style. But, despite the fact that many whites enjoy a living standard which is the second or third highest in the world, South Africa *is* a society under stress. Is it partly due to international pressures and urban terror, or is it caused by the universal urban maladies of unemployment, inflation and rising mortgages? How important is the embryonic war psychosis, engendered by militarisation and call-ups?

Afrikaners clearly prefer beer and *braais* (barbecues) to military parades. They are not Prussians. Reference was made earlier to the "dreadful calm" apparent on the surface of white society, and yet the government has used the media to whip up war fervour. Can both be true? The answer is yes. It may be a typical sociological evasion to say that white society (and South African society in general) is very complex, but that, like nearly every cliché about the country, is nonetheless true. "White society" is itself a misnomer. The Greeks, Jews, Portuguese, English, Scots, Irish, Welsh, Germans and French do not comprise a "nation". Despite apartheid, which has worked because it has kept people apart, the Zulu middle-class doctor usually has more in common with a fellow white professional than either have with a Xhosa peasant or Afrikaner railwayman from the backwoods. Afrikaner society is more cohesive, yet even here there are many contradictions. An Afrikaner is a rugged individualist (or so he says) whose past has been nourished by adversity and the tales of Blood River, yet he is also the soft, urbanised organisation man, brimming with deference for his religious, political and social structures. Take the Afrikaner on the ultra right, typically the most bellicose of his "tribe". According to Denis Beckett, the editor of *Frontline* magazine and a seasoned observer: "The CPs are terrified of blacks, so terrified they can't see straight. They're a walking mass of schizophrenia. They spend half their time bragging about their relations with black individuals; the other half forcing everything from science to religion to fit the conclusions their terror motivates."(23)

The CP or AWB supporter might swagger and declare: "If it comes to it, there's no problem. Each white will shoot five blacks,"—and then lean over confidentially or assert boldly, depending upon the venue, "and we can do it—and that's the problem solved." At the other extreme, at the comfortable dinner parties of the northern suburbs, the same discussion emerges: the if, when and where of emigration and whether one can survive without a maid. The majority of whites, however, the local variants of Middle America, have no intention of leaving the country they love so much. They try not to think too much about the future.

The economy. A type of military-industrial complex has surfaced in South Africa, as the earlier examination of Armscor suggested. The drive for military self-sufficiency has distorted the economy. For example, in the late 1970s the SADF helped to persuade the government that South Africa needed its own diesel capacity. The country now produces diesel engines at about one-third more than an imported model.(24) In fields where total self-sufficency is not possible, Pretoria has co-opted, and compromised, many foreign firms by forcing them into security collaboration. The National Key Points Act, the various amendments to the Atomic Energy Act, the National Supplies Procurement Act and other legislation have required private companies to maintain secrecy about their production levels, sources of supply, trading partners, etc., all of which compounds the siege mentality.(25) The position of the oil majors is particularly sensitive. Even the major international car manufacturers have been discouraged from publishing statistics of car sales and production.

Partisan Politics. Under SADF regulations, permanent force personnel are not allowed to be members of political parties, nor can they take part in party political activity. The SADF offers itself as a professional, non-partisan force, despite its frequent identification as the fighting wing of the ruling party. Yet there have been a number of examples of overtly partisan behaviour. In 1980, details of a document, *Psychological Action Plan: Defence Budget Debate*, were leaked to the newspapers. The document outlined covert steps to manipulate the news media so as to nullify the opposition's criticism of defence measures proposed by P W Botha. A parliamentary row ensued, the story was denied and some of the officers involved were quietly (and temporarily) promoted sideways.

This incident was a minor one compared with the later dirty tricks organised by the SADF. In 1988 the SADF found itself in the dock in three major legal cases. Two involved SADF officers and men accused of murdering civilians and stabbing to death a SWAPO leader in Namibia. The third was concerned with harassment of the End Conscription Campaign, as part of the SADF's campaign to promote conscription. The SADF was forced to admit that, *inter alia*, it had put posters up in Cape Town bearing the slogans "ECC are yellow", "ECC does it from behind" and "ECC believe in fairy tales". The SADF also used a helicopter to drop anti-ECC pamphlets over an ECC fair. In Cape Town Supreme Court, in an affidavit, Lieutenant General Jan van Loggerenberg, the head of the air force, confirmed that such methods were necessary as South Africa was on a "war footing". Defending the ECC, in its application for an interdict restraining the SADF from harassment, Sydney Kentridge, SC, said that the SADF had effectively declared martial law. "These are the pretensions of a junta of South American generals in a country in which the army acts as an independent force... There has seldom been a more dangerous assertion of power by the army," maintained the eminent lawyer.(26) As Kentridge noted, it was ironic that the SADF said it needed martial law and underhand tricks to deal with the ECC when subsequently it was restricted anyway under the emergency regulations.

After the involvement in full-scale fighting in the neighbouring states and the blood spilt in the townships, such actions as dropping pamphlets by air, printing T-shirts and putting up posters, with homosexual innuendoes, against the ECC seem almost benign in comparison. Yet the public airing of the SADF's view on the military situation of the country, as well as the publicity given to Kentridge's condemnation, was significant. Both the ECC case and the 1980 budget incident were rare documented evidence of the SADF's frequent manipulation of white political activity. Few scruples have been displayed, of course, about SADF intervention in black politics.

Praetorianism in Pretoria?

A number of writers have commented on the militarisation of South African politics: the terms "creeping" or "silent" coup have become commonplace.(27) In an incisive critique of this view, however, Annette Seegers argued that the emphasis on militarisation purely from the 1960s is possibly a mistake.(28) She stressed the continuity of military influence by asking: "If one accepts that Afrikaner/Boer societies have, almost from the start, exhibited illiberal and martial tendencies, on what grounds are post-1960 developments exceptional?" (29) She suggested that militarisation could develop "deep within a society's history and culture", not just from the exceptional pressures imposed more recently on the apartheid system. In the previous "age of the generals" soldier-statesmen, such as Generals Louis Botha, Barry Hertzog and Jan Smuts, were not, however, career soldiers or graduates of accredited military academies. They returned to their civilian professions. The earlier tradition was that of an (Afrikaner) nation-at-arms, which allowed for easy transition from military to civilian roles. (On the other hand, in the continuous violence of the nineteenth-century frontier wars, professional British officers performed dual roles as soldier-administrators.) But because of the relentless contemporary centralisation of economic, political and military power, there is no precedent for today's professional standing core of politically influential senior officers. The Afrikanerisation of the security elite in tandem with the rise of the NP has created a uniquely powerful and (largely) partisan senior officer corps.

Despite the fact that total strategy jargon deploys the language of military science in homogenous societies, the SADF is not a nation-at-arms in the traditional French or even Israeli sense. Notwithstanding its careful, if limited, incorporation of other races, the SADF is essentially an instrument of white domination. Despite the sophistication of its short-term strategy of containment, it bears repeating that there is no overarching vision to unify South Africa's generals. This study has outlined some of the divisions within and between the SAP and SADF on the best policy of repressive reform. It is impossible to be definitive about group politics within such secretive bodies, but there appeared to have been serious differences, for example, between military intelligence and the security police over the lifting of the state of emergency in March 1986. In early 1986, during the EPG period, the head of the SAP, General Johan Coetzee, may have lined up with the NIS and foreign affairs to favour further negotiation. Hawks within the SAP and SADF prevailed with the May raids. By 1987, citing the SAP's failures during the unrest, the SADF gained an ascendancy on internal security matters; hence the extra influence of the SADF-dominated NSMS. Although by 1988, and the acknowledged defeat of the resistance, the SADF's grip on the NSMS seemed to have loosened (perhaps deliberately). The police, under the forceful hardliner, General Hennie de Witt, regained some of the initiative.

The NP's influence at the senior levels has been monitored by Adriaan Vlok, the law and order minister, although in the lower to middle ranks, particularly of the SAP, the CP and AWB have gained a growing following. The army, apparently far less prone to ultra-right "entryism", also found itself divided in the late 1980s on the question of the return to orthodox, tough counterinsurgency. Orthodoxy was perhaps best represented by Major General K van der Waal, the general officer commanding special forces, and Major General A J M Joubert, in charge of the Reconnaissance Commandos. A second group, on the other hand, supported the bottom-up, hearts-and-minds approach, which was probably best epitomised by Lieutenant General Charles Lloyd. (30) In short, the high command was vitiated by major differences on strategy, as well as the common police/soldier and army/navy/air force rivalries common to all security forces.

One of the persisting themes has been the SADF's criticism of the SAP's role in both Namibia and the townships and the reluctance of both senior army strategists and individual soldiers to "do the SAP's job for them" in the townships. An anecdote, repeated throughout the army messes in 1986, illustrates this point:

> P W Botha is angered by a crocodile that's eating too many people. He instructs the SADF and the police to stop the "croc". The SADF sends in a high-level aerial photographic unit with in-flight computers, then analyses the pictures, puts in a ground-level reconnaissance crew and, finally, after sifting through the data, plans a detailed operation and despatches a team of "Recce" commandos who grab the crocodile and deliver it, carefully trussed up, to the president.
>
> The police, meanwhile, send out two constables who grab the first lizard they can find and beat it until it confesses to being a man-eating crocodile.

Anecdotal evidence perhaps, but the gusto with which this sort of criticism was articulated in the army against the police is significant. Philip Frankel, in his important study, *Pretoria's Praetorians*, develops this point. He is worth quoting at length:

> Professional militaries...are almost always deeply averse to performing the role of "common" policemen in cases where government policy has totally lost legitimacy in the eyes of the politically aware civilian population. The race gap between the South African military and the broad masses eases the task of domestic control, yet a certain proportion of the Defence Force (the top professional-technocratic officers, relatively uninstitutionalized Citizen Force units and, above all, black recruits) could conceivably experience considerable compunction at the prospect of using heavy fire-power on civilian demonstrators along the lines of the French Army in Algeria, the Colombian military in 1953 and the Turkish military seven years later. In the last two instances, the military not only refused to violate their corporate integrity by taking on police functions to quell public disorder but subsequently displaced the existing government at the height of the disturbances. Militaries, in the last analysis, have their own institutional interests which do not always coincide directly with those of the ruling government or state. In the case of the South African military, its self-perpetuation as a corporate entity in its present form depends on the pre-existence of the white state. Yet the SADF is also at the dangerous point in the development of military institutions where it is neither professional enough to resist crisis calls for political action to save the white state nor primitive enough to be oblivious to notions of institutional identity and corporate interest. In this adolescent position, the advent of extensive public disorder in the form of simultaneous urban terror, rural insurgency, townships riots and widespread industrial action on a scale exceeding the control resources of the "first line of defence" (the police force) could well trigger military intervention, not only in the limited sense of strategic action to uphold the existing government, but in the more fundamental sense of displacing civilian authority as a demonstrably incompetent mechanism for upholding the state and the interests of the military within it.(31)

As in many stale and introverted oligarchies, especially in Africa, fundamental change often comes from the armed forces. So what are the chances that South Africa might have its own version of the Petrograd garrison, the cruiser *Aurora* or Lisbon 1974?

Certainly the role of the ruling party, as a party, had declined under P W Botha. It was suggested earlier that economic liberalisation implied the limitation of the political clout of those who were most likely to suffer the most: poor whites, who have defected to the CP. P W Botha's personal, authoritarian style of rule and the new powers of the presidency further eroded the stature and influence of both parliament and the NP. Anthony Heard, the former editor of the *Cape Times*, noted the decline of parliamentary rule:

> Parliament is as overworked as it is out of touch with real issues. While Pretoria, the administrative capital, decrees without debate that the state of emergency shall be extended for another year and tightened, Cape Town, the legislative capital, sees Parliament enthusiastically discussing the use of sugar cane-based ethanol as fuel. Indeed, Pretoria rules. (32)

But who ruled in Pretoria? In the same week that Heard made this point, Ken Owen, the Cassandra of South Africa, observed in his newspaper, *Business Day*: "The Army doesn't serve us anymore. We serve them." That might have been a (not uncharacteristic) overstatement. Throughout this study, however, the tendency for the military to usurp *some* political functions, especially during the destabilisation policy in the frontline states, has been described in detail. The SADF's "illegal" support for Renamo in 1985 is the prime example. But there are numerous obstacles in the way of a *putsch*.

Firstly, the armed forces have no single voice, or clear alternative leader, such as a Spinola. (General Malan has many critics within the SADF; he is often seen as a NP man, not the military's formal representative in the government.) The SADF is by no means monolithic, despite the single, technocratic, modern image it likes to portray. As Jack Spence, a British authority on South African strategic affairs, noted: "Technocracy, like patriotism, is rarely enough." (33) The SADF leadership has a variety of opinions on military questions, let alone political, economic and social issues. A gaggle of retired senior policemen have stood in elections for the CP, while, in the run-up to the 1989 elections, a number of retired high-ranking SADF officers (most notably Lieutenant General Bob Rogers, the former head of the air force) offered themselves as candidates for the Democratic Party, the newly-aligned liberal opposition. But, for the present, most senior SADF officers appear to

PLATE 17.1 *The Star* used the famous World War I poster, with Minister of Law and Order Le Grange substituted for Lord Kitchener (1985).

support the NP. The trend for retired officers to go into public life is increasing, but more significant, of course, is the behind-the-scenes influence of serving officers. The military already exert tremendous sway, so why become *putschists*? Military prerogative is already institutionalised in the SSC, which is both a sounding board for, and a check on, the military.

Secondly, the civic culture is deeply rooted in Afrikaner society. The NP *apparatchiki* are deeply hostile to any notions of Bonapartism, not least because they would lose their jobs. And, despite press reports to the contrary, South Africa is not a banana republic. The top echelons of all branches of the security forces share the government's dedication to white rule. Unlike many Latin American ruling oligarchies, the South African government is not frail, indecisive or soft. There is no question (now) of praetorian soldiers waiting to "clear out the mess" in Pretoria. The NP administration is ruthless and determined, albeit marginally corrupt. It may have lost faith in its ideology, but not in white rule.

Thirdly, South Africa is an advanced industrialised society. The small regular officer class, however technocratic in outlook, knows it could not cope with the political conundrum on its own, although a few senior policemen might be prepared to try, under certain circumstances.

Moreover, a military coup would be a diplomatic disaster, possibly too much for a pariah state to bear.(34)

Until 1989 the SADF had the ready ear of P W Botha: their man was in the presidential palace already. Defying the will of his own party in early 1989, the ailing president clung doggedly to power, apparently encouraged to stay on by some elements in the military and the presidential aides. And yet the military leadership appears to have accepted F W de Klerk, an outsider to the clique of securocrats. The nature of this succession must undermine the arguments of those who insist that the military runs the show entirely in South Africa.

And yet military authority had grown. That is indisputable. Even if military influence has always been a part of South African tradition, today there is more of it. And, although it was suggested earlier that there is not necessarily a direct ratio between security crises and military solutions, in the South African context it may be correct to assume that Pretoria will continue to evade the central issue of majority rule. Military "solutions", therefore, will continually be applied. Military power will not *necessarily* expand, especially under a new president, but further expansion is *possible.*

If the above analysis is correct, then it is apparent that no concerted conspiracy exists to establish some kind of military apartheid. Frequently, discussions of possible or actual military interventionism have been clouded by naive conspiracy theories. The assumption, for example, that security forces are merely extensions of "international imperialism" is as doctrinaire and simplistic as some senior officers' perception that nearly all populist demands, especially in the third world, are inevitably inspired by an international communist conspiracy. As in Rhodesia, the South African military gained political authority haphazardly, almost by default, in incremental stages, because of the political leadership's lack of farsighted political strategy and vision. The politicians had no choice, then, but to call in the military to contain popular revolt. Unlike the Rhodesians, the SADF does possess a doctrine and practice of white counter-revolution. Whether the total strategy, now unmentionable in Pretoria, was intended as a Machiavellian means to secure for the SADF a bigger arsenal and more privileges, and as a means of mobilising the white "masses", or whether it constituted originally an article of faith is a moot point. It was probably a little bit of each, but it snowballed into a convenient, catch-all credo as the South African crisis spiralled. And, unlike Rhodesia, the SADF, because of the politicisation inherent in their style of counterinsurgency, adopted the "new professionalism" described earlier.

Despite the important differences, the Rhodesian experience is perhaps the best model for comparison with civil-military developments in South Africa. In the 1970s Rhodesia passed through what is termed in civil-military relations theory a "fusionist" phase: the ruling party, senior civil servants and the security forces coalesced to form a unified strategic system designed to counter the menacing guerrilla insurgency.(35) By June 1979, and the premiership of Bishop Muzorewa, fusion had been replaced by what may be termed a "military-supportive regime".(36) By late 1979, as the most militant Rhodesian Front leaders still called for all-out war and military victory, *some* prominent security officials, such as Lieutenant General Peter Walls and Ken Flower, the intelligence chief, realised that only a political compromise could avert military defeat. Rhodesia was by then what might be called a "military-dependent regime", with 90% of the country under martial law.(37) Walls and Flower acted as "praetorian arbitrators", but there was no intention to set up military rule.(38) They reversed the 80:20% axiom: the more prescient members of the security elite spent more time knocking political sense into RF *bittereinders* than in hopelessly trying to stem the tidal waves of guerrilla incursions.(39) A coup attempt was forestalled. This was an example where a military establishment's influence can be at its greatest when its proposals are negative, that is, when it recommends *against* the use of certain types of force.(40) Thus, the erratic development of inadvertent Rhodesian praetorianism played a crucial "swansong" role in negotiating an end to white rule, without intervening overtly in politics as the French generals did, for very different reasons, in Algeria. The latter *grande folie* sealed the fate of the country and resulted in the panic-stricken exodus of more than a million white settlers. In Rhodesia, Walls displaced Ian Smith as the last great white hope and, briefly, ensured the (relative) success of the transition to majority rule. Zimbabwe emerged and half the whites stayed. In short, the Rhodesian military, or a part of it, also ensured that the primacy of the political process prevailed. Ironically, it required political action by individual senior military and intelligence leaders for the Clausewitzian paradigm to survive: the verdict of the ballot box was not usurped by the last-ditchers in the officers' mess and in the smoke-filled rooms of jilted politicians.

This very brief (and arguable) sketch of the frenetic last days of white Rhodesia suggests that, in major crises, growing military influence *may* be beneficial. South Africa is nowhere near the Rhodesian crisis of 1979-80. And even if it were, then the other important demographic, economic and political differences would intrude. Granted these qualifications, what kind of military intervention might occur in South Africa, if indeed there were the intention and means to do so? It is a truism that for a successful revolution to take place the *ancien régime's* security forces (or a large part of them) have to be defeated, suborned or change sides. The white-dominated security forces in South Africa would never defect to the ANC side, although, *in extremis*, in the future, elements of the inevitably larger black force of soldiers and policemen might. If half the SAP is now black what will the ratio be like in ten years time, given the demographic factors? The larger black soldiery might be treated, and act, differently from the loyal black troops in, say, the Rhodesian African Rifles, who were never asked to fire upon masses of their fellows in urban environments.

Would the security forces swing left or right, or split, if the security crisis started to overwhelm them and if overt intervention resulted? Military interventionists are rarely progessive, although one commentator noted drily that many military officers would be reformist, provided social change was orderly.(41) Major social transformation, of course, especially during unrest and war, is rarely orderly. If reform and real change, two different things, stall in South Africa and another —and worse—1984-86 rebellion erupted, would a *verligte* SADF element intervene to force the pace of political change or would the hawks erect a stonewall junta? After all, military intervention is almost the standard method of changing governments in Africa. Why should Pretoria be any different?

To sum up, militarisation in South Africa is more an erratic process rather than an accomplished fact.(42) That process is likely to gain momentum if the war on apartheid escalates. And despite the very major current restraints on the possibility of direct military intervention, in the longer term, without a settlement, the security forces might act as "iron surgeons", either to extend the life of apartheid or to excise the cancer of white supremacy. Less dramatically, the military may act behind the scenes to force their political partners to see the futility of an endless war on the majority of the state's inhabitants.

References and notes:

1. The term was first developed by Harold Lasswell; see "The Garrison State," *American Journal of Sociology*, 46, 1941; also *idem*, "The Garrison State Hypothesis Today," in S Huntington, (ed), *Changing Patterns of Military Politics*, Free Press of Glencoe, Illinois, 1962. For an early application of the garrison state thesis to South Africa, see P Moorcraft, "Towards the Garrison State," in F Clifford-Vaughan, (ed), *International Pressures and Political Change in South Africa*, Oxford University Press, Cape Town, 1978. For a discussion of the "siege culture",

see D Baker, "Race, Power and White Siege Cultures," *Social Dynamics*, 1:3, 1975. For a theoretical study of the white siege culture (or mentality) in Rhodesia, see P Moorcraft, "The Fall of the Republic: The Collapse of White Power in Rhodesia (1976-1980)," unpublished doctoral thesis, University of South Africa, 1987.

2. See A Stephan, "The New Professionalism of Internal Warfare and Military Role Expansion," in A Stephan, (ed), *Authoritarian Brazil*, Yale University Press, New Haven, 1973.
3. H Adam and K Moodley, *South Africa without Apartheid*, Maskew Miller Longman, Cape Town, 1986, p. 66.
4. G Cawthra, *Brutal Force*, International Aid and Defence Fund, London, 1986, p. 26.
5. A Stadler, *The Political Economy of Modern South Africa*, Croom Helm, London, 1987, p. 83.
6. For a useful summary of these developments see M Swilling, "WHAMMING the Radicals," *Weekly Mail*, 26 May 1988, and J-A Collinge, "Start to be made on 'Politics' of Negotiation," *The Star*, (weekly edition), 20 October 1987.
7. For summaries of the NSMS, see A Harber, "The Uniformed Web that Sprawls across the Country," *Weekly Mail*, 3 October 1986, W Ebersohn, "How South Africa Fights the 'Total Onslaught,'" *The Star* (weekly edition), 16 November 1988, "Inside the JMCs," *Southscan*, 13 January 1988, and J Spence, "The Military in South African Politics," in S Johnson, (ed), *South Africa: No Turning Back*, Macmillan, London, 1988.
8. Quoted in S Reiss, "Botha's Carrot and Stick," *Newsweek*, 20 June 1988.
9. James Selfe, a researcher for the PFP, wrote a Master's thesis on the NSMS at the University of Cape Town.
10. Selfe quoted in D Breier, "Guns or Butter: that will be the Choice," *The Star*, (weekly edition), 2 February 1988. See also J Selfe, "South Africa's National Management System," in J Cock and L Nathan, (eds), *War and Society: The Militarisation of South Africa*, Philip, Cape Town, 1989. Selfe argued that the NSMS would survive P W Botha's departure because it was an intrinsic part of white supremacy. See P Moorcraft "The Soft War Specialists," *Southern African Review of Books*, December 1989/January 1990.
11. See Spence, *op. cit.*
12. "Third of SADF are Dual EC Citizens," *Southscan*, 12 October 1988.
13. S Robinson, "Call-up is Bar to South Africa Coup," *The Sunday Telegraph*, 7 August 1988.
14. A Horne, *A Savage War of Peace*, Penguin, Harmondsworth, 1985, pp. 537-8.
15. See the debate on conscription in *Frontline*: H-R Heitman, "Why Conscription Must Continue," December 1985 and R Luyt, "You cannot ignore the Morality," and P Moorcraft, "Black Army to Defend Apartheid," March 1986.
16. Quoted in J Frederikse, *South Africa: A Different Kind of War*, Ravan, Johannesburg, 1987, pp. 8-10.
17. I would like to acknowledge the patient and expert assistance of at least one excellent regular officer in the SADF PR section, (the then) Colonel F van Oudtshoorn, and also (the then) Captain Leonard Knipe of the Cape Town SAP. Knipe, in some ways a model policeman, assisted this writer in making a documentary film on the SAP and, briefly, advised on a popular book on crime: P Moorcraft and M Cohen, *Stander*, Galago, Alberton, 1984.
18. For two interesting opinion poll surveys of white opinion, see the two analyses by D Geldenhuys, *What Do We Think?: A Survey of White Opinion on Foreign Policy Issues*, South African Institute of International Affairs, Johannesburg, 1982 and 1984.

19. F Van Zyl Slabbert, *The Last White Parliament*, Sidgwick and Jackson, London, 1985, p. 105.
20. Interview with author, 1980.
21. In discussion with author, 1985.
22. R Cohen, "Apartheid's Sour Fruit," *The Observer*, 24 July 1988.
23. D Beckett, "The Battle For Boksburg," *Frontline*, April 1989.
24. K Grundy, *The Militarization of South African Politics*, Oxford University Press, Oxford, 1988, p.68.
25. *Ibid.*, p. 69.
26. Quoted in "SADF in the Dock," *Weekly Mail*, 2 September 1988.
27. For example, Grundy, *op. cit.*; D Geldenhuys and H Kotzé, "Aspects of Political Decision-making in South Africa," *Politikon*, 10, 1983; and R Jaster, "South African Defense Strategy and the Growing Influence of the Military," in W Foltz and H Bienen, (eds), *Arms and the African*, York University Press, New Haven, 1985.

    A more iconoclastic view of civil-military relations was published in the *Financial Mail* (which reprinted it from *The Spectator*): "Of Bullies and Banana Republics," 30 August 1985. It commented on the aftermath of the Rubicon speech and the debate about the military's ongoing involvement in Renamo:

    > The whole lot of them out there [Afrikaner leaders] are compulsive liars all the time, or [PW] Botha doesn't know what the boys are up to (which makes him an idiot, especially as he used to run Defence), or he does know and secretly lets them get on with it (which means you can never believe another word he says), or he knows about it, genuinely doesn't like it, but is powerless to stop it. The last possibility—a president impotent in the face of cheeky opposition (which just happens to be an army full of thick officers) is the interpretation that alarms the visitor most.
28. A Seegers, "The Military in South Africa: A Comparison and Critique," *South Africa International*, 16:4, April 1986.
29. *Ibid.*
30. For a summary of civil-military relations in 1988, see "South Africa: Security Tensions under the Emergency," *Africa Confidential*, 17 June 1988. The article outlines politically influential soldiers and policemen under the rubric: "Security: Soldiers with Political Punch". Although this writer does not necessarily agree with the details or the assumptions of this list, compiled in mid-1988, it is worth summarising:

— General "Jannie" Geldenhuys, aged 52, commander of the SADF. Under him are the four service chiefs:

— Lieutenant General Andreas Jacobus "Kat" Liebenberg, 49, head of the army, former director of special forces;

— Lieutenant General Denis Earp, 57, then head of the air force. Succeeded by Lieutenant General Jan Petrus van Loggerenberg, then chief of staff (operations), now air force chief;

— Vice Admiral Glyn Syndercombe, 56, navy chief;

— Lieutenant General Daniel Pieter Knobel, 52, head of the medical services. [The inclusion of the commander of the medical services is unusual; this small service has little political clout.]

— Lieutenant General Ian Rimbault Gleeson, 53, chief of the defence force staff;

— Lieutenant General C J van Tonder, who replaced Vice Admiral "Dries" Putter as head of the SADF directorate of military intelligence;

— Lieutenant General Charles M Lloyd, appointed in 1987 as the secretary of the SSC. He replaced Lieutenant General Pieter van der Westhuizen, who became ambassador to Chile;

— Major General Rudolph "Witkop" Badenhorst who became the SADF chief of staff (operations);
— Major General K van der Waal, general officer commanding special forces; and
— Major General A J M Joubert, commander of the "Recce" commandos.

31. P Frankel, *Pretoria's Praetorians*, Cambridge University Press, Cambridge, 1984, pp. 170-1.
32. A Heard, "Where the Blind Lead the Mute," *The Observer*, 19 June 1988.
33. Spence, *op. cit.*
34. *Ibid.*
35. For a discussion of fusion in South Africa, see Frankel, *op. cit.*, pp. 134-5; for a general comment on the subject, see C Enloe, *Ethnic Soldiers*, Penguin, Harmondsworth, 1980, pp. 160-185; for an analysis of the theory in the context of Israel, see A Perlmutter, *Politics and Military in Israel*, Yale University Press, New Haven, 1981.
36. The term is Finer's; see S Finer, *Comparative Government*, Penguin, Harmondsworth, 1970, p. 535.
37. P Moorcraft, "The Fall of the Republic"..., *op. cit.*, p. 223.
38. A Perlmutter and V Bennett, (eds), *The Political Influence of the Military*, Yale University Press, New Haven, 1980, p. 9
39. See P Moorcraft, "Day of the Generals," *Financial Mail*, 23 September 1988.
40. Perlmutter, *op. cit.*, p. 205 and R Betts, "Soldiers, Statesmen and the Decision to Go To War," doctoral dissertation, Harvard University, 1975, p. 209.
41. J Johnson, *The Military and Society in Latin America*, Stanford University Press, Stanford, 1964, p. 147.
42. Grundy, *op. cit.*, p. 58.

18

The major fronts

South Africa faces current threats on a number of fronts: conventional war; rural insurgency; urban warfare; trade union militancy; social action by churches, students and other community-based groups; and economic warfare, such as sanctions.

The conventional threat

The SADF's withdrawal from Angola has altered the conventional war pressures on the republic. If Namibia's path to independence is relatively smooth, the SADF will redraw its defence lines in the northern Cape. Although this may reduce short-term manpower commitments, the costs of rebuilding the Namibian defence infrastructure farther south will be high.(1) The current reduction and planned withdrawal of Cuban and Russian forces should reduce Pretoria's fears of a landward invasion from Angola, which had been given prominence in 1988. Russia's embryonic detente with South Africa might remove the last vestiges of the red invasion scares which have fired the imagination and bigotry of Afrikaner backwoodsmen and propagandists. It had once been naively believed by many white South Africans that, when the chips were down, the US 7th Cavalry would ride in at the last minute to save righteous Christian capitalists from the godless communist hordes intent on sweeping the whites into the sea. Even if there had been an inkling of truth in such a notion, today the successors of the 7th Cavalry comprise soldiers and non-commissioned officers who are 65% black Americans. In the 1990s there is more chance of the USA and USSR cooperating *against* South African militarism.

Nor could the OAU or frontline alliance cobble together a conventional force which could replace the Cuban/Russian/East German capabilities. Many of the OAU nations are army-based states which could ill afford to risk their precarious domestic stability by sending large elements of their armies out of the country. The armies of the OAU lack a common military organisation, military doctrine, leadership, training methods, deployment plan and general staff. And the frontline states would find it almost impossible to coordinate a conventional military threat. Namibia, economically almost totally dependent on South Africa, will spend a decade, at least, nation-building. Mozambique is in ruins. Only Zimbabwe has efficient armed forces and a common border. The Zimbabwe National Army, overcommitted in Mozambique, has always adopted a defensive posture on its southern border.

It was only in the last stages of the Angolan war that the SADF faced a possibility of serious conventional reverses. This was part of the reason for the 1988 agreement to withdraw from Angola and to allow the UN plan for Namibia to proceed.

The terrain, two oceans, deserts and mountains, provides defensible topographical boundaries for South Africa. If an invasion should ever materialise, South Africa—60 times larger than Israel—has the room for manoeuvrability and a defence-in-depth, unlike the Jewish state. The new defence perimeter in the northern Cape will be easier to guard than northern Namibia: largely open, flat scrubland and desert in southern Namibia will provide excellent opportunities for armoured thrusts and aerial interdiction of any invading columns. But South Africa has extensive land borders to defend: with Botswana (1,105 miles), Namibia (601), Mozambique (305), Swaziland (267) and Zimbabwe (140). If the patchwork-quilt "independent" homelands and Lesotho are included that amounts to about 14,000 miles of border to patrol.

The conventional reaction forces face a number of problems in the 1990s. One is equipment. Angola no longer provides mountains of captured (often outdated) weaponry. That is a minor issue compared with the need for modern equipment, such as advanced combat aircraft and air defence systems. Armscor can produce airframes and most of the electronics, but the deficiency appears to be jet engines. Israel (just possibly, despite US safeguards) and Taiwan (more likely) might circumvent these shortages. Sixty per cent of the total 1989-90 defence budget (R10.25 million, just over £2 billion) was scheduled to be spent through the special defence account (not subject to public audit) which is generally used for secret arms purchases and for Armscor. This 20% increase on the previous budget suggests that an intensive modernisation and procurement programme, particularly for aircraft and helicopters, is underway.(2) Such an increase (even allowing for the official inflation rate of 15% and the lead times for development of weaponry) is large, bearing in mind that the de-escalation of the Angolan war removed the major conventional threat. Presumably, like the ANC, the SADF is preparing for the long haul.

The standing forces also face a number of manpower problems, ranging from the shortage of skilled technicians and the difficulty in retaining quality noncommissioned officers to morale problems associated with regular call-ups, especially for duty in the townships. The end of the current bout of township insurrection has reduced this difficulty and, overall, the SADF does not suffer from major challenges to its morale, for the time being. Nor has the withdrawal from Angola, and later Namibia, appeared to have affected the SADF in the way that retreat from Egypt (in 1974), and later from Sinai, afflicted the Israeli army.

A seaborne invasion is an alternative, albeit a far less likely one than an assault by land from the north. A 1965 report, *Apartheid and United Nations Collective Measures*, envisaged the possibilities of a full-scale naval and air invasion of South Africa.(3) It estimated that 100,000 UN soldiers would be required, with possible casualties ranging from 19,000 to 38,000 men. The SADF is very much stronger today than in 1965. Also, the possible use of South African tactical nuclear weapons (if indeed it has them) would seriously compound the calculation. If they were deployed it would "probably make a 'D-Day' landing of the kind practised in Normandy in 1944 as obsolete as a charge of armoured knights at the battle of Agincourt".(4) And should such an invasion ever succeed, then the tasks of occupying a country the size of South Africa would be daunting indeed.

It seems more than likely that the SADF would resist a conventional invasion, by sea or land, with all its extensive resources, but a naval blockade would require, probably, a political rather than a military response. Pretoria would be extremely loathe to risk a conventional or nuclear war with a great power fleet lying offshore. The SADF, with its tiny navy, would not be able to match the conventional technology of the kind found in the NATO and Warsaw Pact inventories, such as sophisticated nuclear submarines or jet-fighters aboard aircraft carriers. Given the political consensus, a sort of anti-apartheid popular front on an international basis, it would be technically possible to blockade the five or six major South African ports. Britain's Beira patrol, to stop Rhodesian sanctions-busting, was largely a symbolic gesture by one state. A truly international blockade of South African harbours, sanctioned by the UN, might be the short, sharp action that might force the obdurate Afrikaners to negotiate. *Might*. A blockade would involve very serious political and logistical challenges, but they would not be insuperable. Such gunboat diplomacy would obviate the major arguments against current sanctions (discussed in more detail later), namely, the long-term damage inflicted on blacks in the whole region, the South African economy and black-white relations during a lengthy siege.

Guerrilla warfare

Unlike Mozambique, Rhodesia or Angola, South Africa is not suitable for classical African insurgency. Except for a few areas, such as Northern Natal, it is a developed country with few wild, inaccessible places. Nevertheless, the triumph of the bush struggles in the neighbouring states have influenced the morale and the tactics of South African insurgents. Guerrilla warfare, however, is not infallible, even in backward, remote territories, let alone in more industrialised societies. There partisans have usually succeeded only with the backing of more conventional formations: Tito's forces with the support of the Red Army; the South Vietnamese irregulars with help of the North Vietnamese army. Even well-organised, large groups of partisans in Russia could do little to impede the German army, whose insane atrocities had already outraged the local population. Mugabe's guerrillas relied heavily on the Frelimo army in the last years of the Rhodesian war, but the ANC is unlikely to receive the direct assistance of the frontline armies, at least in the foreseeable future. Indeed, Pretoria's agreements with Luanda and Maputo resulted in the removal, directed by the Angolan and Mozambican security forces, of ANC guerrilla facilities. Yet, both the PAC, which has adopted at times a Maoist line, and the ANC have attempted to fight their wars in the countryside as well as in the cities. The ANC's deployment of landmines from 1985 was one phase of its rural strategy.

The SADF's containment policy has concentrated on the borders and the interior, its "area defence". According to General Johan van der Merwe, the head of the security police, 49% of the insurgents who were killed or captured inside South Africa, during the 18 months prior to August 1988, had infiltrated from Botswana. A further 13% came through Swaziland, 9% through Lesotho, 5% via Zimbabwe and less than 1% through Mozambique. The entry point of the other 23% was unknown.(5) The Swazi route had been largely disrupted by the local police and Lesotho's access curtailed soon after the 1986 coup.

The SADF has reacted in a number of ways to this infiltration: by punitive raids on the frontline states, diplomatic and economic pressure,

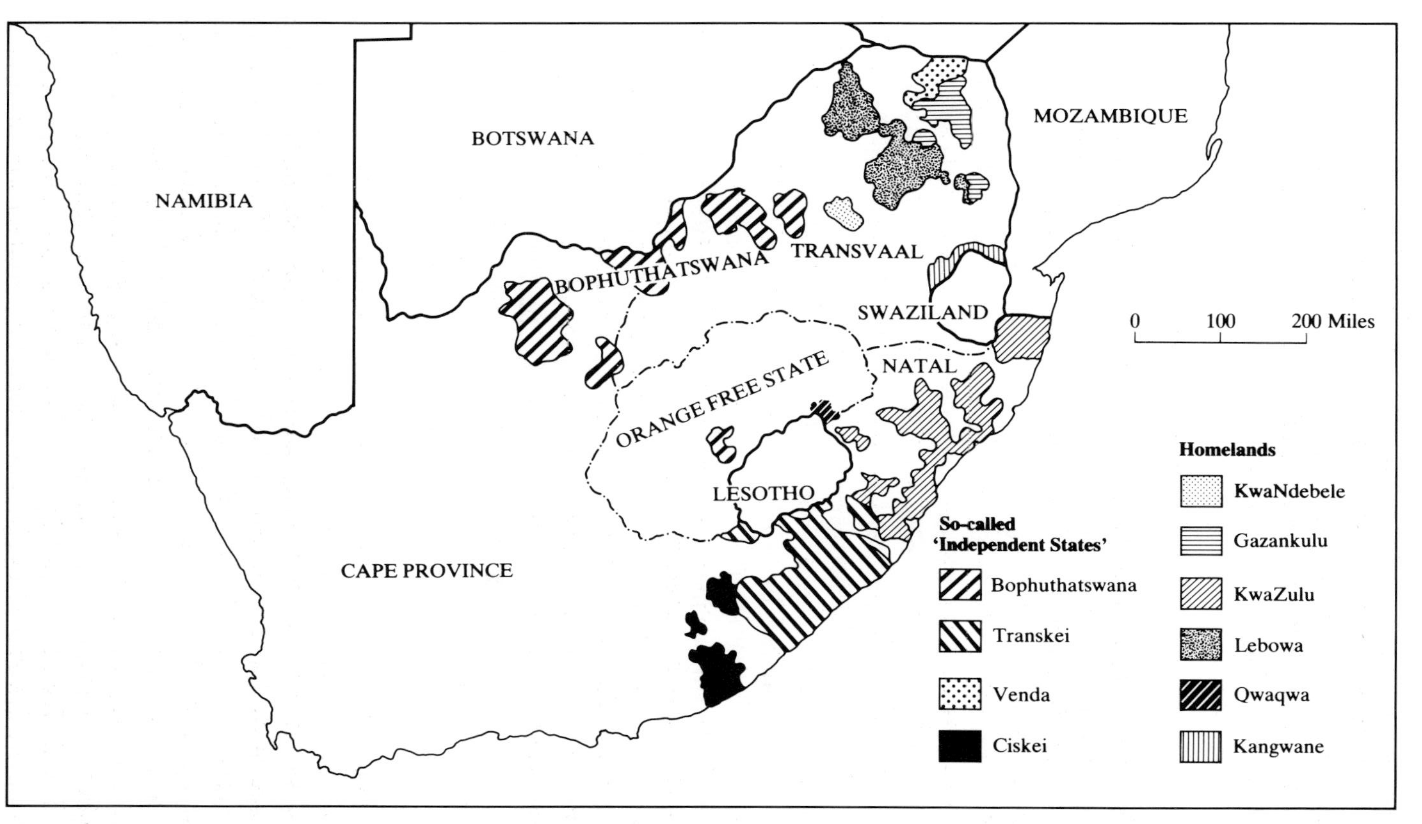

MAP 17 Black homelands

large-scale patrols and the erection of physical barriers. Electrified fences (known as "Caftan") traverse sensitive sections of the Mozambique and Zimbabwe frontiers. In 1986 it was reported that the costs of the fencing, carrying a lethal 4,000 volts, was R130,000 per kilometre.(6) According to the SADF, 70 people were killed on these fences in 1988. Many were refugees attempting to flee from Mozambique. These fences have been criticised but, unlike the Berlin wall, which tried to keep people in, Pretoria's "ring of steel" tries to keep people, including armed enemies, out. The weak point is clearly Botswana. Of the 99 insurgents arrested or captured in the first six months of 1988, 47 had come through Botswana. The borders with Botswana are long, very thinly populated and often present inhospitable terrain. The SADF regards the Botswana security forces as either lax or in cahoots with the ANC. Patrolling these borders uses up extensive manpower and is very tedious, as are minesweeping duties in other parts of the Transvaal.

The second line of protection against infiltration is area defence. The farming areas in the northern Transvaal have suffered far more grievously from depopulation, debt and drought than from insurgency. But a zone depopulated by whites is an invitation to further guerrilla encroachment. Pretoria has tried to get whites back into the border areas with various incentives, including offers of subsidised land and facilities for ex-soldiers (and ex-Rhodesians who seem to cling nostalgically to the peripheries of the "old country"). The paraphernalia of farm defence is very reminiscent of the Rhodesian war, including the MARNET (Military Area Radio Network), an updated version of the Rhodesian Agric-alert. But, again, helping the farmers to fortify their homes and providing mineproofed vehicles is costly.

Behind the farmers stands the commando system. Reservists in the countryside are often "area-bound": they do their call-ups in their own areas because of their local knowledge and their obvious interest in protecting their own properties and families. They also guard key points such as dams and power installations. Although many rural commandos are volunteers, expanding conscription has undermined the original "spirit of voluntarism" which has been an important component of the ethos of rural commandos. Partly because of this, many of them are understrength.

Another weak point in area defence is the proximity of so many bits of the various homelands, which have their own autonomous security forces of varying quality. Originally, homelands were seen as the solution to the apartheid dilemma; now they are part of the problem. Poverty, unemployment, acute soil erosion because of overcrowding, land dispos-

PLATE 18.1 *The Star*'s comment on Russian backing for Cuban forces in Angola: Malan and Savimbi, it suggests, are no match for the Kremlin. (1986).

PLATE 18.2 *The Star* (1986).

session, corruption and repression have turned the four independent bantustans into coup-ridden hotbeds of discontent. Even the "model" homeland, Bophuthatswana, inspired a short-lived military coup, which was rapidly suppressed by the SADF and a highly embarrassed Pretoria. Likewise, the non-independent homelands have also become further breeding grounds for radical discontent. In some white areas adjacent to homelands (and Lesotho) crime, such as stocktheft, has distracted the security forces as much as possible guerrilla infiltration.

In theory, Ciskei or Transkei—when they are not threatening to invade each other—could invite in, say, Cuban troops. Pretoria would act immediately to stop them. But the point is that the homelands are already becoming mini-sanctuaries for insurgents (both local and foreign-trained cadres). And they are a lot nearer to Pretoria than bases in Angola or Mozambique. The police forces in the homelands are often more ruthless than their counterparts in the SAP but, if guerrilla theoreticians such as Carlos Marighela are correct, then this repression will feed the incipient peasant rebelliousness.

In the countryside, liberated areas run by guerrilla warlords are not a feasible proposition. But in the 1984-86 unrest small towns and villages in the *platteland* caught the epidemic of revolt. Trade union activists are also trying to organise and mobilise the (frequently) exploited and, so-far, non-unionised farm workers. The ANC sees the countryside as part of the revolutionary struggle. The occasional landmine or town-riot may not compensate for the absence of the (apparent) romance of bush warfare, or a local Che Guevara to lead it, but the current costs of containing a (very) low-level area war is a contributory strain on the SADF's manpower and treasury. Guerrillas rarely win wars; their adversaries lose them. This may in time become as true of the *platteland* as the cities.

Urban warfare

The urban campaign may be extended by the ANC to strike more often at white soft targets, despite the political fallout naked terrorism could cause. This would certainly sharpen racial polarisation and lead to more black and white vigilante violence. Whites could adapt to this, as the citizens of Belfast have, or as Londoners did during the Blitz. But few Britons had the option to emigrate in 1940. Urban terrorism could be demoralising, especially if white schools are hit, for the more than 1.5 million whites who have or can get foreign passports. They *can* emigrate. It was white emigration that did so much to undermine the economic and military effort in Rhodesia. The exodus of the intelligentsia, business managers and many other middle-class professionals further weakens the economy. By 1988 the migration rate had tailed off, however: immigrants outnumbered emigrants by 10,400 to 7,767, according to the Central Statistical Service.(7) The brain drain has declined from its peak in 1986. The figures, however, can be misleading, not least because young people, with little capital, especially males of military age, leaving to go "on holiday" or "to study abroad", often do not bother to go through the cumbersome emigration procedure. Although the ANC has recently urged its white supporters to stay inside South Africa, the emigration rates, particularly in the English-speaking community, are likely to continue to peak and trough with the recurrent waves of crisis. The majority of whites, however, even those holding foreign passports, are locked into the system. Many are "currency detainees", because of the restrictions on taking out money. The determined and those with marketable skills will always be able to quit. And simply counting heads of immigrants takes no account of the quality of the emigrants. One management expert, in 1986, described the brain drain as a form of "socio-economic suicide".(8) Probably, though, unlike Angola or Algeria, the majority of whites will see it through, unless a second Beirut, not Belfast, beckons. Then, to use the local parlance, the proverbial "chicken run" will become an "owl run".

Even if urban insurrection remains confined largely to the black areas, a scenario of barricades going up and revolution being built from within the ghettos is unlikely. Townships like Soweto are not the same as the urban jungle of Algiers: the small detached houses are laid out in stark, long, straight lines with streets wide enough for armoured cars to patrol and with little cover to prevent the deployment of helicopters. Most black townships were designed with both political and military containment in mind. Riots in Soweto may help to mobilise the masses and are bad for the government's PR, but they are not the ideal means to take over nearby Johannesburg or Pretoria.

Urban counterinsurgency, however, is often demoralising, sometimes dangerous and certainly exhausting for young conscripts. Fighting on your own doorstep against your fellow countrymen is a far cry from the *skiet-en-donder* (action-packed) adventures of repelling Cubans on the northern borders. Before October 1984 an average of 1,500 men failed to report for duty at each call-up. In the first call-up after the troops were sent into the townships, this number rose by 500%, according to the SADF's own figures (later retracted). Attendance at "camps", the call-ups after the two years of national service, was also generally between 40% and 60%. These figures do not indicate that all absentees were opposed on political grounds to call-up, in the townships or elsewhere. Sickness, change of address, deferments, etc. would explain a large percentage. But there is likely to be a correlation in the rise of absenteeism and increasing opposition to the army's occupation of the townships. The increase in conscientious objection, (despite the public obloquy and stiff penalties for those who fail to qualify for the narrow definition of religious objection which permits an alternative community service), and the growth of South African war resisters' groups in Europe confirm this trend.(9)

Limpet mines seem to be the favoured weapon of the urban guerrilla. Their use in urban business areas in 1988 and 1989 rose dramatically. In the first eight months of 1988, for example, 17 people were killed and nearly 200 wounded in bombings in restaurants, shops and cinemas. (10) Such random carnage is difficult to prevent. Western European nations find it hard to cope with the blight of terrorism (or guerrilla struggle, depending on the perspective) in the big cities, where such actions are supported by a tiny minority of the population. This contrasts with South Africa where opinion polls indicate that Nelson Mandela is the most popular of all politicians. Thus, ANC combatants will continue to operate in a comfortable sea of urban fish with potentially majority support, or, almost as effective, neutrality.

Trade union militancy.

A detailed analysis of the trade union movement would transcend the scope of this study. Nevertheless, organised labour is likely to continue to play a major role in opposing apartheid. Before 1979 blacks were excluded from both economic and political power. "No other workforce in the history of industrialisation has been so excluded for so long from the system it made possible."(11) The Wiehahn Commission of 1979 led to the incorporation of organised black labour into the economic—but not the political—system. The more radical unions were, therefore, bound to flex their new economic muscles to press for political incorporation as well. (Initially, some unions, rejecting Lenin's advice that all available political platforms should be exploited, opposed registration under the Wiehahn plan because they regarded it as collaboration.)

Throughout the 1984-86 insurrection, the major unions tried to mobilise the factories and mines and to liaise with parallel movements in the townships. This caused a major rupture in the union movement: between the "workerists" (who wanted to concentrate primarily on shopfloor issues) and "populists" (who emphasised primarily political and community issues).

The biggest union confederation in South Africa is COSATU (Congress of South African Trade Unions), established as a "super-union" amid much fanfare in November 1985. COSATU has identified itself with the ANC and the UDF. Its main rival is NACTU (National Council of Trade Unions), a merger of CUSA (Council of Unions of South Africa), which had a workerist bias, and AZACTU (Azanian Confederation of Trade Unions), which supported a black consciousness/ Africanist line. On the right, Inkatha sponsored UWUSA (United Workers Union of South Africa), which supported the "free market" and attacked COSATU's espousal of sanctions and disinvestment. There are also a large number of independent unions.

The labour movement is clearly riven by ideological divisions. The ANC/PAC/Inkatha splits are compounded by the workerist versus populist debate which rages *within* the various affiliated unions of the confederations as much as *between* the big confederations themselves. There are also divisions along the lines of skills, religion, education, language, race, class, ethnicity, regions and migrants versus settled labour. Much, although not all, of this diversity is the product of apartheid's divide-and-rule tactics. Apartheid quite deliberately tried to create a tame "insider" black class with residential rights (under the former, notorious section ten of the pass laws) separate from the migrant workers. The latter were forced to live in abysmally cramped, single-sex hostels in mine compounds. Part of the reason was to discourage the unionisation of mine workers: migrant workers, the majority of the mine workforce, could easily be sent back to their homelands or neighbouring states at the least sign of militancy. Migrant workers often felt alienated from, and betrayed by, the more comfortable workforce settled, with their families, in the townships. According to one migrant worker: "Township workers have been corrupted by rich whites and blacks, by teachers and bad priests. They don't believe in the brotherhood of workers."(12)

Besides these difficulties, the black labour movement has had to contend with state repression, the constant detention of union leaders, massive unemployment, which has offered plentiful scope for scab labour, and the general poverty of resources in the organisational structure of the unions (alleviated somewhat by a corps of white intellectuals working as union advisers). In the face of a mountain of obstacles, the labour movement has become a focus of black aspirations. Despite the emasculation of its leadership during the first national state of emergency, in 1987 COSATU claimed 750,000 members. By the late 1980s perhaps 25% of the black workforce in the modern sector of the economy was unionised. COSATU has tried to reduce the fragmentation of its affiliates by forging the confederation into fewer larger unions on the principle of one industry, one union. The emerging pattern seems to be that of a smaller, but better-paid, union-protected labour force in the modern, formal sector of the economy, a burgeoning non-unionised black economy, and a growing army of urban unemployed and rural masses living at, or below, subsistence level.

To avoid being tagged an insider, collaborative body, COSATU has cautiously adopted a wider perspective by trying to organise among the unemployed and to pay court to the UDF and ANC. Despite its sympathies with the ANC, many in COSATU, and in the labour movement as a whole, are wary of entanglement for ideological and practical reasons (to avoid being completely banned, for example). In the post-apartheid society, COSATU has no wish to become a tame labour appendage so typical of one-party states.

Despite police harassment, new political forms of industrial action have been conducted by the unions: such as factory and underground sit-ins, sleep-ins, go-slows and overtime bans. Obviously, the most important weapon is the strike. Black strikes, once illegal, typically were of short duration and localised. From 1987 strike actions became longer and bigger. The most significant strike, in the economy's most vulnerable sector, was one called in 1987 by the country's largest union, the National Union of Mineworkers, led by the indefatigable Cyril Ramaphosa, the general secretary. Over 340,000 miners came out on strike for three weeks. Led by Anglo, the Chamber of Mines, the toughest of the employer federations, eventually managed to force the NUM back to work, with very few union gains. Anglo initially dismissed 36,000 of the strikers.(13)

Anglo American, the biggest mine-owner, was showing what critics call its "multifacialism": on the one hand, displaying a liberal face, offering "stakes" (shares) to its workers and yet maintaining a hostel system, with built-in security measures to match many top-security prisons. Despite their claims to be world-leaders, wage and safety conditions in South African mines leave much to be desired.(14) Anglo had encouraged a dialogue with the unions, but on the other hand (not surprisingly) rejected their pretensions to represent the political aspirations of their workers as well. Anglo was trapped in the dilemma facing all major businesses in South Africa: without politial emancipation, economic confrontations must become politicised. It has been the sole legal route for organised black pressure. And it is bad for profits. Anglo's reaction to the mine strike confirmed, to some critics, the conspiracy theory that Anglo and Pretoria were in bed together. "Like distracted lovers, they may not have always enjoyed each other's company but they were bonded by inseparable interests." (15)

The South African economy has three main pillars: the state sector, the three insurance-based groups (Sanlam, SA Mutual and Rembrandt) and the mighty Anglo American Corporation. Big business, especially Anglo, might advocate reform, but economic liberalisation without political representation could make the factories and mines, not the townships, the epicentre of the liberation struggle. There are clear limits to the (self-)interest big business can display in reform without harming its short-term profit margins. Yet, without industrial peace today and some kind of political settlement in the future, capitalism itself is endangered. The common thrust of the labour movement is, unsurprisingly, socialist, sometimes rabidly so.

After the collapse of the 1984-86 insurrection many blacks decided that unions could do a better job than the comrades. Certainly the unions offered an organisational backbone and discipline which mass protest lacked. If they take up this challenge, they may well overextend their limited resources and lose ground on the shopfloor as well. It is a lot to ask of a fractious, harassed labour movement that it should try to break the apartheid rock on its own. The union movement still has to set

PLATE 18.3 The mines could hold the key to domestic revolt.

its own house in order. The NUM, for example, has not yet been able to stop the savage tribal faction-fighting among miners which has little to do with politics. And ruthless intimidation has also been a hallmark of strike "solidarity".

Nevertheless, the state cannot simply ban the labour movement; it is too integrated into the economic structure. Frequently, the major employers' organisations have cajoled Pretoria into releasing senior unionists from detention because they were needed to maintain industrial peace. Nor can the state enforce stable industrial relations or simply gazette higher productivity. The unions, particularly if they can present a more unified front, are likely to expand their implicit political influence. Whether the strike can replace the AK is highly debatable. It could easily complement it. In Marxist-Leninist terms, South Africa today is ripe for a workers' revolt. It has an efficient vanguard communist party, a large disgruntled urban proletariat, an aggressive union movement, a massive *lumpenproletariat* and an army of impoverished peasants. That makes South Africa in the 1990s much more susceptible —theoretically—to a classical urban revolt than Russia was in 1917. As the previous chapter made clear, however, the crucial difference is the nature of state power in South Africa today.

If a workers' revolution is not imminent, attempts to coordinate nationwide strikes are a regular feature of union activity. On Labour Day and 16 June (to celebrate the beginning of the Soweto uprising) massive stay-aways are common. But strikes have not yet been really effective as direct political instruments. There are options, such as a sustained long-term strike in the mining industry, especially in the gold mines. But that would merely increase the value of Pretoria's hoard of the precious metal. More effective would be a transport and harbour strike. Both a mine strike and a long transport strike were attempted in 1987. Both were, on the surface at least, aimed at improving wages and conditions. But nearly all major strikes by blacks in South Africa have an implicit political agenda. At present, the unions appear to lack the strength, will and organisation for a sustained, national strike aimed at bringing down the government. The 1926 general strike in Britain lasted only nine days and backed down before a far less authoritarian but still resolute government. But, as an eminent British historian noted, "that strike brought out two things very clearly: the enthusiasm for a common cause, and the genius for improvisation and organisation shown by local trade union groups".(16) The 1926 strike centred on the resolution of the miners; the same may prove to be true of any South African general strike. A more relevant parallel may be the Polish workers. In the end, the Solidarity union federation, the sole surviving political opposition to the government, did manage to pressurise the authorities into sharing power with it.

Churches *et al.*

Along with the unions, the churches were one of the few legal outlets for protest against apartheid. Nevertheless, the state has continuously banned churchmen and their organisations, at one stage almost going as far as banning public prayer. During the 1984-86 unrest two whole congregations, in Elsies River and Graaff Reinet, were detained. Pretoria particularly resents many of the churches' advocacy of the "just war" concept, and the doctrines of liberation theology which are often associated with it.(17) With their purported biblical justification of apartheid, it was the three Dutch Reformed Churches that did the most to discredit religion in the eyes of blacks. In 1974 the South African Council of Churches (SACC), however, said that the SADF was defending "a fundamentally unjust society". After the Soweto rebellion, many blacks tended to feel that any church which did not actively support their struggle was against them. Some churches, especially the (apparently) conservative, three-million strong Zionist Christian Church, remained aloof from the call to action, but many clerics responded with alacrity. In 1981 the Presbyterians called on their ministers to ignore the Mixed Marriages Act and to marry couples regardless of race. In 1982 the Catholic bishops lambasted the SADF as "an army of occupation" in Namibia; later that year 123 dissident Dutch Reformed ministers signed a document condemning apartheid. In 1983 the World Alliance of Reformed Churches, with local prompting, declared apartheid a heresy. In 1985 over a 100 theologians and prominent Christians signed the Kairos Document which branded Pretoria as "unreformable" and the enemy of the people of God.

Pretoria retaliated particularly against the SACC, which represented 22 of the country's main churches. It banned, detained and harassed its leaders, including Beyers Naudé, an heroic Afrikaner, and Frank Chikane, who has close ties with the ANC. As Chikane put it in 1987: "In 1982 I believed that protest could be non-violent, but now the government has closed the space for non-violence."(18) Some less prominent churchmen have died in detention or been killed mysteriously outside prison, but the most prominent clerics such as Archbishop Tutu and the Reverend Allan Boesak, a patron of the UDF, because of their international prominence, have developed a degree of inviolability.

Individual churchmen have had a dramatic effect on mobilising blacks, particularly during the highly charged atmosphere of mass funerals, as well as, in some cases, urging moderation—for example, Tutu's condemnation of the necklace. Nonetheless, as in the case of the union movement, the churches in South Africa are divided. Many conservative churchmen oppose liberation theology. The Zionist church is deliberately apolitical. Some of the fundamentalist "born-again" faiths are ultra-conservative crusaders against "communism". In Latin America liberation theology is embedded in a centralised Catholism. There is no equivalent in South Africa. In short, Pretoria has its allies as well as its enemies in dog collars.

The more radical churches are, however, enmeshed in a wide network of other important anti-apartheid groups: civic associations, student bodies, educational organisations such as the National Education Crisis Committee, women's organisations and the Black Sash, to name but a few. State repression and more subtle, divide-and-rule tactics, as well as internal divisions, however, may well prevent the emergence of unified, mass social protest.*

Economic weapons

Politicians and academics have quarrelled endlessly about the efficacy of sanctions, most notably in the case of South Africa. An historical survey of the 100 or so examples of sanctions imposed since 1914 would confirm the commonsensical conclusion that sometimes they work and sometimes they do not. The massive body of literature on the subject tends to suggest that, apart from the purely punitive and symbolic considerations, sanctions have not been useful devices *on their own* to induce, persuade or compel a targeted state to comply. The theory of sanctions is straightforward: economic sanctions = economic deprivation = political change. The effectiveness of the first leg of the formula obviously depends on how comprehensive the sanctions are. The second element relates to the strength of the sanctioned economy and its abilities to evade and/or retaliate. The third, political results, depends largely upon psychological factors. Above all, to be effective, sanctions should have a clear political goal. The more specific that is, the more likely it is to be achieved.(19)

*In late 1989 the internal anti-apartheid groups, especially those which supported the ANC, regrouped themselves into the "Mass Democratic Movement". They did not, however, adopt any new tactics, although the unbanning of the ANC in February 1990 might dramatically alter the climate of mass protest.

So far, sanctions against South Africa are nowhere near comprehensive, the state's long-term ability to survive and/or retaliate is unclear, and, although the Afrikaner backlash has clearly begun, no one can prophesy where it will end. But what are the precise aims of anti-apartheid sanctions? Presumably, they are intended to induce a "change of heart" in the Afrikaner citadel of power, and, in the interim, weaken the state machinery's ability to suppress blacks. Many advocates of sanctions, however, do not want to change Afrikaner hearts eventually; they want to move their backsides now from the seats of power. Sanctions have become all things to all men. They are seen as both a means to encourage revolution and as a mechanism to induce a negotiated settlement. Sometimes they have little to do with change in South Africa and rather more to do with creating a "feel-good" posture in Western domestic politics.

One important argument against sanctions is that economic progress alone will undermine apartheid. The debate on this point is complex, but, in sum, the liberal capitalist argument is that trade = economic growth = black mobility = more black political rights. Therefore, if economic development eats away at racial domination, then sanctions are counter-productive. Since the 1960s there has been a major intellectual controversy as to whether economic rationality can undermine state ideology. Not all economists, however, were prepared to predict the victory of the market over ideology. Neo-Marxist scholars insisted that capitalism and apartheid are essentially collaborative and that, *in extremis*, white capitalism would accept diminished profitability in return for the preservation of white supremacy. They pointed to the fact that rapid economic growth in the 1960s coincided with the "high apartheid" period.(20)

The debate, polarised by liberal and Marxist academics, centred on the issues of whether apartheid was an irrational historical aberration or a rational system of economic exploitation and whether apartheid was an inflexible ideological belief system, like Nazism, or a cynical and pragmatic means of domination which could adapt.(21) Despite the pros and cons about whether apartheid and economic growth have been complementary, contradictory or relatively independent variables, sanctions have become a major weapon in the anti-apartheid arsenal.

Supporters of sanctions argue that the alternative is economic warfare, blockade and direct military intervention. Sanctions can, they say, cut short the war, save lives and bring forward the process of negotiations. Pretoria does not have a moral leg to stand on: it deployed sanctions, very forcefully, against Rhodesia and Lesotho, for example. And it has imposed mandatory, and almost comprehensive, economic, social and political sanctions on its black subjects since 1948. Nor, they argue, was Margaret Thatcher's stand against sanctions consistent: she had imposed them on a wide range of states from Argentina to Libya. The practical impact of sanctions will make apartheid that much more expensive to sustain. Crucially, sanctions send a message to whites that their racialism puts them beyond the moral pale and also sends a message to the oppressed majority that the world has not forgotten them.

The latter points are refuted most strongly by the anti-sanctions lobbies. Whites are being driven into the proverbial laager, they say, not to the conference table, and blacks are suffering, not whites, from sanctions and disinvestment. And blacks in the frontline states will suffer, too, from extensive sanctions. Blacks in South Africa do not want sanctions, which threaten their jobs, despite what the Tutus and Boesaks say. Such is the essence of Pretoria's case.(22)

Whether a majority of blacks want sanctions or not is a moot point. "In the South African context, there are lies, damned lies and public opinion surveys on black attitudes to sanctions."(23) The majority of black elite opinion, with the obvious exception of Chief Buthelezi, appears to favour sanctions (even though it is illegal to publicly advocate such economic measures). They are not swayed by the blacks-suffer-most argument. "When the ladder is falling, surely it's those at the top who will get hurt most, not those at the bottom," has been Archbishop Tutu's regular rejoinder. The major black unions also officially support sanctions (although there has been some disquietude about disinvestment). Many outside the unions find it hard to believe that unionists are prepared to sacrifice their jobs for the bigger cause. When the COSATU information officer, Frank Meintjies, was asked how workers would survive if all foreign companies shut shop and left, he turned the question around: "Perhaps the question should be, if the factories close down, would the government be able to survive?"(24) Whether union solidarity would hold under such circumstances, especially with a current (unofficial) tally of four million unemployed, is improbable. Nevertheless, the thrust of the argument of politically conscious blacks inside South Africa appears to be: we are already suffering, so sanctions might help to shorten our misery.

The don't-hurt-the-blacks argument looks shabbiest when it is paraded by foreign businessmen who have never shown the slightest interest in black welfare before. (25) And saying we must not pressurise Pretoria because it might lead to retaliation against blacks is a classic concession to blackmail. A better argument is that sanctions would shatter the feeble economies of the frontline states, as Pretoria passed on the hardships. But the black neighbours—or at least their authoritarian leaders—say they are prepared to make sacrifices too.

In the end the crucial variable is the psychological effect on the white supremacists. Sanctions may be a useful talisman of international opprobrium, but symbolism has its limits. They can also backfire: an even more ruthless Afrikaner oligarchy, sustained by a siege economy, might emerge. This supposition rests largely upon two premises: sanctions will not destroy or drastically enfeeble the economy and, even if they do hurt rather than topple the government, the ruling Afrikaners would rather commit tribal suicide than accept black rule.

Taking the first premise, in some cases, sanctions have not been effective. The arms embargo is one obvious example. Further trade sanctions could likewise be turned around: some of the frontline states could be transformed into sanctions-busting casbahs. Pretoria could then go back to its up-beat domestic propaganda messages of the "prepare to meet thy boom" type. Yet other sanctions have worked, especially when they have been specifically targeted. The sports boycott, for example, resulted in rapid racial integration in most, if not all, areas of South African sport. But sport is not political power. A more powerful example is the refusal to roll over loans in 1985. One man in Chase Manhattan Bank set off a massive financial crisis. And this was triggered by a conservative American banker, not a hostile Soviet manoeuvre. As one writer observed: "It is difficult to see the directors of Chase Manhattan, etc. as the footsoldiers of Lenin."(26) Chase not only torched Pretoria's propaganda agenda, but also emphasised that private commercial anxieties and government-imposed sanctions feed off each other. The 1985 crash was a combination of hard-nosed foreign business concern at the level of profitability in South Africa, moral impulses generated by the anti-apartheid lobbies abroad, the resulting so-called "hassle factor" in the boardrooms and long-term disinvestment, not as a protest against apartheid, but from fear of possible conditions under a future black-ruled government.

"Private" actions by foreign companies, especially the banks, have produced far more dramatic effects than official UN sanctions, partly because UN strictures can be easily evaded in a way that bank loans cannot. There is a domestic variant to the interplay of private and public sanctions: consumer boycotts. These boycotts have been sporadic and largely localised, but sometimes effective, especially in the Eastern Cape. The aims have been to secure local political concessions (for example, the release of political organisers from detention), to alienate white businessmen from the state and to mobilise local communities. "Domestic" sanctions, especially if they are better organised and on a national scale, may become increasingly effective because they are so hard to repress. "The state can ban organisations and meetings, it can clear the streets and change the details of funerals, it can detain people and it can even shoot them, but it cannot force people to buy if they do not want to do so."(27) Consumer boycotts are triggered at one end, while international investors, for usually entirely different reasons, tug at the other end.

The often haphazard combination of international and domestic economic weapons have "worked", in some respects. The time scale is important, though. Sanctions against Rhodesia were said to have failed. Indeed, in the short to middle term, the Rhodesian economy went through an exuberant phase of growth generated partly by import-substitution and swashbuckling sanctions-busting. But in the long term—the growth stage of a siege economy is said to be typically about eight to ten years—the economy ran right down.(28) Sanctions complemented the insurgency in forcing the Rhodesian government to the conference table. Sanctions, if not comprehensive, take time.

The argument in South Africa has shifted ground. From the braggadocio of "sanctions will be a joke", South African businessmen concede that sanctions are hurting, and will hurt more in the long run, but that their effect is counter-productive. Of course, local businessmen can hardly argue for sanctions which will make them poorer, (although the bigger fish are swallowing up, at bargain-basement prices, foreign companies which have disinvested). The argument that sanctions will drive Afrikaners into a suicidal bunker is an unprovable one. It boils down to an assessment of the group psychology of this isolated oligarchy.

To assume that Afrikaners, nuclear bomb in hand, will pull down the pillars of the temple on top of themselves is to assume that South Africa's ruling tribe is as capable of collective madness as it is of collective guilt for the injustices of apartheid. It is not madness, but merely human nature to worry about living under the conditions prevalent in most of black Africa. English, Greek, Portuguese and Jewish South Africans have the same anxieties. Like their English-speaking white compatriots, Afrikaners have now become part of a cosy, spoilt, gadget-festooned suburbia, whose economic pain threshold might be lower than the rugged trekkers of the last century. That may be one interpretation, at least, of the white response to the black consumer boycotts.

Clearly, the sanctions debate is filled with imponderables. The lesson of sanctions on other states suggests that they can be misguided rockets, often hitting the wrong targets. It is particularly ironic that it is socialist governments and parties abroad who so eagerly threaten to impose a siege economy on South Africa as the most effective weapon against apartheid. It is precisely this mechanism most of them use to prop themselves up. It is a further irony that swallowing up the companies offered on a plate by disinvestment (and, more expensively, by domestic privatisation) could further enlarge the £5 billion Anglo American Corporation which stands like a colossus over the South African economy. Sanctions could, in this sense, actually boost the fortunes of monopoly capitalism, the very bulwark of apartheid, according to some Marxist analysts. This might further entrench the racial (and class) polarisation which sanctions could make worse: to most blacks, the destruction of capitalism might become the precondition of freedom.

Economic pressures abound in hypocrisy: one man's sanctions, of course, are another man's business opportunity. As with Rhodesia, often the most noisy and pious sanctioners, especially in the Eastern Bloc and Africa, are the biggest sanctions cheats. Perhaps if the OAU spent as much time studying some of the more enlightened and efficient aspects of the South African economy as it does in drafting resolutions condemning apartheid, the various member states might grow strong enough to use their own weight to lean on Pretoria to escape from its prison of racism. Now, they can hardly argue by example.

Yet despite all its glaring deficiencies, the sanctions programme is usually preferred to military intervention. The suffering induced by sanctions is a small price to pay (especially in the salons and chancelleries of the West) for ending the savagery of apartheid. But there are strong arguments against sanctions, as Helen Suzman, for one, has shown. High-minded principles are at stake on both sides of the sanctions fence. Nevertheless, support for sanctions has become a litmus test of morality. Short of real negotiations, sanctions are here to stay, and they could become more comprehensive.

At issue (until Nelson Mandela's release) was how to make sanctions more watertight. Gold, the mainstay of the economy, is an obvious target. Surprisingly, the conservative *Economist* magazine came out with interesting (if unlikely) proposals to run down the value of gold to undermine rapidly the South African government.(29) More rigorous embargoes on oil and high-tech goods have also been suggested. If blacks are not to suffer, then largely anti-white sanctions could be imposed. All international flights to South Africa could be banned, for example. Whites using the frontline states as alternative staging points could be forced by visas to spend at least three days in a black-ruled country. (This idea, intended to demonstrate the blessings of multiracialism, could well deter even the most liberal white South African from looking forward to majority rule, especially if he had to sojourn temporarily in Lusaka, as opposed to Gaborone, for example.) Another option sometimes advocated, despite the contravention of one the first major international agreements, is the ending of all communications, especially mail, an important conduit for the approximately two million whites of recent European extraction. A small number of states have already done this.

In the final analysis, the logical extension of sanctions brings us back to a blockade. This could include satellite observation, naval patrols (involving submarines or aircraft carriers) around the five or six major South African ports, and careful scrutiny at all large ports and airports for illegal South African goods. Such old-fashioned gunboat diplomacy would require a (very) unusual degree of political consensus, to say the least. But there was a precedent, on a smaller scale, in the joint naval patrols to counter slavery in the nineteenth century. Moreover, hostility to apartheid is the one thing that everyone can agree on at the UN. Also, Pretoria has displayed a rare genius for regularly outraging world opinion. Widespread random killings of blacks by white vigilantes (although not vice versa)—almost a certainty if white schools, cinemas and churches are continually attacked by the ANC—*could eventually* create the right mood for international action.

A naval blockade, or "quarantine" as John F Kennedy preferred, might seem bizarre now. At present "official" sanctions are largely symbolic. If they become more extensive, there is the likelihood that all apartheid's many opponents, and its few allies, might be forced into adopting a maximalist position: that sanctions would only be lifted when a fully-fledged black government, like Mugabe's, came to power in Pretoria.

That day may be a long way off but, as Thatcher has realised, this is the likely terminus of the sanctions route. In essence, sanctions are idealistic: they want Afrikaners to change their minds about their racism. Most Afrikaners see the issue as being asked to change their minds about survival. Nevertheless, sanctions are beginning to make the whites choose between economic comforts and white domination. They used to have both. "The ox-wagon was also a bandwagon," as Conor Cruise O'Brien aptly put it.

Conclusion

In each front, taken *individually*, countervailing factors favourable to Pretoria can be discerned. But *combined*, over a period of time, these fronts are certain to erode white domination—unless all the pressures are magically removed. That seems unlikely, given Pretoria's almost medieval obduracy. Black rule—eventually—is inevitable. The question is: how to get from the present to the inevitable?

Four general scenarios immediately present themselves: a negotiated settlement; a long, partly successful holding operation by the whites; a degenerative collapse; and a revolution. These may develop as progressive stages on a time-scale of, say, 20 years, or elements of each may work in tandem to produce an untidy "solution". All the scenarios point in the same direction. The stages depend largely upon the white psychological reaction to the growing siege and to black responses: more and more blacks could be induced to work within a (radically) modified system of white control, operate in a semi-legal underground or opt wholeheartedly for the armed struggle.

Negotiation. The search for a negotiated settlement and analyses of post-apartheid society have generated a veritable solutions industry. A whole new breed of white prophets has arisen; an anxious white populace has often turned their frequently unprofound placebos into bestsellers. Some of the technocratic prophets of boom have suggested, *inter alia*, a "high road" to the South African version of Japan and a modification of the Swiss cantonal system.(30) Clutching at such straws may well be what Gramsci termed "morbid symptoms of the interregnum", especially if one considers that these best case solutions *followed* catastrophic defeat in a nuclear war in Japan's case and civil wars in Switzerland's. Denis Beckett's compelling solutions book, *The Fallacy of Heroes*, however, offers a more down-to-earth South African attempt to reverse the whites' tendency to think with their blood and to reject the future as almost unthinkable.(31) Yet even his quasi-cantonal model, for all its blazing sincerity, is Utopian. At least these popular books have attracted a wide audience. Many whites seem to avoid thinking about the future at all. As Joseph Lelyveld observed, many white South Africans regard revolution in the same way that Californians regard earthquakes—they try not think about it.

A less publicised technocratic "solution" is big business's espousal of privatisation. But this has been rejected by the black resistance leaders as an attempt by capitalism to transform the large state-controlled sector, a form of ethnic socialism perhaps, into future safeguards against a radical black government. For all the intellectual attractions, the solution industry is seen as a white sideshow to distract blacks from the real issue of the transfer of power.

The key to this is not the modification of apartheid. Van Zyl Slabbert neatly summarised the necessary steps as "unban, release, dismantle and negotiate". The essential first step was the release of Mandela and then the unbanning of the ANC.

But Mandela's release could cause as many problems as it solved. Pretoria had demanded a renouncement of violence by the ANC before any serious negotiations could begin. The armed struggle, however, is the movement's main card. Why throw it away in advance? During the 1986 EPG mission, the right word was sought: "suspend" perhaps rather than "renounce" violence. In mid-1989 the government appeared to soften its line on the ANC's ending of violence. The new phrase became "a contribution to the creation of a climate which would promote peace in South Africa". Mandela's first official press release from prison, in July 1989, precisely endorsed these words. This statement followed Mandela's talk over tea at P W Botha's official residence, perhaps the most dramatic move ever made by any Afrikaner leader. Botha had, in effect, become Mandela's prisoner. This was Moses and the Pharaoh: the theme of the obsessive tyrant pleading with his prisoner to set him free has reverberated through the ages.

Mandela's release, however, could become a public symbol of white capitulation to many Afrikaners. The AWB might decide that the time had finally come to take up arms. After Mandela's release, would the radical right (or left) try to assassinate him, if he stayed in the country? Whoever killed him, Pretoria would get the blame. Or would he go into external exile and possibly spark off a leadership crisis in the ANC, as Pretoria hoped when it freed Herman Toivo ja Toivo? Pretoria had argued that the ANC *wanted* Mandela to remain in prison (thus tacitly accepting that the government had breached Machiavelli's maxim: an enemy should be destroyed or bought—and never made a martyr). So long deified, once Mandela stepped down from the cross to become an active politician, his infallibility ended.(32) His calls for internal and external black unity may not be heeded, once the honeymoon period is over. The PAC, at least, would want the erstwhile saint cut down to size. To them, Mandela is the Nkomo, not the Mugabe, of the struggle.(33)

Presume that somehow a "national convention" of all the major parties—it could not simply be a NP v ANC fixture—were brokered, probably by international diplomacy. If it showed a deft touch (despite its past performances), Pretoria could manipulate the current divisions within black ranks. It could talk to the ANC just to kill off the movement's credibility. Pretoria is committed to splitting the "nationalists" from the "communists" within the ANC. Trying to woo the nationalists—if Pretoria's distinctions have any validity—may prove short-sighted, not least because the Communist Party may be much more pragmatic and moderate, especially on the question of violence. The divide-and-rule tactics may be more generally counter-productive too. Pretoria may well come to need a powerful, united and obedient movement behind a single leader like Mandela to ensure that any command to end the guerrilla war would be heeded. Trying to negotiate later with a cacophonous chorus of rival black warlords might prove impossible. Many of the black youngsters already regard the ANC as too moderate, as the black equivalent of the National Party. For the moment, probably, Mandela's word will command the attention, if not always the obedience, of the masses. The very act of negotiation would probably undermine his support among some of the more radicalised sections of the black population. ANC hardliners want talks only about the mechanics of the transfer of power.

This potential dilemma may not be acute for the simple reason that neither side, possibly, is ready for serious negotiation. Despite the conventional wisdom that it may be too late to talk; on the contrary, it may be too early. Both chief antagonists, the ANC and the NP, think they can win. Victory is possible.

All the white leaders in the region have made an instinctive assumption about the righteousness and inevitable victory of their causes. This was true of Ian Smith as much as of Vorster and P W Botha. As one American scholar opined:

> For African Blacks seeking self-rule, political rights, and majority rule, theirs is a "just war." For white regimes defending their embattled community or "volk", protecting "Western" and "christian" [*sic*] civilization, it is a fight to the death. The tendency of each leader to see his or her territory as the lynchpin [*sic*] of the region and the region as the key to the greater contest for world control adds to the aura of holy war which suffuses the southern African struggle. (34)

Even if Pretoria did see the futility of a holy war and made real concessions regarding "power-sharing"—which may in itself be an impossible contradiction—Tambo and/or Mandela still might fall victim to the Kerensky syndrome.

Negotiation and the peaceful creation of a "democracy" would be to the common good; at the very least it could save lives. The country needs a unifying vision of the future, one which does not rely on pitting parts of South Africa against the others for fear of the whole. Unfortunately, as in all wars, fear, passion and prejudice predominate over reason. The besieged Afrikaners may yet see reason, as they did in 1902, despite the *bittereinders* who wanted to fight on. Nonetheless, this war could continue. As Stanley Uys concluded:

> The longer a negotiated settlement is delayed in South Africa, the more fragmented both the white ruling class and the black opposition will become, and the more the question of legitimacy will arise: who speaks for whom. White and black leaders alike will become less, not more, representative of their people, and a negotiated settlement will become less, not more, accessible. (35)

Holding operation. If the National Party is not prepared to negotiate its abdication—for that is what is at issue—what then? The answer is obvious. It will hold on to power for as long as possible, as Ian Smith did. It is a truism that very few (or perhaps no) privileged oligarchies have given up without a fight; and, to add a cliché to a truism, "especially in Africa". For the moment, indisputably, the last white tribe holds the field: guns will possibly decide much of the outcome, not morality or fancy franchises.

How much—militarily—has the ANC achieved after nearly 30 years of armed struggle? What precedents are there for a guerrilla army overthrowing a modern industrial state? The ANC loses nearly every contact with the SAP or SADF. Only a small proportion of the external ANC insurgents manage to operate inside the country. And its conventional allies, the Cubans, are departing. In military terms, the SADF's counterinsurgency has been very successful. Pretoria cannot be defeated militarily in the foreseeable future. Simply because the apartheid system is morally untenable, that does not mean it may not be militarily tenable. It is weak or indecisive, not cruel, governments that fall. Pretoria has no external patron to pull the rug from under its feet as Vorster did to the Rhodesian Front. South Africa is not a colony in any meaningful sense of the term. There is no imperial metropole to summon home the legions. In R W Johnson's impressive book, *How Long Will South Africa Survive*?, published in 1977, he suggested that Pretoria could develop a kind of metropolitan relationship *vis-à-vis* Washington, which could exert sufficient political leverage at the dramatic moment of truth. The imposition of sanctions and the resulting reduction in American influence has largely demolished Johnson's interesting thesis.

Pretoria does seem set for a long holding operation, which could defend white supremacy well into the twenty-first century. South Africa is today a ruthless authoritarian state, not yet a military dictatorship. A fully-fledged siege state could shift South Africa from a half-free oligarchy to a third world police state, as classical apartheid mutates into crude racial despotism.

Of course, Pretoria would try to daub over this a black veneer. Finally, perhaps, it could pull an internal settlement rabbit out of the hat. The whites would get half-security for offering half-citizenship to a black elite. The kingpin would have to be Buthelezi. His vanity and ambition might tempt him eventually to join other "moderate" blacks in a super-cabinet. (That could be sooner rather than later. Mandela's imprisonment had always been the main stumbling block preventing Buthelezi's acceptance of Pretoria's courtship.) The American right has always looked for heroes in southern Africa. It graced Savimbi and Buthelezi with its special favours. Unlike Muzorewa, Buthelezi in Pretoria may secure some kind of creeping recognition and perhaps a stay of execution on further sanctions from Washington and London. Behind the black facade, with perhaps some real attempts at corralling the elusive beast that is power-sharing, the security forces would deal extra harshly with the blacks who attacked the collaborators. Perhaps Pretoria would use its doublespeak to dub them "progressives" to replace the disgraced term "moderates". The more truculent leaders of the internal resistance could simply become *los desaparecidos* in an African version of Argentina's dirty war. Except that this time it would be fought in the name of a multiracial Pretoria. To sustain its military position blacks, especially Zulus, would be offered the franchise if they joined the army. "If blacks are good enough to fight and die for our country, surely they can vote for it?" In the waning days of the US civil war, the confederate leaders offered freedom to any slave who would fight for the southern cause. They had begun the war (partly) to maintain slavery, but they ended it by offering to abolish slavery so as to continue the war. As in Rhodesia, the white siege state would have to incorporate more and more blacks into the political, economic and military machinery so as to survive, thus diluting the original purpose of the war.

Eventually the containment policy would collapse because of the weight of its own contradictions. Rhodesia won nearly every battle, but lost the war. Despite the increased African soldiery, the SADF could find itself overloaded, especially if it got sucked deeper into the administration of the country as well as fighting a war. There is a substantial myth in South Africa: "Pretoria has not yet begun to use its real naked power." The regime could kill a lot more blacks and thus hasten the polarisation, but it also found itself overstretched in the 1984-86 period. Would it be able to cope with greater unrest in 1994-96 or 2004-2006? Would Mirages be used against stonethrowers (or more likely AKs) in Soweto streets? Or tactical nuclear weapons to deter a peasant revolt? Pretoria has reserves of ruthlessness, no doubt, but often insufficient reserves of manpower. And morale, as every general knows, is as vital as bullets. The white army conscript would not be impervious to the angst enervating the general white population. Iran is one example where a government was toppled while the army remained intact and, for the large part, loyal. The Shah's regime was was not steamrollered by turbulent priests and their fanatical followers. It ended when the army and the police refused to take further action against the crowds. Nor were the military defeated in the Philippines, when President Marcos fell. Even if the SADF remained totally cohesive under the strains, it might become like another impressive war machine, the *Wehrmacht*, in the service of an unjust—some would say suicidal—regime. Under such circumstances, a President Buthelezi, for all his abilities, would not make it to the Finland Station. He would "probably end up a loser, a sort of cross between Zimbabwe's Joshua Nkomo, driven back to a tribal constituency heavily outnumbered by a combination of other blacks, and Bishop Muzorewa, suffocated to death by white kisses".(36)

There are at least two variations on this theme. One could be that a frustrated Buthelezi cuts his losses, turns his back on his ambitions to seize national power and, instead, develops the Natal "Indaba" into an effectively independent Zululand. This could be done with the connivance of white businessmen in the region, if violence in the rest of South Africa became intense. Natal's whites, the majority of whom are English-speakers, have a history of separatist tendencies, and a long suspicion of Afrikaner rule in Pretoria.(37) The second, more likely, variation could be the possibility that Buthelezi's theory of working within the system to destroy it might become a reality. If his national administration got up enough steam, Buthelezi might ditch his white allies and do a straight deal with the external ANC (or the alleged moderates in the movement). That would be the equivalent of Muzorewa pulling off a deal with the Patriotic Front, or at least Nkomo. In mid-1989 there were hints of a rapprochement between Inkatha and the ANC at a diplomatic level, although the fighting on the ground in Natal continued. But the Buthelezi-going-it-alone scenario would depend ultimately upon the military's acquiescence. Unless it had been driven into impotency, the SADF would probably prevent any independent manoeuvre by the Zulu leader which threatened white interests.

A ruthless siege state may survive for a long time—maybe 20 years, but possibly for much longer. The repression-reform-reaction cycle, meeting fire with fire, would cause many traumas for a black/white coalition government backed by the SADF. Police repression could recruit more volunteers for the resistance. The SAP, in 1976-77 and 1984-86, recruited more troops for *Umkhonto* than the underground organisers had managed in the previous ten years. And police brutality ensures more support for trained guerrillas when they return "on mission". Whenever the government closes schools and colleges, this disperses an increasingly revolutionary elite throughout the rural areas. But if the schools are left open, they become centres for radical mobilisation. The same goes for white military recruitment. Granting deferments to allow young men to attend university encourages, in some, liberal attitudes and sympathy towards the anti-war movement. But the phasing out of deferments antagonises young men who feel their careers may be blighted. This in turn encourages emigration. Or if they do their national service first, some of the ex-soldiers later enter college with anti-war sentiments, which fuels the cycle of white resistance. (Many, though, enter university as much more mature, experienced—and right-wing—students.) Continued or extended conscription will further disrupt the white core of the economy, and lead gradually to its substitution by blacks. The alternative, discussed earlier, would entail a largely black army, which *could* turn on its masters. For all its efficiency, the National Security Management System faced a deployment dilemma. To keep on top of the alternative urban structures and to prevent the emergence of underground liberated zones in the cities, it needed to saturate the townships. Isolated farms would have to be guarded as well. Such constant vigil and regular dispersal would not only provide information on the pattern of deployment, in itself useful to the ANC, but also further strain army morale. (38)

This would amount to a no-win war. A long holding operation is not a "permanent transition" nor "violent equilibrium", a current description of the late 1980s. It is rather an euphemism to disguise the ebbing away of the white military power. There is violence, but it is not in equilibrium. The turning point has already been passed and the scales are weighted in favour of the gathering momentum of the majority.

Degenerative collapse. Degenerative collapse, the third possible scenario, is a less successful, more bloody version of the holding operation just described. This scenario, suggested by a number of writers, would entail the hyper-inflation of a Robinson Crusoe economy, massive external white emigration and internal migration to the Cape. Things could get so desperate that panicky whites would even sack their domestic servants, thus swelling the army of unemployed. Lebanon-style anarchy could surface, with the security forces regularly engaging in blood-stained power-brokering with local black and coloured warlords.(39) As in Cyprus, India, Beirut, Germany and Korea, *de facto* and "legal" partition could ensue. *In extremis*, a "whitestan" could result in the Cape, an ironic and logical fulfilment of grand apartheid. Like Israel, this state, would be nuclear-armed. Whites would constitute a "majority", but in alliance with coloured and Indian conservatives. The whitestan could survive, surrounded in a hostile or semi-hostile sea of a black confederation of states.(40) Today, partition-in-war may seem to be the "bellicose frivolity of senile empire", to borrow Barbara Tuchman's phrase, but such a Kahnesque scenario, while unpleasant and improbable, is not unthinkable.

Revolution. A fourth option could be a more rapid "solution": revolution. All revolutions are improbable until they happen; then in academic retrospect they are looked upon as inevitable. Analyses of revolutions often depend upon whether the analyst subscribes to a "great man" theory of history or the concept of sweeping historical forces.(41) A great leader could arise. Mandela might be the man, despite his age. On the other hand, Afrikaners have a long revolutionary heritage, on the right and on the left. The real white Terreblanche (or his replacement) could displace for a time the long-awaited "black Terreblanche".

The white-led Communist Party seems to have turned its back somewhat on its lodestar of revolution. The SACP, nothing if not slavish to Moscow, must be taking its cue from Gorbachev's new thinking. Although the SACP is the oldest and most loyal communist party in Africa and South Africa has the largest and most sophisticated black proletariat, Moscow appears to have reined in its disciples. Part of the reason must be the fact that Moscow takes an extremely pragmatic view of its own economic self-interest. Far from practising a strategy of resource denial, the arrangement with Pretoria is resource cooperation. The long-term and cosy gold and diamonds deals have been noted earlier. Moscow, arguably, has more vested interest in the status quo in South Africa than Washington has. A black radical government, eager to pay for economic reconstruction, could dramatically increase its mineral exports and could, therefore, play havoc with the markets in gold, diamonds and platinum. What would an (apparently) ideologically agnostic regime like Gorbachev's gain in material terms from a maverick in the minerals market?(42)

A classical revolution along the lines of the American, French and

Russian models seems unlikely. Nevertheless, the proverbial spark, the assassination of F W de Klerk or Mandela by one of the innumerable edgy Rambos in the AWB could trigger off a tidal wave of popular emotion. The death, rather than the leadership, of a "great man" may, in the usual convoluted South African fashion, generate a tidal wave in the flow of social forces.

Unsuccessful wars are often the antechambers of revolutions. At the time of writing, the SADF has largely extricated itself from the wars in Angola, Mozambique and Namibia. Those not ignominious military exits were quite rapid, and so could be the re-entry. Yet for all the qualifications of the truism, it still seems that a classical revolution in South Africa requires the defeat, defection or demoralisation of a large part of the SADF. The core would probably hold, but there could be an erosion around the edges. Defection from the black component would depend upon the ratio of blacks in the army, its loyalty, treatment and the nature of its incorporation. The white conscripts, however, could become increasingly dissaffected, assuming that Pretoria has not switched to the alternative strategy of a largely black professional army. The conventional wisdom should, therefore, be modified, especially if the examples of Iran and perhaps the Philippines in 1986 are taken into account. To avoid a revolution: firstly, the loyalty of the armed forces must remain intact; and, secondly, the armed forces must be convinced of their moral right to use whatever amount of lethal force is required, especially against civilians.(43) Thus, under extreme stress, the commitment of some black and some white conscripts might be questionable.

A classic revolution in South Africa is not likely, although a rebellion by attrition is. Short of peaceful negotiation (possible) and revolution (unlikely), the probable outcome may be a type of degenerative collapse. This might take two forms: a Beirut-style anarchy, or a well-managed siege state which could survive well into the twenty-first century. The end result would still be defeat for the whites, but the surrender in the latter case might be a more orderly one, especially if it were brokered and guaranteed by the great powers. South Africa's peculiar variation of the revolutionary experience will be one of slow, but fatal, erosion by defection. The important segments of society, possibly including elements of the army, will turn their backs on white supremacy. Implosion will kill apartheid, not Tambo's tanks rumbling through Pretoria's Church Square.(44)

The white die-hards will prolong the end game at all costs. They will fight hard against history, numbers and reason. But it will all be in vain.

An astute Afrikaner journalist has summed up the probable ungrand finale: "Perhaps it can best be described as a mighty upwelling of black rage that, over the years rather than months, will sap and haemorrhage the white power structure until it falls in on itself."(45)

This will be no easy walk to freedom for black or white. Stephen Davis, a not unsympathetic chronicler of the ANC, suggested a Pyrrhic future, "in which neither side can muscle the other out of contention, yet neither side can willingly give ground without pain. When peace arrives, it will probably not be through conquest. Rather, it will come grudgingly, and after seasons of bloodshed, as a fruit of exhaustion."(46)

But what then? What kind of society is likely to emerge from the death throes of apartheid? As one South African mused: "Everybody's trying to tell the whites to get off the tiger's back. No-one's telling them how they survive once they've done so."(47) That very much depends upon the nature of the transition.

References and notes:

1. "Fight them on the Fences," *Financial Mail*, 26 August 1988. About R129 million was scheduled to be spent on the withdrawal, according to SADF figures.
2. "Pretoria steps up Secret Buying of Weaponry," *The Times*, 20 March 1989; H-R Heitman, "$2.28 billion Defence Budget," *Jane's Defence Weekly*, 1 April 1989.
3. L Gann and P Duignan, *Why South Africa Will Survive*, Tafelberg, Cape Town, 1981, p. 193.
4. *Loc. cit.*
5. Most were ANC cadres; the others were PAC and Black Consciousness Movement of Azania insurgents. Figures quoted in "Terror Trail to South Africa leads through Botswana—SA Police," *The Star*, (weekly edition), 31 August 1988.
6. "Fight them on the Fences," *op. cit.*
7. M Chester, "SA has crucial Talent Gain through Immigration Turnaround," *The Star*, (weekly edition), 3 March 1989.
8. M Chester, "Exodus of Brainpower," *The Star*, 7 March 1986. See also, M Bole-Richard, "Racial Strife tempts more South Africans to the 'Chicken Run,'" (translated), *Le Monde*, 30/31 March 1986; "Locked in and Bolted Down," *Financial Mail*, 18 October 1985; C Bauer, "The Chicken Run," *Weekly Mail*, 23 August 1985.
9. For a discussion of these figures see L Nathan, "Resistance to Militarisation: Three Years of the End Conscription Campaign," in *South African Review 4*, Ravan, Johannesburg, 1987.
10. "ANC making good Bloody Bomb Boast," *The Star*, (weekly edition), 8 September 1988.
11. H Adam and K Moodley, *South Africa without Apartheid*, Maskew Miller/ Longman, Cape Town, 1986, p. 22.
12. A Sitas, "African Worker Responses on the East Rand to Changes in the Metal Industry, 1960-1980," unpublished doctoral thesis, University of the Witwatersrand, 1983, p. 413, quoted in A Stadler, *The Political Economy of Modern South Africa*, Croom Helm, London, 1987, p. 175.
13. D Beresford, "South African Mines Strike Collapses," *Guardian Weekly*, 6 September 1987.

14. J Leger, "From Hlobane to Kinross: Disasters and the Struggle for Health and Safety on the Mines," in *South African Review 4, op. cit*. The excessive security has also been attacked. The large force of mine police has been described as a means of privatising repression. According to one source, Gold Fields operates it own armoury of 6,000 shotguns, *has patented its own rubber bullet*, and runs a mine-security training camp for other mining houses. (K Philips, "The Private Sector and the Security Establishment," in J Cock and L Nathan, (eds) *War and Society: The Militarisation of South Africa*, Philip, Cape Town, 1989, p. 214.)
15. D Pallister, S Stewart and I Lepper, *South Africa Inc: The Oppenheimer Empire*, Simon and Schuster, London, 1987, p. 24. See also "The Oppenheimer Empire," *The Economist*, 1 July 1989.
16. C Mowat, *Britain between the Wars*, Methuen, London, 1966, p. 313.
17. For a discussion of liberation theology in the South African context, see J Leatt, T Kneifel and K Nürnberger, (eds), *Contending Ideologies in South Africa*, Philip, Cape Town, 1986, pp. 285-302.
18. Quoted in A Sampson, "Banned but Unbowed," *The Independent*, 30 September 1987.
19. For a useful summary of the "naive" theory of sanctions, see J Galtung, "On the Effects of International Economic Sanctions," *World Politics*, 19:3, April 1967; for a rebuttal see P Wallensteen, "Economic Sanctions: Ten Modern Cases and Three Important Lessons," in M Nincic and P Wallensteen, (eds), *Dilemmas of Economic Coercion*, Praeger, New York, 1983.
20. For an excellent summary of the debate, see T Davenport, *South Africa: A Modern History*, Macmillan, Johannesburg, 1987, pp.571-7; see also P Berger and B Godsell, "South Africa in Comparative Context," in *idem*, (eds), *A Future South Africa*, Human and Rousseau/Tafelberg, Cape Town, 1988. For a comprehensive discussion, see L Schlemmer and E Webster, (eds), *Change, Reform and Economic Growth in South Africa*, Ravan, Johannesburg, 1978.
21. For a summary of the ideology versus pragmatic domination debate, see P Moorcraft, "Towards the Garrison State," in F Clifford-Vaughan, (ed), *International Pressures and Political Change in South Africa*, Oxford University Press, Cape Town, 1978. The seminal text is H Adam, *Modernising Racial Domination*, University of California Press, London, 1971.
22. In addition, the anti-sanctions lobbies in the USA and Europe emphasised that sanctions ran counter to their free trade traditions; also, more specifically, they said, sanctions could destroy the South African economy and create a wasteland for the post-apartheid society. Russia would benefit, especially if a Marxist system crawled out of the ashes. Moreover, argued the Thatcher government, sanctions removed the Western leverage over Pretoria to modify its repression. An extra layer in the anti-sanctions armour was Thatcher's argument that perhaps as many as "250,000" Britons could lose their jobs as a result of destroying trade links with South Africa. On this point, see R Moorsom, *The Scope for Sanctions*, Catholic Institute for International Relations, London, 1986.
23. J Hanlon and R Ormond, *The Sanctions Handbook*, Penguin, Harmondsworth, 1987, p. 10. For a interesting opinion poll, see M Orkin, *Disinvestment: The Struggle and the Future*, Ravan, Johannesburg, 1986. For a rebuttal, see the summary of the poll conducted by *The Independent* and ITN, "Most SA Blacks Oppose Sanctions," *The Star*, (weekly edition), 5 April 1989.
24. Quoted in A Singh, "The Politics of Sanctions," *Frontline*, August/September 1987.
25. For an excellent summary of the sanctions debate as it stood in 1986, see X Smiley, "South Africa Survey," *The Economist*, 1 February 1986. For an American perspective on sanctions, see W Minter, *King's Solomon's Mines Revisited*, Basic

Books, New York, 1986; for a South African perspective, T Koenderman, *Sanctions: The Threat to South Africa*, Ball, Johannesburg, 1982.

26. J Spence, "Jan Smuts Notes," *International Affairs Bulletin*, Johannesburg, 10:1, 1986.
27. J Pieres, *Rhodeo*, (Rhodes University student newspaper), June 1985, quoted in K Helliker, A Roux and R White, "*Asithengi!* Recent Consumer Boycotts," in *South African Review 4*, *op. cit.*, p. 34. *Asithengi* means in Xhosa "We do not buy".
28. For a useful summary of this growth stage in Rhodesia, see E Cross, "Economic Sanctions as an Instrument of Policy," *International Affairs Bulletin*, 5:1, 1981.
29. Editorial, "Go for Gold," *The Economist*, 19 July 1986.
30. Clem Sunter (*The World and South Africa in the 1990s*, Human and Rousseau/ Tafelberg, Cape Town, 1987) advocated, *inter alia*, the Japanese model; Leon Louw and his wife, Frances Kendall, wrote the bestselling *South Africa: The Solution* (Amagi, Bisho, 1986) which suggested the Swiss example. Louw and Kendall were nominated for the 1989 Nobel Peace Prize.
31. D Beckett, *The Fallacy of Heroes*, Saga, Johannesburg, 1988.
32. See R Johnson, "If Mandela Goes Free...," *The Times*, 18 October 1988.
33. N Mathiane, "The Swing of the Pendulum," *Frontline*, October 1988.
34. K Grundy, "The Social Costs of the Armed Struggle," *Armed Forces and Society*, 7:3, Spring 1981, p. 464.
35. S Uys, "Whither the White Oligarchy?" in J Blumenfeld, (ed), *South Africa in Crisis*, Croom Helm, London, 1987, p. 75.
36. X Smiley, "South Africa Survey," *op. cit.*
37. P Moorcraft, "Dividing the Kingdom," in A Johnston and F Clifford-Vaughan, (eds), *Devolution: Natal's Case*, University of Natal, Durban, 1978
38. See K Gottschalk, "State Strategy and the Limits of Counter-Revolution," in *South African Review 4*, *op.cit.*, pp. 496-98.
39. For a summary of this scenario, see "Degenerative Collapse," *The Sunday Star*, (review), 25 August 1985.
40. For a discussion of the partition thesis, see P Moorcraft, "Towards the Garrison State," *op. cit.* and *idem*, "They do their own Washing Up in the Cape Free State," *Frontline*, July 1982, for a Utopian projection of the partition model.
41. In popular terms there are said to be two theories of history, the conspiracy and the "cock-up". The latter would seem to apply to South Africa.
42. K Campbell, *Southern Africa in Soviet Foreign Policy*, Adelphi Paper No. 227, International Institute for Strategic Studies, London, Winter 1987/8, pp. 37-45.
43. See A Joes, *From the Barrel of a Gun*, Pergamon-Brassey's, New York, 1986, pp. 204-14.
44. See R Levgold, "The Soviet Threat to Southern Africa," *International Affairs Bulletin*, 8:1, 1984.
45. S Uys, "Blacks Now Know They are going to Win," *Guardian Weekly*, 1 June 1986.
46. S Davis, *Apartheid's Rebels*, Yale University Press, New Haven, 1987, p. 214.
47. D Beckett, "Wrath of a Peaceful Man," *Frontline*, January 1989.

19

Waiting for the barbarians*

The direction of the future is clear: black rule. By the late 1980s the centre of gravity had already shifted towards majority rule. Despite the collapse of the 1984-86 revolt, a qualitative change in black political dynamics was evident. But, as Gramsci put it, "the old is dying and the new cannot be born". The South African interregnum will probably be a lengthy one, despite what Van Zyl Slabbert dubbed "the five-minutes-to-midnight-heavy-breathing politics".

Pretoria will wriggle for a long time, hooked on a Catch-22 dilemma: political stability is needed for reform, it says, but its repression fuels instability. There is no escape. Reform raises up black hopes, then the jackboot crushes them; an almost deliberate formula for revolution. Centralisation and militarisation of state power will march in tandem with attempts to decentralise and depoliticise some aspects of economic power. A siege economy will crank up centripetal forces. A temporary growth bubble may pop up under a command economy. The government, however, realises it cannot, on its own, build the golden bridge to provide all the goods required for the black co-option programme. Therefore, privatisation (for example, in transport services) and deregulation will generate centrifugal strains also. Sanctions will help to grind down the economy. Pretoria's friends will become even fewer. By 1989 even the Conservative government in London was distancing itself from an Afrikaner leadership that had shown less than Thatcherite zeal in getting on with the job of reform. The West will continue to move the goalposts, no matter how far the de Klerk presidency goes in the 1990s.

---

*The title refers specifically to the South African writer J M Coetzee's novel, *Waiting for the Barbarians*, Penguin, Harmondsworth, 1982. This remarkable allegory describes the evils inherent in all types of authoritarianism: the real enemy is fear.

Afrikanerdom has already used up much of its remaining political capital in Western conservative circles, just as it is using up its future inside South Africa. Pretoria was creating—until the release of Mandela—its very own hothouse effect by depleting the thin layer of hope. The end result still could be a classic justification of the tragic theory of bargaining: with its power drained away, Pretoria could have nothing left with which to negotiate. It will have painted itself into a corner. In particular, the lessons of white regimes in Africa indicate that the longer the conflict goes on, the more radical the eventual victor will be. In Rhodesia, the whites' most detested opponent triumphed because of white intransigence.

The analogy game

So far, so clichéd. It can easily be argued that South Africa is not Rhodesia writ large. Rhodesians said they were "different" from white Kenyans. They were wrong. South Africans say they are "different", a unique case. Every war is *sui generis,* of course. And, yet, many of these analogies are unhelpful. As the previous chapter indicated, South Africa is not a case of retarded colonialism, despite some of the internal trappings of settler colonialism. In many ways it is inaccurate to regard South Africa as the last act of the decolonisation drama. Afrikaners cannot go home. They *are* home. "This is not a nation needing liberation from an alien ruler, but rather a nation yet to be forged."(1) There might come a day of liberation, but not an Independence Day.

A more common form of comparison is the almost instinctive American habit of viewing South Africa through the prism of the US civil rights movement. Yes, of course, South African blacks demand civil rights, but the other parameters, most obviously the black/white ratio, are incomparable. The civil rights model is a classic example of a projection "of pathology from a particular Western society to a rather conveniently distant place".(2)

Pretoria plays the game too. It says it is like Britain in the nineteenth century: moving towards democracy by gradual enfranchisement of the underclasses. South African whites also readily deploy the North-South/first-third world metaphors. South Africa is, therefore, like "Australia superimposed on Nigeria". The children dying of starvation in the homelands (the third world) are a distant tragedy for the first world whites. The suffering is taking place not in another country, but in another *world.* This political simile provides all sorts of psychic balm: this is a universal problem, not susceptible to quick fixes and, besides, white South Africa is giving more "aid" to *its* third world (the majority of its own people) than any other developed country.(3)

There are no easy analogies. It *is* dangerous to argue by historical analogy. When it comes to analysing the future, however, what else is there but the past?

Numerous parallels have been drawn with the apartheid imbroglio. To take a number of examples briefly:

Historical nationalism: South African black nationalism is an integral part of the broader African, often anti-colonial, tide. It is different from the particularist nationalisms found in, say, Quebec, Nigeria or Yugoslavia. South African blacks want the opposite: the reintegration of apartheid's Balkanisation.

US civil war: The Confederacy ultimately lacked the cohesion to sustain a civil war in defence of its privileges. One writer compared the 1984-86 revolt with the 1862 Battle of Antietam. Greater battles followed. Arguably, in terms of generalship and tactics, the South came out slightly ahead. But Dixie was doomed. "White-ruled South Africa, like the Confederacy after Antietam, is finished. All that remains to talk about is the terms."(4) Some of the bitterness of the US civil war still lingers. Imagine the legacy of hate if that war had raged for 20 years. South Africa's armed struggle is now 30 years old.

The Russian revolutions: R W Johnson, for example, has argued that South Africa may experience a series of 1905s without a 1917 denouement.(5)

The Spanish civil war: The war against apartheid, to the present generation of the left, is the moral equivalent of the anti-Franco crusade. The comparison holds in so far as it is likely that more foreigners (and local whites) will become involved in the South African struggle.

Algeria: Judging by the many references made by black and white intellectuals to Horne's *A Savage War of Peace,* Algeria appears to be a tempting analogy. The ethnic proportions and the manacled social structure bear comparison. The polarisation is similar as well: compare the widespread view among blacks that only violence can change the system and its white counterpart that blacks respect only force. The AWB could perhaps emulate the *Organisation Armée Secrète*, an indication of how a small core of reactionaries could impede the transition. (Horne, incidentally, refers to a possible South African offer of support for the OAS *putsch.*)(6) On the other side of the obduracy equation, the *Front de Libération Nationale's* lesson for the ANC might be: keep on being stubborn, do not deviate from the maximum terms. The rebels lost the Battle of Algiers (read 1984-86?), but they won international support.

The French (Afrikaners) gave too little, too late and locked up the only people they could negotiate with. But, according to Lelyveld, the comparison breaks down because "there is no other country, no De Gaulle waiting in the wings, and no way for the whites to wash their hands of the problem without relinquishing their privileges and power".(7) The fact that the *pied noirs* could leave is an argument that cuts both ways, however. Did the French fight so ferociously *because* they could quit? Ultimately, they did have the "suitcase or coffin" option. Afrikaners, who have to stay (presumably), know that in the end—like the post-Antietam Confederacy—they must do a deal. That could (eventually) temper the repression and prevent some of the worst excesses of the Algerian war being replayed. That might be one of the more hopeful lessons of the Algerian savagery.

Israel: This is the foremost paradigm for Afrikaners. The crucial differences, however, are the approximate balance of Jewish and Palestinian populations; and, more important, America is a military guarantor of the state.

Lebanonisation: The term is frequently used to describe a possible degeneration of South Africa into battling fiefdoms run by local warlords. The Muslim versus Christian passions, to name but one factor, are absent in South Africa.

Northern Ireland: Urban warfare in South Africa is often compared with the long and bitter Ulster crisis. The vital contrast is that, for good and bad, the Irish communities have a referee (of sorts), the UK, in place.

The fall of the Shah: Iran in the late 1970s suggests some striking parallels with the South Africa of the 1980s: powerful, "reformist", rich and armed to the teeth. But the Shah's regime, when it came to the crunch, was indecisive. Unlike South Africa, Islam was important. And, despite its power, the armed forces wavered in the end. None of these factors apply to South Africa, although the army's reluctance to continue firing on the protesters may be relevant, in the future, to South Africa.

The Philippines: Winnie Mandela was formerly compared with Corrie Aquino, acting as a substitute for a martyred husband. The defection of senior military leaders, a reaction against a riotously corrupt dictatorial regime founded on one family, was a key factor. Although some of the generals' commitment to reform may have some relevance to South Africa, the pivotal role of the Marcos family does not.

Bobby Godsell and Peter Berger introduced two new variations: Deng Xiaoping's China and the Meiji restoration in Japan.(8) The first example has been overtaken by events, especially the barbarism of the Tiananmen Square massacre. The Japanese model is interesting. The 1868 transformation involved change from within the elite and, crucially, it was predicated upon giving the warrior caste an important role in the new order.

Some of the salient features of these international comparisons confirm the trends discussed in the previous chapter. As we have seen, unlike the colonial wars, South Africa does not have a metropole. No *deus ex machina* hovers. It is not a colony, but a sovereign state. There is no massive, unified religious opposition. And South Africa does not have a guarantor, as in the case of Israel, nor a referee to hold the ring. The Algerian saga suggests (perhaps) that the no-alternative-but-to-stay predicament could induce an eventual compromise rather than a finger-on-the-button nihilism. The rapid fall of the Shah and Marcos (and "Baby Doc" Duvalier) was dictated by a vacillating army and defection of senior military personnel. In the post-Franco transition and the 1868 Japanese example, the military gave their nod to a reformist transition.

Despite their intrinsic intellectual attractions, what do these comparisons tell us about the possible future shape of South Africa? It may be very little. The Shah's fall was sudden, but Franco's regime lasted for nearly 40 years. Although the outcome of wars and revolutions may be highly variable, there is no necessary correlation between repressive regimes and instability. The regimes of Salazar's Portugal, Stalinist Russia and a number of South American dictatorships lasted for three decades or more. And there is the customary cautionary tale: not only do revolutions regularly devour their children, but often repressive systems are replaced by even worse ones. Fundamentalist Iran is an obvious example. Evil regimes can be repressive and stable over a long period. South Africa could indeed survive a series of 1905s.

African models

The preceding analysis could be used to confirm or disprove the four scenarios sketched in Chapter 18. Specifically *African* examples may be more useful signposts. One example is the Rwanda-Burundi analogy. The Rwanda model is total black victory in a long war. Radicals demand unconditional surrender. A new tyranny exacts massive reprisals against the defeated whites. The Burundi scenario is the obverse: the incumbent regime totally defeats the insurgents. White supremacy reasserts itself along with the massacre of the defeated rebels.(9) A less dramatic model is the Mauritius option: a muddled, but multiracial, democracy.

It could be argued that the South African regime is a white "segment" of Western Europe. Pretoria has always insisted that it is defending Western civilisation on a dark continent. In that case, Pretoria's human rights' record must be judged by Western standards. Apartheid apologists play the field both ways here: South Africa should be compared with the appalling examples to be found elsewhere on the continent. In this perspective, "apartheid is not a concept which divides South Africa from the rest of Africa: on the contrary, it is the local expression of the African ideological personality". Such was Paul Johnson's verdict.(10) He argued that South Africa shares six major characteristics with the rest of Africa: accelerating population growth; tribalism; rapid urbanisation—many African governments use bulldozers against squatters; nearly all have repressive security apparatuses—South Africa boasts the most efficient, if not the largest; all African societies are "racist" in that they discriminate (though not by law) against whites, Muslims, Indians, rival tribes, etc.; and most have eccentric political ideologies, although the general trend seems to be moving away from an addiction to "isms", as in South Africa.

Many of the political problems in Africa are caused not by apartheid, but by the absurd legacy of the old colonial borders. Few African societies are homogenous. Much of the nationalism without nations is bogus, artificially inspired. If the OAU had been truly committed to "throwing off the colonial yoke", it would have tried to redraw the colonial boundaries along the lines of tribal/national identity. This would, no doubt, have opened up Pandora's box. So, instead, the colonial borders were enshrined as the OAU shibboleth and set in concrete. This is part of the reason for the OAU's antipathy towards the homelands.

It is not surprising that South Africa, with 75% of its population comprising Africans, should reflect African traditions, although Johnson's argument that apartheid, a white artifice, is also intrinsically "African" is a trifle perverse. Johnson also maintained that South Africa is different in a number of important areas: wealth, the modern economy, and its large black middle class. South Africa is also distinct, he said, because "it is in many respects a free country... Like Britain [in the nineteenth century] , and unlike the rest of Africa now, it has been moving toward democracy rather than away from it."(11)

It is not necessary to agree with Johnson's thesis to suggest that African models may be more suitable indicators of South Africa's future. Three possible options can be immediately identified. For the

PLATE 19.1 During the 1983 referendum, the Herstigte Nasionale Party wanted a no vote to secure the future. Today the right wing is still vetoing the future. (The sign above the poster says "Dutch Reformed Church" in Afrikaans; the central poster says: "For our future, vote No"; the obscured poster says: "No to Indians and Coloureds in parliament".)

sake of convenience, let us call them the Botswana, Zimbabwe and Mozambique scenarios. The variants on a time-scale of, say, 20 years roughly equate with the probabilites of negotiation in the near future to a siege lasting ten years and finally collapse in 15-20 years. The time scales could, of course, be much longer. The following summary is taken from a 1990 base.

Botswana option	Zimbabwe option	Mozambique option
3-5 years	10-15 years	20 years
Capitalist economy	Mixed economy	Devastation

The road to the South African future could take an entirely different route, but these three options, particularly the Rhodesian/Zimbabwean precedent, may be the best available indicators. The assumption is based partly upon a racist premise: the longer the transition, the less whites will end up in central government; and partly on the reasonable assumption that the longer the war, the greater the economic damage.

Botswana option: Kenya (and perhaps Namibia) may also be precedents. A "grand *Indaba*" (convention) in South Africa, including the ANC and NP, could possibly conjure up a multiracial coalition which could lead to a stable multiparty democracy. This may be an optimistic, even Utopian, scenario.

Zimbabwe option: Although there are many contrasts, the psychology of white supremacy in both Rhodesia and South Africa can be compared. The less ideological and perhaps also less committed Rhodesian whites fought a 15-year war which cost a total of 30,000 black and whites lives. Considering the different ratios of commitment, weaponry and populations, that could mean that 250,000 South Africans of all races—the equivalent of the white population of Cape Town—will die in the South African war. Tens of thousands have died already as a direct or indirect result. And even then, this might be an optimistic scenario. The imperial power, Britain, held the ring in the final round and avoided—just—a real bloodbath. A Lancaster House-type settlement is anathema to Pretoria today. One day it might beg for such a compromise.

Mozambique option: The third is the most ghastly option: a long war, perhaps lasting another 20 years, ending in total collapse, anarchy and the wasteland that is Mozambique now.

An immediate rebuttal of the these scenarios is, of course, that they were colonial transitions. Botswana achieved independence without war. Rhodesia, however, was *de facto* independent. And, in Mozambique's case, it could be argued that there are parallels between pre-revolutionary Portugal and contemporary South Africa.(12) A key variable is the role of the security forces. Here the Rhodesian precedent may prove instructive.

Rhodesia revisited

The debate about the Rhodesian parallel has been rehearsed endlessly. There is no need to go into detail here. In short, the anti-sanctions lobby trots out the fact that South Africa has stockpiled and is ready for tough sanctions; the world needs South African minerals more than it needed

Rhodesia's; and the apartheid economy is much more sophisticated. On the other hand, South Africa has crucial potential weaknesses in the acquisition of capital goods, high-technology and oil. Stockpiles and SASOL cannot last for ever: there might come a day when there is just enough fuel to keep the Casspirs running. And, although it is true that South Africa is more industrialised, the possibility of large-scale union disruption, throwing a spanner into complicated works, could counteract this advantage. In swashbuckling around sanctions, initially the South Africans will no doubt prove the equal of the Rhodesians. But Salisbury had a big brother in Pretoria; South Africa stands alone. Rhodesian sanctions evoked little genuine moral fervour beyond the immediate protagonists. The apartheid pariah, however, is everybody's favourite villain.

Pretoria has drawn heavily on the Rhodesian experience, but so has the ANC. They are applying some of the same ground rules. The ANC has *said* it is not ready to contemplate a ceasefire until the potential for negotiation is well advanced. The precedent of Rhodesia (and Vietnam) was that agreement preceded a ceasefire, and not *vice versa.* And, as with the Lancaster House conference, the ANC has said that negotiation can only take place on the understanding that the principle of the transfer of power to the majority has already been agreed. Short of that principle, formal negotations *may* be premature.

Perhaps the parallel was most aptly summarised by Winnie Mandela when she explained why she supported sanctions: "We are asking the international community to assist us in saving the lives Ian Smith could have saved if he had listened during the Tiger talks."(13)

According to R W Johnson,

> ...already the three most important features of Rhodesianization are in place: a growing militarization of society, and large-scale draft-dodging; a currency which has collapsed to the point where the main economic activity is import substitution and foreign travel for South Africans is almost an economic impossibility; and a large, steady haemorrhage of emigration, most marked among the economically vital (and expensively educated) professional classes.(14)

In 1965 sanctions were the *first* and main pressure on Smith's rebellion. Insurgency—in remote areas—did not begin to be dangerous until 1972. Whereas in South Africa, the main challenges (conventional war on the borders, rural and urban insurgency, trade union militancy and endemic, if sporadic, township unrest) are already in place, *before* the advent of a determined sanctions campaign. "Private" sanctions, disinvestment and the original *threat* of comprehensive sanctions have caused emigration rates to spiral before Rhodesian-style punitive measures have been imposed. Unlike Rhodesia, South Africa has a large "poor white" component: these whites are already suffering economic hardships and unemployment (although domestic factors contribute to this malaise). A Zimbabwean authority on sanctions estimated that sanctions cost Rhodesian whites approximately Z$10 per head per year during UDI.(15) Therefore, it could be argued that, in terms of rand depreciation, migration patterns, white unemployment, disinvestment, etc., South Africa has *already* suffered more than Rhodesia did from economic and political pressures. But Pretoria still rules. What is missing in the equation is the same degree of military pressure.

The military lessons of Rhodesia are twofold: they concern the role of the great powers and the possibility of the security forces promoting and then guarding a transition to majority rule. If South Africans, of all races, cannot agree among themselves to end their civil war, some kind of forceful international intervention may well result. As in Rhodesia, Pretoria could eventually accept outside mediation as an alternative to imminent collapse or defeat. Alternatively, a Lancaster House might be imposed, after such extreme resorts as a naval blockade. Many experts reject the possibility of great power intervention, although sanctions themselves are obvious forms of economic intervention.(16) The principle has been established. The drama inside South Africa as well as the escalating "logic" of sanctions may suck in the great powers willy-nilly.

If the South African security forces are swamped rather than defeated, the SADF could survive a Lancaster House process largely intact, like the Rhodesian army. The retention of (temporary) white military power might be the main precondition for the whites' (very grudging) acceptance of black political power. The continued presence of the white generals may be a vital psychological component of a relatively bloodless transition. Whether Malan could substitute for Walls, however, is a moot point. Some farsighted—or treacherous, depending on the perspective—military and intelligence personnel might cooperate clandestinely in arranging the mechanisms of the international supervision of the end game. Some extra inducements will be necessary. A number of sophisticated buy-out plans have been suggested for the most despairing whites who might be induced to take their money and run rather than stay and fight.(17) Kissinger suggested in 1976 just such a Rhodesian plan, with sliding scales of compensation to encourage whites to stay on longer by providing some financial reassurance. More

PLATE 19.2 Can the small core of young white males provide the military manpower to deter domestic and international pressures well into the 21st century? (SADF).

important might be a nuclear deal: Lancaster House revisited might go hand-in-hand with the surreptitious denuclearisation of the new black state.(18) The South African military interlocutors (*cf* Walls and Flower) could help to organise the details of any international monitoring force (a Commonwealth presumably, rather than a UN, force) to supervise a one man, one vote election or referendum.

Such military details would have to be arranged concurrently with a political compromise. No doubt, Pretoria's interlocutors—politicans or generals—would push for some kind of "second-best" deal. The British made it clear that if the Patriotic Front did not settle, London would recognise Muzorewa's internal settlement. Buthelezi would be the replica perhaps. If the ANC stalled, the great powers could arbitrate over the heads of the movement, as they did with SWAPO in the Namibian settlement, provided that the transfer of power was an *implicit* part of the understanding. Russia and America found enough common ground to jointly compel the smaller powers to settle in Angola/Namibia. Washington and Moscow could do the same with a South African settlement. A joint naval force would be the most extreme sanction, but deft joint manipulation of the gold, diamonds and platinum markets might do the trick as well.

Superpower intercession on this scale would demand an unprecedented political consensus. Massacres, severe sabotage of the economic infrastructure or highly provocative raids on the neighbouring states, especially if they involved the small contingents of Western instructors, could add up to an armed démarche. Such military intervention would probably come a long way down the road of civil war. The Caesarian birth of the new state would be better than a fight to the finish and economic devastation. Better Rhodesia than Mozambique revisited.

Post-bellum South Africa

Calamity may be brewing in South Africa. There is absolutely no comfort for anyone, certainly not the Soviets, in a protracted war. That could inspire the first example of an accession to power of a guerrilla movement in a nuclear-armed state. Like Vietnam, a radical South Africa (or "Azania") could enforce a new regional hegemony; such a state could also boast a nuclear-tipped army. How would such a potentially dangerous state relate to East-West relations as it straddled the Cape sea route and dominated a vast mineral empire?

The inescapable logic is that a rapid transition to black rule is in the interest of the West. In moral and practical terms, the conservative Western powers have backed the wrong horse in South Africa. The Tar Baby is still sticky. In military terms, the best course of action would be to help create a pro-capitalist constituency among the black nationalists. The sooner-the-better rationale is the most hard-headed argument for sanctions. Sitting on the sidelines could eventually flush out another Gaddafi, Khomeini or Amin.

The leaders of the ANC do not, however, look like aspiring tyrants. There is nothing to suggest that either Tambo or Mandela are racist madmen. Mandela is "left wing"—how could he not be?—but not, apparently, a communist. Tambo sent his son to a well-known private school in England, not to a collective in Cuba.(19) There may well be a nationalist-communist clash in the leadership if the ANC gets into power. And Mandela may well play a Kerensky to a new Lenin waiting in the wings (Chris Hani perhaps). Nonetheless, as the ANC edges closer to power, it is likely to moderate its stance. The leadership has refined the vague Freedom Charter and tried to fill in some of the many gaps in its proposals for the post-apartheid state.(20) Despite their oppression, it appears unlikely that the majority of blacks would voluntarily rally to the communist banner. It is more feasible that the ANC will rapidly come to terms with big business; the result would be a mixed economy—with the whites largely running it at first. Mugabe learnt from the exodus of whites from Mozambique. Tambo* and Mandela, or their successor, will need white skills to rebuild the economy.

Major psychological adaptions will have to be made by the whites. It will truly be a black country, with black holidays, celebrating black heroes. They will have to get used to the term "comrade". In exchange, the whites will benefit by the end of sanctions, being able to send teams to the Olympics, membership of the Commonwealth and British Lions' rugby tours; generally a return to the community of nations.

Unless there is the agony of a protracted war, the apartheid-free South Africa will be neither nirvana nor Armageddon. All modern revolutions have resulted in further concentration of state power. It would be naive to expect an ANC government, once in power, to be any keener on Western-style political pluralism than any other African nationalist movement. The ANC will inherit the massive panoply of draconian laws which the whites may find turned against them, especially if last-ditchers resort to resistance tactics. Even the pragmatic Mugabe retained Ian Smith's security legislation and the permanent state of emergency. Whatever its current image of moderation and tolerance, the ANC in Pretoria or Egoli (Johannesburg) will jealously guard their monopolistic power over the press, the security forces and the judiciary. If some of the hard men in the ANC leadership take over the reins from the current aged, moderate generation, the less accommodating whites could find themselves beginning to pay a little for their arrogance. Apartheid decontamination along the lines of de-Nazification could take place. Generally, though, skilled whites, whatever their old beliefs, will be courted rather than purged. In one sense, apartheid racism imprisons whites as much as blacks. As in Rhodesia, many whites may feel a burden removed, especially once Pretoria's tissue of lies, propaganda and indoctrination is revealed for what it really is. Azanian TV may broadcast programmes on history and politics to try to deprogramme a whole generation of whites lobotomised by the Afrikaner thought police. Yet, despite the legacy of bitterness, the gap between blacks and whites (especially Afrikaners) is not as wide as it is in rest of Africa. As Jan Smuts so passionately desired, a real South Africa could be born, but this time it would encompass the whole "nation".

The real problems

An apartheid-free society is merely the first step in solving South Africa's *real* problems: overpopulation, unemployment, soil erosion,

*At the beginning of 1990 Tambo was hospitalised in Sweden, after suffering a serious stroke. Some sources suggested that he would be unable to resume an active political life.

health (especially the AIDs pandemic in the region), education, land redistribution and tribalism. Immediate *post-bellum* issues such as political restructuring and the rehabilitation of the war-wounded and the army of ex-prisoners pale into insignificance compared with the long-term challenges. In this perspective at least, the civil war is so totally unnecessary. South Africa could become the breadbasket of Africa, not another basketcase; the engine for continental renaissance, not its holocaust.

References and notes:

1. P Berger and B Godsell, "Fantasies and the Real World," *Frontline,* August/ September 1987.
2. *Ibid.*
3. J Lelyveld, *Move Your Shadow,* Abacus, London, 1987, p. 79.
4. S Barber, "Soweto 1986 could tip South Africa into Isolation," *Business Day,* 9 June 1986.
5. R Johnson, *How Long Will South Africa Survive?* Macmillan, Johannesburg, 1977.
6. A Horne, *A Savage War of Peace,* Penguin, Harmondsworth, 1985, p. 445.
7. Lelyveld, *op. cit.,* p. 204.
8. P Berger and B Godsell,(eds), *A Future South Africa,* Human and Rousseau/ Tafelberg, Cape Town, 1988, pp. 267-98.
9. See H Kotzé, P du Toit and J Gagiano, "Sanctions and South Africa: On Dealing with Desperate Men—Some Options for the US," *International Affairs Bulletin,* 12:1, 1988.
10. P Johnson, "Who will Win the Race for South Africa?" *The Sunday Star* (review), 24 November 1985.
11. *Ibid.*
12. See, for example, A Thomashausen, "Experiences and Parallels of Political Change in Pre-Revolutionary Portugal and in South Africa," *South Africa International,* 13:4, April 1983; for a rebuttal, see L Gann and P Duignan, *Why South Africa Will Survive,* Tafelberg, Cape Town, 1981, p. 205.
13. Quoted in *The Star,* 7 April 1986. For other examples of the comparison, see P Moorcraft, "The Truth Leaks Out," *Frontline,* February 1989; F Cleary, "Here we are again—at Five Minutes to Midnight," *The Star,* 7 January 1987; J Bloomfield, "Does South Africa really want to go through the same agony as the Whites in Rhodesia did?" *The Sunday Times* (Johannesburg), 10 August 1986.
14. R Johnson, "When Whites Cry Freedom," *The Times,* 5 August 1988.
15. E Cross, "Economic Sanctions as an Instrument of Policy," *International Affairs Bulletin,* 5:1, 1981.
16. For example, J Spence, "Superpowers won't Impose a Solution," *Sunday Tribune,* 19 March 1989.
17. For example, N Macrae, "Colonial Hangover that makes Africans Poorer," *The Sunday Times,* 2 April 1989.
18. K Campbell, *Southern Africa in Soviet Foreign Policy,* Adelphi Paper No. 227, International Institute for Strategic Studies, London, Winter 1987/8, p. 67.
19. X Smiley, "South Africa Survey," *The Economist,* 1 February 1986, p.60.
20. S Johnson, "Charting a New Course for the Charter," *Weekly Mail,* 12 August 1988; V Mallet, "ANC looks beyond the Freedom Charter," *Financial Times,* 14 June 1988.

20

Conclusion

The South African war is about ending apartheid. After more than 40 years, the central issues remain essentially the same: how to end white, especially Afrikaner, supremacy. Despite reforms, the main legislative pillars of racial domination are still intact: racial classification at birth and group, rather than individual, rights, or rather the lack of them. Whites control the economy, the polity, the land and the security apparatus. Dominance, despite the different nuances, is still the same cooperative venture between Boer and Briton.

Apartheid's phases have been stamped by Afrikanerdom's great men: Malan preached Afrikaner unity, Strydom the republican ideal; Vorster's rule was marked by pragmatism and tough security laws; and P W Botha's era was distinguished by the total onslaught and militarism tinged with reformism. The beginning of the F W de Klerk period suggested a new flexibility regarding negotiations with the ANC and Mandela.

But the war on apartheid is a long way from over. Black leaders emphasise the morality of their cause and the strength of world opinion, while whites rely upon their economic and military power. The equation is not simply justice versus tanks: each side has tragically underestimated and misunderstood the other's real strengths and goals. Only in the unfolding of the drama will they become fully apparent. It is so often said that South African blacks have not learned from the mistakes made in the 50 other states on the continent, but nor have the whites. They are both condemned to repeat them—perhaps.

The South African war has been fought on two main fronts. The second front, destabilisation, amounted to the convenient export of South Africa's domestic troubles. The meddling in the Angolan wars compounded the strains of Pretoria's imperial overstretch. In a mercantilist interpretation of strategy, it could be argued that every weapon used in foreign wars was one less tool to repress liberation in South Africa. In this perspective the forward strategy was the supreme achievement of the South African Communist Party. While the legions rampaged on the peripheries, the heartland of white power began to crumble. The South African armies have withdrawn now from the Angolan border. The SADF is losing its empire, but it has not yet found a role.

The implicit theme of this study has been that the long series of interrelated conflicts in southern Africa have tended to militarise the political process. War is a great auditor of political institutions. The Portuguese and Rhodesian polities were found wanting and the generals stepped into the breach. Political action by the military in Lisbon in 1974 ended the colonial wars in Angola and Mozambique. The Rhodesian security chiefs, often inadvertently, guided and guarded the transition to majority rule, despite the vacillation of the Rhodesian Front. The invasion of Angola in 1975 was a setback for the SADF. The final stages of the fighting in Angola in the 1980s demonstrated the limits of South Africa's conventional military power. The fall of Rhodesia, however, was more a psychological than a military blow to Pretoria. Mugabe was the shape of things to come. Nujoma was next.

Few sane men want the war in South Africa to continue. It may just be possible that the leopard can change its spots. At the time of writing, there is euphoria about F W de Klerk's rapid march to end apartheid. The war could wind down and the road to peaceful democratisation might be opened up. But it could also be a false dawn, as in early 1979 in Rhodesia, when Muzorewa's election victory encouraged some observers to advocate an end to sanctions.

With luck, however, F W de Klerk's presidency might herald an outbreak of lasting peace. But if Pretoria does not achieve a comprehensive settlement with its black antagonists, particularly in the ANC, the long civil war could resume with magnified intensity. Then the militarisation of South Africa would be likely to increase, especially if another variant of the internal settlements in Rhodesia and Namibia fails, as it is almost bound to do. Pretoria would again bolster its security apparatus: its prime principle is not to be forced into making political concessions because of military weaknesses. The black resistance would plug away at its—so far—ineffectual armed struggle, and the outside world will try to seduce or persuade Pretoria to "share" power. That is a euphemism for abdication. It may be impossible to persuade Afrikaners to accede to black rule. Sadly, only force, not reason, will work then. The secret is cutting short that attrition so as to save lives. Paradoxically, if the preceding assessment of trends in southern Africa is correct, the SADF might yet be an instrument of salvation.

No one expects the SADF leadership to undergo a sudden Pauline conversion. Yet there were hard men in Lisbon and Salisbury too. If the South African war escalates, not to a Russia in 1917 but to a Rhodesia in 1979, the South African military *may* play a similar role in guaranteeing the transition. For once, the SADF could defend the defensible.

The previous chapter searched for ways out of the apartheid maze. A settlement in the near future may be unreachable. The war, if it continues, might make *any* settlement impossible. It is always assumed that all political problems have solutions. There simply may be no solution to the South African puzzle: the sorcerer may never return to undo the mayhem of his apprentice. Whatever the final outcome, it seems likely that it will become progressively more difficult for the whites to unscramble survival from domination.

Long ago the whites were warned by P W Botha that they had to "adapt or die". Their response has not been entirely promising. As one of South Africa's most controversial playwrights put it: "People have adapted a little...and died a lot. And we have swapped a laager for a bunker."(1) The "just" war against Hitler led to that final bunker. Yet, despite the popular analogies, Afrikaner supremacists are not Nazis. There is room for pity as well as *Schadenfreude* over their self-induced predicament. That is the classic definition of a Greek tragedy. A settlement may avert a fight to the finish. Nevertheless, the hubris of the apartheid warriors has created the conditions for their own requital. As a distinguished French philosopher, Raymond Aron, observed: "When a party gives itself the right to use force against all its enemies in a country in which to start with it is in a minority, it condemns itself to perpetual violence."(2) That is a truly African nemesis.

References:

1. P-D Uys quoted in *The Star,* 7 April 1986.
2. R Aron, *Democracy and Totalitarianism,* Weidenfeld and Nicholson, London, 1970, p. 200.

Postscript

African Nemesis was completed in August 1989. In the preface I talked about a log jam; since then the floodgates of change have burst open. Eastern Europe has experienced a series of dramatic revolutions. Forty years of ideological concrete melted away, almost like ice in the sun. In South Africa the release of Nelson Mandela can be equated with the collapse of the Berlin Wall.

His freedom suggests that the negotiation scenarios outlined earlier might now become more possible. A way out of the apartheid maze may be discovered. With the deadlock apparently broken, both sides are now playing for very high stakes. Once Mandela and F W de Klerk enter formal negotiations, they will be able to back out only at great cost to their own positions. Militants stand waiting in both wings. The struggle, as Mandela indicated in his first speech, is far from over. In many ways the crucial contest is about to take place: how to transfer power from the minority to the majority. There will be many more skirmishes: across the conference table, in the bush and in the suburbs. The battles against white supremacy will continue.

The countdown to Mandela's release was rapid in the last months of 1989. In August a curmudgeonly P W Botha quit after a row about the alleged security aspects of F W de Klerk's trip to see Kenneth Kaunda. The old, finger-wagging warrior had risen and fallen over the question of national security. His useful role in South African politics had ended five years before when he had decided to put "security" before reform.

In September de Klerk won a general election, but with a reduced majority. The Conservative Official Opposition almost doubled its number of MPs, but the biggest surprise was the success of the liberal Democratic Party. P W Botha would have said that 70% of the white electorate (NP and CP) had voted against the radical left. De Klerk, however, argued that 70% (NP and DP) had voted for reform. And reform there was to be, despite the initial murmurings that de Klerk was a closet conservative. Indeed, he was soon hailed as South Africa's Gorbachev.

De Klerk moved fast. In October he released ANC leader Walter Sisulu and seven other prominent political prisoners. In November, after some huffing and puffing by Pik Botha, Pretoria stood back to watch SWAPO win the UN-supervised elections in Namibia. But SWAPO did not quite match up to the UN epithet of "sole and authentic voice" of the Namibian people. SWAPO took 41 of the 72 seats in the new assembly, while the DTA bagged 21. SWAPO's 57% of the vote prevented it from dictating the new constitution (for which it needed a two-thirds majority). Alliance and bargaining, not Marxist domination, seemed to be the order of the day as the new state marched towards independence in March 1990.

De Klerk also had the courage to reverse the militaristic trends which had characterised his predecessor's rule. Defence spending was reduced and the initial conscription period was halved. He restored the primacy of civilian and parliamentary rule. The cabinet reverted to its pre-1978 status. The State Security Council was demoted. Indeed, the whole National Management System, that sinister octopus which had inveigled itself into every nook and cranny of power, was dramatically downgraded and transformed into apparently harmless regional coordinating committees. General Malan also stated that the security forces would no longer take part in the neighbouring wars in Angola and Mozambique. As the Angolan war edged into its thirtieth year, the MPLA tried to move in for the kill as Savimbi sought to compensate for the loss of SADF logistical support in the south. In Mozambique Renamo fought on, while also negotiating with a reformist Frelimo. These developments tended to undermine the white ultras who had begun to exert undue influence in the National Management System. Nonetheless, last-ditch white opponents of de Klerk still survive in the military and particularly the police. When the bloody truth about the police death squads finally emerged, the new South African president initially refused to allow a judicial enquiry.

Previously the National Party has legalised social changes which had already happened. The pass laws, for example, had been overwhelmed by the black influx into the cities. Pretoria was trying hard to keep ahead of the game, but the government was beginning to find itself increasingly overtaken by events. This was certainly true of Eastern Europe where desperate communist administrations dumped the ideological baggage of 40 years. Meanwhile, behind the scenes, the exponents of two failed ideologies, Soviet bloc-style socialism and apartheid, were trying to come to terms: the ANC and the NP groped to find each other in the dark. Moscow urged moderation on the ANC, which could not fail to be influenced by the collapse of communism in Europe. The armed struggle wound down another ratchet, as ANC guerrillas moved from Angola into bases even farther from South Africa. Zambia too ran down its support of the armed struggle. The closest (official) ANC military bases now appeared to be in southern Tanzania, 800 miles from the South African border.

One of Pretoria's persistent goals had been to split the ANC: to separate the so-called "nationalists" from the more radical communists, and to encourage a compliant "internal" ANC as distinct from the hard-line exile wing in Lusaka. Pretoria had always insisted that the imprisoned ANC leàders had to renounce the armed struggle. With a few exceptions, they had always refused. Mandela had never compromised on this crucial ANC position. Rejection of violence had to precede talks, said Pretoria. Nevertheless, South African government leaders, including de Klerk, were busy negotiating with the world's most famous political prisoner.

On 2 February 1990 F W de Klerk finally dragged his party across the Rubicon. In a major speech he announced, *inter alia*, the unbanning of the ANC, the PAC and the Communist party, although the state of emergency was not lifted. It looked as if "normal" politics could begin again in South Africa. On 11 February the black messiah was finally freed after 27 years in prison. In his first speech, in Cape Town, Mandela—while conceding de Klerk's sincerity—warned: "We have waited too long for our freedom; we can no longer wait. Now is the time for intensifying the struggle on all fronts. Our march to freedom cannot be stopped."

The Mass Democratic Movement, the internal groups allied to the ANC, ecstatically welcomed their hero back into public life. But the ANC in exile remained cautious. True, Mandela had been released, but some political prisoners languished in jail. And the state of emergency still gave the government vast and draconian powers, they complained. But most of the world's major leaders hailed de Klerk's historic steps. Margaret Thatcher, out of step with the EC and Commonwealth as usual, removed some of the minor "voluntary" sanctions against Pretoria. Some activists argued that now was the time for the quick kill: short, sharp, comprehensive sanctions could finish off the apartheid beast, while it was reeling on the ropes. Thatcher, however, argued that unless de Klerk was rewarded with some concessions for his boldness and courage he could fall victim to a purge from the reactionary right.

It was from this perspective that de Klerk and Gorbachev were often compared. Both possessed the same combination of steel and charm. Like Mandela, Gorbachev and de Klerk's professional training had been in law. Both presidents were struggling to install the rule of law in their oppressive systems. Nonetheless, the tempting Eastern European analogy may be an inaccurate signpost for South Africa. While both presidents could be said to be walking a tightrope of reform while clinging to power, de Klerk's position looks far more stable. While the supporters of Mandela may shout *amandla*! (power), it is clear that real *amandla* belongs, for the moment, to the state. By 1990 the armed struggle had been relegated almost to the level of mere nuisance. There may be political discontent in the security forces, especially among the police, but de Klerk can still command a large and powerful military machine, which remains immune from defection, at least to the left. Gorbachev may perhaps be toppled by a palace coup, but in political and military terms de Klerk looks like hanging on to power long enough to handle the lengthy negotiations with the ANC and other political parties. Unless an assassin's bullet stops him (or Mandela).

Despite the valid optimism engendered by Mandela's release and the beginning of negotiation politics, great potential for continuing violence in South Africa persists. The whites will haggle, or fight, long and hard before they give up power, especially if they feel that a new constitution will swamp minority rights. It is important that Mandela and de Klerk have met and fostered, it seems, mutual respect. But even if both leaders accomplished a total marriage of minds, they might not carry their parties with them. Even if they do, "negotiations" are not simply a deal between the ANC and the NP, with the possibility or even likelihood of one dictatorship replacing another. A settlement in South Africa, if it comes, must involve a wide array of parties, including Inkatha and probably the homeland leaders. Instead of forming a patriotic front, as in Rhodesia, the resurgent PAC, with its chilling slogan of "one settler, one bullet", might fight on. It could be marginalised; or it could become like the Provisional IRA in Northern Ireland, while the white neo-Nazis could parallel the Ulster Loyalists. In this scenario elements of the security forces could back the white extremists. Pretoria's *perestroika* might yet be a Prague Spring.

At the time of writing this postscript, however, the future looks less gloomy in South Africa. The dangers of a bloody cataclysm prompting international intervention have receded for the time being. Pretoria has adopted its own version of Eastern Europe's "Sinatra Doctrine": black and white South Africans are trying "to do it their own way". Here of course the crucial difference with Europe surfaces. Communism claimed to be a universal credo; like Ulster Unionism, apartheid has been a specific response to unique conditions. But South Africa is an even more complex and dangerous phenomenon than a divided Ireland. We should be wary of undue optimism in South Africa, despite the seismic events surrounding the long-awaited release of Mandela. As the myth becomes man, no matter how great, the original problems remain.

South Africa is a microcosm of every conflict known to man: black versus white, terrorism versus militarism, socialism versus capitalism, tribalism versus nationalism, group identity versus individual rights, to name but a few. And the proferred solutions have varied. According to a common generalisation, there is said to be socialism for the Afrikaners, capitalism for the English-speaking whites and Indians, and fascism for the blacks. That of course is a gross simplification. Yet, as the serious politicking begins with the unbanning of the major black parties, the enormous complexities of South Africa will become even more obvious: not least the issues of land and wealth redistribution, nationalisation and minority rights. The bitter anti-apartheid campaigns have been rich in slogans, but poor in offering sophisticated solutions. Now, at last, Mandela's release affords some hope of jawing rather than warring towards a settlement. Power will pass to the majority, but there is still a long, hard walk to freedom.

Paul Moorcraft. February 1990

APPENDIX 1

SOUTH AFRICA'S WARS

Khoisan wars
Khoikhoi wars
1st Khoikhoi war (1659-1660)
2nd Khoikhoi war (1673-1677)
San wars (1668-1861)
The Frontier wars
1st Frontier war (1779-1781)
2nd Frontier war (1789-1793)
3rd Frontier war (1799-1803)
4th Frontier war (1811-1812)
5th Frontier war (1819)
6th Frontier war (1834-1835)
7th Frontier war ("War of the Axe") (1846-1847)
8th Frontier war (1850-1853)
9th Frontier war (1877-1878)
British occupation of the Cape
Cape Frontier rebellions (1795-)
Mfecane (also known as Difaqane)
Battles of The Great Trek (1836-1840)
Voortrekkers versus British conflict in Natal (1842)
Voortrekkers versus British conflict in the Orange Free State (1845-1848)
Basotho wars (1851-1868)
Cape versus Basotho wars (1879-1898)
Boer-Pedi war (1847-1852)
Makepane war (1845)
The Mahura war (1858)
Venda and Sotho wars (1859-1867)
Pedi civil war (1861)

South African Republic-Pedi war (1st Sekhukhune war) (1876)
Anglo-Pedi war (2nd Sekhukhune war) (1878-1879)
Langalibalele war (1873)
Anglo-Zulu war (1879)
Zulu civil war (1883)
Zulu uprising (1888)
Zululand rebellion (1906)
Griqualand West rebellion (1877-1878)
Tswana Frontier wars (1881-1885)
South African Republic-Mabhogo war (Mapoch war) (1882-1883)
South African Republic-Lobedu (Modjadji war) (1890)
South African Republic-Lobedu war (1894-1895)
South African Republic-Malaboch war (1894)
South African Republic-Venda war (1898)
Transvaal civil war (1862-1864)
Jameson raid (1895)
First Boer war (1st War of Independence) (1880-1881)
Boer War (2nd War of Independence) (1899-1902)
Marengo raid (1907)
Participation in the *First World War* (1914-1918)
The Rand Revolt (1922)
Participation in the *Second World War* (1939-1945)
Participation in the *Berlin Blockade* (1948-1949)
Participation in the *Korean war* (1950-1953)

COLONIAL WARS

Involvement in the "colonial" wars in *Angola* (1961-1975), *Mozambique* (1964-1975), *Rhodesia* (1965-1980), *Namibia* (1966-1989).
Invasion of Angola (1975-1976)

DESTABILISATION WARS

Involvement in civil wars in *Angola* (1975-1988) and *Mozambique* (1980-1988?).

Support for dissident movements in *Zimbabwe*, *Lesotho* and *Zambia*.

HOME FRONT

Counterinsurgency war against the ANC and PAC.

NB. This is a summary of the main conflicts. Various peasant revolts have not been mentioned, nor more contemporary adventures, for example, in the Biafran and Congo wars. Some of the conflicts in South Africa in the nineteenth century have differing titles, depending on the political/racial perspectives. I have tended to use the most common description. For example, the 1899-1902 war has been termed the "Boer War", "The South African War" and "The Second War of Independence", depending upon historical perspective.

The National Security Management System:

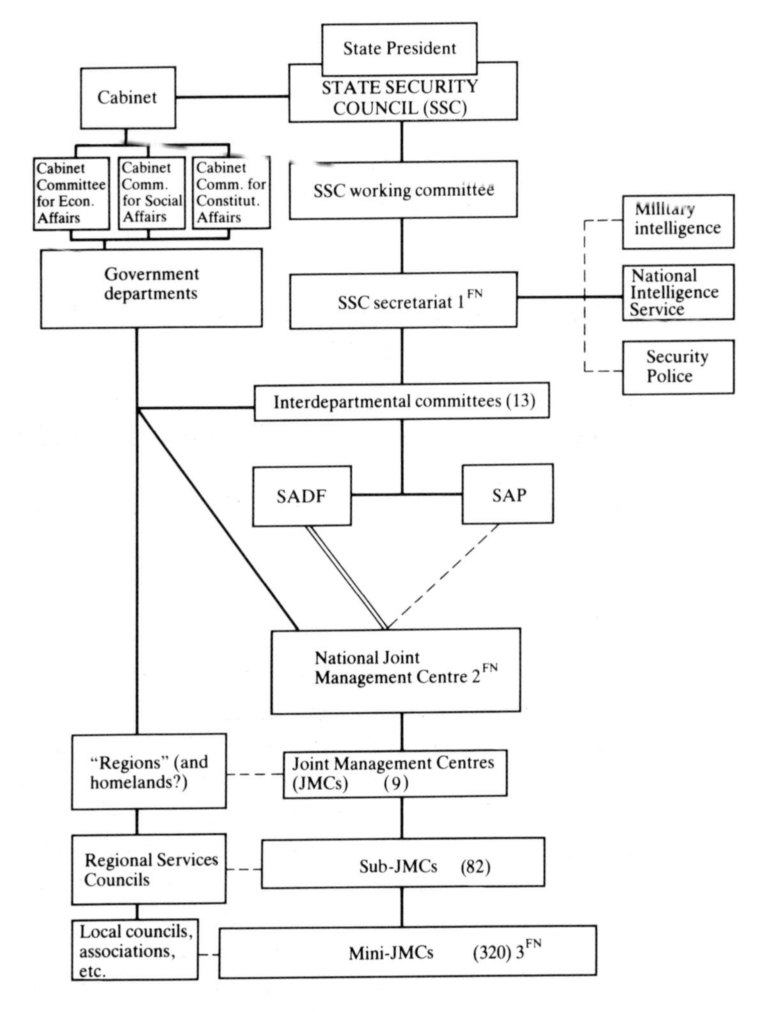

1. The secretariat has four main branches:
The National Intelligence Interpretation Branch;
The Strategic Communications Branch;
Strategy Branch;
Administration Branch.

The JMCs, sub-JMCs and mini-JMCs operated committees which roughly corresponded with the three main branches of the secretariat:
Joint Intelligence Committee;
Communications Committee;
Constitutional, Social and Economic Committee.
These committees were commonly referred to by their Afrikaans acronyms, respectively; GIK, KOMKOM, SEMKOM.

2. Like much of the system, some of its operational machinery was clouded in secrecy. The workings of the National Joint Management Centre were unclear.

3. The estimates of the number of mini-JMCs and sub-JMCs have varied.

FIG. 1

APPENDIX 2

THE STRUCTURE OF THE SOUTH AFRICAN SECURITY SYSTEM

NB: The independence of Namibia and the reforms of F W de Klerk brought major changes to the South African defence structures. The following information is a guide to the system which pertained during the most important wars covered in this book, namely during the period of P W Botha's dominance.

Political control

Until the 1989 changes the complex security system comprised the SADF, Armscor, the South African Police (SAP), the three intelligence services, affiliated security forces in the homelands and Namibia and, technically, the Prison Service. Security policy was generated by the State Security Council (SSC), in theory, for cabinet appraisal. The SSC consisted, usually, of senior ministers holding such portfolios as defence and foreign affairs, plus the chief of the SADF and the commissioner of police. It was chaired by the state president. Various senior civil servants and the head of Armscor, for example, were also invited to attend, as relevant, from time to time. The SSC was the pinnacle of the National Security Management System (NSMS).

The SADF structure

All the various members of the "defence family" have their own hierarchy. The SADF structure is headed in practice by the SSC. The chain of command is: president → SSC/cabinet → minister of defence → chief of the SADF → various councils/committees → the commanders of the four wings of the SADF (the army, navy, air force and medical services). The main SADF planning organs are the Defence Command

The formal political structure:*

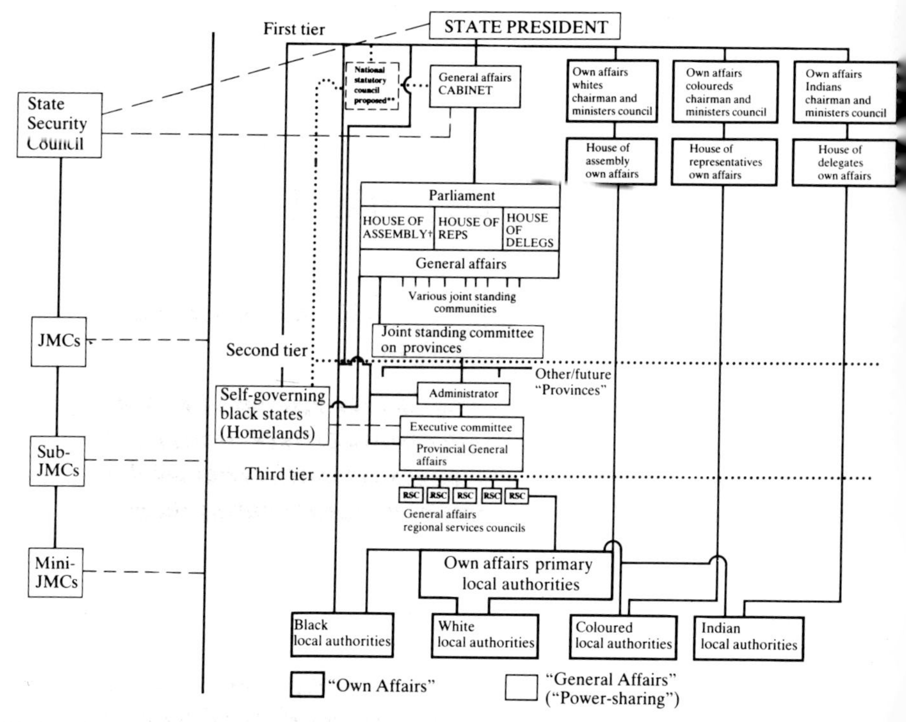

* This diagram is based upon the 1983 constitution, which was considerably revised by the late 1980s.
** The National (Statutory) Council was the proposed vehicle to bring blacks into central, first-tier government, at advisory level.

† The white House of Assembly is the dominant legislature. It consists of 178 members. Twelve are nominated and 166 are directly elected by the white electorate. The September 1989 election results were: 93 seats, National Party; 39 seats, Conservative Party; 33 seats, Democratic Party. One seat was tied and was recontested.

FIG. 2

Council (DCC), the Defence Planning Committee (DPC) and the Defence Staff Council (DSC), all chaired by the chief of the SADF. The DCC manages overall strategy. The DPC is concerned with financial management and liaison with Armscor. The DSC coordinates the various branches of the SADF. Direct military command is exercised by the chief of the SADF via the chiefs of the four services and through joint force commanders when there is a large combined operation in progress. All the services have their main HQs in Pretoria, the "military capital".

The branches of the SADF:

The army

The army is by far the largest section of the SADF, employing over 80% of total manpower. The army is divided into three main components: the conventional force, the territorial force and a largely training element.

The structure of the South African Defence Force:

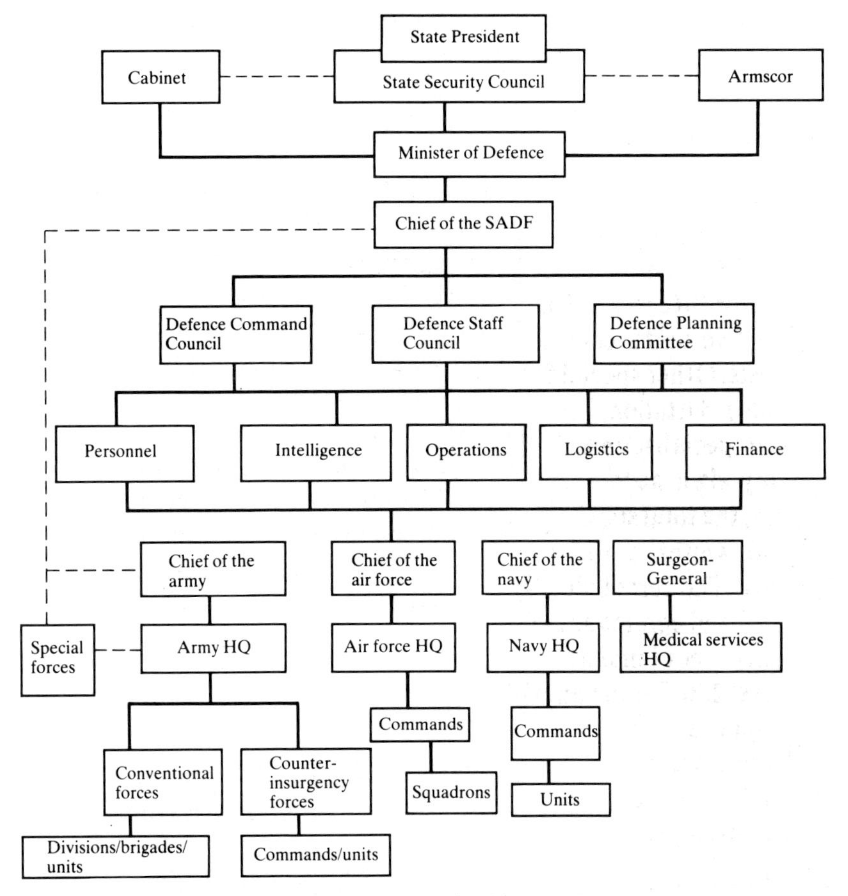

FIG. 3.

The conventional force comprises two mechanised divisions (each of which has one armoured and two mechanised brigades) and the parachute brigade. Permanent force (PF) officers and some national servicemen form the skeleton of the conventional force, but the flesh is largely made up of citizen force (CF) reserve units. The army emphasises rapid deployment and combat mobility, since the conventional force is both the ground deterrent and large-scale offensive force for previous operations in Angola. After some difficulties experienced in Angola in the early 1980s, the parachute brigade is unlikely to be used en masse in large paradrops, but is deployed in smaller raiding or "stopper" groups.

The territorial force is concerned mainly with internal counterinsurgency . This force, comprising largely the CF and commandos, is organised into ten regional commands as well as Walvis Bay. The operations, using light infantry techniques, support the police in case of serious guerrilla incursions. The territorial force also performs disaster relief and "civic action" (hearts-and-minds) roles.

Special forces

Special forces could be said to operate as a distinct fifth wing of the SADF. The army's special forces are directly responsible to the chief of the SADF. The elite special forces unit is the Reconnaissance Commandos or "Recces". This SAS-style force, founded in 1972, now consists of five units, each with its own speciality. They include PF and reservists. Other special force units are the 44 Parachute Brigade and 32 (Buffalo) Battalion, in some ways South Africa's foreign legion. There are also specialist units in the SAP.

Army size: according to the International Institute for Strategic Studies, the total standing force is 77,500. The PF complement is 19,900 (12,000 whites, 5,400 blacks and coloureds as well as about 2,500 women). The remainder is made up of about 58,500 national servicemen, CF and commandos (*ie* reservists).

Main army equipment:

Tanks: 250 Centurion/Olifant;

Armoured cars: 1,600 Eland (of various types, with 90mm gun and 60mm mortar);

Infantry combat vehicles: 1,500 including Ratel, Wolf, etc.;

Armoured personnel vehicles: 1,500 including Buffel, Hippo, Rhino, etc.;

Towed artillery: 175 25-pounder, 30 144mm, 75 G-2, 40 G-5;

Self-propelled artillery: 10+ G-6 155mm;

Surface-to-air missiles: 20 Cactus (Crotale), 54 Tigercat, plus various captured Soviet types such as SA-8/9/13/14. The Soviet ZU-23-2 AA gun is also in service;

Multiple rocket-launcher: 80 Valkiri 127mm.

Air force

The South African Air Force (SAAF) was organised into two regional commands (Western and Southern Air Commands) and four functional commands (Logistics, Air Space Control, Tactical Support and Training). Western Air Command, with its HQ in Windhoek, was concerned with the war in Namibia. Southern Air Command has its HQ at the Silvermine complex near Cape Town. It is responsible for maritime operations in South Africa, including fisheries patrol, air-sea rescue and the helicopters that operate from naval vessels. Air Space Command is tasked with early warning and air defence provided by Mirage F-1 and 111 aircraft, plus mobile SAM and AA systems. Tactical Support Command provides temporary air bases wherever the SAAF needs them. Logistic and Training Commands speak for themselves.

SAAF size: 11,000 (4,000 conscripts and perhaps 400 women).

Main SAAF equipment:

A total of 338 combat aircraft (including 116 operated by CF units) and 14 armed helicopters.
Bombers: 5 Canberra, 5 Buccaneer;
Fighter/Ground attack: 29 Mirage F-1AZ, 80 Impala;
Fighters: 14 Mirages F-1CZ, 19 Mirage 111 CZ/EZ (being converted to Cheetahs, perhaps 27 of the latter in service);
Attack/Training: 24 Impala;
Reconnaissance: 7 Mirage 111;
Electronic warfare/Intelligence: 4 Boeing 707;
Reconnaissance/Maritime: 8 C-47, 20 Albatross P-166S;
Anti-submarine warfare: 8 Wasp HAS-1, 6 Alouette 111;
Transport: 7 C-130B, 9 C-160Z plus various VIP transports;
Helicopters: 14 Super-Frelons, 50 Pumas (some converted to Puma XTP1), 80 Alouette 111;
Liaison: 60 light aircraft of various types;
Training: 130 Harvards, 39 Impala 1/11, 14 Mirage 111, 30 Alouette 11/111.
Air-to-air missiles: R-530, R-550 Magic, Sidewinder, Kukri V-3B;
Air-to-surface missiles: AS-20/30.

Navy

The navy is the Cinderella of the SADF in terms of resources. It is organised into two sections: the Naval Command West with its HQ at Silvermine and its major base at Simonstown, and Naval Command East with Durban as its HQ. The main operational units are:

The Strike Craft Flotilla. Based at Salisbury Island, Durban, the flotilla operates nine Israeli-designed, 430-ton, Minister-class strike craft, armed with Skerpioen ship-to-ship missiles, similar to the Israeli Gabriel. The missiles have a range of 26 nautical miles.

Submarine Flotilla. The primary conventional maritime deterrent is based upon the three French Daphné-class boats.

Mine Warfare Flotilla. Four locally built mine-countermeasure vessels and four Ton-class minesweepers.
Various support and in-shore coastal protection vessels.
The South African Navy does have two frigates, modified Whitby-class. The one, SAS *President Steyn,* has been stripped of its main components. The other, *President Pretorius,* is also now in mothballs. The third of the frigates, SAS *President Kruger,* was sunk in an embarrassing accident with SAS *Tafelberg,* a replenishment ship, in 1982.
SAN size: 6,500 including 900 marines, 1,500 conscripts and 300 women.

Medical service

The 8,000-strong service is organised territorially to support all three fighting wings of the SADF.

Allied forces

The South West Africa Territory Force

The SWATF was established on 1 August 1980 as the basis for an independent Namibian security force. Until late 1989 it was controlled and commanded by the SADF. The SWATF was similar to the SADF structure in that it was militia-based. It possessed both an area-bound COIN element (area force) and a mobile conventional warfare section (reaction force).

The SWATF had 22,000 members. In theory, all race groups were subject to two years' conscription. In fact, the majority ethnic group, the Ovambos, was not conscripted, although some Ovambos volunteered. Originally the Namibian units were organised mainly along ethnic lines (for example, 201 [Bushman] Battalion, 101 Battalion in Ovamboland and 202 Battalion in the Kavango homeland). These units were largely officered by SADF and Namibian whites. Later, there were attempts to create a more unified, integrated army. The SWATF had a number of specialised sections, notably the army's Specialist Unit and the deadly *Koevoet* police COIN unit. By late 1989, parts of the SWATF were being demobilised in preparation for Namibian independence. The future of the SWATF looked decidely uncertain.

Homeland "armies"

The four so-called independent homelands each have their own security forces: Bophuthatswana: 3,100 men under arms; Ciskei: 1,000; Transkei: 2,000; Venda: 1,500. Most have various light aircraft and armoured vehicles. Despite attempted and actual military coups in three of the homelands, Pretoria holds nearly all the reins of real military power. There are also ethnically based army/police units in the non-independent homelands. The KwaZulu paramilitary police is probably the most powerful.

The South African Police

The SAP and the SWA Police are paramilitary forces. Both undergo very similar COIN training to that of the SADF. The most active COIN units were *Koevoet* in Namibia and the various specialist task forces in the SAP. There are a confusing array of police forces in South Africa:

National:
South African Police (incorporating the former South African Railways and Harbour Police);
Police Reserve (ex-members of the regular force, part-time);
Reserve Police Force (part-time volunteers, mainly white but some Asians, coloureds and blacks);
South African Police *Wachtuis* (part-time volunteers, serving, for example, as radio operators).

Regional/local:
Provincial Traffic Police;
Municipal Traffic Police;
Area Defence Units (voluntary part-time rural militia).

African areas:
"Independent" homeland police;
"Non-independent" homeland police (and paramilitary forces);
Township Municipal Law Enforcement Officers;
Township "Kitskonstabels" ("instant" police, trained for three weeks).

Besides the above, there are numerous private "police" forces, ranging from the mine police, paid and controlled by the mining companies, to the hundreds of private security firms which guard white residential and commercial areas. Private security is one of South Africa's few growth industries. According to *The Star* (editorial, 5 April 1989), there are 200,000 private security officers, almost three times the size of the regular police. All the above wear uniforms of various types. There are civilian vigilante groups ranged across the political spectrum who act as neighbourhood "guards". One of the best known types is the *Makgotla,* run by traditionalist elders in Soweto particularly. They have been largely displaced by the "comrades" on the left and the right-wing vigilantes, for example, the *witdoeke* and the "fathers", who are said to be supported by the SAP.

Civil Defence Network

While not officially part of the SADF or SAP, a civil defence network operates nationally. In 1984 there were 646 civil defence units. Some are moribund, others are quite active. The capital city, Pretoria, appears to have a very sophisticated system which can mobilise a large number of civilians down to individual street level.

Intelligence Services

South Africa has three intelligence services. One, the National Intelligence Service (NIS), is an independent body, while the security police is part of the SAP and the directorate (or department) of military intelligence is an integral section of the SADF.

Until 1978 the most influential intelligence body was the Bureau for State Security (BOSS), founded in 1969, and led by the powerful General Hendrik van den Bergh. "South Africa's very own Heinrich Himmler," as Helen Suzman called him, he was said to be the *êminence grise* behind John Vorster. Van den Bergh's empire collapsed in 1978 during the Muldergate scandal. BOSS, the security police (SP) and military intelligence had a very long and bitter history of inter-agency feuding. The rivalry was so intense that they spied on each other and obstructed each other's covert operations. The sharpest antagonism was between the military and BOSS. When P W Botha became premier he abolished BOSS and set up the Department of National Security (DONS), which was renamed the National Intelligence Service (NIS). NIS is headed by a young Free State political science professor, Lukas Daniel Barnard. The NIS fell into temporary disfavour, partly because of its involvement with the Seychelles fiasco in 1981. Military intelligence (specifically its counter-intelligence section) was also criticised when Navy Commodore Dieter Gerhardt, the commander of Simonstown base, and his wife, Ruth, were found guilty of spying for the Soviet Union in 1983. They were alleged, *inter alia,* to have passed on NATO secrets to Moscow; in itself not only an interesting comment on Afrikaner solidarity, but also on Pretoria's connections with Western intelligence.

The NIS today operates as a general think-tank. It plays an important role in preparing the agenda of the State Security Council and is heavily involved with the running of the SSC secretariat. The security police is concerned mainly with field intelligence. Throughout the 1960s and 1970s it kept a meticulous record of the activities of black nationalist groups throughout southern Africa. Its performance was very impressive from a security standpoint. Since the 1984-86 domestic unrest it has lost some ground because of the damage done to its extensive informer network. In the late 1980s, however, some aspects of this network were restored apparently. The SP monitors all internal dissidence, across the political and racial spectrum.

The dominant service in the 1980s was military intelligence, partly because of P W Botha's close relationship with the military in general. In the 1970s the (then) much smaller SADF military intelligence directorate did not perform well, according to its counterparts in Rhodesia and elsewhere. But, under Botha, its size, power and resources were rapidly expanded. It developed a "strategic intelligence function", similar to the CIA's, and it controlled the military aspects of regional destabilisation.

As in Western intelligence agencies, there is still feuding within and between the three agencies over turf. Duplication and competition, however, to some extent was reduced by the centralisation of command and control initiated by the SSC and the National Security Management System.

Manpower

The core of the SADF is the regular professional element, the permanent force. The PF and civilians employed by the SADF make up about 10% of total strength. National servicemen comprise another 10%, while the rest is composed of the citizen force, about 47%, and the commandos (33%). There are four basic periods of military commitment:

1. All fit white male South Africans are liable for service from 18-55. National servicemen were conscripted initially for two years full-time. In 1990 it was reduced to one year.
2. They are then liable for 12 years in CF units. They are supposed to be called up for annual "camps" (periods of further training or oper-

ational duty for up to three months, which should amount to a total of 720 days). The alternative is 20 years part-time duty in a commando for those declared area-bound, such as farmers. There are three main types of commando duty: rural, urban and industrial. Urban commandos assist with crowd control, roadblocks, curfew enforcement, etc. Industrial commandos protect "key points", important commercial facilities. The most common form of commando duty, however, is rural COIN.

3. Then follows five years in the Active CF Reserve. Call-up in this category is usually only during a national emergency.
4. Finally, Controlled National Reserve for those who have completed the previous periods in a CF or commando unit are liable to 12 days call-up a year in an emergency until aged 55. Some volunteer to serve until 65.

The above call-up requirements were reduced in the aftermath of the withdrawal from Angola and Namibia.

There are deferments from national service for a variety of reasons, including full-time study. There are also (strict) provisions for conscientious objection on formal religious, but not political, grounds. Opposition to the draft has grown, particularly among young English-speaking South Africans. The reasons are various: political opposition to apartheid, the disruption of their careers and the social discomfort of the privileged, often middle-class, English-speaking elite who are often more discomfited by running around in the bush with Afrikaner railway workers than by occupation duty in the bleak African townships. Draft-dodging and emigration to avoid conscription have increased. National service also imposes a major strain on the economy, because of the drain on the limited pool of white skilled manpower. Some companies provide "make-up" pay to supplement employees who are called-up. Perhaps one-fifth of private companies pay full salaries. Although there are government guidelines which encourage companies to supplement national servicemen's pay, there is no legal obligation for them to do so.

The obvious alternative sources of manpower were white female and black, coloured and Asian volunteers. About 3,200 white women are serving in uniform in the SADF. The Cape Corps for coloureds was revived in 1963. A compulsory scheme for coloured cadets was introduced, but it met with great opposition and was abolished in 1979. A small number of Indians have volunteered for service in the navy. When coloureds and Indians were allowed to vote for the tricameral parliament in 1984, the government hinted that the vote entailed conscription obligations. The Indian and coloured parties in parliament strongly opposed the draft. So far, only whites have been conscripted. A volunteer black unit, 21 Battalion, based at Lenz near Johannesburg, was set up in 1974. It serves as a training school for the various homeland forces.

There have been partly successful attempts to remove discrimination in pay and career prospects in the SADF. The SWATF had and SAP have black colonels. About 20,000 blacks, coloureds and Indians serve in the SADF and allied homeland forces. Besides this, at least half (11,000) the SWATF was black; and about half (33,000) of the SAP complement is staffed by non-whites. That added up to a total of approximately 64,000 blacks helping to defend the system, for a variety of reasons. Black servicemen in South Africa have often suffered in their own communities because of their alleged collaboration with apartheid. Some black policemen are motivated, it appears, by a (brave) sense of commitment to service in their own community. Some stress their political detachment and say they are concerned only with fighting crime. Mass unemployment is one obvious inducement to join the ranks. Blacks in Namibia, however, complained about being placed in the frontline as cannon fodder to reduce white casualties.

The SADF, particularly during the manpower overstretch of the mid-1980s, began to search for more drastic ways of increasing its pool of personnel. It suffered, like many NATO armies, from a crucial shortfall of skilled technicians and good noncommissioned officers. The SADF could not compete effectively with the wage levels in the civilian sector. Although the question of establishing a better-paid, all-regular force was debated, it was decided to maintain conscription. As in Rhodesia, the SADF pushed up the age limits of white call-ups, and turned to immigrants. In 1984 it was made compulsory for immigrants between 15½ and 25 to take up citizenship after five years' residence, thus making themselves liable for military service. This discouraged fresh immigration (and thereby diluted the pool of white skilled workers) and caused a large number of expatriates, with sons, to quit South Africa, but the SADF stood to gain 45,000 new recruits. A small number of "mercenaries", variously defined, serve in the SADF. Most of them are Americans, British and Rhodesian professionals who had fought in the Rhodesian forces, as well as black and white Portuguese troops from Angola and Mozambique. Although other foreigners from Israel, Europe and Latin America are sometimes recruited, the SADF is rather wary of absorbing foreigners because of the bad publicity surrounding the handful of mercenaries who have deserted (especially from 32 Battalion) and sold sensational stories to the press.

Manpower structure (1989):

	Total	Standing
SADF PF	39,000	39,000
National servicemen	64,000	64,000
CF	175,000	45,000
Active CF Reserve	150,000	
Commandos	c.130,000	c.8,000
Independent Homelands	7,600	7,600
SWATF	22,000	15,900
Total military:	587,600	179,500
SA Police (regular)	c.66,000	c.66,000
Reserves	37,000	c.1,000
Auxiliary police	c.10,000	c.10,000
Homeland police	c.5,000	c.5,000
SWA Police	c.10,000	c.10,000
Total police:	128,000	92,000
Grand total:	715,600	271,500

(Not included are Armscor, SADF civilian employees, Prison Service personnel or "allied" guerrillas, Unita and Renamo. These figures, in some cases based upon rough estimates, can vary enormously according to the political and military situation.)

The force levels should be compared with the overall population estimates:

Total population: 35,364,00 (including 6,360,000 in the "independent" homelands).

Black: 24,719,000; white: 6,295,000: coloured: 3,324,000; Asian: 1,026,000.

Main published sources: *The Military Balance, 1989-1990,* IISS, London, 1989; Helmoed-Römer Heitman, *South African Arms and Armour,* Struik, Cape Town, 1988 and *South African War Machine,* CNA, Johannesburg, 1984; G Cawthra, *Brutal Force: The Apartheid War Machine,* International Defence and Aid Fund, London, 1986; P Moorcraft, *Africa's Superpower,* Sygma, Johannesburg, 1981; annual *Race Relations Survey,* South African Institute of Race Relations, Johannesburg, various; J Brewer, "The Police in South African Politics," in S Johnson, (ed), *South Africa: No Turning Back,* Macmillan, London, 1988.

APPENDIX 3

FRONTLINE FORCES

Angola:
Population: c. 9,560,000.
Total armed forces: c. 100,000.
Reserves: 50,000 militia
Botswana:
Population: 1,210,000.
Total armed forces: 4,500.
Lesotho:
Population: 1,660,000
Total armed forces: 2,000
Malawi:
Population: 7,983,000
Total armed forces: 7,250
Reserves: c. 1,000
Mozambique:
Population: c. 15,000,000
Total armed forces: 71,000
Tanzania:
Population: 24,333,000
Total armed forces: 46,700
Reserves: 10,000
Zambia:
Population: c. 8,000,000
Total armed forces: 16,200
Zimbabwe:
Population: 9, 520,000
Total armed forces: 49,500

Swaziland also has a small paramilitary force.

Source: *The Military Balance 1989-1990,* International Institute for Strategic Studies, London, 1989.

SELECT BIBLIOGRAPHY

This is a summary of the main sources. The following are some of the most up-to-date, concise or most easily available references. For full details see the endnotes.

South African history

Probably the best and most up-to-date history is:

Davenport, T *South Africa: A Modern History*, Macmillan, Johannesburg, 1987.

Colonial wars

Angola

Marcum's two-volume work provides an exhaustive background to the Angolan war:

Marcum, J *The Angolan Revolution: Vol 1, The Anatomy of an Explosion (1950-1962), Vol 2, Exile and Guerrilla Warfare (1962-1976)*, MIT, Cambridge, 1969, 1978.

See also:

Bender, G *Angola under the Portuguese*, Heinemann, London, 1978.

Hallett, R "The South African Intervention in Angola, 1975-76," *African Affairs*, 77:308, July 1978.

Kapuściński, R *Another Day of Life*, Picador, London, 1987.

Porch, D *The Portuguese Armed Forces and the Revolution*, Croom Helm, London, 1977.

Stockwell, J *In Search of Enemies*, Deutsch, London, 1978.

Namibia

The most comprehensive text is:

Du Pisani, A *SWA/Namibia: The Politics of Continuity and Change*, Ball, Johannesburg, 1986.

Also:

Katjavivi, P *A History of Resistance in Namibia*, Currey, London, 1988.

Mozambique

Beckett, I "The Portuguese Army: The Campaign in Mozambique," in I Beckett and J Pimlott, (eds), *Armed Forces and Modern Counter-Insurgency*, Croom Helm, London, 1985.

Hanlon, J *Mozambique: The Revolution under Fire*, Zed, London, 1984.

Isaacman, A and B *Mozambique: From Colonialism to Revolution*, Zimbabwe Publishing, Harare, 1983.

Munslow, B *Mozambique: The Revolution and its Origins*, Longman, New York, 1983.

Rhodesia

Perhaps the most concise political history is:

Meredith, M *The Past is Another Country: Rhodesia: UDI to Zimbabwe*, Pan, London, 1980.

Also:

Astrow, A *Zimbabwe: A Revolution That Lost Its Way*, Zed, London, 1983.

Caute, D *Under the Skin: The Death of White Rhodesia*, Lane, London, 1983.

Cilliers, J *Counter-Insurgency in Rhodesia*, Croom Helm, London, 1985.

Cole, B *The Elite: The Story of the Rhodesian Special Air Service*, Three Knights, Amanzimtoti, 1984.

Cowderoy, D and R Nesbit *War in the Air*, Galago, Alberton, 1987.

Evans, M *Fighting against Chimurenga*, Historical Association of Zimbabwe, Salisbury, 1981.

Flower, K *Serving Secretly*, Murray, London, 1987.

Frederikse, J *None But Ourselves*, Ravan, Johannesburg, 1983.

Martin, D and P Johnson, *The Struggle for Zimbabwe*, Faber, London, 1981.
Moorcraft, P *A Short Thousand Years*, Galaxie, Salisbury, 1980.
Moorcraft, P and P McLaughlin, *Chimurenga: The War in Rhodesia*, Sygma/Collins, Johannesburg, 1982.
Ranger, T *Peasant Consciousness and Guerrilla War in Zimbabwe*, Zimbabwe Publishing, Harare, 1985.
Reid-Daly, R as told to P Stiff, *Selous Scouts: Top Secret War*, Galago, Alberton, 1983.
Sprack, J *Rhodesia: South Africa's Sixth Province*, International Aid and Defence Fund, London, 1974.
Verrier, A *The Road to Zimbabwe*, Cape, London, 1986.

Destabilisation

General texts on the subject are:

Hanlon, J *Apartheid's Second Front*, Penguin, Harmondsworth, 1986.
Hanlon, J *Beggar Your Neighbours*, Catholic Institute for International Relations, London, 1986.
Johnson, P and D Martin, (eds) *Destructive Engagement*, Zimbabwe Publishing, Harare, 1986.
Johnson, P and D Martin, *Apartheid Terrorism: The Destabilization Report*, Commonwealth/Currey, London, 1989.

Also:

Adam, H and S Uys, "From Destabilisation to Neocolonial Control: South Africa's Post-Nkomati Regional Environment," *International Affairs Bulletin*, Johannesburg, 9:1, 1985.
Brittain, V *Hidden Lives, Hidden Deaths*, Faber, London, 1988.
Jaster, R *South Africa and its Neighbours: The Dynamics of Regional Conflict*, Adelphi Paper No. 209, International Institute for Strategic Studies, London, 1986.
Jenkins, S "Destabilisation in Southern Africa," *The Economist*, 16 July 1983.
Jenkins, S "America and South Africa," *The Economist*, 30 March 1985.
Martin, R "Regional Security in Southern Africa," *Survival*, September/October 1987.

Angola

Bender, G "Angola: The Continuing Crisis and Misunderstanding," *International Affairs Bulletin*, 7:1, 1983.

Bridgland, F *Jonas Savimbi: A Key to Africa*, Macmillan, Johannesburg, 1986.

Somerville, K *Angola*, Pinter, London, 1986.

Steenkamp, W *Borderstrike*, Butterworths, Durban, 1983.

Namibia

Manning, P and R Green "Namibia: Preparations for Destabilisation," in Johnson and Martin, *Destructive Engagement, op. cit.*

Stiff, P *Nine Days of War*, Lemur, Alberton, 1989.

Toase, F "The South African Army: The Campaign in South West Africa/Namibia since 1966," in Beckett and Pimlott, *Armed Forces and Modern Counter-Insurgency, op. cit.*

Mozambique

Grest, J "Mozambique Since the Nkomati Accord," in *South African Review 4*, Ravan, Johannesburg, 1987.

Martin, D and P Johnson "Mozambique: To Nkomati and Beyond," in Johnson and Martin, *Destructive Engagement, op. cit.*

Minter, W *The Minter Report*, Holland Committee on Southern Africa, Amsterdam, 1988.

Moorcraft, P "The Savage, Silent Civil War," *Army*, 37:14, April 1987.

Moorcraft, P "Mozambique's Long Civil War—RENAMO, Puppets or Patriots?, *International Defense Review*, 20, October 1987.

Seegers, A "Revolutionary Armies of Africa: Mozambique and Zimbabwe," in S Baynham, (ed), *Military Power and Politics in Black Africa*, Croom Helm, London, 1986.

Wheeler, J *RENAMO: The Mozambique National Resistance*, mimeo, report prepared for the Foreign Policy Research Institute, California, June 1988.

Zimbabwe

Barber, J "Supping with the Devil—Zimbabwe-South Africa Relations," *International Affairs Bulletin*, 6:1, 1982.

Martin, D and P Johnson "Zimbabwe: Apartheid's Dilemma," in Johnson and Martin, *Destructive Engagement, op. cit.*

Patel, H "Zimbabwe", *Survival*, 30:1, January/February 1988.

South Africa

Military

Baynham, S "Political Violence and the Security Response," in J Blumenfeld, (ed) *South Africa in Crisis*, Croom Helm, London, 1987.

Cawthra, G *Brutal Force: The Apartheid War Machine*, International Defence and Aid Fund, London, 1986.

Cock, J and L Nathan, (eds) *War and Society: The Militarisation of South Africa*, Philip, Cape Town, 1989.

Coker, C "South Africa's Strategic Importance: A Re-assessment," *Royal United Services Institute Journal*, December 1979.

Coker, C "South Africa: A New Military Role in Southern Africa, 1968-82," *Survival*, 25: 2, March/April 1983.

Davis, S *Apartheid's Rebels*, Yale University Press, New Haven, 1987.

Evans, M and M Phillips "Intensifying Civil War: The Role of the South African Defence Force,"in P Frankel, N Pines and M Swilling, (eds) *State, Resistance and Change in South Africa*, Croom Helm, London, 1988.

Frankel, P *Pretoria's Praetorians*, Cambridge University Press, Cambridge, 1984.

Frederikse, J *South Africa: A Different Kind of War*, Ravan, Johannesburg, 1987.

Geldenhuys, D *South Africa's Search for Security Since the Second World War*, South African Institute for International Affairs, Johannesburg, 1978.

Grundy, K *The Militarization of South African Politics*, Oxford University Press, Oxford, 1988.

Heitman, H-R *South African War Machine*, Central News Agency, Johannesburg, 1985.

Heitman, H-R *South African Arms and Armour*, Struik, Cape Town, 1988.

Jaster, R *South Africa's Narrowing Security Options*, Adelphi Paper No. 159, International Institute for Strategic Studies, London, 1980.

Jaster, R "South African Defense Strategy and the Growing Influence of the Military," in W Foltz and H Bienen, (eds), *Arms and the African*, Yale University Press, New Haven, 1985.

Leonard, R *South Africa At War*, Hill, Westport, 1983.

Moorcraft, P "Defending the Indefensible," *Army*, 39:3, March 1989 and "The Adversary Within," *Army*, 39:4, April 1989.

Rogers, B and Z Cervenka *The Nuclear Axis*, Friedmann, London, 1978.

Seegers, A "The Military in South Africa: A Comparison and Critique," *South Africa International*, 16:4, April 1986.

Spence, J "South Africa's Military Relations with its Neighbours," in Baynham, *Military Power and Politics in Black Africa, op. cit.*

Spence, J "The Military in South African Politics," in S Johnson, (ed), *South Africa: No Turning Back*, Macmillan, London, 1988.

General

Adam, H *Modernising Racial Domination*, University of California, Berkeley, 1971.

Adam, H and K Moodley *South Africa without Apartheid*, Maskew Miller/Longman, Cape Town, 1986.

Attwell, M *South Africa*, Sidgwick and Jackson, London, 1986.

Beckett, D *The Fallacy of Heroes*, Saga, Johannesburg, 1988.

Benson, M *Nelson Mandela*, Penguin, Harmondsworth, 1986.

Berger, P and B Godsell, (eds), *A Future South Africa*, Human and Rousseau/Tafelberg, Cape Town, 1988.

Campbell, K *Southern Africa in Soviet Foreign Policy*, Adelphi Paper No. 227, International Institute for Strategic Studies, London, 1987/8.

Cobbett, W and R Cohen, (Eds), *Popular Struggles in South Africa*, Currey, London, 1988.

Cohen, R *Endgame in South Africa*, Currey/Unesco, London, 1986.

Gann, L and P Duignan, *Why South Africa Will Survive*, Tafelberg, Cape Town, 1981.

Geldenhuys, D *The Diplomacy of Isolation*, Macmillan, Johannesburg, 1984.

Geldenhuys, D "South Africa's International Isolation," *International Affairs Bulletin*, 11:1, 1987.

Geldenhuys, D "The International Community and South Africa: Penetration, Intervention and Isolation," *International Affairs Bulletin*, 12:1, 1988.

Hanlon, H and R Omond, *The Sanctions Handbook*, Penguin, Harmondsworth, 1987.

Holland, H *The Struggle: A History of the African National Congress*, Grafton, London, 1989.

Johnson, R *How Long Will South Africa Survive?*, Macmillan, Johannesburg, 1977.

Koenderman, K *Sanctions: The Threat to South Africa*, Ball, Johannesburg, 1982.

Lapping, B *Apartheid: A History*, Paladin, London, 1986.

Leach, G *South Africa*, Century Hutchinson, Bergvlei, 1986.

Lelyveld, J *Move Your Shadow*, Abacus, London, 1987.

Lodge, T *Black Politics in South Africa*, Ravan, Johannesburg, 1983.

Lodge, T "State of Exile: The African National Congress of South Africa, 1976-86," in Frankel, Pines and Swilling, *State Resistance and Change in South Africa, op. cit.*

Louw, L and F Kendall, *South Africa: The Solution*, Amagi, Bisho, 1986.

Mandela, N *No Easy Walk to Freedom*, Zimbabwe Publishing, Harare, 1983.

Mandela, W *Part of My Soul*, Penguin, Harmondsworth, 1988.

Maré, G and G Hamilton, *An Appetite for Power*, Ravan, Johannesburg, 1987.

Meli, F *South Africa Belongs to Us*, Zimbabwe Publishing, Harare, 1988.

Meredith, M *In the Name of Apartheid*, Hamish Hamilton, London, 1988.

Minter, W *King Solomon's Mines Revisited*, Basic Books, New York, 1986.

Mission to South Africa: The Commonwealth Report, Penguin, Harmondsworth, 1986.

Moorcraft, P "Towards the Garrison State," in F Clifford-Vaughan, (ed), *International Pressures and Political Change in South Africa*, Oxford University Press, 1978.

Motlhabi, M *Black Resistance to Apartheid*, Skotaville, Johannesburg, 1986.

Murray, M *South Africa: Time of Agony, Time of Destiny*, Verso, London, 1987.

Omar, I *Reform in Crisis*, Ball, Johannesburg, 1988.

Omond, R *The Apartheid Handbook*, Penguin, Harmondsworth, 1985.

Pienaar, S "South Africa from Paragon to Pariah," *International Affairs Bulletin*, 9:3, 1985.

Pallister, D, S Stewart and I Lepper, *South Africa Inc.*, Schuster, London, 1987.

Sampson, A *Black and Gold*, Hodder and Stoughton, London, 1987.

Saul, J and S Gelb, *The Crisis in South Africa*, Zed, London, 1986.

Schlemmer, L and E Webster, *Change, Reform and Economic Growth in South Africa*, Ravan, Johannesburg, 1978.

Smiley, X *South Africa Survey, The Economist*, 1 February 1986.
South Africa: The Sanctions Report, Penguin, Harmondsworth, 1989.
Spence, J "Why is South Africa so Unpopular?" *International Affairs Bulletin*, 10:3, 1986.
Spence, J "Foreign Policy: Retreat into the Laager," in Blumenfeld, *South Africa in Crisis, op. cit.*
Spence, J *The Soviet Union, the Third World and Southern Africa*, South African Institute of International Affairs, Johannesburg, 1988.
Stadler, A *The Political Economy of South Africa*, Philip, Cape Town, 1987.
Uhlig, M *Apartheid in Crisis*, Penguin, Harmondsworth, 1986.
Van Vuuren, D, J Latakgomo, H Marais, and L Schlemmer, (eds), *The South African Election 1987*, Burgess, Pinetown, 1987.
Van Zyl Slabbert, F *The Last White Parliament*, Sidgwick and Jackson, London, 1985.
Venter, Al J, (ed), *Challenge*, Ashanti, Gibraltar, 1990.

Index